THE AYENBITE OF INWYT

EARLY ENGLISH TEXT SOCIETY

No. 278

1979

DAN MICHEL'S
AYENBITE OF INWYT

VOLUME II

INTRODUCTION, NOTES
AND GLOSSARY

BY

PAMELA GRADON

Published for
THE EARLY ENGLISH TEXT SOCIETY
by the
OXFORD UNIVERSITY PRESS
1979

Oxford University Press, Walton Street, Oxford OX2 6DP

OXFORD LONDON GLASGOW
NEW YORK TORONTO MELBOURNE WELLINGTON
KUALA LUMPUR SINGAPORE JAKARTA HONG KONG TOKYO
DELHI BOMBAY CALCUTTA MADRAS KARACHI
NAIROBI DAR ES SALAAM CAPE TOWN

ISBN 0 19 722280 3

*Printed in Great Britain
at the University Press, Oxford
by Eric Buckley
Printer to the University*

PREFACE

THIS volume is a complete rewriting of the apparatus in Morris's edition of the *Ayenbite of Inwyt*, published by the Early English Text Society in 1866. A corrected reprint of the text was made available by the Society in 1965 and this volume is intended as a companion to that text. Although completely rewritten, the apparatus follows the same pattern as that of Morris, for whose pioneer work all students of the text must be grateful.

I wish to thank the staff of those libraries in which I have worked and especially those of the British Library, the Bodleian Library, and St. John's College, Cambridge. I am also grateful to the numerous libraries which have supplied me with microfilms, the British Library, Corpus Christi College, Cambridge, the Bibliothèque Nationale, the municipal libraries of Angers, St. Omer, and Tours, Valencia University Library, and the Public Library in Leningrad. I am indebted also to the Institut de Recherche et d'Histoire des Textes in Paris for providing me with photographs of the manuscripts of the *Somme* in the Mazarine, Arsenal, and Ste Geneviève libraries, and to Mademoiselle Brayer for allowing me to consult her unpublished thesis on the *Somme*. I have also to thank Mr. N. R. Ker and Mr. M. B. Parkes for help with palaeographical matters, Dr. A. M. Hudson for checking a number of passages in the Bibliothèque Nationale as well as for other assistance and advice and the Press reader for some valuable suggestions.

The checking of this book has been arduous and I should like to record my gratitude to Mr. Gert Rønberg and Mr. David Yerkes for unstinting help with this task. To Mrs. Wallenberg I owe a copy of *The Vocabulary of Dan Michel's* Ayenbite of Inwyt, which has been invaluable in the preparation of this book. I gratefully acknowledge, too, a grant from the English Faculty Board which covered the cost of typing and assistance with checking.

Finally I must record my gratitude to the Early English Text Society for initiating this work and particularly to the Director, Professor Norman Davis, for his invaluable assistance and advice.

P. O. E. G.

St. Hugh's College
Oxford

CONTENTS

ABBREVIATIONS

EDD	*The English Dialect Dictionary*
Godefroy	*Dictionnaire de l'ancien langue français*
IMEV	Brown & Robbins, *Index of Middle English Verse*
MED	*Middle English Dictionary* (Michigan)
ODEE	*Oxford Dictionary of English Etymology*
OED	*Oxford English Dictionary*
PNK	Wallenberg, *Place Names of Kent*
SIMEV	*Supplement of the Index of Middle English Verse*

SUPPLEMENTARY CORRIGENDA
TO THE TEXT

3/25	*supply* 37b
6/7	*for* ssepere *read* sseppere
7/9	*for* ssepere *read* sseppere
7/31	*for* uore *read* uor
8/27	*for* writing *read* writinge
8/30	*for* bereth *read* berþ
9/5	*shoulder note: omit* [Fol. 2.a.]
9/11	*for* dyadliches *read* dyadliche
9/17	*for* suiche *read* zuiche
10/27	*for* wiþoute *read* wyþoute
11/24	*for* zenȝeþ *read* zeneȝeþ
12/6	*for* saynte *read* zaynte
12/13	*for* Ion *read* Ion/
13/5	*omit comma*
13/10	*for* sixte *read* zixte; *for* is/ *read* /is
13/12	*for* he *read* [he]; *for* .to *read* /to
13/24	*for* ande *read* and
13/25	*read* belongeþ/
14/27	*shoulder note should read* Matthias *for* Matthew
14/30	*for* sseawyinges *read* sseawynges
15/16–17	*for* uorȝuelze *read* uorzuelȝe
15/26	*for* heuedes zeuen *read* zeue heuedes
16/6	*for* zeuen *read* zeue
16/16	*for* enmi *read* emni
19/3	*for* consenteinens *read* consentemens
22/3	*for* mimþ *read* nimþ
23/2	*for* sriinges *read* friinges
23/12	*for* red; *read* red.
24/1	*for* men *read* man
28/15	*for* afterward *read* efterward
29/12	*for* benimeþ *read* benimþ
29/12	*for* as *read* ase
30/4	*for* felounye *read* felonye
30/26	*for* uolke *read* uolk
32/22	*for* long *read* longe
32/24	*for* nis *read* ne is
37/13	*for* and *read* an
38/27	*for* tornees *read* coruees
39/29	*for* ziȝt *read* riȝt
41/16	*for* kueade *read* kuead

41/29   *for* seynte *read* saynte
44/15   *for* as *read* ase
60/1   *for* good *read* guod
60/36   *for* hi *read* hit
65/24   *read* þes *and omit superior number and footnote. Cf. note to this line*
74/32   *for* þanne *read* þanne
76/21   *for* bezuyke *read* bezuyke
76/27   *for* uram *read* uram
82/9   *for* ane *read* an
83/5   *for* sostyeneþ. *read* sostyeneþ/
83/8   *for* tyeaers *read* tyeares
88/36   *for* aud *read* and
89/34   *add virgule after* paul
90/15   *for* huo *read* hou
90/21   *for* na t *read* naȝt
109/34 *for* /naȝt *read* naȝt/
112/13 *supply virgule after* zueteliche; 113/14 *supply virgule after* loue
124/6   *supply virgule after* oþer
128/10 *for* ne *read* he
128/34 *for* elyuans *read* elynans
136/12 *for* matiere *read* materie
137/13 *for* zayd. *read* zayde
147/6   *for* him *read* him
150/12 *for* ȝefþe *read* yefþe
156/4   *delete question mark though in MS.*
159/13 *read* clenȩ *in foot-note*
159/17 *for* huy *read* hy
175/6   *supply point after* sautere
176/1   *for* dyakne *read* dyakne
180/20 *for* ouercomeþ *read* ouercomþ
184/13 *move inverted comma to after* þe[1]; 35, 36 *inverted commas after* waye *and before* on
185/16 *for* þe[1] *read* be; *for* waye[1] *read* waye:
191/3   *read* testament
192/5   *for* hel *read* he (*MS.* hel)
192/20 *omit colon*
194/2   *supply point after* zayþ; *move inverted comma before* þet[1]; *supply virgule after* yeuere
199/17 *for* him *read* him
200/34 *for* knawe *read* knawe/
202/18 *omit bracket; MS has* his
204/24 *read* nere
209/17 *read* health *for* help *in the shoulder note*
214/5   *for* þinge/ *read* þinge
215/29 *for* him-zelue *read* him-zelue
218/32 *for* ȝigge *read* zigge
222/4   *for* sacramens *read* sacremens
224/fn. 1 *read* ssoruede

225/3 *for* bidde *read* bidde/
228/6 *for* he *read* hi
231/22 *for* me *read* ne
238/14 *for* be *read* þe
242/10 *for* aven *read* ayen
245/8 *for* he *read* þe
246/8 *for* yuele *read* yuele/
248/16 *for* sayþ *read* zayþ
250/21 *for* alone *read* a loue
251/3 *for* end *read* and
255/25 *for* nede *read* hede

Read u *for* v *or* v *for* u *in the following*: leave 1/17, 20; servi 7/9, 14; virtue 14/11; yeve 14/15; zeve 14/35; him-zelve 15/2; diverse 15/9; vor 16/15; ham-zelve 16/26; y-yeve 18/24, 20/13; zevende 26/20; gavelinge 35/28; tavernyers 44/24; levedi 47/20; uridom 86/21; ulesslich 146/14; ssrive 173/29; vor 196/30; covay[ti]se 197/3; y-proved 199/33; Under 221/35; contemplative 245/18; uram 270/17; *read* þ *for* th *in the following*: the 7/11, 11/32, 12/14, 21, 36, 14/26, 22/25, 23/29, 34/19, 257/9; byeth 11/29; ylefth 50/34; profiteth 185/28; troubleth 250/24; *for* in *read* ine *at* 12/10, 14/25, 28/13$^{2\&3}$, 38/16; *for* ine^1 *read* in *at* 14/25

Morris has tacitly emended the following:
6/31, 7/17   MS dyadlich
11/25   MS tuels
13/15   MS sanyt
30/10   MS wreþuollo
42/33   MS oịmchenlich
77/1   MS emer/roydes
77/1–2   MS childrren. (*but cf. note to* 77/1)
92/26   MS geste
116/1   MS of of
121/35   MS assuo
122/10   MS lyermeþ (*cf. note*)
128/9   MS hē
128/36   MS hohi
130/1   MS repe?
131/12   MS hi
142/16   MS wordþe
143/31   MS os
159/31   MS ansuerịeþ
170/4, 8   MS zayte
191/11   MS chld
196/2   MS sanyt
196/20   MS riȝ/uol
198/13   MS giniiynge
206/3   MS uorhay
207/21   MS uesste

208/32	MS clilde
216/30	MS hert
229/1	MS word/dle
254/23	MS man
262/21	MS choystre

INTRODUCTION

THE MANUSCRIPT

1. *Provenance and Date*

MS. Arundel 57, in the British Library, is dated, on folio 94, by
a colophon in the same hand as the text. The colophon runs as
follows: *Ymende. þet þis boc is uolueld ine þe eue of þe holy apostles
Symon an Iudas | of ane broþer of þe cloystre of sa(yn)t austin of
Canterberi | Ine þe yeare of oure lhordes beringe. 1340.* On the
second folio recto, the writer tells us that *þis boc is dan Michelis of
Northgate | ywrite an englis of his oȝene hand. þet hatte*: Ayenbyte of
inwyt. *And is of þe bochouse of saynt Austines of Canterberi.* This
part of the manuscript is thus known to have been written at St.
Augustine's, Canterbury, and to have been finished on 27 October
1340. Dan Michel of the Northgate was probably born within the
parish of St. Mary Northgate in Canterbury.[1] It is usually assumed
that 'ywrite of his oȝene hand' refers to the writing of this manu-
script as well as to the composition of the translation, though this
is not necessarily implied by the colophon.[2] The translation,
however, even if not the work of Dan Michel, cannot be much
earlier than 1300, since it is a rendering of the *Somme le Roi* of
1280.[3] The second folio recto of the manuscript has the press-mark
of St. Augustine's: *Distinctio xvi Gradus iiii.*[4]

Nothing is known of the early history of the manuscript. The
Arundel Collection was made by Thomas Howard, the second Earl
of Arundel, not by the first Earl of Arundel, many of whose books
came into the Lumley collection.[5] It seems likely that the manu-
script may, at one time, have been in the possession of the Royal

[1] I am grateful to Dr. William Urry for information on this point. I have
generally used the English form *Michel* rather than the form *Michael* of the
Latin inscriptions.   [2] See discussion, pp. 10–11.

[3] For this dating see E. Brayer, 'Contenu, structure et combinaisons du
Miroir du Monde et de la *Somme le Roi*', *Romania*, lxxix (1958), 1–2.

[4] See M. R. James, *The Ancient Libraries of Canterbury and Dover* (Cam-
bridge, 1903), p. lx; N. R. Ker, *Medieval Libraries of Great Britain* (2nd edn.,
London, 1964), p. 40.

[5] See Sears Jayne and Francis R. Johnson, *The Lumley Library: the Cata-
logue of 1609* (London, 1956), pp. 2–6.

Society. Henry Howard, who entertained the Royal Society at Arundel House after the destruction of Gresham College in the Fire of London, gave to it, in 1666, a part of the collection of printed books and manuscripts formed by Thomas Howard, the second Earl of Arundel. The growth of specialization eventually made the collection useless to the Royal Society and it came into the possession of the British Library in 1830.[1]

2. *Contents*

(a) The main body of the text, written by Dan Michel, consists of:

1. ff. 13–94:   *Ayenbite of Inwyt*
   incipit Almiȝti god / yaf ten hestes
   explicit Ine þe yeare of oure lhordes beringe. 1340

2. f. 94:   *Pater Noster, Ave Maria*, and Creed in English
   incipit Vader oure
   explicit lyf eurelestinde. zuo by hyt

3. ff. 94[v]–96[v]:   Pseudo-Anselm, *De Custodia Interioris Hominis* in English[2]
   incipit Uorto sseawy þe lokynge of man
   explicit himzelue wende. zuo by hit

4. f. 96[v]:   Treatise on the difference between men and beasts
   incipit Nammore ne is betuene
   explicit þet he arere to god. zuo by hit

5. f. 96[v]:   *Ave Maria* in English
   incipit Hayl godes moder
   explicit of þyne wombe yblessed. zuo by hit[3]

6. f. 96[v]:   *Ave Maria* in English[4]
   incipit Mayde and moder mylde
   explicit ase ich þe bydde can. Am*en*

(b) Dan Michel also wrote the list of contents which, together with Morris's text 1/1–1/20, appears at the bottom of the pages of

---

[1] See A. Esdaile, *The British Museum Library* (London, 1946), pp. 31, 65, 254–6; *DNB* HOWARD, HENRY, sixth duke of Norfolk.

[2] See *Memorials of St. Anselm*, ed. R. W. Southern and F. S. Schmitt (London, 1969), pp. 355–60.

[3] R. Morris prints this and the following item as part of 3; but the *amen*s suggest that they are probably separate.

[4] See IMEV 2034.

the first quire. These endleaves, ff. 1–12, were clearly added later and consist of a discarded copy of part of Aristotle's *De Anima* with glosses.[1] These leaves also contain the inscription of ownership and the shelf-mark.[2] The Aristotle fragment seems to have been copied in the second half of the thirteenth century and the glosses are in an English cursive hand of the late thirteenth century.[3]

(c) Miscellaneous prophecies, written in a later hand, were added in vacant spaces in the first gathering, probably some twenty to forty years after Dan Michel had completed the *Ayenbite*. They are as follows:

1. f. 4ᵛ: Versus Gylde de proph*etia* Aqu*ile*[4]
             incipit Tolle cap*ut* martis bis
             explicit Bubo necabit apem

2. ff. 4ᵛ–5   Versus Northmannie
             incipit Anglia t*ra*nsmittet leopardu*m* lilia galli[5]
             explicit dabit hinc heremita

3. f. 5:   Eleven hexameters
             incipit Gallorum leuitas[6]
             explicit gloria cleri

4. ff. 5–8: Exp*os*i*tio* v*er*suu*m* gylde de prophecia aqu*ile* et
             heremit*e*
             incipit Continet*ur* int*er* d*i*cta h*er*emite satis
             explicit britonu*m* est ore dictu*m*

---

[1] Cf. Albertus Magnus, *De Anima*, ed. C. Stroick (*Opera Omnia*, ed. B. Geyer, Aschendorff, 1968), pp. 61–133. This gives a text very close to Arundel 57. Dr. Malcolm Parkes has kindly pointed out to me that this manuscript is not recorded in G. Lacombe *et al.*, *Aristoteles Latinus* (Rome, 1939—Cambridge, 1955) or in the Supplements by L. Minio-Paluello (Bruges, 1961) and that the text and glosses correspond with those of the *De Anima* preserved as part of the *Corpus Vetustius* in C.C.C.O. MS. 114 (Lacombe, no. 359). The text thus represents a fragment of one of the early translations which formed part of *Corpus Vetustius* which was superseded by that of William of Moerbecke.

[2] See page 1.

[3] I am grateful to Malcolm Parkes for dating the hands in the text.

[4] For this and the following prophecies see H. L. D. Ward, *Catalogue of Romances in the Department of Manuscripts in the British Museum* (London, 1883), i. 307–8; R. Taylor, *The Political Prophecy in England* (New York, 1911; repr. 1967), pp. 56–7, n. 11. For item 6, see Taylor, pp. 160–4.

[5] H. Walther, *Initia Carminum ac Versuum Medii Aevi Posterioris Latinorum: Alphabetisches Verzeichnis der Versanfänge Mittellateinischer Dichtungen* (Carmina Medii Aevi Posterioris Latina 1/1), 2nd. edn. Göttingen, 1969, No. 1026.

[6] Walther, No. 7015.

5. f. 8ᵛ: Thomas de Erseldoune's prophecy of Edward II[1]
incipit To ny3t is boren a barn
explicit seme of hwete

6. ff. 8ᵛ–10ᵛ   The prophecies of Merlin
incipit Vn aignel
explicit toutz iors

7. 10ᵛ: *incipit* Anno mille
explicit destante perito[2]

8. f. 11   E. ssel uordo þ'(?) þor3 vi3t / and strengþe of
almi3t / Er m. þri croked / xl. alle bihoked / ssel
diuerse an daunce / þet neuir wes ymad ine fronce

(d) Commentary on St. Matthew with Prologue: s. xiii ex.–
s. xiv in.[3]

1. f. 97–98,   *incipit* [M]atheus ex iudea
     col. 2   *explicit* hoc debent facere exemplo nostro. nobis
enim 7 cetera

2. f. 98–108ᵛ   *incipit* [L]iber generationis ihesu *Christi* filii
dauidis filii abraham
explicit eius ritem quod si dum

3. *Number of leaves and foliation*

There are two sets of foliation, a medieval one, used by Morris,
and a modern one in pencil from 1 to 108. The medieval number-
ing, in Dan Michel's hand, extends from 13 of the modern
numbering to 96. Thus both the first and last quires have no
contemporary foliation. All references in this description are
to the modern numbering. On f. 2, the number 57 in ink, presum-
ably the press-mark, has been crossed out in pencil. On the fly-leaf
at the end is written '108 fols. examined and corrected RPS. May
1884'. The last two leaves are numbered in pencil, 50 and fol. 50
respectively.

4. *Collation*

The manuscript measures 30·5 cm. by 19·5 cm. The written
space is 24 by 15 cm. The quiring is in twelves. Pencilled quire
signatures appear at the bottom right-hand corner of folios 25 (b
ii), 37 (c iii), 49 (d iiii), 61 (e v), 73 (f vi), 85 (g vii). Catchwords

---

[1] IMEV 3762.   [2] Walther, No. 1139.
[3] Probably Johannes de Rupella, *Com. on Matthew*. Cf. F. Stegmüller,
Repertorium Biblicum Medii Ævi (Madrid, 1951), 3, 4898.

appear on ff. 12ᵛ, 24ᵛ, 48ᵛ, 60ᵛ, 72ᵛ, 84ᵛ, 108ᵛ. The catchword on f. 60ᵛ represents the last words on the page and not the first word on the next. That the manuscript is not complete is shown by the appearance of a catchword at the bottom of f. 108ᵛ. It is also to be noted that the quire signatures refer only to the text from f. 13, but later arabic numbers in pencil, including the first quire, appear at the bottom left-hand corner on ff. 25 (3), 37 (4), 49 (5), 61 (6), 73 (7). They may be the work of the pencil foliator. It is likely that the text of *De Anima* was used only as scrap parchment. Comparison with the text in Stroick shows that the text has been copied in the wrong order, a section of f. 3ᵛ being out of sequence. This may well be why the copying was abandoned and the parchment thus became available to Dan Michel for the writing of his preface and list of contents at the bottom of the pages where the gloss was not written in. Since these items are not included in his foliation they were presumably added later.

5. *Writing space, ruling and lines of writing, colouring, guide letters*

There are forty lines of writing to the page except on ff. 35ᵛ and 36, which have 41. The writing starts below the first ruled line.[1] Prickings are visible in the bottom half of ff. 2ᵛ–12ᵛ at the outer margin. These were, perhaps, intended to serve as guide-lines for the pencil grid used for the glosses on the *De Anima*. Much of this grid has been drawn. The grid at the top of the pages, however, has been drawn without prickings. There are a number of red and blue paragraph marks and initials. In the main text, paragraph marks are often followed by a red line under the heading. Guide letters are visible on ff. 16ᵛ, 21ᵛ, 26, 31, 50, 64, 68, 91, 94ᵛ, 96ᵛ. These have sometimes been erased as on ff. 23ᵛ, 24ᵛ, 30ᵛ, 58ᵛ. The last item has rubricated headings.

6. *Abbreviations*

The abbreviations in the English part of the manuscript are as follows:

(a) *Suspensions and contractions*

(i) The nasal sign is commonly used in English words and also in *optime* in *Nota per optime* in the margin of f. 26.

[1] For the significance of this see N. R. Ker, 'From "Above Top Line" to "Below Top Line": A Change in Scribal Practice', *Celtica*, v (1960), 13–16.

(ii) The horizontal stroke is also used to indicate the abbreviation of -*cio(u)n* as in *adopcion* (f. 42ᵛ) and *temptacionem* (f. 47ᵛ).

(iii) A tilde is used in *amen* (f. 96ᵛ); *bene* (frequently in the margins in the phrase *Nota bene*); in (*pater*) *noster* as, for example, at 34ᵛ; and in *spiritum* (f. 65ᵛ); *gratiam* (f. 65ᵛ); *dominum* (f. 65ᵛ); *uindicte* (f. 66).

(iv) A stroke through the ascender of the *h* in *Ihesu* (f. 2).

(v) A loop is used in *Distinctio* (f. 2); *salomon* (f. 56); *et cetera* (65ᵛ); it is often used for *er/re* as in *pater noster* (41ᵛ, 43ᵛ); *materie* (f. 48), *efterward* (f. 58ᵛ); *propreliche* (f. 59ᵛ).

(b) *Superior letters*

(i) Superscript letters are used as follows: superscript *a* as in *nostra* (f. 46), *grat* (58ᵛ); superscript *e* as in *sacremens* (15ᵛ); *greuousliche* (f. 25ᵛ), *treupe* (f. 31); superscript *i* as in *priour* (58ᵛ), *uirtue* (f. 59ᵛ); superscript *o* as in *gromes* (f. 46); superscript *u* as in *ycrucified* (f. 87); superscript two-shaped *r* is used for *ur* as in *purchacep* (f. 24ᵛ); *sanctificetur* (f. 44), *norture* (f. 46); superscript *a* and *i* are used for *ua*, *ui* after *g* and *q* as in *quaynteliche* (f. 25ᵛ), *quikke* (f. 41ᵛ), *anguisi*, *anguice* (f. 57; cf. note to 146/32), *sanguinien* (f. 60ᵛ). Superscript *i* is used in *hic* (f. 19, 76ᵛ); superscript *c* in *peccata* (f. 65ᵛ); superscript *a* commonly in *Nota* and in *Gradus* (f. 2).

(c) *Special signs*

(i) A nota sign consisting of three dots surmounting a vertical stroke is common in the margins.

(ii) *p* with a stroke through the descender is used for *per*, *por*, *par* as in *persone* (f. 14ᵛ), *paradys* (f. 33), *parfitliche* (f. 65), *tempore* (f. 66); *p* with a loop through the descender is used for *pro* as in *propreliche* (f. 21ᵛ), *prouendres* (f. 22).

(iii) A curl is used for *con-*, *com-* as in *consenti* (f. 14ᵛ), *compleccioun* (f. 20ᵛ). When followed by a superscript *a* it stands for *contra* and not *conra* as Morris and Wallenberg thought.[1] So *contrarie* (f. 15ᵛ), *contrarious* (f. 20). At 260/13, however, the *t* is written in *contrarie*.

(iv) *3* is used for -*us* in *debitoribus* (f. 46), *tribus* (f. 95ᵛ); for *que* in

---

[1] J. K. Wallenberg, *The Vocabulary of Dan Michel's* Ayenbite of Inwyt (Uppsala, 1923), p. 62.

*ne*que (f. 66); a curl is used for *-us* in *dimittim*us (f. 46), *meditat*us (f. 65ᵛ), *august*in (f. 65ᵛ).

(v) *n.* is used for *enim* (f. 66). Morris's expansion to *nam* is wrong.

7. *The script*

Malcolm Parkes has noted that the script represents an idiosyncratic variant of the earlier engrossing hand and marks a stage towards the later Anglicana Formata.[1] The same kind of idiosyncratic variation can be seen, in his view, in Ashmole 43 and in the Auchinleck manuscript. Mr. N. R. Ker has also pointed out to me in private correspondence that the writing represents a transitional style especially in regard to the ascenders, which belong to the older book-hand (*textura*) tradition. C. E. Wright draws attention to the following characteristics of the script:[2] the use of *ȝ* for spirantal sounds, a well-formed *þ* still in use (although Dan Michel uses *th* to spell his own name), a dotted *y*, and *i* indicated by a slanting stroke; two forms of *r* are used, the two-shaped *r* being correctly used after *o*; both long and round *s* are used; the *a* is very elaborate, the top bow being carried exaggeratedly above the line and then brought down to touch the lower bowl; the ascenders are usually a split wedge-shape, this being due to a quirk at the top; both *w* (but not *wynn*) and *ȝ* are used.

8. *Punctuation*

The usual marks of punctuation are the *punctus elevatus* and the virgule. The point is also used as, for example, after *manhode* at 12/15 (f. 15); after *ende* at 14/18 (f. 15ᵛ) and so on; a raised point is used after *þanne is* at 16/33 (f. 16) and in *red; conspiracions. strif.* at 23/12–13 (f. 18). Morris's reproduction of these points often makes the text difficult to read, since, in accordance with normal medieval practice, they often appear in the middle of a sentence. It will also be noted that Morris sometimes renders the points by a stop and sometimes by a semi-colon. The *punctus elevatus* he usually renders by a colon.

9. *Capitalization*

This has often been normalized by Morris. For example, on f. 1

[1] M. B. Parkes, *English Cursive Book Hands 1250–1500* (Oxford, 1969), p. xvii, n. 1.

[2] C. E. Wright, *English Vernacular Hands from the Twelfth to the Fifteenth Centuries* (Oxford, 1960), No. 12.

the manuscript has *dan michelis of Northgate, Holy Archangle Michael, Almiȝti kyng.*

10. *Corrections*

The manuscript has been corrected with great care by the author although, inevitably, a number of errors evaded his vigilance. Words are cancelled by subpuncting, deletion or both. Additions are often inserted in the text with a caret mark or a tag (or sometimes with neither) or else they are put in the margin. It appears that the correct word was sometimes written in the margin as a guide and then inserted on an erasure. Such would seem to be the case at 145/4 (f. 56ᵛ) where *charitable* is written in the left-hand margin with an insertion mark, *and charitable* appearing in the text on an erasure. Similar cases appear at 158/14 (f. 61), where *god* appears in the right-hand margin and is also inserted above the line in the text, and at 50/34 (f. 26ᵛ), where *ylefþ* is squeezed in over an erasure and written also in the margin. On the same page, *heþ* (50/19) is in both the margin and the text. At 61/13 (f. 29ᵛ) *efterward* has been inserted after *and*, but the letters *ter* are blotted out and the whole word has been written again in the margin with an insertion mark. Sometimes there was not room to insert the whole word in the text. Thus at 95/26 (f. 40ᵛ) the text has *alwe* altered to *alowe*; the margin has *alouwe*; at 106/29 (f. 44), *out of* is on an erasure and *smak* is added in the margin. All such correction, whether in the text or in the margin, Morris tacitly incorporates in the text.

Corrections are very numerous. In some cases, the corrections and additions seem to reflect uncertainty about the correct translation. Such cases may be divided into the following categories:

1. One word has been written over another. These cases have been indicated by Morris by printing one word after the other in square brackets.[1] Thus at 7/6 (f. 13ᵛ), *Zeterday* is over *sabat*;[2] at 7/12 (f. 13ᵛ) *diȝte* is over *ordaynede*; at 21/2, 12 (f. 17ᵛ) *despit* is written over *onworþnesse*; at 32/4 (f. 21) *arȝnesse* is written over *litel wyl*. Most usually, as one would expect, an English word is inserted over a French one. Thus, in addition to the examples cited above, at 43/22 (f. 24) we find *bezuykinge* written over *traysoun*; at 64/17

---

[1] But at 32/17 (f. 21), *ontrewe* cannot gloss *sleuuol*. See note to this line.
[2] But cf. 7/5 (f. 13) where *i. Zeterday* is in the margin.

(f. 31), *ydelnesse* over *uanite* which is subpuncted; at 66/28 (f. 31ᵛ), *atwyt* over *reproueþ* which is subpuncted; at 66/30 (f. 31ᵛ), *lac* is written over *defaute* which is subpuncted as Morris notes; at 70/5 (f. 32ᵛ), *awrekþ* over *punyceþ* which is subpuncted; at 76/31 (f. 34ᵛ), *haþ* is written over *fortune*. At 76/21 (f. 34ᵛ), *begyled* is written in the text but *zuyke* in the margin; at 83/18 (f. 36ᵛ), there is a cross over *preus* (and in the margin) but no alternative has been supplied, and at 85/25 (f. 37ᵛ), a cross has been put over *empirete* and in the margin; but even this double reminder failed and no English equivalent was supplied. Similarly, a cross marks an unfamiliar form, but no alternative is supplied, at 38/27 (f. 22ᵛ), *coruees*; 59/23 (f. 29), *forre*; 83/28 (f. 36ᵛ), *prous*; 93/21, 22 (f. 40), *uile, vile*; 130/22 (f. 51ᵛ), *cornardyes*; 155/3 (f. 60), *foru`i'ons*; 155/4 (f. 60), *soigneus*; 247/30 (f. 89ᵛ), *abandones*; at 157/8 (f. 60ᵛ), *paye, condecendre* have crosses over them and against them in the margin. Dan Michel seems also to have had doubts about *aperteliche* (96/33, f. 41). He put over it a cross which he subsequently erased. An obscure case occurs at 129/20 (f. 51ᵛ) where *ca arrieres* (not *ta arrieres* as Morris thought) has been written on an erasure with a cross above it and in the margin. Possibly the intention was to translate it. The erasure may have been of a translation subsequently considered incorrect.

2. A gap is left and the French is in the margin at 150/32 (f. 58ᵛ), *boune*; 159/18 (f. 61ᵛ), *quarteus*; 159/26 (f. 61ᵛ), *cerceaus*; 195/11 (f. 73), *forriers*; 244/30 (f. 88ᵛ), *foleant*; 250/36 (f. 90ᵛ), *mares*; 251/19 (90ᵛ), *fanc*; 253/8 (f. 91), *apeluchier*; 258/11 (f. 92ᵛ), *bougeren*. In these cases, it is probable that the gap was left for the insertion of the correct translation when this had been ascertained. Morris's tacit insertion of these French words gives a misleading impression of Dan Michel's vocabulary. Cf. *ine ariere* (f. 63).

3. Dan Michel has often been blamed for the literal nature of the translation. But the manuscript gives evidence that this was, in some cases, at least, deliberate. Thus at 22/21 (f. 18), *de ceus* is first translated *to ham* and then altered to *of ham*; at 24/18 (f. 18ᵛ), *par uaine gloire* is first rendered *of ydele blisse* and then altered to *be ydele blisse*; at 24/24 (f. 18ᵛ), *ou hautis* is translated *an heȝþe* and then altered to *to þe heȝþe*. At 55/36 (f. 28) *ine þo blisse* as a rendering of *en la gloire* is altered to *ine þe blisse*. At 202/8 (f. 75), *lykeþ god* is altered to *lykeþ to god* in line with *plest a dieu*. He also seems

to have given careful thought to the choice of synonyms in some passages. Thus at 27/24 (f. 19ᵛ), *fortune* is rendered *opcomynge*. This is then subpuncted and *hap* substituted. We may compare 30/19 (f. 20ᵛ), where *strif* is written and then subpuncted and *chidinge* written over the top. At 39/29 (f. 23), *barres e delais* is translated *strif and respit*; *strif* was then deleted and *wypsettigges* written in the margin. These cases seem to suggest that Dan Michel aimed to translate 'word for word' rather than 'sense for sense', but also that he gave some thought to his choice of words.

The same care has been expended on the orthography, a matter of some importance for the philologist. Thus we find at 8/22 (f. 13ᵛ), *schele* altered to *skele*; at 8/24 (f. 13ᵛ), *scele* altered to *skele*; at 16/6 (f. 16), *zeuen* to *zeue*; at 44/31 (f. 24ᵛ), *scriuens* to *scriueyns*; at 103/24 (f. 43), *boystose* to *boystoyse*; at 103/35 (f. 43), *streche* to *strechche*; at 186/32, 34 (f. 70), *faleþ* to *faileþ* (cf. *yfaled* 187/3 (f. 70)); at 253/3 (f. 91), *flechi* to *flechchi* and so on. Of particular interest are the cases where Dan Michel has corrected to characteristic spellings. As examples may be cited the following: *gode* is altered to *guode* (7/27, 53/26; ff. 13ᵛ, 27); *byualde* to *byuealde* (8/31; f. 14); *kuede* to *kueade* (10/27; f. 14ᵛ); *beleua* to *beleaue* (11/33; f. 14ᵛ); *sleuþe* to *sleauþe* (16/3; f. 16); *gratte* to *greatte* (25/12; f. 18ᵛ); *heued* to *heaued* (29/26; f. 20); *queantise* to *queayntise* (37/16; f. 22ᵛ); *leues* to *leaues* (59/8; f. 29); *nesseþ* to *nhesseþ* (94/32; f. 40); *yleue* to *yleaue* (112/4; f. 46); *stremes* to *streames* (121/6; f. 48ᵛ); *chyst* to *chyest* (126/33; f. 50ᵛ); *ssewy* to *sseawy* (127/26; f. 50ᵛ); *sseweþ* to *sseaweþ* (134/3; f. 53); *greten* to *greaten* (139/12; f. 54ᵛ); *godes* to *guodes* (on erasure) (139/28; f. 54ᵛ); *heape* to *hyeape* (139/33; f. 54ᵛ); *grete* to *greate* (152/16; f. 59); *þewes* to *þeawes* (153/14; f. 59ᵛ); *nesse* to *nesssse* (153/20; f. 59ᵛ); *lirni* to *lierni* (209/7; f. 77).

The evidence afforded by the corrections and additions to the manuscript is difficult to interpret. The corrections from a more usual to a more characteristically Kentish spelling could be taken to suggest that the scribe was copying from an exemplar which did not have the Kentish spellings. It seems to suggest, at least, that they were not part of the original orthographic system. They may thus indicate a regard for what Dan Michel thought to be correct orthography. Dan Michel's spelling of his own name with *th* while the copied texts gave *þ* for the dental fricative may also point to the text's being a copy only. Some of the manuscript corrections are also difficult to understand except on the assumption that Dan Michel was merely the copyist. Thus, at 252/30 (f. 91) *boue* is altered to *aboue* for no apparent reason. Some corrections may betray original non-Kentish features. Thus *þat* is altered to *þet* at 203/9 (f. 75ᵛ). At 54/1 (f. 27ᵛ) *ymaked* is altered to *ymad*. At 194/27 (f. 72ᵛ) *zaule* has the *a* erased, possibly because the original had *zoule*. The correction of *zych* to *zuych* at 260/31 (f. 93ᵛ) may point in the same direction, although, since there is a large number of cases in which a *u* is omitted, this example cannot be regarded as more than suggestive. On the other hand, the gaps in the manuscript, and the glosses and emendation of French words, seem rather to suggest an author's copy. If we assume that Dan Michel was merely the scribe of the text, then we must assume that he copied these features from an exemplar, an eccentricity not unparalleled in other manuscripts; or they may indicate an intention to emend his copy. All the author tells us is that the manuscript was written *of his oȝene hand*, which could mean as well that he merely copied it as that he translated it. Equally ambiguous is Dan Michel's statement, to be found in the concluding verses, that he 'made' the book (262/14–15).

11. *Marginalia*

(a) Numbers are often written in the margin to indicate the progress of an argument. Thus at 12/4, 7 (f. 14ᵛ); 17/30, 18/30, 19/11 (ff. 16ᵛ–17) and so on. Sometimes numbers are written over words in the text. Thus at 46/24 (f. 25), .1. and .2. are written over *auerst* and *efterward*; at 46/25 (f. 25), .3. and .4. are written over the two instances of *efterward*; at 46/26 (f. 25), .5. is written over *efterward*; at 46/32 (f. 25), .1. and .2. are written over *of herte*[1] and *of bodie*; at 46/32–47/10 (f. 25), the numerals 1–4 are written in the margin against the four steps of lechery of heart.

(b) *Nota* marks are frequent in the margins.

(c) There are numerous marginalia, reproduced by Morris in his shoulder notes. He has omitted only two: at 50/35 (f. 26ᵛ) *a strif* is in the margin and at 53/32 (f. 27ᵛ), the margin has *Nota a stryf*. Morris sometimes takes a marginal note as a heading. Thus, on p. 33 (f. 21) *þe peril of slacnesse* and *þe 6 poyns of sleuþe: þet brengeþ man to his ende* and on p. 57 (f. 28ᵛ), *þe zennes of þe tonge*. These are, in fact, marginal annotations and there is no reason to treat them differently from the rest.

12. *The author*

Dan Michel has been identified with a secular clerk whose
ordination as priest in 1296, to the title of St. Sepulchre's Priory
for female religious at Canterbury, is recorded in the Register of
Robert Winchelsey.[1] He seems to have been ordained deacon the
preceding year, 1295.[2] It would appear, however, from the colo-
phon to the *Ayenbite* that in 1340 Dan Michel was a brother of the
cloister of St. Augustine's and so he must, as Emden points out,
have entered religion some time before that date. There has been a
persistent tradition that Dan Michel was an Augustinian Canon,
but evidence for this seems to rest only on the fact that he was 'of
the Northgate'. Here Lanfranc had built a hospital, and opposite it
the church of St. Gregory, in which he placed Augustinian Canons
who were to minister to the hospital. But as a brother of St.
Augustine's, Dan Michel would have been a Benedictine monk
and cannot have been an Augustinian Canon.[3] Assuming Emden's
identification to be correct, Dan Michel must have been an old
man when he wrote the *Ayenbite*. If he was ordained a priest in
1296 at the age of 32, he would have been 76 in 1340, and even if
he had a dispensation to be priested younger, he must, at any rate,
have been about 70 when he wrote the text. This would explain
both the somewhat archaic nature of his script and the conservative
nature of his language. It is tempting to suppose that the verses at
the beginning of the work refer to himself as being *zeuenty zer al
round*. But the verses as a whole certainly cannot be taken as auto-
graphical, since they conflict with the explicit statement that he
wrote the text *of his ozene hand*. He could scarcely have done this
had he been, like the writer of the verses, *blind and dyaf and alsuo
domb*. It is much more likely that he was using a traditional verse
which had marginal reference to his own advanced years.

Our other source of information about Dan Michel is the list of
twenty-four books he gave to the library of St. Augustine's.[4]

---

[1] A. B. Emden, *Donors of Books to St. Augustine's, Canterbury* (Oxford
Bibl. Soc., Occasional Papers, No. 4, 1968), p. 14; *Reg. Winchelsey, Cant.*
(Canterbury and York Society, 52, 1956), p. 914.

[2] *Register*, p. 907.

[3] See *The Victoria County History; The County of Kent*, ed. W. Page (Lon-
don, 1926), ii. 211; David Knowles and R. Neville Hadcock, *Medieval Religious
Houses: England and Wales* (London, revised edn. 1971), p. 61.

[4] See M. R. James (1903), pp. lxxvii, 197–406, and catalogue nos. 69, 647,
649, 767, 782–3, 804, 841, 861, 876, 1063, 1077, 1155–6, 1170, 1267, 1275, 1536,
1548, 1595–7, 1604, 1654.

These include a number of scientific books as well as the usual patristic and didactic works. Three of these books have been identified as Cambridge University Library Ii. 1. 15,[1] Bodley 464,[2] and Corpus Christi College, Oxford D. 221.[3] The first of these contains treatises on arithmetic and astronomy and a treatise on the sacraments. Dan Michel proclaimed his ownership of the book several times. On the fly-leaf, written in Dan Michel's hand, are the words: *Liber fratris Michaelis de Northgate de Librario Sancti Augustini Cant*uariensis *Distinctio xiii gradus iiii. In quo continen*tur *subscripta etc. Liber cu*m *P*; to the right is a large P. Underneath is the list of contents. Facing the list of contents is a red monogram consisting of a large capital M surmounted by a capital I while above is repeated the information: *Collectiones cu*m *.p. dist*inctio *xiii^aG.^aiij* [sic]. The first folio of the text has the words *Liber michaelis de Northgate* in red and again on f. 3, the first of the text. This manuscript is thought to have been 'mostly written in the xivth century'.[4] The Corpus manuscript, formerly owned by John Dee,[5] and dated as xiith and xivth centuries,[6] has miscellaneous contents. It has the usual inscription, *Liber michael Northgate (m. Nor(t)hgate) Cum I Distinctio xiii^a gradus 3°.* Bodley 464 is dated circa 1318[7] and contains astrological and astronomical works. Most of this manuscript seems to be in Dan Michel's own hand except ff. 1–4 and the tables on ff. 4^v–57, although he may have written the annotations to these tables. He also wrote the inscription: *Cum G Almanach michaelis de Northgate de Libris Sancti Augustini Cant*uariensis.

Folios 1–67 of the Corpus manuscript may also have been written by Dan Michel. He supplied a list of contents in all three manuscripts and red section headings in CUL Ii. 1. 15 on ff. 3–7. In the latter manuscript he has copied a poem on f. 53^v and possibly the notes at the bottom of f. 20^v and the last line of a poem on 48^v.

---

[1] See James (1903), No. 1155.
[2] ibid. No. 1156.   [3] ibid. No. 1170.
[4] *A Catalogue of the Manuscripts preserved in the Library of the University of Cambridge*, iii (1858), 328–9. For the significance of the classifying letters see James (1903), p. lx.
[5] See M. R. James, 'Lists of Manuscripts formerly owned by John Dee', *Suppl. Trans. Bibl. Soc.* No. 1 (1921), 31. I am grateful to Mr. Andrew Watson for confirming this identification.
[6] See Coxe's *Catalogue* of Oxford College Manuscripts (Oxford, 1852), ii, MSS. Coll. Corp. Christi, pp. 87–8.
[7] *Summary Catalogue*, No. 2458.

He may also have supplied the notes at the bottom of the *Tractatus de Spera*.[1] These palaeographic details are of some interest as showing that Dan Michel not only owned but also copied and studied some, at least, of the manuscripts he possessed and later bequeathed to his house. They also show that he was a practised copyist and could well have copied a translation of the *Somme* rather than translated the text himself.

THE LANGUAGE OF THE *AYENBITE*

A. *Vowel Quantity*

The most recent study of the phonology of the text[2] points out that vowel quantity can be ascertained from spelling in only a limited number of categories: (i) the spelling *ou* indicated [u:]; on the other hand, the spelling *o* is ambiguous in regard to quantity. Not only does it spell [ǫ], [ǫ:], and [o:] but, in the French manner, [u], when Magnusson thinks it always represents a short vowel. But it seems that this could, occasionally, be used in Middle English for a long vowel as well.[3] There are, however, a number of corrections in the text which possibly support Magnusson's contention. Thus *dost* is emended to *doust* (108/11); *floreþ* to *floureþ* (28/20); *ho* to *hou* (20/24, 117/13, 14, 173/7); *hose* to *house* (110/23); *no* to *nou* (170/32, 217/13); *os* to *ous* (118/5, 212/3); *preciose* to *preciouse* (152/36); *þo* to *þou* (11/6, 21/11, 31/18, 270/25). (ii) OE [ea:] is spelt *a* when shortened.[4] (iii) OE [ɑ:] when shortened usually appears as *a* but sometimes as *o* by a later shortening.

(1) *Shortening*

The text shows shortening of Old English long vowels, as we should expect, before double consonants and consonant clusters

---

[1] I am indebted to Mr. N. R. Ker for confirming my identification of Dan Michel's hand in these manuscripts.

[2] Ulf Magnusson, *Studies in the Phonology of the 'Ayenbite of Inwyt'* (Lund Theses in English, I, 1971), pp. 37–8.

[3] Cf. Olof von Feilitzen, *The Pre-Conquest Personal Names of Domesday Book* (Uppsala, 1937), p. 54. It may be noted here that the spellings *ou* and *o* are sometimes preferred by the corrector. Thus *lhude* is corrected to *lhoude* (212/34) and *onbuȝsamnesse* to *onboȝsamnesse* (33/28).

[4] In Magnusson's opinion, *e* also indicates the shortening of an Old English diphthong. This matter will be discussed in the section on diphthongs.

other than *st*;[1] in words of three or more syllables; in weak stress; and, sporadically, in monosyllables, especially before dentals as in (*be*)*hat*, *grat*, *ssat*.[2] This latter tendency may, perhaps, be compared with the spellings *blud*, *gud*, *mud*, *stud*, *wud* in the lyrics of Arundel 248, a manuscript which seems to derive from East Anglia.[3] That these spellings do not simply indicate /o/ seems to be suggested by the use of the letter *o*, not *u*, for long open *o*, and for long close *o* in open syllables, as in *blode*, *glod*, *gode*, *maidenhod*, *rode*.[4] The most likely explanation seems to be a raising and shortening of long close *o* before a final dental.[5]

Certain irregularities of length require comment:

1. In some cases, spellings which seem to imply short vowels may be merely errors; others may be genuinely indicative of an original shortening due to lack of stress. Thus *abote*, (*al*)*paȝ*, *bote*, *copen*, *ore*, *os*, *þo*; but more doubtfully *moþe*, *þosend*. Probably analogical are the vowels in *grate*, *grater*, *kuade*.[6] The form *to*(*a*)*yans*, which occurs twice in the text, is probably an error, since the form can only be otherwise regarded as having shortening of Old English *ēa*. But the Kentish form would be *ongen*, not *ongean*. Wallenberg tried to show that Kentish had diphthongization after initial palatals[7] but his evidence is not convincing. The form *amote* (OK *ēmetan*) may be a loan-form.[8]

2. Spellings seeming to imply a long vowel in trisyllabic forms, or before double consonants, may have arisen by analogy in: *beloukþ* (from **belouke*?); *bouȝþ* (from *bouȝe*), cf. *boȝsam*, *boȝsamliche*, (*on*)*boȝsam*(*nesse*); *cheapfares* (from *cheap*); *deadlich* (from *dead*); *greatte*; *house*(*bounde*) (from *house*), cf. *hose*(*bounde*); *kueadhedes*, *kueadliche*, *kueadnesse*, *kueaduol* (from *kueade*); *leazinge*, where we

---

[1] Cf. *doust*, *cheaste*, *yeast*, *gost*. See Luick, § 352 (b) & n. 3; Jordan, § 23.

[2] Cf. Luick, § 388; Jordan, § 35, n. 2; S. Rubin, *The Phonology of the Middle English Dialect of Sussex* (Lund Studies in English, 21, 1951), 185; E. J. Dobson, *English Pronunciation, 1500–1700* (Oxford, 2nd edn., 1968), § 24.

[3] I am indebted to Professor E. J. Dobson for information on this point.

[4] See *English Lyrics of the XIIIth Century*, ed. Carleton Brown (Oxford, 1932), Nos. 45, 46, 47.

[5] Cf. Rubin, pp. 153–4; Flasdieck, however, thought that the spelling was probably a Gallicism (See 'Studien zur me. Grammatik', *AB*, xxxiv (1923), 314–9.

[6] See Magnusson, pp. 39–43. For *gra*(*t*)*ter*, *gra*(*t*)*teste* etc. see p. 42, n. 4.

[7] Wallenberg, p. 105, n. 2. For *ayeanward*, *toyeans* see p. 35.

[8] Cf. Luick § 363 (3). Wallenberg (p. 9, n. 2) supposes an OK form with *ā* instead of the usual *ē*; but it may have shortening of non-Kentish *ǣ*².

might expect shortening in a trisyllabic form, may have retained
length by analogy with the verb; *namecouphede* (by analogy with
coupe); *þreapni, þreapneþ, þreapninge* may be by analogy with the
noun or with the verb without the nasal infix. The latter is not
recorded in the *Ayenbite* but is well evidenced elsewhere in Middle
English;[1] *uoulhede, uoulliche* (from *uoul*); *uourtaʒte, uourti* (from
uour); *zoucþ* (from *zouke*). In the case of (*house*)*bounde*, (*neʒe*)*boures*
(cf. *neʒybores*), a secondary stress may have preserved the length of
the penultimate vowel.[2] The form *zouteres*, with its long root syl-
lable in a trisyllabic form, is unexplained. The form *beat* may be by
analogy with *beate* but shortening before dentals is not invariable.

3. There is a group of words in which OE *ā* does not appear to
have been shortened. These are (i) *holyiste, holyliche, holylaker,
holyhede, holinesse, hollyche, yholnesse*; (ii) *oʒeneres, oʒninge*; (iii) *oxi*;
(iv) *toʒte, ytoʒte*; (v) *betocneþ, betoknede, betokned, tocne, tocnen,
tokninge*. The first, second, and last groups could be by analogy
with *holy, oʒen*, and *token*. The second and last could also be
explained by the conjunction of stop and nasal in syncopated
forms.[3] The other forms are not so easy to explain. The forms
toʒte, ytoʒte have been thought to be due to the influence of the
final vowel which, on this view, inhibited shortening just as it
facilitated lengthening before lengthening groups.[4] They have also
been explained as by analogy with such forms as *zoʒte, þoʒte*,
which is perhaps the most probable explanation.[5] The form *oxi* may
be supposed to be due to the influence of an unmetathesized form
with medial *sk* which did not cause shortening. This was followed
by cross-analogy between *ăxen* and *ōsken*.[6]

4. The form *blepeliche* constitutes a special problem. An analogical
reformation on the basis of an association with *bleaþ* is suggested
by OED;[7] with *blessen, bletsian* by Dolle.[8] But both phonology and

---

[1] See *OED* THREAP *v.*   [2] See Magnusson, p. 40.
[3] And cf. Luick, § 352a. He points out that, in such cases, length is usually
maintained.
[4] M. Konrath, 'Zur Laut- und Flexionslehre des Mittelkentischen', *Archiv*,
lxxxix (1892), 159; Wallenberg, p. 238, n. 3.
[5] Cf. Konrath (1892b), 159; H. Jensen, *Die Verbalflexion im 'Ayenbite'*
(Kiel, 1908), p. 59.
[6] Cf. L. Morsbach, *Mittelenglische Grammatik* (Halle, 1896), § 63; Luick
§ 352d; H. M. Flasdieck, 'Die Entstehung des engl. Phonems /ʃʃ/', *Anglia*,
lxxvi (1958), 408–9.   [7] See *OED* BLETHELY.
[8] R. Dolle, *Graphische u. lautliche Untersuchung von Dan Michels 'Ayenbite
of Inwyt'* (Bonn, 1912), § 84.

semantic considerations seem to be against such an assumption. It is more likely that, as Wallenberg suggests, we have shortening in a polysyllabic form accompanied by slackening and lowering of the vowel.[1] It should be noted that the form appears in non-Kentish texts such as *William of Palerne* and *The Parlement of the Thre Ages* and cannot, therefore, be assigned to specifically Kentish conditions. Other cases of the lowering of *ĭ* to *ĕ* will be noted in the section on qualitative changes.

(2) *Lengthening*

(a) *Before consonant groups*

It is a characteristic feature of the *Ayenbite*, as of other Kentish texts, that lengthening before consonant groups does not occur in monosyllables.[2] Most of the exceptional cases can be explained as due to cross-analogy from other forms of the paradigm. Thus *bold*,[3] *doumb*, *grihound*, *strongliche*, *hond*, *long*, *ueleuold*, *wrong*[4] with unexpected vowel length; and *dombe*(?), *yhanged*, *stranger*, *wonde(n)* (?), *wonder* and derivatives(?) with unexpected short vowels. The derivatives of *hard* are peculiar in never showing lengthening. Various explanations seem possible. In spite of the occasional change of *er* to *ar* in the *Ayenbite* which will be discussed later, the consistency of the forms makes such an explanation unlikely here. It is possible that analogical shortening from the nominative, or from forms with a third consonant, are in question, but it seems

[1] Wallenberg, p. 35, n. 5; he compares *stefhede, stefliche* but these may derive, not from OE *stif*, but from a variant root. Cf. *OED* STEEVE; Konrath, on the other hand, compared KGl. *lecetere* and thought that a spelling for *bliþeliche* was in question (see M. Konrath (1892a), 172).

[2] This was first pointed out by Konrath (1892a), 50–1. For a more recent view see N. E. Eliason, 'Old English Vowel Lengthening and Vowel Shortening before Consonant Groups', *SP*, xlv (1948), 1–20. It should be noted that, although the change took place in the Old English period, it has been thought to have affected French loans. Thus *rond/rounde* perhaps, although the form *rounde* could be explained as due to the coalescence of vowels in hiatus in French (cf. M. K. Pope, *From Latin to Modern French* (Manchester, 1934), § 242); *ournemens* is another possible example although Dolle (§ 154) thought this might be an error.

[3] We should expect the forms to be *bald, bealde* as *ald, ealde*. The *o* may represent the rounded form of an analogical *ā*. Cf. Wallenberg, p. 18, n. 4. So, too, *ueleuold* below.

[4] Wallenberg (p. 288, n. 2) points out that, with one exception, *wrong* appears after a preposition and he thinks the forms are for *wronge*.

more likely that the forms have been influenced by French *hardi*, and probably also by polysyllabic forms such as *hardliche*, *hardnesse*, as well as by polysyllabic forms from French, such as *hardyesse* (French *hardiesce*) and the blend form *hardiliche*. The single case of *yhanged* against *o*-forms elsewhere may be simply an error, although Wallenberg suggests that it may be either a loanform or due to occasional weak stress.[1] The form *warningges* probably shows shortening in a trisyllable.[2] It may also be noted that the forms *rearde* and *uor(e)werde* (OK *reard, foreweard*) appear to have lengthening before a final vowel of secondary origin.[3]

A special problem arises with a group of words containing the clusters *rk*, *nk*; namely, *spearken*, *þonki*, *þonkeþ*, *yþonked*, *þonke*, *þonkes*. Much ingenuity has been expended on these forms. In regard to *spearken*, Konrath thought that it should be compared with forms such as *ceapfares* where he supposed the spelling with *ea* to indicate a somewhat fronted short sound.[4] But the form *ceapfares* is probably analogical. Wallenberg, on the other hand, argued that the root vowel was long because of the final vowel.[5] It is tempting to suppose that *spearken* should be connected with similar forms in place-names. Thus, for example, *Spercheforde*, 1086; *Sperkeford* 1205, 1213, 1214 etc. from Somerset and *Sperkeford* 1284 etc. from Hants.[6] The element *mearc* also shows a development to *merk* in place-names in southern counties, although this may be explained, as Löfvenberg suggests, by an antecedent form *gemirce*, *gemerce*.[7] But these place-names more probably owe their root-vowel to a spelling confusion between *er* and *ar* than to a lengthening of the root before the cluster *rk*.[8] Indeed the form *spearken* may well be an error, although a sporadic lengthening is not impossible on the assumption that we have a conditioned lengthening, depending perhaps on intonational variation.

[1] Wallenberg, p. 125, n. 3.   [2] Magnusson, p. 63.

[3] Wallenberg (p. 270, n. 2) points out that KS. also have *forewerde*. He suggests that the final vowel maintained the diphthong which was, however, finally shortened to *e* in reduced stress.

[4] Konrath (1892a), 52.   [5] Wallenberg, p. 222, n. 1.

[6] See H. Hallqvist, *Studies in Old English Fractured* ea (Lund Studies in English, 14, 1948), pp. 23–4, 27.

[7] See M. T. Löfvenberg, *Studies on Middle English Local Surnames* (Lund Studies in English, 11, 1942), p. 130; Hallqvist, pp. 21, 23, 26, 27, 30–6; Rubin, p. 160.

[8] Cf. von Feilitzen, p. 44. But they may witness a sporadic development of OE *ea* to *e*, since the *e*-spellings are not limited to cases before the group *rk*. Cf. Hallqvist, p. 50.

A similar explanation has indeed been assumed for the cases with medial *nk*. Morsbach argued that spellings in the Kentish Glosses such as *pinc, anbidinc, leccinc, wordlunc* were back-spellings resulting from a voicing of *nk* to *ng*.[1] To this view Wallenberg objected that in Middle Kentish we never find the spelling *nk* where *ng* is followed by a vowel; nor do we find the spelling *ng* in words with medial *nk* such as *drinke*.[2] But, in fact, KS show not only *kink* (38) but *offrinke* (34, 36).[3] Nevertheless, these spellings can as well be explained by unvoicing of final *ng* >*nk* as by voicing of medial *nk* to *ng*. There does seem to be some evidence, however, of the voicing of medial *nk* to *ng* in Middle English and this is not incompatible with final unvoicing.[4] That the *Ayenbite* has final unvoicing of *g* it is impossible to demonstrate.[5] It does, however, occasionally confuse *nk* and *ng* medially as in *dringþ, þengst, þengþ, (uor)þin(n)gþ*.[6] Rather than assume that the language had final unvoicing of *ng* to *nk* which is never expressed in spelling, and that these are back-spellings, it seems simpler to suppose that special phonetic circumstances affected the group [ŋk]. It may well be that Kentish and other South-Eastern dialects had at one period final unvoicing and medial voicing in the group [ŋk], [ŋg] so that the two were in complementary distribution and that vowels lengthened as a result of this tendency in Old Kentish were later shortened in a way analogous to later shortening before [ŋg]; namely because the conditions favouring lengthening were no longer maintained. If this is the explanation, the forms *þonki* etc.

---

[1] Morsbach, § 94, n. 2. Konrath (1892b, 156) assumes lengthening before *nk* + vowel.

[2] Wallenberg, p. 247, n. 4.

[3] References to the Kentish Sermons are to the text in J. Hall, *Early Middle English* (Oxford, 1920), No. xxiii.

[4] See K. D. Bülbring, *Altenglisches Elementarbuch* (Heidelberg, 1902), §§ 286, 489; Luick, § 369; E. Ekwall, *English Place-Names in* -ing (Skrifter utgivna av kungl. Humanistiska Vetenskapssamfundet i Lund, vi, 1923), 29; O. S. Anderson Arngart, *The Proverbs of Alfred* (ibid. xxxii, II, 1955), §§. 194, 206, 207; the Fairfax manuscript of Gower twice has *þong* for *þonk* as well as regular *thonk(e)*.

[5] But it does have examples of unvoicing of final *d* in *yhet, ysset, ofdret, ywent* whence *wente*. Cf. Wallenberg, p. 108, n. 2. The unique *ant* may be, as Wallenberg suggests, a scribal error (*s.v.*) but *saynd* for *saynt* is possibly a back-spelling again indicating that *d* was unvoiced finally; but for another explanation see p. 53 (e).

[6] Cf. *The Owl and the Nightingale*, MS. C, *þungþ* 1473; *þing(þ)* 1694; cf. *strncþe* 1226 for *strengþe*: Jensen (p. 9) suggests that *dringþ* shows the Kentish change of *nk* to *ng*.

would suggest that this shortening took place after the rounding of OE [ɑ:] to [ɔ:].[1]

(b) *Lengthening in open syllables*

It seems likely that the vowels *a, e, o* had been lengthened in open syllables in the *Ayenbite* but evidence is not easy to find. There is a small number of words with double spellings, namely, *bloode, graate, exaamened* but Wallenberg may be right in supposing that they are errors.[2] In any case, only two of the three examples could indicate lengthening in an open syllable as *bloode* has an original long vowel. A more promising area of investigation is the treatment of verbs in Class II where the ending is to some extent dependent upon the length of the root. In particular, the verbs *maki* and *waki*, as we point out in the morphology section, seem to give evidence of such lengthening. That there is virtually no spelling evidence of this lengthening is what we should expect in view of the retention of final -*e* in the text.[3]

B. *Vowel Quality*

(1) *Short Vowels*

The following short vowel phonemes, deriving mainly from English and French sources, may be assumed for the *Ayenbite*:

/i/	/u/	late OK	/i/	/u/
/ɛ/	/ɔ/		/e/	/o/
/a/				/ɑ/

At a high level of abstraction this implies the same pattern of contrasts for the *Ayenbite* as for late Old Kentish; but, at a lower level of abstraction, it may be assumed, as Magnusson points out,[4]

---

[1] *smertnesses* is perhaps by analogy with an MK noun or verb *smerte*; or due to a change of *ĕa* to *e*. It is not likely that it shows lengthening before *r*+*t*. Cf. Wallenberg, p. 219, n. 2.

[2] Wallenberg, pp. 38, n. 3, 87, n. 3, and 96, n. 2; so too the spellings *byyleaue, niymþ, uiyʒt,* and *wyiɲ* (cf. *purgatoriie, worþssipij*); for *graate* cf. also B. Sundby, *Studies in the Middle English Dialect Material of Worcestershire Records* (Norwegian Studies in English, 10, 1963), p. 175. The cases with short vowels are clearly errors.

[3] Cf. E. J. Dobson, 'Middle English Lengthening in Open Syllables', *TPS*, 1962, 124–48; 'Notes on Sound-Change and Phoneme-Theory', *Brno Studies in English*, viii (1969), 43–8; A. S. Liberman, 'On the History of Middle English *Ā* and *A*', *NM*, lxvii (1966), 66–71. It is possible that this lengthening was not yet phonemic in Gower. Cf. Dobson (1968), § 148, n.   [4] See Magnusson, p. 151.

that the *Ayenbite* differs from Old Kentish in that the short vowels are more open[1] and that the low vowel [ɑ] has moved towards a more front articulation and has possibly become [a].[2] The relationship, however, between the Old Kentish short vowels and the short vowels of the *Ayenbite* is not in every case a symmetrical one. There are two reasons for this: re-alignment of phonemes and analogy.

The re-alignment of phonemes is due to both combinative and isolative changes. Thus (i) (a) OK *eo* has been monophthongized and joined /e/ which subsequently became open. It is thus a member of the phoneme /ε/. The same development occurs after an initial palatal as in *yend, yeȝepe, yeue*.[3] (b) When followed by [χ] +consonant, however, it joins the phoneme /i/ if no velar follows as in *kniȝt, riȝt, uiȝt* etc. (c) In the combination *weor* it joins /u/ as in *work, wors(i), yworþ, zuord*,[4] etc. (ii) (a) OK *ea* has joined /a/ as in *ald, half, hard*, etc. This is also the case after palatals as in *chald, ssarp(nesse), yalp*. There is no evidence of southern smoothing after palatals.[5] (b) When followed by [ç], [k] +consonant, final [χ], it has joined /ε/ as in *eȝte, eȝtende, ulexe, wex, izeȝ*, etc. The forms *(man)slaȝþe* are probably by analogy with *slaȝe*. (iii) In some cases, OK [i] seems to have been lowered in the *Ayenbite* especially before *r* and thus joined /ε/. Thus *berne*,[6] *cherche*,[7] *(a)uerst(e)*,

---

[1] That this opening has taken place is suggested by the forms *layt* (OK *leȝet*), and *draye* (OK *dreȝe*).

[2] For discussion of the value of this vowel in Middle English see Dobson (1968), § 59. For French [a] + nasal group see pp. 39–40.

[3] For *yue* see p. 32. The form *yeȝeþe* is to be compared with KGl. *giogeþe* (cf. pp. 30–1). There is no need to assume with H. Cornelius (*Die AE. Diphthongierung durch Palatale* (Studien zur engl. Philologie, xxx, 1907), p. 174) that it is by analogy with OK *geng*. The *Ayenbite* form in any case is *yong*. In open syllables, an allophonic lengthening probably took place as we have already said.

[4] In *wors(i)* we probably have forms with exceptional breaking. We should, accordingly, posit OK* *weors(i)a(n)* for expected *wors(i)a(n)* (Cf. KGl. *werstum* and A. Campbell, *Old English Grammar* (Oxford, 1959), §§ 149, 201, 1). But *querne* (OK *cwěorn*) may be from a lengthened form *cwiorne* which gave rise to s new nominative *cwěorn*. Cf. Wallenberg, p. 199, n. 1.

[5] See Hallqvist, pp. 119–20, 122–5.

[6] This form must be treated with caution, however, since it may have been confused with the transitive *berne*.

[7] Cf. *cherche*, the regular form in Gower, Luick (§ 285, n. 1) suggested that the vowel in this word was rounded to [y] and then unrounded to [e]; but this seems unlikely. It may be noted that South-Eastern place-names show a good deal of variation in their spelling of this and other words with OE [i], *e*-forms being not uncommon. Cf. Cheriton (*PNK* 442–3); Dymchurch (*PNK* 462); Eastchurch (*PNK* 246); Ivychurch (*PNK* 479); Newchurch (*PNK* 470);

yerne.[1] Lack of stress, or early lowering of *i*>*ĕ*, may explain the forms *ywreʒe* (OK *ʒewriʒen*) and *seruese*; *smerieles* is probably from OK **smerels*, not *smirels* as Wallenberg seems to imply.[2] Some interchange of *e* and *i* may be due to the uncertain incidence of velar umlaut in Old English or to a retention of *ĭo* in Kentish. Thus we have *nime, nimeþ* but *nemeþ* occurs at 92/17; *hire* occurs beside *here* for the genitive pl. of the personal pronoun; *nykeren* and *ziker* show *i* where *e* might have been expected. Wallenberg[3] may be correct in suggesting that KGl. *ofsticōð, ficol* indicate that velar umlaut was not always carried through in Old Kentish before *k*; but we shall suggest later that Old Kentish had *ĕo* beside *ĭo*. Other cases of *i* where *e* might have been expected have been explained etymologically. Thus *ysliked* and *ripe* may have had original long vowels,[4] (iv) (a) OK *e+r* may have been lowered to *ar* in *harkni* so that, in this case, /ɛ/ joined /a/.[5] (b) on the other hand, [e] appears, in some cases, to be raised to [i] before palatals and *n*. Thus *nhicke*,[6] *onderuing*,[7] *zigge*.[8]

St. Mary in the Marsh (*PNK* 479); Upchurch (*PNK* 272); Woodchurch (*PNK* 364); for other counties cf. Löfvenberg, pp. 33–5, 57, 80, 139; Rubin, p. 63–4. It is difficult to ascertain how far these are graphic and how far phonetic. Cf. von Feilitzen, pp. 50–1.

[1] Cf. KGl. *irnn, irnð*. But the initial glide may suggest OK *eorne* in spite of the forms in KGl.

[2] Cf. Wallenberg, p. 215, n. 2; p. 219, n. 1; it is a possibility that *ywreʒe* might be by analogy with the past plural, *wreoʒon*; on the other hand, Wallenberg suggested analogy with an original *yzeʒe* (p. 289, n. 1).

[3] Wallenberg, p. 170, n. 1. On the other hand, *ssepe* (OE *scipe*) is common in Middle English. Cf. Wallenberg, p. 229, n. 1.

[4] See *OED* SLICK *v.*, REAP *v.* It may be noted here that *i* sometimes appears for *e* in unaccented syllables, as in the plural ending *-in* for *-en* or the verbal ending *-iþ* for *-eþ*.

[5] Wallenberg suggests an ablaut variant as the basis (p. 111, n. 1) but this is unnecessary. Early examples of the writing of *ar* for *er* are to be found in place names. Cf. Barksore (*PNK* 248–9); Dernedale (*PNK* 385–6); Luick, § 430; Jordan, §§ 67, 270; Rubin, pp. 43, 204; it is possible, however, that a spelling rather than a sound change is in question. See von Feilitzen, p. 44. It may be noted nevertheless that a change of *er* to *ar* occurs in Anglo-Norman. See Pope, § 1147.

[6] Luick (§ 379, n. 2) suggested that double forms existed already in Old English and cites German *Genick* as evidence of a mutated form. But we should expect a palatalized consonant. Wallenberg, on the other hand, assumes sound substitution (p. 169, n. 1). But a raising before *k* seems more likely. Cf. KS *wrichede* (59) and *Ste. Iuliene, rikenin* (S. T. R. O. d'Ardenne, *Þe Liflade ant te Passiun of Seinte Iuliene* (Liége, 1936); reprinted EETS 248, 1961), § 6.

[7] The forms *king, uorþingþ* may have had unrounding already in Old English. Cf. KGl. *hinraþ*; but Luick (§ 183, n. 3) suggests dialect borrowing. The *Ayenbite* also shows *litel* (KGl. *litel, litlum*) and *uorbisne* (cf. Wallenberg, p. 267,

Footnotes 7 and 8 continued opposite

In a number of cases, analogy explains the realignment of phonemes. Thus *atamed* (OK *atemod*) is from *tam*; *blake* (OK. *blec*) from *blacum*; *gate* (OK *get*) from Norse or, more probably, from the plural; *gledye* (OK *gladian*) from *gled*; *hate* (OK *hete*) from *hatian*; *leme* (OK *lim*) from *leomu*; *losteþ* has been influenced by *lost*; *nyteþ* is perhaps from *witeþ*; *prikieþ* (beside *prekieþ* from OK. *preokiaþ*) from *prikke*; *wem* (OK *wamm*) from *wemman*; *workeþ* from *work*; *uader* for the expected *ueder* may belong here. Wallenberg assumed the influence of an oblique case.[1] This seems more likely than that it is an ecclesiastical loan as Luick thought.[2]

Three other words, which seem to show a raised vowel in a palatal context, may be discussed here; they are *esssse*, *keste*, *wesse*. The form *esssse* was explained by Morsbach as showing the raising effect of the sibilant.[3] The normal Old English forms are *axe*, pl. *ascan*, *axan* where presumably *axe* is from *æsce* by analogy with the plural. The fronted form we might expect in the singular, *æsce*, is, indeed, recorded twice in Old English in an oblique case and is implied by the forms *e(a)scan* in VP. This is, no doubt, the ancestor of *Ayenbite esssse*.[4] It is not, therefore, necessary to assume raising. The form *keste* (ON *kasta*) has been variously explained. Luick thought that it was by analogy with verbs such as *lesten*, pa. t. *laste*;[5] but, as d'Ardenne points out, this is unlikely in view of the tendency in Northern texts, for example, to favour *e*-forms in the preterite. In any case, as far as the Kentish form of the pa. t. is concerned, it would be *leste* from OK *lēste* and not *laste* from *lǣste*. D'Ardenne suggests that both AB *keasten* and *Ayenbite*

n. 3) On the other hand, *þonneliche*, if correctly derived from OE *þynne*, has retained a rounded vowel. See, however, the note to this line.

[8] It has been thought that this form should be compared with KGl. *slicc*, *twiicce*, *wige*. For a different view of the alternation of *i* and *e* see Campbell, § 310 and n. 1. The form *uorzuylþ* may belong here but is obscure. Cf. Wallenberg (p. 271, n. 1). On the other hand, Senff (*Die Nominalflexion im 'Ayenbite of Inwyt'*, Jena, 1937, p. 72) is probably right in supposing that *zuyche* and *zueche* derive from OE *swilc* and *swelc* (cf. KGl. *swilc*) although Wallenberg (p. 298, n. 5) thinks that the final vowel inhibited raising.

[1] Wallenberg, p. 257, n. 1; cf. also H. C. Wyld, 'South-Eastern and South-East Midland Dialects in Middle English', *Essays and Studies*, vi (1920), 115; Rubin, pp. 31, 33; the Kentish Sermons also have *uader*. For *prodeþ* see note to 79/11.   [2] Luick, § 364, n. 2.

[3] Morsbach, § 87, n. 3. In favour of this view it should be pointed out that place-names with OE *hrysc*, OK *hresc* sometimes show raising before a sibilant. Cf. Rishfords (*PNK* 216–7); Rushmore Wood (*PNK* 226).

[4] Cf. Dolle, § 1, n. 2; for the OE see Bülbring, § 250.

[5] Luick, § 382, n. 2.

keste derive from an OE **cæstan* from ON *kasta* by sound substitution.[1] This seems more probable than the suggestions put forward by Wallenberg that we have the analogy of such forms as *wax* pa. t. *wex*; *wass* pa. t. *wess*; *late* pa. t. *lete* with transference of *e* to the present stem;[2] but it might be due to the raising influence of the sibilant as Morsbach thought.[3] The form *wesse* is not so easy to explain. Old English *wascan, waxan*, should have given *Ayenbite wasse* (or *wassse*) not *wesse*. Wallenberg proposed analogy from such forms as OK *wesc* (sb.) and the pp. OK *gewescen*; or compounds such as OK *weschus*; analogy from other verbs in the same class such as OK *hebban, hlehhan, sceppan* he also regards as possible.[4] But it seems more probable that Morsbach was right in thinking raising caused by the sibilant is in question.[3] We should, therefore, perhaps assume that a fronted [a] was liable to raising in certain palatal contexts in MK.

Finally some mention must be made of the forms *pans* and *dane*. It is used to be assumed that these forms were characteristic of the Essex and Middlesex dialect and Luick suggested that, in other areas, they were dialectal borrowings.[5] Wallenberg thought them church loans[6] but this is an unnecessary assumption. A good deal of evidence has been assembled to show that they are, in fact, of much wider distribution; that they are, indeed, South-Eastern. Zachrisson drew attention to examples in Kentish documents and thought that they represented local speech habits.[7] Förster, also, drew attention to such forms in the south and south-east and suggested that the *e*-forms were proper to rising intonation and the *a*-forms proper to falling intonation.[8] This would, of course, explain the sporadic nature of the forms in counties such as Kent. Löfvenberg likewise added to the place-name material for the south-eastern counties. Thus we find in Sussex and in Surrey at the same period forms such as *de la Blakefanne* (1341); *atte Danne* (1327); *ate Trandle* (1327).[9] It has also been pointed out

[1] *Ste. Iuliene*, pp. 159–61.   [2] Wallenberg, p. 135, n. 1.
[3] Morsbach, § 87, nn. 2 and 3.
[4] Wallenberg, p. 277, n. 4.   [5] Luick, § 363, 1 and n. 2.
[6] Cf. Wallenberg, p. 69, n. 4.
[7] R. Zachrisson, 'Notes on the Essex Dialect and the Origin of Vulgar London Speech', *ESt*, lix (1925), 349–51.
[8] M. Förster, *Der Flußname Themse und seine Sippe* (Sitzungsberichte der Bayerischen Akademie der Wissenschaften, Phil. Hist. Abt., 1941, 1), 470–8.
[9] Löfvenberg, pp. 15, 50, 214; cf. A. Mawer, F. M. Stenton, and J. E. B. Gover, *The Place-Names of Sussex* (EPNS, vi, 1929), p. xxvii; J. E. B. Gover, A. Mawer,

that in the late Old English period the mutation of *an* to *æn* spread far beyond the boundaries of Essex.[1] The evidence for Kent is certainly limited but it is interesting to note that, while a considerable number of names with the elements *fenn* and *denn* have forms in *e*, the *a*-forms are mostly to be found in the area of the North Downs, especially the Eastern end.[2] But whether we assume that the forms *pans* and *dane* are due to local variation in Kent, or to intonational variation as Förster suggested, it seems legitimate to suppose that they are genuine Kentish forms.

(2) *Long Vowels*

The following long-vowel phonemes (derived mainly from English and French sources) may be assumed for the *Ayenbite*:

/iː/	/uː/	late OK	/iː/	/uː/
/eː/	/oː/		/eː/	/oː/
/ɛː/	/ɔː/			/ɑː/[3]
	/ɑː/?			

As in the case of the short vowels, there has been some re-alignment of the Old Kentish phonemes. The problem of the OK diphthongs *īo*, *ēa* will be discussed later, but the following cases may be noted here: (i) *īo*: before [ç] + consonant has joined [iː] and then as in *liȝt*, *aliȝte* is shortened. (ii) *ēa*: before [ɣ] and [χ] joins [eː] as in *heȝ*, *eȝe*, *leȝe*.[4] The form *þaȝ* has reduced stress.

Two special problems arise in connection with the long vowels [eː] and [oː]. It seems that these sounds develop a glide before them in certain cases. Thus *hyer*, *hyere* (v.), *zuyetnesse*[5] and the French words *chiere*, *clier*, *clyerliche*, *clyernesse*, *clyerer*, *fyeble*. Similar spellings appear in other Kentish or partly Kentish texts;

and F. M. Stenton in collaboration with A. Bonner, *The Place-Names of Surrey* (EPNS, xi, 1934), p. xxiii; for *dane* forms in Sussex cf. also Rubin, pp. 45–51.

[1] See C. and K. Sisam, *The Salisbury Psalter*, EETS, 242 (1959), pp. 13–14.

[2] Cf. Dane Court (*PNK* 301, 373, 585, 603); Dane Farm (*PNK* 542); Denwood (*PNK* 383); Fanscoombe Wood (*PNK* 386;) High Halden (*PNK* 361); Little London (*PNK* 551); Lyddendane (*PNK* 425); Poppington Farm (*PNK* 305–6); Small Dane (*PNK* 292); Syndale Bottom (*PNK* 226).

[3] Cf. Magnusson, p. 152. My diagram differs from his, since I assume /ɛː/ from OK /eaː/. Whether or not one assumes that vowels lengthened in open syllables had become phonemic makes no difference to the long-vowel structure except in regard to /ɑː/.

[4] Cf. Rubin, pp. 187–90. For the forms *beaȝ*, *fleaȝ* see p. 34, n. 3.

[5] Wallenberg, however, regards this as a scribal error. See p. 298, n. 4.

for example, KH *dieð* (233/31); *sielpe* (233/28); *rien* (233/27) etc.;[1] KS *apierede* (7). The *Ayenbite* also shows occasional *i/y* spellings as *clyre*. A number of explanations have been produced for these spellings. Some scholars have thought that a spelling device was in question. Konrath, for example, suggested that the spelling *hi/hy* might sometimes be for [jh][2] or some weakened form of it; Dolle that, in some cases, at least, the purpose was to distinguish synonyms such as *hyer(e)* 'here' from *her* 'hair' and *here* 'to hear';[3] Wallenberg that they are on the analogy of French spellings such as *chere/chiere*.[4] Other scholars have tried to explain them by reference to a sound change. Thus Luick suggested that in Kentish [e:] was diphthongized after *h*, *cl*, the diphthong being, in the first instance, rising and then falling.[5] But, as Wallenberg points out, this does not explain the lack of diphthongization in comparable forms,[4] unless it be supposed that these too underwent the change. Flasdieck thought that, while some cases after *cl* might show French spellings, the native examples demonstrated an (East) Kent change of $\bar{e}$ (from mutation) $> \bar{\imath}\partial > \bar{\imath}$.[6] This theory, however, does not explain the form *hyer* which does not have mutation; nor does it explain the lack of the change in forms such as *depe*, *smech*, *strepe*, *leue* which do have mutation.[4] Dobson suggests that a change of $\bar{e}$ to $\bar{\imath}$ might be in question but he notes also the existence of *j*-glides in early Modern English and connects them too, hesitantly, with the *Ayenbite* forms.[7] It is impossible to reach a conclusion on these spellings without a consideration of comparable spellings for the OE diphthong $\bar{\imath}o/\bar{e}o$. But it may be noted here that the *Ayenbite* uses three graphs for OK $\bar{e}$ and for OK $\bar{\imath}o/\bar{e}o$; namely, *e*, *ie/ye*, *i*. But the spelling *ie/ye* is also used occasionally for *i* as in *tuyegges*, *hiealdeþ*, *hieaþ* for *tuigges*, *hialdeþ* and *hiaþ*. Such spellings are probably to be connected with Anglo-Norman spellings such as *chief/chif*; *chier/chir*, *matiere/matire*; *piece/pice*,[8] and it may well be

---

[1] *Kentish Homilies*, ed. R. Morris, *Old English Homilies* I. ii; EETS, os 34 (1868), 217–45.

[2] Konrath (1892a), 159–60.

[3] Dolle, § 75a.   [4] Wallenberg, p. 121, n. 2.

[5] Luick, § 405, 1.

[6] H. M. Flasdieck, (1923), 25–32; 'Ein südost-mittelenglischer Lautwandel', *ESt*, lviii (1924), 15–18 posits a similar south-eastern change.

[7] Dobson (1968), § 430, n. 2.

[8] Cf. W. Schlemilch, *Beiträge zur Sprache u. Orthographie spätaltengl. Sprachdenkmäler der Übergangszeit, 1000–1150* (Studien zur engl. Philologie, xxxiv, 1914), 36; F. J. Tanquerey, *Recueil de lettres anglo-françaises, 1265–*

that, while spellings such as *clyre* are purely Gallicisms, there was a spelling confusion of *i*, *ie*, *e*. It has indeed often been pointed out that the *ie/ye* spellings could represent [e:] because of the monophthongization of *ie* to *ē* in certain contexts. But it is equally true that the pronunciation [je:] was maintained in French into the later Old French period and the digraphs could equally well have represented the sound [je] or even [ie]. On these grounds it is likely that the spellings such as *hyer* represent a sporadic glide development.

Such a supposition is supported by the use of the spelling *uo* for *ō*. This spelling occurs in (a) *guo*, *buope*, *buones* all with *ǭ*; (b) *guod*, *guos*, with *ǭ*; (c) *guodes* (40/30) (gen. sg. of *God*).¹ Comparable spellings are to be found in other Middle English texts, most notably the Laud 108 manuscript of the *Southern Legendary* from the early fourteenth century. This shows many such spellings. Thus, for example, *bringue*, *finguer*, *guod*, *pingue* and so on.² Sporadic examples occur in other texts; for example, *guod*, *guodehede* in the Douce manuscript of *Amis and Amiloun*;³ *gwon* from *Sir Amadace*;⁴ *ygwo* from the Burton manuscript.⁵ As in the case of the *ie/ye* spellings, opinion has been divided as to whether the *u/w* graph is purely an orthographic device or whether it has phonetic value. Flasdieck suggested that, like the spellings in the Laud manuscript, the spellings in the *Ayenbite* are due to French orthographic habits.⁶ But Wallenberg rightly points out that we do not find, in the *Ayenbite*, the use of *gu* before *e* which is so characteristic of the Laud manuscript.⁷ Moreover, the spellings occur after *b* as well as *g* in the *Ayenbite*. It seems therefore, more likely that the spellings indicate some kind of sound development. Whether it is a vocalic or consonantal glide it is difficult to determine.

1399 (Paris, 1916). Many of these letters are associated with Canterbury. Cf. also *Boeve de Haumtone*, edited A. Stimming (Halle, 1899), p. 202; Pope, §§ 510, 513.

¹ But this may be an error. Similar spellings for *God* have been corrected by elimination of the *u* at 23/32, 102/2, 113/26, 209/33, 265/21.

² *The Early South-English Legendary*, ed. C. Horstmann, EETS, 87 (1887), 11/349, 33/131, 5/134, 12/378.

³ MS. Douce 326, ll. 16, 2393.

⁴ *Sir Amadace*, ed. C. Brookhouse (*Anglistica*, xv, 1968), l. 670 (p. 130).

⁵ *Religious Lyrics of the XIVth Century*, ed. Carleton Brown (2nd edn. rev. G. V. Smithers, Oxford, 1952), No. 87, l. 14. For other examples see Jordan, § 46; M. L. Samuels, 'Kent and the Low Countries: some linguistic evidence', *Edinburgh Studies in English and Scots* (ed. A. J. Aitken, A. McIntosh, and H. Pålsson, London, 1971), pp. 9–10.

⁶ Flasdieck (1923), 20–5.   ⁷ Wallenberg, p. 100, n. 3.

Konrath assumed the fracture of [oː] to [uo];[1] Luick that we have first a rising and then a falling diphthong;[2] Wallenberg also assumes the development of a diphthong.[3] On the other hand, Mařik supposed that the spelling indicated a consonantal glide in the cases of the open vowel, but a spelling for *ū* where the vowel was close.[4] Dobson also suggests that we have a consonantal glide favoured by the rounding influence of *b* and the high tongue position of *g*.[5] This seems to me much the most probable explanation, especially in view of the probable glide development before *ē*. Such glides may be observed in modern dialects.[6] It is, also, possible that we should assume a glide development to explain the forms *muekliche*, *mueknesse*, and *zuolʒ* (OE *sulh*). In regard to the first two, Konrath compared Shoreham *pustre*, *muknesse*,[7] and supposed that the *Ayenbite* forms had a rounded vowel [u] or [y].[8] But the Shoreham forms could have shift of stress and shortening and raising before a dental or guttural. Wallenberg compares *Ayenbite preus*, *proeue*, and *moyrdrer* (OF *mordreour*) to support the idea of a rounded vowel in *muekliche*, *mueknesse*.[9] But these are French loans and Dan Michel demonstrably takes French words into the text. The form *poer* at 170/19 is another example. They cannot therefore be regarded as evidence for the pronunciation of a word of Norse origin. The form *moyrdrer*, in any case, may well be an error for *mordrer*. It seems much more likely that *muekliche* and *mueknesse* have a labial glide after the initial labial. The form *zuolʒ* is surprising as we should expect *zolʒ* with Dan Michel's usual spelling of [u] by *o*. This form too may be an error. There is, how-

---

[1] Konrath (1892a), 66.

[2] Luick, § 405, 2; cf. Jordan, § 46.   [3] Wallenberg, p. 100, n. 3.

[4] J. Mařik, *W-Schwund im Mittel- u. Frühneuenglischen* (Wiener Beiträge, 1910), 83, 94–5. For raising of *o*: to *u*: in Middle English cf. Rubin, 148–54 and refs.; Dobson (1968), 158, and nn. 2, 4. But there is no evidence of it in the *Ayenbite* and Mařik's view cannot be sustained.

[5] Dobson (1968), § 431, n. 2.

[6] Cf. B. Widén, *Studies on the Dorset Dialect* (Lund Studies in English, 16, 1949), 54–5, 77. It may be assumed that the glide combined with the vowel to form a rising diphthong. Cf. Samuels, pp. 9–10.

[7] *The Poems of William of Shoreham*, ed. M. Konrath; EETS, ES 86 (1902), v, 130, i, 1034.

[8] Konrath (1892a), 168; cf. P. H. Reaney ('On Certain Phonological Features of the Dialect of London in the Twelfth Century', *ESt*, lix (1925), 343–5) for rounding of *eo* in the London area, Essex and perhaps Kent.

[9] Wallenberg, p. 166, n. 2. The forms *efterwuard*, *irchouon* (for *irchoun*) and *ouot* (for *out*) *spuoshod* are most probably errors although Wallenberg (p. 81, n. 4) thinks that the first of these shows a glide (cf. note to 175/29).

ever, to my mind, no doubt that the language of the *Ayenbite* shows both palatal and labial glides before the vowels $\bar{e}$ and $\bar{o}$.[1]

We turn now to the development of the OK diphthongs $\bar{e}a$ and $\bar{\imath}o/\bar{e}o$ in the *Ayenbite*. Let us consider first the treatment of OK $\bar{\imath}o/\bar{e}o$. This appears in the *Ayenbite* spelt *e*, *i*, *ye/ie* as in *leue* 'dear', *chise*, *chyese* etc. and initially in *yerne*.[2] Other Kentish texts show similar spellings as, for example, the Digby manuscript of the *Poema Morale* (PMD):[3] *ben* (14), *deuel* (104), *biede* (128); KS *deueles* (241), *frend* (221), *sike* (58),[4] *dieule* (61), *liese* (16); KH *chiesen* (219/20), *diercynne* (225/18); Sh *nides* (VII 439), *þyster* (VII 146). Opinion has varied widely as to the value of the *ie*, *ye* spellings. Konrath[5] argued that the medial spellings indicated a monophthong [e:]; the initial spellings, [je:]. Most scholars, however, have thought that either a diphthong or a glide development was in question. Heuser argued that the graphs represented rising diphthongs[6] and Morsbach that OK $\bar{\imath}o$, $\bar{\imath}a$ (and more rarely $\bar{e}o$) became [iə], [i:] and sometimes [e:].[7] Luick, on the other hand, thought that [io:] when medial became [ie:]. This diphthong had level stress and underwent a double development; either to a rising diphthong [i̯e] from which perhaps developed [e:]; or to a falling diphthong [i̯ẹ], [i̯ə] which developed to [i:] especially when final.[8] Magnusson also assumes that the spellings *ie*, *ye* stand for a diphthongoid [iə].[9] On the other hand, it has been claimed that they represent monophthongs. Thus Taylor,[10] and later, Wyld,[11] argued that the graphs were mainly spelling devices for monophthongs. More recently, Berndt supposed that the ultimate development was to [e:], although [i̯ẹ́] remained for some time medially,

---

[1] Cf. the place-name Little Gussels, about 8 miles south-west of Canterbury, which contains the element *gos* and has such early spellings (1334–8) as *de Gwosole* (*PNK* 379). For *bouerʒe* see note to 134/16.

[2] But see p. 22, n. 1.

[3] See J. Zupitza, 'Zum Poema Morale', *Anglia*, i (1878), 5–42. The citations from Kentish texts are selective only. Full lists appear in the articles of Konrath already cited.

[4] The form *sik*, however, is common in Middle English.

[5] Konrath (1892a), 63–5, 169–71; H. Sweet (*History of English Sounds*, Oxford, 1888, § 683) proposed 'diphthongic (jee)' in all positions.

[6] W. Heuser, 'Zum kentischen Dialekt im Mittelenglischen', *Anglia*, xvii (1894), 81. [7] Morsbach, § 9b (11b).

[8] Luick, § 359, 2. Cf. also the discussion in Wallenberg, pp. 309–11.

[9] Magnusson, p. 92.

[10] A. B. Taylor, 'On the History of Old English *eā*, *eō* in Middle Kentish', *MLR*, xix (1924), 1–10.

[11] H. C. Wyld, *A Short History of English* (London, 3rd edn. 1927), § 169.

especially after dentals.[1] Even more recently, a Lithuanian scholar has proposed a development from [io:] to [je:] to [e:] with the graphs *ie*, *ye* maintained traditionally for the monophthong aided probably by the French graph *ie*, *ye* for *ē*.[2]

Before these divergent views can be discussed, however, a fundamental point of Old English philology must be considered. According to Luick, late OK had only the diphthong *īo* and not the diphthong *ēo*.[3] On this assumption it is very difficult to explain the forms with *e* in Middle Kentish. But it is not clear that such an assumption is necessary. The evidence for this assumption is to be found mainly in the late Kentish texts in Cotton Vespasian D vi, the Kentish Glosses, the Kentish Psalm, and the Kentish Hymn.[4] It is true that the Kentish Hymn and the Kentish Psalm have the spelling *io* for the long diphthong except for the form *befreo* in the Kentish Psalm; but they also have spellings with *io* for the short diphthong which, according to Luick's view, should have a lowered first component in late Kentish. Thus we find forms such as *hiofena*, *hiofen(rices)* in the Kentish Hymn and in the Kentish Psalm *hiofenum*, *sioðða̅n*, *hiom*, *hiora*, *hiofenrices*, *mild-hiortnesse*, *hiorte*, *giogeða*.[5] The Kentish Glosses, on the other hand, have a number of cases in which the long diphthong is spelt *eo*. Thus *freondscipas*, *deohlum*, *beoð*, *forleose*, *steopfeder*, *-sunu*, *-dohter*. The evidence for the localization of Cotton Vespasian D vi is the press-mark which shows that it once belonged to St. Augustine's, Canterbury.[6] But the press-mark is not contemporary and, in any case, the texts could have been copied from an exemplar in another dialect; indeed, in the case of the Kentish Psalm, this is certainly so. It is perhaps interesting that the text which shows least evidence of contamination, the Kentish Glosses, is the text which shows most examples of the graph *eo* for the long diphthong. Some of these certainly may have undergone shortening but this cannot be the case with a form such as *beoð*. It is also possible that some of the forms are back-spellings, or, indeed, some

---

[1] R. Berndt, *Einführung in das Studium des Mittelenglischen* (Halle, 1960), p. 50. He supposes the *i*-spellings to reflect a development from [ie̯] to [ia̯] to [ī].

[2] A. Steponavičius, 'Sud'ba drevneanglijskikh diftongov (e̯a) (e̅o) (i̯o̅) v kentskom', *Kalbotyra*, xiii (1964), 225–34.

[3] Luick, § 260.

[4] See H. Sweet, *Second Anglo-Saxon Reader* (Oxford, 2nd edn. 1887) No. X; *Anglo-Saxon Reader* (Oxford, 15th edn. revised D. Whitelock, 1967), No. XXXVII; *ASPR*, VI pp. 87–8.

[5] Cf. p. 21, n. 3.   [6] See Ker (1964), p. 43.

may be West-Saxon forms. It seems, therefore, that the evidence for the universal raising of the first component of the OK long diphthong *eo* is somewhat ambiguous. It may also be noted that the usual development of the long diphthong in Kentish place-names is to *e*.

It is perhaps simplest to consider first the development of the diphthong when final. In the *Ayenbite* it is, with one exception, always to [i:].[1] This is, however, probably not the case in the earlier Kentish documents where it is also spelt *ie* as, for example, PMD *ibie* (66) (but also *bi*, *si*); KS *bie* (156), *hye* (87) (but also *hi* (8)); KH *besie* (231/21), *hio* (223/26) (but also *hi* (223/18), *isi* (241/27)); Sh *hye* (V, 195) (but also *be* (IV 126), *fre* (I, 1787), *by* (V, 41), *byvly* (V 280), *hy* (V 26), *ysy* (IV, 180)). On the evidence of these forms it seems reasonable to suppose that, when final, the diphthong was so tense that the development was either from [e:o] > [e:] > [i:] or, by a process of raising, from [i:o] > [i:e] > [i:]. On either assumption, the earlier Kentish texts witness an earlier stage in the development than the *Ayenbite* which has, in almost every case, reached the stage [i:]. It is, also, probably correct to suppose, as Steponavičius does, that the development is conditioned by a narrowing of the first component of the diphthong [e:a] which thus began to converge upon [e:o], [i:o].[2]

The development of the OK diphthong *ēo/īo* has sometimes been associated with a change of *īo* (*eo*) to *īe* to *i* posited by some scholars for the South-East[3] but the frequent *e*-spellings in place names make it difficult to assume that this was a universal development in Kentish.[4] The evidence can, perhaps, most convincingly be interpreted as follows: if we consider first the spelling of OK *ēo*, *īo* when final, we observe that in the Kentish texts antecedent to the *Ayenbite* the spelling is often with *ie* as well as with *i*.

---

[1] The subj. pl. *be* at 16/9, 10 may be an error or due to lack of stress as Wallenberg suggests (p. 32, n. 1).

[2] Steponavičius, loc. cit.

[3] Cf. Flasdieck (1924), 1–23; A. Mawer and F. M. Stenton, *The Place-Names of Bedfordshire and Huntingdonshire* (EPNS, iii, 1926), 149; E. Ekwall, *English River Names* (Oxford, 1928), p. 424; *Early London Personal Names* (Skrifter utgivna av kungl. humanistiska vetenskapssamfundet i Lund, xliii, 1947), 189–90; von Feilitzen, pp. 64–5; H. Bohman, *Studies in the Middle English Dialects of Devon and London* (Göteborg, 1944), pp. 136–7; Rubin, pp. 203–4.

[4] Some *ie*- and *i*-spellings occur but some of the *i*-spellings may be shortenings. See Deerton Street (*PNK* 279); Leaveland (*PNK* 286); Lewsome Farm (*PNK* 224); Liverton Street (*PNK* 224–5).

It might be argued that the *ie*-spelling was simply a rendering of *i*: on the analogy of the Anglo-Norman variation of *chief/chif* which we have already noted. But the lack of such spellings finally in the *Ayenbite*, when the same text uses them as the normal rendering of the OK diphthong medially, makes this seem unlikely. It thus seems clear that in the *Ayenbite ie/ye* do not normally render [iː]. Two points perhaps indicate that the graph *ye* is for [i̯eː] or [i̯e]. In the first place, it is so used initially in such words as *yerne*, *yerpe*;¹ in the second place, it is used in a number of instances for the product of OE *ēa* where, in my view, it interchanges with the graph *ya* which I take to represent [i̯a] or possibly [i̯e]. It may also be added that the comparative rarity of its use for OK *e*: suggests that it cannot be purely a graph for *ē*; further, if Dan Michel was familiar, not only with the Anglo-Norman pronunciation in words such as *chef*, but also with the central French pronunciation, he could just as well have used *ie* as a graph for [i̯e] as for [eː]. The further development could be indicated by the evolution of words such as *yeue* in the *Ayenbite*. This verb appears also in the form *yue* (cf. KS *iyue* (133)) and, in view of forms in earlier Kentish texts such as *forȝiet*, *ȝif*, *ȝieue*, *–ȝiete*, *ȝiet* (KH 235/5, 231/20; PMD 17, 21), it seems likely that the combination *i̯e* in Middle Kentish sometimes developed a glide after the initial palatal which then caused raising of the following vowel and loss of the initial palatal.² The final stage of the process is to be compared with the loss of an initial palatal before *i* seen in words such as *icicle* or in the place-name Ipswich or in the form *ildhall* recorded in London documents, for example, for *gildhall*.³ It may well be

¹ Magnusson (p. 92) argues that the graphs *ye/ie* cannot stand for [i̯e] because initial *i* spells [dʒ] in the *Ayenbite*. But initial *ye* certainly spells [i̯e] and the use of the graph *y* for [dʒ] in *yewes*, *yoyes*, *yyoyned*, *yesu*, *yesse* suggests that the graph could have more than one value. The use of the letter *g*, normally a spelling for a guttural stop, for [dʒ] would be another case of a double phonetic value for a single letter. Thus *ganglinde*, *goye*, *geus*, *gyewes*. These examples show that it was quite possible to use an English spelling with one sound value and, at the same time, to take over a spelling from French with a different sound value.

² Campbell (§ 300, n. 1) suggests that a different root is in question. The *i* could also have come from the third person present but here the *e* is frequently restored (cf. Campbell, § 733b). But in view of the early Middle Kentish forms, it seems more likely that we have a glide development. Cf. Flasdieck (1923), 32; Wallenberg, p. 106, n. 3.

³ Cf. Luick, § 750. For comparable developments in place-names cf. from OE *geoc*, Ickham (*PNK* 521); ? Icknor (*PNK* 231); from OE **g(i)edda* (?), Idleigh Court (*PNK* 37); from OE *geoguð* (?), Iffin Farm (*PNK* 502); from OE

that the development of Kentish medial *ie* from OK *īo* is ana-
logously from *ie* to *ii* to *i*:, the final stage being reached perhaps
in some words already in the *Ayenbite*.[1]

On the other hand, it is, I think, to be assumed that Old Kentish
may have had also the diphthong [e:o] in certain phonetic contexts
and that this developed to [e:] and thus fell in with OK original
[e:].[2] A special case is the development before *w*. In some instances
the development is conditioned by a shift of stress. Thus, on the
one hand, we get the forms *trau, traue* and *onzauwed* (OK *onsio-
wan*) and, on the other, the forms *uour, uourti, uourtaȝte, you,
youre* (cf. KS *furti* (266)). In the first group, the shift of stress has
given a diphthong [ou] which is then unrounded to *au*.[3] In the
second group the development is from [ou] to [u:], the difference
being due to lack of stress and, in the case of the numeral, the
initial labial.[4] In the majority of cases, however, the spelling is
with *ew* or *yew, iew* as in *trewe, chewynge, trieweliche, chyewe*.
Similar spellings appear in earlier Kentish texts. Thus, for example,
PMD *rewen* (170), *ȝeu* (75); KH *bereuseð* (245/11), *ȝeu* (223/20;
KS *biknewe* (8), *newe* (134); Sh *trewe* (V 207), *reuþe* (VII 454).
Wallenberg's view is that the spelling *ew* probably represents a
development of OK *iw* to *ew*.[5] Magnusson, also, on the basis of the
treatment of *iw* (OK *i*+*w*) in words such as *besnewed*(OK *besniwed*),
hewe (OK *hiwan*), supposes the value of the spellings *eu, ew* to be
[iu].[6] It is surely easier to assume that *w* favoured a low vowel and
that consequently the combinations *i*+*w* and *īo/ēo*+*w* became
[eu]. The two instances of the spelling with *ye/ie* Magnusson
suggests may represent conservative spellings or stand for a
conservative pronunciation; but I prefer to suppose that they
represent the development of a glide before the root vowel and

---

geld?, Ileden (*PNK* 557); Guildsted (from OE *geld*) had a form Hildestede
from 1198 (cf. *PNK* 231). For forms from elsewhere in the South-East cf.
PNSr. (Elm Bridge) p. 230; P. H. Reaney, *The Place-Names of Essex* (EPNS,
xii, 1935), (Ealing Bridge) p. 37; Löfvenberg, xliii.

[1] The use of *ie, ye* occasionally to spell *i*, already noted, may perhaps be due
to such a raising. It must, however, be remembered that some of the *i*-forms
may be due to shortening. Cf., for example, *uil*.

[2] Some of the forms with *e* may have shortening. This may be the reason for
the predominance of *e*-forms in place-names, since place-names are commonly
compounds and therefore peculiarly likely to contain shortened forms.

[3] Cf. Konrath (1892a), 179–80; Jordan, §§ 109, n. 2; Dobson, (1968) § 241.
For the shift of stress cf. KH *trowes* 223/20 etc.; Sh *trou* VII 604, *trowes* VI
662 etc.   [4] Cf. Jordan, loc. cit.; Dobson (1968), § 173.

[5] Wallenberg, p. 313; cf. Luick, § 399, 4 and 5.   [6] Magnusson, p. 97.

thus represent as elsewhere in the text [i̯e].[1] I, therefore, presume
that the OK diphthong *ēo/īo*: (i) joined the phoneme /e:/ (ii)
developed to a rising diphthong [i̯e:] (iii) joined the phoneme /i:/
when final and possibly in other cases (iv) combined with a
following *w* to form a diphthong /ɛu/ (v) when it underwent stress
shift, when under low stress, or after a labial, joined the phoneme
/u:/; otherwise the phoneme [au].

We pass next to the development of OK [e:a]. This appears in
the *Ayenbite* with the following spellings: (i) *ea* as in *dead, deaþes,
greate, teares*, etc. This is the majority spelling. (ii) *ya* as in *dyad,
lyaf, tyares*. (iii) *ye* in *hyeldeþ, lyesinges, tyeres, uaderlyese*; *ye*
initially as in *yere, yestre*. (iv) *yea, iea* in *dyead, dyeaþ, lyeaf, hieaþ,
tyeares*; initially in *yeast*.[2] Comparable forms appear in the other
Kentish texts. Thus, for example, PMD *breade* (92), *deade* (92),
deað (94); KH *æac* (221/9), *deade* (237/28); *hunitiar* (217/27–8),
niatt (233/25); KS *beleaue* (45), *great* (169), *greater* (267); *beliaue*
(41), *diadliche* (150), *griat* (201); Sh *deade* (I 884), *deaþes* (V 189),
forbead (VII 672), *great* (I 1949); *diaþ* (I 683), *groundlyas* (VII
767), *lias* (VII 767), *sennelyas* (r.w. *was*; IV 101). Numerous views
have been expressed as to the significance of these spellings.
Konrath thought that the medial graphs indicated [æ:]; the initial
graphs [jæ:]. In support of this view he adduces (amongst other
evidence) the rhymes used at 262/14–17, and the use of *ea* as a
graph for an original monophthong as in *year* (OK *gēr*); *yeaue* (OK
gefon); *leawed* (OK *lewed*); *sleaupe, sleauuol* (OK *slewþe*).[3] To those
may be added *cheake*. Heuser, on the other hand, writing a few
years later, posited also a rising diphthong [eæ] as the product of
OK *ēa*.[4] Morsbach thought that there were two diphthongs dis-
tinguished by having a lower and a higher first element; namely,
[ē̯ə] (ē̄ⁱə) and [iə] beside a monophthong [ɛ] or [e:].[5] Luick sup-
posed the development of a level diphthong which then split so
that it became, according to sentence stress, on the one hand, [ɛ̯a]
and then after dentals [i̯a] (spelt *ea, ya, yea*); and, on the other, [ɛ̯ə,

---

[1] Magnusson, loc. cit. The form *ieu* 'Jew' etc. belongs here and possibly
lheucliche.

[2] Forms with *a* such as *chapfare, grat, gratne, hauedzennes*, etc. are due to
shortening. See discussion pp. 14–15. Similar forms appear in, for example,
KH *brad* (233/8), *gelafen* (227/6), *grate* (231/13), *hapes* (219/9); KS *belaue* (67).

[3] Konrath (1892a), 61, 65–6. To these should, perhaps, be added *beaȝ,
fleaȝ*. The lack of digraph spellings in other words of this kind suggests that
smoothing took place in OK. Cf. Campbell, § 314 and n. 1 and p. 25.

[4] Heuser, pp. 76–7.   [5] Morsbach, §§ 9(b), 11(b).

eǝ] and then [e:] (spelt *ea, e*).[1] Wallenberg assumes, like Luick, that there was a stage at which *ea* was a level stress diphthong, especially after dentals, but, perhaps, also in other positions. In his view, the first element had a slightly palatal colour and was phonetically [i̥] or [i] and he posits the diphthongs [ea], [ia] (of which *e* was a reduction) and the spelling *yea* he assumes to be a compromise between *ea* and *ya* but admits the possibility of a triphthong [iea] of which [ie] would be a reduction.[2] The possibility of the spellings representing triphthongs was also considered by Hallqvist who supposed the spellings *ea, ya, yea, ye* to denote, at least medially, a falling series of diphthongs or triphthongs, in the latter case [ēi̯a] or [i̯i̯a] (ēi̯ǝ, i̯i̯ǝ) rather than [īea]. The spelling *yea* when used initially may indicate prosthetic *j* but medially *yea* must stand for a falling diphthong [ēa] [ia] [iǝ] or triphthong [ēi̯a] [i̯i̯a]. He is insistent that the spellings cannot represent a rising diphthong.[3] Berndt supposes a development [ę̄æ] > [i̯æ] > [i̯ǽ] > [i̯ę́] or [ji̯ę́] (spelt *ea, e*) which later became [ɛ:]/ except after dentals. The spellings *ia, ya* he regards as of uncertain significance.[4] Steponavičius assumes a development from [eæ] to [ɕæ], [i̯æ] to [jæ], [æ].[5] On the other hand, Magnusson assumes that we have the sound [eǝ] with variants [jeǝ] and [ja].[6]

It seems most likely, in my view, that the spelling *ea* represents a monophthong, [ɛ:]. In support of such a view a number of points may be made. In the first place, there is the evidence of the spelling, noted by Konrath, of OK [e:] by *ea*. The use of a graph proper to an open vowel for a close vowel may be due to the progress of the narrowing of open vowels before certain consonants in later Middle English[7] which led to spellings such as *cheat* and *seat*

---

[1] Luick, § 359 and n. 1. The spelling *ye* he thinks may represent [iǝ].

[2] Wallenberg, pp. 307–8.   [3] Hallqvist, pp. 76–7.   [4] Berndt, p. 49.

[5] Steponavičius, p. 229. The monophthong theory has also found support in recent years in *Early Middle English Texts*, edited by Bruce Dickins and R. M. Wilson (Cambridge, 1951), pp. 144–5 and *Early Middle English Verse and Prose*, edited by J. A. W. Bennett and G. V. Smithers (Oxford, 2nd edn. 1968), pp. xl–xli.   [6] Magnusson, pp. 88–91.

[7] See Dobson (1968), § 106 ff. Evidence of such narrowing may be seen in local developments of OE [e:a] to [i:] as Bincombe, Byncroft, Bynsted (Sx, Do) from OE *bean*; Chipstead (Kt) from OE *ceap*; (Grene)lif (Sx) from OE *leaf*; Helebym (cf. atte Byme) (Sx, Do); Holebym (De) with an OE *beam*; Ydy, Isteton (Sx) with OE *eadig, east*; Lykfoldbrigge (Sx) with OE *leac*; Quidhiwis (De) with OE *cwead*); Rydeston (De); Ride (Sx) with OE *read*. See Bohman, pp. 291, 292, 296, *PNK*, Hallqvist, p. 53, Rubin, pp. 169–73. Some scholars have assumed a development in these words of [e:a] to [i:e] to [i:] but they have

in Modern English. In the second place, spellings such as *an-cheaysoun* and *zeayde* for *ancheysoun* and *zeyde* suggest that *ea* was a graph for *e*. The rhyme *yzed*: *bread* (262/14–15) I take to show a late shortening in a monosyllable before final *d*. This also suggests that the OK diphthong has developed to the monophthong [ɛ:]. On the other hand, forms such as *grat* can best be explained as shortening of [æ:]. Lastly, the evidence for the development of OK *ēa*: when final, though very slight, suggests that this was to a monophthong. The instances are the infinitive *sle*, *slea* from OK *slean*. Clearly not much reliance can be put on these forms since *sle*, the only example, could be an error. Nevertheless, analogy with the development of OK *īo* when final may be held to support the view that when final OK *ēa* became [ɛ:]. It will be noted that while the OK diphthongs become increasingly tense, the short vowels, including those due to shortening, are further contrasted with the long vowels by their slack articulation.

Alongside the development of the monophthong, however, there was another development in Middle Kentish in which the first component of OK *ēa* appears to be raised as clearly indicated by the spellings *ya*,[1] *ye*, and *yea* (most simply explained as a graphic variant of *ye*). These, too, commonly occur in place-names.[2] They may be associated with the tendency to shortening, especially in conjunction with dentals, in which environment the *ya*-spellings are common. Later shortenings would produce [i̯e], spelt *ye*, *yea*. The development, in fact, is to be associated with the tendency to develop glide vowels which we have already noted in discussing the long vowels. But it should be noted that the development does not usually occur before original short vowels. Whether this tendency

also been regarded as showing spellings for close *e*. Some of the forms cited above, however, probably have shortening. For discussion see Löfvenberg, xliii, 7–8, 89; Bohman, pp. 121–9; also Hallqvist, pp. 53–8; B. Sundby, *The Dialect and Provenance of the Middle English Poem 'The Owl and the Nightingale'* (Lund Studies in English, 18, 1950), pp. 152–3; Rubin, pp. 185–7. The separation in Gower of rhymes with lengthening of *e* from rhymes with OE *ēa* supports the view that [ɛ:] was narrowed and thus closer than the vowel resulting from lengthening. But cf. Dobson (1968), § 148 n.

  [1] The spelling *ia* appears only in two loans, *diakne* and *triacle* which probably have /ia/.

  [2] Cf. Holebyem (De); Hyantona (Ox) (Hallqvist, pp. 19–20); Snotb(y)am (*PNK* 149); Olebiame (*PNK* 296). Eyastmunton (*PNK* 416) seems to be due to the develpment of a glide between the components of the diphthong unless it is merely a spelling error. There are also frequent spellings with *ie*, *ye* in Kentish but since these are ambiguous they are not cited.

coincides with the tendency to raise the first component of the diphthong it is difficult to say.[1] The development of the two long diphthongs is thus essentially the same. In both cases, there is a dual development; on the one hand, a gradual monophthongization with increasing tenseness of articulation as [i:o] (and perhaps [e:o]) and [e:a] converge on [i:] and [e:] respectively. Both show the same tendency to develop a form with a glide followed by a short vowel as an alternative to the tense monophthong. The development initially is also similar to that of OK [i:o]. Initial glides appear in *yalde*, *yealde*, *yeare*, *yeren*, and may, perhaps, be compared with forms in PM McClean[2] *ʒedi* (213), *ʒeplete* (70) (OK *eaplete*) in which the spelling with *ʒ* indicates that we have an initial consonant and not a vowel. These forms thus seem to confirm the supposition that the spellings *ya*, *ye*, *yea* indicate a development to the rising diphthongs, [i̯a], [i̯e:], [i̯e].

Finally, the development of OK *ēa* before *w* must be considered. The spellings here are (i) *ea* as in *deau*, *deawe*, *sseawy*, *þeawes* (cf., for example, PMD *veawe* (168); KH *feawe* (237/7), *unþeawes* (239/10); KS *feaue* (224), *seawede* (39); Sh *scheaweþ* (IV 149), *þeawes* (I 1516) (ii) *ew* as in *ssewy*, *þewes* (cf., for example, KH *forescewede* (227/24); Sh *yschewed* (IV 277) (iii) *ya* as in *dyau* (cf., for example, PMD *viawe* (167))[3] and (iv) *eau* as in *þeauwes*. In the case of the spellings *ew*, *eaw*, I should assume a graph for [εu]. The graph *yau* is a spelling for [i̯au]. The spelling *eauw* is probably an error.

It thus appears that the OK diphthong *ēa* produces the phoneme /ε:/ in the first instance but, by the time of lengthening in open syllables, it may have become tense. It also develops to the rising diphthongs [i̯a], [i̯e:], and [i̯e]. On the other hand, before *w*, as in the case of OK *īo/ēo* we have the development of a diphthong; in this case [eu] or [i̯au]. Thus the two OK diphthongs *īo/ēo* and *ēa* when followed by *w* join the diphthong phonemes to which we now turn.

[1] The form from KGl *smyagenne* is ambiguous. It may have *y* for *e*. In general, in Kentish *ia* is a graph for OK /io:/.

[2] See Anna C. Paues, 'A Newly Discovered Manuscript of the *Poema Morale*', *Anglia*, xxx (1907), 217–37. A consonantal glide before *e* appears in KH *ʒeie* (225/34, 233/22).

[3] Similar forms appear in place-names. Thus Biauford (De); Beauford (De) with OE *beaw*; Dyaudone (De) with OE *deaw*. See Hallqvist, pp. 18–19; Kentish examples are Byauesbergh; Byauesfelde, Biawesfeld; cf. *PNK* 558 ff., 565 ff., Hallqvist 21.

(3) *Diphthongs*

The *Ayenbite* lacks many of the diphthongs which arose in Middle English from vocalizations and glides. Thus (i) we have in general no evidence of diphthongs developing from secondary palatals. Thus *weʒe, neʒen, lyeʒe*. Exceptionally, however, we find *wraye* (OK *wreogan*); *playe* (OK *pleogan*). The form *wraye* is probably due to those forms which had a front vowel in Old English such as the present third singular. *Play(e)* may be due to such forms as *plegstow, pleghus*, as Wallenberg suggests.[1] Other analogical forms are *wayes* (OK *weogas*) from the singular; *ywryʒeliche*, on the other hand, with *ʒ* where we might expect an Old English palatal. In *weʒe* the guttural has been generalized throughout the paradigm. The same is true of *waʒe* (OK *weg*) where we might expect in Middle English *way*. The form is, in fact, probably from a strong feminine **wagu* or a weak feminine **wage*.[2] (ii) Glide vowels do not appear between a vowel and [χ], except, perhaps, in *nauʒt*.[3] Thus *boʒte, doʒter, eʒte, ynoʒ*, and so on. (iii) There is no spelling evidence that vocalization of [ɣ] has occurred. Thus *draʒe, daʒes, uoʒel*. An exception is *wyndowes*[4] which may have been imported, as Wallenberg suggests, from another dialect.[5]

The following diphthongs may be assumed:

1. *ǫi* from French loans. Thus *anioynj, anoy, anoyþ, anoylinge, asoyli* and so on. The forms *uile, vile* beside *oyle* probably indicate the diphthong *ui*.[6]

2. *ai* from OFr. *ai, ei* and from OK *ĕ+į* as in *day, eyr, pays*,[7] *tuaye, way*. Dan Michel has few *ei*-spellings, from which it may be inferred that the opening of short vowels and the consequent development of [ɛi] to [ai] has taken place.[8] In a number of cases, the *ai*-diphthong appears as *a*. Thus, for example, *fali, ymamed, master, prazeþ, uariste* and so on. In Wallenberg's view, these

---

[1] Wallenberg, p. 191, n. 1. Cp. Playstow (*PNK* 10).
[2] Cf. *OED* WAW *sb.*[1]   [3] Cf. note to 120/4.
[4] The form *uelaʒe*, also from Norse, has retained the guttural. Rubin (p. 223) points out that in Sussex place-names, the *gh*-spelling is maintained throughout the fourteenth century.   [5] Wallenberg, p. 280, n. 4.
[6] See Dobson (1968), § 256; Magnusson, p. 171.
[7] But the smoothed form *pes* also occurs.
[8] Much has been made of the spelling *crayme* (cf. Wallenberg, p. 65, n. 1). But it is probably a mere spelling variant resulting from the change of pre-consonantal *ai > ę* which facilitated the interchange of *ai* and *e* as spelling variants (cf. Pope, § 529). Godefroy records one example of *craime* for OFr *cresme*.

spellings represent a genuine phonetic reduction of the diphthong.[1]
It should be noted, however, that a considerable number of such
spellings have been corrected. Thus, *agrayþed* 14/18; *asayleþ*
157/27; *faileþ* 186/32, 34; ?*failinde* 32/18; *maydenhod* 228/15,
231/6; *maister* 239/20; *playneþ* 181/1; *plaiteres* 39/35; MS. *saileþ*
210/6; *uaire* 47/20, 110/13; *uayreþ* 95/23; *wayteþ* 253/29, 254/9;
zainte 241/16; all these words had simply *a* in the root syllable
before correction.[2]

3. The diphthongs [eu] and [ɛu] have already been discussed on
pp. 33–4, 37.

4. *au* occurs by unrounding in words containing OK *ā+w*, *īo+w*
as *beknauþ*, *blauþ*, *trau*, *zaule* and so on; in words with OK *a+w*
as *clauen*; in French words as *cause*, *defaute*; also Anglo-Norman
[ã]+nasal group as *adaunteþ*, *graunteþ*, etc. Pope argued that the
spelling *au* in such words indicated a monophthong and supposed
that the development was from nasalized *a* to a nasalized long
open *o*. In her opinion, such a view could be sustained by spellings
such as *daunyer*, *dauneour* for *donier* and *doneour* in Bozon and the
Ayenbite spellings *chonge*, *penonce*.[3] It seems unlikely, however,
that *au* monophthongized in the *Ayenbite* in view of the lack of
spellings with *o* for the diphthong arising from OK *ă+w*. More-
over, Dan Michel uses the digraph *au* for the unrounding of *ou*
which can hardly be other than [au]. It seems, therefore, reasonable
to suppose that the *Ayenbite* has a diphthong arising from the
development of a glide although this glide was often not expressed
in spelling as shown in *abandones*, *chambren*, *granteþ*, *sanguinien*,
etc. Whether these spellings indicate diphthongs or monophthongs
it is impossible to determine. The spellings with *o*, such as
auonci, *chombre*, *chongi*, *lompe*,[4] etc., are more difficult to explain.

[1] Wallenberg, p. 154, n. 1. According to Dolle (p. 90) *fali* etc. are due to the
influence of Latin *fallere*. The forms *master* (*mester*) are possibly genuine al-
though sometimes corrected in the manuscript. Cf. Luick, § 427, 4.

[2] Reduction of other diphthongs is even more problematic. Corrections of *e*
to *ey* occur in *eyder* 66/7; *meyster* 65/24; *scriueyns* 44/31; of *o* to *oy²* in *boystoyse*
103/24. cf. Wallenberg, p. 39, n. 2. It will be noted that the last two examples
occur in weak stress. The form *pes* beside *pais* is, of course, due to Anglo-
Norman 'smoothing'. *Zayde* and *zede* are in origin Anglian and south-eastern
forms. This is the only word which keeps both forms. *Mayde* occurs but not
mede while *rene* occurs at 130/1 as a rhyme word. In *regne*, *regneþ* the French
spelling has been maintained. Cf. Wallenberg, p. 202, n. 1; p. 294, n. 1.

[3] See Pope, § 1152.

[4] Here, perhaps, belong *plonteþ* in which OE *plantian* seems to have been

Wallenberg suggested that they might represent a reproduction of
French nasalized *a*;[1] Pope that they represent long nasalized open
o;[2] Bliss that they represent the shortening of [ɑ:], the product of
Anglo-Norman *a*+nasal.[3] The problem, however, is that the forms
with *au* and the forms with *o* appear from the first part of the
thirteenth century.[4] It is difficult accordingly to assume that they
represent borrowings at different stages of the Anglo-Norman
sound development. On the other hand, the forms with *o* seem to
offer no special conditions favouring shortening. It seems possible
that the *o*-forms derive from the central French nasalized *a*.[5] The
forms in *au* would then be Anglo-Norman existing perhaps along-
side forms without the glide containing a sound approximated to
the native vowel /a/. On this view, words containing French *a*+
nasal group exhibit the following phonemes in the Ayenbite: /au/,
/ǫ/, ?/a/. The diphthong phonemes in the *Ayenbite* may thus be
summarised as follows: /eu/, /ɛu/, /(y)au/, /ǫi/, /ai/, /ui/. To these
must be added the rising diphthongs already discussed, [i̯a],
[i̯e:], [i̯e], but it is not clear that these had phonemic status.

(4) *Consonants*

(i) *Long consonants*[6]

The *Ayenbite* shows long consonants medially after short vowels,
corresponding, in most cases, to OE long consonants.[7] Thus *asse*,

influenced by OFr. *plante* (cf. Wallenberg, p. 191, n. 3). The form *scoldeþ*
may give evidence of *o* as a spelling for /au/. But, more probably, Wallenberg
(p. 212, n. 3) is correct in assuming that the form is by analogy with such words
as have OE *a*+*ld*; the *l* may be of Norse origin. Cf. Luick, § 418, n.

[1] Wallenberg, p. 303.   [2] Pope, § 1152.
[3] A. J. Bliss, 'Vowel-quantity in Middle English Borrowings from Anglo-
Norman', *Archivum Linguisticum*, iv (1952), 142–5.
[4] Wallenberg (p. 303) suggests that the *o*-forms are earlier than the *au*-forms.
But his own figures (p. 301) do not really support this view. According to Luick
(§ 414, n. 2) the *au*-spellings appear in English and Anglo-Norman in the first
half of the thirteenth century.
[5] Cf. Wallenberg, p. 303; for the French development see Pope, § 667 and
refs.; the form *soui* may also be regarded as a borrowing from a French form
with a rounded monophthong from an earlier *au*. As Pope points out (§ 535),
there is some evidence that the change is earlier than the main body of evidence
would suggest.
[6] For the discussion of the exact phonetic nature of these consonants see
H. Kurath, 'The Loss of Long Consonants and the Rise of Voiced Fricatives
in ME', *Language*, xxxii (1956), 435–45.
[7] The spelling *ngg* which occurs, for example, in *acsingges*, *blondingges*,
warningges, is obscure. Magnusson (pp. 121–2) suggests that it might be a spell-

becleppe, habbe, sterre, strechche, þridde, ualle, wynne, wreþþi, zigge, and so on.[1] Long consonants seem also to appear in French loan-words such as *cellen, dette, fyebble* (beside *fyeble*), ?*markatte, robbi, somme,* and so on.[2] There are, however, a number of cases in which single writings appear. After an unstressed vowel, it seems likely that these indicate a genuine simplification of the consonant group. So, for example, *amide, habe(þ), hede, huane, huerine, wyleþ.* Other instances are not so easy to explain. Some, no doubt, are errors and, as such, will be discussed in the notes to the text.[3] There are, however, three consonant clusters which require mention here. They are cases in which the double spellings are in a minority even though the Old English antecedent may be supposed to have had a long consonant. These are the spellings *chch, sss,* and *ȝȝ.* The first of these appears in words which had a doubled consonant as *wrechche* (OE *wrecca*) but, also, in French loan-words as *flechchi, grochchinge,*[4] *techches.* But there are also a number of cases with single spellings such as *grochinge* (beside *grochchinge*); *wychen, wychecreft* (beside *wychche*); *wreche, wrechide* (beside *wrechche*); but the forms *esssse, nesssse, uisssse* are the only representatives of this long consonant when intervocalic.[5] The spelling *ss* after a short vowel appears in *bissop, englisse, nhesseþ, resse, vissere, wesse.* The spelling *ȝȝ* is used in *l(h)eȝȝe, neȝȝeboures* as compared with *leȝinge, lheȝinges, neȝybores, neȝebo(u)res.* In regard to the short spellings, Magnusson assumes that they are merely spelling inconsistencies[6] but it seems more likely that they are errors. As far as *ss* is concerned

ing for /ŋg/ as against /ŋ/. The forms with *gg* (as *blondigge, costnigge, grauntigge,* and so on) are probably errors.

[1] But, also, sporadically where they would not occur in Old English.

[2] But some French words have a double consonant in English corresponding to a single grapheme in French as *gabbeþ, cockou (coccou), contackes, felle, iuggi, lessoun;* these appear to have fallen in with the native pattern VC:V in contrast with forms such as *age, yobliged, rage, stages.* The form *outtrage* may be an error. Native words such as *quikke, smackes* which have a single consonant in Old English seem to have conformed to the same pattern. *Smakinde* beside *smackinde* may be an error. For *markatte* see *MLR,* xlvii (1952), 152–5.

[3] In some cases single consonants are corrected, however. Thus *alle* 34/13; *habbeþ* 41/23, 86/26; *hedde* 198/13, 251/13; *myddelguodes* 136/21; *stoppeþ* 257/28; *strechche* 103/35; *weddes* 102/15; *werreþ* 29/3; *wylleþ* 55/19, 165/17; *wyttes* 128/8. All were first written with a single medial consonant.

[4] Bliss ((1953), 30) suggests that the short vowel in *grucche* is due to levelling from the past tense.

[5] For the doubling of /ʃ/ after a short vowel when medial see Luick § 691; Jordan § 181.

[6] Magnusson, p. 115.

it may be, as Magnusson suggests,[1] that, since *sk* was not doubled in Old English, there was no phonematic distinction between the long and the short consonants and the expression in spelling was therefore erratic. But it would seem possible that the clumsiness of this spelling and of the spelling *chch* may have had something to do with their comparative infrequency.[2]

Long consonants also appear in words which in Old English had consonant lengthening before a liquid or nasal. Thus *briddle*, (beside *bridle*), *eddre*, *lheddre*, *little* (beside *litle*).[3] By analogical transference such long consonants also appear medially between vowels as in *eppel*, *middel* (beside *midel*), *gratter*, *smaller*[4] and single consonants appear before liquids and nasals as in *bridle*, *litle*, *midleste*. According to Kurath, the variation in spelling is due to 'the phonematically ambiguous status of phonemically long stops and fricatives in a position in which phonically short consonants did not occur.'[5] Thus, as Magnusson points out, 'the variant forms then become allomorphs with long and short contoid respectively'.[6]

Long consonants are shortened before consonants other than liquids or nasals. There is, however, a small group of instances which show a double spelling in a consonant group. Thus *effterward*, *kennd*, *onderstonndinge*, *ssriftte*, *ssriffþe*, *þinnge*, *þinngþ*, *worddes*, *yeffþe*, *zellue*. Magnusson suggests that these spellings may indicate that the preceding vowels are short; in other cases, that they are purely errors.[7] The forms *godsspellere*, *godsspelle* are, no doubt, to be compared with the spellings *sslaȝt* etc. discussed in a later section and do not belong here.

We may then conclude from the material that the *Ayenbite* probably had long and short consonant phonemes preserved, which is what we should expect in view of its retention of final *e*.

[1] Magnusson, pp. 111–12. But analogy may play a part. Cf. Magnusson, p. 124, n. 7.   [2] Magnusson, p. 112.

[3] The form *worddle* beside *wordle* may be an error.

[4] The comparatives *smaller*, *gratter* (beside *grater*) seem to owe their double consonants to doubling before *-ra*. These were then preserved, perhaps by analogy with other double consonants, after the conditioning factor was removed (cf. Magnusson, p. 119). The forms *greatte* and *gratteste*, *gretteste* (beside *grateste*, *greteste*) are probably analogical also.

[5] Kurath, p. 436.

[6] Magnusson, p. 118.

[7] Magnusson, pp. 59, 120. The forms *delles* (cf., 164/17 n.), *goddes*, *þrelles* may also be errors. For *kennd* see the note to 189/24; for *childrren* and *emerroydes* see notes to 77/1.

(ii) *The short consonants*

Most of the consonant phonemes offer no problems. We may assume 1. voiced and voiceless plosives /p/, /b/, /t/, /d/,[1] /k/, /g/;[2] 2. the affricates /ʧ/, /dʒ/; 3. nasals /m/, /n/, /ŋg/, /ŋk/ (see pp. 19–20); 4. liquids /l/, /r/; 5. semi-vowels /j/, /w/; problems arise, however, in connection with the spirants, the groups *hl*, *hn*, *hw*, and the sibilants.

(a) *The voicing of initial spirants*

Initial spirants in the *Ayenbite* have undergone southern voicing and the originally voiceless *f*, *s* are spelt *u*, *z*, except in the case of French loan-words.[3] The only exceptions in this category are *ulatours, ulateri, ulaterie* and *zaint* which may have derived from OE **flaterian, sanct*.[4] It is probably to be presumed that *þ* was also voiced initially and in the combination *þr, þw*, but the lack of a distinctive spelling makes certainty impossible.[5] In combination the position is more ambiguous. The labio-dental spirant was voiced before liquids as *beulaʒe, uleʒe, uless, urend*, etc. but *s* appears to have remained unvoiced in combination as in *slac, sleauþe, smal, snode, spade, stape, stede*. The spellings are, however, ambiguous as the letter *s* is not infrequently used medially in native words for what can hardly have been anything but a voiced sound. It must, therefore, be assumed that *s* could be used, no doubt under the influence of French, as a graph for the voiced sound. The same variation is observable in French loan-words as, for example, *desert* as against *dezert*. We even find *s* initially in *som(e)* from *zom* (OE *sum*) spelt as though the initial sound were

---

[1] Final unvoicing of *d* occurs occasionally. Cf. p. 19, n. 5. It should be noted that *d* represents not only OE *d*, but also OE *ð* in *ayder, berdone, huader, lodliche*; cf. Luick, § 724, 1; 725 & n. 1; but *wydoute, wydstonde* may be errors. Cf. Samuels, pp. 11–14. But his lists give no examples of these words. The apparent unvoicing in *plaity* (OFr. *plaidier*) is due to analogical reformation on *plait*.

[2] Magnusson (pp. 114–15) is, no doubt, correct in supposing that /g/ had assumed phonemic status.

[3] See Luick, § 703; but an earlier dating has been suggested by W. H. Bennett, 'The Southern English Development of Germanic Initial [f, s, þ]', *Language*, xxxi (1955), 367–71. He suggests it might be a continental development preceding the Anglo-Saxon invasion of England. Cf. Samuels, p. 8.

[4] See Wallenberg, p. 263, n. 3, p. 209, n. 1; the apparent exceptions, *uals* and *feure* are to be otherwise explained: *uals* is probably from OE *fals*; *feure* from a blend of OE *fefor* and OF *fieure*. Cf. Wallenberg, p. 89, n. 1, p. 258, n. 2. Magnusson (pp. 187, 207), suggests voicing of French loans, with the spelling retained from the French.　　　　[5] Cf. Luick, § 703 (3); Magnusson, p. 200.

identical with the sound in *summe* (Fr *summe*). The frequent spellings with *z* both initially and medially suggest plainly that the sound was indeed voiced in both these positions. In view of this statistically impressive testimony, it is probably best to assume, as in the case of *þ*, that where the graph *s* is used, it is merely either an error or a variant due to the French use of *s*, when medial, for the voiced sound. Whether this is also true of the sound in combination with another consonant is not so clear. The spellings *ssla3t, sslepe, ssmak, ssmelle, sspeke* may indicate a shift from [z]+ consonant to [ʃ]+consonant but the forms may be merely errors.

The solution of this problem depends to some extent upon whether the voiced sounds [z], [þ], [y̯] are phonemic in the *Ayenbite*. Magnusson argues that they are merely allophonic variants of the voiceless sounds and he, therefore, assumes that even the French loan-words have initial voicing although it is not expressed in the spelling.[1] This implies that the usual assumption, namely that the realization of initial *f* as a phoneme in southern texts was the result of French loans, is no longer relevant.[2] It seems odd, however, if this is the case, that the sounds are expressed in most cases by spellings distinguished according to language of origin. The use of *z* medially, moreover, in such words as *arizinges*, an obvious innovation on Old English usage, and one which could hardly be attributed to French influence, seems to suggest that *s* and *z* had been realized as separate phonemes although *s* was sometimes still used for the voiced sound on the analogy of both Old English and French spelling habits. It seems likely, therefore, that we should assume the spirantal phonemes /f/, /þ/, /s/ and /y̯/,[3] /ð/, /z/.

(b) *The guttural spirants*[4]

The *Ayenbite* apparently uses the symbol *3* for several sounds: 1. for [ç] as in *ui3t, li3t, e3te* etc.; 2. for [χ] as in *a3t, beca3t, do3ter,*

---

[1] Magnusson, p. 197. The odd spelling *stryfinge*, which might support this view, is probably, as Wallenberg suggests (p. 236, n. 3), due to the influence of *stryf*. But cf. *wefde* as compared with *weuede*.

[2] See Kurath, 439, n. 7; Magnusson, pp. 199–200.

[3] There is some evidence that the change of [y̯] to [w], well-evidenced in place-names, may have occurred in the *Ayenbite*. Cf. *(e)wangelist(e), wi3te, wyndeþ, wizage, wor* 121/2 (cf. *vord*). Cf. Wallenberg, p. 262, n. 1; B. Sundby, 'Middle English Overlapping of *v* and *w* and its Phonemic Significance', *Anglia*, lxxiv (1956), 438–44. For the dialect evidence see Löfvenberg, pp. 64–5; Rubin, p. 222.   [4] Cf. discussion in Magnusson, pp. 113–15, 197.

alþaჳ, ynoჳ, boჳ. These two must have represented, as in Old English, allophonic variants of the phoneme /χ/; 3. possibly a voiced sound [ɣ] as in *draჳe, uoჳel* and a sound which may have represented the voiced equivalent of [ç] in situations in which a secondary palatal would have developed, namely [ẏ]. So *weჳe, lyeჳe, eჳe.* That this last sound was not [i̯] is suggested by the fact that it is not spelt with *y*. It presumably represents an allophonic variant of [ɣ], itself originally an allophone of /χ/. The apparent ambiguity of the spelling in the *Ayenbite* suggests that all these sounds are merely allophonic variants of each other.[1] The interpretation of initial *h* is less certain. Magnusson argues that the initial sound is also /χ/, the distinctive spelling being due to the influence of French scribes, who identified this sound with their own initial *h*, but used ჳ for the unfamiliar spirantal sounds medially.[2] The realization of initial *g* as a separate phoneme he believes to have depended to some extent upon the fact that it slotted into and completed the bundles /p/–/b/; /t/–/d/; /k/–(/g/).[2] No such function in the phonemic pattern can be discovered for an aspirate which, in any case, may well be confined to initial position.[3] Nevertheless, the clear orthographic usage inclines me to think that the initial sound may be a distinctive phoneme /h/. Thus we have the phonemes /h/, /χ/.

The problem is associated with the development of the groups *hl, hn, hr.* The most usual view is that the spirantal element had been weakened and a voiceless liquid or nasal had developed and that these voiceless liquids and nasals were spelt *nh, lh.* Thus *nhicke, nhesseþ, lhade, lheaþe* besides forms with *n* and *l*. On the other hand, Dan Michel spells *raþe, raþre, reuþe,* etc.[4] Magnusson, however, argues that not voiceless sounds, but consonant clusters are in question. If, however, we assume that the initial sound is not

---

[1] See Magnusson, p. 115. The spelling *wykhed* for *wycked* is probably by analogy with the suffix *hed(e)*.

[2] Magnusson, loc. cit.

[3] Possible cases of the loss of initial *h*, or the addition of an inorganic *h*, may suggest that the initial sound was an aspirate rather than a guttural spirant. For example, we find *alfpeny, are* (182/16), with loss of initial *h*, and *hihere, his* with inorganic *h*. Initial *h* in French loans is also precarious. Thus *(h)eresye, (h)eretik(s), (h)eritage, hermite, ermitage, (h)oneste, onestete.* Sometimes *h* has been added by the corrector as in *halt* 146/19; *ham* 189/2; *hester* 216/8. On the other hand, *houre* is corrected to *oure* at 54/9.

[4] Such spellings for liquids and nasals appear elsewhere in Middle English. Cf. Orm's spelling *rhof.* Löfvenberg records *atte Nhutbyme* for Sussex in 1332 (p. 138). Cf. Luick, § 704; Magnusson, pp. 188–9, 201–3 for discussion.

/χ/ but /h/ it would seem more probable that the development is to voiceless sounds; sounds, however, which are rapidly voiced as is indicated by the normal use of *r* rather than *rh* in the text and the use of single *l* or *n* as well as *lh* and *nh*. I would, therefore, suppose that the opposition between the voiced and voiceless liquids and nasals was rapidly being neutralized in the *Ayenbite*. The group OE *hw*, however, is a different matter. Here the spellings are consistently *hu* and it is likely that we have indeed a consonant cluster rather than a voiceless sound [ʍ].[1]

(c) *The sibilants*

There is considerable inconsistency in the use of symbols for sibilants in the *Ayenbite*. The usage may be summarized as follows: (i) the letter *s* is used (*a*) in the combinations *sm*, *st*, *sp*, as in *smal*, *ston*, *spade* (*b*) to render OE final *sc* in *englis*, *ules*[2] (*c*) for the intervocalic sibilant in English and French words as *ariseþ*, *useþ*, *desert* (*d*) for OFr initial [s] as in *sacrifice*, *seconde* (*e*) for French palatalized [s] in *anguisi*[3] (*f*) for initial [s] as in *senne* (170/15), *set* (260/31). (ii) the letter *ʒ* is used to spell (*a*) an OE initial sibilant as in *ʒayl*, *ʒeche* (*b*) an OE and OFr medial [z] as in *ariʒinge*, *haʒard* (*c*) an OE initial [s]+consonant as in *ʒuift*. (iii) *ss* spells (*a*) OE [s]+consonant in *godsspelle(re)*, *sslaʒt*, *ysslaʒe*, *sslepe*, *ssmak*, *sspeke*, *ssmelle* (cf. *desspendour*) (*b*) OE [s:] as in *blisse*, *-nesse*, *messe*, *asse* (*c*) OE [sχ] as in *ssine*, *sso*, *sseþ* (*d*) OF [ŝ] as in *passion* and the verbal suffix *-iss* in *ioisseþ*, *marissi*, *punissi*; also in the suffix *-esse*[3] (*e*) for OFr [s] as in *lessoun*,[4] *dissiplines*. (iv) *ssss* is used to spell an Old English geminate as in *nesssse*, *uisssse*, *esssse*.[5] (v) *ce*, *ci* spell OFr [ŝ] and [s] as in *anguice*, *office*, *seruice*, *-cion*.

The interchange between *s* and *ʒ* in spelling is, no doubt, due in part to the conditioned distribution of [s] and [z] in this dialect; partly to the use of French *s* for the voiced sound; partly to traditional spellings of words containing a medial sibilant in Old English. The interpretation of the spellings with *ss* is more contro-

---

[1] Cf. Luick, § 704; Dobson (1968), § 414; and R. J. Vachek, 'On Peripheral Phonemes of Modern English', *Brno Studies in English*, iv (1964). There is however, a possible example of loss of the guttural component in *wet* for *huet* at 265/17.

[2] The spelling *sel* (189/25) for *ssel* is probably an error unless it is due to lack of stress. For the development of OE *sc* cf. Luick, § 691.

[3] Cf. Pope, § 315. For the form see note to 146/32.

[4] Cf. Pope, § 308 (i).   [5] Cf. Magnusson, pp. 110–12.

versial. It has been argued that the spelling represents [s] and such a view has the advantage that it reconciles the use of the graph in such words as *blisse, lessoun, sslepe* with its use in such words as *ssine*.[1] A second view is that the spelling represents a palatal [ŝ].[2] But there is no evidence of a phoneme [ŝ] and it seems that such a sound, if it ever existed in English, would be rapidly absorbed into either the phoneme /s/ or the phoneme /ʃ/. It seems unlikely, for example, that the spellings *cherice, cherisse, cherissheth* in Chaucer conceal three distinct phonemes /s/, /ŝ/, /ʃ/. It is more likely that in *cherisse* the spelling *ss* is simply taken over from French as a spelling for [is], the normal Central French derivative of [ŝ].[3] The view most commonly accepted nowadays is that the *ss* spelling represents [ʃ].[4] It may be noted, in addition to the points made above, that Dan Michel never uses *ssss* for words such as *blisse, asse* which he might have done had the graphs *s* and *ss* been interchangeable. Nor do we ever find *ss* initially in French loans.[5] Such an assumption implies that Dan Michel's spelling system is not consistent, but this can be demonstrated in a number of cases. It thus seems probable that the graph *ss* represents [ʃ] as well as [s:] The use of the graphs *s, ss* was not unknown in Middle English for the Old English [sχ] and was, no doubt, due to the lack of the sound in French. French scribes consequently equated the sound with *s* and devised a spelling for it which indicated this affinity. On the other hand, it is, perhaps, worth noting that in late Middle English there was a sporadic change of [s] to [ʃ] and this may explain the use of *ss* in such words as *russoles, parosses*.[6] The spelling of the French verbal suffix with *ss*, alongside the alternative pronunciations, suggested by Chaucer's spellings *cherisseth, cherissheth,* may also have led to spelling confusion. It seems

---

[1] Cf. J. M. Booker, *The French 'Inchoative' Suffix* -iss *and the French* -ir *Conjugation in Middle English* (Heidelberg, 1912), pp. 50–1. Booker thinks that the writing -*iss* for the French suffix spells [s]. But his reliance on rhymes makes the Kentish evidence particularly weak. Cf. Wallenberg, p. 216 on the use of *ss*+C in native words.

[2] Cf. E. Slettengren, 'On the Development of OE Initial *sc*', *Studier i modern språkvetenskap,* xv (1943), 45–50; C. T. Onions, 'An Experiment in Textual Reconstruction', *Essays and Studies* xxii (1936), 101.

[3] Pope, § 315; Pope points out that the palatalized sound remained longer in the north-east and east and became /ʃ/.

[4] Cf. Wallenberg, pp. 314–7; Flasdieck (1958), 361, 391; Magnusson, loc. cit.

[5] Cf. E. Björkman, review of Booker, *ESt*, xlviii (1914), 159. We may also note the spelling *noriches* in which the graph *ch* may represent /ʃ/.

[6] See Dobson (1968), § 373 and n. 3; Wallenberg, p. 203, n. 3.

reasonable, therefore, to assume three phonemes for sibilants: /s/, /z/, /ʃ/.

(d) Consonant groups

(i) Old English consonant assimilations are maintained in the *Ayenbite*:

1. in the pr. 2 sg. of verbs with syncope as follows: (i) (consonant +) *d, t, þ+st* appear as (consonant +) *-st* in *bezest, bist, est, onderstanst, prest, vinst, worst*; (ii) /χ/+*st* appears as *kst* in *izixt*;[1] Middle English innovations appear in *ss(l)ast* (56/8), (cf. KGl *slehst*) and *zentest* for OE *sendest* pa. t. 2 sg.

2. in the pr. 3 sg. of verbs with syncope: (i) (consonant +) *d, t, s* +*þ* appear as (consonant +)-*t* in *abit, ablent, agelt, aliȝt, anhet, arist, atwyt, azet, beat, behot, chyest, diȝt, dret, et(h), gret, halt, hat, kest*[1&2]*, ilest, let(h)* (for the forms in *-eþ* see pp. 98–9), *let lhest, liest, met, miswent, (mis)ret, oplet, slyt, smit, spret, ssent, sset, stant, todiȝt, ueth, viȝt, uint, uorbyet, uorlet, uoryet, went, wesst, wext, writ, zent, zet*; (ii) *k+þ* appears as /χ/+*þ* in *tobreȝþ, uorzaȝþ (uorzakþ)*.[2] Consequential back-spellings are *wecþ* (beside *weȝþ*), *wrikþ* (beside *wriȝþ*) and *zicþ* (beside *ziȝþ*)[3] (iii) exceptionally *adraynkþ* (iv) *þ+þ* appear as *pt* in *ssept (ssepþ)* (but cf. *ssefþes* for *sseppes*) (v) /χ/+*þ* appear as *ȝt* in *beulyȝt (beulyȝþ), draȝt (draȝþ), sslaȝt (slaȝþ*;[4] the forms *prittaȝte* and *zixtiaȝte* (OE. *þritiogoþa, sixtiogoþa*) represent Middle English developments. (vi) assimilation of a spirant and stop appears in *ssrif(f)þe* beside *ssrift(t)e*.

3. in the past tense and pp. of weak verbs (i) (consonant +) *þ, t, k, s, +d(e)* all appear as (consonant+)-(*t*)*t(e)* in *adreynten* (cf. *adrayngt, adreynct*), *agelt, aliȝt, anhet, beclepte, beclept, bisset, bezet, ydept, idiȝt, ykest, keste, ykuenct, lheste, ysset, ssette, þresten, ueste, westen, zette, yzet*; (ii) later developments are represented by the assimilation of *vd* to *ft* in *yblefte(n), ybleft (ybleued)*; *rd+d* to *rt* in *gerten, ygert, yhert*; *nd+d* to *nt* in *ybent, miswent, wente(n), ywent, zente(st), yzent*.

---

[1] Cf. Campbell, § 481, 4.

[2] Wallenberg (p. 242, n. 1) suggests that these forms may be analogical but this is unnecessary. Cf. Sievers-Brunner, *Altenglische Grammatik* (Halle, 1951), § 395, 5.

[3] The forms *wriȝþ* and *ziȝþ* represent OK *wrihþ* and *sihþ* (cf. Campbell, §§ 306, 310). The spelling *awrecȝþ* represents a blending of the two. Cf. Luick, § 718. 2.   [4] Cf. Sievers-Brunner, § 359, n. 9.

These may be due to analogical extension from forms where the consonant was final in the past participle. The form *prette* is anomalous. Cf. Wallenberg, p. 194, n. 2.

(ii) The simplification or assimilation of consonant groups; consonant loss

1. *l* is lost in *chid* (180/10), *haf, hyeade* (54/26, 62/4), *midehede* (133/8), *ofheadeþ* (39/4), *ssode* (127/21). Luick draws attention to the Middle English loss of *l* after *a* and *o*. He inclines, nevertheless, to regard *haf* in the *Ayenbite* as a scribal error.[1] The form *ssode* could be due to weak stress. It should be noted that forms such as *hyeade, mydenesse, ssode* are from time to time corrected but this may only indicate that the forms were regarded as slipshod. Nevertheless, it seems likely that most if not all of these cases, with the possible exception of *haf* and *ssode*, are errors.

2. *r* is lost or assimilated in *clegie* (16/5), *copereaus, efteward* (24/33, 110/4, 184/4), *meci* (189/12), *mosseles, norþene, ondestonde* (57/24), *ssappnesse* (232/17), *stanglaker* (17/17), *yesteneuen*. The form *mosseles* is well authenticated.[2] The forms *copereaus, meci, norþene, yesteneuen* appear also to be genuine although in some cases the evidence comes to light at a date rather later than the *Ayenbite*.[3] The other words are dubious although they may have lost the *r* as part of a consonant group. The form *stanglaker* is probably a mistake. It may be noted that compounds with *onder-* frequently have the *r* supplied by the corrector.

3. *t* is lost in *briȝnesse* (121/32, 266/23); *liȝliche* 207/8, 223/5, 249/8, *þos, þosses, ryȝnesse* (265/28, 36), *riȝuol(le)* (196/20, 269/23), *riȝuolnesse* (3/30, 29/13 etc.), *zuyfliche* (194/26); finally in *miȝ* (114/34, 141/25), *naȝ* (45/11, 156/4 etc.), *zayn* (12/13, 23). The forms *þos, þosses* are undoubtedly genuine.[4] The forms *briȝnesse, liȝliche, riȝnesse*, etc. and *zuyfliche* may show reduction of a triconsonantal group. The omission of a final *t* may be a sandhi phenomenon (cf. pp. 52–3); or it may be due to lack of stress. It may be noted that the form *naȝ* is often corrected as is *riȝnesse* at 264/2.[5]

4. *d* is lost in *guonesse* (244/17), *hanlinge* (46/28), *harnesses* (181/2), *milhede* (132/1), *worle* (86/22, 164/27, 241/12), and finally

---

[1] Cf. Luick, § 502, n. 3; § 770, n. 1.   [2] See *OED* MORSEL *sb.*
[3] Cf. Luick, § 738, 2, & n.; §§ 760, 772d.
[4] Cf. *EDD* s.v.; Dobson (1968), § 406.   [5] Cf. Luick, § 779; p. 53.

in *efterwar* (172/9, 175/34), *onderstan* (160/15), *pouzen*.[1] Corrections of *harnesse* and *worle* to *hardnesse* and *wordle* occur in the manuscript. *An* is common for *and* and, although often corrected, is probably a genuine form.

5. *þ* is lost in *onwornesse* (20/22), 196/34), *worssipe*, *wynimþ* (17/3), *wyoute* (37/34, 54/19 etc.), *wystondinge* (29/13). The first two forms are genuine;[2] the last three are probably errors. There are many such forms corrected in the manuscript. The form *sudyakne* (pl. *suþdeaknes*) is a special case. It shows the Anglo-Norman development of *z*+voiced consonant to *ð* and then to *d*.[3] This has then been lost in conjunction with the following dental.

6. *g* has been lost in *archanle*, *stranliche* (233/26); notwithstanding corrections of *strenþe* at 21/21, *þenþ* at 24/22, and *dinnetes* at 42/24, the form *stranliche* may be genuine.[4] In that case, Wallenberg is wrong in supposing *archanle* to be an error.[5]

7. *ȝ* is lost in *brytnesse* (82/1n., 142/4), *bryte* (156/20), *knyt* (168/24), *knythod* (161/34, 162/7), *myte* (267/17), *nat* (210/25), *nyt* (52/22), *ryuolliche* (265/29), *zoruollaker* (90/20). Notwithstanding the correction of *myte* at 82/12, the forms may be genuine and represent a French type of spelling.[6] *ryuollyche* seems to be an error for *ryȝuollyche* unless we assume that, after the loss of *t*, the guttural has become palatalized and then been absorbed by the root vowel. The forms *uorzuelþ*, *uorzuylþ* represent OK *forswelþ* and do not belong here.[7] The form *nat* is due to low stress.

(e) *Loss of final nasals*

After an unstressed vowel *n* is often lost except in the plural of weak nouns where it is always maintained. In verbal forms it is always lost in the infinitive, subjunctive plural, and past participle but often retained in the preterite plural, partly, no doubt, because of the functional load, since in weak verbs the nasal alone distinguished the singular from the plural. In the dative singular and plural of pronouns a nasal is often but not always preserved. The nasal ending is characteristic of pronominal as distinguished from adjectival usage. The reason is probably to be found in the

---

[1] Cf. Luick, § 764, 2; 779. Cf. p. 52. [2] Cf. Luick, § 779, n.
[3] See *OED* SOUTH-², SUBDEAN; Pope, § 1175 (ii), § 1177.
[4] Cf. Luick, § 764, 3. It may be an attempt to distinguish [ɲ] from [ŋg].
[5] Wallenberg, p. 14, n. 1. [6] Cf. Luick, § 57, n. 1; § 769, 3 & n. 1.
[7] For the form *neȝleþ* see p. 98, n. 7.

close conjunction of noun and adjective and the tendency of pronominal forms to occur in hiatus. Wallenberg notes that only the form *zeuen*, with a retained nasal, occurs in independent usage and is here in contrast with the form *zeue*.[1] Thus, in spite of the following aspirate a nasal has been deleted in *þise zeue heauedes* (*15/26*, 16/6). On the other hand, nasals have been deleted before consonants in *were þe* (13/6); *þise zeue gostes* (119/10–11); that the final nasal has not purely a phonetic function is suggested by the correction of *eȝen is* to *eȝe is* at 159/9; on the other hand, at 264/3 *eche his* is emended to *echen his*. Further details of usage will be found in the morphology section. It may be noted here, however, that the *Kentish Sermons* are slightly more conservative, as we should expect in view of the earlier date. Thus we find that a final nasal is sometimes kept in the infinitive of verbs and in the past participle although it is always lost in the subjunctive plural. In nominal and pronominal forms a final nasal is usually lost except in the plural of nouns. It is sometimes retained in the dative plural of nouns as *daghen* (252); *haleghen* (146). It also appears in pronominal forms before a vowel as in *ayen þan euen* (206); *toyenes þan euen* (235); the form *himseluen* used as a nominative (183) may suggest that the function of the final nasal was becoming primarily phonetic except in the plural of nouns. The usage with the possessives and indefinites in the *Ayenbite* is by no means consistent. Thus, while we find a strongly marked tendency to retain the nasal only before a vowel or *h*, there are a number of exceptions as: *non guod man* (32/15–16); *non zuo guod man* (33/2); *non drede* (63/9); *non uayr body* (81/8); *non zoþe lhordssip* (84/27); *non misual* (86/28); *non noblesse* (87/18); *non guod* (89/24, 91/16); *non comparisoun* (92/34–5); *non uondinge* (116/21–2); *non bost* (139/15); *non spousynge* (227/33); *non wantrokiynge* (265/1); *non lessynge* (269/12); *non uallynge doun* (269/12–13); *on god* (12/1); *at on tyme* (78/20);[2] *uor on paternoster* (102/25–6); (*þe*) *on leme* (147/15, 148/5, 12); *on mere* (185/34); *þe on stat* (122/16–17); *þe on uot* (149/2); *ine on stat* (155/23); *on time* (239/3); *on guod* (244/31); *on wyfman* (258/34); *þin riȝt hand* (146/36); *þin name* (107/9). The contrast

---

[1] Wallenberg, p. 293, n. 1. The form *petren*, if not an error, may also be a hiatus form. It occurs before *and*. The form *saren*, a post-prepositional form, however, occurs before a consonant. It is, of course, anomalous as a substantival form. Cf. *euen*, *marþen*, *tobyen*.

[2] In the case of *at on tyme* and *ine on stat* the forms may have been influenced by Fr. *un*, but the others render a Fr. *uns* or *une*.

between the forms *non* and *on* and the article *a(n)* may be that the former cases are stressed and therefore tended to keep the nasal in spite of the following consonant (cf. *morȝen, to morȝe*). At 202/8 *non chastete* is corrected to *no chastete*; at 186/9 *on body* to *o body*. It should also be noted that, while we find a number of instances of the retention of the nasal before a consonant, we find no cases of forms without the nasal before a vowel or *h*. The unstable situation is illustrated by the use of *euen* before a consonant and in hiatus at 113/11, 168/29, 191/25; *eue* before a vowel at 262/19.

(f) *Sandhi phenomena*

(i) Elision of a final vowel before a following vowel or *h* is common in the text; for example, *bot a* for *bote a* 72/2; *þe wangeliste* for *þe ewangeliste* (112/29); *yefþ of* for *yefþe of* (144/27); *clen* (MS clenę) *and* for *clene and* (159/13) etc. (Cf. *of anę epple (82/9)*). A final *e* has sometimes been restored by the corrector as in *huanne hy* (36/34); *uele oþre* (40/9); *yefþe of* (42/31); *zenne him* (51/18); *ssole yzi* (96/33); *oure herten* (98/19); *þe ilke orible bosyne* (137/22); *more ynoȝ* (137/28); *þane oþrene* (180/18); *guodness is* is corrected to *guodnesse is* nineteen times.[1]

(ii) Elision of consonants:

(a) *d* has been restored in *and* *ᵈemþ* (125/1); *d* has been lost before *z* in *þouzen ziþe* (75/18).

(b) *þ* has been restored in *makeᵇ þet* (31/7); *makᵉᵇ þe* (39/11); *byeᵇ þe* (47/35); *deᵇ þe* (111/2); *zayᵇ þe* (112/23); *conceyueᵇ þe* (136/7); *doᵇ þe* (212/32). The phrase *lyese þe* is for *lyeseþ þe* (40/3); *sterf þet* for *sterfþ þet* (70/26); *by þe* for *byeþ þe* (142/5n.); *com þer* for *comþ þer* (180/22); *conneþ þe* is perhaps for *conne þe* (46/18, 249/27);[2] *onderstonde þe* for *onderstondeþ þe* (74/28n.); *sterf þerinne* for *sterfþ þerinne* (202/15); *and de* is for *and þe* (162/17);[3] *zay saynt* for *zayþ saynt* (250/8).

(c) a dental spirant has been restored before *h* in *makeᵇ hy* (36/35); *nolleᵇ hise* (38/6); *spekᵇ huanne* (163/4–5); *sseweᵇ his* (237/5). Cf. *ylef ham* (60/27).

---

[1] *þane ylych* (64/13–14) may be for *þan ylych*. An accusative form has been erroneously substituted for the dative. The sense suggests that it is plural, but it could be singular.

[2] Wallenberg, p. 60, n. 1.

[3] But for another explanation see Samuels, pp. 11–13.

(d) a dental spirant has been lost before *t* in *bouʒ to* for *bouʒþ to* (246/34-5).

(e) *t* has been lost before a dental stop or spirant in *sayn simoun* (14/9); *miʒ do* (114/34); *miʒ þou* (141/25); *worþssipes þe* (188/23-24); *naʒ to* (196/27); *onderstans þet* (270/10); a *t* has been restored in *hue^t þet* (20/16); *loues^t to* (254/25); *t* has perhaps been assimilated to a following /dʒ/ in *saynd Ion* (88/13).[1]

(f) *t* has been lost before /dʒ/ in *sayn Ion* etc. (12/13, 23; 149/10; 180/16); *sayn Iude* (14/12); *sain Ierome* (210/7).

(g) *l* has been lost in *sse loki* (234/18). A similarity of articulation makes credible the assumption of a phonetic loss in these cases. Other instances are more difficult to assess. There seems no reason, for example, for the loss of *t* before a vowel in *naʒ o del* (175/21); *naʒ onlepiliche* (222/9); similarly, while the loss of final t before /dʒ/ is easily explicable, the collocations *sain bernard* (153/33); *sain gregorie* (199/34), *sterf ne* for *sterfþ ne*[2] (75/2) or *worþssipes god* (188/24), for example, are less so. These and similar cases may be colloquial forms arising from the conjunction of consonants; but they may be unstressed forms or merely errors.

The French and Latin sources

Since in the following discussion of the morphology of the *Ayenbite* reference has frequently been made to the French and Latin sources, it would seem appropriate to preface the morphology section by a brief account of these sources and their use by Dan Michel. By this means we can obtain some indication of their value as evidence.

The library of St. Augustine's, Canterbury, possessed in the Middle Ages two copies of the *Somme le Roi*. One of these belonged to Dan Michel himself. It is described in the late-fourteenth-century catalogue printed by M. R. James as follows:[3] *Liber Michaelis de Northgate cum titulo* Amen *in quo continentur | speculum sancti Edmundi Archiepiscopi Cantuariensis | liber quem compilauit quidam frater predicatorum ad rogatum philippi Regis francorum | Prouerbia diuersorum auctorum | Signa misse et quid significant | de penis purgatorii | Canticus dei genetricis Marie plenus pietate et dolore qualiter demonstrauit passionem dilectissimi*

---

[1] But cf. p. 19, n. 5.
[2] For the examples with *sterf(þ)* see note to line 70/26.
[3] See James (1903), No. 1548.

filii sui et | confessio Sancti Edmundi Archiepiscopi in gallico 2⁰ fo. *partient.* The second manuscript is recorded as *Liber Th. Abbatis in gallico quem compilauit quidam frater ad instanciam philippi Regis francie 2 fo. in libro* iors.[1] No manuscript has yet come to light which contains the items listed in the first of these manuscripts. The second, however, has been identified as Cotton Cleopatra A. v which on the second folio of the text of the *Somme* (f. 13) has indeed the word *iors*.[2] Nevertheless, this text, although very close to the text of the *Ayenbite*, is not that from which it was translated. Francis thought that Dan Michel's source was most probably either the exemplar or a copy of Cleopatra. It certainly seems probable that the manuscript belonged to an insular type represented by St. John's College, Cambridge, S. 30, a manuscript connected with Peterborough,[3] and by Ste Geneviève MS 2899. This manuscript has a colophon which runs as follows: *Cest liuere resingna Frere Jordan de Kyngestone a la commune de Freres meniers de Suthamptoun par la volunte le graunt Frere Williame de Notingham Ministre de Engletere dunt la commune ad sa lettre Lan de grace M⁰c⁰c⁰c⁰ xvij*.[4] This manuscript can thus be shown to have been in England in the fourteenth century. These two manuscripts share a number of errors with Cleopatra. Moreover, Ste Geneviève, like Cleopatra, lacks the section on the Branches of Mercy.[5] Both the similarity to manuscripts known to be connected

---

[1] James (1903), No. 1504.

[2] See W. N. Francis, 'The Original of the *Ayenbite of Inwyt*', *PMLA*, lii (1937), 893–5. James (1903, lxxii–lxxiii) argued that Abbot Thomas might have been Thomas Findon (1283–1309). Thomas Poucyn (1334–1343) and Thomas Hunden (1405–1419), however, were also donors of books and Francis thought the owner was Thomas Poucyn. Unfortunately, the date of the manuscript is unclear. Dr. Malcolm Parkes tells me that he would date it in the first half of the fourteenth century although, in his view, the dating would vary somewhat according to whether the manuscript was written in England or France. If this dating of the hand is correct, then the owner may have been Thomas Poucyn rather than Thomas Findon. Cf. Emden, pp. 3–4.

[3] See M. R. James, *Catalogue of Manuscripts in St. John's College, Cambridge* (1913), No. 256.

[4] The William of Nottingham referred to is probably the seventeenth provincial (1316–30?); cf. Beryl Smalley, 'Which William of Nottingham?', *Med. and Renaissance Studies*, iii (1954), 200–38. Jordan of Kingston may have been a friar at Kingston-upon-Hull. But he could have come from any of the numerous Kingstons scattered throughout English counties. His name is not recorded in Emden's Registers for Oxford or Cambridge.

[5] Paris BN 939 lacks some of the Branches but it is a late manuscript and possibly defective. St. John's S. 30 is incomplete and it is therefore impossible to tell whether it ever contained this section.

with England, and the demonstrable connection with Canterbury, justify the use of Cotton Cleopatra in the discussion of the morphology of the *Ayenbite*.

Moreover, the closeness of the translation makes such a procedure relevant. The following passages show the nature of the translation:

Le premier *com*mandement que dieu fist ⁊ *com*manda est cestui. Tu nau*r*as pas diuers dieus. Cest a dire. Tu nauras dieu fors moi. Ne aoureras ne seruiras. Et ne mettras pas tesperance fors en moi. Car cil qui met sesperance principaument en creature⸱⸴ pecche morteument. ⁊ fait contre cest *com*mandement. Tel sont cil qui aourent les ydoles. ⁊ font lor dieu de creature q*ue*le quele soit. Contre cest *com*mandement pecchent cil qui trop aiment lor tresor. Or ou argentz ou autres choses terrienes. Qui en ces choses trespassanz mettent tant lor cuer ⁊ lor esperance quil en oublient lor creatour. ⁊ laissent celui q*ui* touz ceus biens lor a prestez. Et por ce le deuss*en*t seruir ⁊ mercier. ⁊ sor toutes choses amer. ⁊ honurer; sico*m*me vous enseigne cis premiers *com*mandemens.

þe uerste heste þet god made / and het: is þis. 'þou ne sselt habbe / uele godes'. þet is to zigge / 'þou ne sselt habbe god / bote me. ne worssipie / ne serui. And þou ne sselt do þine hope / bote ine me'. Vor þe ilke / þet deþ his hope / heȝliche ine sseþþe: zeneȝeþ dyadliche. and deþ aye þise heste. Zuiche byeþ þe ilke / þet worssipeþ þe momenes. and makeþ hire god / of sseþþe / huich þet hit by.

Aye þise heste / zeneȝeþ þo / þet to moche / louieþ hire guod. gold. oþer zeluer. oþer oþre þinges erþliche. Huo þet/ ine þise þinges agelteþ: zetteþ zuo moche hire herte / and hire hope: þet hi uoryeteþ / hire sseppere. an leteþ him / þet alle þise guodes ham lenþ. And þeruore / hi ssolden him serui / and þonki / and toppe alle þinges / louie / and worssipie / alzuo þe tekþ / þis uerste heste.

It will be observed that, while rendering the French very closely, the *Ayenbite* is translated into a generally acceptable English as far as morphology and syntax are concerned. On the other hand, consideration of the two texts indicates certain problems inherent in such a comparison. For example, Dan Michel has rendered the French *trespassanz* by *agelteþ*; that is to say, he has not only

assigned the wrong meaning to the French, but has misunder-
stood the construction. In a number of such cases investigation
of other manuscripts suggests that Dan Michel was, in fact, only
following an error in his original. In other words, close though
Cleopatra is to Dan Michel's text, it is not the manuscript from
which he worked. Its evidence, therefore, though often illumina-
ting, must always be used with caution.

The text of the *De Custodia*, being much shorter, provides less
valuable evidence. The textual situation is much like that of the
Somme. The manuscripts that have been consulted are clearly
closely related in spite of some variation. The text from St.
Augustine's, Canterbury, now Corpus Christi College, Cambridge,
154,[1] is not in fact as close to Dan Michel's text as the continental
group, St. Omer, Bibliothèque Municipale 86; Tours, Biblio-
thèque Municipale 317; and Paris BN lat. 392, all from the twelfth
century.[2] As in the case of the *Somme*, the translation is close and
can throw useful light on the text and language of the *Ayenbite*.

Morphology
Nouns
The nominative

The inflection of nouns in the *Ayenbite* falls into two main
categories: a consonantal declension, marked by a zero ending in
the nominative, and a vocalic declension, marked by the ending
-*e* in the nominative. The vocalic declension comprised a large
number of feminine nouns including many which, in Old English,
had a zero ending in the nominative. Thus we find in this de-
clension:

1. Old English ō-stems: (*ded, ynoȝ)bote, cheaste, mede, (on)treuþe,
pine, rearde, sleauþe, þiefþe, uorwerde, uelþe, wombe, wonde,
wordle*(?), *zaule, ziȝþe, zorȝe* and the suffix -*inge*.[3] Exceptionally
half and *pors* remain in the consonantal declension.[4]

---

[1] Ker (1964), p. 40.
[2] As well as these manuscripts, Hereford Cathedral Library MS. P. I i and
Bodleian MS. Laud misc. 264 have been consulted. See Southern–Schmitt,
Memorials, p. 355.
[3] The form *makying* at 1/13 is a rhyme form.
[4] Senff (p. 15), however, points out that, according to Holthausen, *half* can
be masculine and feminine in Old English. The forms *dissuol, handuol* (120/1,
77/35) may belong here.

2. Old English *jō*-stems: *blisse, berdone, candele,*[1] *helle, reste,* *(uore)speche, wreche* (OE **wræc), zenne*[2] and the suffix *-nesse.* Exceptions here are *ssarpnes* (226/24), *polemodness* (265/20), *zuetness* (92/8), the first and the last of which are due to elision. It should be noted that there are many examples of manuscript corrections in which a final *-e* has been added to this suffix. This suggests either that Dan Michel's exemplar had the final vowels or that he regarded them as morphologically significant. On the other hand, the post-prepositional case of this suffix sometimes appears also without a final vowel. Thus *guodnes* (191/33), *mildenes* (231/14), and *pyesterness* (189/29). Senff assumes these forms to be errors,[3] but the first is more probably due to elision and the last to elision or to a misunderstanding of the construction. The second form may indeed be an error. There are thus only two genuine cases of the loss of final *-e* in this suffix. The nouns *heg,* *wen, yerd* have remained in the consonantal declension.

3. Old English feminine and neuter *i*-stems; *bene, (mis, ouer)dede,* *(be)heste* (OE *hæs), kende* (cf. *kennd* and note to 189/24), *myzte,* *yefpe.* But Old English *nied* has generally remained in the consonantal declension.[4]

4. Old English masculine and neuter *a*-stems, ending in a liquid or nasal, and liable to syncope, sometimes assume a final vowel. Thus *(arch)angle,*[5] *tocne;*[6] the form *vlindre* may belong here but its etymology is obscure.[7]

5. The Old English masculine *u*-stem *drugoþ* and the *i*-stems *scrift* and *(man)sliht* appear in the *Ayenbite* as *druzþe, ssrifte,*[8] and *(man)slazte.*[9] These may be by analogy with other abstract

---

[1] But influence from AN *candeile* is possible. Cf. Wallenberg, p. 46, n. 6. The use of *zy þet (cele qui)* as a relative at 102/7 may confirm the feminine gender.

[2] The form *zen* (262/12) is a rhyme form.

[3] Senff, p. 16.

[4] The one example of *niede* (201/5) may be an error but the accusative *niede* perhaps suggests a double inflexion. *(Be)heste* may be by analogy with words ending in *-te*. See *OED* BEHEST *sb.*

[5] The root vowel has been influenced by Latin *angelus.*

[6] Senff (p. 9) assumes extension from inflected forms.

[7] Wallenberg (p. 265, n. 2) derives tentatively from an OE **flinder* but it is perhaps rather to be compared, as Wallenberg admits, with Du. *vlinder.*

[8] Cf. Senff (p. 16) who suggests that *ssrifte* has become feminine. The feminine *hi* is used as a pronoun of reference at 172/7. As Senff points out, however, the pronoun could depend on the French *ele.*

[9] The root vowel is from the verb. Cf. Wallenberg, p. 156, n. 4.

nouns which, already in late Old English, had assumed a vocalic ending.

6. The Old English neuters *get* and *lim* have assumed the forms of the plural and appear as *gate* and *leme* from Old English *gatu*, *leomu*.[1]

7. Some nouns have a final vowel through the loss of a nasal. Thus *geme*, *mayde*, and *melle*. The suffix *-hede* may belong here, but it could represent a mutated form of the OE suffix *-had*, or be due to the influence of *-rede*.[2]

8. *drede* is derived from the verb and has no OE antecedent.

9. The Norse loans *boþe*, *rote*, *skele*, *sleзþe* (O.E.Norse **boð*, *rot*, *skiæl*, *søgð*) belong here. The word *skiæl* is neuter in Norse, but in the *Ayenbite* its qualifiers are masculine, but its pronouns of reference usually feminine. Senff suggests that it may have been regarded as a feminine abstract noun but this is difficult in view of its masculine qualifiers.[3] The reason for its inflection is obscure.

10. OFr nouns in *-e* and *leuayne*. *Prouesse* shows forms both with and without final *-e*.

In some cases, anomalies of inflexion may be due to a double declensional pattern in Old English. The variants *kuen*, *kuene* may go back to OE *cwen/cwene*, but *kuen* may be due to elision. The form *heuene* probably derives from an Old English weak type evidenced by the formula *heuene blisse* in Middle English. Similarly, *(ayen)wyзte* may derive from OE *(ge)wihte*.[4] We have already pointed out that *waзe* is probably from an OE **wagu* or **wage* and not from *weg*.[5] The vocalism of *snode* suggests that it is not from OK *sned* but may rather be from a weak form **snoda*.[6] Also probably from OE variants are *play* and *yefþe*. It has already been pointed out that OE *plega* should have given **pleзe* in the *Ayenbite*. The actual form may come from an OE **pleg*.[7] As for the form *yefþe*,[8] the simplest explanation is that it is a reformation

---

[1] The form *gate* is more credibly so derived than from Norse. Cf. Senff, p. 9. Cf. also p. 23.

[2] See Wallenberg, p. 45, n. 1 and Senff, p. 18, n. 1.

[3] Senff, pp. 9–10.   [4] See Senff, p. 18.   [5] See p. 38.

[6] At 111/3 this word has a masculine qualifier, *þane*. We have thus assumed a masculine Old English antecedent.

[7] See p. 38.   [8] The two occurrences of *yefþ* are before a vowel.

of OE *gefu* to **gefþu* on the pattern of other abstract nouns. The noun *anliche* is of dubious etymology but may belong here.¹

The consonantal declension derives mainly from Old English masculine and neuter nouns, excepting those that ended in a vowel, such as weak nouns and certain masculine *ja-*, *i-*, and *u-* stems.² This declension also included French nouns ending in a consonant. There are, however, some cases in which a word, having originally in Old English or Old French a final vowel, appears with a zero ending in the *Ayenbite*. Thus *arblast*, *bargayn*, *best*,³ *ewangelist*,⁴ *mostard*, *lhordssiþ* (but cf. *worþssiþe*), *serayn*, *scarlet*, *stech*, *yolk*.⁵ Elision may, however, account for *mostard*, *scarlet*, *stech*, and *yolk*. With the exception of *best*, which occurs three times, these cases, of which there is only one instance each, may be errors.⁶ Manuscript corrections may also be held to support this conjecture. Thus, at 32/7, *drede*¹ (acc.) was first written *dred*; at 42/31, *yefþe* was first written *yefþ* (elision); at 47/30, *dede* was corrected from *ded*; at 51/18, *zenne* from *zenn* (elision); at 54/34, *strengþe* (acc.) from *strengþ*; at 92/31, *blisse* (p.c.) from *bliss*; at 121/2, *guodnesse* from *guodness* (elision); at 148/12, *hede* from *hed*; at 169/2, *prouesse* from *prouess* (elision); at 183/27, *yefþe* from *yefþ* (elision); at 217/18, *uestinge* from *uesting* (elision). It is significant that there are no examples of the addition of a final *-e* to a word which we should expect to belong to the consonantal declension. They are all feminine nouns which would normally have a final *-e* in early Middle English. The only exception is the French word *prouesse* and this preserves a final *-e* from the French except at 166/18. It seems, therefore, more likely that the few cases which seem to show loss of final *-e* may well be errors.

The coincidence of the pattern discernible in the *Ayenbite* with the normal early Middle English pattern, as well as the evidence of the corrections in the manuscript, suggest that the final *-e* has still at least a lexical if not a morphological function.

¹ *OED* regards this form as an absolute use of the adjective OE *anlic*. Wallenberg, however, compares with OE *gelica*, *gelice* (p. 12, n. 2).

² It is to be noted that the form *liue* is an error. See note to 155/4–5.

³ At 182/12 this word is neuter; hence, perhaps, its transference to the consonantal declension.

⁴ This may be from Latin *euangelista*. Cf. Wallenberg, p. 87, n. 2.

⁵ The form *halʒen* is remarkable. It may be by analogy with forms such as *gamen*, *tacen*, *wolcen* as Wallenberg suggests (p. 109, n. 2).

⁶ Cf. Senff, p. 38–9.

We can therefore conclude that the *Ayenbite* maintains a twofold declensional system with the nominative marked either by zero or *-e*. The former declension includes those Old English nouns, mainly masculines and neuters, which ended in Old English in zero, or French words which originally ended in zero; the latter, the vocalic declension, comprises mainly Old English feminine nouns and masculines and neuters which in Old English ended in a vowel (or the oblique cases of which ended in a vowel), and French words which originally ended in a vowel.[1]

The accusative

The accusative of nouns is usually identical with the nominative except for *niede* (90/31, 34, 95/15) and *manhode* (19/13, 15, 118/29). In regard to the first, if we accept the nominative form *niede* as genuine, this may represent the normal accusative. The second form may, as Senff suggests, have become feminine and joined the vocalic declension;[2] or it may have been influenced by the suffix *-hede*. But, since the nominative is not recorded, it is impossible to determine its declension with any certainty. Further, the only instance of a p.c. in zero, a possible indication of the consonantal declension, is due to elision. If, as is possible, the nominative was *manhode*, the accusative then coincides with the nominative in the normal way.

The genitive

This usually ends in *-es*, or *-is*. The form *heuene* in *heuene blisse* may be the remains of the original weak ending in *-an*. Wallenberg assumes that the *e* is purely a link-vowel as it is in *housebounde*.[3] The nominative *heuene*, however, makes this improbable. An endingless genitive appears in *by myne uader zaule* (64/13).[4]

The dative and post-prepositional cases

The use of a dative case in *-e* is not common in the *Ayenbite* but is regular in *manne*. After prepositions, on the other hand, a final *-e* is very common. The consonantal declension has the allomorphs zero and *-e* in this position. Senff calculated that the

---

[1] But it must be noted that there is a large number of nouns for which only the p.c. is recorded. The declension of these cannot be determined.
[2] Senff, p. 20.   [3] Wallenberg, p. 120, n. 1 and p. 127, n. 2.
[4] For *þine nixte* see note to line 11/7.

proportions were about half and half except for original neuter *a*-stems.[1] In the vocalic declension, with a very few exceptions which are probably errors, the dative and post-prepositional case always ends in *-e*. The forms *bench* (130/3) and *rod* (1/2) (which as *i*- and *ō*- stems probably had *-e* in the nominative) are rhyme forms; and *quen* (216/8) and *manhod* (224/8) have elision. Both may, in any case, represent a nominative in zero. Surprisingly, however, *half* never has *-e* after a preposition. That the prepositional case was a morphological reality is suggested by the addition of the morph *-e* to a number of French words as *arblaste*, (*consayle*),[2] (*desspendoure*), (*dragoune*), *fornayse*, *gardine*, *gerniere*, *glotoune*, (*heyrone*), (*leuele*), *messagere*, *poynte*, *sautere*, (*sopiere*); others, like nouns of English origin, show both *-e* and zero. Thus *best*, *castel*, *fisicien*, *fol*, *lioun*, *pays*, *poynt*, *prison*, *sergont*; corrections to the manuscript also suggest that the final *-e* was not entirely otiose. Thus an *e* has been added by the corrector in *echedaye* (93/34), *strengþe* (117/11); *ate ende* (128/29), *messedaye* (175/32), *lompe* (186/28), *kueade* (188/7), *goste* (211/15).

The plural

The plural endings are *-es* (*-is*), *-s*, *-en* (*-in*, *-on*, *-n*), zero, and exceptionally *-e*. The distribution of the *-es/-en* endings appears to be without regard for the original declension. For example, the *-en* plural may appear in an original masculine *a*-stem as *crouchen*, *dyeulen*, *nykeren;* or in Norse words as *carten*, *roten*, *wyngen*; or in French words as *cellen*, *chaynen*, *chambren*, *lompen*, *stablen*, *tronen*, *werren*. The following words show only this plural: *bryest*, *broþer*, (*calketreppen*), (*carten*), (*cellen*), *child*, *chombre*, (*clauen*), *cou*, (*crouche*), *dyeuel*, *doȝter*, *eare*, *eȝe*, *aye*, (for *halȝen* see p. 61), (*hennen*), *hand*, (*ympen*), *kempe*, *lamb*, (*lenden*),[3] (*lippen*), *lompe*, *messe*, *moder*, (*net*(*t*)*len*), *nhicke*, (*nykeren*), *oxe*, (*reuen*), *rote*, *snode*, (*spearken*), (*stablen*), *sterre*, *tocne*, *tonne*, *trone*, (*ueperen*), *uleȝe*, *uo*, *welle*, *wychche*, (*wyngen*), *wyse*, *wodewe*, *wombe*, *wonde*, *wrechche*, *zoster*; the following have both *-en* and *-es* plurals: *bene*, *blisse*, (*chaynen*), *cherche*, *dyacne*, *drope*, *eddre* (cf. 203/18 n.), *elmesse*, *heaued*, *herte* 'heart', *pine*, *tonge*, *uorbisne*, *werre*, *zaule*, *zenne*, *zide*.

---

[1] For masculine *a*-stems he calculated the proportion of forms with *-e* as 327:301; for neuters, 471:172; for neuter *ja*-stems, 39:33; for *wa*- masculines, 1:1; for masculine long *i*-stems, 7:4; for neuter long *i*-stems, 24:3.

[2] Words in brackets are found only in the oblique case.

[3] This form is a reduction of OE *lendenu*.

Most nouns showing an -en plural either belong to the vocalic declension or had, in OE, a weak plural or a plural ending in a vowel.

The majority of nouns in the *Ayenbite*, whether of French or English origin, have a plural ending in -es. In French loan-words, nouns spelt with a final -e end in -es except in the case of *heretike*, pl. *eretiks*. Consonantal nouns show -es and-s. Dan Michel also uses a number of French-style plural forms. French nouns ending in *d* or *t* have a plural in *s*. Thus *condwys, consentemens* (see list on p. ix), *enchauntemens, lipars, momenes* (beside *momenettes*),[1] *ournemens, poyns, prelas* (beside *prelates*), *presens, prouos* (beside *prouostes*),[2] *ribaus, sacremens, sergons, seruons, stas* (beside *states*), *tyrans, tornemens, truons, uestemens*.[3] The French plural is kept in *ioiax, ioyaus* beside *iueles*.

The ending zero is limited, with four exceptions, to English neuter long stems. Thus, *hors, hous, marc, pond, ssep, þing (þinges), yer (yeres)*,[4] *zuyn*. In addition two French words, *cas, payre* appear in this category; and one native word, *halȝen*.[5] *Uolc* is a special case. It takes a plural verb and (or) qualifier as, for example, at 53/2–3, 197/7, 207/2–3, 239/25–6, 243/9–10, 255/8 (Fr. *mout de genz*). But the singular seems also to be used as a collective plural. So *þet uolc . . . . . zeneȝeþ* 52/18–20 (cf. 195/35–6, 196/26–7, 211/7–8, 242/14–15). For *guod* see note to 100/9.

A plural in -e appears in *þinge, uolke,* and *ziþe*. The last is probably derived from the dative plural, as Senff suggests,[6] since it occurs in adverbial phrases. The form *þinge* may also derive from the dative or genitive plural but may also be an error.[7] It should be noted, however, that plurals *siþe* and *þinge* occur in the *Orrmulum*.[8] The form *uolke* at 39/22 is ambiguous.

---

[1] Wallenberg (p. 165, n. 2) points out that we should expect **momes, momettes*. The extant form may be due to a blending of *maumet* with a form such as ME. *mahun*.

[2] Wallenberg (p. 197, n. 2) points out that this could come from OE *profost* or OF *provost*; but the plural form *prouos* suggests the latter.

[3] The form *gromes* comes in this category if it is correctly derived from OF *gromet*. But the etymology is uncertain. Cf. Wallenberg, p. 100, n. 1. *Ches*, listed in this category by Senff (p. 42), is borrowed into English as a singular (see *OED* Chess).

[4] Wallenberg notes (p. 105, n. 2) that the uninflected form is used after numerals.   [5] See p. 59, n. 5. For the form *wyf* cf. note to 9/8.

[6] Senff, p. 8.   [7] See note to 83/19.

[8] See M. Lehnert, *Sprachform und Sprachfunktion im Orrmulum (um 1200)* (Berlin, 1953), p. 57. For *yefþe* see note to 3/21; for *guode* see note to 74/29.

It may be plural. At 74/29, 244/26, 261/31, *guode* may be plural. But cf. note to 74/29.

The *Ayenbite* retains the mutation plurals *men* and *uet* as well as the double plurals *children*, *ken*, and *lambren* already noted as having plurals in *-en*.

Genitive plural

The genitive plural appears in *manne* and *wermene*.

The noun declension in the *Ayenbite* may thus be summarized as follows:

1. *Consonant declension:* NA. zero; G. zero, *-es*; D., PC. zero, *-e*; PL. *-es* (*-is*), *-en* (etc.), *-s*, zero, *-e*, mutation and double plurals; GPL. (*-e*, *-ene*).

2. *Vocalic Declension:* NA. *-e*; G. *-es*, (*-e*); D., PC. *-e*; PL. *-es* (*-is*), *-en* (etc.), zero.

The adjective

A. Strong adjectives

The nominative

The nominative of adjectives, like that of the noun, generally ends in *-e* or zero[1] according to etymology. Thus, adjectives such as *clene*, *zuete* go back to OE *i-* stems with a final vowel, while those with zero go back to OE forms with zero. The form *sleȝe* from Norse always shows a final *-e*.[2] There are, however, some cases in which the nominative has a final *-e* in spite of an etymon with zero.[3] The examples may be classified as follows:

(a) *attributive use*

(i) preverbal: *fole opnymynge* (*fole emprise*) 83/26;[4] *guode herte* (*bon cuer*) 251/15;[5] *liȝte couaytise* (*couoitise legiere*) 11/15;

---

[1] Some adjectives end in *-i* as *almiȝti, bisi, holi, onlosti, yredy, onlepi*. Of these only *bisi* shows inflection. *Onlepi* inflects the first element. The form *ydele* in the collocation *ydele blisse* is invariable and the forms are not noted.

[2] Forms with a final *-e* in the masculine in French, such as *poure, tendre*, remain vocalic. Final *-e* has been lost in *chast, colrik, scarlet*. The form *line* (OE *linen*) retains *-n* in the inflected cases. But *line* is weak at 178/15. Cf. *oȝe* (17/5, 48/23) and Senff, p. 54. Obscure are *lheuc* and *scallede*. Cf. Wallenberg, pp. 145, n. 3; 211, n. 3.

[3] Note, however, the deletion of final *-e* in *uayre* (145/1).

[4] The form *fole* may, however, be for *foli*; cf. *MED* FOLI adj.

[5] But cf. note to 251/14–16.

ry3(t)uolle loue 269/23;[1] *linene kertel* (236/20) may belong here but may be dative or weak.

(ii) postverbal (subject or complement): *yblissede bleuinge* (*beneure acheuance*) 168/22; *blisfolle uela3rede* (*gloriouse compaignie*) 75/4–5; *fole bezechinge* (*fole priere*) 116/35–117/1; *fole opniminge* (*fole emprise*) 22/1–2; *fole ssame* (*fole uergoigne*) 26/21; *fole wylninge* (*fole baerie*) 22/34; *guode tonge, rearde* (*bone langue, uoiz*) 24/5–6; *zuo harde todelinge* (*si dure departie*) 189/34; *he3liche clom* 264/12;[2] *lo3e clopinge* (*humble abit*) 226/31; *ri3te beleaue* (*droite foi*) 207/21; *wyckede drede* (*mauuaise paour*) 17/27; *zor3uolle yelpinge* (*dolourouse uantance*) 59/35; *zope blisse* (*uraie gloire*) 83/12, 89/19; *zope blisse and ziker* (*uraie ioie parfaite*) 93/18–19; *zope mildenesse* (*uraie humilite*) 144/8; *non zope lhordssip* (*uraie seignorie*) 84/27; *zope ssrifte* (*uraie confession*) 202/22; *zope pouerte* (*uraie pouerte*) 241/25.[3]

(b) *predicative use*

ypocrisye . . . *fole* (*sote*) 25/34; *bezechinge* . . . *guode* (*bone*) 98/14; *cas* . . . *guode, kueade* (*bone, male*) 168/5; *kertel* . . . *huyte* (*blanche*) 236/20; *zenne* . . . *kendeliche* (*selom nature*) 176/3; *vi3t* . . . *riotouse* (*rioteuse*) 170/17; *bezechinge* . . . *ssorte, uayre* (*brieue, bele*) 98/14; *speche* . . . *uayre* (*bele*) 57/21; *guodes* . . . *zope* (*uraie*) 76/19;[4] *loue* . . . *zope* (*uraie*) 121/18.

With the exception of *he3liche* and *riotouse* all these adjectives have a recorded nominative with a zero ending. The forms with -*e* cannot, therefore, be due to a shift from the consonantal to the vocalic inflection. On the other hand, the majority of cases render a French feminine adjective and may be purely errors resulting from the influence of the French. It should also be noted that the majority of cases are either predicative or, if attributive, follow the verb. In the latter instances, the adjective may have been felt to be accusative; in the former, it is possible that, since predicative adjectives were often uninflected, this may have been a category in which it was felt that -*e* and zero were allomorphs.

---

[1] But this may be due to a misunderstanding of *uor*; *a li3te scele* (250/12) is an error; see the note to this line. This list should, perhaps, include the numerous cases of *zaynte*. See note to 13/15.

[2] Senff (p. 55) assumes this to be an error for *þe he3liche clom*.

[3] The rather frequent use of *zope* as a nominative and accusative form may be due to the influence of the adverb. [4] See note to this line.

The accusative

The accusative usually coincides with the nominative. But there are a considerable number of cases where the accusative ends in *-e* as against a nominative in zero.

(a) *attributive use*

(i) postverbal: 1. the adjective precedes: *aperte miracle (le miracle apert)* 134/29;[1] *clenliche clopinge (honeste abit)* 216/22; *ane dyaue (.i. sourt)* 211/8–9;[2] *ane greate zenne dyadlich and orrible (i. grant pecchie mortel 7 horrible)* 43/4–5; *ane wel greate hete (une tres grant ardour)* 111/17; *greate blisse (grant ioie)* 135/7; *ane zuo greate herte*[3] *(un si grant cuer)* 143/25; *zuo greate zikernesse (une si grant seurte)* 143/27; *zuo greate scole (si grant escole)* 34/22; *meste greate tresor (le plus grant tresor)* 112/5;[4] *ane greate hete (une grant ardeur)* 166/26; *greate penonce (grant penitance)* 179/15; *greate drede (poor grant)* 231/20; *ane guode iornee (bone iornee)* 113/9; *guode beleaue (bone foi)* 207/23; *guode hope (bone esperance)* 207/30; *kueade anginnynge (mal commencement)* 31/7–8; *more kueade amendinge (plus mal amendement)* 31/8; *ozene wyl (propre uolente)* 109/24; *ozene wyt (propre sens)* 109/24; *ouerlyche hezhnesse (souraine hautesce)* 123/23–4; *ouerliche guodnesse (souraine bonte)* 123/24–5; *ouerliche mageste (souraine maieste)* 123/24; *principale dette (principal dette)* 35/14; *rizte byleue (droite foi)* 126/22; *rizte mesure (droite mesure)* 249/30; *riztuolle knaulechinge (droite conoissance* 250/25; *ane rounde figure (une figure reonde)* 234/22; *sceluolle mesure (mesure resnable)* 259/33–4; *ane speciale coroune (.i. especial corone)* 234/34; *ane speciale ouercomynge (especial uictoire)* 235/1; *none ualse wytnesse (faus tesmoin)* 10/5; *ualse moneye (fause monoie)* 26/7; *ualse monaye (fause monoie)* 62/22; *ualse wytnesse (faus tesmoignage)* 64/35–65/1; *ueste bileue (ferme foi)* 207/25; *uolle elde (parfait aage)* 259/24; *uoluelde . . . louerede (parfete . . . amistie)* 149/5; *zikere blisse (parfaite ioie)* 93/19–20; *zope loue (uraie amour)* 91/12; *zope beknawynge (uraie conissance)* 126/23; *zope ssriffpe (uraie confession)* 179/2.

[1] Senff (p. 55) suggests emending to *þe aperte miracle*, and this is conceivable as are his readings *þe meste greate tresor* (112/5) and *þe ozene wyt/wyl* (109/24).
[2] This may be weak, but the substantivalized adjective after *an* is usually strong (cf. p. 67); or it could be dative.
[3] Cases after *zuo* and *non* may be due to an extension of the weak forms but have been regarded as strong.
[4] For *meste* see p. 70.

2. the adjective follows: *charite guode* (*charite parfaite*) 90/29; *mesure sceluolle* (*mesure resnable*) 250/7; *alle blisse clene and zope of herte* (*toute ioie pure e uraie de cuer*) 93/22–3.

(ii) preverbal object: *ane zuo greate hope* (*une si grant fiance*) 143/28; *none guode techinge* (*nule bone doctrine*) 69/20; *greate glednesse* (*grant ioie*) 240/9; *heȝe cleregye* (*haute clergie*) 81/32; *kueade anginnynge* (*mal commencement*) 31/9; *kueade uelaȝrede* (*mauuaise compaignie*) 177/34.

(b) *predicative use*

þane þet . . . anlyke (*semblant*) 227/15; *mesure(s) . . . ane little . . . ane scarse, guode* (*une petite . . . une escharse, bone*) 53/24–6, 54/2, 3.

The adjectives *grat, guod, hard, kuead, uayr, uest, ziker, zop,* when used attributively, all show accusative forms in zero. The forms in *-e,* which co-exist with the zero forms, may in origin have been feminine accusative forms, since they frequently qualify nouns belonging, in the *Ayenbite,* to the vocalic declension and many of them were originally feminine. The accusative ending *-ne,* on the other hand, qualifies originally masculine nouns of the consonantal declension. Thus *ane fieblene castel* (227/20); *ane gratne viss* (238/32); *ane gratne dyeuel* (239/5); *ane guodne man* (238/28); *ane newene kniȝt* (162/1); *ane strangne uend* (227/20–1); *þane ualsne peny* (24/14); *ane yongne boryeis* (162/1); and in predicative use *uiss . . . ane littlene* (238/32). Senff points out[1] that the forms are always preceded by *ane* or *þane* and suggests that the ending might be by analogy with the qualifiers. But this seems unlikely (despite the irregular *þane ualsne peny*) in view of the maintenance of the historical ending *-ne* in pronominal forms. The use of *ane* with an apparently masculine ending arises from a falling together of OE **anne* and *ane* in unstressed position.[2]

The genitive

A genitive in *-e* (possibly weak in origin) occurs in *yonge Thobyes wyf* (48/30, 223/16). *Zaynte* (13/34, 35) relates to the nominative in *-e.*

Post-prepositional case

The endings are zero and *-e* as in nouns. The zero ending is especially frequent with common adjectives such as *guod, grat,*

[1] Senff, p. 51.
[2] KS have *ane* as acc. sg. masc. at 213, 214, 216.

kuead, riȝt.[1] The adjectives *riȝt* (as in *a riȝt half*) and *left* are uninflected; perhaps because the phrases in which they occurred were felt to be compounds.

The strong adjective can be used substantivally with the indefinite article. Thus *a dyad* (258/20); *to ane kueade* (62/4). For *ane dyaue* see p. 65 and note 2.

B. *The weak adjective*

The weak adjective maintains to a considerable extent, as elsewhere in Middle English, the functions which it has in Old English. Thus it is used:

(a) for the vocative as in *leue uader* (109/3); *vayre uader* (110/13–14, 139/1); *vayre zone* (187/6).

(b) to form substantivalized adjectives. Exceptions here are *þe couaytous* (80/24), *þe enuious* (9×);[2] *þe riȝt guod*(103/21); *þe lostuol* (80/25); *þe wel strong, þe wel special ald* (16/27, see note); *þe riȝt wys* (103/21).[3]

(c) after a demonstrative or possessive adjective or the definite article. There are, however, a number of cases where the weak form is not used. So *þet commun profit*[4] (147/31); *þin euel wyl* (114/19); *þe general ariȝinge* (14/13); *þe gentyl hond* (75/32–3); *þe gentyl kende*(89/18–19); *þet his oȝene guod wyl*(109/21–2); *to þine left hand* (147/1);[5] *of þe litel childe* (137/4–5); *þe ilke litel bal* (179/7–8); *þe litel child* (134/10);[6] *ine þe middel stat*[7] (122/23); *oure principal desyr* (106/5–6); *þe principal yefþe* (106/13); *þin riȝt hand* (146/36); *þi riȝt hand* (196/6); (in verse) *þe wycked uend* (1/3); *þe zeuend boȝ* (43/2); *þe zeuend stape* (260/1). The number of cases is not great and any or all of them may be errors.

When the adjective is postponed we find both usages. Thus *þet bread bodylich* (111/27–8); *þet liȝt bodilich* (200/21); *of þe wyfman grat myd childe* (82/20); *of oure uader gostlich* (87/28–9); *þet bread*

---

[1] The corrector sometimes added a final -*e* to an adjective after a preposition. So *heȝe* (164/25).

[2] Senff suggests (65) that French adjectives do not take a final -*e*. But *þe enuiouse* occurs in the text.

[3] At 167/1, *þe uerþ stape* is corrected to *þe uerþe stape*.

[4] Senff points out (p. 64) that 65 per cent of attributive adjectives of French origin show the weak inflection after articles, demonstratives, or possessives.

[5] *þi left hand* (196/6) may be due to elision but *left* does not usually show weak forms. Cf. Senff, p. 63.

[6] *þe litel amote* (141/24) is probably due to elision.

[7] Cf. Senff, p. 64.

lostuol (110/27); *þe broþerrede ulesslich* (146/13–14); *of þe uader ulesslich* (87/27); *of his moder poure and zik* (197/23–4); on the other hand, *þe zeuende boʒ heʒliche* (26/27);[1] *to þe liue restuolle* (199/32–3); *þe uayriste lyf an þe zykeriste* (78/2).[2]

The plural

The plural of adjectives ends in *-e*. Cases of a zero ending in attributive usage are rare and may be errors.[3] Thus *diuers colurs* (15/9); *zuo grat amendes* (113/27);[4] *grat guodnesses* (18/15–16); *þe midel guodes* (79/21); *þe middel þinges* (136/25); *alle uenyal zennes* (74/11); when postponed, both inflected and uninflected forms occur as *þe þinges bodilich* (200/22); *be biddinges dreduolle* (42/9–10); *biddingges dreduolle oþer ulessliche* (42/4–5); *to oure uaderes gostliche* (8/10). As in the singular, predicative forms are often uninflected. Forms without a final vowel also occur when the adjective is used substantivally as in *þe couaytous* (154/31); *to þe couaytous* (189/11–12); *þe bysye oþer þe melancolien* (253/9–10); *þe men* (122/7); but also without the article in *zuyche religious* (243/14).[5] The first example, however, may have elision.

In some cases a French plural in *-(e)s* appears: 1. most commonly these are postponed as in *þe uour uirtues cardinales* (3/25, 124/1, 2); *uirtues contraries* (123/3–4); *þe kuede humours and corruptes* (128/31–2); *uele þoʒtes newe diuerses & wyluolle* (162/2); *þe þri boʒes principales* (34/29); *þe oþre (seconde) guodes principals* (209/29); *nyedes seculeres* (215/9); *ypocrites sotyls* (26/7–8); *uele notes sotiles an zuete* (105/15); (*þe*) *uelaʒredes suspiciouses* (226/8–9, 231/28); *þe zennes uenials* (178/16–17); *þoʒtes, wordes uenimouses* (27/14, 35); 2. predicative usage appears in *cardinals* (123/10, 124/8); *contraries* (123/7; *rebours and rebels* (68/34); *rebels* (69/7); *þe preciouses, þe viles* (76/27); 3. pre-nominal attributive use in *zeuen principals doles* (17/20–2); *þe zeuen principals uirtues* (159/30–1); *uour wel preciouses þinges* (96/5–6). Both the ending *-e* and the ending *-s* are used in the

---

[1] The French shows this to be an adjective and not an adverb. Cf. note to 26/27.   [2] Cf. Senff, pp. 54, 64.

[3] The following cases in which a final *-e* has been added by the corrector may be noted: *diverse* (15/9); *manye* (31/25); *greate* (38/30, 78/14); *ualse* (48/20); *heʒe* (139/30); *þe couaytouse* (209/29–30, 210/3–4); *wordeliche* (210/19).

[4] But the form may be due to a feeling that the sense is singular; or the ending-less form may be due to elision.

[5] See Senff, p. 65. In *clerkes an lewede and religious* (34/25) the form *lewede*, with its adjectival plural, suggests that *religious* is also an adjective and belongs here.

formation of substantivalized adjectives. Thus *þe kuede* but also *þe fiebles* (148/32–3); *of priues* (37/18), *his priues* (184/28). The form *wrechchen* (187/18) as an adjectival plural arises from the use of the weak form as a noun. There is then confusion between the adjective and the noun.

The dative plural

A dative (p.c.) plural in *-en* appears when the adjective is used with substantival function. Thus *of þe greaten* (139/12); *to þe guoden* (72/31); *amang þe holen* (205/23); *to pouren* (190/7–8); *ate yealden* (184/16).[1]

Comparative and superlative

The comparative of adjectives ends in *-er*. This is not usually inflected. Exceptions are *heȝere* and *leuere*. The former is probably plural at 176/2; at 122/4, it may be weak or it could be an example of the earlier form of the ending, *-ere*. The latter probably shows the earlier form of the ending, stereotyped because of the idiomatic nature of the phrases in which it normally occurs.

The superlative usually ends in *-este*, (*-iste*). This ending could derive either from the Old English weak ending *-esta* or from the strong form *-est*. Since, however, the forms in the *Ayenbite* are mainly weak or plural, the latter seems more probable. This view is supported by a few cases of the ending *-est* (*-ist*): *heȝest* (124/8; or elision), 244/32; *loȝest* (122/4); *alast* (69/10; or elision); *lodlakest* (49/23).[2] *Holyist* (54/36) may be an error for *holyiste*, as Morris supposed, since it follows a demonstrative and we should expect it to be weak. A special case is the form *wors* (OE *wersa*). It may be due to confusion with the adverb just as *mo* is often used as an adjective in the *Ayenbite*, a usage arising from the loss of the genitive inflection which syntactically distinguished the adjective from the adverb in Old English.[3] On the other hand, the form could be due to elision, since it occurs in the phrase *þet wors is* and in *wors endinge* (31/9). The expected form *worse* occurs, however, at 17/32, 265/14.

[1] For *of þe newen* see note to 99/5; *þe wrechchen* (188/1, 189/11) are ambiguous. They could be substantival or adjectival.

[2] Cf. *bleþelaker* (180/1) where the French suggests that an adjective is required. The form is due to confusion with the adverb. Cf. Wallenberg, p. 322.

[3] The form *mo* is sometimes corrected to *more*. So at 21/11 and 213/9. The contrary confusion may appear in *worse* (213/9) but it could be a plural adjective.

It may be noted that the adverb *mest* seems to be inflected like an adjective (wk. and pl.) after *þe*. Thus *þe meste periluse ziknesse* (16/33); *þe meste guode men* (25/13); *þe meste wyse* (72/5–6); *þe meste poure makynge* (92/21–2); *þe meste profitable red* (185/1); *þe meste gentile guodes* (89/35–90/1); at 112/5 *meste greate tresor* should perhaps read, as Senff suggests (p. 55), *þe meste greate tresor* (Fr. *le plus*).

Demonstratives, possessives, and indefinites and the definite article

The morphology of demonstrative, possessive, and indefinite adjectives corresponds in many regards to that of other adjectives. The words considered in this section are: *al, an, ech, eni, eurich, min, non, on, (an)oþer, þellich, þin, (þes), zom, zuich*. The corresponding pronominal forms will be considered later, as will the derivatives of OE *se, sio, þet*.

The nominative

As in the case of other adjectives, a few instances with an unhistorical final -*e* occur. Thus *ane holy ssamnesse (une)* 142/31;[1] *þine eȝe* (159/9; cf. note); *þise uirtue (ceste)* 146/28, 250/9;[2] *þise uorbisne (cest)* 191/30; *zuyche difference (tele)* 210/32. It will be noted that the majority of these forms refer to nouns either originally feminine or belonging to the vocalic declension. Some, however, may be due to the influence of the French or merely errors. The proportion is statistically very small. The adjective *al* is a special case. As in Gower, the form *alle* is used when no other qualifier occurs in the collocation. Thus *alle triacle* (17/1); *alle manere* (34/23); *alle heȝnesse* (97/3–4) etc. but *al þe herte* (109/7–8); *al guod red* (185/3); *al his mayne* (239/6) etc. The only exceptions are *al uolc* (155/17) and *alle þe uerste uondinge* (168/10). In view of the large number of instances it may be assumed that these exceptions are errors. The accusative follows the same pattern.[3]

---

[1] At 131/5, *ane ze* is strictly governed by the preposition *bote*. It is, however, separated from it by a number of phrases and it is not clear whether *ane* should be regarded as post-prepositional. For 142/31 cf. note.

[2] But the form may be due to taking the preceding *Vor*, an adverb, as a preposition.

[3] Note that, at 16/19, *alle his uelaȝrede* has been emended to *al his uelaȝrede*. See Senff, p. 62. The collocation *al day* is exceptional.

The accusative[1]

As with other adjectives, there are more cases of the morph -*e* than in the nominative. Thus:

1. *ane* is the usual form of the accusative of *an*; *a* is used (a) with original Old English neuters as *corn* (37/1); *child* (58/31, 98/32); *lyte* (73/15); *stech* (62/6); *trau* (95/14, 185/25); *uer* (67/13); *wyl* (166/26); *wyt* (257/22–3); *zeluer* (36/33), (b) also with the Old French masculine substantives; *paradis* (95/11), *sautyer* (91/9), and an OE masculine in *a day* (73/17, 74/21), (c) Old French feminine substantives *best* (14/31–2); *pater noster* (91/9).[1] Of these, *best* and *pater noster* occur with neuter qualifiers in the *Ayenbite*. It will be noted that all the instances belong to the consonantal declension. The reason for the dominance of the form *ane* is, no doubt, the convergence of OE **anne* and *ane* in weak stress. This meant that originally *ane* referred to both masculine and feminine nouns and *a(n)* to neuter ones.

2. *eche manyere* occurs at 70/17–18, *eche niȝt* at 171/12,[2] and *enye elmesse* at 194/4. All three nouns are originally feminine.

3. *mine* occurs before the following nouns which, with one exception, were originally feminine: *bene* (211/30); *couche* (171/12); *matire* (262/2–3); *rearde* (211/31); *uader* (219/28–9);[3] *ziȝþe* (267/2).

4. *none* appears before (a) the originally feminine nouns *beste* (201/24; but this may be dative); *miȝte* (170/23); *reste* (29/33–4); *ssame* (135/27, 139/24, 196/32); *strengþe* (149/24); *techinge* (69/20); *þiefþe* (9/23); *uelaȝrede* (254/11); *uirtue* (126/23); *wytnesse* 10/5); and the consonantal *enchesoun* (217/2) (b) English and French masculine nouns *sacrefice* (192/13); *time* (90/33); (c) *drede* (128/18, 254/9). All, except *enchesoun*, belong to the vocalic declension. The -*e* is retained before vowels or *h* in *none arizinge* (147/8); *hede* (5 ×); *ydele blisse* (195/32–3); *onderstondinge* (201/27); *ou(t)trage* (54/18, 110/16–17).

5. *one* appears before (a) original feminines *herte* (145/9); *loue* (145/9–10); *yefþe* (115/12); *zenne* (52/7, 86/8),[4] (b) an original masculine *beleaue* (145/27). All belong to the vocalic declension.

[1] The form *an* before words beginning with a vowel or *h* is ambiguous since elision is common in the *Ayenbite*. Thus *an eddre* (or dative ?) (61/16); *an eppel* (84/12); *an hondred ziþe* (134/30–1). At 62/10 *ane mes* is corrected to *a mes*.

[2] *eche daye* presumably represents OE *ælce dæge* and not an accusative.

[3] But this may be dative.

[4] *on zenne* (acc.) is corrected to *one zenne* at 52/7.

6. *oþre* occurs with *lac* (66/30); *speche* (211/6). The latter is an original feminine. Of *oþre lac* Senff (p. 76) conjectured that the form of the qualifier was due to the French *defaute* which DM first wrote and then corrected to *lac*. This may be correct.[1] The compound appears with a final vowel in *anoþre empire* (85/15); *anoþre time* (220/13) and doubly inflected in *ane oþre speche* (110/5). The latter qualifies a feminine noun; the two former cases nouns originally masculine which belong to the vocalic declension.

7. *þellyche* qualifies *uorbysne* (263/11), a feminine noun.

8. *þine* qualifies *bene* (102/25); *chastete* (205/28); *gost* (74/34); *klennesse* (205/28); *moder* (8/3); *noblesse* (100/24); *playnte* (99/34); *richesse* (100/2–5); *sseppere* (7/9);[1] *strengþe* (54/34); *time* (71/27, 129/22); *uader* (8/2, 210/20);[1] *uayrhede* (100/24); *wil* (114/16); *yefþe* (194/16); *zaule* (73/2). The majority of these either are feminine or belong to the vocalic declension. In some cases *þine* appears before a word beginning with a vowel or *h*. Thus *þine herte* (73/3, 114/15, 133/32);[2] *hope* (5/22); *emcristen* (10/8).

9. *þise* is the most common form of the accusative; *þis* is most common when the accusative precedes the verb and then most frequently when the noun which it qualifies ends in a vowel. *þise* qualifies 43 original feminines and one vocalic noun, *office*. *þis* qualifies 22 original masculines or neuters and 3 original feminines *yefþe*, *heste* (2×). The latter instances may be due to elision, however.

10. *zuiche* qualifies *blisse* (244/27); *dede* (47/35); *dette* (222/32–3); *fourme* (220/23); *mesure* (53/28); *manere* (54/12); *seruice* (236/4); *speche* (211/2–3); *uelaȝrede* (254/8–9). Of these only *seruice* is in origin masculine.

11. *zome* qualifies *cortaysye* (36/34); *prowesse* (168/7). Both nouns are original feminines. An ambiguous case is *uor zome grace to bidde* (214/36–215/1). This should probably be interpreted as *zome grace uor to bidde*, since *bidde* is not usually construed with *uor*. *Grace* is an original feminine.

12. As in the nominative, *alle* is the form used without, *al* the form used with, a qualifier.

---

[1] But this form may be dative.

[2] The text has *of þine herte zuo moche ouercome* where *of* governs the infinitive. But DM may have thought *þine herte* was post-prepositional.

The Old English masc. acc. sg. suffix -ne occurs in the following instances: *alneway* adv.; *anoperne way* (162/6); *nenne bend* (48/6), *gelt* (30/27), *man* (8/19–20), *oprenne* (175/5, 237/26), *skele* (86/13); *enne day* (91/6), *god* 'God' (244/13), *gost* (145/9), *yhanged* (241/9), *sseppere* (145/15); *perne*[1] *(ceste) ansuere* (214/22), *dyap* (72/30), *mete* (111/5, 11), *paske* (133/20), *viȝt* (181/16), *uridom* (86/5–6, 14–15), *way* (165/15–16); *perne (cest) gardyn* (94/30–1). In this last group, all are original masculines except *viȝt*, an original neuter, and *ansuere*, *paske*, original feminines. In Old English, *bend* could be masculine, feminine, or neuter. The problems associated with *skele* we have already discussed.[2]

The genitive

A genitive in -e occurs in *ane payenes zone* (239/2); *eche dayes* (112/11, 262/25); *by myne uader zaule* (64/13); *none mannes speche* (267/36); *pine neyȝbores wyf* (10/22); *pine nixte* (11/7) is a dubious case; cf. note to this line.

The dative and post-prepositional cases

Except that *al* and *alle* are distributed as in the nominative and accusative,[3] the pattern is the same as for nouns and other adjectives. The endings are -e and zero.[4] It may be noted that the forms *mine* and *pine* not infrequently occur before a word beginning with a vowel or *h*. Thus at 103/11, 157/3–4, 216/13–14 and 10/5, 22, 20/10, 11, 114/16 etc. On the other hand, at 233/13, *mid ale pin wylle* has been corrected to *mid ale pine wylle*. Some exceptional cases occur. The forms *enne* and *nenne* are used as post-prepositional forms in *bote enne moup* (249/22); *uor nenne wynd* (168/3–4); *uor nenne man* (256/15). These may be errors or may point to a contrast between forms with and without final -e so that the morphologically significant element is no longer -ne but -e. A dative *none manne* appears at 213/34.

---

[1] This form is possibly made up of the suffix -ne and the old genitive and dative *per* which otherwise occurs only in *perhuile*, *perhuils*. For other suggestions see Wallenberg, p. 250, n. 1.

[2] See p. 58.

[3] Exceptions are: *of al kueade* (16/9); *of alle his guode* (18/29); *mid ale pine wylle* (233/13). These may be errors.

[4] Wallenberg (p. 10, n. 3) suggests that *a(n)* occurs when the following word is inflected.

Weak forms

A weak form *oþre* (nom. and acc.) appears with the nouns *bene* (107/33, 34); *manere* (35/24, 44/21); *werre* (30/3); *zyde* (89/9), all feminines. A weak form *oþrene* appears in *þan oþrene urydom* (87/14); *of þane oþrene dyaþ* (180/15–16); the accusative form at 87/14 may have the masculine suffix -*ne*; the post-prepositional cases may have the suffix -*n* with a further -*e* added. In other instances *oþer*, not *oþre*, appears after demonstratives.

Plural

The plural of these words ends in -*e* as other adjectives.[1] It may again be noted that this ending is maintained before a vowel and *h* as in *mine ealde wones* (166/7); *þine eȝen* (156/15); *þine honden* (218/3); *þine earen* (257/5). The plural *þis* (73/12) may be an error.

Pronominal inflection

The demonstratives (except derivatives of OK *se, sio, þet*), indefinites, and possessives are inflected as follows:

The nominative

The nominative forms usually end in zero. Thus *al, on, ech, eni, eurich, min, non, anoþer, þin, þis, þes, zom, zuich*. Exceptionally, however, we find cases with -*e*. Thus *one of þe guode doȝtren* (140/34); *one of þe uariste doþter* (142/31); *anoþre (ypocrisie)* 25/34; *(hate)* 29/28;[2] and after the article *þe one* (86/2, 120/34); *þe oþre (cas)* (42/24); *(manere)* (86/2); *(boȝ)?* (62/5 n., 67/24.)

The accusative

As in the adjectives, there are three allomorphs: zero, -*e*, and -*ne*. All the words in question show a zero ending in the accusative but the following show the other two endings also: (a) -*e* in *anoþre (mesure)* (53/25); *enye (kenne)* (49/8); *none (wyfman)* (49/8); and after the article, *þe oþre* (68/1); *þanne oþre* (102/22);[3] (b) -*ne* in *eurinne* (134/33, 136/26); *nenne* (10/8, 22/30, 48/12, 136/11, 157/4,

---

[1] The forms *al* for normal *alle* at 76/2 and 102/9 may be errors or due to elision. Note that at 54/35, 109/33, 117/15, 125/22, 130/21 *þis* (pl.) has been corrected to *þise*. The last example is a pronoun.

[2] At 27/20 it is not clear whether *zome* comes in this category. See the note to this line.

[3] For *ane (little)*, *ane (scarse)* see note to 53/24.

34); *nenne oþrenne* (175/5, 237/26); it will be noted in this last example that *oþer* has a distinctive ending with syncope. This word (and the compound *anoþer*) show a number of variant forms. Beside the regular *oþrenne* already noted, we find (*þe, þann*) *oþren* (46/12, 66/9, 102/21, 135/33); (*leme*) (147/15) (but this example may be dative); (*broþer*) (186/21); *anoþrene* (155/25); *ane oþrene* (*viȝt*) (180/21); and, after the article, *þan*(*n*)*e oþrene* (66/20, 222/21).

The genitive

The forms *oþres* and *anoþres* occur at 27/1, 2, 136/16, 175/12, 197/21.

The dative and post-prepositional case

The endings are zero and *-e*. Zero endings appear for *al, on* (before vowels), *oþer*. It must be remembered, however, that the total number of pronominal forms is very much smaller than that of adjectival forms. These forms may not, therefore, give a true picture of the system. Forms with *-e* occur in *enie* (5/7); *one* (205/34); *oþ*(*e*)*re, anoþre, þise*. Forms in *-en* (*-in*) appear in *echen, echin; eurichen; nonen; onen;*[1] *oþren; anoþren, þisen*. The possessive pronouns also have forms with final *-n* when post-prepositional. Thus *þinen* (194/29); *hiren* sg. & pl. (38/30, 60/21, 111/32 n.)[2] (but *hare* 'theirs' (144/16, 241/29); *hyre* 'hers' (96/27); *youre* 'yours' (265/18)) and, without inflection, *of his* (22/13, 54/3). Exceptionally we find *enne* in *wyþ enne* (102/32); *be enne of his angles* (129/9).

The plural

In the nominative, the plural ends in *-e*. Thus *alle*,[3] *enye, none, oþ*(*e*)*re, þise*,[4] *zome, zuiche*. The accusative plural also ends in *-e* except that we find *oþren* used as an accusative plural.

Dative and post-prepositional case

Alongside forms with *-e* we find forms ending in a nasal. Thus *allen, oþren, þisen, zuichen*. The reason for the retention of the

---

[1] The form *onenen* (91/6) is probably an error.
[2] For discussion of the origin of these forms see Wallenberg, p. 112, n. 1.
[3] The plural *al* (119/11) may be an error.
[4] The plural *þis* (11/20) may be an error. The form *þos* (5 ×) usually renders French *cil* and should perhaps be regarded as the plural of *þe ilke* in spite of being the historical derivative of OE *þas*. The form has, however, been recorded under *þis*.

nasal in pronominal forms, and not in adjectival forms, is no doubt that the close conjunction of adjective and noun favoured the loss of the nasal.

The development of adjectives and pronouns

The most problematic endings are those which end in -e. It is not easy to assess the function of this final vowel. It must first be considered whether it is purely random. On the whole, the evidence suggests that this is not the case. In the first place, if we consider the noun declensions we find that, in the great majority of instances, allowing for the normal early Middle English extension of final -e in certain categories, the final vowel is remarkably stable in nouns of French, English, and also Norse origin. As we have already indicated in our discussion of the nouns, exceptions are rare except in the dative and after prepositions. In the second place, if we look at verbal forms, we find that infinitive, subjunctive, weak preterite, and strong past participle almost always retain their final -e. In the third place, unexpected final -e is rare in other words. The following examples may be noted: *ake*, *ane* (prep.), *ere*, *hiere*, *huere*, *iche*, *myde*, *þere*, *zainte*. Some of these are susceptible of other explanations. Thus *ake* may be, as Wallenberg suggests, by analogy with *bote*.[1] It occurs four times after a clause containing a negative. *Ane* occurs most commonly when a weakly stressed word such as *þe* or *his* (+subst.) follows.[2] It may be original or by analogy with *in(n)e*. *Huere* and *ere* may also be analogical.[3] The form *myde* is used when it is placed after the word it governs and appears to be a genuine adverbial form.[4] The form *zaynte* may be a derivative of OE *sancta*. It is not uncommon in the *Orrmulum* where its use seems to be dictated by rhythmical considerations.[5] The forms *beuor*, *bodilich*, *bot*, *cherch*, *neuremor*, *tuay*, *zuetelich* lack final -e. Of the two instances of *tuay* one (72/12) is due to elision. The other (30/19) may have been error or by analogy with *tuo*. *Bot*, also, has elision. The other examples are few in number and may be errors.[6]

---

[1] See Wallenberg, p. 2, n. 3.   [2] Cf. Wallenberg, p. 10, n. 1.

[3] *beuore*, *auore* may have provided analogies for *ere*. See Wallenberg, p. 85, n. 1.

[4] Cf. *OED* MIDE and Wallenberg, p. 161, n. 3. The KS also have *mide* (55).

[5] See Lehnert, pp. 32–3.

[6] But for the form *neuremor* see Wallenberg, p. 168 n. 2. Corrections suggest that the final vowel was not optional. Thus the final -e in *diverse* (15/9); *manye*

They certainly do not provide substantial evidence for a random use of final -e as a graph following on the loss of its phonetic identity. Corrections in the manuscript may point in the same direction.

It seems, therefore, reasonable to assume that final -e is pronounced in the text. It follows from this that the large number of instances in which the adjectival declension shows the morph -e, especially in the accusative, plural, and weak forms, must have some historical explanation. In regard to the plural and weak forms there is, of course, no problem. They derive from the equivalent Old English morphs. The accusative forms are not quite so easy to explain. The usual assumption is that they represent the Old English feminine accusative ending. It is certainly true that in a large number of cases they qualify words which were originally feminine, but this is not always true. Some other factor should probably be sought. It should perhaps be noted, firstly, that, in a number of instances, the text tends to preserve the Old English contrast between the nominative and accusative of adjectives. This was normal in Old English except in the case of feminines, whose nominative ended in -e, and of neuters. In Old English nouns, on the other hand, such a contrast was less common and was usually obliterated in early Middle English. This difference between the noun and adjective declensions in Old English is still reflected in the *Ayenbite*. There may, therefore, be a purely historical reason for the maintenance of a distinctive accusative ending in adjectives. The dominance of -e, however, is odd. Why, for example, should there be so many cases of the morph -e and comparatively few of -ne? One factor in the situation may have been the gradual loss of final nasals as a result of which the weak declension simply ended in -e. There were thus a large number of forms ending in -e which may have encroached upon the strong forms. This seems to be so particularly where the noun belongs to the vocalic declension. Since a large number of feminine nouns which in the accusative would have had a qualifier marked by -e, ended in -e, it is not improbable that, by a simple harmonic principle, nouns ending in -e tended to be associated with this ending

(31/25); *Waynye* (88/7); *greate* (38/30, 78/14); *dede* (47/30); *ualse* (48/20); *strengþe* (acc.) 54/34; *þise* (54/35, 109/33, 117/15, 125/22, 130/21); *zoþe* (89/11); *blisse* (92/31); *heʒe* (139/30, 164/25); *hede* (148/12); *kueade* (188/7); *couaytouse* (210/4); *wordleliche* (210/19); *zome* (213/31), etc.

in the qualifier. Thus the system moved towards an accusative in -e for adjectives which qualified nouns with a vocalic ending. The same tendency may explain the appearance of a nominative in -e.

On the other hand, the system appears to be unstable. We observe, for example, that closely tied forms are more conservative than forms not linked in fixed collocations. Thus the predicative adjectives more often have zero endings than attributive forms. The zero forms are more common in pronouns than in adjectives. Rhythmical factors may also play a part. The invariable zero form of *al* when followed by a qualifier may be due to some such principle.[1] But a structural principle is probably the most important. A large number of -e forms in the singular vitiate the contrast between singular and plural. The almost total lack of zero forms in the plural suggests that the system was moving towards the simple contrast between *singular* zero: *plural -e*.[2]

The somewhat different treatment of the pronominal forms is, no doubt, due to their use in independent function and consequently often in hiatus. Most notable is their retention of final -*n* in the dative and post-prepositional case.

The normal inflexion of adjectives is thus: N. zero, -*e*; A. zero, -*e*, -*ne*; G. zero, -*e*; D., PC. zero, -*e*; PL. -*e*, (-*e*)*s*; WK. (zero), -*e*. The pronominal inflection differs from this; firstly, in the comparative rarity of the -*e* inflection in the accusative. Thus, for example, the accusative of *þis* (pron.) is *þis* while the accusative of *þis* (adj.) is usually *þise*. In the second place, the pronouns retain final -*n* in both the dative post-prepositional singular and plural in a number of instances.

The Derivatives of Old Kentish se, sio, þet

The development of the Old English demonstrative presents one of the most difficult problems for the student of morphology of the *Ayenbite*. The pronoun *þis* (*þes*), the inflection of which we have already discussed, presents no serious problems. It represents the French pronoun *cist* in the majority of cases and can, no doubt, be taken as broadly representative of the Modern English *this* as it is historically of Old English *þes, þios, þis.*

[1] It is odd that *ane* (prep.) seems to demonstrate the opposite principle, its dissyllabic form being used when a qualifier follows.

[2] The plural ending is the most stable; next come the weak forms of which there are quite a number without final -*e*, and then the dative and prepositional cases and the accusative.

The other demonstrative, however, is more difficult to assess. The fundamental problem is the development of the Old English demonstrative *se, sio, þet* which presents a number of peculiar features. The development appears to be as follows:

When used as qualifiers, not only the reduced form *þe*, but also the forms *þane* and *þet*, appear to function as a definite article. Thus out of 257 examples of *þane* only 8 translate French demonstratives; of 419 examples of *þet* only 42 translate a French demonstrative, 13 of these occurring before *stat* for reasons which I have been unable to determine. Given the word-for-word nature of the translation, even allowing for some textual variation, it is difficult not to accept the view that Dan Michel regarded *þane* and *þet* as allomorphs of *þe*. This view is supported by the translation of the *De Custodia* where nouns without a qualifier are usually rendered by the equivalent noun preceded by *þane* and *þet*. Thus, for example, *galeam* is translated by *þane helm* and *scutum* by *þane sseld*. On the other hand, there appears to be a distinction in the post-prepositional case between the demonstrative and the article. Thus, where the English *þet* renders the French article after a preposition, the form is *þet*; when, however, the French has a demonstrative after a preposition, the form is *þo* or *þan*. In other words, while *þet* is a definite article, *þo* and *þon* are demonstratives.[1]

It might be argued that this situation could be partially explained by assuming that the *Ayenbite* had no definite article and that *þet* and *þe* represented simply the unaccented and accented forms of the Old English article/demonstrative forms. They thus did duty for both the French article and the French demonstratives. But, in fact, French *cil* (and in 41 cases *cist*) is translated by *þe ilke* (occasionally *þet ilke*). The purely demonstrative nature of this collocation seems to be indicated by the use in the *De Custodia* of *þe ilke* for *ille* (or occasionally *hic* or *ipse*) while *idem* is rendered by *þe ilke zelue* except at 263/20 where *þe ilke* renders *eiusdem*. In the same way, at 185/33–4, *cel liure meismes* is rendered *þe ilke zelue boc*.[2]

---

[1] The position of *þo* (acc.) is unclear. In two cases, 143/30 and 225/6, it renders French *cele*. At 130/23 it renders the French article. The accusative pronoun *þo* is a demonstrative and the adjective should probably be regarded as demonstrative also.

[2] It may be noted that a similar system seems to operate in the first Kentish Sermon in which derivatives of OE *se, sio, þet* render the definite article in French and *þo il(e)ke* (59) renders a French demonstrative *ices(tes)* (*e celes* in

It may be supposed that the development was somewhat as follows: the Old English paradigm would provide the form *þe*, either by analogical extension of *þ* to the masculine *se*, or by weakening in low stress of the neuter *þet*.[1] The neuter *þet* remained as a stressed form. The form *þane* also remained as the masculine accusative supported, no doubt, by the analogy of *he/hine* which was now neatly parallel to *þe/þane*. These forms seem to have been used as a definite article. On the other hand, it emerges from a comparison with the French that, in an overwhelming majority of cases (and there are a great number of examples), the adjectival forms *þo* and *þan* (OE *þa*, *þam*) are demonstrative in usage, since they render French demonstratives. The development is in fact analogous to that of the Old English indefinite and interrogative *hwa*. As is well known, the oblique cases came to be used as part of the relative system because of the convenience of having inflected forms for the invariable *þat*. A paradigm thus arose which historically blended two originally distinct words and *huos*, *huom* functioned as the genitive and dative of *þat*. In the same way, it seems, *þo*, *þon* (*þan*) were used as part of the demonstrative *þe ilke*.

So far we have considered the development of OE *se*, *sio*, *þet* in general terms. We must now consider some of the differences between the adjectival and pronominal uses. The differences concern the distribution of the derivatives of Old English *se*, *sio*, *þet*. The form *þe ilke* is used for both the demonstrative adjective and pronoun in all cases and genders. On the other hand, the following differences of usage may be observed between adjective and pronoun. 1. While the adjective *þet* is a definite article, *þet* is common as a demonstrative pronoun. For example, it frequently renders French *ce* in such phrases as *þet is to zigge* (*cest a dire*); *þet is to wytene* (*cest a sauoir*); *þet byeþ* frequently renders French *ce sont* 'namely'. In general, *þet* is neuter while *þe ilke* can be used for animates and inanimates. 2. In the oblique cases, the pronoun differs from the adjective in that the form *þane* is used as a demonstrative in the compound relative *þane þet* (*celui qui*) alongside

Hatton). In the other Sermons the French article is usually translated by a derivative of *se*, *sio*, *þet* but sometimes the French demonstrative also. The demonstrative *þis* is used normally for French *cest*. It may also be noted that in some instances in which comparison with Cotton shows a discrepancy, other manuscripts of the *Somme* provide the expected form.

[1] OE *se*, *sio* remain, however, in the relative collocations *ze þet*, *zy þet*.

þe ilke þet.[1] We thus have an asymmetrical relationship between *þane* adjective and *þane* pronoun. 3. In the post-prepositional case and the dative, the pronoun retains a final nasal. The forms are thus *þan* in the singular and *þan* and *þon* (as well as *þo*)[2] in the plural while the adjectival forms are *þo*, *þa* in the singular and *þo* in the plural. The form *þet* can also be used after a preposition to form conjunctive phrases. Thus, beside forms such as *to þan þet* 'in order that'; *ine þan þet, uor þan þet* 'because'; *mid þan* (234/ 19) 'in addition'; *er þan* 'before'; *be þan þet* 'according as' and so on, we find phrases as *ine þet þet* (*en ce que*) 'in so far as' (105/26); *ine þet* (*en ce que*) 'because' (134/9); *to þet* (*a ce que*) 'in order that' (111/20).

The forms may be summarized as follows:

The article: N. *þe, þet*; A. *þe, þane, þet*; D., PC. *þe, þet*; PL. *þe*.
The demonstrative adjective, 'that': N. *þe ilke*; A. *þe ilke, þo*(?); D., PC. *þe ilke, þo* (*þa*); PL. *þe ilke, þo*.
The demonstrative pronoun, 'that': N. *þe ilke* (animate and inanimate), *þet* (inanimate); A. *þe ilke, þane, þo*; D., PC. *þan* (*þet*); PL. *þe ilke, þo*; D., PC. *þon, þan*.

In addition to the uses discussed above, the descendant of OK *þet* has a number of other functions:

(i) It is used as a relative. As such it is invariable but some idiomatic uses deriving from Old English may be noted here. 1. It is used as a compound relative 'that which', 'what'. It is usually neuter but is used with a masculine antecedent at 37/13[3], 78/4, 103/14. At 162/11, it means 'those who' notwithstanding the antecedent is strictly *manere*. 2. The compound relative can be expressed also by *þet þet* rendering French *ce que*. 3. Where Modern English requires the relative governed by a preposition, we find constructions similar to those used in Old English. Thus *ine þo half þet* 'into that part in which' (13/5–6); *to ham þet me ssolde . . . bou3e* 'to those to whom one should submit' (20/8–9); *to ham þet þou ssoldest* 'to those to whom thou shouldest (pay respect)' (20/19); *of þinge þet me nis na3t ziker* 'concerning something of which one is not certain' (64/8–9); *of oþre zennes þet he ne*

---

[1] For *þo* (acc.) see note p. 79, n. 1.
[2] After prepositions *þan* is the usual form but *þo* is also used as in *of þo þet* (59/14); *ayen þo þet* (189/1). For *þane ylych* (64/13) cf. p. 52, n. 1.
[3] Cf. note to this line.

is naȝt gelti 'of other sins of which he is not guilty' (70/22); *ine time þet* 'at the time at which' (224/20–1); the words *to, inne* are postponed in *þet me may to hopye* 'to which one can aspire' (89/2–3),[1] and *þet . . . inne* 'in which' (225/7–8). 4. The form *þet* is dative in function in *hit behoueþ . . . þet* 'it is necessary . . . for him who' (159/6–7). 5. It can be governed by a preposition as *ine þet* (*en ce que*) 'in that which' (32/27, 86/10, 183/34); *be þet* (*selom ce que*) 'according to that which' (13/3, 24, 14/23); *to þet* (*a ce que*) '(to) that which' (127/1, 5, 242/27); *uor þet* (*por ce que*) 'for that which' (127/4); *of þet* (*de ce que*) 'of what' (183/31, 246/17); *bote þet* (*fors qui*) 'except that which' (183/13).[2] 6. The collocation *þet þet* can also be governed by a preposition. Thus *be þet þet* (*selom ce que*) 'concerning what' (20/2, 188/5). 7. *Be him þet þe wordes byeþ* (64/20–1) 'by him whose the words are' is a calque on the French.

(ii) it is used as a conjunction (*a*) to introduce a noun clause (*b*) to indicate result (*c*) to indicate purpose (*d*) to indicate reason (*e*) in the collocation *þet. . . ne* 'but that' (*f*) as a subordinating particle in such collocations as *huo þet, huanne þet, huyche huet þet* (*quiex que*); (*toyans*) *huam þet, ase þet, be zuo þet*. The particle indicates conjunctive usage.

These latter constructions are, of course, in line with Middle English developments elsewhere. Early in Middle English *þe* and *þet* were more fully equated in conjunctival uses than they were in Old English. Thus in the *Lambeth Homilies* we find the frequent substitution of *þat* for *þe*. For example, Old English *ær þam þe* is rendered *er þon þet* 'before'; on the other hand, *þe* is, on numerous occasions, substituted for the conjunction *þet* as well as being employed as a subordinating particle in phrases such as *seoþþan þe* 'since' and *þer þe* 'where'. Later in Middle English, *þat* superseded *þe*, and this seems to be the case in the *Ayenbite* in spite of a number of cases in which *þe* has been emended to *þet*. In regard to the asymmetrical development of the adjectival and pronominal forms, it may be surmised that it was caused, in part at least, by the retention of grammatical gender. As *þet* remained as a neuter qualifier in such phrases as *þet trau* it was not possible for a simple bifurcation into *þe man* 'the man'/*þet man* 'that man' to take place. Thus, while *þet* is predominantly neuter

---

[1] Cf. note to this line.   [2] For *þet uram* (*a cui*) see note to 189/16–17.

when used as a pronoun and renders to a considerable extent the French neuter *ce*, when used as an adjective it has the force of an article. Thus instead of a split into *þe man/þet man* we get *þe man/ þe ilke man*. On the other hand, the OE *þæm* was not gender distinctive to the same extent as *þet* and thus the derivative *þon*, *þan* could stand in contrast with *þe* and was used as a demonstrative.

The personal pronouns

The paradigms are recorded in the glossary and here it will be sufficient to note some points of particular interest. On the whole the personal pronouns are remarkably conservative. They can be seen to descend quite regularly from their Old English equivalents if it is remembered that the forms *ha*, *hare*, *ham* are weak stress forms.[1] Certain innovations, however, may be noticed here:

1. The third person accusative singular feminine and plural, *his(e)* is a preverbal form in the *Ayenbite*. It may represent an extension of the OE accusative singular feminine and plural *hi*, which was highly ambiguous. It could, on the other hand, be by analogy with *þise*.[2] Whatever its origin, however, it corresponds in the great majority of cases to the French preverbal *la* (fem. sg. acc.) and *les* (pl. acc.). Only in one case does the plural render French tonic *eus*; on the other hand, French *eus*, *leur*, *lor* are usually translated by *ham*, while, in the feminine, *lui* and *li* are usually rendered by *hire*. Only occasionally is *hire* used as a preverbal form. Nor are these forms ever used as reflexives.

2. The neuter *hit* does not usually have a distinctive dative or post-prepositional form. These cases are characteristically supplied by forms compounded with *þer-*. Thus *þerof* 'of it'; *þerto* 'to it' and so on. This idiom also renders constructions with the French neuter *ce* after a preposition and includes a range of meaning which in Modern English would be kept separate. Thus *hyerof* 'concerning this' (190/2); *þerof* 'from this', 'because of this' (31/12, 134/24); *þerto* 'in addition (to this)' (169/3); *þerby* 'because of this' (85/20), and so on.

Reflexive and emphatic pronouns

The *Ayenbite* has two forms of the reflexive pronouns like other Middle English texts; either the simple personal pronoun in the

---

[1] The forms *here* and *hem* may show lowering of OK *hiora*, *hiom* to *heora*, *heom*. Cf. Wallenberg, p. 114.
[2] For other theories see Wallenberg, p. 114.

accusative or a form compounded with *zelue*. There is a tendency for *him* to render *se* and *himzelue* to render *soi*. The compound reflexives also render a French pronoun compounded with *meismes*. The compound forms in the *Ayenbite* are always formed with the inflected element *zelue*. The forms are thus *mizelue*, *þizelue*, *himzelue*, *hirezelue*, *hamzelue*. The form *himzelue* is also used for the impersonal 'oneself'.

The neuter pronoun *hit* is not used as a reflexive. *Him* and *hire* (*hare*) are the only forms used in the third person. Von Glahn[1] pointed out that *him* is used, not only for masculines and neuters, but also for feminines. In a few cases where the substantive is an abstract or a concrete inanimate, or where a woman is in question, *hire/hare* is also used. Wallenberg, however, points out that this can go with a feminine noun; so, *hy hare sseweþ* (131/32–3) refers to *uirtue*; *hy hyre sseweþ* (260/22) refers to *uirtue; hy ne yeue hire naʒt* (254/30) refers to *herte*. On the other hand, the use of *him* for feminines as, for example, *him* referring to *zenne* at 21/23, 22/11 is probably simply due to loss of feminine gender as Wallenberg suggests;[2] or, more properly, the loss of grammatical gender in pronouns of reference.

The emphatic pronouns

The emphatic pronoun is formed with the element *-zelf*. It is inflected in the oblique cases, where it is identical with the reflexive. Thus *þizelf* (*þezelue*, *þizelue*), *himzelf* (*himzelue*), (*harezelue*, *hirezelue*), (*hamzelue*). The form *zelf* (*zelue*) is also used by itself to render French *meismes* as in *þe wordle zelf* (*li siecles meismes*) 59/6; *god zelf* (*dieu meismes*) 93/25, 149/19, *þe(t) ilke zelue* (*celui meismes*) 156/14, 190/30; *of one zelue þris* (*d'un meisme þris*) 186/12; *þis ilke zelue* (*ce meismes*) 236/33. It may be noted that, as elsewhere in Middle English, the emphatic pronouns can function without an antecedent. This is especially true of the oblique cases, so that the *Ayenbite* does not distinguish between 'he said it to him' and 'he said it to himself'.

The relative pronouns

The relative form *þet* has already been discussed. The forms

---

[1] N. von Glahn, *Zur Geschichte des grammatischen Geschlechts im Mittelenglischen* (Anglistische Forschungen, 53, 1918), pp. 88–90.

[2] Wallenberg, p. 112, n. 1. Cf. also the discussion of gender pp. 85–97.

huet and *huich* are also used as relatives. *Huet* is used as an invariable compound relative 'what', 'that which' at 115/14, 196/6, etc. It most commonly introduces an indirect question.[1] *Huich* is used as a relative at 7/11, 52/1, 154/5, etc. Unlike *huet*, it has an antecedent which can be animate or inanimate, singular or plural.

As elsewhere in Middle English, *huo* is not usually a relative but its oblique cases are. It is difficult to judge how far it is tied to gender in the *Ayenbite*. It refers to inanimates at 21/30, 69/7,[2] 96/3, 148/8, 168/24, 202/21, 203/8, 9, 260/12 but the gender confusion in the text makes it difficult to draw any firm conclusions. No doubt, in a number of cases, confusion also arose because of French *qui*, which was used to refer to inanimates as well as to animates. In general, the neuter inflections are rendered by compounds of *huer*. Thus *huerinne* 'in which', *huermide* 'with which', *huerof* 'of which', 'concerning which', and so on. Thus we may summarize the main *Ayenbite* usages as follows:

Who: SG. (*huo*), *þet*, *huas*, *huam;* PL. *þet*, *huiche(n)*, *huam*
Which: SG. *þet*, *huam*, *huich(en)*, *huer-;* PL. *þet*, *huiche(n)*
What: *þet*, *huet*

Interrogatives and indefinite pronouns and adjectives

The interrogatives are *huo* 'who', *huet* 'what', *huich* 'which'. The indefinites are *huo* (*þet*), *huet* (*þet*), and *huich* (*þet*) 'whoever, whatever, of whatever kind'. A demonstrative or personal pronoun+*þet* is often used as an indefinite. Thus *þe ilke þet*, *he þet* 'whoever'.

Gender

A number of forms in the *Ayenbite* have been thought to be gender markers. These must be considered in turn. 1. Adjectives and pronouns with the suffix *-ne* usually qualify or refer to masculines. The only exception is: *nenne skele* (86/13); forms such as *oþren(e)*, *ane* may belong here but are not included. 2. *þes* (adjective and pronoun) refers to original masculines (16×). The only exceptions are *god* 'benefit',[3] an original neuter which, however,

---

[1] At 186/22, *huet þe urend is* should probably read *huo þe urend is*. See note to this line.
[2] It seems most likely that the antecedent is *heste* and not *lhorde*.
[3] Cf. Wallenberg, p. 94, n. 1.

has *he* as a pronoun of reference; *yefþe*, an original feminine which is often masculine in the *Ayenbite*, perhaps under the influence of French *don*. But it should be noted that the unaccented feminine could also give *þes* (OK *þeos*). At 62/13, *þes* refers to *þe scorpioun*; at 53/26 to 'man'; at 62/4 perhaps to *boȝ* or *ȝenne*. The names of animals are usually masculine in the *Ayenbite*. 3. *þis* (OE *þios* f. and *þis* neut.). Wallenberg[1] regards *þis* as the feminine and neuter form. In the nominative, both the adjective and the pronoun qualify or refer to feminines[2] and neuters quite frequently (113 ×). The form *þis* also refers to masculines as *article* (4×); *boȝ* (2×) (at 17/30 *he* is used as a pronoun of reference); *name* (1 ×); *stat* (1 ×); *vridom* (1 ×). 4. *þis* (acc.) might reasonably be expected to refer to neuters only since it represents the OE neuter *þis*. Out of a total of twenty-six adjectival and pronominal uses, however, only seven refer to or qualify original neuters. Use with the feminine *heste* (2×) and the masculine *article* (10×) might be due to elision of *þise heste*, *þise article*. But the form occurs also with an original feminine, *yefþe* (1 ×), and with the masculines *cloþ* (1 ×), *lhordssip*[3] (2 ×), and *mes* (1 ×). 5. The form *þerne*, which shows the distinctively accusative masculine ending -*ne*, is recorded with masculine nouns (8×) but also with feminines *ansuere* and *paske*, and with a neuter *viȝt*. 6. *þo* (acc. adj. pron.) qualifies or refers to a feminine three times (*contraye*, *bene*, *dede*) and a masculine (*byleue* 143/30) once. The latter may be due to the influence of French *cele foi*.[4]

It seems probable that the asymmetrical relationship between, on the one hand, the nominative *þis* which serves to contrast the feminine and neuter with the masculine *þes*, and, on the other, the accusative *þis* which serves to distinguish the neuter from the masculine and feminine, led to the supersession of **þos* (OE *þas*) and the recession of the masculine *þerne*. The former is replaced by *þis* or *þise* and the latter to a considerable extent by *þis*. It seems, therefore, doubtful whether *þis* can be regarded as a

---

[1] Wallenberg, s.v.

[2] At 163/28, 30, it refers to a feminine, *uirtue*, but the pronoun of reference is *himȝelue* (cf. p. 84). At 226/25, the text is corrupt. See note to this line.

[3] For discussion of this form see p. 89, n. 4.

[4] Wallenberg (p. 246, n. 3) points out that *tuay(e)* is restricted to masculines and only twice occurs with feminines, namely *lettres* (1/18) and *manere* (212/29); *tuo* is used for the feminine and neuter and OF feminines. But it is also used with the masculines *nykeren* (61/9); *ssetteles* (94/29), and with *yefþe*, an original feminine which is usually masculine in the *Ayenbite*. For *þan(e) oþrene* see p. 89.

gender marker. The partial retention of the derivatives of OE *þone, þa, þet* in the accusative means that, in spite of the falling together of *se* and *sio* in *þe, þet* remained a neuter form and there was not the same impetus towards its extension into other genders. 7. The qualifier *þane* (OE *þone*) is generally used with masculine nouns. Exceptionally it refers to original feminines, *loue* (2×), *yefþe* (2×) and to neuters, *scele* (13×), *viʒt* (4×), *weued* (1×), *zuelʒ* (2×), *zoþ* (1×).[1] If we subtract from the total the words *spot, smel, smite, snegge, snode, strok* as being of uncertain etymology and gender, we have 25 exceptions out of 260 examples, or 7 exceptional cases out of 88 words.[2] 8. The position with regard to *þet* is somewhat more complicated, since Old French nouns had no neuter gender. It seems best, therefore, to consider words of native or Norse origin and words of French origin separately. The results of such an analysis are as follows.

1. English and Norse words

If we include in our count the substantivalized adjectives, *greate* ('gross'), *guod(e), kuead(e), uayreste, uerste*, and the points of the compass *norþ, yeast, zouþ*, the number of cases in which *þet* is used as a qualifier is 419. Of these, all are original neuters except (i) the Old English feminine substantives *boc* (1×), *dong* (1×), *prede* (1×) (ii) the Old English masculines: *angel* (1×), *colt* (1×), *del* (2×), *doʒ* (1×), *hod* (1×), *smech* (1×), *stor* (1×).[3]

2. French words

(i) The following Old French masculines are qualified by *þet*: *barat* (1×), *cas* (2×), *cheker* (2×), *comfort* (1×), *frut* (14×), *gernier* (1×), *hauberk* (1×), *iowel* (1×), *lauor* (1×), *mestier* (1×), *mortyer* (1×), *peril* (1×), *profit* (1×), *sacrament* (1×), *stat* (7×), *strif* (1×), *tornoyment* (2×), *tresor* (8×), *uenym* (2×); *scot* (1×) may belong here but could represent ON *skot* n. (ii) Old French feminines: *best* (1×), *colour* (1×), *flour* (7×), *pays* (5×), *pater noster* (7×).

---

[1] Wallenberg (p. 94, n. 1) suggests that the masculine qualifier is due to 'God' in the next clause.

[2] This includes the perhaps doubtful examples *þane fleumatike, colrik, melancolien, sanguinien, laʒre, sleuuolle*.

[3] At 247/28, *þet god* is probably an error. See the note to this line.

3. In addition there are words which have two different qualifiers. Thus (a) masculine: *clop* (*þane* 1×; *þet* 1×); *fol* (*þane* 1×; *þet* 1×); *lost* (*þane* 3×; *þet* 1×); *pot* (*þane* 1×; *þet* 1×); *red* (*þane* 2×; *þet* 4×); *wode* (*þane* 1×; *þet* 1×); (b) feminine *loue* (*þane* 2×; *þet* 1×); (c) neuter *viȝt* (*þane* 4×; *þet* 1×). Some, at least, of the cases of *þet* with a feminine or masculine noun may be errors for *þe* but the total number of examples would seem to forbid this as a general explanation. Out of 419 examples, 82 instances of *þet* qualify original feminines or masculines. From this total we should, perhaps, subtract the 50 instances of French masculines, which would mean that, out of 370 examples in all, 32 qualify words not neuter; 1 neuter is also qualified four times by *þane*; 10 instances occur in which *þet* qualifies masculine or feminine nouns which are qualified also by *þane*. It will be seen that the statistics suggest that the forms where *þet* qualifies an original neuter, or *þane* an original masculine, cannot be taken as random. They must be supposed to suggest that they derive from a linguistic situation in which grammatical gender still obtained. How far such a situation still obtained in the *Ayenbite* is, of course, a different question and one to which we shall return. It has been customary to assume that deviations from the original gender indicate a change of gender. But they may merely indicate a changed function of certain allomorphs originally gender markers. It is noteworthy that while the originally masculine accusative forms *þerne* and *þane* and the originally feminine accusative form *þo* can be used to qualify words of a gender to which they were not originally appropriate, they are never used as nominative forms. In the same way, the form *þes* may occasionally be used to qualify words which are not masculine in origin but it is not used as an accusative. This may imply that there was a tendency, as Charles Jones has suggested, to regard these forms as tied to case rather than to gender.[1]

The pronouns of reference are a distinct problem. The instances may be considered under the following headings:

1. Some cases may be explained by reference to the French. Thus

ayenwyȝte n. (*he:il*) 247/20;
beleaue m. (*hi:ele*) 123/15 n.;

[1] Cf. Charles Jones, 'The Grammatical Category of Gender in Early Middle English', *English Studies*, xlviii (1967), 289–305; N. S. Baron, 'A Reanalysis of English Grammatical Gender', *Lingua*, xxvii (1971), 113–40.

(*þet*) *body* (*he:il*) at 54/17,[1] 81/13, 154/5–6 are perhaps due to French *il*;

charite f. (*hi:ele*) 90/33, 34, 91/4, 5, 7; 123/20 n., 21; (*hire, his: son*) 90/34, 35;

(*þane, þerne, þes*) *dom* (*hi:ele*) 124/18;

(*þane*) *drope* (*his:la*) 91/31; (*þet hy:quele*) 92/7[2] may be due to the gender of the French but *drope* is referred to also as *he, hine* (91/33);

grace f. (*hi:ele*) 128/28; (*him:se*) 184/7;

guod is usually neuter and both *þes god* (200/19) and *he* (79/25, 200/19) are probably dependent on the French *cil don* (cf. note to 200/19); *ce bien:il*; *cil don:il*. But later in the passage (79/28–31) it is also referred to as *hy* perhaps by confusion with *yefþe* (but this is often masculine); perhaps because it was thought to be a feminine abstract noun; or in the later examples in this latter passage its antecedent may have been thought to be *grace*;

(*þane, þes*) *kertel* (*hi:ele*) 236/20; but, at 236/21, where there is no French equivalent, it is referred to as *he*. The form *hi* could be due to the French, an error for *he*, or it might be plural. At 236/21 the pronoun of reference is *him* (NF);

(*þet*) *inwyt* (*hi:ele*) 7/18;

lecherie f. (*him:se*) 47/27;[3]

lhordssip m. (*hi:ele*) 84/29;[4]

(*þet*) *leme* (*he:il*) 147/2, 148/6;[5]

(*þet*) *lyf* (*hi:ele*) 199/9, 12, 14, 15, 18; *him* (NF) 199/13;

maydenhod m. (*hi:ele*) 228/11; at 228/6 *he* (*ele*) is an error. The manuscript has *hi*;

ssrifte m. (*hi:ele*) 172/7;[6]

(*þet*) *trau* (*his(e):les*) 97/31, 32, 33. The text, however, is corrupt and the forms may be plural;[7]

uayrhede (*hy:ele*) 81/19;[8]

uirtue f. (*he:*NF) 147/13; at 124/31, *he* refers to 'man' rather than

---

[1] See note to this line.

[2] But it might refer to 'sweetness'. Cf. von Glahn, p. 75 and note to this line.

[3] Cf. p. 84 for *him* as a reflexive referring to feminines.

[4] Von Glahn (p. 78) suggests a change of gender. He points out that the *Vices and Virtues* treats nouns in -*ssiþe* as feminine.

[5] At 148/14, 15, the reference is unclear. If *he* refers to *leme*, the metaphor is odd. It may rather be impersonal 'one', or refer to *herte* (see below).

[6] But this can be masculine or feminine in Old English.

[7] See the note to 97/29–30..

[8] This noun, however, may be feminine. Cf. p. 58.

'virtue'; *his* (gen. sg.) renders a French plural possessive at 131/30, 32, 35. In a number of cases, however, the pronouns are feminine. Thus *hi* renders *ele* at 83/33, 131/32, 132/3–4, 145/4, 248/23, 260/22, 27; it has no French equivalent at 166/3; also feminine, as the French, are *his*:*la* (248/23); *hyre*/*hare* are reflexive (131/32, 260/22) but *him* is used at 146/29;

(*þet*) *uless* (*hi*:*ele*) 181/2 n.; but, at 181/1 DM has *him* (*s'*) and, at 181/3, where there is no French equivalent, DM has *ha*;

welle f. (*hi*:*ele*) 251/20, 22; (*hym*:*se*) 97/34;

(*þet*) *weter* (*hi*:*ele*) 93/3. But the text is corrupt and the referent unclear;[1]

(*þet*) *wyf* (*him*: *lui*) 49/12; *wyf* is immediately afterwards referred to as *hi* and it seems unlikely that the pronoun *him* reflects the original gender;

(*þet*) *wil* (*hise*:*la*) 109/23; (*hi*:*ele*) 109/25–6 but *he* (NF) at 109/23 as well as the ambiguous *him* (*li*) at 158/18, 253/14. The passage, 109/23–6, is involved and unclear and it is probable that DM simply followed the French pronouns where these were available[1] (at 125/24–7 *hi* (*ele*) probably refers to *scele, loue, wyl*);

wylninge f. (*he*:*il*) 163/19 but also *hi* in the same line;

(*þet*) *wyt* (*he*:*il*) 83/3;

wombe f. (*him*:*le*) 50/33, 34;

zaule f. (*he*:*il*) 143/14;[2] (*him*:*li*) 81/20, 142/30, 36, 143/15, 18, 22, 24, 32; (*his*:*son sien*) 81/21, 158/15 but *he* (NF) at 143/19 and *his* (*sa*) at 81/20, 24, 105/31, 143/22 (*le sien*). Also, however, it is referred to as *hire* (*lui, ele*) 142/35, 143/7 and *hi* (*ele*) 105/30, 142/35, 36, 143/8, 9, 21, 22, 26, 29, 30, 31, 197/27 and so on (cf. 3 below);

zenne f. (*he*:*il*) 21/22, 22/11, 29/3; (*him*:*se*) 17/19, 21/23, 22/11, 27/5, 48/3, 20 etc. In spite of French *il*, however, feminine pronouns are also used at 16/25–6, 28/29, 48/21, 59/1, etc. A French possessive may also sometimes be responsible for an apparent change of gender. Thus, at 57/21 and several times at 152/28–33, *speche f.* is referred to as *hi*. Nevertheless, it has *his* as its possessive and not *hire*. But the French *son*, of course, agrees with the noun it precedes and not the noun it stands for.

Some nouns with unoriginal gender markers in the *Ayenbite* come also in this category. Thus

---

[1] See the note to these lines.
[2] See the note to 143/14–32.

(*pet*) *del m.* under the influence of the French is referred to as *hi* (*ele*) at 165/10;

(*pet*) *flour f.* is referred to as *hi, hire* (*ele, la*) at 230/24, 25. Von Glahn suggests that the pronouns here may refer to *maydenhod*[1] but as *maydenhod* was originally masculine this does not solve the problem and the pronouns are more probably due to the French;

(*pane, pet*) *loue f.* is referred to as *hi* (*ele*) at 83/4, 121/17, 250/29, 251/1, 2 (for 125/26 see *wil* above);

(*pet*) *pays f.* is referred to as *hi* (*ele*) at 261/33, 34. This could be personification, however;

(*nenne, pane*) *skele n.* is referred to as *hi, hire* (*ele, la*) at 151/19, 20, 25, 35 (for 125/25 see *wil* above);

(*pane, pes*) *yefpe f.* is referred to as *he* (*il*) at 127/32, 144/27, 150/13, 14, 151/23, 33, 152/17, 247/4; but *hi* (*il*) at 150/19. This may have a genuine change of gender but the use of *pise* (acc.) at 106/17, 144/32, 184/23 could reflect the original gender.

2. Some cases are probably mechanical errors. Such is certainly the case at 139/15 and 181/2 where *man* is referred to as *hi*, certainly an error for *he*;

merci f. is referred to as *ha* at 174/9 but as *hi* (*ele*) at 191/31. It is possible that *ha*, which is not in the French, means 'the man' and not 'mercy';

onderstondinge f. usually referred to as *hi* (159/17 n., 22, 24, 25) is referred to as *he* (*il*) at 159/22 but here again the sense is probably 'the man'. At 103/35 it is referred to as *him* (*se*);[2]

ziknesse f. (*him:y*) 22/31 may be an error for *hire*;

(*pet*) *uolk* (*hi*) 184/11 may be, as von Glahn suggested, an error for *hit*.[3]

3. In some cases DM's exemplar may be in error. This is apparently the case at 143/14 where, as already mentioned, *he* referring to the usually feminine *zaule* seems to be due to a misunderstanding of French *il*. Errors in the French may explain *perne* (*ceste*) *paske* (133/20) and *his* (*sa*) referring to the feminine *zaule*; on the other hand, *perne ansuere* (214/22) cannot be so explained as there is no French equivalent. At 102/33, *auarice* is referred to as *hi* (*il*) and DM's exemplar may have read *ele*.

---

[1] Von Glahn, pp. 82–3. At 233/30 *hi* probably refers to *lylye*.
[2] Cf. p. 84 for discussion of *him* as a reflexive referring to feminines.
[3] Von Glahn, p. 68.

Cleopatra is here correct; the sense is 'a man' not 'avarice.'
At 34/26 *him* is used as a reflexive referring to *auarice*.

4. In some cases, personification may explain the irregular gender.
Thus perhaps *hope*, an original masculine, referred to as *hi* (*il*)
at 123/17 n.; *ordre* (*hi*:NF) at 151/9 n. may reflect the original
gender. The word later became masculine in French, however,
under the influence of Latin;[1] (*pet*) *prede f.* is referred to as *hy*
(*ce*) at 17/8 but at 127/33 as *his* (*son*). The feminine pronoun could
reflect the original gender or be personification. On the other
hand, *his* is probably due to French *son*.

5. Association with related words may sometimes explain an
unexpected gender. For example, von Glahn suggests that the
feminine pronoun *hise* (*le*) referring to (*pane*) *time* m. at 214/3
may be due to confusion with the feminine *tide*.[2] But *time* is re-
ferred to as *hine* at 52/22, 207/3 and DM's text may have been
corrupt.

6. Some cases defy simple explanations and may be due to a
number of factors. Thus, *bene*, an original feminine, appears to
keep original gender qualifiers; so at 211/12, it is qualified by *þo*
(*cele*). But much uncertainty appears in the pronouns of refer-
ence. Thus, at 99/22, 219/13, *he* (*ele*) and at 217/22, *him* (*la*);
but *hi* (*ele*) at 209/17, 211/19, 21, 217/19, 219/5 and, without a
French equivalent, at 102/5; the reflexive *hire* (*soi*) occurs at
217/20. Von Glahn suggested that the pronoun *he* might be from
OE *heo*[3] but this does not seem probable even though forms in
low stress sometimes, in the *Ayenbite*, show the development of
OK *io* to *e*. Nor would it explain the other gender confusion already
mentioned.

Similar confusion appears also in the case of the noun *herte* (*f.*).
In origin feminine, it occurs with a number of feminine pronouns
of reference. Since French *cuer* is masculine, these are usually
independent of the French. Thus *hi* (*il*, *i*) 94/34, 95/10, 106/15,
109/5, 111/20, 150/19, 202/10, 250/35, 252/4, 13, 254/18,
19, 20, 30, 260/29; *hi* (*le*) 95/10;[4] *his*(*e*) (*le*, NF) 58/1, 5, 106/15, 26,
107/1, 116/25, 26, 144/33, 250/24, 254/14; *hire* (*le*, *l'*) 144/31, 201/14,
251/32; *hire* (*ses*) 58/4. In some cases, however, the pronoun of

[1] See Pope, § 777 (iv).   [2] Von Glahn, p. 78.   [3] Von Glahn, p. 79.
[4] A doubtful case is *hi* (*ele*) 94/34. *Ele* refers to *terre bone* (*land*). But it seems
unlikely that *hi* refers to *land*.

reference is masculine perhaps owing to the influence of the French. Thus *he* (*il*) at 88/8, 136/31, 33, 34, 148/14, 252/17, 18, 254/15; *him* (*lui*) 148/14, 15;[1] *him* (*le*, *li*) 250/25, 29, 251/31, 32, 252/16; but there are cases in which the masculine gender does not appear to depend upon the French, although allowance must always be made for the possibility of a different reading in DM's French text. Such cases are: *he* (*qui*) 87/17; *his* (*ses*, *son*) 136/31, 32, 250/30, 260/29; *himʒelue* (*soimeismes*) 136/34; *ha*, *he* (NF) 88/9–10 (cf. note), 251/15,[2] 252/15; *him*, *himʒelue* (*soi*, *se*) 250/26, 251/15, 16, 252/15, 260/29; *hire* (*s(e)*) 251/9 n., 254/20, 30; *hireʒelue* (*soi*), *hire* (*son*, *sa*) 251/9, 10, 260/30.

A special category consists of the names of animals. They are usually referred to as *he*, *hine*. Thus (*pane*) *asse*, *bere*, *cat*, *dogge*, (*pane*) *hond*, *hare*, *heyrone*, *lyoun*, *oxe*, (*pane*) *uoʒel*: some are feminine as *cou*, *eddre*, *mere*, *ulindre*; variable gender appears in *mous* (*his*, *hire:la*); *turle* (*he*, *hi*, *hare*); *pornhog* (*he*, *hit*); *uleʒe* (*hi:ele*; *his:son*). Possibly on the analogy of the masculine names of animals, *best(e)* qualified by *pet* at 182/12, is referred to as *he* at 15/33.

Nevertheless, when all dubious instances have been excluded, there is still a considerable number of cases in the *Ayenbite* where the pronouns of reference retain the original gender. Some of these correspond to the French but some do not. Thus

(a) original masculines: (*pes*) *boʒ* (*he*:NF) 17/30; (*fieblene*, *pane*) *castel* (*he:il*; *him:se*) 240/29, 31; *chalis* (*ha:il*) 167/22; (*enne*, *pane*) (*Zon*)*day* (*hine:le*) 7/22; (*perne*, *pane*) *dyap* (*he*) 264/16, 17, 18; (*pane*) *eppel* (*he:ele*) 205/24; (*pane*, *perne*) *mete* (*he:il*, NF, *ele*) 112/35, 36; (*pane*, *ualsne*) *peny* (*ha:il*) 91/2; (*pane*) *spot*(?) (*he*:NF) 238/19; *sseawere* (*him:li*) 158/8; *mirour* (*hine:le*) 158/10; *sso* (*he:il*) 220/24; (*pane*) *uot* (*him:li*) 149/3; (*anoperne*, *pane*, *perne*) *way* (*hine:la*) 60/12;

(b) original feminines: *beheste* (*hi:il*) 225/26; *blisse* (*hi:ele*) 93/20; *hy* 269/4; *boʒsamnesse* (*hi:ele*) 140/12; (*hise:l'*) 140/15; (*hire:la*) 140/11; *chastete* (*hy:ele*) 220/25; *cherche* (*hy:il*) 51/3; *cite* (*hise:la*) 195/27; *coupe* (*hi:ele*) 167/21; *dette* (*hi:ele*) 163/11 (or refers to *riʒtuolnesse*);[3] (*his:la*) 145/31; *drede* (*hi:ele*) 231/23; *elmesse* (*hi:ele*) 192/3, 4; (*his:la*) 192/3 ff., 193/23, 196/11; *errour* (*hi:ele*)[4]

---

[1] But the passage is ambiguous. See p. 148 n. 14.
[2] But cf. note to this line.   [3] But see *OED* s.v.   [4] See Pope § 777 (iv).

83/25; *erþe* (*hy*:*ele*) 89/6; (*hise*:*la*) 143/10 n; *face* (*his*:*la*) 88/9; *hand* (*hire*:*se*) 149/4; (*rote*) *herbe* (*hi*:*ele*) 153/9; *ypocrisie* (*hire*:*se*) 25/32; *laȝe* (*hi*:*ele*) 97/12–13, 97/15; (*his*(*e*):*la*) 97/21, 22; (*harezelue*:NF) 97/15;[1] (*hise*:*en*) 126/21; ?*lilye* (*hi*:*ele*) 233/30; *lompe* (*hi*:*ele*) 232/24; *manere* (*hi*:*ele*) (but cf. *lyf* page 89); *mildenesse* (*hy*:*ele*) 140/15; (*hire*:*ses*) 140/15; (*perseuerance*) (*hi*:*ele*) 232/35;[1] *riȝtuolnesse* (*hi*:*ele*) 125/32; *robe* (*his*:*la*) 167/25; *sobrete* (*hi*:*ele*) 248/29. 249/3; *speche* (*hi*:*ele*) 57/21; *ssame* (*hy*:*ele*) 26/26; *tale* (*hi*:*il*) 234/21; *uondinge* (*hi*:*ele*) 116/14; (*his*:*la*) 176/9; *wordle* (*hi*:*il*) 162/17; (*hire*:*sa*, *laquele*) 82/4, 248/8;[1] (*hi*:NF) 87/12 n., 164/36; (*his* acc.: NF) 243/17; *ȝe* (*hi*:*ele*) 119/8.

There are, if we omit those cases in which there is no French or Latin equivalent, three situations here: (*a*) French loan words (17×). The agreement between the English and French may only show that DM is simply following the French. (*b*) English words (i) whose pronouns of reference coincide with the original gender and with the French (19×); (ii) whose pronouns of reference correspond to the original gender but not to the French pronoun (5×). While, given the nature of the translation, the evidence must be regarded with the greatest caution, it is difficult to assume that all indications of grammatical gender in the *Ayenbite* are purely due to the French text. The translation is literal, but not in the way in which the Early Version of the Wyclif Bible is literal. It is true that pronouns of reference tend to be separated from the noun to which they refer and therefore are more susceptible to this kind of influence than qualifiers, but the qualifiers also suggest that the text contains relics of the older gender system. The problem is to assess precisely the function of these forms in the economy of the morphological system as a whole. To do this we must consider the cases in which *hit* is used as pronoun of reference. Leaving aside those instances in which *hit* refers to neuters, the instances may be classified as follows:

1. (a) *hit* refers to nouns not originally neuter which, however, have no indications of gender in the *Ayenbite*: (i) original masculines: *paradis* 138/32; *spoushod* 221/27–32, 222/3, 9; (ii) originally feminine nouns are: *armure* 171/4; *blissinge* 245/12 n.; *clergie* 99/2, 3; *clopinge* 217/11; *dignete* 215/23; *ymage* 242/14;[2] *oyle* 186/32;

---

[1] But cf. note to this line.　　　[2] See Pope, § 777 (i).

pouerte 138/22; ? *reste* 133/30–1; *slacnesse* 33/11; *sseppe* 6/2; *vileynie* 18/17.[1]

(b) *Hit* confirms an apparent change of gender from masculine to neuter: *þet frut* 229/24; *þet peril* 173/35; *þet stat* 227/15; (*þet*) *strif* 22/4; *þet tresor* 232/22, 23; (*þet*) *uenym* 27/33; from feminine to neuter: (*þet*) *pater noster* 99/6 etc.

2. *Hit* coincides with the original but not the *Ayenbite* gender: *þornhog* (*he*) 66/14–18.

3. *Hit* coincides with part only of the gender indications: (i) original neuters: (*þet*) *body* (*he*) 20/33, 34, 36, 221/24, 237/5; (*þet, þes*) *g(u)od* (*he, hi*) 94/21; (*þane, þet*) *pot* (206/15); (*þet*) *trau* (*his(e)*)[2] 131/27, 185/28; (*þet*) *wyl* (*he, hi, him, hise*) 109/16; (ii) original masculine and feminine substantives number only two, both French loans; (*þet*) *beste* (*he*) 14/35, 15/23, 32; (*þet*) *flour* (*hi, hire*) 230/27.

4. *Hit* conflicts with gender indications in the *Ayenbite* (i) original masculines preserved in the *Ayenbite*: (*þane*) *bal* 179/9; (*þane, þerne*) *dyaþ* (*he*) 72/32, 33; (*þane*) *lost* 179/22; (*þane, þerne*) *mete* (*he*) 111/6, 8; (*þane, þerne, þes*) *uridom* 86/12; (ii) feminine preserved: *blisse* (*hi*) 14/15; *chastete* (*hy*) 227/1; *elmesse* (*his, hi*) 192/6, 11, 194/11, 195/34, 196/8; *uayrhede* (*hy*) 100/30; (iii) original gender partly preserved: (a) masculine: (*þane*) *time* (*hine, hise*) 214/16; (b) feminines: *merci* (*ha, hi*) 187/25; *wylninge* (*he, hi*) 163/20; *zenne* (*he, him, hi*) 16/33, 49/20, 27; (*þane, þes*) *yefþe* (*he, hi*) 192/19; (iv) *Hit* refers to an original masculine which has a feminine pronoun: *lhordssip* (*hi*) 85/1; *maydenhod* (*hi*) 232/33; (v) *Hit* refers to an original feminine which appears to have become masculine: *dede* (*him*) 47/30, 31.

It seems probable that these instances represent, in the majority of cases, an encroachment of the neuter *hit* as a pronoun of reference for inanimates.[3] Nevertheless, the very wide use of feminine and masculine pronouns of reference for inanimates in the text, even though these may in some cases be due to the French, must suggest that grammatical gender was in some sense

---

[1] Here may belong also *chasthede* 230/35; *uayrhede* 81/10, 13 (for the reference at 81/19 see p. 89 and von Glahn, p. 85). For nouns in -*hede* cf. p. 58.

[2] The form *his(e)* may be plural however. See note to 97/29–30.

[3] At 8/17 *hi* (*onboȝsamnesse*) has been emended to *hit*.

a reality still in the *Ayenbite*. We should expect on the analogy of other texts that the weakest link in the system would be the pronouns of reference. This we have shown to be the case. Yet there were perhaps two other factors in the process. In the first place, we have already noted that an adjectival accusative in *-e* is frequently used with original feminines. Moreover, even where it is used with original masculines, these tend to be words which have assumed a final *-e* in the *Ayenbite*. Thus there seems to be a tendency to align the substantival and nominal declensions by a simple process of harmonizing the endings and in some cases of discrepancy this principle may be at work. Thus *loue*, an original feminine, has feminine pronouns of reference and adjectival qualifiers ending in *-e*. But it is qualified by *þet* and *þane*. The former we shall deal with later, but it may be suggested here that *þane* may simply be due to the harmonic principle already mentioned. On the other hand, *þane time*, an original masculine, has adjectival qualifiers in *-e* and *hise* and *hine* as pronouns of reference. Here again the harmonic principle may have undermined the original morphological structure. The original feminine (*þes, þane*) *yefþe* (*he:il*) has adjectival qualifiers in *-e* which may merely indicate that the noun belongs to the vocalic declension. Possibly a mere error is the accusative *þine gost* (74/34) which conflicts with the qualifiers *enne, þane, þes*. Moreover, it may be noted that the use of an adjectival qualifier in final *-e* coincides with other marks of feminine gender in: *blisse, charite,*[1] *chastete, dette, grace, manere, riƷtuolnesse, speche, ssame, ssrifte*.

The second factor which tended to undermine the system of grammatical gender was probably the development of the invariable *þe* which is in common use in the *Ayenbite*. We probably have in the *Ayenbite* a process of convergence as follows: 1. The neuter-tied *þet*, as *hit* is increasingly used for all genders, is identified with *þe* which in the *Ayenbite* is the only masculine and feminine nominative form. 2. In the accusative, *þet* is partly in contrast with *þane*, a masculine tied form; with adjectives in *-ne*; with the rare feminine *þo* and with *þe* in all genders. But the forms in *-e* were liable to erosion from the harmonic principle and *þo* had already been almost entirely merged in *þe*. With the weakening of these contrasts *þet* again tended to merge with the genderless *þe*.

[1] At 123/20, *hi* (*charite*) is altered from *he* (*il*).

A third source of confusion may be convergence of *he* and *hi* for purely phonetic reasons. These factors may explain the case of *loue* to which we have already referred. An original feminine, it has adjectival qualifiers in -*e* as well as some feminine pronouns of reference. On the other hand, it is qualified by *þet*[1] and is also qualified by masc. *þane*. It thus partakes of three different systems: 1. It has the nominative/accusative qualifier *þet* 2. It is a vocalic noun and thus has qualifiers ending in -*e* 3. It participates in the masculine system with *þane*. Some old neuters might be analysed in a similar way. Thus for example, *þet wil*, an original neuter, has adjectival qualifiers in -*e* and both masculine and feminine pronouns.[2] Here, if our understanding of the situation is correct, the rare examples of the adjectival qualifier in -*e* may be errors.

Thus it seems that, while much of the apparatus of grammatical gender is maintained in the *Ayenbite*, it is subject to erosion from a number of conflicting systems: the substantival declension; the development of the invariable *þe*, in the first instance merely an unstressed form; the use of *hit* as pronoun of reference, in the first instance a symptom of erosion rather than a cause, but one which hastened the downfall of the system, by the introduction of a conflicting system, that of natural gender.

Verbs

1. *The present tense*

A. The endings of verbs belonging to this class are as follows: INFINITIVE -*e*;[3] INDICATIVE SG. 1. -*e*, 2. -*st*,[4] 3. -*þ* (-*t*);[5] PL. -*eþ*;[6] SUBJ. SG. and PL. -*e*; IMP. SG. zero, PL. -*eþ*;

---

[1] The single example could, however, be an error.

[2] But at 109/16 *hi* (*ele*) referring to *wyl* has been corrected to *hit*. Cf. 57/18–19 where *hi* (*ele*) referring to *word* has also been corrected to *hit*.

[3] Corrections of endingless forms to forms with -*e* in *benime* (112/9); *onderstonde* (263/29); *zeche* (80/16) may indicate a tendency to lose the final vowel or be merely due to carelessness. For *poruay* see note to 152/23.

[4] Cases of a 2 sg. pr. ending in *s* appear to be due to sandhi. Thus *worþssipes* (188/23, but not 24) is probably, as pointed out on p. 53, due to the following *þe*; cf. *onderstans* for *onderstandst* (270/10). At 254/25, *loues* is corrected to *louest*. The loss of the final dental was caused by the dental of *to* which followed.

[5] For consonant assimilations see pp. 48–9. OK also shows an interchange of -*þ* and -*t*. Cf. Wallenberg, p. 108, n. 2.

[6] The forms *byet* (66/27), *habbet* (126/14, 21) may be errors or French spellings (cf. Wallenberg, p. 108). The form *bied* (138/30) may be an error due to the proximity of *accorsed*. On the other hand, *sostinet* (39/35) may be by dissimilation from the following *þe*. Cf. Wallenberg, p. 32, n. 1 for *byet* and *bied*.

PR.P. -*inde*[1]. To this class belong (a) OE strong and weak-strong verbs (b) OE weak verbs of the first class except those which, like *herian*, had a short vowel followed by *r*[2] (c) *habbe, libbe, zigge* (d) *playe* from weak class II (e) *prede, ssmelle* from the same nouns (f) contract verbs *beulaʒe, slaʒe, sle*(*a*), *uly, wry* (g) French verbs whose stem ended in a vowel.[3] Thus (*aspiþ*),[4] *alowe*, (*anoyþ*), (*asayþ*), (*astruþ*), (*brayinde*), (*condueþ*), *destrue, edefie*, (*fyeþ*), *glorifie*, (*multepliest*), *paye, poruay*(*e*),[5] *remue, reneye* (h) the Norse verb *keste*(1). The following exceptional cases may be noted:

1. In the imperative singular, *habbe* and originally weak verbs with short stems show -*e* and a single consonant as in *haue, ssete, zele* (beside *zel*),[6] and *zete*. The forms *arere, miswende, ssylde* are historically incorrect and, no doubt, owe their final vowel to analogy. For *brenge* see the note to 1/10.

2. Contract verbs show the normal phonological developments from Old Kentish bearing in mind that in 2 and 3 sg. Kentish often retained a guttural, whence such forms as *wriʒþ*[7] in the *Ayenbite*. In the imperative, the forms *beuli, ysy* are analogical but a historically correct form is preserved in *yziʒ* (OK *gesih*). Also analogical are the forms *beulaʒe, slaʒe* (inf.), *sslast, slaʒþ, sslaʒt* (2, 3 sg.) and *beulaʒeþ* (pl.) and the participles *ulyinde, zyinde* (OK *flionde, sionde*).

3. A number of verbs have been thought to show a 3 sg. in -*eþ* instead of, or in addition to, syncopated forms. Thus (a) of the originally strong, or weak-strong verbs: *clepeþ*,[8] *comeþ, eteþ, lyeʒeþ, oþbereþ, oþhebbeþ, sseppeþ, wyndeþ, yeldeþ, yerneþ, arereþ*

---

[1] Verbal substantives follow the pattern of the present participle. Thus *heryinge* but *bezuykinge* analogous to **heriinde* and **bezuykinde*. The form *bezuykyinge* (28/5) may be due to shortening as Wallenberg suggests (p. 31, n. 2). Cf. *groniynge* (Wallenberg, p. 100, n. 2) and *tidyinges* (Wallenberg, p. 240, n. 2); for *porueynde* see note to 265/19; *sseawyinges* is an error. See list of corrigenda.   [2] See Class B below.

[3] See Jensen, p. 31.

[4] Round brackets indicate that no infinitive form is recorded.

[5] See p. 97, n. 3.

[6] Jensen (p. 28) explains *zel* as due to analogy with the long forms but it is probably merely due to elision. Cf. Wallenberg, p. 291, n. 2.

[7] The form *neʒleþ* (OK *niohlecþ*) is perhaps on the analogy of such forms as *yzycþ/yzyþ*. Cf. Wallenberg, p. 167, n. 4.

[8] See Wallenberg, p. 55, n. 2 and note to 207/36.

(b) of original weak verbs: *beggeþ, bestrepeþ, brengeþ, ledeþ, leueþ workeþ, zelleþ* (c) of French loans: *condueþ, fyeþ, glorefieþ, multi-plieþ, payeþ*. It is possible, however, that some or all of these are errors.[1] In the 2 sg. we find *leuest, multepliest*.

B. The endings of verbs belonging to this class are as follows: INFINITIVE *-ie*; INDICATIVE SG. 1. *-ie*, 2. *-est*, 3. *-eþ*; PL. *-ieþ*; SUBJ. SG. and PL. *-ie*; IMP. SG. *-e*, PL. *-ieþ*; PR.P. *-iynde*. To this class belong (a) OE weak verbs of Class I which had a short stem ending in *r* (b) some verbs, such as *clepie*,[2] *resye*[3] belonging to Class II (c) the French loans *abatye, ascapie, astonie, (blamyeþ), blasfemie*,[4] *cachie, studie* (d) *wayuye* from ON *veifa*.[5]

The following dubious cases may belong here also: (i) *werie* shows forms coinciding with those of Class A. Thus *werþ* (3 sg.) beside *wereþ*, and *wereþ* (pl.) beside *weryeþ*.[6] (ii) it is not clear to which class *worþssipie* belongs. We should expect, since it has a disyllabic stem, that it would probably belong to the next class and it may be that, as far as the infinitive is concerned, *worþssipij* is merely a variant of *worþssipi*. But the majority of forms have the suffix *-ie*. The present plural, on the other hand, appears twice as *worþssipeþ* which may, however, be an error for *worþssipieþ*; (iii) The form *glede* in *glede we* may be for the subjunctive *gledye we* or by confusion with A. (iv) *zuerie* has 3 sg. *zuerþ* at 6/24.

C. The endings of this class are as follows: INFINITIVE *-i*;[7] INDICATIVE SG. 1. *-i*, 2. *-est*, 3. *-eþ*; PL. *-eþ*;[8] SUBJ. SG. and PL. *-i*;[9] IMP. SG. *-e*, PL. *-eþ*; PR.P. *-inde*. The distribution of verbs between the last two classes is a matter of some difficulty.[10]

---

[1] See the glossary and relevant notes.

[2] The apparently plural form *clepeþ* (17/25) is in fact an error. See note to 17/25.

[3] See Wallenberg, p. 203, n. 1.

[4] Cf. the correction of *blasfeme* to *blasfemie* at 70/11.

[5] Cf. the correction of *wayny* to *waynye* at 88/7 and note.

[6] Cf. Jensen, p. 27; Wallenberg (p. 276, n. 1) suggests analogy with *zuerie*.

[7] Cf. the corrections of *harm* to *harmi* (10/8); *lok* to *loki* (224/22); *mak* to *maky* (64/15).

[8] The plural *seruyeþ* is probably an error but it might be due to assimilation to Class B.

[9] The forms *lyerne, scorne* (subj. sg.) may be errors or due to assimilation to Class B.

[10] Classes B and C correspond to d'Ardenne's IIa and IIb. I have avoided this terminology because of its historical implications, which are not entirely relevant to the *Ayenbite*.

The simple pattern demonstrated for AB is not entirely applicable to the *Ayenbite*. Nevertheless, the length of stem is, as in AB, an important factor in the morphological structure. Thus, to this class belong:

1. (a) OE Class II verbs with a long vowel and single consonant or whose stem ended in a lengthening group. Thus, for example, (*belongeþ* pl.), (*clopeþ* pl.), *endi, greny,* (*handleþ* pl.), (?*hordeþ* sg.), (*hongi*), *liki, loki, lyerni,* (*ymende* imp.), *mildi,* (*oneþ*), *onworþi, pini, ssewy,* (*stoupi* subj. sg.), *tyeny, uondi, wyui,* (*wondreþ* pl.), *yealdy* (b) verbs derived from other parts of speech as *anlykny, anheʒi,* (*bedeaweþ*), *loʒy, medi, mori, strengþi, wreþi*[1] (c) verbs based on disyllabic roots as *cristni, gaderi, openi, rekeni, wetery* and perhaps (*betokneþ* pl.), (*emteþ* pl.), *halʒy.*

2. Verbs with Middle English short vowels before two consonants. Thus *acsy,* (*borʒeþ* pl.), *clensi, harkni,* (*harmeþ*), *emni,* (*helsny*), *lessi, naʒti,* (*offre* imp. sg.), *rocky, smacky, stoppi, þonki,*[2] *þreapny, uanni, uerri, uestni, uetti, uolʒy,* (*waleweþ* pl.), *wylny, zeneʒy,*[3] *zorʒy.* The following belonged to Class II in Old English but have no distinguishing features in the *Ayenbite*: (*baþeþ*), (*plonteþ*), (*ualouweþ*), (*uayreþ*) all 3 sg.; (*waggeþ*).[4]

3. Verbs with original short stems as (*aslaky* subj. sg.), *poty,*[5] (*spari* subj. sg.).

4. Some verbs with short stems show a mixed type of conjugation. Thus *maki* has subj. sg. *makie* and *maki*; pr. p. *maki(i)nde*; *waki* shows imp. pl. *wak(y)eþ.* Cf. *waki(i)nges.*

5. Some originally Class I weak verbs show this type of conjugation as *nemni, resti,* and perhaps (*losteþ* sg.) but this should probably be included in 2 above.[6]

6. The majority of French loans belong to this class whether the stems are long or short. It should be noted here that French *blamer,* which must have had a long vowel after the loss of *s,* appears in the previous class. This seems to suggest that it was

---

[1] This is from the noun *wrĕþ(þ)u* and has a double consonant in *wreþþi* (subj. pl.).   [2] But see discussion on pp. 18–19.
[3] The form *zeneʒþ* may be an error due to partial assimilation to Class A.
[4] See *ODEE* s.v.
[5] OE has two forms of this verb: *pŭtian or *pūtian* and *potian* (see *ODEE* s.v.). The *Ayenbite* form probably comes from *pūtian* or *potian.*
[6] It is probably derived from the sb. *lost.*

borrowed before lengthening in open syllables took place and
that it was thus subject to sound substitution. On the other hand,
it would seem that English verbs with short stems such as *maki*
and *waki* were in transition from the one class to the other as a
result of lengthening in open syllables.[1]

7. Also to this class belong verbs from Norse as *agrayþi, herberȝi,
trosti,*[2] *(uelaȝest, uelaȝeþ), wypscore* (imp. sg.).

8. Possibly the following verbs of uncertain origin: *(godeleþ* sg.),
(lackeþ sg.), *(lyexneþ* 66/7 n.), and *lourinde.*[3]

The preterite

Class A is subdivided according to whether the preterite forms
are weak or strong. The strong forms represent quite faithfully
the ablaut classes of Old English.[4] The weak forms have syncope
with consonant assimilation where appropriate. The past tense
endings are as follows: INDICATIVE SG. 1. 3. *-de, -te,* 2. *-dest,
-test;* PL *-de(n), -te(n);* SUBJ. SG. and PL. *-de, -te.* The past
participle ends in *-d, -t.*[5] The only exceptions are *arered(e),
asterued, bebered, ybleued* (beside *ybleft), ycrucefied, yglorefied,
yleued(e), yrymed, spended;*[6] *awarȝede* may derive from an Old
English *wargian* or it may be direct from the noun *wearȝ.*[7] In
either case we should expect it to belong to Class C. The forms
besmet, besmetted are problematic but it seems most likely that
the word derives from an Old English *besmyttan* (cf. *OED* SMUT
v.), giving a regular *besmet* (cf. *yzet*). The form *besmetted* may be
compared with the irregular *arered* or may be from an Old English
form **besmyttian.*[8] The endings of the verbs of Classes B and C
are the same as those of Class A except that they do not show
syncope. Thus the endings are *-ede* etc., *-ed.*[9] The past participle

---

[1] The slightly earlier Kentish Sermons have *makie* as the infinitive.
[2] This verb has an irregular imp. sg. *trost.*
[3] For discussion see *ODEE* and Wallenberg s.vv.
[4] The following analogical reformations of the past tense and past participle
may be noted: *beaȝ, slaȝe, steaȝ, uleaȝ, yzoȝe.*
[5] Cf. Campbell, § 751(3).
[6] It seems possible that, as Wallenberg suggests (p. 223, n. 3), the verb is an
aphetic form of *despendre,* but cf. *ODEE.*
[7] Cf. discussion in d'Ardenne, p. 184, n. 3.
[8] For a different view see Wallenberg, p. 27, n. 2.
[9] The form *becaȝt* (cf. *cachie*) instead of **becached* is probably an analogical
formation. Cf. *OED* s.v.

usually retains the *y*-prefix except (i) when preceded by *by* when elision takes place (ii) where the verb begins with *y* as in *yemd*, *yeue*, *yolde*, but also *y-yeue*, *yyolde* (iii) a few cases of *bi* for *ybi*.[1]

The modals[2]

SHALL

We may note the following uses of the modal *shall*: 1. It is used to express obligation. Here it regularly renders the parts of French *devoir*. 2. It expresses indebtedness. 3. It is used to express futurity as in 178/6–7 (*neuremo*) *ssel wende* (*retornera*) or 264/16 where *ssel come* renders *aderit*. When the sequence of tenses requires it, it is, of course, used in the past e.g. 223/19 *þet hise ssolde habbe to wiue* 'who was to marry her', 'who was going to marry her'. The past here is purely dependent on the past tense in the main clause and is distinct from modal uses of *ssolde* which are discussed below. 4. It seems to be used to express a contingent future. That is to say, it has a modal as well as a temporal function (cf. *OED.* SHALL 10). It is not always easy to distinguish this from the temporal sense but such a meaning is often suggested by the French. In any case, the senses of futurity and the senses of contingency so merge that a precise translation is sometimes impossible to come by. For example, at 107/12, 13, 14 the simple future makes good sense but it renders a French subjunctive and should perhaps be translated as 'might be' rather than 'shall be'. (Cf. 264/3 where *ssel zitte* renders *sedeat*). At 179/7 the translation should be 'that he may not bark' rather than 'so that he will not bark' and at 228/27 the sense again is 'may not be' rather than 'will not be'. The French here has the conditional, *seroie*. At 116/35, 118/7 the translation of *we ne ssolle by uonded* is probably 'we be not tempted' or perhaps 'we may not be tempted' rather than 'we shall not be tempted' and *we ssolle by delyured* 'we may be delivered' rather than 'we shall be delivered'. At 137/30 *ne ssel by exaamened* is probably to be translated 'be not examined' and 188/1 *þet hi ssolle by* by 'that they be not'. All these render a French present or imperfect subjunctive (cf. 264/19, 269/1).[3] In other cases, we have the use of *ssel* rendering a French future tense where English would more usually have a present tense. For example, at 70/27–8

---

[1] Cf. Wallenberg, p. 32, n. 1.

[2] For general discussion see F. T. Visser, *An Historical Syntax of the English Language* (Leiden, 1969), pp. 1581–1734.

[3] Cf. the note to 265/9–10.

Vor non wel libbe ne ssel conne: þet to sterue ylyerned ne heþ (Car nus bien uiure ne saura qui a morir apris naura). This could be rendered either 'For no one knows how to live well who has not learnt to die' assuming that the future is a gallicism; or 'For no one shall know how to live well' etc. assuming a modal implication. Or at 93/2–3 *Huo þet ssel drinke . . . of þe wetere þet ich wylle y(e)ue him: hi ssel* etc. 'Whoever shall drink' . . . or 'Whoever drinks of the water that I shall give him shall become' or 'will become' etc. We may compare 120/10–11, 146/7–8 n., 150/33, 181/32, 183/16–17, 196/9, 247/26, 261/25; at 258/34 *ssel habbe* (Fr. *aura*) could possibly be translated *has* and the *ssel* taken as a gallicism. A third category is that in which the English *ssel* appears to indicate a contingent future and renders a French *devoir*. Here we should perhaps translate with the modal 'shall' but various shades of meaning are involved. Thus *þe more gratter ssel by þe zorȝe* (171/7–8) (where the French reads *tant doit estre li duels plus granz*) is largely future in implication. In *H(u)anne a riche man ssel (doit) come to ane toune* (195/7–8) the sense seems to be 'is due to come'; but in *þet þing / þet me ssel (doit) weȝe* (44/26–7) it is rather 'which is to be weighed'. A fourth category of problematic cases is that in which Dan Michel has rendered a French future or conditional by a present instead of the preterite we might expect. Thus 105/8 *Huo þet heþ wel þise uour þinges . . . he ssel by yblyssed* (French *aura . . . seroit*); it is difficult to tell whether the sense of *ssel* is modal or purely future. We could thus translate either 'Whoever has these four things . . . he shall be' or 'he will be blessed'. Slightly different cases occur at 117/1–2 and 197/10 where the French has a conditional in both clauses; thus *ase þe zone of a guod man þet ssel by a newe knyȝt him bezekþ* (French *seroit, prioit*) 'as the son of a good man who is to be a new knight beseeches him', or 197/9–11 *vor yef hi sterueþ ine zuich stat: hire elmesse ne ssel ham naȝt wytie* (French *moroient . . . garderoient*) 'for if they die in such a condition their alms shall not protect them'. The more precise translation of the latter would be *yef hi storue ine zuich stat hire elmesse ne ssolde ham naȝt wytie* 'if they should die in such a condition their alms would not protect them'. Compare also 162/23–4 *huo þet þise þri þinges may (porroit) winne: he ssolde by (seroit) more þanne emperour* and 257/25–6 *huo þet stoppeþ (estoupereit) þet on eare mid erþe . . . he ne ssolde habbe (naroit) non hede* etc. At 256/23–4, the conditional is rendered by a present subjunctive: *non ne ssolde by misziggere: bote þer by an hyerere* (*sereit, uoudreit*). In other cases (56/10–11, 219/13–15) both the French and DM have a present or future in the main clause and DM has *ssolde*+inf. rendering a conditional in the subordinate clause or a subjunctive present.

On the other hand, DM also uses *ssolde*(*st*) for French *dois, doit*; so 18/5, 19/22, 26, 20/19. Here the sense is one of obligation and the implication seems to be 'ought to' rather than 'must'; but this is not a distinction which can be generally observed. Apart from the use as a preterite tense of *ssel, ssolde* is thus used as a modal auxiliary. So at 71/4–6: *Vor al þet lyf of ane manne þaȝ he leuede a þousond year: þet ne ssolde by bote onlepy prikke: to þe zyȝþe of þe oþre lyue* 'For the whole life of man, though he lived a thousand years, would be but a single point in comparison with that other life . . .'; cf. 12/35, 13/2, 31/19, 33/3, 75/13–14, 95/16, etc. As is to be expected, it usually translates a French conditional, although at 33/3 the verb is impf. subj. It is also used to translate the French present or imperfect subjunctive in final clauses as 60/10–12: *Hy smerieþ þane way of helle mid hony . . . uor þet þe zeneȝere hine ssolde guo* (*uoisent*) *þe hardylaker* 'They smear the way to hell with honey . . . in order that the sinner should go more confidently' (cf. 135/28); moreover, at 214/8 the meaning of *ssolde do* (*deust faire*) seems to be 'should have done'. Where a sense of obligation is in question, the distinction between past and present is not easy to make. Thus at 256/27–8 *þise greate men hi ssolden* (*deureient*) *wel ham loki þet hi hiereþ and þet hi leueþ* 'These great men ought to be very careful in regard to what they hear and believe'. It seems likely that the preterite, like the French conditional it renders, here has a modal function; *ssolle* would have rather the force of 'must'. Similarly at 258/13–16: *Me ssolde him wel hyealde* (*tendroit*) *fol þet were proud to bere þe ssredinge. þet ne ssolde by* (*seroit*) *bote a tokne. and a bepenchinge of þe ssame of his uader / and of his oȝene* 'One ought to consider him a fool who would be proud to wear clothes which should be but a token and a reminder of his father's shame and his own'.

WILL

The verb *wille* has two main senses, futurity and volition, and translates the French and Latin future and *vouloir, volo* in a great number of cases. The distinction is clearly seen in *ich wille zigge* (*je veus dire*) 'I mean' and *ich wille zigge* (*je dirai*) 'I shall say'. There is, however, a tendency, at least, to distinguish between the future with *shall* and the future with *will*. The future with *will* tends to have an implication of volition, whereas the future with *shall* has, as well as the contingent senses already discussed, the sense of necessity, deriving naturally from the sense of obligation which this verb has. To some extent there seems to be a pressure from the semantic system to keep separate the senses of volition and obligation. Thus we sometimes find *shall* used where *will* might imply an inappropriate implication of volition. The following passages illustrate the distinction between the two futures clearly; '*Huo þet ssel drinke*', he *zayþ*, '*of þe wetere þet ich wylle y[e]ue him, hi ssel become a welle þet him ssel do lheape into þe lyue eurelestynde.*' (*beura, dourrai, deuendra, fera*) (93/2–4) Here *ssel drinke* is clearly required since the implication is not that the person wants or intends to drink but that he shall have done so. That is to say, the future is contingent; *ssel become* and *ssel do lheape* have implications of a contingent action in contrast with *wylle y[e]ue* which has an element of volition or intention. Or at 70/31–4, *Yef þou wylt* (*ueus*) *libbe vriliche. lyerne to sterue gledliche. Yef þou me zayst | hou me hit ssel lyerny: ich hit wyle þe zigge an haste. Þou sselt ywyte þet þis lyf: ne is bote dyaþ;* (*dirai, dois*); 'If you want to live in freedom, learn to die gladly. If you say to me, "how must one learn it?"; I will tell you straightway: you must understand that this life is but death.' Another example is 161/22–3: *Vor he wyle zuo wypi hare eʒen | þet neuremo ne ssolle wepe | ne ne ssolle yuele kuead ne zorʒe; ac euremo ssolle by myd god ine paise etc.* (*essuiera, plorront, sentiront, seront*). Here again the futures *ssolle wepe, ssolle yuele, ssolle by* are necessary results of the willed action of *wyle wypi*. There are, however, cases which are less clear-cut than these. One problematic case is at 220/18–20 and 22–3; *þet child lyerneþ ine his yeʒeþe: he hit wyle healde ine his elde* and *Huo þet tekþ colte endaunture: hyalde hit wyle þerhuyle hit ilest.* The Latin of the biblical original has *non recedet ab ea* (future), the French *uelt.* We might here expect *ssel,* but the English translation may have been influenced by the French *uelt.*

An interesting case is 197/22–3; *Non ne wolde zigge þet yef he were reupeuol . . . þet ne ssolde habbe reupe of his moder poure and zik.* The French has *Nul ne diroit que cil fust piteus ne misericors*

qui naroit pitie de sa mere poure et malade. Dan Michel appears
to have mistaken *cil* for *si il* and his sentence as it stands means
'No one would say that if a man were merciful he ought not to
have pity on his mother.' But the French means 'No one would
say that he was merciful . . . who would not take pity on his mother'.
The English should thus read: *non ne wolde zigge þet he were
reupeuol . . . þet ne wolde* ('who was not willing to') or *ne ssolde*
('who were not to') *habbe reupe of his moder poure and zik.* In this
instance the difference of meaning between *ssolde* and *wolde*
is not evident in the French. This appears also from such an
example as: *Huo þet wyste huet day he ssolde sterue: he hine wolde
agraypi ase zone ase he miȝte* (173/32–4); *wyste, ssolde sterue,
wolde agraypi* render *sauroit, morroit, apparilleroit.* The sense
of *wolde agraypi* could be 'he would be willing to prepare himself'
or 'he would prepare himself'.

The preterite is used to render a French imperfect subjunctive
or conditional, when the sense is hypothetical, or in a rejected
condition. Thus at 52/4, we find *huerof hi ham / wolden loki*
(French *gardassent*) 'from which they would have abstained' or
57/7–12, *yef me ham zede oþer dede asemoche ssame to hire uader . . .
ase me deþ to hire uader of heuene . . . mochel hi wolden ham wreþi
(courrouceroient) and oþer red hi wolden do (mettroient);* cf. 254/17 ff.;
*þe herte is ase þe uoȝel þet wolde (uelt) vly to his wylle and bote hy by
ofhealde (nest retenuz) be þe ges of beleaue . . . hy ulyȝþ perilousliche.*
Dan Michel has here cast the sentence in a more hypothetical
mood than the French, as he has done at 210/9 where *uoudras*
(future) is translated *woldest.* It is possible, however, that Dan
Michel's text had *uoudroies.*

The past modal of *wille* is sometimes used to translate a French
imperfect. For example, *yef God wolde (uoloit) usy to yelde dom*
(113/30); 'if God were accustomed to render justice'.

MAY

The basic sense of the verb *mai* is 'am/is able'. It normally
translates the French and Latin verbs *pooir, possum.* The preterite
miȝte(n) renders the French conditional in accordance with the
usual English idiom already noted in connection with *ssel* and
wille. It should also be noted that the subjunctive *moȝe* is used in
clauses in which we should expect a subjunctive such as final
clauses; that is to say, modal *may* is not usually employed in such

constructions but where these are required the subjunctive is used. On the other hand, the subjunctive *moȝe* is used with only slight modal implications in some instances. Thus at 10/1–2, *yef he hit wot and moȝe (puet) hit do*. The indicative form *wot* as well as the French *puet* suggest that a formal subjunctive is not in question. The implication is 'if he knows and (provided that) he can do it'. Another example is found at 193/8–9, *þanne me yziȝþ þe nyede and me hit moȝe do* 'When one sees the need and (provided that) one can do it'.

The English *may*+infinitive can, however, be used to render a French subjunctive.[1] In some of these instances some kind of modality seems to be in question. Thus, at 63/19–20, *ac naȝt uor þan | þet ine no poynt me ne may (puist) zuerie*; 'but not because one may never swear'; but the sense 'can' is acceptable at 89/2, 92/24, 121/12, 135/23, 141/20 even though all these render a French subjunctive; that is to say, though they render a subjunctive, *may*+infinitive does not usually seem to be a subjunctive equivalent.

In a number of cases, *may* renders *porroie, porroit*. *May* has, perhaps, some modal force in these instances also; but the rendering 'can' is possible in all of them; cf. 17/20, 27/15, 39/33, 60/2, 144/21, 148/8, 166/6, 244/18, 20, 261/34; cf., also *miȝt* for *porroies* at 31/17, 179/16. Rather more surprisingly *may* can render a French future as at 137/35, 157/5, 6, 181/35; cf. *miȝt* rendering *porras* at 133/34, 187/6.

As with other modals, the preterite *miȝte* is used to indicate a modal preterite 'could have'.

---

[1] Cf. 264/8 where *moȝe telle* renders *narrent*, and *may awaki, valeant*.

BIBLIOGRAPHY

d'ARDENNE, S. T. R. O., *Þe Liflade ant te Passiun of Seinte Iuliene*, Liége, 1936; reprinted EETS 248 (1961)

BERNDT, R., *Einführung in das Studium des Mittelenglischen*, Halle, 1960

BLISS, A. J., 'Vowel-Quantity in Middle English Borrowings from Anglo-Norman', *Archivum Linguisticum*, iv (1952), 121–47; v (1953), 22–47; 'Quantity in Old French and Middle English', vii (1955), 71–86

BOHMAN, H., *Studies in the Middle English Dialects of Devon and London*, Göteborg, 1944

BOOKER, J. M., 'The French "inchoative" suffix -*iss* and the French -*ir* Conjugation in Middle English', Heidelberg, 1912

BRAYER, E. 'Contenu, structure et combinaisons du *Miroir du Monde* et de la *Somme le Roi*', *Romania*, lxxix (1958), 1–38, 433–70

DANKER, O. *Die Laut- und Flexionslehre der mittelkentischen Denkmäler*, Strassburg, 1879

DOBSON, E. J., 'Middle English Lengthening in Open Syllables', *TPS*, 1962, 124–48

—— *English Pronunciation, 1500–1700*, Oxford, 2nd edn. 1968

—— 'Notes on Sound-Changes and Phoneme-Theory', *Brno Studies in English*, viii (1969), 43–8

DOLLE, F. W. R., *Graphische und lautliche Untersuchung von Dan Michels 'Ayenbite of Inwyt'*, Bonn, 1912

Early Middle English Verse and Prose, ed. J. A. W. Bennett and G. V. Smithers, Oxford, 2nd edn., 1968

EK, K.-G., *The Development of OE ӯ and ēo in South-Eastern Middle English* (Lund Studies in English, 42, 1972)

EKWALL, B. O. E., *English Place-Names in -ING* (Skrifter utg. av kungl. Humanistiska Vetenskapssamfundet i Lund, vi, 1923)

—— *English River Names*, Oxford, 1928

—— *Early London Personal Names* (Skrifter utg. av kungl. Humanistiska Vetenskapssamfundet i Lund, xliii, 1947)

ELIASON, N. E., 'Old English Vowel Lengthening and Vowel Shortening before Consonant Groups', *SP*, xlv (1948), 1–20

EMDEN, A. B., *Donors of Books to St. Augustine's Abbey, Canterbury* (Oxford Bibliographical Society, Occasional Publications iv, 1968)

EVERS, R. W., *Beiträge zur Erklärung und Textkritik von Michel's 'Ayenbite of Inwyt'*, Erlangen, 1887

von FEILITZEN, O., *The Pre-Conquest Personal Names of Domesday Book*, Uppsala, 1937

FLASDIECK, H. M., 'Studien zur me. Grammatik', *AB*, xxxiv (1923), 20–32, 314–19

—— 'Ein südost-mittelenglischer Lautwandel', *ESt*, lviii (1924), 1–23

—— 'Die Entstehung des engl. Phonems /ʃ/', *Anglia*, lxxvi (1958), 339–410

FÖRSTER, M. T. W. 'Die Bibliothek des Dan Michael von Northgate', *Archiv*, cxv (1905), 167–9

—— *Der Flußname Themse u. seine Sippe* (Sitzungsberichte der Bayerischen Akademie der Wissenschaften, Phil.-hist. Abt., 1941)

FRANCIS, W. N., *The Original of the 'Ayenbite of Inwyt'*, *PMLA*, lii (1937), 893–5

von GLAHN, N., *Zur Geschichte des grammatischen Geschlechts im Mittelenglischen* (Anglistische Forschungen, 53, 1918)

GOVER, J. E. B., A. MAWER, and F. M. STENTON, in collaboration with A. Bonner, *The Place-Names of Surrey* (EPNS, xi, 1934)

HALLQVIST, H., *Studies in Old English Fractured ea* (Lund Studies in English, 14, 1948)

HEUSER, W., 'Zum kentischen Dialekt im Mittelenglischen', *Anglia*, xvii (1894), 73–90.

JAMES, M. R. *The Ancient Libraries of Canterbury and Dover*, Cambridge, 1903

—— 'Lists of Manuscripts formerly owned by Dr. John Dee', *Suppl. Trans. Bibl. Soc.* No. 1, 1921

JENSEN, H., *Die Verbalflexion im 'Ayenbite of Inwyt'*, Kiel, 1908

JONES, C., 'The Grammatical Category of Gender in Early Middle English', *English Studies*, xlviii (1967), 289–305

JORDAN, R., *Handbuch der mittelenglischen Grammatik*, 2nd edn. rev. H. C. Matthes, Heidelberg, 1934

KER, N. R., 'From "Above Top Line" to "Below Top Line": A Change in Scribal Practice', *Celtica*, v (1960), 13–16

—— *Medieval Libraries of Great Britain*, 2nd. edn. London, 1964

KONRATH, M. 'Zur Laut- und Flexionslehre des Mittelkentischen', *Archiv*, lxxxviii (1892), 47–66, 157–80; lxxxix (1892), 153–66

KURATH, H., 'The Loss of Long Consonants and the Rise of Voiced Fricatives in Middle English', *Language*, xxxii (1956), 435–45

LEHNERT, M., *Sprachform u. Sprachfunktion im* Orrmulum (Zeitschrift für Anglistik und Amerikanistik, 1, Berlin, 1953)

LÖFVENBERG, M. T., *Studies on Middle English Local Surnames* (Lund Studies in English, 11, 1942)

LUICK, K., *Historische Grammatik der engl. Sprache*, Stuttgart, 1914–40; revised reprint, Oxford, 1964

MAGNUSSON, U., *Studies in the Phonology of the 'Ayenbite of Inwyt'* (Lund Theses in English, I, 1971)

MAWER, A., and F. M. STENTON, *The Place-Names of Bedfordshire and Huntingdonshire* (EPNS, iii, 1926)

MAWER, A., F. M. STENTON, and J. E. B. GOVER, *The Place-Names of Sussex* (EPNS, vi-vii, 1929–30)

Memorials of St. Anselm, ed. R. W. Southern and F. S. Schmitt, London, 1969

MORSBACH, L., *Mittelenglische Grammatik*, Halle, 1896

PARKES, M. B., *English Cursive Book Hands, 1250–1500*, Oxford, 1969

POPE, M. K., *From Latin to Modern French*, Manchester, 1934

REANEY, P. H., 'On certain Phonological Features of the Dialect of London in the twelfth Century', *ESt*, lix (1925), 321–45

—— 'The Dialect of London in the thirteenth Century', *ESt*, lxi (1926), 9–23

—— *The Place-Names of Essex* (EPNS, xii, 1935)

RUBIN, S., *The Phonology of the Middle English Dialect of Sussex* (Lund Studies in English, 21, 1951)

SAMUELS, M. L., 'Kent and the Low Countries: some Linguistic Evidence', *Edinburgh Studies in English and Scots*, ed. A. J. AITKEN, A. McINTOSH, and H. PÁLSSON, (London, 1971), 3–19

SENFF, H., *Die Nominalflexion im 'Ayenbite of Inwyt'*, Jena, 1937

STEPONAVIČIUS, A., 'Sud'ba drevneanglijskikh diftongov (ĕa) (ĕo) (ĭo) v kentskom', *Kalbotyra*, xiii (1964)

SUNDBY, B., *The Dialect and Provenance of the Middle English Poem 'The Owl and the Nightingale'* (Lund Studies in English, 18, 1950)

—— 'Middle English Overlapping of V and W and its Phonemic Significance', *Anglia*, lxxiv (1956), 438–44

—— *Studies in the ME Dialect Material of Worcestershire Records* (Norwegian Studies in English, 10, 1963)

TAYLOR, A. B., 'On the History of Old English ēa, ēo in Middle Kentish', *MLR*, xix (1924), 1–10

VACHEK, J. 'On Peripheral Phonemes of Modern English', *Brno Studies in English*, iv (1964), 1–100

VARNHAGEN, H., 'Beiträge zur Erklärung und Textkritik von Dan Michel's "Ayenbite of Inwyt" ', *ESt*, i (1877), 379–423; ii (1879), 27–59

WALLENBERG, J. K., *The Vocabulary of Dan Michel's Ayenbite of Inwyt*, Uppsala, 1923

—— *The Place-Names of Kent*, Uppsala, 1934

WIDÉN, B., *Studies on the Dorset Dialect* (Lund Studies in English, 16, 1949)

WRIGHT, C. E., *English Vernacular Hands from the Twelfth to the Fifteenth Centuries*, Oxford, 1960

WYLD, H. C., 'South-eastern and South-east Midland Dialects in Middle English', *Essays and Studies*, vi (1920), 112–45

—— *A Short History of English*, 3rd. edn., London, 1927; revised 1951

—— *A History of Modern Colloquial English*, 3rd. edn., Oxford, 1936

ZACHRISSON, R. E., 'Notes on the Essex Dialect and the Origin of Vulgar London Speech', *ESt*, lix (1925), 346–60

PREFATORY NOTE TO ANNOTATIONS

1. *The source*

It has been impossible to consult all 113 manuscripts of the *Somme le Roi*. All the known thirteenth-century copies, however, have been consulted except Ashburnham–Barrois 246[1] which was sold to Maggs in 1901. This I have been unable to trace any further. A few fourteenth-century manuscripts have also been collated for the same passages as the thirteenth-century manuscripts. These manuscripts form the group designated E and consist of the following:

(a) *thirteenth-century manuscripts*

Paris, BN, f. fr. 938	P1	
1824	P2	
13304	P3 (contains only the section up to and including the seven deadly sins)	
n.a. fr. 10875	P4	

Paris, Bibliothèque Mazarine 870   M (dated 1295)
Paris, Ste Geneviève 2899[1]   G1
Angers, Bibliothèque municipale 264   An
Valencia, University Library 863[1]   V
Leningrad, Public Library F.v. XVII. I[2]   Ld
London, British Library, Egerton 945 (Pater Noster only)   Eg1

(b) *fourteenth-century manuscripts*

Paris, Bibliothèque de l'Arsenal 6329	A2 (dated 1311)	
Cambridge, St. John's College B9	Ca1	
S30[3]	Ca2 (stops at the middle of p. 126)	
London, British Library, Cotton Cleopatra A.v[3]	C	
Additional 28162	Add1	
Royal 19 C. ii	R1	
Egerton 745[1]	Eg2 (Commandments only)	

---

[1] I am grateful to Mademoiselle Brayer for drawing my attention to these manuscripts.

[2] Mr. Ker kindly dated this manuscript for me.   [3] See pp. 53–6.

Lambeth Palace 298 — L (to the fourth branch of Simony)

Oxford, Bodleian Library, Fr. f. 1 — F1 (Pater Noster only)
Rawlinson D 913 — Ra (fragment only from sixth degree of Prowess)

A number of other manuscripts have been consulted in cases of special difficulty. They are:

(a) *fourteenth-century manuscripts*

Paris, BN, f. fr. 409	P5
943	P6
1767	P7
1895	P8
22932	P9
24780	P10
Bibliothèque de l'Arsenal 2318	A1
Ste Geneviève 24	G2
792	G3
2897	G4
2898	G5

(b) *fifteenth-century manuscripts*

Paris, BN, f. fr. 939	P11
940	P12
942	P13
958	P14
959	P15
24781	P16
London, British Library, Royal 16 F. v[1]	R2
Additional 24125	Add2

Since the references are necessarily incomplete, readings do not, of course, imply anything about the genetic relationships of the manuscripts. It should also be noted that, since the later group has only been consulted on points of special difficulty, failure to refer

[1] Mademoiselle Brayer kindly gave me this reference.

to these does not imply that they do not contain the reading in question.

For the *De Anima* the following manuscripts have been collated:

(a) *twelfth-century manuscripts*

Paris, BN, lat. 392	P
St. Omer, Bibliothèque municipale 86	O
Tours, Bibliothèque municipale 317	T
Hereford Cathedral Library P. I. 1.	H

(b) *fourteenth-century manuscripts*

Cambridge, Corpus Christi College, 154[1]	C
Oxford, Bodleian Library, Laud misc. 264	L

The following English versions of the *Somme* have been consulted:

The Book of Vices and Virtues[2] (fourteenth century)	VV
London, British Library, Add. 37677 (first half of s. xv; incomplete)	En3
Royal 18 A. x (first half of s. xv; incomplete)	En4
Cambridge, Corpus Christi College 494 (s. xv)	En5
Oxford, Bodleian Library, Ashmole 1286 (*c.* 1400; incomplete)	En2
e Musaeo 23 (1451)	En6
Caxton's Royal Book (1486)[3]	En7

2. *The references*

The majority of the biblical references have been supplied, and such of the patristic references as I have been able to identify. For the biblical sources of the *De Anima* the reader is referred to the Southern–Schmitt edition.

---

[1] For this manuscript's association with St. Augustine's, Canterbury, see N. R. Ker (1964), p. 40.

[2] Edited W. Nelson Francis, EETS 217 (1942).

[3] Manuscript references in brackets indicate that the manuscript so marked substantially supports the reading in question but does not correspond word for word with the other manuscripts showing the reading.

NOTES

1/1–4. *Zuete iesu . . . ende*: these lines should be set out as verse. Cf. *SIMEV* 3238.5.

1/4. Morris does not print the press mark that follows *zuo by hit* in the manuscript. For this press mark see Introduction, p. 1.

1/8–11. See *SIMEV* 1227.

1/10. *ye brenge*: (cf. 1/13 *þou bryng*; 271/15 *þou . . . ssylde*). For the preceding pronoun see T. F. Mustanoja, *A Middle English Syntax*, I (Helsinki, 1960), pp. 475–6. The ending may derive from the Old English form without the final dental in spite of the inverted order. From an Old English point of view the order should be *brenge ye*.

1/12–13. See *SIMEV* 1961.3.

1/13. *bryng*: this verb usually shows *e*-forms, and the form here is due to the exigencies of rhyme (cf. Wallenberg, p. 44, n. 1).

1/14–15. See *SIMEV* 539.5.

1/20. read *oþer half*.

2/17. *toknen*: the meaning is not clear. It is, perhaps, *OED* TOKEN *sb.* 2. 'a sign or mark indicating some quality, or distinguishing one object from others'. Thus the 'tokens' of the beast of hell are those sins which indicate its presence.

2/20. read *todele*.

2/36. *noster*: superscript *e* usually indicates *re* and this is perhaps for *nostre*. Cf. p. 3 n. where the MS reading is perhaps *nostreer*.

3/21. *yefþe*: cf. 120/30, 31. We should, perhaps, emend to *yefþes* but the form might be singular or it might represent an OE *gefþa*.

4/5. *ynoȝbote*: read *ynoȝ bote*; cf. *ynoȝ amendement* 171/1.

5/14. *hatte*: Wallenberg (p. 126, n. 3) points out that the sense requires the meaning 'calls'; but the examples in the section of *OED* to which he refers (HIGHT *v.*[1] I 4) are not strictly analogous. It seems that either the form is an error for *het* or, more probably, as Jensen (p. 26) suggested, the construction is imprecise. The object precedes the verb and thus it was easy to write *þis boc hatte* when grammar required *þis boc het*.

5/23. *heȝliche*: 'chiefly', 'principally', rather than 'completely', 'fully'. The French has *principaument*.

6/5. *huo þet*: C *qui* is plural but DM has perhaps taken it as singular.

6/5. *agelteþ*: C *tres/passanz*; it seems that DM did not know *trespassanz* in the sense of 'fleeting'. The erroneous translation creates an anacoluthon. Read *pasinde* for *agelteþ* (cf. H. Varnhagen, 'Beiträge zur

Erklärung und Textkritik von Dan Michel's *Ayenbite of Inwyt'*, *ESt*, i (1877), 386). Cf. 72/15, 104/16.

6/9. Cf. note to 19/24.

6/17. *ine guode skele*: C *o bone cause*; this contrasts with 14 and should read *wiþ guode skele*. Cf. 6/19.

6/18. MS *oþ of soþe*: this is the correct reading. Morris's emendation is unnecessary. C reads *serement de verite* (cf. Varnhagen (1877), 386).

6/19–20. *in oþre guode skele. and clenliche and skeluolliche*: C *en autres bones causes 7 honestes 7 profitables*; read *skeles*.

6/20–1. *ne is no riȝt to zuerie*: C *ne lit pas iurer*; translate 'nor is there any justification for swearing'. Cf. 8/24. For *zuerie . . . þane name* see *OED* Swear *v.* I 7.

6/24. *zuerþ*: Varnhagen ((1877), 387) suggested reading *zeneȝeþ* since the French texts read *pecche*. He also points out that, at line 29, DM reads *zuereþ liȝtliche* where the French has *peche ueniaument* and this should be emended to *zeneȝeþ liȝtliche*.

6/27. Wallenberg does not record *zoþ adv.* But, in view of the clearly adverbial use at 26/17, it seems possible to take this example also as an adverb (cf. *OED* Sooth *adv.*). C had *uoir*. Cf. 51/33, 60/31 for further examples.

6/31. *bote yef him ne loki*: Varnhagen pointed out ((1877), 387) that this lacks a subject. C reads *qui ne sen garde* '(for) whoever does not guard himself from it'. DM has misunderstood *qui*, understanding it, possibly, as Varnhagen suggests ((1877), 387–8), as *quin*, whence the rendering *bote yef*. Read *uor him þet him ne lokeþ þerurom*.

7/7. *miȝt*: C *sues* 'thou art accustomed'.

7/8. *þe yeme*: C *entendre*; the pronoun is redundant and may be an error for *te*. The meaning of the French is 'give one's mind, attention'.

7/12–13. *þis heste | uoluelþ gostliche | him þet lokeþ*: C *Cest commandement acomplit espiriteument cil qui garde*; Varnhagen ((1877), 388) pointed out that DM had wrongly taken the French *cest commandement* as the subject and *cil* as the object. Emend *him* to *he*.

7/18. *hi*: *inwyt* is usually neuter. The form may be due to French *ele* but may be merely an error for *he*. Cf. Glossary and p. 89.

7/24. *ope þe woke*: this is a calque on C's *seursemaine*. Cf. Varnhagen, (1877), 388.

8/27–8. 1 John 3: 15.

9/8. *oþre manne wyf*: C *autrui femme*; *wyf* could be plural but it is not usually so in DM and is here, no doubt, singular in a distributive phrase. Possibly DM took *autrui* as plural but kept *femme* as singular. Read *oþres mannes*.

9/13. *al[l]e*: C *du tout*; DM's form should, perhaps, be emended to *of alle*. The form *ale* may be unstressed but, at 34/13, *ale* has been corrected to *alle* and Morris's emendation may be necessary. In that case, *ale* at 233/13 should also be emended. Cf. pp. 40–1.

10/8–9. *lede . . . in wytnesse*: this renders C *mesdie . . . en tesmoin* and, although it makes sense of a kind, it may be an error, due, as Varnhagen ((1877), 390) suggested, to confusion of *mesdie* with *mener*. The reading *lede* should, perhaps, be emended to *miszigge*; *in wytnesse* would then mean 'in testimony'.

10/14. *hire dedes*: C *les fez*; as Varnhagen ((1877), 392–3) pointed out, DM has rendered *ses fez*.

10/22. MS *neȝybores*: Wallenberg (s.v.) rightly keeps the manuscript reading, as Morris does at 30/16.

10/28–9. *of zuyche manere*: C *de tele maniere*; the correct reading is possibly *matiere* as all E manuscripts except A2, G1, An, V.

11/1–3. Matthew 5: 28.

11/7. *þine nixte*: C *a ton proeme*; for *þine* as a genitive cf. p. 73; but it is doubtful whether *nixte* is a genuine genitive and *of* should, perhaps, be supplied; or the phrase might be dative.

11/13–14. *Consentement | and þe þoȝtes þerto*: C *consentement certains et apenses i est*; DM has omitted *certains* and *est*. It seems that, as at 115/13, he has misunderstood *apenses* 'intentional'. The English could be brought into line with the French by reading *consentement ziker and wyluol biþ þerto*.

11/21. *diȝt* is plural and should be emended to *diȝteþ* in both instances. C has *ordenent*.

11/22–3. *þise ten hestes | byeþ to echen . . . yhyealde to conne*: C *Ces .x. commans est chascuns . . . tenuz a sauoir*; DM has taken *Ces .x. commans* as the subject and therefore put the verb in the plural and made *chascuns* dative. Read *þise ten hestes | is ech . . . yhyealde to conne*. Cf. Varnhagen, (1877), 393.

11/28. *huanne*: the sense here is 'since'. Cf. 32/16 and note to 246/26.

11/31. *wyleþ*: the forms with a single consonant are probably due to lack of stress. Cf. p. 41.

11/32–3. *þe zeuende: to þe zone. þe uerþe | to þe holi gost*: C *Li .vii. au fil Li .iiij. au saint esperitz*; the sense is that seven articles belong to the Son and four to the Holy Spirit. Thus, in spite of the French text, *þe zeuende* should read *zeue* and *þe uerþe* should read *uour*. Cf. Varnhagen (1877), 393.

12/2–3. For the association of the twelve apostles with the articles of the Creed see C. F. Bühler, 'The Apostles and the Creed', *Speculum*, xxviii (1953), 335–9. The order of the *Ayenbite* appears to be that in *Sacramentarium gallicanum* (Mabillon, *Museum Italicum*, Paris, 1687–9) I², 396.

12/10 ff. There seems to be haplography here. C has *Je croi en iesu crist nostre seignor fiz dieu le pere. En ce doit on entendre 7 croire que il est semblables 7 egaus au pere en toutes choses* qui *apartienent a la deite*. DM has jumped from the first *pere* to the second.

12/14. *þe vifte*: C *li quint*; as at 11/32, DM has an ordinal where a cardinal numeral is required. Read *uif*. Cf. Varnhagen (1877), 393.

12/34. *zoþe* is written over *guode* and should be substituted for it. C has *en uraie foi*.

12/35–6. *uor þe zenne*: this should read *uor uor þe zenne*. Cf. Varnhagen (1877), 395.

13/15. *saynt*: Morris's emendation of this word is highly inconsistent. Thus *sanyt* here and at 196/2 is tacitly emended to *saynt*, but, at 121/2, it is retained; the form *sanyn* at 14/30 is retained but should be emended to *sayn*; *sain* is usually unemended but emended at 210/7 to *sainte* perhaps because the MS has *sain-* suggesting that the scribe meant to write *sainte*. *sanynte* (126/19) and *sanynt* (262/21) should be emended to *saynte* and *saynt*. At 170/4, 8, Morris tacitly emends *zayte* to *zaynte*, an emendation indicated in the text at 143/4, 148/28, 221/18, 244/11, 253/25; but the form is unemended at 253/8; *saynyte* (123/22) should read *saynte*.

13/20. *made*: C *sist*; DM has misread *sist* as *fist*. Read *zette* for *made*. Cf. Varnhagen (1877), 391.

14/1. *cherch*: the form without a final vowel, which appears again at 42/24, may be an error. Cf. Wallenberg, p. 50, n. 2.

14/22. *huer he ssel habbe an*: C *ou il aura uescu* 'in which he lived'. DM has not understood the construction and has confused *vescu* 'lived' with *vestu* 'clothed'. (Cf. Wallenberg, p. 10, n. 2) Read *huer he ssel habbe yleued*. For the beast see Apocalypse 13.

15/2. *hedde miȝte of him-zelve to viȝte*: C has *auoit pooier de soi combatre*. Varnhagen ((1877), 395) assumes that DM's translation is incorrect, but he is probably translating a French *auoit pooir de soi de combatre* 'he had power within himself to fight'.

15/23–4. Apocalypse 13: 7.

15/30–1. *also moche ase may*: a rendering of C *tant comme il puet*.

16/4–5. C has *Li quins auarice*; DM has added a gloss.

16/20, 21. *ondeþ, brekþ*: the verbs are singular but the sense requires a plural. C reads *deffont, brisent*. Read *ondoþ, brekeþ*. Cf. Wallenberg, p. 43, n. 3.

16/22–3. *oþer . . . byeþ worþ*: C *li autre . . . ualent*; *oþer* does not occur as a plural in the *Ayenbite* and the form is probably an error for *oþre*.

16/27. *ald*: C *uins*; as Varnhagen pointed out ((1877), 391), DM's form is due to confusion between *uins* 'wine' and *uius* 'old'. Cf. 48/10.

16/28. *begyleþ*: C *en iure*; Wallenberg (p. 22, n. 1 and p. 318) suggests that DM has assumed that *eniure* 'intoxicates' is part of the verb *engign(i)er* 'to deceive'. The text should read *adrengþ*. The error, no doubt, arises from the misunderstanding of *uins* in line 27.

16/30. *generalliche*: *MED* (GENERALLI adv. (a)) renders 'universally etc.' but the contrast with *specialliche* suggests rather that it means 'in general' as contrasted with 'in particular'.

16/32–3. *ne yzeþ / hire misdedes / ne hire folies / ne hire wyttes*: DM has slightly altered the sense. C reads *nen uoient lor meffais nen lor folies se sens no*n; 'they see nothing in their misdeeds and their folies but wisdom'. Cf. Wallenberg, p. 318.

17/6. *kende*: C *heritage*; the same rendering appears at 84/13. Cf. *MED* KINDE n. 12.

17/6. *of his guode*: C *de ses biens*; the sense appears to be 'because of his goodness'.

17/15. MS *huā last let*: C *qui darrain le laisse*. The sense is 'which leaves him last'. Varnhagen ((1877), 396) pointed out that DM seems to have taken *qui* as accusative but it is, in fact, nominative and refers to *zenne*. Emend to *þet last him let*. *þane kniȝt oure Lhord* is a calque on the French *le cheualier nostre seignor* 'the knight of Our Lord'. The form *huā* should be expanded to *huam*.

17/22. *of ane wyckede rote*: the sense requires 'from one evil root'. Accordingly, *ane* should be emended to *one*. The error arises from a failure to distinguish between French *uns* 'one' and *uns* 'a'. Cf. 107/2, 109/11, 117/20, 146/12, 153/8, 202/31, 238/25.

17/24–5, 25–6. MS. *we clepeþ, we clepieþ*: C *nous apelons* in both cases. Morris suggests emending to *me* but, in view of the French, we should probably emend the first instance to *we clepieþ*.

17/28. *byþ*: this should perhaps be emended to *byeþ*. Cp. 18/27, 26/11, 102/16, 156/23, 208/28.

17/32. *Þo oþer*: *worse*: the form *þo* for *þe* occurs before a word beginning with *o* also at 41/19, 47/4 and before *spoushod* at 225/34. Cf. Wallenberg, p. 249, n. 1. It should be emended to *þe*. Cf. *opo* (39/18); *bohote* (65/19); *bolongeþ*, *bouore* (234/13); these are all probably errors. The proper names *Iocob* (102/23), *Iorome* (229/19) may derive their form from the source. Such assimilations are not uncommon in Anglo-Norman (cf. Pope, § 1139).

18/6. *yeldeþ*: C *rent*; Wallenberg (p. 104, n 1) regards the form as plural and argues that the following *ous* indicates an implied subject *we*.

18/14. We should expect an object for *useþ* (C *en use*). Varnhagen ((1877), 396) pointed out that DM. elsewhere misses out the French *en*. We should, perhaps, supply *ham* after *useþ*.

18/19. *onderuangþ:* C has *receit on* and Varnhagen ((1877), 396) proposed reading *me onderuangþ*. But the omission of subject pronouns is not uncommon in Middle English.

18/29. *vor guodnesse*: *oþer askeþ*: 'for one good turn deserves another'.

18/32. *wext*: C *nest*; Varnhagen ((1877), 397) pointed out that we should expect *is*. *Wext* is written above the line in the manuscript and there is an erasure between *þanne* and *ariȝt*. DM may first have written *nis* as a translation of the French *n'est* but, not perceiving that the sentence was interrogative, he expected an affirmative verb and thought that this was to be found in the form *nest*. This is the negative of the verb 'to be' but he took it as from *naistre* and translated *wext*. Emend to *þanne nis he naȝt ariȝt þe ilke fol* 'is he not then truly foolish' . . .

19/4. *wasteþ, despendeþ*: C *gastent, despendent*; Wallenberg is right in taking these as singular in spite of the French. The subject is *he* and C appears to be in error. The verbs are singular in E except An, V, Ca2, P4.

19/15. *alzo moche ase of him is* renders C *quanque est de lui*.

19/24. *alsuo*: this could be an adverb but in view of the parallelism is more likely to be a conjunction. Cf. *alzuo* 6/9.

19/25. *leȝers*: emend to *lyeȝeres* or *leȝeres*.

20/1-4. Translate 'And though it be true that no mortal sin is without contempt of God, nevertheless, in respect of that which we say here of contempt, man may here particularly commit this sin in three ways.'

20/11-12. *þet þou hest / ine herte þe ilke / þet more byeþ worþ þanne þou / onworþest*: C *que tu as en ton cuer ceus qui mielz ualent de toi despis* 'that thou hast in thy heart despised those who are of greater worth than thou'. Emend to *onworþed*.

20/23. *onworþnesse*: C *irreuerence*; the repetition of *onworþnesse* is perhaps an error.

21/11. *y-zeneȝd*: read *yzeneȝed*.

21/12. *þet* in the sense 'than' is a calque on the French. Cf. *OED* THAT *conj.* 9.

21/16. *opniminge* seems to be a literal rendering of French *presumpcion*.

21/19. *oþer*: here and frequently the manuscript has *oþe* corrected to *oþer*. The form *oþe* may be simply an error, or OE *oþþe*. Cf. 30/6.

21/21. *strengþe*: C *forteresce*; cf. *OED* STRENGTH *sb.* 10.

22/1-2. Cf. Prov. 25: 8.

22/2-4. *þet is to zigge . . . hit uolȝeþ*: not in the French.

22/9. *þis zenne is ybounde ine þan*: C *Cist pecchies est lies en celui*; the reading *lies (en) (ybounde (ine))* is perhaps an error for *lienz, laïs* adv., the reading of P1, 2, A2, An, Ca1, 2, Add1; G1, R1 have the reading of C.

22/13. *redeþ / and yefþ ham of his*: C *louent 7 lor donent le leur*; read *yeueþ ham of hare* (cf. Wallenberg, p. 319). Wallenberg also points out that *redeþ* is not a translation of *louent* and it should perhaps be emended to *prayseþ*; nor is *of his* a rendering of *le leur*, which should read *of hare* as we have pointed out. The sense is that the sin is doubled in those who pay boasters and flatterers to give them the praise they would not dare to give themselves.

22/15. *noblesse*: C *oublees*; the French can only mean 'offering' and seems likely to be a mistake. Cf. 60/5. VV (17/35) has *nobeleies*.

22/17. *ouerwen[er]e*: the emendation is supported by C's reading, *sorquidier* 'an arrogant person'. But Wallenberg (p. 183, n. 3) may be right in supposing that DM took the form as verbal.

22/21–2. *of ham*: C *de ceus* depends on *se moke 7 chuffle*; but the English *bisemereþ and scorneþ* should take a direct object.

22/27. *þet guod | him wolde*: C *qui son bien li vuelent*; the text should perhaps read *willeþ*.

22/31. *him*: C *i*; the reference may be to the sick person.

22/32. *to þan | þet alle medicines*: C *a ki toute medecine* 'for whom all medicine'. Read *medicine*.

23/7. *uor þet me ssel him hyealde*: C *þor ce que on le tiegne*; the modal may here represent the subjunctive. But cf. the indicative after *uor þet* 'in order that' at 26/5, 59/33, 60/17, 156/25, 32, and notes to these lines.

23/10. *arereþ . . . wylneþ*: C *lieuent . . . desirrer*; the correct reading appears to be *(a)leuer, esleuer* (so E manuscripts except P2, G1, Ca2, and M which omits) . . . *desirrer* (so E manuscripts except P3). DM's text presumably had *lieuent* as P2, G1, C, Ca2; *desirre* as P3. The text should read *arere . . . wylni*.

23/17. *wytindeliche*: C *esciousement*; the correct reading is *esioissement* as E. Read *ioye*; *oþer wenþ by*: this goes with what follows; 'or expects to be praised for something' etc.

23/27. for *resye* see Wallenberg *s.v.*

24/8. *onderstondinge* here and at 78/25 renders French *memoire*.

24/9. *kendeliche*: *MED* (KINDELI *adj.* 4(b)) has 'worthy', 'noble'. But the French reads *par quoi li uns est naturelment plus que li autres ou larges ou debonaires* etc. 'By which one man is naturally more generous or compliant than another' etc. DM is following the French closely and the sentence is clumsy; but there is no doubt as to the meaning.

24/14. *werreþ*: C *guerroie*; VV (20/1) reads *warieþ* which gives better sense; but all the early manuscripts support the reading *guerroie*.

24/16–17. *And huo þet . . . by hit zenne*: C *Et qui bien i prent garde ꞏ en touz ces biens de nature que iai briefment conte soient pecchiez*: the Cotton reading, *soient pecchiez* appears substantially in the *sont pecchiez* of G1 and Ca2. The translation is presumably 'there may be (there are) sins'. A better reading, *sieut on pechier*, appears in a number of other manuscripts (P2, 3, 4, 9, 16, A2, M, V, Ca1, G4, L); or possibly *uiennent pechie* (P1, 12, Add1) is correct. DM has, in any case, mistranslated; *by hit zenne* should read *moȝe by zenne*. The passage can then be rendered thus: 'And a perceptive man will observe that, in regard to all these gifts of nature which I have briefly narrated, there may be sins' (*or* 'man is accustomed to sin' *or*, 'sins come') etc. The text could be emended by reading *me useþ to zeneȝi* for *by hit zenne* or, keeping the reading of C, by reading *moȝe by zenne*.

24/20. For *þet* 'than' see note to 21/12.

24/22–6. C reads *Car quant dame de fortune a sa roe tornee a lome 7 leuee 7 assis ou haut de sa roe* comme *molin a vent. 7 la haut monte: iloec ventent tuit li .xij. uens de vaine gloire*; Varnhagen ((1877), 399) pointed out that DM has (i) taken *a*, in *a lome*, as a preposition (ii) not realised that *a vent* belongs to *moulin*, and that *monte* is factitive; thus he translates *a* by *to* and takes *a vent* to depend on *tornee*; *monte* he has rendered by *ycliue*; nor has he perceived that the erroneous *7 leuee* (*eleve*) does not refer to *roe*; nor that *la* is for *l'a*. The passage should read: *Vor huanne þe lheuedi of haþ heþ hire hueӡel ywent, heþ þe man arered and yzet to þe heӡþe of hare hueӡel ase wyndmelle, and him heþ heӡe ydo cliue, þere blaweþ alle þe tuelf wyndes of ydele blisse.* Morris's addition of *þe* before *melle* is unnecessary.

24/27. *þet* in line 27 should be omitted. Cf. the reading of An, R1; *Car quant cil est si haut montes en prosperite* (*si*) *pense en son cuer.*

24/35. *wyþ eyse of loste*: C *ou uaisselement de liz*; DM has taken *de liz* as *deliz* 'pleasure' whence, perhaps, *eyse* for *uaisselement*. He has probably been misled by a reading *de liz* (as in G1, Ca2, and C) for the reading *en liz* of other early manuscripts. Read *wyþ zelure, wyþ beddes*. (Cf. Wallenberg, p. 319.)

25/16. *yherþ*: C *sesioist*; Wallenberg points out (p. 319) that the French verb is from *esjoier* 'rejoice' and not from *ouïr* as DM seems to have thought. Read *him ioisseþ*.

25/25. *properliche*: Morris usually expands as *propreliche*. Cf. 34/30, 140/11, 235/15.

26/2. *berieles*: Matthew 23: 27 suggests that this is plural. Cf. *smeryeles* and Wallenberg, p. 26, n. 2; Dobson (1968), § 270.

26/4. *penonces / an guode*: C *penitances 7 bones*; the reading *penitances e de bones oeures* in P1, 3, 4, A2, M, G1, An, V, Ld, Ca1, Ca2, L, Add1, R1, R2 may represent the original reading. The reading of C, however, makes adequate sense.

26/5. *halt*: C *tiegne*; DM may have confused the subjunctive with the indicative *tiegn*; but cf. note to 23/7.

26/22. *huane*: is an unstressed form. Cf. Magnusson, p. 117, note to 131/2 and discussion pp. 40–1.

26/27. *heӡliche*: the French shows that this is an adjective and not an adverb. For the form compare 264/12 where *heӡliche clom* renders *summum silentium*. Cf. note to 27/6 and pp. 64, n. 2 & 68, n. 1.

27/3. *nanmore*: Wallenberg (p. 167, n. 1) is perhaps correct in rendering the nasal sign as *m*. The word shows assimilation elsewhere. Cf. 270/1.

27/6. *heӡliche*: the French *principaus* shows that this is an adjective and not an adverb. Cf. note to 26/27.

27/13–15. *and of al . . . may telle*: C *7 de tout fait son domaige tant a ou cuer del enuious pensees enuenimouses de faus iugemenz que on ne les porroit nombrer*; a new sentence begins after *harm*. DM has taken *a* as a preposition and has misunderstood *tant*, which he renders by *zuo moche* 'to such an extent' whereas the sense requires *zuo uele* 'so many'. Thus *zuo moche þet to* should be emended to *zuo uele heþ*. For the phrase *of al makeþ his harm* cf. VV, 22/29–30: *of al þat he doþ hymself harme*.

27/20. *zome | þet me hyelde guode men: ys y-blamed*: C *aucuns que len tenoit a prodome: est blamez*. The form *zome* (*aucuns*) should be singular. The verb *hyelde* must be subjunctive but an indicative is required. Emend to *zom þet me hild guod man is y-blamed*.

27/34. *mo[u]þe*. It is probably unnecessary to emend. See p. 15.

27/35–28/1. Psalm 9 (10): 7.

28/21. *rebeleþ*: C *rebee*; Wallenberg points out (p. 319) that the verb *rebeer* means 'to covet'.

28/29. *contrarious*: cf. p. 6. At 123/4, 7 and 136/17, 261/13 Morris has emended comparable forms unnecessarily.

28/30–3. Matthew 12: 32.

28/33–4. *and me ssel ine þet | hollyche onderstonde*: C *7 doit on ce sainement entendre*; Varnhagen ((1877), 401) pointed out that *ine þet* may be due to confusion of *on* with *en*. *Ine* should certainly be omitted. *MED* (HOLLI adv. 3 (a)) renders *hollyche* by 'completely', 'fully' etc. but *sainement* means 'wisely', 'sensibly', and *hollyche* here is simply a literal rendering of the French. Cf. VV, 24/15 ff.: *but euery man schal wisely vnderstonde þat þer is no synne so gret þat* etc.

29/1. *him uorþingþ | and byt merci | uor þe zenne þet werreþ*: C *se repente de cel pecchie. qui guerroie*; as Varnhagen ((1877), 401) pointed out, R1 reads: *repent de bon cuer mes a paines auient que l'en se repente de tel pechie qui guerroie*. This reading appears also in M, Ld, and may represent the original reading. The reading of the majority of the manuscripts could be due to homoeoteleuton.

29/30. *werreres*: C *guerroiers*; the sense requires the reading *guerres* which appears in E (except that P3 has *ires*, L *graces*, and G1, Ca2 read *guerroiers* as C). The text should read *werres*.

29/31–3. *uor huanne man | him berþ . . . and þet body*: C *car quant ire seurporte lome au torment 7 lame 7 le cors*; Varnhagen ((1877), 403) pointed out that DM has (i) confused *seurporte* and *se porte* whence *him berþ* (cf. the reading *semporte* of G1, Ca2); (ii) confused the grammatical function of *ire* and *lome*. The subject is *ire* and not *lome* as DM's rendering suggests; (iii) not observed that *lame* and *le cors* are genitive. Furthermore, C's reading must be corrupt since it has no main verb. R1 reads *au torment elle tormente* for C's *au torment* which looks like conflation. The majority of early manuscripts omit *au torment*. Thus P1–4, A2, V, Ld, Ca1, Add1 read *elle* (*li*) *tormente* while M reads *7 li tormente* and An *7 le tourmente*. Whatever the precise original reading, it seems clear that a verb is required. The text could be emended to read: *uor huanne ire opbereþ þone man hi tormenteþ and þe zaule and þet body*. It may be noted that G1, Ca2 share with C the erroneous reading *au torment*.

30/4. *opereþ*: Wallenberg (p. 180, n. 3) notes that this is a literal rendering of *seurporte* and supposes the plural form to be due to the double subject; but *nimþ* is singular and *opereþ* may be singular. Cf. p. 98.

30/36–17. *to his nixte*: C *a ses proismes*; the French shows that the form is plural. Cf. 78/12.

30/20. The French has *rancune . . . haine*; accordingly, the second *wreþe* should be emended to *hate*.

30/21. *efter*: C *apres*; the English should perhaps read *efterward*. Cf. 249/21.

30/33. *þet byeþ to ham helpinde*: *MED* (s.v. 1. (c)) regards this as reflexive but C has *qui lor sont en aide* which must mean 'who help them'. This suggests that *byeþ helpinde* is an expanded tense even though such tenses are not usual in the *Ayenbite*.

30/34. *an ine zuyche nyede*: C *7 en tele besoigne* seems to follow on from *qui lor sont en aide*. VV 26/19 has *in suche doynges* and begins a new sentence at *And þerfore þei beþ* etc. The 'and' appears to be superfluous in the French and the English. Read *ine zuyche nyede*.

31/1–2. See Whiting, Y 17. Cf. 137/36, 218/13–15.

31/10. *þonneliche*: C *tenuites*; C's reading means 'thinness' (cf. Godefroy, TENVETE). It is clear, both from the French and from the use of the noun *arȝnesse* at 31/14, that we should expect a noun here. The French shows that *OED*'s rendering of *þonneliche* as 'in that case' cannot be correct. Wallenberg (p. 253, n. 2) thinks that DM has translated *tenurement* in the next line and that the word is an adverb. But this does not explain the vowel unless it represents an unmutated OE form. The correct reading may be that of Ca1, *tiedetez* 'tepidity'. This is the sin which makes a man love *lheucliche* instead of *bernindeliche*. For *þonneliche* we should perhaps read *lheucnesse*.

31/13. *to alle guodes* / *to done*: C *a touz biens faire*; omit the first *to*.

31/15. *huerine*: the form is unstressed. See Magnusson, p. 117 and discussion p. 40–1.

31/29–30. *nyedes* / *þet*: C *besoignes que*; there is an omission here. The French should read *besoignes dou monde mais il sont endormi aus besoignes dieu (car)* for *besoignes que*; so substantially E except P1, Add1; G1, Ca2 share the omission of C.

32/15. DM has understandably taken the French *de mauuais sergant* as singular but the French verb *font* is plural. But DM has not noticed that the pronoun in line 16, *his* (French *les*) is plural and does not match the singular *kuead seriont*. It should be noted, however, that the French changes number later in the sentence and the evil servants are referred to as *il est* (DM. *he is*, l. 17).

32/16–18. C reads *quand il est de la gent nonchalant. oublieus. perreceus. lasches. 7 defaillans*. The reading *nonchalant, oublieus, perreceus, lasches, defaillans* is confirmed by the majority of the manuscripts, although there are minor variations of order in some. It would seem that DM's *uoryetinde* represents *oublieus*; *slak*, *lasches*, and *perreceus*; and *fallinde* (or *failinde* with an *i* or *l* above the line), *defaillans*. The reading *de la gent* appears also in P1, 4, 5, 7, Ca2, Add1 but would appear to be erroneous. G1 has *de la gent* subpuncted and *deslele* substituted in the margin. This corresponds to the common reading *desloiaus* in a number of manuscripts (P3, 6, 10, 11, 13, 14, M, An, V, L, Ld, Add2, R1). It may be supposed that DM's *ontrewe* thus represents an alternative to *sleuuol* and reflects some such correction in his exemplar. Thus *sleuuol* would seem to represent the reading *de la gent*. This, however, makes little sense and probably represents a corruption of the reading *delaianz* (P2, 8, 9, 12, A2, G4, 5, Ca1). (Cf. note to 32/18.) If this is correct, then the mysterious *onssriuel* represents *nonchalant*. Morris proposed emending to *onssriuen* and so also Dolle (§ 44). Wallenberg (p. 177, n. 2), however, objects that the strong past participle usually has no final *n* in the *Ayenbite*. He prefers a later suggestion of Morris, namely that it is from OE *scrifan* 'to care for' and shows the kind of *l*-formation apparent elsewhere in the text. He suggests the general sense 'careless' rather than the more precise meaning given by *OED* (SHRIVE *v.* under UN-*prefix*[1] 3) 'neglectful of confession'. The surmise is supported by ME *shryue of* 'concern oneself about'; cf., for example, *Kyng Alisaunder*, 3892.

32/18. *ontreuþe*: C *desloiautes*; the reading of C is that of all E manuscripts other than P2, A2, Add1. These have the reading *delaiance* which the sense requires, a reading which appears also in P9, 12. Cf. 32/24.

32/22. *he hi*m / *onwoneþ*: C *le desacoustume*; omit *he*.

32/24. *deþ hit auerst*: C *fait delaiement*; *auerst* usually means 'at first' and we should perhaps read *a uerst* 'a delay' in which case *hit* would seem to be redundant. At 161/14, *deþ auerst* means 'delays' but an adverbial combination *auerst(e)* 'tardily' seems possible here.

32/30–1. *of uoryetynge*: C *de negligence 7 de oubliance*. DM has only one sin but both sense and the manuscript evidence require two. Emend to *of sleuþe and of uoryetynge*.

33/12. *op let*: read *oplet*. As Wallenberg points out (p. 180, n. 5), it translates French *sormaine* 'wears out', 'wearies'. The English appears to be due to a misunderstanding of the French. Read *trauayleþ*.

33/16. *toualþ ine þa slacnesse*: C *de chiet en tel peresce*; the sense requires *ine zuiche slacnesse*. DM has read *tel* as *cel*. *Toualþ* is a literal rendering of C's *de chiet*. Cf. Wallenberg, p. 244, n. 1.

33/17. *smak*: C *sauoir*; Wallenberg (p. 319) points out that DM has rendered *sauour*, the reading of P1–3, A2, M, An, V, Ld, Ca1, Add1. P4, G1, and Ca2 have *sauoir* as C.

33/22. *kan*: DM derives *sieut* from *savoir* and not from *soloir*. Cf. 67/10, 80/17, 115/8, 118/10, 156/30, 176/25, 209/22, 246/32. Cf. also 77/33, 103/26, 206/14, 252/10.

33/23. *uol-serueþ*: C's *par sert* suggests that Wallenberg (s.v.) is right in assuming that *uol* is a verbal prefix and not an adverb as suggested by *MED* FUL adv. I (a).

33/27. *brengeþ*: C *met*; the text should read *brengþ*.

33/29. *oþer me*: C *ou se len*; supply *yef* after *oþer* or understand *huanne*.

34/8–9. *him hasteþ and wylneþ*: C *se haste et desirre*; the text is corrupt here. The correct reading may be *soushaide 7 desirre* (P2, 3, 4, A2, M; *rev.* An, V); G1, Ca2 have the reading of C which may be a corruption of *se het et desirre* (Add1). The text could be emended either by reading *desireþ and wylneþ* or *him hateþ and wylneþ*.

34/16. *poyns*: seems to refer to the dots on dice. See *OED* POINT *sb.* B I 3 g.

34/20–1. 1 Timothy 6: 10.

34/26. *zuo disordene*: C *cil desordenemens*; DM seems to have read *cil* as *si*. The text should read *þis disordenaunce*.

35/15. *þer is anoþer lenere corteys . . . leneþ*: C *il i a uns autres presteors cortois . . . prestent*; read *þer byeþ oþre leneres corteys*.

35/16. *in heȝinge*: C *en attendant*; Wallenberg (p. 117, n. 1) suggested that DM read *en accendant*. But the correct reading is probably *en attendant les bontez* (so E except G1, An, Ca2 which read as C). Cf. Varnhagen, (1877), 405–6. *Chapfare* in line 16 seems to mean 'a formal compact'. VV, 30/36, has *couenaunt*. These lenders bargain, but not officially or professionally.

35/19. *seruices ulessliche*: C *seruises. coruees*; a *corvee* was a day's work of unpaid labour which a vassal owed his overlord. DM apparently thought that the word had some connection with *caro* (cf. Varnhagen (1877), 406). *MED* (CORVE n.) suggests reading *coruees* (cf. 38/27).

35/21–2. *and oueral to gauel | huanne me hit nimþ | by þe skele | of þe lone*: C *e par tout a usure quant on le prent par la raison du prest*; it seems best to take French *a* as a verb and not a preposition. If we emend DM's *to* to *biþ* the sentence can be translated 'and always there is usury whenever he takes it (i.e. the service) by reason of the loan'. That is to say, the unofficial loan is usury if some return is expected for it (cf. Varnhagen (1877), 409).

36/3–10. Francis (pp. lx–lxi) explains the implications of this passage. What is meant is the selling of goods on credit. It comes under the heading of usury because the extension of credit raises the price and is in reality a device for concealing interest. It is thus a double transaction, consisting of the sale of goods, and the option on the purchase price in return for an agreement to pay a larger sum later. It is indeed a medieval equivalent of our 'hire purchase'. VV 31/28 adds that this is *aȝens þe statute of marchaundes*. For DM's *Vor hire time-zettinge* the French has *Car por leur termoiemens* and *be* should, perhaps, be supplied after *vor*.

36/7–8. *þe derrer tuyes | oþer þries zuo moche | þane*: C *plus chier .ii. tant ou .iii. tant que* 'two or three times more dearly than'. DM seems to have misunderstood *tant que* (= *tans que*). Read *ziþe* for *zuo moche*. Cf. 36/17 *tuyes zuo moche | oþer þries*: C *.ii. tans ou .iii.*

36/12. *hy*: C *lor* 'to them (the usurers)'; *hy* should read *ham*.

36/13. *þet naȝt him ne aquytteþ*: C *qui point ne saquite* 'which (the mortgage) is never discharged'. *Him* is neuter reflexive.

36/16. *þet he payþ*: C *quil paient*; the text should read *þet hi payeþ*.

36/21. *alhuet hi*: C *ou tans queles*; Wallenberg (p. 319) points out that DM has rendered *ou tans que* as *tant que*. The English should read *huanne hi*.

36/27. *uelaȝe*: *MED* renders 'accomplice', 'accessory' but the sense is rather 'partner'. See *MED* FELAU(E n. 7.

36/28. *to þe haluedele*: the reference is to the *métayage* system by which the farmer pays rent in kind to the owner of the land and the owner provides stock and seed. Translate 'they give their beasts by the *métayage* system on condition that their value be maintained; that is to say, if they die, the tenant will have to replace them by others of the same value'. *To þe haluedele* is a literal translation of French *moiteerie*.

36/29. *fer pris*: C *fer*; *pris* is inserted above the line and, according to Morris's usual practice, should be enclosed in square brackets. As Wallenberg points out (p. 88, n. 5) *fer* is for French *fuer* 'price', 'value'.

36/30. *ine mene-time: do*: C *li moitoiers mettra*; DM has not understood the meaning of *moitoiers* 'the tenant who goes halves', 'the *métayer*'. The text should read *þe haluedelere ssel do*.

36/31 ff. *þe pans* (l. 36) should read *uor þe pans*; C *por les deniers*. Translate 'The seventh kind consists of those who set their poor neighbours to work for them and (this) because they have lent them a little money or corn or done them some favour. And, when they see them poor and necessitous, they make with them a bargain to work for them and because of the money which they previously lent the poor man (or because they lent him a little corn) they gain for one penny three pennyworths of work.'

37/10, 13. *þe þyef*: the French forms *li larron* are plural as appears from the verbs and the pronouns *les, lor* (DM) *hise, hire* (ll. 12, 15). Read *þe þieues*. In line 13, *is* should read *byeþ*.

37/22–3. *rekeneþ more | ine dedes. and ine spendinge*: *dedes* translates C *mises* 'outlay' and is clearly a misunderstanding. DM probably regarded *dedes* as standing in the same relationship to *do* as *mises* to *mettre* (cf. Varnhagen (1877), 412). The meaning seems to be that they claim expenses but withhold rents. The gloss in *MED* is purely contextual (DEDE n. 1a (d)).

37/29. *deþ zuo moche | be hare zenne*: C *fait tant par son pecchie*, 'so contrives by her sin'. DM's literal rendering of the French is hardly English. Cf. 44/26 *makeþ zuo moche þet*; French *font tant que*.

37/30. For *berþ* read *bereþ*. The subject is *þe children*.

38/10. *be hire ssrifteuaderes*: C *de lor* con*fessors*. Emend *be* to *of*.

38/18. *mid hare þyefþe*: C *ou cele le larrecin*; DM has confused *ou* 'or' with *o* 'avec'. His text may have lacked *cele*.

38/29. *zecheþ*: for *zeche* 'contrive' see *OED* SEEK *v*. 7 D.

39/4. *þet hi ofhealdeþ*: read *þet ofhealdeþ*.

39/6. *prela[te]s*. But Morris leaves the French form *prelas* at 49/20, 67/29, 237/6.

39/10. *prouost*: C *prouoz*; a plural is required and we should read *prouos*. Wallenberg (p. 197, n. 2) points out that *prouoz* could also be singular; hence the error.

39/15. *ycontined*: C *continuez*; Wallenberg (p. 61, n. 2) points out that *ycontined* 'contained' could be a variant of the form *ycontyened*; presumably DM would have rendered *continuez* by *ycontyened*. It seems likely, in any case, that textual corruption is in question. At 12/2 and 12/17, *ycont(y)ened* 'contained' renders, correctly, French *contenu*. In the case under discussion *ycontined* renders French *continuez* 'continued' where the sense requires 'contained'. The reading of C appears also in G1, Ca2 but the reading *contenues* appears in the other early manuscripts. It seems probable, therefore, that the form *ycontined* renders a French *contenues* and is not due to the reading *continuez*. This supposition is supported by the erroneous reading *continuees* in G1, Ca2, C at 118/15 for which the correct reading *contenues* appears in P1, 2, 4, A2, M, An, Add1. DM seems to have had this latter reading as he renders by *ycontyened*. At 260/17, *contenues* in the French manuscripts is rendered *ycontynent*, a form which Morris and Varnhagen ((1877), 412) thought to be an error for *ycontyned* but which Wallenberg regarded as due to the influence of the Latin participle. It should be emended to *ycontyned*. For examples of confusion of 'contain' and 'continue' see *MED* CONTINUEN *v*. 6. French *contenues/continues* probably lie at the root of the confusion.

39/18. *opo*: see note to 17/32.

39/24. *lang time*: Varnhagen ((1877), 413) pointed out that the French has *lointains* and conjectured DM read *longtemps*. The reading of VV (35/21), *longe delaies* may support this conjecture but *lointains* can mean 'long-lasting' as well as 'distant'. See Godefroy, LOINTAIN.

39/28. *naȝt*: C *nient*; DM has mistaken the verb for the noun. Read *naȝteþ*.

40/1. *hise beclepieþ*: C *les empeeschent*; Varnhagen ((1877), 413–14) pointed out that two other manuscripts have *bones* between *les* and *empeeschent* which completes the sense (so P1, 3, A2, M, An (*les bons gens*), P2, P4, V (*les bonnes querelles*), Ld, Ca1, L, Add1, R1 or reverse). The erroneous reading of C is shared with G1, Ca2. The text should read *þe guode beclepieþ*.

40/3. *lyese*: for *lyeseþ*. See p. 52.

40/5. MS *doȝ*: here and at 91/7, Morris's reading *doþ*, *deþ* should be accepted; cf. *heʒ* 145/25; *ouercomʒ* 181/16; *kuelʒ* 248/2; *zekʒ* 253/10; *zyeʒ* 244/4; *zeneʒeʒ* 222/22; and the reverse spellings in *doþter* 142/31; *naþt* 197/17; *zorþe* 202/30 all of which should be emended. Cf. *ydiʒt* for *ydiʒt* 217/4.

40/36. *halʒede þinges*: C *saintuaires* 'sanctuaries'. DM's rendering is an error.

41/16. *naþemo*: *OED* (Nathemo(re *adv.*) cannot be correct in translating 'never the more'. The French has *ausi* and the sense required is 'furthermore'.

41/19. *þo*: see note to 17/32.

42/13. *leteþ*: C *laissent*; the meaning must be 'leave' rather than 'let' as *MED* (Leten v. 2 (a)) suggests.

42/27. *religon*: Wallenberg (p. 202, n. 2) suggests that the manuscript reading should be retained. But there is no evidence for such a form. Cf. 48/12.

42/30–3. The reference is to Canon Law. See *Corpus Iuris Canonici, Decretum* C. 1. q. 1, 114 (ed. A. Friedberg (Leipzig, 1879), I, cols. 402–3).

43/3. *wychkedhede*: the spelling may show confusion with *wychche*.

43/4. *dyeuel*: is here used adjectivally. Cf. *dyeules tormentors* for *tortores diabolici* (265/12 and note to that line); and *men apostles* for *viri apostolici* (267/23–4).

43/22. *grochinge*: C *murtre*; DM has rendered *murmure*, a reading which appears in R1. Cf. Wallenberg, p. 319.

43/35. *c[h]alengeþ*: restore *calengeþ*, a Norman form.

44/1. *raymi*: C *raimbre*; for the sense 'plunder' see *OED* Raim *v.* 2.

44/1. *kueadliche lede*: C *malmener*; the English is a calque on the French.

44/20–1. *beggeþ . . . zelleþ*; C *achate . . . vent*; read *bayþ . . . zelþ*? But cf. p. 99.

44/34–5. *maki/ porchaci*: C *faire e porchascer*; supply *and* between the two verbs.

44/35. *makeþ uor to ssewy*: C *appareillent por sembler*; Varnhagen ((1877), 414–15) pointed out that Add1 and R1 read *apere*, which clearly makes better sense. All the E manuscripts read *apere* (*apert*) except G1, Ca2 which agree with C. The English should read *ssewy*.

45/9. *hysians*: read *hiriaus*. Wallenberg (p. 124, n. 1) points out that this is an error for the French *hysiaus, hiziaus*, which is itself an error for *hiriaus* 'herald'.

45/15. *byeþ*: read *biþ*.

45/24. *to eʒte daʒes*: C *a .viii. iors* 'in eight days'; in the previous line DM renders *a (.i. mois)* as *uor (ane monþe)*.

45/28. *to lite*: C *aperte*; emend *to lite* to *aperte*. Wallenberg (p. 319) points out that DM has rendered *petite* for *aperte*.

46/9. *y[e]ue*: there is no need to emend here or at 93/3, 114/3, 116/4, 152/34, 165/20, 198/28, 219/7, 229/34 (see p. 32).

46/34. *becleppe*: DM has confused *embraser* 'kindle' with *embrasser* 'embrace'; cf. 66/1, 88/30. The text should read *aliȝte*.

46/35. *likinges*: C *figures*; read *likninges*.

47/1. *makeþ penche*: C *i fait penser* makes better sense and the English should probably read *makeþ penche þerof*.

47/4. *þo*: see note to 17/32.

47/12–13. *þet sseweþ ham* . . . *hy sseaweþ*: C *parees e* . . . *se parent*; Wallenberg (p. 320) points out that DM has rendered *parees* 'adorned' and *se parent* 'adorn themselves' as part of *aparoir*. The text should read *agrayþed and* . . . *ham agrayþeþ*.

47/14. *honesteliche*: C *deshonestement*; DM's text seems to have had *honnestement* (R2). But the sense requires *deshonesteliche*.

47/21–2. This seems to be a gloss on Ecclesiastes 7: 27.

47/30. *hue* is OK *hwe*. Morris's conjecture is mistaken.

47/31–2. 1 Corinthians 7: 2.

47/34. *him arist*: the reading of C, *se muet* substantiates the translation 'is aroused'.

47/35. *dede*: C *œure*; the sense of the French is 'things'. Read *þinges*.

47/35–6. *þe mochele drinkeres. and eteres*: C *li outrageus de boire e de meng*er; the sense requires *outrages* etc. 'excesses of eating and drinking'.

48/4–5. *an heȝ*: C *en montant*. The meaning is 'progressively' as *MED* suggests (HEIGH adj. 8b. (f)).

48/6–7. *ne of wodewehod*: C *ne de veu*; as Wallenberg points out (p. 320), DM has rendered *vedve* 'widow'. Read *oþ* for *wodewehod*.

48/10. *ald*: C *uiex*; the reading *uiex* (G1, C) confuses the word 'old' with *uieus, uis, uils* 'vile'. For *ald* read *uyl*. Cf. 16/27.

48/19. *desertesoun*: C *desheritemens*; Wallenberg (p. 72, n. 3) points out that the French means 'disinheritance' not 'desertion'.

48/23. *heþ*: is a misreading of French *a* 'to'. Read *wiþ*.

48/24–5. *ordre and of spoushod*: C *dordre de mariage*; read *of ordre of spoushod*.

48/27–8. Genesis 38: 8–10.

48/28–30. Tobias 3: 7–9.

48/35. *godzybbe*: C *marraine*; *OED* (GOSSIP *sb.*) regards the form as feminine. For a contrary view see Wallenberg, p. 95, n. 1.

49/2. *nyeȝ oþer uer*: *MED* (FER adv. 2 (a)) takes *uer* as an adverb. But it is surely an adjective. The sense is 'whether it be a close or distant relationship'.

49/10. *of þe half of*: Varnhagen ((1877), 415) rightly points out that the

French *a* is a verb, not a preposition. Read *heþ part ine*. The sense of the phrase is elucidated by VV 45/27: *takeþ anoþer of hire kyn*.

49/12. *mid him*: C *a lui*; C is wrong here. The sense requires *li*, the reading of P1–3, An, Add1, R1. The English should read *mid hire*.

49/31 ff. Genesis 19.

50/15–18. Matthew 8: 30–2; Mark 5: 11–13; Luke 8: 32–3.

50/18–19. *þet þe glotouns . . . to guo in ham*: C *que es glotons qui mainent uie de porciaus : a li diables congie dentrer*; DM has misunderstood the construction. The text should read; *þet into þe glotouns þet ledeþ lif of zuyn þe dyeuel heþ yleaue to guo*.

50/21. *tocleue*: C *creuent*; read *tocleueþ*.

50/27–8. Genesis 3.

50/30. *chinne*: Varnhagen ((1877), 415–6) pointed out that DM has mistaken *emecon* 'a hook' for *menton* 'a chin'. Given the similarity of *c* and *t*, if his manuscript read *lemecon*, DM may have thought that a nasal sign had been omitted from the word *menton*; cf. 248/20.

50/34. *ylefþ*: C *crient*; Varnhagen pointed out that DM has translated *croit* ('Dan Michel's *Ayenbite of Inwyt*', *ESt*, ii (1879), 53). For *ylefþ* read *dret*.

51/6. *ssolle . . . uynde*: C *trouera*; a subjunctive is out of place here. There is probably confusion with the preceding *ssolle we*. Read *ssel . . . uynde*.

51/13. *þous to þe kueade zayþ*: C *ci a malvais dit*; 'here is an evil speech'. Read *Hyer biþ kuead word*. Cf. Varnhagen (1879), 53.

51/18–19. Cf. Gregory, *Moralia* Bk. XXXI, cap. xlv (PL lxxvi, col. 621) and *In Primum Regum Expositiones*, Bk. II, cap. iii (PL lxxix, col. 110).

51/34. *heþ ymad þet kuead*: C *li a fait le chief mauuais*; Varnhagen, ((1879), 54) pointed out that DM first wrote correctly *heued* after *þet* and then deleted it. Read *him* before *heþ* and *heued* before *kuead*.

52/6. *þet hi doþ: propreliche*: C *que il font proprement*; P1–4, A2, An, Ca1, Add1, R1 have the reading *que il font (il) font proprement* which the sense requires. Cf. Varnhagen, (1879), 54.

52/17. *and alsuo*: C *ausi*; omit *and*.

52/18–20. *þet uolk . . . louieþ* etc.: for the number of *uolk* see p. 62.

52/23–4. Isaiah 5: 20.

52/36–53/1. *þe kete of his sperringe*: C *li goufres de satalie*; Francis (note to 49/28–30) followed Varnhagen ((1877), 416) in supposing that the reference is to the Gulf of Satalieh, or Adalia, on the southern coast of Asia Minor. This may be correct, although a large number of manuscripts read *saternie*. The reading of the *Ayenbite* is a mystery. Varnhagen ((1877), 416; (1879), 55) suggested that DM took *satalie* to mean *sa talie* 'his stick, rafter' and that *sperringe* is from *sperren* 'to close' but with the sense of the noun *sparre* 'log, trunk'. The translation *kete* 'kite' he

thinks to be due to a confusion of *goufres* with Latin *vultur* but Wallen-
berg (p. 224, n. 2) is probably right in suggesting that DM more probably
confused it with French *voutre* 'vulture'. Nevertheless, as Wallenberg
points out, a vulture swallowing a rafter is a striking phenomenon. He
proposes that *sperringe* is rather to be connected with OE *spyrran* 'to slit,
tear to pieces' and that DM has taken *sa talie* as the possessive and a
noun *talie, taillee,* 'incision, act of cutting' and that *sperringe* would be
related to this word as *þenchinge* is to French *pensee*. But it is possible that
sperringe means rather 'fastening' (cf. *OED* SPAR *v.*¹ 1). DM's manuscript
possibly had some such reading as A2's *li goufre de sa cheine* (probably for
satheine). This could have suggested the idea of the bird swallowing
everything including its chain or fastening rather than 'that which it has
torn asunder' as Wallenberg renders it.

53/2–3. *moche uolk sterueþ. and ofte þer comeþ*: C *mout de genz en moerent e
souent en uient*; read *moche uolk sterueþ þerof and ofte þerof comeþ*. For
the number of *uolk* see p. 62.

53/6–8. Regularize to singular or plural.

53/10–12. Romans 8: 13, Philippians 3: 19.

53/15–16. *hyealde | hire fole uelaȝredes*: *MED* (HOLDEN v. (1) 20 (a))
implies 'engage in their foolish activities'. But cf. 54/26 where the sense
seems to be 'keep company'. This also seems to be the natural sense of the
French *tenir . . . compaignies*. Translate 'maintain their foolish friend-
ships'.

53/24–5. *ane little | and ane scarse*: this is ambiguous. It probably means,
however, 'a little one and a sparse one' rather than 'one little and one
sparse', since we should expect *one little and one sparse* if this were the
sense.

53/27. *þe ilke þet couaytyse ledeþ*: C *cil* qui *auarice mainent*; *þe ilke* is the
subject, not *couaytyse*, and the citation in *MED* LEDEN v. (1) 4 (a) should
be transferred to LEDEN v. (1) 9 (c). The usage is probably a calque on the
similar use of French *mener*.

54/1. *be wyȝte ymad*: C *par þais faisant*; the sense of the French is 'in
order to make peace' viz. between the belly and the purse. DM, no doubt,
had the reading *þois* for *þais* which appears in Ca2. Cf. Varnhagen
(1877), 416–7. Read *uor þais to maki*.

54/3. *of his*: this is a calque on French *ou sien*. 'in his own (house)'. The
English should read *ine his*. For the idiom cf. 111/32, 194/28–9.

54/8. *to þe wordle*: C *au siecle* 'in the world'. Read *ine* for *to*.

54/16–17. *Þo þet habbeþ þe lhordssip | ope þe bodyes*: C *Cil ont la seignorie
sor le cors*; DM has taken *cil* to mean 'those who' instead of 'those people'
and has taken *cors* as plural. Emend to *þo habbeþ þe lhordssip ope þe
bodye*. Cf. Varnhagen, (1879), 56.

54/20. *uor þet*: C *por ce que* seems to be an error for *par ce que* 'by that
which', the reading of P1, Ld, R1. P4 has *selonc ce que*. Emend to *bi þet*.

54/24–5. *þet yef*: C *se*; omit *þet*.

54/34–5. Cf. Psalm 58 (59): 10.

54/35. *cleuiinde*: *MED* (CLEVEN v. (1) 6 (c)) renders, here and at 98/14, by 'memorable', 'convincing'; *OED* (CLEAVING *ppl. a.*²) by 'abiding', 'lasting', 'persistent', and so at 107/20. The French has *attaignans* and, at 98/14, *atteignant* 'convincing'; at 103/34, *attaignaument* is rendered by *cleuiyndelyche*. At 107/29, *cleuiynde* renders French *aerse* 'attached'.

54/36. *operhuyl*: C *a la fois*; Varnhagen ((1879), 57) suggested that DM confused *a la fois* with *quelquefois*. But the reading makes good sense.

55/2. *hes*: it seems best to accept Zupitza's suggestion that this is OK *es* 'carrion', an interpretation which is supported by French *charoigne*. Wallenberg (p. 119, n. 5) thinks that the form may have arisen in an alliterative phrase such as *ase deþ þe hond to þe hes* but DM does show some confusion in the spelling of words with initial *h*; cf. p. 45, n. 3.

55/7. *ethe metes*: C *toutes uiandes*; Varnhagen ((1877), 417) read *eche* but this is uncertain. In any case, however, the French suggests that emendation may be required. The choice is between assuming a plural *eche* or amending to *alle*. E. Einenkel (*Geschichte der englischen Sprache: historische Syntax* (Strassburg, 1916), p. 146) draws attention to a few cases of 'each' as a plural but none is exactly parallel (cf. Wallenberg, p. 80, n. 3). The form may be due to *ethe* above and it is probably best to emend to *alle*.

55/13. *wyþ-oute*: C *saous*; read *ynoȝ* for *wyþoute* (cf. Varnhagen (1877), 392). Other manuscripts confirm the reading of C here.

55/18. *of þise zenne*: C *est li pecchies*; the English requires a verb. Read *is þe zenne*.

55/20. *uelle hare glotonye*: C *lor goule emplir*; *uelle* must mean 'satisfy' unless DM's exemplar was in error.

55/30. *to þe delit*: C *les deliz*; omit *to*.

55/34–5. *mid grat lost*: C *ou grant delit*; the text should read *ine þe grat lost*. Cf. Varnhagen (1879), 58.

56/1. *þet miȝte telle*: C *qui porroit raconter*; omit *þet*. The sentence is a rhetorical question.

56/2. *to*: as Varnhagen ((1877), 417–18) pointed out, DM has confused the verb *a* with the preposition. Read *heþ*.

56/4. *uor hare uoule lost*. C *por lor palais deliter*; Varnhagen ((1877), 418) was probably right in suggesting that DM has confused *palais* with *lais* or he had a defective manuscript at this point. Read *uor hare zuelȝ to liki*.

56/7. *him uoryet* renders *soublier* 'to forget to do what one should do'.

56/8. *ssast*: read *sslast*.

56/9. *lyckestre*: C *lecheresse* means 'harlot'. The English is a calque on the French. Literally it would mean 'a female licker'.

56/12. *recorder*: this should, of course, read *recordy*, the English form.

56/13. *nykken of crane*: C *col de grue*; the manuscript has *nykken* with the final *n* added above the line. In fact, a singular is required but the plural is, no doubt, due to *hi hedden*.

56/35. *þer he ret*: C *i list il?* read *ret he þer?*

57/18. *yef*: C *si* 'indeed'; emend to *zuo*, DM's usual rendering of the French particle. Cf. Varnhagen (1877), 418.

57/20. *of heauede*: as Varnhagen ((1877), 418) pointed out, this is a calque on French *derechief*; accordingly, *of heauede* does not mean 'in the first place', 'principally' as *MED* (HED n. (1) 6 (b)) suggests. But DM translates *derechief* correctly by *alast, ate laste* at 100/14, 104/8. Cf. Varnhagen, (1879), 30.

57/35. *nimeþ*: C *perdent*; as Wallenberg points out (p. 320), DM had rendered *prenent*.

58/5. *velþ*: this is the spelling of the marginal insertion. The text has *uel* with *þ* squeezed in between *l* and the following word. The verb should be plural as in the French.

58/6. *beuor*: read *beuore*.

58/15. *yef hi spekþ*: C *si resont*; DM has again mistaken the particle *si* for the conjunction. Varnhagen ((1877), 418–19) also pointed out that DM has misunderstood the meaning of French *resont* 'come forth' and erroneously added *hi*. The verb should also be plural. Read *zuo comeþ uorþ*.

58/15. *bisye*: C *curiouses*; Varnhagen (loc. cit.) suggested that the meaning of the French *curiouses* is here 'inquisitive', a sense which he regards as inadequately rendered by *bisye*. The meaning, however, is rather 'well-calculated' (cf. *MED* BISI adj. 5(g)) VV, 55/33 has *sliȝe*.

58/27. *draȝe to hare corde*: C *a leur corde traire*; 'engage in their interests', 'bring under their influence'; cf. Wallenberg, p. 62, n. 4.

58/28. *habeþ*: cf. 114/24. The form may be an error but could be due to lack of stress as Magnusson (p. 116) suggests. Cf. *habe* 69/16; *hede* 190/33, and discussion p. 41.

59/5. *he miȝte . . . hi yeueþ*: the change of number is in the French also.

59/7. *ham*: C *le*; this refers to *zenne* (French *pecchie* is masculine). The text should read *hit*.

59/14. *payeþ*: Wallenberg (pp. 184, n. 3, 320) points out that the French reads *painent*. The English should read *payneþ*.

59/23. *ich wylle awreke forre*: C *Je vengerai forre*; a proverb meaning 'I will achieve the impossible'.

59/23–4. *wille maki*: C *ferai* seems to mean 'will bear away' of which the English is an imprecise rendering.

59/27. *ase riȝt naȝt ne him prayseþ*: C *ausi come riens ne se preist* 'as though it were of no value at all'; the English is a literal rendering of the French.

59/30. *hi hit makeþ a naʒt*: C *il le font a rebours* 'they do quite the contrary'. DM's rendering is loose as Wallenberg points out (p. 320).

59/33. *hereþ | and hyealde*: C *lot e tiegne*; DM has not recognized *lot* as present subjunctive. Cf. note to 23/7.

59/34–5. Bernard, *Sermones, 11 in Psalmum 'Qui Habitat'* (*Opera*, ed. J. Leclercq and H. M. Rochais (Rome, 1966), iv. 451).

60/5. For the rendering *noblesse* for French *oublees* cf. 22/15.

60/15. *beuly*: DM has mistaken *chuer* 'fondle' for *eschiver* (cf. Varnhagen, (1877), 420). Read *ulateri*.

60/16. *him*: C *le*; *him* is probably an error for *hit*. Cf. 196/15.

60/17. *heþ*: C *en ait*; *þerof* should be supplied. For the indicative as a rendering of the French subjunctive see note to 23/7.

60/19–20. *ydo oþer yzed: hy leueþ* etc.: the forms *fait ou dit* in C are indicative present but DM has taken them as participles (cf. Varnhagen (1877), 392). Read *doþ oþer ziggeþ*. The subject, French *lor enfant*, is singular but DM has taken it as a plural. Moreover, as Wallenberg points out (p. 320), *hy leueþ* renders French *croissent* (from *creistre* 'increase') and not, as DM seems to have thought, a form of the verb *creire* 'believe'. Accordingly, *leueþ* should read *moreþ*.

60/29. *þanne þet hi useþ*: C *que ce que il vsent*; the reading *en sent* for *vsent*, which appears in P1, An, Ca1, Add1 (or the reading *en set* of P2, 3, 4, R1) gives better sense than the reading of C. The English could be emended to read *þanne þet he bi hym onderstondeþ* (or *knauþ*) 'than that which he understands [or "knows"] concerning the matter'.

61/1–2. *þe blondere defendeþ | and excuseþ | and wryeþ*: C *li flateor defendent e excusent e cueurent*; read *þe blonderes defendeþ* etc.

61/7. *bezuykinge of tedraʒynge*: C *leur tricherie de detraction*; this reading, which appears also in P1, Add 1, G1, Ca2, incorporates a heading *De detraccion* which appears as such in P3, A2, M, Ca1, R1.

61/8 ff. The two beasts are the sirens. For the development of the sirens from half man, half bird to half woman and half fish see F. McCulloch, *Mediaeval Latin and French Bestiaries* (Univ. of N. Carolina Studies in the Romance Languages and Literatures, 33, Chapel Hill, 1962), pp. 166–9. Some manuscripts, while maintaining the original description in the text, have illustrations showing a creature which is part woman, part fish, and part bird. Cf. *A Thirteenth Century Bestiary*, ed. E. G. Millar (Roxburghe Club, Oxford, 1958); *The Bestiary*, ed. M. R. James (Roxburghe Club, Oxford, 1928).

61/12. *zuetelich*: read *zueteliche*.

61/14. *uorzuelʒþ*: C *deuorent*; read *uorzuelʒeþ*.

61/16. For the serpent *sirena* see Isidore *Etymologies* XII, 4, 29 (PL lxxxii, col. 446); McCulloch, pp. 169–70.

61/17. *vleþ* is plural like the French *uolent*. The whole sentence should be

singular or plural. DM has translated literally the French, *Il resont .i.
serpent qui ont a non seraines qui corent plus tost que cheuaus. e a la foiz
uolent*, except that having mistakenly assumed *.i. serpent* to be singular
he has made *yernþ*, in line 16, singular also. He no doubt did not realise
that *.i. serpent* was plural. For *uns* as plural see L. Foulet, *Petite syntaxe de
l'ancien français* (Paris, 1930), § 87). Cf. 76/18, 19.

61/20–1. Cf. Ecclesiastes 10: 11.

61/25. *eteþ*: C *meniue*; read *et* as the sense requires.

61/34. *leaჳinges*: ჳ is here written for *z*. It may be due to the influence of
French orthography but should probably be emended to *leazinges*; or
there could be confusion with *lyeჳinges*.

62/4. *hise deþ hyealde to ane kueade*: C *les fait tenir a maluais* (cf. 51/13);
there is confusion here owing to the reading *a maluais*, common to
Gı and C. The alternative reading *pour maluais* (as in other E manu-
scripts) is to be preferred. Wallenberg (p. 320) suggested that the reading
of DM was for *hyealde uor kueade men* but, in view of the testimony of the
French manuscripts, it is better to read *hyealde ase kueade*. The whole
phrase is then to be translated 'makes them be considered evil men'.
For *hyeade* see p. 49.

62/5. *þe oþre ne eteþ* etc.: it is not clear whether this is singular or plural.
The form *oþre* occurs occasionally as a singular and the verbs *byt*, *nimþ*
are singular. The French has *li autres ne le maniue*. The sense is ambiguous
but the French suggests that we should probably emend to *þe oþre ne eth*
etc. but cf. p. 98. For *oþre* see p. 74.

62/10. *ames*: C *.i. mes* 'a "but" '.

62/12. *zuich* is perhaps an error for *zuich and zuich*; cf. 103/20–1, 132/26–7.

62/14. *enueymeþ*: read *enuenymeþ*.

62/33. *heþ ech manere colour / þet ne heþ non his oჳen*: C *a chascune colour
que il uoit mue la soue* 'at each colour that it sees changes its own'. DM
takes the preposition *a* as a verb. Thus, the first *heþ* should be emended
to *at*. In regard to the second part of the sentence, Wallenberg suggested
(p. 320) that DM read *mue* as *mie*. This reading, in fact, appears in Ca2.
The words *ne heþ* may represent an attempt to make sense of the passage.
The clause could be emended to *þet hit ziჳþ chongeþ his oჳen*.

63/1–5. Cf. *Sermons*, lxxxi 5 (PL xxxviii, cols. 502–3) but especially *De
Mendacio*, xi (PL xl, col. 501). For the 'helpful lie' see more generally
De Mendacio and *Contra Mendacium* (PL xl, cols. 489–548).

63/2. *ase moche ase*: C *combien que* 'notwithstanding that'. The English is a
calque on the French.

63/5. *hyeჳinges*: C *menconges*; read *lyeჳinges*. Cf. Wallenberg, p. 146,
n. 2. For *h* for *l* cf. note to 74/6.

63/23. *zuereþ . . . boldliche*: C *pecche len en sairemens . . . ardanment*; *zuereþ*
should be emended to *zeneჳeþ me ine oþe* which gives better sense. Wal-
lenberg (p. 320) suggests that DM has rendered *hardiement* for *ardanment*.

63/25–7. *þeruore hit uorbyet saint Iacob . . . uor to zuerie*: C *Por ce deffent saint iakes ne uoel iurer* 'For' *quant besoins est mais la uolente:* est *la leccherie de iurer*; the reference is to James 5: 12: *Ante omnia autem, fratres mei, nolite iurare, neque per caelum, neque per terram neque aliud quodcumque iuramentum. Sit autem sermo vester: Est, est: Non, non: ut non sub iudicio decidatis.* In the phrase *mais la uolente est la leccherie de iurer*, DM has correctly rendered *ē* (*est*) (which occurs also in G1) as *is* and he may, indeed, have had the reading *est* which appears in Ca2. But the sense requires *and* and the majority of early manuscripts have, in fact, *e*(*t*). Moreover, the French text has confused direct and indirect speech in the first part of the sentence. The words *ne uoel iurer* are a rendering of *nolite iurare* and the influence of the Latin may explain the appearance of this reading in G1, Ca2, C. But the majority of the E manuscripts read for these words *ne mie le iurer*, which is clearly correct. The text could be emended to *þeruore ne uorbyet saint Iacob naȝt to zuerie huanne hit is nyed ac þet wyl and þe lecherie uor to zuerie*: 'therefore St. James does not forbid swearing when it is needful but the desire and the lust to swear'. It may be noted that the added *For* of C appears as *fors* in the text of G1, Ca2.

64/10. *zikerliche*: C *certeinement*; the meaning seems to be 'confidently' rather than 'bindingly' as *OED* (SICKERLY 5b) suggests.

64/14–15. *Vor þet ich ssel maky ziker: ich ne ssel naȝt draȝe to wytnesse | bote þane heȝe zoþ. þet is god þet al wot*: C *car a ce que ie di* (read *doi*) *confermer: ie ne doi pas traire a tesmoin fors la souraine uerite. cest dieu qui tout set* 'for I must not call to witness, for that which I must affirm, other than the high truth, namely God who knows all things'.

64/20–1. *me zuereþ be him | þet þe wordes byeþ | and byeþ ywryte*: C *on iure par celui qui paroles sont qui sont escrites* 'one swears by him whose are the words which are written'. Read *me zuereþ be him þet þe wordes byeþ þet byeþ ywryte*.

64/31–2. *þise ne uorbereþ naȝt oure lheuedi*: DM seems here to have had a text superior to C which reads *Cil ne demanderent riens nostre dame*.

65/3–8. The reference is to Canon Law, *Decretum* C. 22, q. 5, c. 13 (ed. cit. I. 886). *Mueknesse* (4) and *muekliche* (7) render French *simplete* and *simplement* (but cf. Psalm 83 (84): 12); *stryf* (7) renders French *barat* 'fraud'. The meaning is that, though a man swear with the intention to deceive, *be art oþer be sophistrie*, God, *duplicitatis aspernator*, will understand the oath in the sense in which a simple and honest hearer accepts it.

65/9–12. C's *tieus hons* is singular but DM has taken it as plural and trans lated by *zuyche men*. He has accordingly converted the singular verbs of the French into the plural but failed to adjust *nele* and *him* in lines 11 and 12. He reverts to the singular in line 13. The text should read *zuych a man . . . zuereþ . . . he wot . . . behat . . . he nele . . . him*.

65/12. *þet*: C *quant*; the following clause depends upon the main clause. The sense is 'Great is the mercy of God that the devil does not strangle straightway the man who swears' etc.

65/14. *and he lyeȝe*: C *e il ment*; in view of the French, the correct reading may be *lyeȝeþ* (for the loss of *þ* before *h* see p. 52; but the text could be rendered 'if he lie'.

65/19. *bohote*: see note to 17/32.

65/24. *þes meyster*: C *cist mester*s; 'this occupation'. DM first wrote *þis mester*. He then added a *y*, changing *mester* to *meyster*, and also altered *þis* to *þes*. Wallenberg (p. 154, n. 1) thought that DM supposed *meyster* to be more suitable in the context; but it is possible that DM confused the French forms and decided on second thoughts that the word meant 'master' not 'occupation'.

65/25. *huerof ne is non drede*: C *dont nest pas doute*. The phrase should perhaps be read as a parenthesis *herof ne is non drede*. As it stands it seems to combine two constructions.

66/1. *becleppe*: see note to 46/34. The text should read *aliȝte*.

66/2. *cheaste*[2] is perhaps an error. For the first the French has *contens*, for the second *tencon*.

66/7. *eyder lyexneþ oþren*: C *il dementent lun lautre*; the etymology of *lyexneþ* is obscure; cf. discussion in Wallenberg, p. 147, n. 3. The lack of grammatical concord results from the rendering of *il* by the singular *eyder*.

66/7-8. *oþer greate wordes*: C *ou dient grosses paroles*; supply *ziggeþ* after *oþer*. Ca1, Ca2 omit the verb and DM may have used a manuscript of this type.

66/9. *peyneþ*: Wallenberg (p. 185, n. 1) points out that this translates French *poignent* 'combat, attack'.

66/20. For the meaning of *godeleþ* see Wallenberg, p. 94, n. 2.

66/21-2. Cf. Psalm 100 (101): 5.

66/22-3. Perhaps an imprecise rendering of Ephesians 5: 5. For the number of *uolc* see p. 62.

66/24. *ase þe wyȝte þet ualþ ine hot weter*: C *ausi come li pos qui bout*. Francis (note to VV 64/15) points out that DM's original possibly had *pois* for *pos* hence *wyȝte*. DM may have had a corrupt manuscript or, having misunderstood the meaning of *pos*, invented a passage to fit in with the second part of the sentence. The verb *bout* is from *bouillir* 'boil' (cf. Wallenberg p. 320). Read *ase þe uet þet boilleþ*. The image was perhaps suggested by Proverbs 15: 2: *Os fatuorum ebullit stultitiam*.

66/34. *sostyeneþ*: C *suscitent*; Wallenberg points out (p. 320) that DM has rendered the verb *sustenir* for *susciter*.

67/8. *Vor*: C *por ce*; the text should read *þeruore*.

67/11-15. Numbers 26: 9-10.

67/15-22. Numbers 11: 21, 26: 51, 65.

67/24. *regneþ*: C *raigne* 'argues'. DM's form may be due to a misunderstanding of the French or, possibly, an early example of the verb *raign*. See *OED* RAIGN *v*.

67/31. *þe grochinges*: C *cist murmures*; read *þis grochinge*.

67/35. *alle þe wylles*: C *toutes lor uolentez* makes better sense; read *hare*?

68/3. *yet nou ynoʒ* renders French *encore assez*.

68/7–8. *pater noster*. *to tokne*: C *pater nostre au singe* "To say the ape's *pater noster*' means 'to chatter with the teeth'. See *OED* APE *sb*. 6. DM has confused *signe* and *singe*.

68/15. *ant*: Wallenberg (p. 11, n. 2) suggests that the form is due to anticipation of the *t* of *out*.

68/29–31. Cf. Wisdom 12: 26–7.

69/6. *erþan*: C *ancois*; Wallenberg (p. 321) points out that DM has mistaken *ancois* 'rather' for *ancois* 'before'. Read *ac* for *erþan*.

69/6. *me gabbeþ of ham*: C *sen gabent de eus*; 'they (the sinners) mock them (those who counsel them).' Read *hi gabbeþ of ham*.

69/9. *of toknen*: C *dessoines*; *toknen* is not a translation of the French and should, perhaps, be emended to *excusinges*. Wallenberg (p. 321) thought that DM has rendered *enseignes*. A2's reading, *denssongnes*, may support this conjecture. Such a form could have been understood as *d'ensoignes*.

69/16. *habe*: cf. 58/28.

69/24–5. *blasfemyes*: C *blasphemes* is singular. Read *blasfemye*.

70/3. *dreduol and zorʒe*: not a precise rendering of French *hidour et horreur*.

70/7–9. Matthew 12: 31–2.

70/12–14. Ecclesiastes 10: 13.

70/16. *him studé deþ*: C *sestudieroit*; this suggests that the correct reading is *him studede*, pa. t. subj., rendering the French conditional.

70/26. *sterf/þet*: as Evers pointed out (R. W. Evers, *Beiträge zur Er-klärung und Textkritik von Michel's* Ayenbite of Inwyt (Erlangen, 1887), p. 70), this is for *sterfþ þet*. Cf. 75/2 (where Morris emends), 202/15, and discussion pp. 52–3. Evers also noted (p. 70) that in the French the passage is metrical and appears as the opening verse in *Enseignement proffitable a toutes gens pour bien vivre et bien mourir*. *Heþ* renders C's *l'a*.

71/5–6. *þet ne ssolde by / bote onlepy prikke*: C *ce ne seroit pas uns seuls momens*. DM's translation is inexact. He renders 'Would only be a single moment' whereas the French means 'Would not be a single moment' (cf. Evers, p. 70).

71/19. *gerlondes*: C *chapiaus*; Evers (p. 70) points out that the translation is imprecise.

71/25. *begonne libbe*: the text should probably read *begonne to libbe* as *begonne to sterue* below.

71/30. *þe clerk zyinde*: C *li clerc uoiant*; Evers (p. 71) pointed out that other French manuscripts have *li cler veant* (P2, 4, 5 A2, M, V, Ca1, Add1,

R1; P1, G1, Ca2 share the reading of C; An reads *certes li clerc*; Ld *li clerrc especialment*); read *clyer* for *clerk*.

71/31–2. Translate 'Day and night they do the same; and the more they do so the less indeed they know'.

72/4. *lyerne*: is probably an error for *lyerni*; but cf. p. 99, n. 9. For the citation see Walther, *Proverbia, Sententiaeque Latinitatis Medii Aevi*, No. 5863.

72/8. *hi westen*: C *socioient* 'slew themselves'; a place was originally left free for *westen* which was filled in later. Evers (p. 71) took it as from a verb *westen* 'to lay waste' (OE. *westan*) and it seems possible that we should read *hi ham westen* 'they destroyed themselves' or, as Wallenberg (p. 277, n. 5) suggests, that DM identified the French verb with *soucire* 'waste away' and that the meaning of *westen* is 'wasted away'.

72/11. *þet louieþ god | and yleueþ | þet*: C *qui dieu aiment e crement qui*; DM has confused *crement* and *croient* as Evers pointed out (p. 71). The relative after *crement* is superfluous. The sentence should run *þe holy men . . . of þri dyeaþes habbeþ þe tuay ypased*.

72/12–13. *Vor þer is dyaþ to zenne*: and *dyad* (MS *dyadę*) *to þe wordle*: C *car mort sont au pecchie e mort sont au monde*; the French is clearly correct and the text should be emended to *vor hi byeþ dyad to zenne and dyad to þe wordle*.

72/15. *agelteþ*: C *trespassent* 'pass over, cross'. DM has assumed the metaphorical sense. Cf. 6/5 where DM renders *trespassanz* 'fleeting' as *agelteþ* and 104/16 where he renders *trespassement* 'passing of time' by *gelt*.

72/17–18. Philippians 3: 20: *Nostra autem conversatio in caelis est.*

72/21–2. *Vor þet is damezele bereblisse | þet þe dyaþ*: C *Car cest damoisele porte ioie que la mort* 'For death is indeed Lady Bring-Joy'. As Evers (p. 72) pointed out, other English translators have also misunderstood the pleonastic *que*.

72/22–3. *corouneþ, doþ, zetteþ*: the subject is *dyaþ*. The French has *coronent* and *met*. Emend to *deþ, zet*. The form *zetteþ* is written in the margin and may be intended as an alternative to *doþ*.

72/28. *of þis half þe streme*: C *deca le ruissel*; DM seems to have taken *þe streme* as p.c. after *of*.

73/5. *ssel[t]*: there is probably no need to emend. Cf. *OED* SHALL A 2 b. But it should, perhaps, be noted that *ssel* has been corrected to *sselt* at 25/13.

73/12. *heȝliche*: C *hautement*; the French means rather 'highly' than 'at great cost, richly', etc., the meaning which *MED* (HEIGHLI adv. 1 (b)) assigns to the English form.

73/25–7. *And þeruore is þe ilke zorȝe . . . And huanne þou yzixt*: C *e por ce est cele paine bien apelee mort pardurable. e quant tu uerras*; Evers (p. 72) pointed out that Cotton has an omission here. The other E manuscripts (except G1, Ca2, P5) read after *mort pardurable*: *Car len vit tous iours en morant et muert len tous iours en viuant*. The same reading as C appears in G1, Ca2. The omission is clearly due to homoeoteleuton. The text could be emended to read after *ende: Vor me leueþ alneway ine steruinde and me sterf alneway ine libbinde*.

73/29. *be vlaʒe quik*: C *escorchier uif*; both the French and the unusual form *be* suggest a compound *bevlaʒe* rather than the passive.

74/2–3. *al þet . . . þoleden þe holy martires*: C *quanques souffrirent . . . li saint de martire*; DM seems to have misunderstood the idiom *quanques de martire* 'whatever torment' and obtains the translation *þe holy martires* by taking the proper subject, *li saint*, as adjectival. Cf. Evers, p. 72.

74/3–4. *of zorʒe*: C *de dolours*; DM has rendered literally not realizing that *de dolours* depended on *quanques* above. Cf. Evers, p. 72.

74/6–7. *ine þe vere | me ne vint lesse þanne yclenzed*: C *ou feus ne trueue mais* que *espurgier*; Evers (p. 72) pointed out that DM has misunderstood the passage: (i) he has mistaken the construction of the sentence and thus takes *ou feus* to mean *au feu* whence *ine þe vere* (ii) he has inserted *me* before *vint* but the subject is *feus* (iii) he has rendered *mais* as though it were *mains*. The French means 'where the fire finds no more to purify'. For *ou feus* An, Ld, R1, V read *au/en feu* and supply a subject for *trueue*.

74/6. MS *ychenzed*: Morris is probably incorrect in reading *yclienzed* here, *cliene* for *chene* at 224/28 (cf. 104/13, 123/9, 125/24), and *clierkes* for *cherkes* at 78/32; it should be noted that *h* is written for *l* in MS *chihd* (101/32); *choystre* 262/21; *onlepihiche* (109/24); *hohi* (128/36); *uorhay* 206/3 and *l* for *h* in *clilde* 208/3; *lolynesse* (222/3). Note also that an *h* has been corrected to an *l* in *ycheped* (80/15), *chepeþ* (81/6); and an *l* to *h* in *madenlhode* (231/13) in which the *l* has been subpuncted. It seems, therefore, improbable that the *h* spellings are for *li* and spellings such as *chene* do not, accordingly, indicate the existence of *ie* spellings in such words but are merely erroneous spellings for *clene* etc.

74/8. *al þet hit vint*: C *que quanqil trueue*; supply *þet* before *al*. DM has omitted *que*.

74/8. *gelte*: C *rooil*; DM's reading may indicate that his manuscript had *vil* as An, Ca1.

74/9. *yerneþ*: C *atourt*; *atourt* is the 3 sg. of *atorner*. DM probably had the reading which appears in Ca2, *acurt*, R1 *acourt*. It is difficult to distinguish *t* and *c* in many of the French manuscripts. Read *went* for *yerneþ*. Wallenberg (p. 106, n. 1) regards the form as plural. The number is, no doubt, due to the double subject, but it should strictly be singular.

74/12. *ofte | and smale*: C *souent e menu*; as at 158/34, DM has not understood *menu*. Cf. Evers, p. 111.

74/13–14. *alle oþre ydelnesses . . . to guo in-to heuene*: C *toutes autres uanites e quele soit digne dentrer ou ciel*; Evers (p. 73) pointed out that DM is close to Cotton here in having an omission. Most E manuscripts read after *uanites*: *tant que en lame uait riens que espurgier*. The shorter reading is common to G1, Ca2, C.

74/18. *ase hi*: C *come sil*; Evers (p. 73) suggested that DM had rendered *come sil* as *come il*. But *ase* here means 'as though'. Cf. Glossary s.v.

74/19–20. *And þeruore þet non*: C *E por ce que nuls*; this goes with what precedes; *And* should be omitted.

74/20–1. Proverbs 24: 16.

74/24. *zuo*: C *ici*; DM probably had the reading *si* as An, V, R1.

74/24. *hi onderstonde to uolʒi*: C *il attendent seurement*. It is possible that, as Evers (p. 73) suggested, DM misunderstood *attendent* as *entendent* and *seurement* as from *suivre*. The use of *onderstonde* to render the sense 'expect', 'await' seems to be due to confusion between *attendre* and *entendre*. This view is supported by the reading *entendre* in V. Cf. 97/6, 123/28, 196/4, 209/1, 245/12 and also 242/5, 247/11 and *onderstondinge* 120/25.

74/28. *onderstonde*: C *concoit on*; the form *onderstonde*, where we might expect *onderstondeþ*, is probably due rather to the following *þe* (cf. p. 52) than to a parallel with the preceding infinitive, *knawe*. At 136/7 DM renders *concoit* as *conceyueþ* which should, perhaps, be substituted here. The sense is that one obtains the holy fear of God, not that one understands it.

74/29. Here and at 244/26, 261/30, *guode* renders *biens* and should perhaps be emended to *guodes*.

75/6. *opwexeþ*: is a loose translation of C's *sorhabondent*.

75/12. *ytake*: is only an approximate translation of French *taste* and should perhaps be emended to *ytasted*. Cf. Evers, p. 74.

75/15. *drede*: C *puors* 'stink'; DM's text probably had the reading *peors, pour, peurs* 'fear' which appears in Ca1, Ca2, R1. The text should read *smelle*.

75/16–17. *and þe ilke to greate . . . him ssolde*: C *e cele tres grant amour quil aroit de la uenir: li feroit*; the English should be emended to *ssolde maki* to render *feroit*. The rest of the passage is more problematic. Evers (p. 74) pointed out that other manuscripts have *et desirriers* after *amour* (so substantially E manuscripts except that G1, Ca1 read as C). The majority reading is probably correct and the reading of G1, Ca1, C, although it makes possible sense, would be improved by emendation. Thus the English text should probably read *and þe wilnynge* after *loue*. The translation would then be 'and that very great love and the desire which he would have to come there would make him' etc.

75/18. *hardiliche*: renders French *ardaument* which DM seems to have taken as *hardiement* (cf. Evers, p. 74).

75/19. *þet is al þe drede of helle*: C *que est toute la poor denfer*; Evers (p. 74) pointed out that other French texts do not have the superfluous *est*. The sense is 'than all the fear of hell'. The erroneous reading of C is shared by G1, Ca2. For DM's rendering of *que* 'than' by *þet* see note to 21/12.

75/26. *ledeþ*: C *maine*; DM probably had a reading such as An, *mainnent*. But the verb should be singular. Read *let*.

75/26. *he zekþ raþre*: C *il queurt plus tost*; DM seems to have had for *queurt* 'runs' the reading of Ca2, *quiert* 'seeks'. Read *he yernþ raþre*.

75/29–30. *þe holy man yernþ*: C *li saint home courent* is plural but DM has taken it as singular although he returns to the plural with *habbeþ*. Read *þe holy men yerneþ*.

75/34. *of gentil herte*: C *as cuers gentils*. Read of *of gentil herten*. The rest of the sentence is plural.

76/3. *wyllis*: read *wyll is*.

76/8. *tekþ*: C *aprent*; here *aprent* has the sense 'learns' but DM has taken it to mean 'teaches'. Read *lyerneþ*.

76/14. *uor to dele*: C *deuiser*; the infinitive *dele* depends upon *conne* in line 12. The words *uor to* according to Evers (p. 74) should, accordingly, be omitted. It should be noted, however, that, while the infinitives *knawe* and *deme*, which also depend upon *conne*, immediately follow the modal, *dele* does not and *uor to* is probably correct.

76/14. *uram þe oþren*: an imprecise rendering of French *del apparant* 'from the apparent (good)'.

76/18. *zeue smale yefþes*: C *vij. petis dons*; the correct reading is *vns petis dons* 'some small gifts' (so E manuscripts except G1, Ca2 which share the error of C). The English text should read *zome smale yefþes*. For *uns* see following note.

76/19–20. *on lite / an oþer grat / and zoþe. An onlepiliche byeþ guodes ariʒt*: C *uns moiens e uns grans e uraie que seulement sont bien adroit*; DM has not understood the use of *uns* as a plural (cf. note to 61/17); the French means 'some moderate, some great and true which alone are really good'. Nor is *lite* a correct rendering of *moiens*. The English should read *opere mene an opere greate and zoþe þet byeþ onlepiliche* etc. DM may have started a new sentence at *An onlepiliche* because, as Evers (p. 75) suggested, he did not realize that *que* was for *qui*.

76/21–3. *Vor hi yeueþ þe great guodes . . . uor þe lesse*: this passage is not in C. Cf. Evers, p. 75.

76/24–5. *fole chapmen. þet of alle þinges / hi knaweþ þe propre uirtue and þet worþ*: C *fous marchanz qui de chascune chose connoist la propre uertu e la ualue*; DM has followed the French closely but a better reading appears in P1, 2, 4, M, An, V, Ld, Add1; *fous mercheanz qui achetent uoirres por saphirs. cuiure por or. vesiees pour lanternes. Mes cil est adroit bons mercheanz qui de chascune chose conoist la propre uertu 7 la ualue*. It is clear that the shorter text must be wrong since it describes the foolish merchants as knowing the true value of everything.

76/30–2. þe guodes of fortune [haþ]. and þe leuedy fortune: went hare hueȝel eche daye / and benymþ / and yefþ: C *les biens de fortune que dame fortune a toute sa roe toute iour e tout e done* 'the goods of fortune; for lady Fortune, with the whole of her wheel, every day takes away and gives.' DM did not perceive that *que* was for *car* (see Foulet § 428); on the other hand, his reading *went* gives better sense than C's reading and may represent a French *atourne*. Cf. Evers, p. 75 and note to 181/20.

77/1. emeroydes: the manuscript has *emerroydes* but this is probably an error arising from a repetition of the *r* at the beginning of a new line. Cf. p. 51.

77/1. iueles: C *ioueles*. VV 75/12 has the reading *trendelen* 'hoops'. It may be that the reading *ioueles* was introduced under the influence of the preceding list of jewels. Wallenberg's reading *childrren* is probably an error. The letter that looks like a two-shaped *r* may be *e* and the reading thus *childeren*.

77/4–5. his. efterward / wayes: C *les aspres uoies*; DM has read *aspres* as *apres* and rendered *les* by *his*, presumably reading *ses*. Emend *his* to *þe* and *efterward* to *bitere*. Cf. Evers, p. 75.

77/6–7. ase deþ þe guode godes knyȝt. þet þane kyngdom of heuene payneþ be strengþe to wynne be his prouesse: C *sicomme font li bon cheualier dieu qui le regne du ciel pernent a force e conquierent par lor proesce*; DM has taken *li bon cheualier* as singular although he returns to the plural later under the influence of the plural French verbs. The verb *pernent* 'take' he reads as *peinent* whence *payneþ* and he does not notice that the verb *conquierent* is finite. Emend to *ase doþ þe guode godes knyȝtes þet þane kyngdom of heuene ouercomeþ be strengþe and winneþ be hare prouesse* (cf. Evers, p. 76).

77/8. ne smale aryȝt: C *ne petit adroit*; a better reading is to be found in other early manuscripts, namely: *ne bien adroit. Car se sont bien adroit* (so substantially E manuscripts with the exception of P4; the reading of C is shared by G1, Ca2). Read *ne guodes aryȝt. Vor ȝif þise byeþ guodes aryȝt*.

77/26–9. Ac þe wyse chapman / þet is þe guode man / . . . þet oueral him knauþ / huet ech þing is worþ / and yzyȝþ hit riȝt wel. Hi onderstondeþ: C *Mais li sage marchant ce sont li prodome . . . qui partout se conoissent qui seuent que chascune chose uaut il le uoient tres bien. Il entendent*; there are a number of errors in this passage: (i) the singular verbs *is, knauþ, yzyȝþ* render French plural verbs because DM has translated the plural subjects *li sage marchant* and *li prodome* as singular. But because of a corrupt reading in his manuscript, he lost the construction and kept the plural in *onderstondeþ*; (ii) the reading of C appears also in G1, Ca2 but other E manuscripts omit *le* before *uoient* and supply *e* after *bien* and *entendent*; DM has telescoped *se connoissent qui seuent* and rendered *il . . . uoient* as if *e . . . uoient*; the meaning of the passage is thus: 'but the wise merchants, that is, good men . . . who are thoroughly reliable judges, who know what each thing is worth; they see well and understand' etc. The text could be emended to read *þe wyse chapmen þet byeþ þe guode men . . . þet oueral ham knaweþ, þet knaweþ huet ech þing is worþ. Hi yzyeþ riȝt wel and onderstondeþ.*

77/31–2. *And þeruore huo þet lokeþ*: C *Et por ce quil regardent*; the sentence is correlated with *Hy makeþ* (34–5) and accordingly *þeruore huo þet* should be emended to *þeruore þet hi.*

77/33–4. Cf. Whiting, G 96.

77/34–5. *Hy makeþ to god ane handuol*: C *il font a dieu une paumee*; 'they make a bargain with God'. Read *Hy makeþ chapfare wiþ God.*

78/5–6. *þet me may hise habbe*: C *qui les porroit auoir*; the *qui* is indefinite and the English should read *huo þet moȝe hise habbe.*

78/9–17. The words *uele oþre* refer not to the patriarchs but to those who know how to profit from the goods of time. All the verbs should be present as in the French.

78/13. *drede. and yleue*: C *cremir e redouter*; *yleue* must be an error, since the words form tautological pairs.

78/18–19. *yef hi wel ham wytyeþ*: C *cist bien se sauuent*; Evers (p. 77) pointed out that DM has read *cist* as *si ils*. Emend *yef hi* to *þise.* The sense is 'these people know well how to save themselves'.

78/25. *zuyfthede*: C *iustesce*; DM read *uistesce* but 'justice' makes better sense since mainly moral qualities are in question.

78/27. *ine alle oþre guodes*: C *En tous autres biens*; the sense requires *e* for *en.* Such a reading appears in P2, 4, A2, M, An, V, Ca1, Add1, R1; G1, Ca2 share the erroneous reading of C. Cf. Evers, p. 77.

78/31–2. *of greate clierkes*: C *de grans clers*; the unidiomatic *of* is added later above the line and is possibly designed to bring the English more closely into line with the French.

79/4–5. *þet þieues ne moȝe stele*: C *ce lerres ne puet embler*; 'though a thief cannot steal'. Read *þaȝ* for *þet.*

79/9–10. *bote hi hise ne wel usy*: C *se il nen usent bien*; for the construction see Evers, p. 77. He points out that DM renders *se il* in four ways: 1. by *bote . . . ne*; 2. by *bote* without a negative; 3. by *bote yef . . . ne*; 4. by *bote yef* without a negative.

79/10. *And huanne hi ham yelpeþ*: is not a new sentence as the capital suggests but depends upon *harmeþ ham.* Cf. Evers, p. 78.

79/11. *prodeþ*: perhaps an error for *proudeþ.* Wallenberg's suggestion (p. 194, n. 2) that it may be by analogy with French *prod* is, however, possible. The form *proudeþ* pl. could be from the adjective *proud* or from OE *prutian* (see *OED* PROUD *v.*). The other forms of the verb, however, would suggest that the former explanation is correct.

79/23. *hise*: C *la*; DM has, perhaps, taken the French *l'a* for *la* and rendered *hise.* The noun *guod* can hardly be feminine. He then supplies *heþ.* Read *hit* for *hise.*

79/28. *alzuo is þe zaule*: C *ausi*; G1 reads *ausi ę lalme* and other E manuscripts read either *ausi lalme* (A2, M, Ca2) or *ausi (morte) est lame (morte)* (P2, 4, Ld, Ca1, V, R1). Add1 agrees with C. DM is clearly not rendering C here.

79/29. *worþssipeþ*: C *aorne*; as Evers pointed out (p. 78), DM has confused *aorer* 'adore' with *aorner* 'adorn'. Read *agrayþeþ* for *worþssipeþ*.

80/4–13. 1 Corinthians 13.

80/15–16. *And hueruore wylt þou þet guod | þet is ycleped riȝt uirtue more louie*: C *Et porquoi que tu uoelles cest bien qui est apeles drois uertus plus amer*; The French means 'In order that you may desire (for *porquoi* for *por que* see Foulet § 427) to love more this good which is called true virtue' etc. DM has clearly misunderstood and *hueruore wylt þou* should read *þeruore þet þou wylle*.

80/17. *þis ich wylle yet eft*: C *te uoel ie encore*; DM has read *ce* for *te*. Emend *þis* to *þe*.

80/21. *Of þe guodes of þe wordle*: this follows on from the previous clause. Lines 20–3 mean 'And thou seest plainly, in regard to the good things of the world, that no one desires or loves anything unless he thinks that it will be either honorific or pleasurable or beneficial for him'. Cf. Evers, p. 79.

80/25–6. *And alle þet þise zecheþ ydelliche: is ine uirtue zopliche*: C *Et quanques cist quierent uainement :' est en uertu uraiement'* 'And whatever these people seek vainly is truly in virtue'; DM has translated *quanques* as plural but kept the singular verb *is*. Emend to *al*.

80/33–4. *Þanne ydele blisse is to moche*: C *dont uaine gloire sourt a plente* 'whence vain glory springs in plenty'. Read *Huerurom ydele blisse arist to moche*. DM has misunderstood French *dont* and rendered *sourt* as *soit*; cf. Evers, p. 79.

81/3. *yef he*: C *car cil*; emend *yef* to *uor þan* 'because'. Evers (p. 79) suggested that DM overlooked *car* and read *cil* as *si il*.

81/3–4. *he . . . þe ilke*: C *cil . . . cele* 'he' . . . 'she', 'man' . . . 'woman'. The usage is odd since *þe ilke* is not usually gender-distinctive and it is possible that DM misunderstood the meaning of *cele* here.

81/7. The form *leucernere* should read *leuceruere*. Cf. Wallenberg p. 142, n. 2.

81/7. *alouer*: C *tout outre*; Wallenberg (p. 8, n. 2) suggests that the meaning is 'quite over'; Evers (p. 79) suggested the meaning 'throughout' and compared the renderings of VV and Caxton. But the sense is rather 'quite beyond'. The lynx can see, not only through the wall, but beyond it.

81/11–12. *anon ase þe zaule him todelþ. al þe uayrhede þet | þet body heþ*: C *tantost comme lame sen depart. toute sa biaute que li cors a*; Evers (p. 79) pointed out that something is missing here. After *depart* the French text should read *toute sa biaute li cors pert*. *Donc* (substantially the reading of P1, 2, A2, M, An, V, Ld, Ca1, Add1, R1). Further, DM seems to have misunderstood *s'en depart*. The text could be emended by reading: *anon ase þe zaule went al his uayrhede þet body lyest vor al. þe uayrhede þet | þet body heþ.*

81/19–20. *hy reformeþ | and agrayþeþ*: C *ele reforme e appareille*; Evers pointed out (p. 80) that other manuscripts read *la* after *ele* (so P1, 2, A2, M, An, V, Ld (*le*), Ca1, Add1, R1; P4, G1, Ca2 have the reading of C). For *hy* read *hy hire*. In line 20, *him* and *his* (*li, sa*) should strictly read *hire*. Cf. p. 89.

81/28. *uayr*: for *uayr* as a noun cf. see 270/6.

82/1. *brytnesse*: this may be a genuine form as Wallenberg suggests (p. 44, n. 4). Morris emends at 142/4 and *bryte* at 156/20. On the other hand, he emends forms without the dental at 121/32 and 266/23. See p. 50.

82/2. *yef*: C *li*; DM had the reading *si* for *li* as G1, Ca2. Emend to *þet*.

82/2–3. 1 Corinthians 3: 19.

82/9. *by*: emend to *of*.

82/14–15. *Efter þe childhede | þet þe wyt of þe wordle*: C *Apres ce est enfance que li sens du monde* 'Then again it is childishness, the wisdom of the world'. Read *Þanne hit is childhede þe wyt of þe wordle*. DM has read *apres cest enfance*. For the pleonastic *que* cf. note to 72/21–2.

82/16. *þet*: C *qui*; Evers (p. 80) suggested that the reading *il* for *qui*, to be found in P1, Add1, was to be preferred to the reading of C. It should be noted, however, that all other E manuscripts except Ld, Ca2 support the reading *qui*. Some sense can be made of this reading on the assumption that the clause introduced by *qui* is parallel to *þet byeþ zuo wyse* although the sentence would strictly be an anacoluthon in which *In zuych uolk* refers back to line 14. The sentence could then be translated: 'Furthermore, it is childishness, the wisdom of the world and those who are so wise in caring for, giving comfort to, and delighting the body, who live like children who seek only the fulfilment of their desire—in such people wisdom is dead.'

82/20–1. *þet more hi uynt smak*: C *qui plus trueue sauour*; Evers (p. 80) suggested that DM read *que* for *qui* but *þet* is the usual rendering of the relative in the text. The *hi* is redundant but may be correct.

82/31. James 3: 15.

82/31–2. *þet eche daye hi*m *uondeþ*: C *qui tous iors se peine*; the verb *uondi* is not usually reflexive and this usage may be due to the French. Cf. *MED* FONDEN -IEN v.

82/34. *þet*: indirect questions are usually introduced by *huet* and text should, perhaps, be emended.

83/1. *þet*: C *que*; the sense requires the meaning 'because'.

83/4. *zoþ þing | and of pris*: C *chose uraie e preciouse*; DM agrees with C here but what follows shows that the Cotton text is incomplete. A number of early manuscripts read *7 douce* after *precieuse* (so P1, 2, 4, A2,

M, V, Ca1, Add1, R1). The erroneous reading of C is shared by G1, Ld, Ca2, while An has an error of its own, reading *chose vraie 7 douce*. The English text should read *and zuete* after *pris*.

83/9–10. *Þet is þe zuete sucre*: C *Cest li sucres dous*; there appears to be an omission in C, G1, Ca2. There is considerable divergence of readings in the E manuscripts but six (P1, 2, M, An, Ld, Add1) have *damer* before the phrase represented in C by *Cest li sucres dous*. The English text should perhaps read *loue, hit is þe zuete sucre*.

83/13. *Efter uirtues / an charites: he yefþ zoþe prouesse*: C *Apres uertus e charites done uraie proesce*; Evers (p. 81) pointed out that DM changed his mind about the translation at this point. He first rendered: *Efterward uirtues / an charites yefþ zoþe prouesse*: 'afterwards, virtues and charity gives true prowess'. He then decided that *Apres* was a preposition and deleted *ward* and supplied a subject, *he* for *yefþ*. He was, perhaps, confused by the singular verb for which P1 has, more correctly, *donnent*. The text, in fact, should read: *Efterward, uirtues / an charite yeueþ zoþe prouesse*. The form *charites* is probably due to the influence of the French. As an English form it can only be plural.

83/16. *Ine prouesse byeþ þri þinges to-deld*: C *En proesce a .iii. choses parties*; Evers (p. 81), is right in suggesting that the French is in error here. Other E manuscripts do not have *choses* and the reading should be *en proesce a .iii. parties*. Read *ine proesse byeþ þri deles*. DM seems to have taken *parties* as the ppl. of *partir*. The error of C is shared by Ca2.

83/19. *to greate þinge ondernime*: C *a grans choses emprendre*; *þinge* could be an erroneous use of the prepositional case after *to* but more probably it is plural. Cf. p. 62.

83/20. *uor to uolȝy . . . uor to uolȝy*: the repetition, based on the French, may be erroneous. For the second instance VV 82/4 has *to brynge it to þe ende*.

83/22–5. Vegetius, *Epitoma Rei Militaris*, I, xiii (ed. C. Lang, Bibliotheca Teubneriana, p. 17, ll. 16–19).

83/23–4. *hou þet hit by uounde myd amendement*: C *coment que soit troue on amendement*; as Evers (p. 81) pointed out, DM has taken *troue* as a past participle. The *myd* is due to confusion of *on* 'one' with the preposition *ou*. Read *hou þet hit by me uint amendement*. Translate 'somehow or other one finds a remedy'.

83/27–8. *þe opnymynges / þet me clepeþ prous*: C *les emprises con apele preuz*; Evers (p. 81) pointed out that other manuscripts have *de cels* (or *de ceus*) after *emprises* and this may represent the more original reading (so E manuscripts except V which reads *des hardiz au siecle que* and P4, G1, Ca2 which share the reading of C). The text makes good sense as it stands, however.

83/31. *lost*: C *los*; the *t* was added later. Presumably *lost* was thought to give better sense, but it is an imprecise rendering of the French.

84/8. *grat herte: herte* here has a double sense of *cuer*, 'courage' and 'heart'.

84/18. *wydstonde* should perhaps read *wypstonde* but cf. p. 43, n. 1.

84/21. *more þanne þer byeþ dropen of rayn ine þe ze*: C *plus que neurent goietes de pluie en la mer*; Evers (p. 82) pointed out that *plus* was lacking in some manuscripts and thought that DM had read the abbreviated form *neurent* as *ne sont*. But it is more likely that DM's manuscript read (*n*)*ont* for *neurent* as P1, 4, M, An, V, Ca1, Ca2, R1. The sense of the whole passage is that sorrows, disasters, and the menaces of fortune have no more power against virtue than drops of rain have in the sea. The text should read *more þanne habbeþ* etc.

84/28. *þet to huam*: C *cil a cui*; read *he* for *þet*.

85/3–4. *him deþ þe wordle onderuot*: C *li met le monde souz pie* 'makes him despise the world'.

85/4. *him deþ wende to heuene*: C *le fait conuerser ou ciel* 'makes him dwell in heaven'. The English should read *him deþ wonie ine heuene*.

85/6. *þanne by þe kyng / of his regne*: 'than the king may be of his kingdom'.

85/8. *wone*: C *usage*; according to Evers (p. 82), the French *usage* means 'tribute' not 'custom' as DM has rendered it.

85/11–12. *of zuo moche makeþ his prou / and of al hire god*: C *de tant fait son preu e de tout loe dieu*; Evers (p. 82) thought that the French *tant* should read *tout* as all E manuscripts, in fact, do (except P2 which omits and G1, Ca2 which share the reading of C). The reading *hire* is no doubt due to a misreading of *loe* as *soe*. None of the E manuscripts, however, has this reading. Thus the English text should read: *of al makeþ his prou and of al hereþ god*.

85/12. *dredeþ*: C *crient*; the French is 3 sg. of *criendre*. Read *dret*. DM seems to have read the form as plural.

85/17. *demþ*: C *iustice*; Evers (p. 82) pointed out that the French here means 'keeps under control' and not 'judges'.

85/19. *bliþe*: C *ioins*; 'united'; P2, A2, Ld, Ca2 read *ioious* which was, no doubt, the reading of DM's manuscript. Read *yyoined*.

85/25. *Ase moche worþssipe / and grat empirete of þe kynge*: C *ausi grant honeur e grant empirete du roi*; Evers (p. 83) pointed out that the reading of C is corrupt. A large number of manuscripts have some form of the future of *doner* instead of *du roi*. A form *donrai* could easily have been corrupted to *dou roi*. It should also be noted that DM has taken *empirete* as one word and put a cross in the margin to indicate that he did not understand its meaning. *MED* (s.v.) assumes a sense 'sovereign power' but the French texts support Wallenberg's view (p. 83, n. 4) that it is *empire te*. *Ase moche* is also incorrect. The text could be emended to *Alzuo grat worþssipe and grat empire ich wylle þe yue*. The reference appears to be to Seneca's *Letters*, 113, 30: *imperare sibi maximum imperium est* (ed. L. D. Reynolds, Oxford, 1965, p. 479).

85/29–30. *þet hyse tormenteþ ofte*: C *que il les tormente souent*; the sense appears to be 'in that they (their hearts) often torment them'. Thus the plural, *tormentent*, which appears in P1, A2, An, V, Ld, Add1 is to be preferred to the singular. Supply *hi* after *þet*.

86/8. *strengþi*: C *efforcier*; Evers (p. 83) suggested that DM had rendered *efforcier* quite literally. *Efforcier* means 'constrain' which is the sense required. This is not the usual sense of *strengþi*.

86/18. *his þrel*: C *ses sers*; the reading *ses sers* is an error common to G1, Ca2, C. *Ses* should be deleted from the French and *his* from the English.

86/18–19. *zuo þet he ne may hit uorþrawe to his wylle* | *þet he heþ ymad zyker*: C *si quil ne sen puet pas gieter a sa uolente quil a ia aseure*; Evers (p. 83) pointed out that the French *se gieter de qch.* means 'free oneself from sth.' Further, *aseure* seems to be a corruption of *aseruie* 'deserved' (the reading of E manuscripts, except P4, which omits, and G1, Ca2, which read as C). Thus the meaning is 'so that he cannot free himself at will from what he has indeed deserved'. The text could be emended to read *zuo þet he ne may him vri to his wylle of þet he zoþliche heþ ofserved*. Cf. Evers, p. 84.

86/35. *stedeuestliche*: here and at 105/23, 26, 27, 28 and 123/4 this word translates French *parfitement*; at 200/7, 8 *stedeuestnesse* translates *perfection* and *stedeuest* at 122/19, 36, 200/6 translates *parfait*. The sense development appears to be from 'firm' to 'immutable' to 'complete' to 'perfect'.

86/36. *leueþ*: C *criement* 'fear'. DM seems to have confused *criement* and *croient*. Read *dredeþ*.

87/2. *nyeȝ*: C *ia*; cf. 87/6. At 87/7 *nou* renders *ia*; *nyeȝ* is presumably a loose rendering of the French affirmative sense, 'indeed', 'certainly', while *nou* renders the sense 'now'; cf. Evers, p. 84.

87/12. *huet hi is y-do*: C *tant soit parfais* 'however perfect he be'. It looks as though DM took the subject to be *wordle*. Emend *hi* to *he*. (Cf. Glossary **he**, and Evers, p. 84). For *ydo* 'perfect' cf. 155/23 *wel ymad bien parfet*). But the forms could be errors for *uoldo, uolmad*. Cf. 28/11, 23, 96/20, 146/7, 260/32.

87/26. *to*: the choice of preposition may have been dictated by Fr. *a*. Cf. notes to 105/24, 246/24.

87/29. *zondes*: Wallenberg (p. 296, n. 2) translates 'messages' because of French *messages*; but OF *messaiges* means 'a messenger'.

88/4–6. *þe holy man . . . deþ . . . his . . . his . . . hire herte*: C *li saint home . . . mettent . . . leur . . . lor . . . lor cuers*; read *men* for *man*; *doþ* for *deþ*; *hire* for *his*; and *herten* for *herte*. Cf. Varnhagen (1879), 51.

88/6–7. *alle zenne to waynye*: C *pecchie du tout espurgier*; DM has misread *du tout* 'completely' as an adjective qualifying *pecchie* (cf. Evers, p. 84). The form *waynye* has given rise to discussion. Morris assumed that it was connected with Old English *wanian* 'diminish' but this leaves the vocalism unexplained. H. Varnhagen (review in *Deutsche Litteraturzeitung*, iv, 1882, col. 1219) and Evers, read *towayuye*. Varnhagen supposed DM to have equated *espurgier* with Latin *dispergere* but

Wallenberg (p. 273, n. 2) rightly objected that this is improbable. Nor, as he points out, is it necessary to assume that *to* is a prefix. He reads *wayuye* and this is probably correct although it is only an approximate translation of *espurgier*. The sense is presumably 'to move', 'send', and thus 'to remove'.

88/9–11. *and þe more þet he his yzyȝþ openliche: þe more he him loueþ þe stranglaker. þe more he him likneþ propreliche*: C *e com plus la uoit ap*erte*ment: e plus laime ardaument tant le resemble il plus proprement* 'and the more openly he sees it, and the more ardently he loves it, the more specifically he resembles him'; the English should read, after *openliche*, *and þe more he him loueþ strangliche* etc. as the French. The pronouns are ambiguous but the sense suggests that *he* refers to *herte*: DM may, however, have intended the sense to be 'he', 'a person'. The pronoun *his* refers to *face*; *him*, in both instances, refers, apparently, to Christ. In fact, *le* in C is probably an error for *li* and refers to *face*. Cf. VV 86/20–3: *For þe more clene and pure þat a mannes herte is, þe more apertly seeþ he þilke faire face and þe more hertely he loueþ it and þe more properly is he like it.*

88/13. *uor þanne*: C *que adonc* is correlative with *quant* (*huanne*) in line 14. The text should read *þet þanne*. The reference is to 1 John 3: 1–2.

88/17–19. 1 Corinthians 13: 12.

88/18. *Vor*: C *mais*; the English should read *Ac*.

88/24–5. Dionysius, *De Caelesti Hierarchia*, VII, ii (PG iii, cols. 220–5).

88/29–32. *uor he his arereþ zuo ine god | and his beclepþ zuo ine his loue | þet al hare wyl | and al hare onderstondinge is | þet is . . . þet is hare beþenchinge þet is ywent ine god*: C *car il leslieue si en dieu e les embrase si en samour que toute lor entente el lor entendement est. ce est lor entencion. toute lor uolente. toute lor memoire. cest lor ramembrance qui est conuertie en dieu*; there are a number of errors in this passage: (i) in the French, *est* (*is*) should be omitted after *entendement* (so P1, 4, A2, An, Ld, V, Ca1, Add1, R1) and *qui* (*þet*) after *ramembrance* (so P1, 4, A2, M, An, Ca1, Add1); (ii) there is clearly an omission in the English, since *beþenchinge* is not a gloss for *onderstondinge*. All the early French manuscripts agree in the last two faculties, namely, *uolente*, *memoire* (*ramembrance*), except that V, R1 omit *uolente* for which Ld reads *uertu*. But there is confusion about the first faculty which P4, A2, An, Ca2, G1, C expand to two; G1, Ca2 read as C, *entente*, *entendement* (*entencion*); A2 reads *entendemens*, *entencions*. The other early manuscripts read *entendement* (*entencion*). The three faculties are desire (or intention), will, and memory; it is, therefore, clear that the consensus is correct. The English text could be corrected by reading after *wyl*: *and al hare entente, þet is hare onderstondinge, al hare memorie, þet is hare beþenchinge is ywent ine god*. It will be noted that the order of items in DM differs from the order in the French manuscripts.

88/30. *beclepþ*: see note to 46/34. The text should read *aliȝt*.

88/32–5. *þis loue . . . oþer þanne god wyle. uor hi ne habbeþ betuene god and ham*: C *Ceste amour e cis desirrers qui en ioint e oint si le cuer a dieu quil ne puet autre chose uoloir que ce que dieu ueut. car il nont entre lui et dieu*; there are a number of points to be noted in this passage: (i) DM has rendered *unist* (as A2, An, Ca1, Ca2) for *oint* in C and G1. (ii) The structure of the sentence is defective. There are three possible ways of construing it: (*a*) 'this love is the desire which joins and unites the heart to God so that it can only desire what God desires'. This involves reading *ceste amour est cis desirrers*, a reading supported by G1 (*b*) 'this love and this desire join the heart to God' etc. This involves omitting *qui* after *desirrers* as in P1, 4, Add1 (*c*) 'this love and this desire which join and unite the heart to God cannot desire' etc. This involves omitting the first *que* and emending *puet* to a plural. There is no support from the early manuscripts for this. In view of the singular verbs *ioint e oint* (*unist*) the first solution seems the most probable. (iii) The second *oþer* in the English should probably be omitted and *þet*, perhaps, supplied after *þanne*. (iv) Evers (p. 85) pointed out that sense requires *il n'a* (P1, Add1, R1) for *il nont*. The sense is 'there is but a single will between the heart and God'. The English should thus read *uor ne biþ betuene god and hire* (or *him* in view of the unusual masculine *he* in line 34).

88/36–89/1. *to þe ymage | and to þe anliknesse of god*: C *a lymage e la semblance dieu*; DM has mistaken the verb *a* for the preposition. For the first *to* read *heþ*. Omit the second. Cf. Varnhagen (1879), 51.

89/2–3. *þet me may to hopye: and cliue*: C *a qui on peust tendre ne monter*; as Varnhagen pointed out ((1879), 51), the translation is loose. *Tendre* probably means 'to take one's way', but DM has taken it to mean 'to aspire'. The French seems to confirm that *to* is an adverb and not a verbal prefix.

89/7. *and hy ham yelpeþ*: C *e se vantent*; no subject is needed for *yelpeþ* which is parallel to *makeþ* in line 4. Omit *hy*.

89/12. *mest*: C *plus*; read *more* for *mest*; cf. 122/6 where DM has again used a superlative before *þanne*. Cf. Evers, p. 86.

89/19. *þerof*: C *dont*; read *huerof*.

89/23. *þet ich leue*: C *ce croi* 'as I think'; omit *þet*.

89/26–34. 1 Corinthians 13: 1–3.

89/31. *slaȝe*: C *martire*; Wallenberg (p. 215, n. 4) interprets this as a noun; more probably it is a verb or an error for *slaȝþe*.

90/2. [*þe*] *porueyonces*: C *porueances*; other manuscripts have *penances* or *penitances* (so E manuscripts except G1, Ca2, which agree with C). This reading makes better sense than *porueances* 'provision', 'foresight'. It is not necessary to supply *þe* but *porueyonces* should read *penonces*.

90/4. Omit *he* before *zayþ*.

90/12. *and . . . þet | þet ne by charite |*: the *and*, though present in the French also, is superfluous and should be omitted. The negative in the second member is due to the French *e ce nest pas doute que ce ne soit charites* etc. The meaning, of course, is positive. Cf. 105/13–15.

90/15. *huo* (for *hou*) *moche*: C *combien que*; DM translates *combien que* 'however much' by *hou moche* at 197/24. For the reading in Morris see List of Corrigenda. *Hou moche* 'however much' is the correlate of *Hou* in line 19.

90/25–6. *yef he is wyþ-oute charite*: C *se ce est sans charite* 'if this (i.e. good works) is without charity'; DM has rendered *il* for *ce* thus altering the sense; cf. Evers, p. 86.

90/27–8. *Vor þeruore . . . þe raþre / yef he sterfþ wyþ-oute charite*: C *car ia por ce plus de merite uers dieu naura. ancois sil meurt sanz charite* 'for indeed he will have no more merit with God on account of this (i.e. austerities); on the contrary, if he dies without charity' etc. DM's *þeruore* is an adverb 'on account of this'; it renders *por ce. Ia* is omitted and *ancois* DM has translated by *þe raþre*; but the position of the virgule suggests that he did not understand the text. The virgule should precede *þe raþre*.

90/31. *grace of blysce*: C *grace de gloire*; the correct reading is *grace* (*los* Ld) *e gloire* (as E manuscripts, except G1, Ca2 which agree with C). Emend *of* to *and*; cf. Evers, p. 86.

91/3–4. *Charité wynþ ine eche þinge. and playntes*: C *charite gaaigne en toutes quereles*; the text should probably read *Charite wynþ in alle playntes* although it is possible that DM had an extended text reading *en toutes choses et en toutes plaintes*.

91/6. *onenen*: is a case of dittography and should be emended.

91/9. *Zygge a pater noster*: C *vne pater nostre dire*; Evers (p. 86) suggested that *a lun* should perhaps be supplied before *vne pater nostre*. This completes the sense but has not much authority from the early manuscripts. Only G1 has *Tant uaut a lun vn pater nostre dire*. Other E manuscripts read (7) *une patre nostre dire*.

91/13–14. *þe balance [zayþ] saynt Michel*: C *la balance saint michiel*; The construction is an appositive genitive and the translation is 'the scales of Saint Michael'. Omit *zayþ*.

91/22. *ine huychen*: C *en cui* 'in whom' (viz. God). DM has assumed that the relative referred to *guodes*. Read *ine huam*.

91/23–4. *þe uerste guod wyþ-oute: byeþ þe vif wyttes of þe bodye*: C *Li uns biens uient par dehors. e par les .v. sens du cors*; DM has been confused by the erroneous reading of C (shared by G1, Ca2). The correct reading is *Li un(s) bien uiennent* etc. (as P1, 2, 4, A2, M, An, Ld, Ca1, Add1). The reading of the insular group combines this reading with the reading *lun bien vient* (V, R1) and reads *li uns biens uient*; but the sense requires the plural. The English should read *zome guodes comeþ uram wyþoute and uram þe vif wyttes* etc. Evers (p. 87) pointed out that there is a gap after *guod* and *wyþ-oute* is on an erasure. This suggests that DM had some trouble in translating this passage.

91/27. *uor to deliti | and uor ham zouke*: C *por deliter le. e pour li aleschier*; DM seems to have confused *aleschier* and *lechier* and wrongly supposed *li* to be plural. He has also omitted *le*, or had a manuscript which lacked it (as P2, 4, A2, M, An, V, Ca1, R1). The English should read *him uor to deliti and him uor to draʒe*.

91/30. *ac*: renders French *mais*; both are superfluous. Cf. Evers, p. 87.

91/34–92/2. *Alsuo þe playinges of þe wordle . . . sseppeþ | and sseaweþ moche of pris*: C *Ausi des desduis du monde e des delis des .v. sens come on les pense e figure e desirre mout apperent precieus*; Evers (p. 87) thought that DM read *les* for *des* (as P1, Add1) and forgot *desirre*. He also regarded *sseaweþ* as an incorrect rendering of *apparent*; but the sense 'appear' is possible. On the other hand, *and* at 92/2 should be omitted.

92/6. *zone comeþ. ine none manere uelle ne may*: C *tost anuient en nule maniere saouler ne puet*; Evers (p. 87) supposed that DM had read *anvienent* for *anuient* 'pall', but it is by no means clear that this is the correct reading. The forms *ennuient, anuient, anient, anienent*, appear in P2, 4, M, G1, Ld, V, C, Ca1, Ca2, Add1; the forms *envient, uiennent* in A2, An, R1. Either makes possible sense. On the other hand, the reading *puet* of G1, C is erroneous. It should be plural as in all E manuscripts except P1, G1, V, Ca2. Thus *may* should read *moʒe*.

92/6–8. *and þet ine one drope is zuo moche zuetnesse | þet hy ssel by þe zuetnesse of al þe welle*; C *e se en une goute a tant de doucour quele iert la doucour de toute la fontaine*; Evers (p. 87) pointed out that DM has rendered the French *se* 'if' as if it were *ce*. Read *yef* for the first *þet*. *Quele* 'how great' he has taken as *qu'ele* and rendered *þet hy*. This should be emended to *huet*.

92/8–10. *þe wyse and þe holy man . . . of þise wordle*: C *li sage e li saint home . . . de ce monde*; DM takes the French noun as singular but leaves the verbs and the pronouns in the plural. Emend to *þe wyse and þe holy men* as Morris suggests.

92/16–17. *myd alle þe honden þet hy moʒe*: C *a tout le mains ce quil puent*; the French means 'as little as ever they can' but DM has taken *mains* (*moins*) as 'hand' whence his nonsensical translation. Read *also litel ase moʒe*.

92/22. *þe spirit of man*: C *que li esperis del home*; Evers (p. 88) pointed out that DM has omitted *que* which depends upon *seuent (wyteþ)*. Supply *þet* before *þe spirit*.

92/32–3. *zuo þet he ne may him hyealde | ne him-zelue yuele*: C *si quil ne se puet contenir ne soi meismes sentir* 'so that he cannot contain himself nor be aware of himself'; *ne him zelue yuele* is a calque on *ne soi meismes sentir*.

93/2–3. *'Huo þet ssel drinke' he zayþ | 'of þe wetere þet ich wylle y[e]ue him: hi ssel become a welle'*: C *Qui beura dist il del eaue que ie li dourrai ele deuendra une fonteine*; see John 4: 13–14; Evers (p. 88) thought that DM had not understood the conditional nature of the sentence; but the

English can be regarded as an acceptable rendering of the French; cf. discussion pp. 103, 105. The form *hi* (*ele*) perhaps refers to the Samaritan woman or to other women who may come to the well; or perhaps it is for *he*. But the gospel text shows that it should refer to *eaue*.

93/8–10. Psalm 30 (31): 20. The text seems to blend the readings evidenced in both the old and new versions of the Vulgate Psalter.

93/9. *þet þou lokest to*: (C *que tu gardes a*) Latin *quam reservasti*.

93/15. *bouteþ*: Wallenberg (p. 39, n. 3) and *MED* (BONTEN v.) read *bonteþ*. This is probably correct. The form *bolt, boult* (see *OED* s.v.) has indeed a variant without the *l* but the forms appear to the Northern. On the other hand, the verb *bunt* (see *OED* s.v.) is recorded by Wright (*EDD.* s.v.) as occurring in the Kentish dialect. *Bonteþ* would be the normal *Ayenbite* spelling of this verb.

93/18. *þet is zoþe blisse*: C *qui est uraie ioie*; the redundant relative should probably be omitted (P1, V, Add1, R1); assuming, however, that *þet* is a demonstrative and not a relative pronoun, the text makes sense.

93/19–20. Whiting J 63.

93/21. *ha clepeþ uile / oure lhord by þe þe profete*: C *apele vile nostres sires par le prophete*; the text is corrupt as Evers (p. 88) rightly noted. It is clear from the citation from Isaiah which follows that the meaning is: 'Our Lord calls it (*blisse*) oil, through the prophet'. The reading of P1, Add1, *lapele* for C's *apele* is clearly to be preferred as it provides an object for the verb. DM has not perceived that the subject is *nostres sires* and *ha* should be emended to *hit*. *Be* is an error and should be omitted. There may, however, be a more deep-seated corruption. E manuscripts other than P1, G1, (Ca1), Ca2, Add1 read *est apelle* for *apele* and *sicom dit* before *nostres sires*.

93/22–3. *wylle*: C *dourrai*; Isaiah 61: 3 *darem eis . . . oleum gaudii pro luctu, pallium laudis pro spiritu moeroris*. DM has omitted to translate the French *dourrai*. Supply *yeue* after *wylle*.

93/25. *god zelf*: C *dieu meismes*; the French should read *deus meismes* and the English *of hamzeluen*. The reading *de eus, dels, deaus, deus* appears in P2, 4, M, An, Ld, V, R1 but P1, A2, G1, Ca1, Ca2, Add1, have *dex, die(u)x, dieu(s)*. Cf. Evers, p. 88.

93/29–30. 1 John 4: 16.

93/30. *þet lif is*: C *cest uie*; omit *is*. But cf. VV 92/4 for another rendering.

93/32–3. *to zeche to habbe*: C *e aquerre? þor conquerre*; DM's text seems to have read *a querre* etc. Read *and zeche to habbe*.

94/4–5. *lyf worþssipuol lyf. lostuol*: C *uie honorable. delitable*; the first *lyf* is inserted later. DM first wrote *worþssipuol* and then altered his translation to fit the French word order. But he failed to delete the second *lyf*. Cf. Evers, p. 88.

94/6–7. *zikerlyche . . . wy[þ]-oute zorȝe*: C *seurement, sagement, ioieusement sanz dolour*; the French text seems to be defective here. It should read *seurement, sagement, ioieusement*; *seurement sanz courrouz, sagement sanz errour, ioieusement sanz douleur* as A2, M, An, Ld, Add1, R1.

94/22–3. *He þet can guod* ... *þer is zenne* / *yef he misdeþ*: C *Qui set le bien e nel fait:* *pecchie i a e si meffait.* The reference is to James 4: 17 *Scienti igitur bonum facere, et non facienti, peccatum est illi.* The French is tautological. The second member of the sentence appears to mean 'there is sin and indeed he sins'. DM has taken the particle *si* to mean 'if'. Read *and zuo he misdeþ*.

94/28–29. Canticles 4: 12.

94/33. *wex ymered*: C *cire meirie*: 'moulded wax'. DM has been influenced by English *amerian* 'to purify'; cf. Evers, p. 89.

95/6. *wocnesse*: C *humour*; Wallenberg (p. 287, n. 4) assumes *wotnesse* from an OE *watnes* 'moisture'. It seems more likely that the word is an error for *wetnesse*. The letters *o* and *e* are sometimes not dissimilar and DM may have written one for the other.

95/8–9. *þise þinges* / *makeþ þe* grace *of þe holy gost mid herte*: C *ces choses fait a la grace du saint esperit ou cuer*; P1, Add1 have a plural verb, *font*, which Evers (p. 89) thought to be correct. It is not clear, however, that a plural verb gives the best sense. Other E manuscripts have a singular verb like C. The problem arises from the grammatical ambiguity of *þise þinges*, which could be subject or object. Furthermore, *mid* is clearly wrong whether the sense is 'These (three) things make the grace of the Holy Spirit enter the heart' or 'These (three) things the grace of the Holy Spirit makes to enter the heart'. The correct reading is *ine herte*. DM has confused *ou = au* with *ou = auec*. The perfect verbal form in C may be wrong. Other early manuscripts have simply *fait la grace*.

95/10. *hi*[1]: C *le*; Wallenberg does not record an accusative *hi* but the French makes it plain that *hi* is accusative in this passage (cf. 151/9). The second *hi* renders French *i* and DM has slightly altered the sense.

95/12. *and of frut* / *and precious*: C *e precieus*; omit *and of frut* which was possibly taken from the line below.

95/15. *hueruore þet*: C *por ce que* 'for the reason that'; read *þeruore þet*. Cf. 264/4.

95/21–2. John 4: 55.

95/23–4. *alle þo ine paradis*: C *tout ce paradis*; DM seems to have read *tous ceus en paradis*. Read *al þis paradis*. Cf. Evers, p. 89.

95/25–6. *al hit ys guod*: C *tout est bon*; cf. 156/28, 168/27 where DM also adds a tautological pronoun after *al*.

95/26. The text reads *alowe* with *o* above the line; the word is also added in the margin in the form *alouwe*.

95/31. *hueruore*: C *dont* is a relative pronoun 'with which'. Read *be huichen*. Cf. Evers, p. 89.

95/34–5. Isaiah 11: 1.

96/1. *becleppinge*: the meaning is 'inflaming'. Cf. 46/34, 66/1 where DM has made the same mistake. C reads *brasier*.

96/5. *þe tyeres*: C *les lermes*; as Evers (p. 89) pointed out, the sense here is not 'tears' but 'sap'. DM had used *zep*, however, for French *gome*. For the sense 'gum, sap' see *OED* TEAR *sb.*[1] 3.

96/15. *euere*: at 220/29, Morris keeps the reading *euerte*. Wallenberg (p. 86, n. 4) rightly pointed out that *euerte* is a genuine form and should be retained.

96/16–17. John 15: 5.

96/22. *priuelyliche*: probably an error for *priueliche*.

96/25. *zeayde*: may be a blend of the spellings *zede* and *zayde* but possibly it is a spelling for *zeyde*. Cf. pp. 35–6.

96/26–34. Matthew 5: 3–9.

96/31. *ssol*: this could be a genuine form of the plural. Cf. 217/13, 236/18, and *OED* SHALL A 3 γ. Compare the following note however.

96/33. *ssole*: the form is corrected from *ssol*. The single consonant may be genuine (cf. 189/25 and p. 41) but could be due to the inadvertence of the corrector.

97/4. *heʒnesse*: *MED* (HEIGHNES(SE n. 3(b)) renders 'ecstasy', 'supernatural perfection' but the French has *hautesce* 'nobility'.

97/6. *onderstonde*: Evers (p. 89) pointed out that some manuscripts have *attendre* for C's *entendre* (so E manuscripts except G1, An, V, and Ca2). Emend to *abide*. Cf. note to 74/24.

97/13. *to þe yewes*: C *as Iuis* is possessive. Read *of þe yewes*.

97/13–14. *hi is zoþliche newe*: C *Ele est uraiement nouele*; DM follows C here but all E manuscripts (other than the pair G1, Ca2, which read as C) have a fuller and better text. They read before *Ele est uraiement nouele*, *Et pour ce que ele fet lame enveilli(r) par pechie rejouenir et nouelle deuenir (par bonnes oeures)*. Ld lacks *ele est uraiement nouele*.

97/14–16. *Laʒe is yzed þeruore þet hy hare-zelue ne bynt. ake þe oþre byndeþ | and þis onbynt*: C *Lois si est dite pour ce que ele ne lie. mais les autres lient e ceste deslie*; Francis (note to VV 95/22) points out that the etymological point is lost in translation. Though, as she says, *lier–loy* is not good etymology it is probably due to a connection between *ligo–legem*; *harezelue ne* should be omitted in the text or emended to *harezelf*. The verb cannot be reflexive. *þe oþre* is plural and refers to other laws contrasted with the law of Christ. Of the manuscripts I have consulted, only Ca2 has the erroneous negative like C.

97/18–19. *to*: C *a*; read *biþ* for *to*.

97/21. Proverbs 29: 18.

97/27. *huo*: C *qui*; read *huet* as a neuter is required.

97/29–30: the subject of the verbs is *þe traw of uirtue*. Accordingly, *traw* must be emended to a plural or the verbs to the singular. It seems to make better sense to take *traw* as singular but the early French manuscripts, in fact, have the plural and on these grounds we should, perhaps, emend to *trawes*. The pronouns in lines 31–3 are also plural.

98/3. *uor*: C *que par*; read *þet* before *uor*. Cf. Evers, p. 90.

98/6–7. *þet is of his grace and of his yefþe ne comþ*: C *se de sa grace e de son don ne uient*; DM has misunderstood the idiom. Read *bote ȝef þet of his grace and of his yefþe ne come* 'unless it come of his grace and his gift'.

99/5. *newen*: a number of French texts read here *noel* (P1, 2, 4, 6, 9, 10, A2, Add1), or *noyel* (P13, 14, Add2) 'a buckle or fastening'. But these clearly do not make sense in the context. The correct reading may be *mouel(le)* 'yolk' (G1, P15; cf. VV. 97/19 ȝelke) or even *nouelon* (G4) 'germ of wheat, stone of fruit' or *noyau* (P12) (cf. *kernel* En5, En6). In view of the similarity of form between *mouel* and *noel*, the majority reading, however, it is probably best to assume that the original reading was *mouel*. The reading *nou(u)el* found in some manuscripts (P5, 7, 8, 16, M, G5, An, V, Ld, Ca2, R1, C), is probably a corruption of this, as is the reading *moien* of F1. The reading *nouel* in C explains DM's erroneous rendering. The English text should probably read *ȝelke*. Cf. 96/3 where *ȝelke* renders *moele*.

99/18–21. Gregory, *Moralia*, XXXIII, xxii (PL lxxvi, col. 701). Cf. 211/34–212/2.

100/9. *alle guod*: C *tuit li bien*; *guod* should, perhaps, be emended to *guodes* but it might be a long-stem endingless plural. Cf. p. 62.

100/15–16. Wisdom 11: 25.

100/22. *Nou ich þe sseawy þanne þis word*: C *Ore te moustre dont cis mos*; as Varnhagen pointed out ((1879), 30–1), *cis mos* (*þis word*) is the subject. Read *þe sseaweþ* for *ich þe sseawy*.

100/24. *of oþerhalf þe zelue*: C *dautre part toi meismes*; DM is rendering a French appositive genitive.

100/25–6. *ne may ich habbe*: C *ne pues auoir*; read *ne miȝt þou habbe*. Cf. Varnhagen (1879), 31.

101/16. *þet þou him uelaȝest*: C *qui tu acompaignes*; read *huam þou uelaȝest*. The clause is an indirect question. Cf. Varnhagen (1879), 31.

101/29–30. Romans 3: 24; Cf. Ephesians 2: 8.

102/1. *huer-of*: C *dont*; 'then', 'accordingly'. Read *þanne*. Cf. Varnhagen (1879), 32.

102/2. *þe cortaysye [of] god*: C *la cortoisie dieu*; as often, DM has rendered the appositive genitive literally.

102/7. *halle and uol of uolk*: C *sale pleine de gent*; as Varnhagen suggested ((1879), 32), *and* should be omitted.

102/11. *louye*: C *deuons amer*; supply *ssolle*.

102/14–17. Romans 8: 15–17.

102/15. *weddes*: C *gages*; the form *gages* is singular.

102/23. James 5: 16. For the form *Iocob* cf. note to 17/32.

102/24. *zuo hit is*: C *si est*; *hit* is redundant. Cf. Varnhagen (1879), 32.

103/1–3. John 14: 15–21; 15: 10.

103/8–15. Exodus 3: 1–14. God, in fact, appeared to Moses in the burning bush on mount Horeb.

103/13. *yef me akseþ*: C *Se on me demande*; DM first translated literally and then deleted the second *me* after *akseþ*.

103/25. *speke we*: C *parlons*; read *we spekeþ*.

103/29. *huer-by me may ywyte hou þet hit by þe man knawe*: C *par quoi on puet* comment *que soit lome conoistre* 'how one may, somehow or other, recognize the man'. Omit *ywyte*.

103/30. *ase*: C *ausi* comme; DM seems to have mistaken the sense here. *Ac ne ziggeþ naȝt ariȝt his name* goes with what precedes. The French *ausi comme* means 'likewise when'. Emend *ase* to *alzuo huanne*. Cf. Varnhagen (1879), 33–4.

103/36. Job 14: 4.

104/6. *And ase zayþ Salomo[n]*: the reference is to Ecclesiastes 1: 2 etc. For C's *e com dist* some manuscripts have *si comme dist*. This may be the correct reading in which case *and* should be omitted here and preserved after Salomon.

104/6. *and naȝt*: C '*e' nient*; cf. Varnhagen (1879), 34.

104/8. *zetnesse an uestnesse*: C *establement e fermement*; DM seems to have mistaken these forms for nouns. He does the same at 104/14 where *zetnesse* again translates French *establement*. Cf. Varnhagen (1879), 34.

104/9–11. James 1: 17.

104/10. *him remue*: *OED* (Remue v. 4) renders 'change'. Thus the passage seems to refer to the divine attributes, impassibility, immutability, and immovability.

104/16. *gelt*: C *trespassement*; cf. notes to 6/5 and 72/15.

104/21. *musy*: *OED* (Muse v. I 1) says that the meaning is 'to ponder' and VV (103/8) has *studie*. But the meaning may be rather 'spend time on something', 'linger'. French *muser* usually means 'idle'. Cf. *EDD* Muse *v.*[1] and *sb.* for a similar sense.

104/26. *þe eldeste*: C *le plus uieus*; the French represents the past participle of the verb 'to see'. Cf. line 30 where DM translates *veus* 'seen' by *ald*. Read *þe mest yzeȝe*; cf. Varnhagen (1879), p. 35.

104/29. *bodyes*: C *cors*; an error for *cuers* which the sense requires. So E manuscripts (R1 *cors 7 cuers*) except that Ld, Ca1, Eg1 omit; P1, G1, Ca2 read *cors* as C.

104/35. *bezide*: C *iustes*; as Varnhagen observed ((1879), 35), DM has confused *juste* = Latin *juxta* with *iuste* = Latin *justus*. Read *riȝtuol*.

105/6. *dyepnesse*: *MED* (DEPNES(SE n. 4 (c)) glosses as 'greatness'. The French, however, has *parfondesce* 'profundity'.

105/7. *he3nesse*: C *hautesce*; the meaning is 'loftiness' rather than 'power', 'majesty' as *MED* (HEIGHNES(SE 2 (d)) suggests. Cf. note to 97/4.

105/8. *zopliche*: C *ataintes*; DM may have read *acertes*. For *zopliche* read *ycome to*. Cf. Varnhagen (1879), 36.

105/13–15. *hit ne is no drede þet . . . ne heþ*: C *nest pas doute que . . . nait*; 'doubtless . . . there are'. Cf. note to 122/2, 143/14–32.

105/16. *lyte lettre*: C *petit de lettres*; read *lettres*. The superscript *e* is squeezed in in the margin. An *s* should have been added.

105/17. *porchaceþ*: C *empetrent* means 'claim' not 'obtain'. The English should read *biddeþ*.

105/23–6. Augustine, *De Trinitate*, iv. 6 (PL xlii, col. 1042) summarizes the psychological trinity as *memoria, intelligentia, voluntas*.

105/24. *þet is be þri*: C *est selom .iij.*; omit *þet* as Varnhagen suggested ((1879), 36). The preposition *to* renders Fr. *a*. Cf. notes to 87/26, 246/24.

105/31. *ne3le[c]þ*: Wallenberg (p. 167, n. 4) is probably mistaken in keeping the manuscript reading. His analogy with (*y*)*zyþ* is not valid. Cf. p. 48.

106/16. *Wysdom is yzed of smac | and of smacky*: this does not, of course, make sense in English although it is true that Latin *sapere* means 'to taste' as well as 'to know'. Hence *sapientia* 'wisdom' is connected with the verb 'to taste'. The French has *Sapience est dite de saueur e de sauourer*. Cf. 245/27.

106/26–7. *ase deþ þet uer [þet] clenzeþ*: C *ausi comme li feus purge*; Varnhagen ((1879), 37) rightly pointed out that, if the text is to be emended, *deþ* should be omitted rather than *þet* supplied.

106/33. *of alle wreþe*: C *de tout corous*; C is wrong here. The correct reading appears to be *de toutes cures* (so P2, 4, A2, An, Ld, Eg1, R1, F1). The erroneous reading of C is shared by G1, Ca2. The text should read *of alle zor3es*.

107/2. *one* 'one' is probably an error for *ane* 'a'. Cf. note to 17/22.

107/7. *depe*: *MED* (DEPEN v. 1 (b)) glosses 'baptize' but *depe* always renders French *taindre* 'immerse', 'dye'. Cf. 107/17 *ydept yne grayne* 'dyed in scarlet'.

107/9. *[he] wyle þis word*: C *veult . . . cis mos*; the subject is *cis mos*. Morris's emendation is unnecessary. Cf. Varnhagen (1879), 40.

107/9. *þin name*: this may be an error or due to nunnation before the initial of *name*. Cf. 146/36 and p. 51.

107/17. *zuo moche ydept yne grayne*: C *taint en graine*; *zuo moche* is superfluous. It looks as though DM had a text which combined the reading *taint en graine* of the majority of E manuscripts with *tant en graine*, the reading of An and Ca2. Omit *zuo moche*.

107/24. *huich*: C *quele*; emend to *þet hi*. Cf. Varnhagen (1879), 40.

107/24. *cryepe*: C *crouller*; *MED* (CREPEN v. 8) suggests that *cryepe* is an error. Wallenberg (p. 68, n. 1), however, thought that DM preferred the sense 'creep' to the meaning of the French 'move', 'shake', because roots creep and he could thus continue the metaphor. This seems far-fetched. It is more likely that DM misunderstood *crouller* or that DM's manuscript read (*se*) *couler* 'slip', 'glide', 'creep'. Unless an otherwise unknown *tocryepe* is assumed, *to* should be omitted.

107/29–30. *þet ne of no þing þenche*: C *quele ne puet a riens penser*; read *hi ne may þenche* for *þenche*. Cf. Varnhagen (1879), 40.

108/1–3. Luke 17: 21.

108/9–10. *þe ilke . . . wyndeþ hi zuo uele defautes*: C *cis qui cuidoit estre tous nes troue lors tant de defautes*; supply *þet* after *þe ilke*; read *wynt* for *wyndeþ*; omit *hi* after *wyndeþ*.

108/12. *þet doust þet byeþ*: C *les poudrettes qui sont*; read *biþ* for *byeþ*.

108/15. *beneþe þe helle*: C *desouz lui enfers*; DM seems to have translated the reading which appears in Ca2, *desouz li enfers* and taken *li* as the article; or he may have had a manuscript which read *le* for C's *lui*. A better reading is *desouz lui* (*li*) *en enfers* (or rev.) as in P1, 2, A2, M, (An), Ld, Add1, F1. Read *beneþe him ine helle*.

108/19. *me zyȝt*: C *uoit*; the subject is 'the heart' and *me* should read *hi*.

108/20. *wynynde*: C *desirrans*; read *willende*. Cf. Varnhagen (1879), 41.

108/31. *benimþ*: the subject is *alle þe uelþes*; read *benimeþ*.

109/10–11. Matthew 13: 44.

109/11. *on* 'one' is possibly an error for *a*. Cf. note to 17/22.

109/20–22. *bote yef we ne habbe . . . and þet he ous wende*: C *se nous nauons . . . e quil nous conuertisse*; 'unless we have . . . and unless he change for us'. DM has rendered the French literally. Cf. Varnhagen (1879), 42.

109/23. *to þe heȝe guode*: C *a la soe bone*; DM's rendering is only a para-phrase. The French means 'to his (God's) own good (will)'. Cf. Varn-hagen (1879), 42.

109/23–6. The pronouns in this passage are confused. In line 23, *hise* and *he* refer to man's will; in lines 24 and 27, *his* refers to the Holy Spirit or to God; in lines 25 and 26, the will of the Holy Spirit is referred to as *hi*, corresponding to French *ele*. For the gender of *will* see p. 90.

109/32–3. *þet guode red*: C *le don de conseil*; DM has read *le bon conseil*. Cf. Varnhagen (1879), 42. Read *þe yefþe of red*.

110/1. *o[u]re*: no need to emend. Read *ore*. See p. 15.

110/4. *Þe oþre vour*: C *Es autres .iiij.*; DM's manuscript seems to have read *Ces* for *es* as M and Eg1; or, possibly, as Varnhagen ((1879), 42) suggested, it read *les*. The text should read *Ine þe oþre vour*.

110/17. [*ac*]: there is no justification for this emendation either in source or sense.

110/21–2. *Huanne me bit þe broþerhede | and þe uelaȝrede*: C *Quant on requiert .i. abbe le pain de sabaie ? on requiert la fraternite et la compaignie*; DM may have had a defective manuscript at this point. Read *Huanne me bit ane abbotte þe bryead of his abbaye me bit þe broþerhede and þe uelaȝrede*.

110/23. *Alsuo hit is huose þet smackeþ*: C *Ausi est ci qui qua lotroi*; 'thus it is here for whoever has the gift' etc. The text should read *Alsuo hit is hyer huose heþ þe yefþe*. DM has omitted *ci* and mistranslated *otroi*. Cf. Varnhagen (1879), 43.

110/25. *and*: is redundant and should be omitted. Cf. Varnhagen (1879), 43.

110/29–32. John 6: 51–2.

111/1–2. Perhaps a reference to Exodus 12: 11.

111/7. *ine grat*: C *en gros*; *MED* (AGRETE) suggests 'in all', 'all told', but the sense here is clearly 'completely'.

111/8. *þet | þet hit is*: C *que cest*; read *þet hit is*.

111/24–5. *him . . . ham*: the French has the plural throughout and *him* should read *ham*. *Knyȝt* should also be plural.

111/32. *of hiren*: C *du sien* 'from herself'. Cf. *of his* 22/13, 54/3, 194/28–9.

111/33–5. The reference is to Leviticus 6: 21 (*quae in sartagine oleo conspersa frigetur*) and only indirectly to the Psalter. Gregory (*Hom. in Ezechielem*, I (PL lxxvi, col. 932)) links Ezechiel 4: 3 (*et tu sume tibi sartaginem ferream*) with Leviticus and with Psalm 68 (69): 10, *zelus domus tuae comedit me* because the metaphor of the pan signified zeal. Cf. Honorius of Autun, *Gemma Animae*, I, xxxi (PL clxxii, col. 554).

111/35. *blode*: C *saim* 'fat'; DM's text reads *sanc* (so V, Eg 1; R1 *sanc 7 sain*). Cf. Varnhagen (1879), 44.

112/10. *of eche daye . . . of eche daye*: C *cotidien . . . de chascon iour*.

112/11. *to his wel wilynde*: the French text has *a ses chanoines* (cf. VV 110/31 *to his chanounes*). The following phrases, *doþ his seruice* and *ziggeþ his oures*, suggest that the reading of the French text is correct.

112/22–4. Cf. Wisdom 16: 20.

112/24. *to gromes*: C *a garconer*; Varnhagen ((1879), 45) thought that the reading of C was inappropriate but it is supported by all the E manuscripts except P4 which reads *a donner a garcons*. DM has read *a garcons*.

112/25. *piecaille, cheuaille*: read *pietaille, chenaille*; cf. Wallenberg, p. 189, n. 2; 50, n. 1.

112/29–30. Matthew 6: 11.

112/34. *wit substances*: C *sens sustancieus*; the correct reading is *s(e)us-(sour)sustancieus* as in E manuscripts except P1, A2, V, R1; Ca2 reads as C; Ca1 is defective. Read *opesubstancial*. Cf. note to line 113/4 below.

113/4. *alsuo*: C *ains* 'but rather'. This looks like an error on DM's part.

He probably read *ausi* for *ains*. Read *þe raþre*. *ope substance* is a mistaken rendering of French *sorsubstancieus* for which see *OED* SUPERSUBSTANTIAL.

113/5–6. *onderstondigge*: read *onderstondingge*. Cf. p. 40, n. 7. Morris usually emends such forms.

113/21. *þet is þet beste wed of þe house*: C *cest le meillor gage del hostel dont*; this appears to go with what follows and we should supply *huerby* after *house* to correspond to the French *dont*. The meaning is that a bargain by which one single sin (a small debt) can send a man to hell (the exaction of an enormous profit) is an excellent bargain for the moneylender. The *hostel* may refer to a money-lending centre in Paris.

114/3. Morris's emendations are unnecessary; cf. note to 46/9.

114/20–1. *huer he al misdeþ*: C *ou il tont mesfait*; cf. 114/23 *þet þe habbeþ misdo* (*qui tont mesfait*) 'who have wronged you'. DM has misread *tont* as *tout* and taken *ou* to mean 'where' instead of 'or' (cf. Varnhagen (1879), 46). Emend to *oþer þe habbeþ misdo*.

114/23–4. *more yet eft*: C *plus encor*; 'yet even more'.

114/25–7. Luke 6: 32, 33. The question mark should be replaced by a stop in line 27. It makes nonsense of the quotation.

114/31. *of ous to uoryeue*: C *de nous pardoner*; Varnhagen's conjecture ((1879), 47) that C's *de nous* is an error for *deuons* is confirmed by the reading of all E manuscripts except A2, M, F1, and Ca1 which is defective. The English should read *ssolle uoryeue*.

115/3–4. Romans 12: 5.

115/8. *zuych can zigge his pater noster*: C *Tiex seut dire sa pater nostre*; Varnhagen ((1879), 47) suggested that the sense required a negative but only P4, A2, M have a negative. The sense is elliptical: 'Such a man may be accustomed to say his Pater Noster but he had better be silent' etc.

115/9. *were betere*: C *mielz . . . uendroit*; the reading *vaudroit* which appears in P1, 2, A2, V, Ld, Add1, Eg1 gives better sense. Cf. Varnhagen (1879), 47.

115/13. *ine þoȝte*: C *apense*; DM seems to have taken *apense* 'reflective' as *a pensees*. Cf. 11/13 and Varnhagen (1879), 48.

115/17. *ywonne*: C *acreu*; Wallenberg (p. 321) suggested that DM derived *acreu* from *aquerir* 'win' instead of from *acroistre* 'increase'; but it is more probably from *acroire*. The sense is 'how much he has here borrowed and how much he owes'.

115/31. *and*: omit.

116/4. *uory[e]ue*: no need to emend here. Cf. note to 46/9.

116/20–2. This seems to be an elaboration of Ephesians 3: 17: *in charitate radicati et fundati*.

116/26. *berþ*: C *porter*; read *bere* as the syntax requires.

116/28. *þe erþe of libbende*: C *la terre des uiuans*: read *of þe libbende*.

116/34. *to hare*: *lor*; Wallenberg (p. 113) is perhaps right in thinking that DM has forgotten that *herten* is plural; *hare* should be emended to *ham.*

117/8–9. *ne heþ þise uondinges*: C *na este temptes*; Varnhagen ((1879), 49) rightly pointed out that DM has translated *ceste* for *este*. Read *ne heþ yby yuonde.* See Ecclesiasticus 34: 9 ff.

117/11. *ne him uestni ine*: C *ne soi enfermer en*; other early manuscripts read *ne senfermete ne* (P1, 2, A2, M, An, V, Ld, Add1, (Eg1), R1, F1). This clearly makes better sense. The English text should read *ne his ziknesse ne* etc. The erroneous reading of C is shared by G1, Ca2.

117/18–19. *al þet is of ous*: C *quant est de nous* 'as far as we are concerned'.

117/20. *ane*: the sense requires *one*. Cf. the note to 17/22.

117/28–32. Cf. Augustine, *Liber de Natura et Gratia*, xxvii. 31 (PL xliv, col. 262).

118/3. *o[u]s*: no need to emend; see p. 15.

118/4. *dy[e]uele*: no need to emend; cf. 189/30.

118/8. *zene*: read *zenne.*

118/15. *y-contyened*: see note to 39/15.

118/17. *materie*: cf. 136/12 *matiere*. In both cases the correct reading is *materie*. The abbreviation is after the *t*. Cf. Corrigenda.

118/25. *and hire brengþ*: C *quil li porte* which makes better sense. Emend *and* to *þet he.*

118/26–8. Isaiah 11.

118/30. *Yef we telleþ*: C *Si nous raconte*; as Evers (p. 91) pointed out, DM has mistaken the French particle *si* for the conjunction 'if' and read *nous raconte* as *nous racontons*. Read *He zuo ous telþ.*

118/32–4. Isaiah 11: 1.

118/34–119/1. *þet is to zigge* . . . *Vor nazareþ*: *is ase moche worþ* | *ase flour* | *and grace. ase moche ase cos*: C *cest a dire la flour des flours. Car nazareth uaut autant come flour e grace. autant comme uns brasiers*; there are various errors in this passage; (i) most early manuscripts read *et jesse (uaut)* before *autant comme uns brasiers* (so P1, 2, 4, A2, M, An, V, Ld, Ca1, Add1, R1). This is certainly correct and G1, Ca2, C have an omission here (ii) DM has mistranslated *brasiers* 'ardour'. He presumably took it to mean 'embrace' and hence 'kiss' (iii) some manuscripts have the following passage after the quotation: *(de) la tres grant charite (clarte) (7) du tres grant brasier de lamour de dieu il nous uendra (dist il) une uierge qui portera la fleur de nazareth* (so P2, A2, An, V, Ld, R1). It looks as though the shorter text may have arisen through homoeoteleuton.

119/2–4. For the gifts of the spirit see Isaiah 11: 2–3.

119/4. *wytte*: C *science*; Evers (p. 91) pointed out that DM normally renders *science* by *connyng* and conjectures that he read *science* as *sens*. But there are a number of cases in which DM uses *wit* to mean 'knowledge'.

119/8–10. John 1: 14, 16.

119/10. *we nimeþ al*: C *nous prenons tuit*; DM has taken *tuit* as the object but it goes with *nous*. Read *alle* here and at 119/11.

119/12–15. *þe graces bodiliche . . . to echin he him sseweþ*: C *les graces corporeus . . . a chascun se moustre*; as Evers pointed out (p. 91), the subject is *graces bodiliche* and the verb should, accordingly, be plural as it is in all E manuscripts except G1, V, Ca2, which share the erroneous reading of C. Both DM and C have an erroneous point before *a chascun* (*to echin*). This phrase, in fact, belongs to what precedes and the point should follow and not precede. It was presumably this erroneous pointing which led DM to assume that the phrase went with what followed and thus to supply a subject for *se moustre*. The text should read *to echin. ham sseweþ*.

119/16. *alsuo is he*: C *Ausi est il* 'likewise is it'; read *alsuo is hit*.

119/18. *be þan þet god him yefþ*: C *selom ce li done dieus*; 'accordingly God gives him'. Read *be þan god him yefþ*. Cf. Evers, p. 91.

119/19–20. *þet sseweþ þis yefþe*: C *se moustrent cist don*; DM has mistaken *se* for *ce*. He has then put the verb in the singular and taken *cist don* as the object (cf. Evers, p. 92). Emend to *ham sseweþ þise yefþes*.

119/21–2. 1 Corinthians 12: 11.

119/23. *sseweþ*: C *moustrent*; Evers was right (p. 92) in preferring the reading of the other E manuscripts, *montent*. Read *cliueþ*.

119/24. *þanne ine wysdome*: C *donques en sapience*; Evers (p. 92) pointed out that *donques* is an error for *dusque* 'up to'. A2, C alone have this error. Read *al to* for *þanne ine*. Cp. 143/8, 144/8.

119/24–5. Psalm 110 (111): 10.

120/2–6. James 1: 17.

120/4. *nauʒt*: the reading *nauʒt* for MS *nanʒt* may be correct although DM does not usually have a glide before a voiceless guttural. Cf. Wallenberg (p. 166, n. 3) who refers to a correction of *nanʒt* to *naʒt* at 230/32. The reading *naʒt* is to be preferred.

120/4. *y-yeue*: C *donet* (so G1, Ca2); Evers (p. 92) suggested that the French word is *donets* 'small gifts' which DM has interpreted as the past participle of *doner* (cf. the reading *donnes, donnez* in P2, 4, A2, V, Ld, R1). This would be supported by the reading of P1, M, An, Add1, Ca1 *donnetes*. But it seems, in fact, that the French is a literal rendering of the Latin: *omne datum optimum, et omne donum perfectum desursum est, descendens a Patre luminum, apud quem non est transmutatio, nec vicissitudinis obumbratio* (James 1: 17). The distinction is between *donum* and *datum* rendered in French by *dons* and *donet*. For *naturalia data, supererogata dona dicantur* see D. O. Lottin, *Psychologie et Morale aux xiie et xiiie siècles* (Louvain, Gembloux, 1949), p. 333.

120/6–7. *þet he ne yefþ him-zelue*: C *qui ne li doint soi meismes*; the English means 'to whom he does not give himself' and may render a

French *cui il ne doint soi meismes* (so P1) rather than the reading of C. Cf. Evers, p. 92.

120/8. *graces*: *MED* (GRACE n. 1 (b)) takes these to refer to divine graces. But the term 'endowment' is nearer to the meaning. The graces in question are those referred to at 119/12, *graces bodiliche*, equally gifts of God, and so graces, but distinct from *grace* in its theological sense. Yet the word cannot be translated 'graces' since this loses the implication of 'a favour', 'something given'; cf. 11/10–12 where the essential contrast is between *guode* and *grace* 'possessions' on the one hand, and 'endowment', 'natural abilities', on the other. Cf. *OED* GRACE *sb.* 2.

120/14. *þer byeþ yefþes*: C *il sont done*; DM has taken the French to mean 'there are gifts'. Emend to *hi byeþ y-yeue* etc.; cf. Evers, p. 92.

120/18. *yzyȝþ*: C *regart*; VV 118/32 has *rewardeþ and ȝeldeþ*. The French must mean 'rewards' not 'regards'. Read *yelt*. Cf. *to þe reward of* 74/4.

120/22. *wyþ-oute yefþe*: C *sans dons*; C shares this erroneous reading with Ca2. The words should be omitted. Cf. Evers, p. 92.

120/25. *onderstondinge*: C *attendre*; DM read *entendre*. Read *abidinge*. Cf. note to 74/24.

120/31–2. *hi byeþ y-cleped / yefþe ... of þe zone*: C *sont il plus apele don ... du fil*; there are a number of errors in this passage: (i) DM has omitted French *plus* which the construction requires (cf. Evers, p. 92). *Raþre* should be supplied before *y-cleped*; (ii) French *don* is plural and *yefþe* may be singular. Cf. 3/21 n. (iii) the French is a question and, therefore, *hi byeþ* should read *byeþ hi*. Supply a question mark after *þe zone* in line 32.

121/1. A verb *byeþ* should probably be supplied before *þe workes* although it is lacking also in the French.

121/2. *vor*: MS *wor* should be retained. See p. 44, n. 3.

121/3. *to lere*: C *esprendre*; Evers (p. 92) was probably right in suggesting that the reading *espandre* 'expend' is correct. This reading appears in all the E manuscripts except P4, G1, Ca2 which share the reading of C. Read *to spendi*.

121/5–6. Romans 5: 5.

121/24. *to þe greate þreste*: C *a la grant mace*; 'with the great cudgel'. DM seems to have confused *mace* with *masse* as well as mistranslating *a*. At 183/7 *þrestes* renders *presses*. Cf. Wallenberg, p. 256, n. 1. Read *wyþ þe greate steue*.

121/26. *arise*: C *leuee*; the reference is to the club raised and ready to strike. Read *arered*.

121/33. *izixt*: C *uois as ielz*; DM has left a gap after *izixt* and put a cross in the margin. Perhaps, as Evers suggested (p. 93), the words *as ielz* were written as one in his manuscript and he thus did not understand them and so omitted them.

121/34–5. *comeþ to þe wordle*: C *uiuent au monde*; emend to *libbeþ ine þe wordle*.

122/2. *heþ*: C *a*; for *heþ* 'there are' compare lines 14–15 (where *heþ* he renders *a il* 'il y a') and note to 105/13–15.

122/2–4. For the grouping of the orders of angels into three hierarchies of descending importance see Dionysius, *De Caelesti Hierarchia*, vi 2 (PG iii, cols. 200–1).

122/4. *men*: at line 8, *midliste* is written above *men* in a somewhat paler ink. DM seems to have been doubtful about the correct rendering of *moien*, although, at line 4, he simply translated by *men*. Cf. Evers, p. 93.

122/6. *þe nixte*: C *plus pres*; for *þe nixte* read *nier*. Cf. Evers, p. 93 and note to 89/12.

122/10. *lyernieþ*: the manuscript has *lyermeþ* or *lyerneþ* with prolongation of the *r*. The form *lyernieþ* would be abnormal in a verb whose infinitive ends in *-i*. Wallenberg (p. 147, n. 1) is, no doubt, right in supposing the correct form to be *lyerneþ*.

122/10–11. *an þet hi hoteþ*: C *ce quil* com*mandent*; the *an* is redundant and should be omitted as Evers suggested (p. 93).

122/12. *þo þet byeþ ine office*: C *li official*; 'officials'.

122/14–15. *heþ he*: C *a il*; the French means 'there are'. Cf. 122/2 and note to 105/15.

122/15. *zone*: should be plural as the French. Read *zones*.

122/15–16. Romans 8: 14.

122/20. *þet ysyeþ*: C *quil uoient*; DM's text had *qui uoient* (so E except that G1 reads as C).

122/23. *Þe þridde byeþ*: C *Li tiers sont*; strictly the verb should be singular.

122/26, 28. *zix* should read *zeue*.

122/27–8. 1 Corinthians 12: 11.

122/31. *bidde*: C *ourer*; DM has confused *ovrer* 'work' with *ourer, orer* 'pray' (cf. Evers, p. 94). Emend to *werche*.

123/12–13. 1 Corinthians 13: 13.

123/14. *hare*: C *lor*; the correct reading is *le* (*les*) as E manuscripts except G1, Ca2 which agree with C.

123/14–15. Augustine, *De Agone Christiano*, xiii (PL xl, col. 299).

123/15–16. *and hi ous deþ beknawe / and to byknawe. to þe lhorde*: C *e le nous fait conoistre e reconoistre a seignor*; 'And faith makes us recognize and acknowledge God as lord'; DM may have meant to write *ayenknawe* for *reconoistre*. The main verbs also require an object and *him* should be supplied after *deþ*; *to þe lhorde* is clearly due to a misunderstanding of the French and should be emended to *ase lhord*. It should be noted that DM's exemplar was superior to C here; C's *e le* should read *e ele le*.

123/17. *Hope: zayþ. hi ous arereþ*: C *Esperance dist il nous eslieue*; DM appears to have read *Esperance, dist, il nous eslieue*. The English should read *he zayþ* for *zayþ. hi*. Cf. Evers, p. 94 and 123/20.

123/19. *þet hi þet paceþ*: C *ce qui passe*; DM first wrote *þet þet* and then inserted *hi* between them. He may have meant to substitute *hi* for the first *þet*. But *hi* is erroneous and should be omitted. Cf. Evers, p. 94.

123/20. *þis zayþ. hi*: C *ce dist il*; DM has misread the French. Read *þis zayþ he*.

123/21–22. Cf. Colossians 2: 2.

123/28. *onderstant*: C *atent*; DM has confused *atent* and *entent* (cf. note to 74/24). Read *abit*. DM's manuscript may have read *entent* although no E manuscripts have this reading.

123/30–1. *ine dede*: C *e œure; ine dede* is on an erasure. As Evers pointed out (p. 94), DM has misread *e* as *en*. Read *and workeþ*.

123/30–2. This passage appears to mean that there are degrees by which one can apprehend the good of another; one can know of it by hearsay. To act on this is to act by faith; or one can expect good of a man, make an intellectual judgement, but not oneself experience the goodness. Then one acts in hope, "following the scent" of one's observation; or, thirdly, one can experience another man's goodness and then indeed one is in true possession of it, one grasps it, experiences it at first hand, and possesses it. This is charity. In line 32 *zikþ* renders French *uoit*; in line 31, *uelþ þane smel* renders *sent lodour*.

124/3–5. This appears to be a general reference to the book of Wisdom. The phrase *spiritus sapientiae* (Wisdom 1: 6) is taken to refer to the Holy Spirit.

124/32. *to þe lyne of scele*: C *a la ligne de raison*; 'by the line of reason'. Emend *to* to *bi*. The reference is to a builder's line. As *MED* points out (LINE n. (1) 3 (a)), it is often difficult to distinguish the figurative from the literal uses. Cf. Glossary **line**. In 124/28–9 the reference is to Cicero's *De Officiis*.

124/34. *by do*: C *uoisent*; DM did not recognize the subjunctive of *aler*. Read *guo*.

125/6. *þise office*: C *ceste uertu*; read *uirtue* as the sense requires. Cf. Evers, p. 95.

125/8. *to louie zikerliche*: C *damerseurement*; the French should read *damesurement* 'of moderation' and not *damer seurement*. The correct reading appears in the E manuscripts P2, M, G1, An, Ld, Ca1, Ca2; P4, R1 read *(de) mesure*. The English text should read *of mesure*.

125/8. *him of scele*: C *lui de raison*; DM renders the reading which appears in G1, Ca2, C. The correct reading may be *le iou de raison* 'the yoke of reason' as in P1, 2, A2, M, An, Ca1, Add1. The English should probably read *þe yok of scele*. It is possible to make sense of C, however, on the assumption that *de raison* is for *deraison*.

125/8–9. *he zet . . . dret*: C *il met . . . doute*; if the reading *þe yok of scele* is adopted we should either read *he him zet* (cf. Add1 *il se met*) or read *dompte* for *doute* (as Harvard MS. cited in VV, note to 123/15–17); in that case the meaning would be 'he puts under the yoke of reason and tames all the desires of the world' instead of 'he puts himself under the yoke of reason and fears' etc.

125/11. *ssent*: C *honissent*; *þise þri þinges* is the subject not *þe wordle*. Emend to *ssendeþ*.

125/11–13. 1 John 2: 16.

125/16. *huo*: C *cuers*; Evers (p. 95) may be correct in assuming that DM has misread *cuers* as *ceus* but his text makes perfectly acceptable sense.

125/17. *No þing hi*m *ne dret*: C *Riens il ne doute*; Evers (p. 96) assumed that DM had translated the French as though it read *riens ne le doute*. When used reflexively, *drede* is usually followed by *of* and the text should perhaps read *of noþing* for *no þing*. But DM may have taken *Riens* as an adverb 'not at all'.

125/20. *wepinge*: C *ploier*; read *bouȝinge*. DM had the erroneous reading *plorer*, which appears in Ld, Add1.

125/22. *armenþ*; read *armeþ*. The error is no doubt due to French *arment* as Evers (p. 96) suggested.

126/2. *ydo*: C *fait il*; the French means 'he says'. Read *he zaiþ*.

126/11. *ne wenden*: C *nequedent*; DM has read *ne cuident* (cp. G1 *nequident*). Emend to *naȝt uor þan*. Cf. Evers, p. 96.

126/12. *be strengþe*: C *a force*; the French is best interpreted as the ppl. of *aforcier* 'compel'. Read *ystrengþed*.

126/16. *yzeȝe þet*: C *ueons que*; *ueons* seems to be an error for *uolons*, the reading of E (except that G1, Ca2 agree with C). The phrase goes with what precedes; *þet* means 'so that'. Read *willeþ* for *yzeȝe*.

126/18–21. Romans 2: 26, 27.

126/24. *moȝe*: C *peurent*; read *miȝten*.

126/27. *uirtue þet is wyþ-oute charité*: C *uertu qui est sans charite*; some E manuscripts add *7 uertu qui est o* (*com, en*) *charite* which completes the sense (so P2, 4, A2, M, An, R1; G1 reverses the order of the two members). The English text should read *uirtue þet is wyþoute charite and uirtue þet is wyþ charite*. Cf. Evers, p. 96.

126/28. *Huer-of*: C *Dont*; DM has confused the adverb *dont* with the preposition. For *Huer-of* read *Þanne*.

126/29–127/6. *De Moribus Ecclesiae*, xv (PL xxxii, col. 1322).

126/34. *and habbe*: C *a auoir*; read *to habbe* as Evers (p. 96) suggested.

127/4. *uor þet he loueþ*: C *por ce quil laime*; the correct reading is *por ce quil aime*, the reading of the other E manuscripts; DM's manuscript clearly differed from C here in having the correct reading.

127/15–16. *þet is þe riȝte þeþ*: C *qui est li drois sentiers*; the correct reading appears to be *qui le maine par le droit sentier* (so E except P1, Add1, and G1, which shares the erroneous reading of C). The passage from Wisdom

(10: 10) reads: *Haec profugum irae fratris iustum deduxit per vias rectas: Et ostendit illi regnum Dei*. The English text should read: *þet him let be þe riȝte peþ*.

127/21–3. *ac wexe* . . . *lyky*: C *mais habonderoit en dieu quil auroit en soi en cui il se deliteroit*; 'but he would abound in God, whom he would have in him, in whom he would delight'. VV (125/25–8) is more explicit: *but euere he scholde wexe more and more in God, þat he schulde alwey bere wiþ-ynne hym, in whom he schulde haue his likynge and his delit*.

127/24. *kende*: C *matire*; as Evers pointed out (p. 97), DM has misread *matire* as *nature*. Read *matere* for *kende*. Cf. 220/15.

127/26–8. *ous teche* . . . : *bestrepeþ* . . . *he zette | and norissy þe zeue uirtues*: C *nous enseigne a moustrer coment il par ces vii. dons estrepe les .vii. uices de nos cuers et i plante e norrisse les .vii. vertus*; Wallenberg (p. 28, n. 3) suggests that *bestrepeþ* is an error for *bestrepe*. But this is unnecessary. The text of C seems to be faulty. The majority of manuscripts read *norrist* for *norisse* and the verbs in DM should probably read *bestrepþ, zet, norisseþ*. The sentence would then run: 'that he teach us, in order to show how he, by these seven gifts, strips the seven vices from our heart and plants there and nourishes the seven virtues'. It may also be noted that DM's manuscript seems to have read *il plante*, as G1 and R1, for the correct *i plante*. For *he* read *þerinne*.

127/35. *þe ribaud and dronke*: C *li ribaus yures*; *MED* does not record *dronke* in the sense 'drunkard' and the *and* should perhaps be omitted. Cf. Evers, p. 97.

128/3. *playneþ*: C *sen plaint*; Evers (p. 97) pointed out that this is on an erasure. The English should read *him playneþ þerof*.

128/10. *huet godes*: C *quiex biens*; the French suggests that *guodes* is plural but it might be genitive singular after *huet*.

128/11–15. Luke 15: 11–32.

128/15. *Atenende*: C *Derechief* 'yet again'. The translation is imprecise.

128/16. *zeneȝeres*: read *zeneȝere* as Morris suggests.

128/16–18. Proverbs 23: 34–5.

128/17. *amide*: see p. 41.

128/22–7. Acts 12: 6–10.

128/24. *him*[1]: C *prouost*; DM has not rendered *prouost*. But since he translates it *prouost* elsewhere it seems likely that it was missing in his exemplar rather than that he did not understand the word.

128/34. *ine uers*: should perhaps read *ine þe uers* as Evers (p. 97) suggests. For Elinand see P. Meyer, 'Les *vers de la mort* d'Hélinand', *Romania*, i (1872), 364–7; F. Wulff and E. Walberg *Les Vers de la Mort* (S.A.T.F. 1905); K. Voretzsch, *Introduction to the Study of Old French Literature* (Halle, 1931) tr. F. M. Du Mont, p. 122.

128/35. *zuich*: C *tiex*; read *zuiche* as the sense requires.

129/2–3. *þet him help*: C *quil le garist*; Evers (p. 97) thought that DM had omitted the subject; but such a construction is possible in Middle English.

129/3–5. Cf. Psalm 140 (141): 5.

129/6–8. Genesis 3: 9.

129/9–10. *þe þierne [of] saynt abraha*m: C *labaiesse saint abraham*; DM has rendered the appositive genitive literally as elsewhere in the text. There is no need to emend.

129/12. *þise þri acsinges*: C *Ces .iij. demandes*; as Evers (p. 97) pointed out, there are four questions, not three. The error may have arisen because the four questions are made up of one question which God asked Adam, and three questions which the angel asked Hagar. But in the biblical text (Genesis 16: 7–8) the angel only asks Hagar two questions and the third may be an error.

129/13. *awakeþ and arereþ*: C *lesueille e resuscite*; supply *hine* before *awakeþ*.

129/18. *not*: C *ne sent*; Evers (p. 97) suggested that DM had read *seut* for *sent*. It is, however, more probable that *not* is a loose translation of the French. DM usually renders *seut* by *can*.

129/20. *ca arrieres*: this is erroneously inserted from the French. DM erased some words and put a cross in the margin. He later inserted the French words into the text over the erasure.

129/24–5. *a-uorye þet body | and a-uorye þe zaule*: C *diuers le cors e diuerse lame*; the majority of E manuscripts have the reading *deuers* which DM renders *auorye* (so E manuscripts except G1). The reading *diuers* 'evil' appears in G1 and C. It makes good sense but, in view of the manuscript evidence, the correct reading is probably *deuers*.

129/35. *lyeȝeþ*: read *lyeȝþ*? Cf. p. 98.

130/5. *domes man*: read *domesman* as 115/9–10. The French text read *la iustice* which DM has rendered as 'judge' and added *zuo stout*. But the meaning here is 'justice'. Although *justice* means both 'judge' and 'justice' in Middle English, DM seems to have understood it as meaning 'judge' (Cf. Ld's reading *iuge*). Thus at 131/17, he renders *la iustice dieu* as *his demere god* (whereas the meaning is 'the justice of God'); at 153/25, he renders *juge* by *iustise*; on the other hand, at 153/26, 28, 154/2, *iuges* is rendered by *demere* in each case written on an erasure.

130/9–10. *[he] yzyþ*: C *regarder*; the *þ* has been added later and is probably an error. Read *yzy* and omit *he*.

130/11. *astoneþ*: read *astonieþ*. The subject is *uour strokes of þondre*.

130/13. *to ziȝþe*: C *regart*; Evers (p. 98) regarded *to* as an error but *toziȝþe* is probably one word. It should be plural.

130/13. *roten*: C *rainsel* 'branches'. Emend to *boȝes* as Evers suggested (p. 98).

130/19–21. *of azemoche ase can habbe. oþer azemoche he is of miȝte. oþer azemoche ase he can conne. oþer ase moche ase can by worþ*: C *ou quanque soit auoir. ou quanque soit pooir. ou quanque soit sauoir. ou quanque seit ualer*; the phrase *azemoche ase (he) can, he is* is, of course, a literal rendering of French *quanque soit* (something or other'), a reading which occurs also in G1. The majority of manuscripts have *que que soit*. The translation is not in any case very precise. French *ou quanque soit auoir* 'either possess something or other' is awkwardly rendered by *azemoche ase can habbe*. The passage could be better rendered by *habbe oþer zom possession huet þet hit by; oþer zom miȝte huet þet hit by; oþer zom connynge huet þet hit by; oþer zom worþ huet þet hit by*.

130/22. *cornardyes*: DM has incorporated the French word and put a cross in the margin.

130/21–4. Zechariah 1: 18–21.

130/25. *efter*: C *apres*; all other E manuscripts (except G1) read *þor*. For *efter* read *uor*.

131/2. *huan[ne]*: there is no need for Morris's emendation. Cf. 56/32, 63/27 where Morris has not emended the form *huan*.

131/17. See note to 130/5.

131/23. *and þet he ne deþ naȝt*: the repetition is an error and these words should be omitted.

131/30. *of his stapes*: C *de ces degres*; all the early manuscripts, except G1, read *a* 'has' for *de* as the sense requires. Some manuscripts (P1, 2, V, Ld, Ca1, Add1, R1) have *.vii.* for *ces* which may be the original reading as it gives better sense than *ces*. In any case, *ces* is, of course, the demonstrative and not the possessive. The English should read *heþ þise stapes*.

131/31. *profiteþ*: C *ele pourfite*; provide *hy* before the verb.

131/35. *keste*: C *giete*; read *kest*.

132/2–4. *Dicta Anselmi*, i (Southern, *Memorials*, p. 111).

132/6–8. Bernard, *De Gradibus Humilitatis et Superbiae*, I. 2, 21–2 (Leclercq, Rochais, iii (1963), 17).

132/8. *Huanne* goes with what precedes.

132/13. *þet he yuele*: C *qui sent*; emend *þet he* to *he þet* and *yuele* to *yuelþ*.

132/15. *zaiþ þet he*: C *qui*; DM does not seem to have noted that this goes with what follows. The French sentence runs: *e qui sent les mauuaises humors ou cors :' lies est quant il les puet purgier*. As Evers (p. 99) pointed out, DM seems to have realized that something was wrong, since he added *zaiþ* over the line. Emend *zaiþ* to *huo* and omit *he*.

132/21. *Ac hi nolden anone manere*: C *mais ne uoudroient a nul fuer* etc.; read *a none manere*. Evers (p. 99) thought that DM has lost the construction and started a new sentence with *ac* and supplied a subject for the verb. But this is not a necessary assumption.

132/22-3. Translate 'therefore the fourth degree of this virtue is to be willing to be known' etc. The curious order is due to the French.

132/26. *a kuead | and zenuol*: C *mauuais e pecchierres*; we should, perhaps, understand *a kueade and a zenuolle*, namely the weak adjective with elision. Cf. *ane dyaue* 211/9.

132/30. *Yhere blepeliche of him-zelue*: C *oir uolentiers de soi meismes*; the reading of E (except G1, V, R1), *oir uolentiers uerite de soi meismes* is to be preferred on grounds of sense. The English text requires *þe zoþe* after *blepeliche*.

132/35-133/3. 2 Samuel 16: 5 ff. and 2 Samuel 19: 16 ff.

133/26-7. *And hou þet þis by | he him sseweþ huanne he zede*: C *Et comment ce soit il le moustre quant il dist*; DM has misunderstood *le* as 'him' whereas it means 'it'. Accordingly, *him* should be emended to *hit*. The sequence of tenses requires *zaiþ* rather than *zede*. Evers (p. 99) suggested reading *voirs* after *soit* as P1, Add1. But this is unnecessary and not supported by other E manuscripts.

133/26. Matthew 5: 3.

133/27-9. Matthew 11: 29.

133/32-3. *of þine herte . . . ouercome*: C *de ton cuer tant uaincre* (MS *uaintre*); *of* governs *ouercome* and is a literal rendering of the French idiom. Translate 'so to overcome thy heart'.

134/6. *be him-zelue of al | ine god y-leue*: C *Par soi du tout en dieu fier* 'by trusting wholly in God'; DM's translation hardly makes sense.

134/16. *bouerȝe*: C *sauuer*; Evers (p. 100) takes this to be for *borȝe*. *MED* (Borwen 3 (a)) reads as *borwen* (OE *borgian*); but OE *borgian* should give *borgi* not *borge* (cf. Jensen, p. 22). It seems more likely that Wallenberg (p. 26, n. 1) is right in thinking that the spelling indicates a glide after *b* unless it is simply an error. On either assumption the verb is *berȝe* from OE *beorgan*.

134/15-16. Cf. Titus 3: 8.

134/22-4. *ac hi ham hyealdeþ | and ȝiggeþ ase þe gauelere he him halt to þe wynnynge þanne to þe simple worde ne wyle nonen yleue*: C *ains se tienent ce dient ausi comme li useriers se tient au gaaing qui a la simple parole ne veut nului croire*; there are a number of problems here (i) C's reading *ains se tienent ce dient* is shared with G1 but appears to be erroneous. The readings of the majority of the other manuscripts at this point divide into two: (a) *il ne (le) croiront ia ce dient* (P1, 12, Add1); (b) *en quanque il dit mais a la uiue raison se tienent (ce ne vaut) ce dient* (P2, 6, 7, 8, 9, 10, 13, 16, M, A2, G4, 5, An, V, Ca1, R1). The latter gives the best sense. (ii) the reading *gaaing (wynnynge)*, shared with G1, is an error for *gage*; (iii) nor is *and ȝiggeþ* an accurate rendering of *ce dient*. (iv) DM's *þanne* is wrong. He has rendered *que* (P1, 12, V, Add1). The text could be emended to *ine þet he zaiþ huet þet hit by. Ac hi ham hyealdeþ to þe kuike scele (þis ȝiggeþ) ase þe gauelere him halt to þe wedde þet to þe simple word ne wylleþ nonen yleue* (Cf. Wallenberg, p. 115, n. 1). *Se tenir* here means 'to stick to', 'believe in'.

134/28. *me*: C *il*; DM has slightly altered the sense by rendering *il* 'he' as 'one'. But he also uses *he* for 'one'. Cf. 237/21.

134/31. *him þet ne may naȝt lyeȝe*: C *ce que cil ne puet mentir*; the correct reading is probably as P1, 2, 4, M, An, V, Ld, Ca1, (R1): *ce que cil dit qui ne peut mentir* (or rev.) 'that which he who cannot lie says'. The English, however, makes sense as it stands. Cf. Evers, p. 100.

134/32. *him-zelue*: C *ce meismes*; the sense of the whole passage appears to be: 'We believe a hundred times more him who cannot lie than we do miracles or reason or even that which we see'. DM has perhaps taken *ce meismes* 'that thing itself' to mean 'he himself'. But it must be remembered that DM uses *him* as the neuter reflexive and thus *him zelue* is probably correct for 'itself', 'that thing itself'.

135/5. *Efterward ase*: C *Apres si*com*me*; the French has a paragraph sign before *Apres* but it would seem to be an error. The sense follows on from what precedes and *Apres* is unnecessary. DM's *Efterward*, a literal rendering of *Apres*, should accordingly be omitted.

135/9. *to*: an odd rendering of Fr. *du*. The English may have been suggested by the sound of *du*; or DM may have intended to supply an infinitive.

135/12. *naȝt of hi*m: C *nient de soi*; the reading *nient de debte* which appears in A2, M, Ca1 gives better sense. The English text should, perhaps, read *naȝt of riȝt*. G1 has the same reading as C.

135/13. *lefþ . . . of*: C *croit . . . de*; some early manuscripts have *trait* for *croit* (so E except G1, An) and *a* for *de* (E except G1). These readings are to be preferred on grounds of sense and the English should read *draȝþ . . . to*. G1 shares the reading of C.

135/18–19. *mid riȝtuolle oninge of herte*: C *de droit assentement de cuer*; as Evers pointed out (p. 101), DM seems to have taken this phrase as parallel to *mid zoþe teares* but it, in fact, depends, like *of godes grace*, upon *comeþ*, Emend *mid* to *of*. The reading *sentement* (P4, A2, M, An, V, Ca1, R1) is perhaps to be preferred to *assentement*.

135/20. *echedaye*: C *tous iors*; the correct reading *touz nuz* appears in all E manuscripts except G1. The English text should read *al naked*. G1 has the erroneous reading of C.

135/23. *endy*: C *finer*; Evers (p. 101) pointed out that *finer* here means 'pay' and not 'end'. Emend to *paye*. *Hit* should read *he*.

135/24. *y-nome and mid mo*: C *pris a plus*; as Evers pointed out (p. 101), DM has erroneously inserted *and* after *ynome*.

135/25. *ine þe nykke*: C *ou col*; the English should read *aboute þe nykke*. Cf. Evers, p. 101.

136/6. *y-rewarded*: C *regarde* 'observes'; the French verb is 3 pr. sg. and both grammar and sense are wrong. The English should read *nymþ hede* and *of* should be supplied before *alle* (5). Cf. Wallenberg, p. 203, n. 5. Cf. 74/4 and note to 120/18 for the confusion of *reward* and *regard*.

136/8. *ondo*: C *refais*; read *ayenimad*. DM's manuscript may have read *defais* as Evers suggested (p. 101).

136/9. *hit is y-bore*: C *est neis*; DM appears to have identified *neis* 'even' with *nez* the ppl. of the verb *naistre*, misled by the erroneous *est* which appears only in G1, C (cf. Evers, p. 101). The sense is 'even of stones and flint can he suck oil'. Friar Lorenz has conflated two passages here; Deuteronomy 32: 13 and Psalm 80 (81): 17.

136/10. *oly*: this form represents an AN *olie*. Cf. *OED* OIL *sb.*¹

136/11. *wille*: C *uoit*; DM seems to have read *ueut* for *uoit*. Emend *wille* to *zizþ*. Cf. Evers, p. 101.

136/22. *ine guode*: C *en bien* 'as good';

136/33. *of asemoche þet*: C *de tant come*; DM's rendering is hardly English.

137/1–2. *and doþ alneway. and makeþ alneway semblont*: C *e font tous iors semblance*; DM has rendered the French twice. Omit *and doþ alneway*.

137/9–10. *ne wenþ*: C *nequedent* 'notwithstanding'; Evers pointed out (p. 102) that DM has read the French as *ne cuident*. Cp. 126/11; *and* in line 10 should be omitted.

137/10–12. Genesis 18: 27.

137/14–17. This seems to be a conflation of a number of passages in Job. Cf. 7: 5, 7; 8: 9; 14: 2; 17: 14; 13: 25; 20: 7; 25: 6; 30: 19.

137/15–16. *smech*: C *fueille*; *gadereþ*: C *escuiele*; both these readings are erroneous; the Latin text has *contra folium, quod vento rapitur, ostendis potentiam tuam, et stipulam siccam persequeris* (Job, 13: 25). For the first, DM probably rendered *fumee*, as Evers (p. 102) suggested. For the second, the correct reading of the French is *estoule, esteule, estouble* etc. 'stubble' (P1, 6, 12, 16, G4, An, Ca1, Add1) of which the readings *escuiele, escuel(l)e*, etc. are simply corruptions (P2, 5, 7, 10, 11, A2, M, G1, Ld, C). DM has supposed the word to be part of the verb *escueillir* as Evers pointed out (p. 102). The reading *escoupe, estoupe* (P8, 9, G5, V, R1) is clearly erroneous.

137/20–3. Cf. Jerome, *Regula Monacharum*, Cap. xxx (PL xxx, col. 417).

137/23. *went*: C *corne*; DM has rendered the French as *torne*. The letters *t* and *c* are alike in most of the French manuscripts. Read *blauþ*.

137/23–5. *And þeruore þe ilke . . . hiere: himzelue to deme*: C *Et por ce quil ne veut pas estre la iugies :' ne se fine onques ci de soi iugier*; 'And since he does not wish to be condemned there, never does he cease from judging himself here.' A more precise translation would be *And þeruore þet he nele nazt by þer demd; endi* should read *endeþ*. Cf. 28–30.

137/31. *ine þe cort of merci*: the punctuation is misleading here. This phrase goes with what follows: 'In the court of mercy, that is, in holy confession; in that court, whoever gives a true account, he is entirely acquitted'.

137/35. *aquitti he ne may*: C *aquiter ne sen þurra*; the intransitive use of *aquitti* is odd and should perhaps be rectified by providing an object as in the French. The text would then read *him aquitti of hit ne may*. Cf. Evers, p. 102.

137/36. See note to 31/1–2.

138/7–8. *bote þe demere . . . yprayzed treweliche*: C *se la iustice nest apres prise loiaument* 'unless justice is afterwards duly exacted'. As Evers (p. 102) pointed out, DM has taken *prise* from *prisier* 'to praise' and *justice* as *justicier*. Read *dom* for *þe demere* and *ido* for *yprayzed*. Cf. note to 130/5.

138/11. *and zuo deþ*: C *ensi en fait*; omit *and* which vitiates the construction as Evers pointed out (p. 102).

138/23–7. Cf. Psalm 13 (14): 6; 67 (68): 10–11; 101 (102): 18 (New Version).

138/27–8. Job 29: 16.

138/28–31. Luke 6: 20, 24.

139/1–3. Luke 10: 21.

139/15. *hi ne zecheþ*: for *hi* read *he* (cf. Glossary **he**); for *zecheþ* read *zecþ*.

139/17. *heþ*: C *a a*; the French is an error which DM at first copied by writing *heþ to*. He then perceived that it was an error and crossed out *to*.

139/19. *biterneses*: C *damertumes*; the manuscript has *biternese* (with final *e* above the line) but Morris's emendation is no doubt correct.

139/28. *do*: C *fait*; *do* should perhaps be emended to *deþ*; but it could represent a subjunctive of unrealized comparison. The meaning would be 'than he would do' etc.

139/31. *dyamod*: C *dyamans*; Evers (p. 102) suggested that the French means 'loadstone' and not 'diamond'. But for the setting of the diamond, or adamant, in gold and steel see P. Studer and J. Evans, *Anglo-Norman Lapidaries* (Paris, 1924), pp. 74, 120. Read *dyamond*.

139/34.–140/1. Matthew 13:30; cf. Matthew 3: 12, Luke 3: 17.

140/21. *niede bote uor him-zelue*: C *que besoigner por soi*; DM probably intended to write *bote niede uor him-selue* 'only need as far as he is concerned'.

140/23. *he y-hyerþ*: C *il oent*; DM no doubt mistook *il* for the singular and altered the verb to match. Emend to *hi yhyereþ*.

140/25–8. *huanne he heþ . . . mid to greate blisse* etc.: C *quant il a le commandement son mestre receu, que les periex e les paines e la mort il recoit auoec a tres grant ioie*; the sentence is awkward but is substantiated by the majority of the manuscripts. The translation appears to be 'when he hath received the command of his master, for he receives with it perils and torments and death with very great joy'.

140/29–31. Psalm 118 (119): 127.

141/7. *mid*: C *ou*; DM seems to have misunderstood *ou* as *ouec* (*avec*); *mid* should be emended to *oþer*. Cf. 161/28, 199/4, 200/17.

141/9–13. Translate 'As the star which is called Saturn does, which traverses as much, with the firmament, in a single day, when propelled by the firmament, as it does in thirty years, in its own circuit, and on its own course'. In line 9 the second *is* should be omitted.

141/16. *lyad. ase þet corn*: C *plonc* com*me or. e le ble*; DM has omitted *or. e*. Read *lyad ase gold. and þet corn* etc.

141/19. Cf. Isaiah 40: 31.

141/19. *nis he naȝt*: C *nest il riens*; 'there is nothing'. Read *nis þer naȝt*. DM has mistaken the neuter *il* for the masculine. Evers (p. 103) noted a cross above *bere* and inferred that DM realized that the sense of the passage was defective.

141/22. *ne þe ȝonne*: C *ne que li solaus*; DM's text must have read *ne li solaus*. Emend to *þanne þe ȝonne*.

141/24. Perhaps a reference to Proverbs 6: 6 where the ant is used as an exemplar of diligence.

141/33. *him pineþ*: C*il se peine*; perhaps read *him paineþ*. Cf. Wallenberg, p. 190, n. 2.

141/34–5. *of him-ȝelue ansuerie*: C *de soi repondre*; Evers (p. 103) suggested that DM had confused *repondre* 'conceal' with *respondre* 'answer'. Emend *of* to *to* and *ansuerie* to *hede*.

141/35–142/1. *þet gadereþ uor þe rage*: C *se coile por lorage*; *OED* glosses *rage* here as 'violence' but the French suggests that the meaning is probably 'storm of wind' (cf. *OED* RAGE *sb.* 4c). DM seems to have read *se* as *ce* (whence *þet*) and *coile* (from *cueillir*) for *çoile* (from *celer*) 'conceal'. Cf. Evers, p. 103. Read *him het* for *þet gadereþ*. The whole passage down to 142/2 depends on Isaiah 32: 2.

142/4–5. Psalm 103 (104): 18.

142/5. *þet by* renders French *ce sont* and should probably read *þet byeþ*. As Wallenberg pointed out (p. 32, n. 1), the loss of final *þ* is probably due to the following *þe*. Cf. p. 52.

142/7. *huerinne resteþ and him deþ þe colure oure lhord*: C *ou se refuient e se repounent li colombiau n*ostre seign*ur; *resteþ* is an imprecise translation of *refuient* 'take refuge'; *repounent* is from *repondre* 'conceal' for which *deþ* is also an inexact translation. The French verbs are plural but DM has made them singular. The phrase *þe colure oure lhord* is an appositive genitive rendering *li colombiau nostre seignur*.

142/10. *heþ ȝuo moche ydo*: renders *a tant fait*.

142/15. *willieþ*: read *wilneþ*.

142/22. *quereles*: C *quereles*; the sense is probably 'debate', 'discourse'. Cf. Godefroy, QUERELE.

142/23. *he him*: C *se deresne*; the reading of C is supported by all the E manuscripts except P4. DM has omitted the verb. Read *spekþ* for *him*.

142/24. *stedeuest*: C *feruanz*; the French means 'fervent', 'earnest', and the meaning of *stedeuest* here is probably 'earnest'.

142/25–7. Cf. Psalm 24 (25): 14 (New Version).

142/31. *ane*: is probably an error for *an*; but cf. p. 70. The form *doþter* should perhaps be plural. C has *une des plus belles filles*. But DM may have intended to write *on þe uayreste doȝter*. For the spelling see the note to 40/5.

142/33. *heþ þanne*: C *quant*; *heþ* is added before *þanne* above the line. It is clearly incorrect and should be omitted.

143/4. 2 Corinthians 12: 2.

143/6–8. *þe ilke holy zaule . . . be-tuene hire | and an holy prede*: C *que cele sainte ame commence a auoir de dieu entre ele en un saint orguel*; as Evers pointed out (p. 104), DM has not perceived that *entre* is here a verbal form and has translated by *be-tuene*. He has also rendered *en* erroneously as *and*. Emend *be-tuene hire | and* to *hi geþ into*, and supply *þet* before *þe ilke*.

143/8. *þanne*: C *duques* 'right to'; emend to *al to*. DM has confused *dusques* and *donques*. Cf. Evers, p. 104 and 119/24, 144/8.

143/9. Isaiah 51: 6.

143/10. *and hise yzyȝþ z[u]o*: C *e la ou uoit si*; the majority of E manuscripts read *e (ele) la uoit si* (so P4, A2, M, V, Ld, Ca1, R1). If this is correct, a new sentence begins at *þanne* (line 13). It is possible that the reading *e la ou uoit* of C, G1 represents *e la o uoit* 'and behold she sees it!'; for *o = es* see Godefroy, ES. There is no need to emend *zo* to *zuo*.

143/11. *zuo y-zicþ*: C *si regarde*; the reading of C (shared by G1) is erroneous as comparison with other early manuscripts shows. The correct reading appears to be *(7 si) laide au regart de* as P1, A2, M, An, V, (Ld), Ca1, Add1, R1. The English should read *zuo onuayr to þe ziȝþe of* etc.

143/14–32. The pronouns in this passage are confused in both the French and the English. The subject throughout is *þe ilke holy zaule* which is referred to as *hi (ele)* throughout the passage. But DM has wrongly rendered *il a = il y a* at 143/14 as *he heþ* (cf. note to 105/15). He also repeats *he* without a French model at 143/19. On the other hand, *li*, rendered at 143/15, 18, 22–32 by *him* is strictly feminine and should read *hire*.

143/20–1. Cf. Romans 6: 11; Galatians 2: 19–20.

143/23. *ayen y-ueld*: C *raempli*; cf. 144/12–13. That the verb is not a compound, in spite of the French, is suggested by 58/5 where *velþ his ayen* renders *raemplent*.

143/27. *Ane zuo greate zikernesse*: C *Vne si grant seurte*; cf. P4, (Ld) *a une si grant seurte*; R1 *li vient vne si grant seurte*. Supply *heþ* after *zikernesse*.

143/30–3. Matthew 17: 19.

144/1–8. Bernard, *Epistolae*, xi (PL clxxxii, cols. 113–14). Cf. *De Dili-gendo Deo*, viii–x (Leclercq, Rochais, iii (1963), 138–44).

144/7–9. Francis (note to VV 142/25 f.) seems to approve Morris's emendation of *god* to *guod* in line 7; but this is wrong. The contrast is with the second stage of self-love in which a man loves God for his own profit. In the fourth stage, he loves God for himself alone. The fourth stage is thus contrasted both with pure self-love and with the love of God for one's own profit, the two stages of self-love. The third and fourth stages of love, on the other hand, are two stages of the love of God; love of God for his goodness and love of God for himself alone. The text here summarizes the last two stages, the love of God in which a man loves neither himself nor God but for God alone. Result clauses usually take the indicative and we should perhaps emend *louie* to *loueþ*; *þanne hyer* in line 8 renders French *dusque ci* 'so far', 'as far as this'. As Evers (p. 104) pointed out, DM has again misread *dusque* as *donques* (cf. 119/24, 143/8). For *þanne hyer* read *al to hyer*.

144/13–15. *uelþ ʒuo moche þet hi uelþ þe mylde. þet hi his makeþ king of heuene*: C *lessauce tant cis qui essauce les humbles que il les fait roi du ciel*; there are a number of errors here: (i) *essauce* means 'exalt' and not 'fulfil' (cf. Evers, p. 104). (ii) *þet hi*[1] should read *he þet* (iii) the second *hi* should also read *he* (iv) the first *uelþ* requires an object. Cotton has *l'* but it should be plural. Thus the whole sentence should read *hise anheʒeþ ʒuo moche he þet anheʒeþ þe mylde þet he his makeþ king of heuene* 'he who exalts the humble so greatly exalts them that he makes them king of heaven'.

144/16. Matthew 5: 3.

144/19. *hou*: begins a new sentence.

145/3–4. *manhede, louerede*: C *humain, amiable*; these readings may be due to DM's having read the French adjectives as nouns (cf. Evers, p. 105) and the forms should, perhaps, be emended to *manli, loueli* 'friendly'. It is, however, worth noting that the noun *louerede* is used as an adjective in the Middle English translation of the *Horologium Sapientiae* (*MED* s.v.) and it is possible that both *manhede* and *louerede* are adjectives here and that *-hede* represents a reduced form of *-hedi*. Cf. Wallenberg, p. 155, n. 5.

145/6–10. Ephesians 4: 3–4.

145/16. *heþ yssape*: C *a forme*; the best reading seems to be *a une forme* (so P4, A2, M, G1, An, V, Ca1; P1, Add1 read *dune forme*; R1 *en une forme*). The English text should read *of one ssepinge*.

145/16–17. John 17: 21–3. The words *þet is þet we by . . . ine his spelle* (16–17) are in parenthesis. *Mochil* in line 18 depends on *þeruore* in line 14.

145/18–19. Ecclesiasticus 13: 19.

145/27. *scele*: *is* should be supplied after *scele* although it is not in Cotton.

145/28–30. Romans 13: 9, Galatians 5: 14.

146/2. *þos*: C *se*; as Evers pointed out (p. 105), DM has misread *se* as *si*. Read *ham*.

146/5. *þet*: MS *þeþ*; the form *þeþ* appears again at 228/20. While a form *þeþ* might occur by assimilation before a dental spirant, it is unlikely to develop before a vowel or *w*. The forms are probably best explained as due to dittography.

146/7–8. *y-hote*: C com*mandee*; P1, M, An, Ld, Ca1, Add1 have (*en*)-*commence* which is clearly the correct reading. Read *begonne*.

146/9. *bodylich*: C *corporelment*; we should expect *bodyliche*. The same form appears at 240/36 and at 200/16 but these are most probably due to elision. It is just possible that the forms are postponed adjectives but, in view of the French, it is more likely that we should emend to *bodyliche*. Cf. Wallenberg, p. 39, n. 1.

146/12. *ane*: the sense requires *one* for *ane*. Cf. note to 17/22.

146/17. *þet we libbeþ*: C *qui uiuons*; the English could mean 'in that we live' but it seems more likely that the addition of *we* is inadvertent and that it should be omitted.

146/32. *angrisi*: C *angoisse*; cf. 147/2 *angrice*. Wallenberg points out that the abbreviation sign is in fact for *ui* not for *ri* and that the forms should therefore be read *anguisi*, *anguice* (see Wallenberg, p. 11, n. 5). Emend *angrisi* to *anguisi* and *angrice* to *anguice*.

146/36. *þin riȝt hand*: C *que ta main destre*; this may be an error for *þi riȝt hand*; *þet* should perhaps be supplied before *þin* but the construction is adequate as it stands. For *þin* cf. 107/9 and discussion p. 51.

147/5. *to uoluelle*: C par*fete*; read *uolueld* 'perfect'.

147/13–14. Perhaps a reference to 1 Peter 4: 8.

147/16. *grochinge*: C *dang*er; Evers (p. 105) suggested that DM's text read *murmure*.

147/18–23. The sentence is awkward. *þanne a man hua*nne is correlative with *Ac þanne* 'when a man . . . then'. This is parallel to C's *Dont uns hons quant . . . Adonc*.

147/19. *him a-cordeþ . . . mid þe helpe*: C *secort . . . du pooir*; DM's manuscript may have had *s'acort* for *secort*. He has also mistranslated *pooir*. Cf. Evers, p. 105.

147/20. *oþer him ret / oþer tekþ*: C *ou il conseille e enseigne*; Evers (p. 105) assumed that the object is missing here and that DM read *il* as *li* and so rendered *him*. It is possible, however, that *þe oþre* (19) should be taken as singular; in that case, *him* would be an appropriate object. DM may have had the reading which appears in R1 : *ou li conseille ou enseigne*.

147/24–6. Perhaps a reference to 2 Peter 1: 3–7.

147/25. *guodnesse*: C *graces*; the text should perhaps read *guodnesses*.

147/28–9. *þe man . . . byeþ beyete*: C *li home . . . sont engendrez*; *li home* is plural but DM has translated as singular with resulting confusion of number. Emend *þe man* to *men*.

147/31–2. A common Pauline image but see especially 1 Corinthians 12: 12 ff.

148/1–2. The 'tuaye offices' are explained below; see 1 Corinthians 12: 26.

148/4. *þo[u]*: there is no need to emend; cf. 51/1, 56/8, 102/26 where Morris leaves the form unemended. Cf. p. 15.

148/14. *ine hi*m: C *a lui*; read *to hi*m.

148/15–17. Cf. Seneca, *De Clementia*, I, xvii, ed. C. Hosius (Leipzig, 1914), p. 234.

148/18. *amendes*: C *correction*; this is an unusual sense of *amendes* although it is not uncommon for *amendment*. *MED* (AMENDE(s n. 5), however, cites *Catholicon Anglicanum, An amendes*: *emenda, emendacio, correccio*. The meaning here, therefore, should probably be accepted. It should be noted, however, that the reading *correption* 'blame' gives better sense (so P1, 4, An, Ld, R1).

148/21–2. *efterward*: C *apres*; Evers (p. 105) pointed out that DM has confused *apres* 'bitter' with the adverb.

148/23. *þe dedes*: C *le fes*; Evers (p. 105) pointed out that *fes* is a miswriting of *fer(s)*, the reading of all the E manuscripts, except Ld, G1, which have the reading of C. Read *þe ysnes*.

148/23. *techinge*: C *discipline*; although 'instruction' is a possible meaning of *discipline*, the metaphor suggests that the meaning here is 'discipline'.

148/23–4. *yef he . . . emparement*: C *sil ne fet se empirier non* 'if he only gets worse'. DM's translation is a word-for-word rendering of the French. Evers (p. 105) suggested that the pronouns *he* and *hit* (24) referred to *herte*.

148/26. *oþer hi*m *do uram hi*m-*zelue*: C *ou laloigner de soi*: possibly a word is missing in Cotton; or *de soi* is a corruption of the possessive *des soens*. VV. reads (147/6–7) *or to do hym fer away out of þe companye* and the sense of *des soens* would be 'from his own (people)'.

148/26–8. 1 Corinthians 12: 25, 26.

148/33. *þos[t]*: no need to emend. See page 49.

149/1. *him zet uor hi*m: C *se met por lui*; DM's translation is a calque on the French.

149/1–2. Whiting F 634 and cf. 186/21–2.

149/5–7. John 15: 13.

149/9–12. 1 Peter 2: 21; 1 John 3: 16.

149/13. *is þet*: C *est il*; read *he* for *þet*.

149/15. *by þe riȝte yblissed*: C *seroit le droit boneures*; the correct reading appears to be *seroit adroit boneures* as P4 (*droitement*), A2, M, V, Ca1, Add1, R1. G1 shares the erroneous reading of C. The text should read *by riȝte yblissed*.

149/16–18. Matthew 5: 4.

149/21. *Ase*: this is not a new sentence as the capital might suggest. It goes with what precedes.

149/22–5. *And þeruor þet god þet is þe land of þe libbinde: he heþ his y-blissed in his saysine. uor hi ne makeþ none strengþe þet quemeþ god ine hire sayzyne / ase zayþ þe sauter*: C *e por ce que diex qui est la terre des uiuanz a les boneurez en sa possession. car il ne font rien de force qui plest a dieu en lor possession sicom dist li sautiers*; reference to other manuscripts clarifies the latter part of this passage. C and G1 have *de force qui* instead of the correct *fors ce qui* of the majority of the manuscripts. These two manuscripts have also omitted *pour ce est drois que il aient dieu* before *en lor possession*. The text should thus read: *uor hi ne makeþ naȝt bote þet þet quemþ god. þeruor biþ riȝt þet hi habbe god ine hire sayzyne*; 'For they do nothing but what is pleasing to God. Therefore it is right that they should possess God.' The passage refers to two Psalter passages: *mansueti autem haereditabunt terram* (Psalm 36 (37): 11) and *Tu es refugium meum, Portio mea in terra viventium* (141 (142): 6 Rev. V.). Augustine (*Enn. in Psalmos*, Psalm 36: 29) identifies the land which the meek shall inherit with the 'land of the living' and in his commentary on 141: 6, the portion in the 'land of the living' is identified with God himself who is the portion of those who love him. Thus the meek possess God (PL. xxvi, xxxvii, cols. 390, 1840).

The former part of the passage, however, is obscure in all the manuscripts. It seems likely that there was a case of homoeoteleuton at an early stage in the history of the manuscripts. It may be conjectured that the French originally read: *et pour ce diex qui est la terre des uiuanz a les boneurez* (or, as some manuscripts, *debonnaires*) *en sa possession [et les boneurez* (or *debonnaires*) *ont dieu en lor possession] Car* etc. This would eliminate the apparent contradiction in the text. DM could then be emended to read: *And þeruor god þet is þe land of þe libbinde heþ his y-blissed in his saysine and þe yblissede habbeþ god in hire saysine. Vor* etc.

149/25–6. *þe milde zayþ / he ssel habbe þet land ine kende*: C *Li deboneire dist il auront la terre en heritage*; this goes with what precedes and refers again to Psalm 36: 11: *mansueti autem haereditabunt terram*. DM has taken it as a new sentence and has thus assumed *Li deboneire* as subject of *dist*. Emend to '*þe milde*', *hit zayþ*, '*ssel habbe* etc.'

149/26–7. Augustine, *De Salutaribus Documentis*, x (PL. xl, col. 1050).

149/27–8. *ine possession. Vor hi byeþ riȝtuolliche lhordes of hire herten. ac ire*: C *en possession ? car il sont droitement seignor de leur cuer mais ire*; G1, Ca1 agree with C in erroneous readings here. All other E manuscripts except P4, R1 read: *en possession qui ne sera premierement en la sieue. Apres li debonnaire ont si la terre de leur cuers en possession car il sont droitement seigneur de leur cuers. Li felon ne sont pas (seigneur de leurs cuers) mes ire* etc.

149/29. *amaystreþ*: both the French text and the sense show this to be plural.

149/29–32. Proverbs 16: 32.

150/5. *þet þet god*: C *que se dieu*; as Evers (p. 106) pointed out, DM has taken *se* as *ce*. Read *þet yef god*. There should be a question mark after *helle* in line 7. The first *þet* is strictly tautological.

150/6. *þe bitere*: C *li auier* 'the avaricious'; DM misread as *amer* 'bitter'. Cf. Evers (p. 106). Emend to *þe wrechchen*.

150/7. *wyþoute*: C *fors* 'except'.

150/13–14. *amesureþ*: C *amesure en*; Evers (p. 106) pointed out that DM took *amesure* as pr. 3 sg. instead of ppl. adj. and left out *en*. Emend to *amesured ine*.

150/21–3. Cf. Apocalypse 4: 6.

150/24–5. Zechariah 3: 9.

150/27. *abo[u]te*: the vowel was originally long and Morris's emendation may be correct; but see p. 15.

150/30. *to wylle*: C *a point*; 'precisely' is presumably the sense which DM assumed. But it seems possible that in view of the following phrases it means 'with a pricker'; that is to say, like the line, the rule, the plummet, and the level, it serves to guide the workman.

150/32. *his pricke and his boune*: C *son point e sa boune*; DM seems not to have understood *boune* as he left a gap in the text and wrote the French word in the margin. Wallenberg (p. 42, n. 5) points out that it is OF *boune* 'boundary stone', 'boundary'. The reading is supported by all manuscripts but one. Cotton seems to begin a new sentence with *Il prent* (*he nimþ* 32) but VV (149/17–19) reads *for it makeþ al þing to þe poynt wel in rule in lyne and leuel; riȝt by þe led first he takeþ his merke and his lyne*. This may be right. If so, we should read for the *Ayenbite*: *and to þe leuele* (*a liuel*) *he nimþ uerst his pricke and his boune* 'and at ground level he first takes his position and his limit'. This fits what follows and gives better sense than the meaning 'plumb-line' suggested by *MED* (BOUNE n.) in spite of the support given by VV *his merke and his lyne*. The quotation suggests that the workman is here measuring out the starting-point and the end of his work. If this is correct, DM has also misunderstood *point* 'position'. Cf. Godefroy and Compl. s.v.

150/33–4. Ecclesiasticus 7: 40: *In omnibus operibus tuis memorare novissima tua*.

150/34. *heauede*: C *chief*; the French here means 'end'. Emend to *ende*.

150/35. *he ne heþ*: C *il ua*; DM has read *ua* as *n'a*. Emend to *he geþ*.

151/3. *man*: C *ouni*; as Evers pointed out (p. 106), DM has read *ouni* 'level' as *omme* and translated 'man'. Emend *man* to *smeþe*.

151/3–4. *be þe commune lyue of þe guode*: C *par la commune uie des bons*; this reading appears also in G1 but other early manuscripts read *car* for *par* and supply *il aime* after *bons* (so P1, 4, A2, M, An, Ld, Ca1, Add1; V, R1 have *hante* for *aime*). This clearly makes better sense than the reading of G1, C. The English text should read *uor þe commune lyf of þe guode he loueþ*.

151/4. *newe hedes*: C *noueletes*; read *newehedes*.

151/9. *deþ hi loki*: C *fet garder*; DM has supplied an object, *hi*, which may be a slip for *him* or *hit* as *ordre* was feminine but later masculine. For *hi* as acc. fem. see note to 95/10. Cf. p. 92.

151/14. *guod wil uelþ*: C *affection sent*; DM seems to have spoilt the sense by substituting *guod wil* 'right intention' for 'affection', 'feeling'. The contrast is clearly put by VV 150/4–5: *and affection feleþ þat þ*ᵗ *resoun vnderstant*.

151/30. *to þe zaule to þe loue of god*: C *a lame. a lamour de dieu*; Gı shares the reading of C. Other early manuscripts read *au salut de lame et qui plus maine a lamor de dieu* (so (P4), A2, M, An, V, Ld, Caı, Addı, Rı; Pı reads between *ame* and *et qui, et por son proisme haidier*). The English text should, perhaps, read *to helpe of zaule and mest let þe zaule to þe loue of god*.

152/3–6. Seneca, *Letters*, 3. 4 (Reynolds, p. 5).

152/6–7. *Efterward wel acsi: wile wel deme*: C *Apres bien enquerre ueut bien iugier*: the sentence means 'after right inquiry comes right judgement'. Evers rightly suggested (p. 107) that the French should read *u(i)ent* for *ueut*. In fact, of the early manuscripts, only Gı shares the reading of C. The others read *uient*. The English text should read *comþ* for *wile*. The infinitive phrase *Wel to deme*, in line 7, functions as a dative governed by *belongeþ*.

152/8. *þanne bote yef me by ziker*: C *dont on ne soit certeins*; as Evers pointed out (p. 107), DM has confused the pronoun *dont* with the adverb. It seems, also, that his text had *se* 'if' before *on* whence *bote yef*. Emend to *and huerof me nis ziker*. Lines 7–8 may thus be rendered: 'It appertains to right judgement that one affirm nothing unless it has been well investigated and of which one is not certain.'

152/10–13. *Þe onderstondinges of herten | of þinges þet ne moȝe torni* . . . *ariȝt ine þe guode half*: C *les entencions des cuers. des choses* con *ne puet torner a destre e a senestre que homme les entende ades en la bone partie*; DM seems to have understood *ades* as *adroit* and *ariȝt* should be emended to *zone*. (Cf. Evers, p. 107.) The rest of the passage, however, can hardly be correct as it stands. Two emendations are necessary in the French: (i) for *des choses* the text should read *les choses* or *e les choses* as the majority of the manuscripts; (ii) the negative should be omitted before *puet* as in a number of French manuscripts (P4–7, 9–13, 15, A2, M, G4, 5, Caı, Addı). The passage then reads: *þe onderstondinges of herten (and) þe þinges þet moȝe torni* . . . *zone ine þe guode half*. It should also be noted that *þe onderstondinges* does not begin a new sentence but is in apposition to *þe þinges anhyalde*. The sense of lines 9–13 is: 'Right judgement will not concern itself with matters not proper to it such as matters arcane, the intentions of men's hearts, and matters morally ambiguous, which must be instantly interpreted in a good sense.'

152/13. *Þanne*: C *Dom*; Evers (p. 107) pointed out that the French represents the pronoun *dont*. DM, however, took it as an adverb and this makes adequate sense. The capital letter and the preceding paragraph sign suggest that C also took it as the adverb. Cf. 155/1.

152/19–20. The reference seems to be to John 14: 26; 16: 13–14. The phrase *he beþengþ to þe manne | al þet him is nyed* renders *il rementoit a lome quanque mestier li est.* This is perhaps a translation of *docebit omnia* in John 14: 26 or *docebit vos omnem veritatem* in John 16: 13. At 152/19, *beþenche* probably means 'reflect' and *beþengþ* 'causes to consider', 'teaches'; *rementevoir a* usually means 'call to mind'.

152/23. *poruay*: emend to *poruaye*. Cf. Jensen, p. 33.

152/28–9. Proverbs 10: 20.

152/34. *ye[u]e*: Morris's emendation is unnecessary. Cf. note to 46/9.

152/35–6. Matthew 7: 6.

153/3–6. *þet is | þet he habbe . . . and þet me yleue . . . ase me ssel*: C *ce est que on aint ce quil doit. e si*com *il doit. e tant* com *on doit. que on crient ausi ce* con *doit. e si*com *on doit. e tant* com *on doit*; DM's text seems to have diverged at several points from C: (i) for the correct *aint* he had *ait*, a reading which appears in P4, 7, 9, 13, G1, G5, V, Add2, R1; *habbe* should, accordingly, be altered to *louie*; (ii) *crient* he has taken from *croire* instead of from *criembre*; accordingly, *yleue* should read *drede*; (iii) a fuller reading appears in many manuscripts: after the words *que on crieme ausi comme on doit ce con doit 7 tant comme on doit* which conclude the passage cited above, they add *Que len nait ioie ne delit fors en ce que len doit | e sicomme on doit 7 tant comme len doit. Et que on nait doleur fors de ce que on doit et si comme on doit et tant comme on doit.* Thus, the four operations of the will, love, fear, joy, sorrow, are to be exercised in three ways: in regard to their proper object; in their proper manner; and in their proper degree. The essential symmetry of the passage suggests that the fuller reading is correct.

153/7. *atamed*: only an approximately correct rendering of French *atrempees*. (Cf. Evers, p. 107.)

153/8. *one . . . one*: *one* is possibly for *ane*. Cf. note to 17/22.

153/10. *ne to wet*: C *ne trop moiste*; P1, G1, Ld, read as C but other E manuscripts read *ne trop moiste ne trop seiche* or the reverse. The English ought to read *ne to wet ne to draye*.

153/14. *þeawes*: C *.iiij. meurs*; DM has omitted the numeral. Read *uour þeawes*.

153/17. *roten*: C *rainsel*; Evers (p. 108) pointed out that here, as at 130/13, DM has mistranslated *rainsel* 'bough'. But here, at least, his text may have had the reading which appears in R1, *racuel*, possibly with the sense of *racine*. Cf. Godefroy, RACHUEL. Read *boȝes*.

153/22. *onlepiliche*: C *oniement* 'uniformly'; the sense is unusual for the English but Wallenberg (p. 177, n. 1) is perhaps right in pointing out that *onhede* means 'unity' as well as 'solitude' and that accordingly it might be supposed that *onlepiliche* could mean 'with singleness of purpose' here.

153/25. *iustise*: see note to 130/5.

154/13–14. *ine hosiynge | and ine ssoinge*: as at 177/16–17, this renders French *chaucer*, as Evers (p. 108) pointed out.

154/15–16. *to moche . . . þe litle*: C *trop . . . poy*; *to moche* could mean 'excess'. Morris's note is probably to be deleted in spite of *þe litle*.

154/24–5. Jeremiah 9: 21.

154/30. *deþ þerto*: C *si met*; Evers (p. 108) pointed out that *deþ* appears to have no object. It seems that DM, having partly rendered *si* (*s'y*) by *þerto*, forgot the reflexive. The text should read *him deþ þerto*.

154/33. Job 18: 9.

154/33–4. *þet to timliche [eyse]*: C *cest as temporeles*; as Evers (p. 108) pointed out, DM has mistaken *c'est* for *cest* and the text should be emended to *þet is to timliche* etc. On the other hand, Morris's emendation is unnecessary. DM has translated French *as temporeles* literally. If emendation is needed it would be better to read *to timliche þinges*. It may be noted, however, that C (and G1) is probably wrong here. Other E manuscripts read *cest aus plez aus querellez*. Cf. 158/33–4 and note.

155/1. *þanne*: C *dom*; as Evers (p. 108) pointed out the French is for *dont* 'wherefore'. Read *hueruore*. Cf. 152/13.

155/3. For *zeneзþ* see Glossary.

155/3. *foruions*: DM did not understand *foruions* and put a cross in the margin to indicate the need for a translation. This, however, he never supplied. *MED* in fact records a Middle English verb *forveien* but, if this were an English form, we should expect *forveieþ*. Clearly, DM has simply copied the French form here with the intention of correcting it later. Evers (p. 109) pointed out that DM seems to have understood the word, however, at 94/24, 160/6 where he translates *mysgeþ* and *guo amis* respectively.

155/4. *þenche, soigneus*: read *þencþ* to match *is*. The form is probably due to the French *pense*. DM put a cross against *soigneus*, indicating that he did not understand it. As in the case of *foruions*, he probably meant to correct it but forgot. Cf. 157/19.

155/4–5. *of al . . . ordayny* 'about the ordering of the whole life'; *liue* should read *lyf*. It is accusative and it is not governed by *of*.

155/8. *hate*: C *corous*; the correct reading is probably *cures* which appears in M, V, Add1. The English text should read *zorзen*.

155/21. *of þan*: C *deceus*; DM has read *deceus* as *de ceus*. Emend to *deceyued*. Cf. Evers, p. 109.

155/21–2. The reference seems to be to the First Conference of Abbot Chaeremon on Perfection (Cassian, *Collationes*, II, xi: PL xlix, cols. 847–70).

155/23. *wel y-mad*: C *bien parfet*; see note to 87/12.

155/24. *willeþ*: C *beent*; it seems that DM has taken *beent* in the sense of 'desiring', 'being envious', whereas the sense seems to be 'they are amazed'. For *willeþ* read *byeþ astoned*.

155/26–7. *hi wylleþ and yerneþ efter*: C *i beent e corent apres*; DM has omitted *i* so that *wylleþ* has no object. Supply *þerat*. For *wylleþ* see previous note.

155/30–1. *ne makeþ bote him weri*: C *ne fet fors soi lasser* 'only makes himself weary'.

155/31 ff. See G. Thiele, *Der lateinische Äsop des Romulus* (Heidelberg, 1910), pp. 64–8.

155/32–3. *of þe asse . . . he yernþ*: C *del asne qui ueoit . . . quil li coroit*; DM has here simplified the construction by omitting *qui ueoit* and starting a new sentence at *þe hond* in line 32.

155/33. *þet he yhyerþ [þet] his lhord comeþ*: C *que ses sires uenoit*; DM seems to have had a different reading here from Cotton, as at 155/35, where he adds *and him froteþ*.

156/14–15. Proverbs 23: 5.

156/25. *be-ulyȝt*: C *fuie*; for the indicative rendering the French subjunctive cf. note to 23/7.

156/26–30. Proverbs 24: 30–2.

156/32. *loueþ*: C *aime*; the indicative is unusual. Cf. note to 23/7.

157/2. *þe kende*: C *la persone*; emend *kende* to *persone*.

157/5–6. *zuich . . . ha*: C *tieus . . . qui*; read *zuich . . . þet*. Cf. 21/11 where *zuich* also has demonstrative force. The sense is 'he . . . who'.

157/8. *a-yens ham paye and condecendre*: C *en uers eus ploier e condescendre*; perhaps DM did not recognize *ploier* (cf. 125/20 where he translates it as *wepinge*). He may have identified it, as Evers thought, with *payer*. But it is possible that he intended the sense to be 'to please' as a rendering of *ploier* 'to be complacent'. The cross in the margin, which Evers (p. 110) assumed to refer to *paye*, refers presumably to the French form *condecendre*. For *ploier = payer* see Godefroy PLOIER.

157/17. *more*: C *poons*; read *moȝe* as Morris suggests.

157/19. *soigneus*: DM did not understand the word and wrote it in the margin with a cross and left a blank in the text; cf. 155/4.

157/33. *uiȝte*: C *plus combatre*; *mo* should perhaps be supplied before *uiȝte*.

157/34. *ine zuyche guod*: C *en tieu bien*; G1 shares the reading of C. The correct reading appears to be *entend bien* as in the other E manuscripts. Emend to *onderstand wel*.

157/34. *spari*: C *espairgne*; the sense requires an indicative.

158/2–3. *Yef þou [wost]*: C *Ses tu*; as Evers (p. 110) pointed out, DM has read *ses tu* 'thou knowest' as *se tu*. Read *wost þou*. This seems to be a reference to the fact that the Book of Job was thought to contain many allegorical types of the devil and his wiles. Leviathan, in particular, was a type of the devil and it was to him that Job referred when he said *Quis est iste qui celat consilium absque scientia* (Job 42: 3) on which the *Glossa Ordinaria* comments: *Absque scientia Leuiathan celat consilium quia quamvis contra infirmitatem nostram multis fraudibus occultetur* (iii. 414).

158/4–6. Cf. *De Caelesti Hierarchia*, III, ii (PG iii, col. 165).

158/30. *þe gostes*: C *touz les esperiz*; *al* should perhaps be supplied before *þe*; the biblical text (1 John 4: 1) has *omni spiritui* and DM's reading is probably erroneous.

158/32. *makeþ . . . guod*: C *ont lor* con*fessor bon*; as Evers (p. 110), pointed out, DM has taken *ont* as *font* and rendered the idiom literally. Read *habbeþ* for *makeþ*.

158/33–4. *ine zuiche þinges timliche*: C *en tiex temporeles*; as at 154/34, *temporeles* is probably a corruption of *quereles*, the reading of all early manuscripts except G1 which shares the reading of C. The reading of C however, makes quite acceptable sense. Cf. Evers, p. 110.

158/34. *ofte/and grat and smal*: C *souent e menu*; the English is only an approximate rendering of *menu* 'minutely'. Evers noted (p. 111) that DM seems not to have understood *menu* which he mistranslates also at 74/12.

159/1–2. Ecclesiasticus 34: 17.

159/2–4. Ecclesiasticus 32: 24.

159/6–7. *þet hit . . . þise uirtue*: C *que il couient auoir qui ueut auoir ceste uertu*; a literal rendering of the French explains the clumsy English.

159/9–12. Matthew 6:22; Luke 11: 34. The manuscript has *þine eʒen* (line 9) with the *n* of *eʒen* subpuncted. The final *e* of *þine* should perhaps have been subpuncted also. Cf. discussion p. 70.

159/12. *þin*: is probably, as Evers suggested (p. 111), a mistake for *þe*. The French has *lentencion*.

159/14. *þise stapes*: C *touz ces degrez*; DM has omitted *touz*. Read *al þise stapes*. At 159/17, *hwy* is for *hy*.

159/18. *quarteus*: C *quarteus*; DM left a blank and wrote *quarteus* with an insertion sign in the margin. At 159/26 he did the same with the French form *cerceaus*. According to *MED* (CERCEAUS n.) the form *quarteus* is an error for *cerceaus*. The words *hop* or *trendle* would have been available to DM; he clearly did not understand the French.

160/1–2. *þise zeue uirtues . . . ledeþ . . . þane gost of wytte*: C *Ces .vii. uertuz garde e conduit mout droit e mult seurement li esperiz de science*; the subject is *li esperiz de science*. Probably DM's *þane gost of wytte* should be emended to *þe gost of wytte* and *ledeþ* to *let*. It should be noted, however, that three manuscripts (P8, Ld, R1) take the seven virtues as the subject and there may be textual confusion at the back of DM's reading. Thus, for example, Ld *Ces uertus gardent 7 conduient mult seurement lesperit de science*; R1 has an extended reading which justifies the plural verb: *Ces vij vertus gardent et conduisent moult droitement et seurement lomme a dieu et les garde et conduit bonnement et saintement li esperis de science* (cf. Francis, note to VV 159/6–9). Thus DM may have had a text which read *Ces vij uertus gardent et conduisent mout droitement e mult seurement lesperit de science* in which *lesperit* was in fact the object. DM did not notice that the text did not make sense.

160/2–3. Proverbs 8: 20.

160/4–5. Cf. Bernard, *Sermones super Cantica Canticorum*, lxxxv. 5 (Leclercq, Rochais, ii (1958), 310): *iram, metum, cupiditatem et gaudium, veluti quemdam animi currum, bonus auriga reget, et in captivitatem rediget omnem carnalem affectum, et carnis sensum ad nutum rationis in obsequium virtutis.*

160/6. *his let and brengþ uorþ*: C *les meine e conduit*: DM here follows the French but, in fact, the subject is *discrecion and scele* (4) and the verbs should be plural.

160/15. *onderstan[d]*: the emendation is probably correct although the manuscript reading may represent a colloquial pronunciation. See p. 50.

160/16. *hi ne is naȝt*: C *il ne dit pas*; the text should read *he ne zaiþ naȝt*. DM presumably assumed that the pronoun referred to *uirtue* which is usually feminine.

160/19. *Vor we ne habbeþ hire onneaþe y-wonne*: C *car la naurions nous gueres gaaigne*: as Evers (p. 111) pointed out, DM has taken *la* as the feminine pronoun instead of an adverb. The rendering of *naurions* by *habbeþ* is also incorrect. Read *Vor þer ne ssolde we onneaþe habbe ywonne*. For *win* as an intransitive verb see *OED* WIN *v.*[1] 4. The sense is, 'For, in that case, we should scarcely have prevailed'.

160/24. *lingne*: the spelling is a Gallicism. Cf. *ingnel* 141/6.

160/25–6. Matthew 5: 5.

160/35. *uor huo þet mest can*: C *que qui plus siet*; emend *uor* to *þet* which the sense requires. Cf. Evers, p. 111.

160/35–161/1. Cf. Ecclesiastes 7: 5.

161/5. *þus þenche. Zix maneres*: C *ci penser .vj. manieres*; in spite of the punctuation, *zix maneres* is the object of *þenche*. Evers (p. 111) pointed out that DM had been misled because he took *ci* 'here' as *si* 'so'. For *þus* read *hier*.

161/11. *wexeþ*: C *naissent*; the sense requires a singular. Read *wext*.

161/20. *be strengþe*: for *a force* 'despite oneself' see Godefroy, FORCE.

161/28. *mid*: C *ou*; as Evers (p. 112) pointed out, DM has translated *o* 'avec' for *ou* (*au*). Read *ine* for *mid*.

161/34–5. *þet lyf . . . Vor . . . borgeysye*: C *que uie dome sor terre est come cheualerie. Car uie dome en terre est come borgesie*; Evers (p. 112) pointed out that this was based on Job 7: 1: *Militia est vita hominis super terram; Et sicut dies mercenarii, dies eius.* The antiphonal variation seems to have puzzled scribes. The majority of manuscripts read *car* as C. This does not, however, represent the sense of the Latin. A better reading is either *et* (as P1, P13) or *que* (as P2, P4, P10, M). In view of the Latin, the reading *et* is perhaps to be preferred although *car* is perhaps a more credible corruption of *que*. *Borgesie* is not a very accurate rendering of the Latin and this may have given rise to the scribal confusion.

162/1–2. *Mochel habbeþ þos of uele þoȝtes*: C *mout ont cist doi pensees*; as Evers (p. 112) pointed out, DM has taken *cist* as *si*, *doi* as *des*, and added *uele*. The text should read *þise two* (*cist doi*) and *uele* should be omitted. *Mochel* is a literal rendering of *mout*. A more natural English rendering would be *manye . . . þoȝtes*. Wallenberg, however, takes *þos* to be a plural demonstrative form (p. 321).

162/2. *diuerses and wyluolle*: C *diuerses e beeries*; *beeries* is a noun and not an adjective as DM supposed. The French text should read (as E manuscripts except P2, 4, G1, V) either *e diuerses beeries* or *e diuerses e diuerses beeries*. The English text could be emended accordingly to either *and wylninges diuerses* or to *and diuerses and diuerses wylninges*.

162/15–16. *byeþ to huam þet*: C *sont a cui*; Evers (p. 112) suggested that the reading should be *byeþ þo þet*. This is more idiomatic but DM's translation is possible.

162/19–20. *þet moȝe by worþ to godes loue*: C *Kalamour de dieu se puet comparer*; the sentence is very awkward. As Evers (p. 112) pointed out, two lines below, DM again translates *se comparer* by *by worþ to* although he generally uses this phrase in the sense 'to be of equal value to'. The verb *anlicni* would have provided a more accurate translation. There is no need to emend *moȝe* as Morris suggests.

162/30. *Hardyesse*: in spite of the capital, which is also in Cotton, the sentence follows on from what precedes. The correct reading, however, is *hardi* as in all other E manuscripts. G1 has *hardi* corrected from *hardiesce*.

162/32. *yblysseþ*: should be emended to *yblyssed*. So at 163/15. (Cf. Wallenberg, p. 37, n. 5.) The reference is to Matthew 5: 6.

162/33–4. Proverbs 12: 26.

163/1–2. *yeldere. and a-yens god of treuþe*: C *detteor e uers dieu de loiaute*: Evers (pp. 112–13) suggested that the original reading for *detteor* was *douceour* as in P1, Add1, R1. But the reference to *þise dette* in line 3 justifies the reading *detteor*. There is, however, uncertainty about the reading of the rest of the phrase. The best reading is that of P4, A2, M, V, Ld, Ca1, R1, *enuers dieu de lui amer*. The English could read *yeldere ayens god to louie hym*.

163/15. Read *yblissed* as at 162/32.

163/19–20. *þet he hit ssewy*: C *quil le moustre*; the French should probably read *quil se* for *quil le* (so E manuscripts except V and G1, which reads as C). The English should read *þet hit ssewy*.

163/20–1. Proverbs 6: 27.

163/25. *be moche . . . to y-leste*: C *par mout souffrir e endurer*; 'by great suffering and endurance'.

163/35–164/1. *alhuet . . . Ac more hi yeden ledinde blisse*: C *adonc quil fusseint de ceste uertu armez. mais puis quil aloient menant ioie*. The reading *puisque* which appears also in G1 is an error for *puis*, the reading of the majority of the manuscripts. It seems likely that DM's manuscript either read *plus*, or read *puis* which he misread as *plus*. The text should read *alhuet . . . Ac þanne hi yeden* etc.

164/4. The reference seems to be to Aristotle's ethical works, which do indeed discuss what later became the 'cardinal virtues'.

164/6. *þise uirtues cliueþ/and profiteþ*: C has the singular; *ceste uertu monte e profite*.

164/11. *zixt*: read *zixte*.

164/17. *delles*: read *deles* as Morris suggests. See p. 42, n. 7.

164/19–21. Augustine, *De Libero Arbitrio*, I. xiii, 27 (PL. xxxii, col. 1235).

164/22–3. Seneca, *Letters*, xxxix, 4 (Reynolds, p. 103).

164/26–7. Isaiah 33: 17.

164/34–5. Ecclesiastes 1: 2,

165/2–4. Perhaps a reference to Psalm 143 (144): 4 *Homo vanitati similis factus est; dies eius sicut umbra praetereunt*. But cf. Psalm 38 (39): 6 *Verumtamen universa vanitas, omnis homo vivens*.

165/7–8. *of þise uirtue. þet hi*m: C *de ceste uertu quele*; *him* is miswritten for *hi*.

165/8–9. *ine ariere*: C *en ariere*; DM left a blank in the text, put an insertion mark, and placed the French word in the margin with a matching mark. Accordingly Morris has inserted it in the text. But presumably DM did not understand the word or he would have either inserted it directly into the text or given a translation.

165/16. *chy[e]zeþ*: there is no need to emend. Read *chyzeþ*.

165/20. *y[e]ueþ*: Morris's emendation is unnecessary. Cf. note to 46/9.

165/24–5. *þet weren vry*: refers to *þo þet* (22).

166/13. *him yefþ*: C *saert*: Wallenberg (p. 321) comments that DM has not realized that *saert* is pr. 3 sg. of *servir*. But the translation is possible.

166/15–16. *may / and can*: C *set e puet*; DM's text presumably read *puet e set*.

166/31–4. See the Passion of St. Agatha in Mombritius, *Sanctuarium*, i. p. 38, 38–9. Morris's shoulder note should be emended.

167/9–10. Psalm 5: 13 (New Version): *Benevolentia, velut scuto, circumdabis eum*.

167/12–13. Romans 5: 3.

167/19. *ate leste*: this is not in the French and it looks as though DM has translated the French *a meins* twice; once as *ate leste* and once as *mid hand*. It is not required by the sense and should be omitted.

167/20. *of strokes of yzen*: C *de fer e de cous*; all E manuscripts (except V which omits) read *feu* for *fer*. This makes better sense than C. The English should read *of strokes and of uer*.

167/32. *him baþeþ*: *MED* (BATHEN v. 6 (a)) renders 'swims' but the French has *se baigne*.

168/9–10. *þe stranger . . . þanne*: C *plus forte . . . que*; omit *þe*.

168/11–13. Psalm 90 (91): 7. Cf. Bernard, *Sermones, In Ramis Palmarum* 2 (Leclercq, Rochais, v (1968), 47): *Cadent a latere tuo mille, sinistro scilicet, per quod signatur adversitas et decem millia, id est multo plures, a dextris tuis, in quibus prosperitas designatur.*

168/17. *and grat*: C *e grant*; other early manuscripts read either *a* for *e* (Add1, R1); or *e a* (P1, 2, 4, A2, M, An, Ca1, R1); or *e en* (V); or *qui a* (Ld); or *es* for *e* (G1). Any of these readings makes acceptable sense. The English text should read either (*and*) *ine grat* or (*and*) *heþ grat*.

168/22. *of heȝe nyede y-blissede bleuinge*: C *de haute besoigne. beneure acheuance*; it looks as though DM may have mistaken the sense of *besoigne* 'enterprise'. The word *bleuinge* suggests that DM's manuscript read, as does A2, *achenance* 'tenacity', 'zeal' or he may have misread *acheuance* as *achenance*. This makes tolerable sense but the correct sense is 'the happy achievement of a lofty enterprise'. Cf. Augustine, *De Diversis Questionibus, lxxxiii,* XXXI (PL xl, col. 21): *Magnificentia est rerum magnarum et excelsarum cum animi ampla quadam et splendida propositione agitatio (cogitatio) atque administratio.*

168/26–28. *alle þe uirtues yerneþ: . . . þet zuord. alle hy viȝteþ: . . . coroune*; C *toutes les uertuz corent? mais ceste gaigne lespee. toutes se combatent mais ceste a la uictoire. e la corone*; cf. 1 Corinthians 9: 24, 25: *Nescitis quod ii qui in stadio currunt, omnes quidem currunt, sed unus accipit bravium? Sic currite ut comprehendatis. Omnis autem qui in agone contendit, ab omnibus se abstinet, et illi quidem ut corruptibilem coronam accipiant; nos autem incorruptam.* The meaning of *bravium* is 'prize' but the French MSS. all gave *espee* except P1, P12 which read *pris*. The French text represents a perversion by the author, or a corruption by the scribe, of the biblical text. St. Paul is not saying that the virtues run and fight.

168/29–30. Matthew 10: 22; 24: 13; Mark 13: 13.

168/32. *mayster*: superscript *e* usually represents *re* and the form should, perhaps, be read as *maystre*.

168/34–5. Possibly a paraphrase of Ecclesiastes 1: 9: *Quid est quod factum est? ipsum quod faciendum est.*

169/10. *ich am*: C *li sui ie*; supply *him* before *am*.

169/16–19. Matthew 5: 6.

169/25–6. The seven rewards offered to the seven churches are enumerated in Apocalypse 2–3. Cf. 170/8–11.

169/26–9. Cf. Bernard, *Epistolae*, PL clxxxii, col. 528.

169/30–1. 2 Timothy 2: 5.

170/1–3. Clearly, Christ cannot be referred to in the Book of Kings and it seems likely that some analogy between Christ and an Old Testament figure is here in question. A clue to the meaning is perhaps to be found in the association of David and Christ with the ceremony of knighting. Such an association of David with the order of knighthood is to be found in the liturgy for the knighting ceremony. Thus, for example, a prayer for blessing the lance invokes the God who *benedixisti . . . David regem . . . triumphales congressus exercentem* (probably a reference to 1 Paralip. 12; for the reference see A. Franz, *Die kirchlichen Benediktionen im Mittelalter* (Freiburg i. Br., 1909), ii. 296). David thus came to be regarded as the prototype of the king in this feudal function (cf. *Piers Plowman* B i. 102–5) and by a further transference was equated with Christ.

170/3–4. 1 Corinthians 1: 9; 10: 13; 1 Thessalonians 5: 24; 2 Thessalonians 3: 3; Hebrews 10: 23.

170/7–8. Cf. 2 Corinthians 12: 9.

170/8–11. Cf. Apocalypse 2, 3. Only one reward is, in fact, a crown. The author seems here to be glossing the text.

170/14–15. *þet nele to senne* consenti: C *qui ne veut a pecche consentir*; there is an omission here. The correct reading appears to be *qui ne ueut. Car qui ne se ueut au pechie consentir* (so the majority of manuscripts except P1, G1, Add1). The English text should read *þet nele. Vor huose nele to senne consenti.*

170/19. *poer*: C *poeir*; this is not, as Wallenberg lists it, the word *pouer* 'power' but the word 'fear'; cf. VV 171/7 *for drede*. The meaning 'power' makes no sense in the context.

170/18–20. Apocalypse 3: 15–16.

170/21. *heþ more strenger to done*: C *a plus fort a fere*; Wallenberg (p. 321) points out that *a fere* = *afaire* 'difficulty'. Thus 'has more difficulty'.

170/30. There are a number of examples of this metaphor in the Pauline epistles. See Romans 13: 12; 2 Corinthians 6: 7; Ephesians 6: 11–17.

171/2. *yhol*: C *enterrinez*; DM appears to have translated *enterin* 'whole' rather than *enterrinez* which must mean 'composed', 'completed'. *MED* (IHOL(E adj. 2 2(a)) translates 'whole', 'in one piece' etc. but this assumes a very odd sentence structure and one which is at variance with the French. Emend *yhol* to *imad*.

171/11–12. Psalm 6: 7.

171/19. *þet . . . wynne*: a reference to the parable of the talents.

171/19–22. *þet byeþ . . . straytliche*: these lines are parenthetic.

171/22. *hise*: refers to *guodes* in line 20, *ine euele wones* is a translation of French *en malueises usages* and *ine* perhaps here means 'in' rather than, as *MED* suggests (IN 21 (b)) 'for the sake of'. For *wone* 'habit' cf. Wallenberg, pp. 321, 325. At 210/2, DM again uses *wone* for *usage* 'use', 'habit'.

171/31–2. *sest geus*: C *sest geuz*; the reading of C is supported by A2, M, G1, V, Ca1, R1 (Ld *a ieu*). The most likely explanation is that *geuz* is the pp. of *gesir*. The phrase is reflexive and means 'has lain'. This conjecture is perhaps supported by the reading *se gist* in P1, Add1, and *cest couchiez* in P4. The author is carrying on the metaphor of the bed. If this is correct, the English should read *huerinne* for *huerof*. For this C reads *ou* (substituted for a subpuncted *qui*). For the metaphor see 31/14–15.

171/35. *chomberier*: C *chamberiere*; *OED* CHAMBERER and *MED* (CHAUMBERER(E n.) regard this word as feminine like the French. Wallenberg (p. 52, n. 4) argues that it is masculine on the grounds that *ssrifte* is masculine. As it stands, the word is masculine but should, perhaps, be emended to *chamberere* to bring it into line with the French.

172/2–3. Psalm 76 (77): 7.

172/15. For Augustine see lines 20–2 and note.

172/20–2. The reference is given in the French text; namely, *De uera et falsa Paenitentia*, cap. X (PL xl, 1122).

172/28–9. Isaiah 38: 15.

172/31. *iogelour*: C *ioglieres*; *MED* (JOGELOUR n. 3) glosses 'parasite', 'deceiver', 'rascal', but the reference is presumably to the nomadic habits and dubious moral reputation of minstrels.

172/36. *heþ day*: C *est aiornez* 'is summoned to appear on a certain day'.

173/12–13. Psalm 118 (119): 62.

173/18–20. Ecclesiasticus 5: 8–9.

173/22. *y-kuegt*: read *ykuengt*.

173/35. *huer hit is*: C *ou il est* 'in which he is'; emend to *huer he is*.

174/5. *þet al may habbe ayen*; C *que il peut tot recouerer* 'all of which he may recover'; emend to *þet he al may habbe ayen*.

174/8. Apocalypse 3. 20. It may be noted that the Latin has *sto ad ostium et pulso* 'I stand at the door and knock', The French, however, has taken *pulso* to mean 'push', 'strike' and rendered *boute* which DM, in turn, renders as *ssofþ*.

174/9. *ha . . . ssriue*: C *le doit haster de confesser*; *ha*, if correct, must refer to the mercy of God but it should perhaps be omitted. Cf. Wallenberg, p. 321.

174/15–16. *late ham ssriueþ*: C *se tardent a confesser*; other E manuscripts except M have a singular verb. Read *him ssrifþ* to bring the number into line with the rest of the sentence.

174/28–9. Boethius, *De Consol. Philosoph.*, Bk. I, prose iv.

174/30. *þe truont þe ssel teche*: C *li truant se doiuent enseigner*; the French appears to be erroneous here. DM's manuscript clearly read *te* for *se* as do all E manuscripts except G1, Ld. He has, however, mistakenly supposed *li truant* to be singular hence the change of number. Read *þe truons þe ssolle teche*.

174/31. *uo[u]leste*: no need to emend. The word has shortening in a trisyllabic form.

175/5–7. Psalm 31 (32): 5.

175/10. *and þerof þet*: C *de ce dont*; as Wallenberg pointed out (p. 321–2), *and* is superfluous.

175/13–14. *zuyche weren þe farizeus . . . zayde his . . . onworþede*: C *Tiels estoit li pharisieus . . . recordoit ses . . . despisoit*; there is only one pharisee in the parable (Luke 18: 10). Read *wes* for *weren* and *zuych* for *zuyche*. The form *farizeus* is probably plural and should also be emended (see *OED* PHARISEE *sb.*). Wallenberg (s.v.) takes *zayde* as plural but *his* shows that DM has reverted to the singular.

175/23. *tales*: C *metoirie* 'division'; *tales* is perhaps a rendering of *matiere*, the reading of P2, A2, An, Ld.

175/29. *Efterwuard*: Wallenberg (p. 81, n. 4) suggests that the spelling may represent a glide after the *w*. Cf. p. 28, n. 9.

175/33. *more yno3*: C *plus assez*, 'considerably more'.

176/3. *kendeliche*: Wallenberg lists this as an adverb but the sense seems to require an adjective. See p. 64 for the inflection.

176/10. *þe uondinge*: C *la temptacion*; this makes dubious sense. P2, 4, A2, M, An, Ld, Ca1 read *entencion* for *temptacion* which is clearly a better reading than that of C and the other E manuscripts. The temptation is the cause. The cause and the motive are in question. The English text should read *þentencion*.

176/10. *comþ*: C *auient*; P2, A2, M, An, Ld, Ca1 read *esmeut* (*esmeuuent*) which clearly makes better sense. The English text should read *meueþ*.

176/18. *of oþre . . . moche*: C *dautres maneres dont il i a trop*; DM's rendering could mean 'of some other kind of which there is too much'; but both the sense and the French suggest that the translation is erroneous. It should probably run *of oþre maneres huerof þer byeþ to moche*. *Manere* as a plural is generally used in conjunction with a noun. Cf. 23/31, 33, 48/1, 91/21.

176/20. *þise*: C *ses*; emend to *his*.

176/26–7. *zet ofte grat cost*: C *met souent . . . grant coust*; *MED* (COST n. (2) 1 (c)) translates 'often spends much money'. In view of the French *met souent grant peine e grant coust*, however, the meaning cited under COST n. (2) 1 (d) 'expenditure of effort' might also be possible.

176/31. *oþer of oþren*: C *ou dautrui*; VV (179/25–6) has more explicitly *& ofte of oþer þing þan of here owne*, referring, presumably, to false hair.

176/34. *trossinge*: C *farder*; Wallenberg (p. 246, n. 1) suggested that DM had confused *farder* 'make up' with *farder* 'load'. But the sense of *trossinge* is probably 'fastening the hair, binding it up with pins or ribbons'. Cf. *OED* TRUSS *v.* 5 and 6.

177/1. *croki*: C *encontrer*; Wallenberg (p. 68, n. 2) suggests that the French is an error for *acoutrer* 'arrange'. The reading of C, shared by G1, is certainly wrong. The early manuscripts (A2, Add1) read *acoutrer*; *assembler* (V, R1); *atorner* (M, An, Ca1), *atierer* (P1), *acointier* (P4). It is possible that DM's manuscript read *atorner* which he understood in the literal sense of 'turn' and thus 'twist', 'crimp'; but *croki* may represent simply a gloss on the general sense of 'arrange'. The form *here* in the same line is probably an error for *her*; *ine* governs the infinitive *to croki* and not the noun.

177/1–3. *to bleue þe strengþe . . . þet is ine tokne of kueadnesse*: C *duire a force . . . qui en seigne de mauueistie*; there are two points of note in this passage; (i) DM seems to have understood *duire* 'lead, train' as *durer* 'endure'; (ii) DM's manuscript may have read *qui est en seigne* as all the early manuscripts except G1 which has the reading of C. The meaning is 'which is an indication of sinfulness'. But cf. Wallenberg, p. 322.

177/10, *ethe*: Wallenberg points out (p. 86, n. 1) that at 248/19, *OED* (EAT *sb.* 1) interprets the form as a substantive. But he rightly draws attention to the French infinitive which the English form renders. The force is gerundial 'eating' and not substantival 'food'. Cf. 221/22.

177/28. *ase me helt uol a pot*: C *Ausi com on espant plein pot* 'as one pours out a pot full (of water)'. Cf. Wallenberg (p. 322).

177/29–35. Translate 'when the water is spilt, there remains no colour as with milk, nor smell as with wine, nor taste as with honey; so likewise one must not retain (anything) of the sin after it has been confessed; neither the colour, that is the evil manner of behaviour which one has had (either in speech or in looking or in following evil company) or in anything else which has colour of sin'. C reads *ne la colour ce est la mauuaise maniere* for *ne þet colour / þet is þe kueade manere*. The words *ce est* are written over a subpuncted *ne*. This represents a correction to the reading of the majority of the manuscripts. Only P1, 12, G1, Add1 have the original reading of C which, while it provides a correlative for the first *ne* which the structure of the sentence requires, does not make good sense. The reading *ce est* is probably correct and the anacoluthon is due to a loose correlation of *ne* with *Efterward* (35). *MED* (COLOUR n. 5 (c)) renders *colour of zenne* as 'manner of sin', but it may simply continue the metaphor.

178/1. *yef*: C *Cil*; DM has taken *Cil* as *s'il*. Omit *yef*.

178/15. *zeche*: C *aquerre*; Wallenberg (p. 322) assumes that DM has confused *aquerre* 'get' with *querre* 'seek'. In fact, A2 reads *querre* and so, no doubt, did DM's text.

178/26. *telle*: C *conter*; cf. *OED* TELL *v.* I 13.

178/28–9. *winne ayen / þet me heþ lesse ynoȝ y-do*: C *recourer ce kon a meins souffisaument fait*; DM seems to have taken *recourer* 'repeat' as *recovrer* 'recover'. The English text should read *do ayen*. The phrase *lesse yno3* is scarcely English and is an obvious calque on *meins suffisaument*.

179/6. *bal*: C *renoille* 'frog'; at 179/8, where the word occurs again, P1, 4, M, Ca1, Add1 read *raine*. It may be that DM was confused by some such form and that *bal* is a guess.

179/8. *þet makeþ*: C *quele fet*; the reading *que(l)le fet*, which appears in all the other E manuscripts, makes good sense and the English text should read *þet hit makeþ*.

179/20–1. *þe þridde kueade loue*: C *La tierce chose est mauuaise amour*; read *þing is* after *þridde*.

179/21. *uorzoke*: C *aleiche*; *MED* (FORSAKEN v. 2 (a)) derives from *uorzake* 'to abandon, cast out'. But it seems that DM has confused *alechier, allécher* 'to entice' with *aletier, allaiter* 'to suckle'; cf. Wallenberg (p. 270, n. 4). Given the similarity of *c* and *t*, such a mistake could easily arise.

179/27. *þou sselt wel come þer to þe to ssriue*: C *tu recouerreras bien a toi confesser*; the meaningless *þer* should be emended to *þerefter* (cf. VV (183/19) which reads *her-after*); *to þe to ssriue* is a calque on *a toi confesser*; *sselt . . . come* is an imprecise rendering of *recouerreras*. DM may have read it as *recouerras*.

180/1. *uorþingþ*: C *repentent*; read *uorþencheþ*.

180/12. *heleþ*: C *enterinent*; *MED* (HELEN v. (2) 1 (a)) glosses as 'cover' but the French suggests that the meaning is 'make complete', 'make up'. Cf. 171/2 where *yhol* glosses French *enterrinez*.

180/14. *And he*: C *Et qui*; read *And he þet*.

180/14–19. Apocalypse 2: 11; 20: 6, 14; 21: 8.

180/25–7. This is perhaps a gloss on Matthew, 11: 16–17 (Luke, 7: 32). Morris's emendation is unnecessary. Cf. p. 45, n. 3.

180/26–7. *nou hi proposent / nou hit is betere*: C *ore proposent ore est mielz*; the form *proposent* is taken direct from French. But the sense of the clause is obscure. VV 184/25–6 has *now þei ben in good purpos, now þei beþ out þerof*. It is to be presumed that the last member of the sentence, like the other two, will form an antithesis and the sense seems to be 'Now they propose and now they deny'. If this is correct, the form *proposent* in DM should read *byeþ ine porpos*. The second part is clearly corrupt as it makes no sense. The French *mielz* is probably a corruption of *nulz*, a supposition which is given credibility by the reading *neant, noient, nient, riens*, of the E manuscripts (other than G1 which shares the reading of C). But it may well be that the original reading was *ore proposent ore nient* 'now they propose, now they deny'; in this case, the English should read *nou hi na3teþ* for *nou hit is betere*.

180/30–3. Apocalypse 3: 12.

180/34. *hi him kepþ*: C *li respont*; DM has assumed the French verb to be *repondre* 'conceal' (of which *respondre* is a possible form) instead of *respondre* 'correspond'. Cf. Wallenberg, p. 134, n. 4. The meaning is 'corresponds to it'. The *he* is redundant.

181/2. *hi*: this should, perhaps, read *he* but Wallenberg (p. 322) points out that it renders French *ele*, referring to the feminine noun *char*. It may thus simply represent an inadvertent translation of the French pronoun. Cf. p. 90.

181/4–5. Cf. Proverbs 19: 13; 21: 9; 27: 15. Read *Salomon*.

181/5–6. 'who behaves worse towards him who indulges her most and (the more he indulges her) the more she opposes him'. *Huo þet* is here used as a dative.

181/8–14. Judges 16: 4–21.

181/16–18. Apocalypse 7: 13–14.

181/20. *mid al hare hueʒel*: C *a toute sa roe*; the meaningless *a toute* (*mid al*) is possibly a corruption of *atourne* 'turns'. Cf. note to 76/30–2.

181/22–3. Cf. note to 168/11–13.

181/30–1. Apocalypse 3: 21.

182/3. *wyteþ*: C *repont* 'conceals'; DM's rendering is inexact.

182/10. *dor*: probably for the subjunctive *dor(r)e* (OE *durre*). Cf. Wallenberg, p. 70, n. 1.

182/11. Supply *he* before *by*; in the French *apeine sosera nuls reclamer crestien* the subject is implicit in the reflexive.

182/16. *defoulent*: C *foulent*; read *defoulieþ*.

182/16. [*h*]*are*: there is no need to emend. Cf. p. 45, n. 3.

182/19. *þolmodnesse*: should probably be emended to *þolemodnesse*.

182/21–3. Apocalypse 2: 26.

183/7. *mid*: C *a*; emend *mid* to *heþ*.

183/11. *liʒtlyliche*: is probably a scribal error. Cf. Wallenberg, p. 148, n. 3.

183/16–18. Apocalypse 2: 7.

183/22–3. Matthew 5: 6.

183/31. *comþ . . . heauede*: C *uient a bon chief*; Wallenberg (p. 323) points out that the English is a calque on the French idiom 'comes to a good end'.

184/4–6. Proverbs 19: 20.

184/8–10. Tobias 4: 19.

184/11. *onzauwed*: C *desconfiz*; DM seems to have read *desconfiz* as *descousiz*, assuming it to be from *descosdre* with the sense of French *décousu* 'fallen apart' (cf. Wallenberg, p. 179, n. 2). The English should read *tobroke*. The reference is to Proverbs 11: 14.

184/13–15. Ecclesiasticus 8: 20.

184/19–22. 3 Kings 12: 1–19; 2 Paralip. 10: 1–19.

184/23. Read *efte[r]ward*. Morris emends at 24/33, 110/4, 184/4 and this instance is probably an oversight. Cf. p. 49.

184/26. *yleue*: C *croire*; the French should perhaps read *croit*, the English *ylefþ*. But the infinitive could depend on *bezyinge* and is supported by the majority of E manuscripts.

184/29–31. Seneca, *Letters*, xvi. 2 (Reynolds, p. 42).

184/34–5. Proverbs 12: 15.

184/35–185/1. Possibly a paraphrase of Ecclesiasticus 21: 18: *Verbum sapiens quodcumque audierit scius laudabit, et ad se adiiciet; audivit luxuriosus, et displicebit illi, et proiiciet illud post dorsum suum.* Luxuriosus in the Vulgate appears as 'a foolish man' in the Syriac text and some such reading may have appeared in the author's Vulgate (cf. *The Apocrypha*, ed. R. H. Charles, Oxford, 1913), I, p. 389.

185/2–4. *þe red of . . . [and] ous brengþ*: C *le conseil que nostre bon mestre iesu crist qui est la sapience dieu le pere de qui uient tout bon conseil nus aporta*; emend *þe red of* to *þe red þet* and omit the *and* supplied by Morris.

185/4–5. Isaiah 11: 2.

185/6–9. Matthew 19: 21.

185/7. *zel*: here and at 187/9 final *e* is lost before a following vowel. Cf. p. 98, n. 6.

185/16. *þe oþre*: C *par autre*; read *be* for *þe*.

185/28. *profiteth*: MS *porfiteþ*; Wallenberg (p. 197, n. 1) points out that the manuscript spelling is probably a genuine form depending on OF *po(u)rfiter*. For the spelling *th* read *þ*.

185/31–2. *þe boc . . . of kende of bestes* is the Bestiary.

186/18–19. *children of [on] uader and of moder*: C *fiz de pere e de mere*; E manuscripts read either *frere(s)* (7) *de pere e de mere* 'brothers on the father's and the mother's side' (P2, 4, A2, M, An, V, Ca1, R1); *fiz de pere e de mere* (G1, C); or *frere dun pere e dune mere* (P1, Add1). The manuscript evidence suggests that the correct reading is *freres de pere e de mere*; the English, in that case, should read *broþren of uader and of moder*. The father is God and the mother Holy Church.

186/22. *huet þe urend is*: C *qui ami est*; the English should read *huo* for *huet*.

186/23–4. *þe heste . . . redeþ and hoteþ*: C *les commandemenz . . . conseillent e commandent*; the text should read *þe hestes* to rectify the concord.

186/25–7. Ecclesiastes 9: 8.

186/30. *op arist*: C *sormonte*; we should probably read *oparist*, assuming a calque on *sormonte* 'rises above'. It seems to be transitive in spite of Wallenberg's observation (p. 323) that *arise* and *arere* are never confused in the *Ayenbite*. The use is, no doubt, due to the French in which *sormonte* must govern *toutes les autres liquors* (*alle þe oþre woses*).

186/34–187/2. 1 John 3: 17.

186/35–6. *he [ne] him yefþ [sset]*: C *li clorra*; DM has misread *clorra* as *dorra* as Wallenberg pointed out (p. 323). The text should read *he him sset*. Omit Morris's emendation.

187/5–8. Tobias 4: 7–9.

187/8–10. Matthew 19: 21.

187/13–14. Hosea 6: 6.

187/14–16. Cf. Augustine, *City of God*, IV, xxiii (ed. B. Dombart (Leipzig, 1909), I, 174).

187/30–4. John 12: 1–6.

188/4–5. James 1: 5.

188/6–7. Matthew 5: 45.

188/7–8. *huo þet is*: C *quil est*; DM has mistaken *quil* for *qui* 'whoever'. The English should read *þet he is*. Cf. Wallenberg, p. 323.

188/10–12. Luke 6: 36.

188/12–13. 1 Peter 1: 13–21 is perhaps referred to here.

188/13–16. Ecclesiasticus 4: 10–11.

188/18–19. Proverbs 14: 31.

188/19–21. Matthew 25: 40.

188/25–6. *þe lhordes sergont . . . to þe sergond*: C *le sergant au seignor . . . au seignor*; the passage is corrupt as Wallenberg pointed out (p. 323). The sense requires *le seignor . . . au seignor*. This reading, in fact, appears in all early manuscripts except G1 which partly shares the erroneous reading of C. The English text should read *þe lhord . . . to þe lhord*.

188/33–5. James 2: 13.

188/35–189/1. The passage is a paraphrase of Matthew 25: 41–6.

189/4–7. Luke 16: 19–31.

189/7–10. Matthew 25: 1–13.

189/16–17. *þet uram reuþe went þane reg*: C *a cui pite le dos torra*; *pite* is the subject. The English should read *te huam* for *þet uram*.

189/22–3. See especially Hebrews 7: 1–3; cf. Psalm 109 (110): 4; Hebrews 5: 5–6; 7: 17–21.

189/24. *kennd*: C *lignage*; Wallenberg (p. 134, n. 1) assumes an error for *ken*; *kennd* would derive from OE (*ge*)*cynd* 'lineage' but it would normally assume a final -*e*. Wallenberg's conjecture may be correct though the form could have elision. For the double consonant see p. 42.

189/27–31. Matthew 25: 41.

190/3. This story is to be found in the *Acta Sanctorum* for 31 July, p. 218 (cf. Sisam, *Fourteenth Century Verse and Prose* (Oxford, 1925), p. 212).

190/4. *ancerne*: an error for *aucerne* as Sisam points out.

190/18. For this story see *Acta Sanctorum*, 23 January, pp. 501–2.

190/20. *A*: C *kun*; supply *þet* before *A*.

190/33. *hede*: cf. 58/28.

191/7 ff. Gregory, *Dialogues*, I, ix (PL lxxvii, col. 197).

191/18. The story is the basis, as Sisam points out, of the fabliau of *Brunain*.

191/20–1. Matthew 19: 29; Mark 10: 29–30.

191/28–9. *þet he hedde y-yolde*: C *que li auoit rendu*; Varnhagen pointed out ((1879), 52) that DM took *que* as accusative and *li* as *il*. Read *þet him hedde y-yolde* (the cow).

191/29. *yloked*: C *aiugiees* 'awarded'; Wallenberg (p. 150, n. 3) draws attention to *OED* (Look *v.* 6 f.) for the sense 'provide', 'decree'.

191/31. *chapuare* renders French *marchande*.

192/1. *hi lyezeþ*: C *perdent*; *hi* is superfluous according to Wallenberg (p. 323). But the idiom is perfectly acceptable.

192/10. *of tol*: C *de tolte*; Wallenberg points out (p. 323) that DM has taken the wrong sense of *tolte*. Here it means 'plundering' not 'toll'.

192/12–15. Deuteronomy 17: 1.

192/15–17. Ecclesiasticus 34: 24.

193/1. *y-yeue*: C *donee*; all the E manuscripts (except G1 which reads as C) read *doit estre donee* which gives better sense. The English should read *ssel by y-yeue*.

193/4. *þet þo þet ne byeþ*: C *qua ceus qui ne sont pas*; the majority of E manuscripts read as C. DM seems to have misunderstood the abbreviation of *qua* as *que*. The text should read *þet to þo* etc. 'than to those'. The phrase depends upon *more* in line 1.

193/5. *wel ich habbe þe eft / yzed*: C *bien le vus a ci recite*; supply *hit* before *þe*. The phrase only occurs in G1, C and looks like a marginal note which has been incorporated in the text.

193/9. *zuo me*: C *son* (*se on*); emend *zuo* to *ȝef*. Cf. Wallenberg, p. 323.

193/12. *Vor*: in spite of the capital *vor* is a conjunction.

193/20. *deþ harm uader oþer moder*: C *fet mal a pere e a mere*; perhaps supply *to* before *uader*; but the forms may be dative.

193/26–8. Gregory, *In Septem Psalmos Paenitentiales*, iv (PL lxxix, col. 595).

193/28–32. Mark 12: 42–4; Luke 21: 2–4.

193/34. *þanne a*: C *que suns*; read *þanne ȝef a*. The French *suns* is for *si uns*.

193/36–194/1. Ecclesiasticus 35: 11: *in omni dato hilarem fac vultum tuum; et in exsultatione sanctifica decimas tuas*. Thus *glede* (194/1) is an adjective and not a verb.

194/1–3. 2 Corinthians 9: 7.

194/7. *wel*: C *bien*; *bien* here seems to be a mistake for *rein*. Read *naȝt*.

194/8–10. Ecclesiasticus 4: 8.

194/12–15. Proverbs 3: 28.

194/15–16. *ne leng naȝt þine yefþe uram þe nyeduolle*: C *naloigne pas ton don au soufraitous*; emend *uram* to *to*. It is then unnecessary to render *leng* as 'withhold' as *MED* (LENGEN v. 4) does. The sense is rather 'delay not thy gift to the needy'; *leng* is a precise rendering of *aloigne*. The reference is to Ecclesiasticus 4: 3: *non protrahas datum angustianti*.

194/21. *beuore er hi*: C *auant quil*; omit *er* which would normally take a subjunctive unless preceded by a negative main clause.

194/22. *to moche hy ham zelleþ*: a calque on the French *trop lor uendent* 'they sell to them at too high a price'. Note that at 194/25 DM renders *trop achate* by *Dyere ha bayþ*. Cf. 198/1.

194/23–4. Cf. *De Beneficiis*, II, iv; ed. C. Hosius (Leipzig, 1898), p. 16. See also note to 198/1.

194/25. Morris's side note is wrong; 'delay' should read 'asking'.

194/27. *ha leueþ and hol*: C *il est uif e sain*; supply *is* before *hol*.

194/27–31. Ecclesiasticus 14: 11–12.

194/28–9. *do guod of þinen*: C *fai bien a toi*; the Vulgate reads *benefac tecum*. DM seems to have assumed that the sense was 'Do good with thy possessions' (cf. notes to 54/3, 111/32) rather than 'Do good to thyself'. The English should read *do guod to þyzelue* (cf. Wallenberg, p. 323).

194/31–2. Ecclesiasticus 14: 13.

194/36–195/1. Matthew 25: 40.

195/6–7. Galatians 6: 10.

195/17. *be þan þet me heþ huerof*: C *selom ce quon a. dont*; it would be possible to translate *huerof* as meaning 'the wherewithal' and so to translate the whole phrase as 'according as man has the wherewithal'; but, in view of the punctuation of the French text, it is perhaps better to supply a full-stop after *heþ*.

195/17–18. Ecclesiasticus 35: 12.

195/19–22. Tobias 4: 7–9.

195/26–30. For this tale see Seneca, *De Beneficiis*, II, xvi, 1–2; ed. cit., p. 33.

195/35–6. *Zom uolk þer byeþ*: for the number of *uolk* see pp. 62–3.

196/1–2. Ecclesiasticus 29: 15.

196/3. *yef he hit zent*: C *cil la uoie*; DM seems to have read the French as *sil lenuoie*. Read *he hit ziȝþ*.

196/4. *onderstant*: C *atent*; read *abit* (cf. note to 74/24). No E manuscripts have the reading *entent*.

196/4–8. Matthew 6: 3–4.

196/8. *þe halt*: C *te rendra*; the Latin has *reddet tibi*. Emend to *þe ssel ayenyeue*. Cf. Wallenberg, p. 115, n. 1.

196/11. *wone*: C *condicion*; the French may mean 'feeling' or 'moral state'. Cf.Godefroy, Compl. CONDICION.The English could mean 'frame of mind'.

196/15. *him*: probably an erroneous rendering of French *le* 'it'. Cf. 60/16.

196/16–17. *uolkerede*: C *genz luire*; the reference is to Matthew 5: 16; *Sic luceat lux vestra coram hominibus*. DM seems to have confused *luire* and *lire*. Cf. Wallenberg, p. 266, n. 2. Read *uolke ssine*.

196/18–20. 'and therefore St. Gregory says that a man may do his works (of charity) openly provided that the motive be right as well'. The reference is to *Moralia*, VIII, xlviii (PL lxxv, col. 853). The English paraphrases *opus ergo nostrum cum hominibus ostenditur, in cordis prius examinatione pensandum est per ejusdem ostensionis studium quid quaeratur; si enim dantis gloriam quaerimus, etiam publicata nostra opera, in conspectu illius occulta servamus*.

196/23–4. Isaiah 58: 7.

196/26. *zom uolk byeþ*: for the number of *uolk* see pp. 62–3.

196/29–30. Job 31: 19; *þe guoinde* renders French *trespassanz* which renders Latin *pereuntem* 'he who perishes, is perishing' of which *þe guoinde* is a dubious rendering.

197/2. *þet* ('than') here refers back to *betere* 196/36.

197/4–5. *and ham makeþ . . . makeþ ha*m: the subject is *manie riche men*.

197/7. *þer byeþ som uolk*: see pp. 62–3.

197/13–17. Cf. Deuteronomy 4: 9.

197/19–22. Cf. *Enchiridion*, lxxvi (PL xl, col. 268).

197/22. *uor*: C *fors*; emend to *bote*.

197/22. *yef he*: C *cil*; DM read *cil* as *s'il*. Omit *yef*.

197/25. *þe ilke þet*: C *que cil*; omit *þet* or read *þet þe ilke* as suggested by Wallenberg, p. 324.

197/32–4. Psalm 40 (41): 1.

197/33. *ham yeueþ*: C *entent*; the English means 'devote themselves' (cf. *OED* GIVE *v.* IV). Here and at 198/19, where DM renders French *entendent* by *doþ ham*, the translation is only approximately equivalent to the French. Cf. 198/5.

198/1. *to moche bayþ/þet byt*: the sense is evident from VV (214/32–3) *Dere he bieþ þ*[t] *askeþ* and from *The Royal Book*: *It is overdere bought that is damaunded*. See Whiting B 636 and note to 194/23–4.

198/11–15. Matthew 25: 41–3. Morris's emendation here and at 198/23 brings the English into line with the biblical text. But Wallenberg points out (p. 324) that the French has *maleurez* and *li beneurez* which DM has faithfully rendered.

198/20. *betake*: C *deliures*; it looks as though DM has taken *deliures* as *liures*; or, possibly, as Wallenberg suggests (p. 324) confused the sense 'set free' with the sense 'hand over'. The dictionaries give no examples of *betake* 'deliver'. The text should probably read *deliured*.

198/21–2. Matthew 25: 34.

198/23–7. *ye yblissede* in line 23 should read *þe yblissede*. Cf. note to 198/8–11. The reference is to Matthew 25: 34, 40.

198/28. *y[e]ue*: emendation is unnecessary. See note to 46/9.

198/30–1. Matthew 5: 7.

199/4. *mid*: C *ou*; DM has mistaken *ou* 'where' for *o* 'avec'. Emend *mid* to *huyder*. The subject is *merci*. Cf. Wallenberg, p. 324.

199/13–14. *to god uor to knawe*: C *a dieu conoistre*: DM has taken *a*, the infinitive sign, as the preposition 'to'. The first *to* should be omitted.

199/18. *y-robbed*: C *rauie* 'ravished', 'rapt'; emend to *yrauissed*.

199/19–21. 1 Thessalonians 4: 16.

199/23. *þe knyȝt*: the French *li cheualier* is plural. Read *knyȝtes* to restore concord.

199/28–31. Luke 10: 38–42.

199/32–4. Cf. Gregory, *Moralia*, VI, xxxvii (PL lxxv, cols. 760–1).

200/6. *þe loue*: C *Le don*; emend *loue* to *yefþe* which the sense requires.

200/16. *ine*: C *e*; DM seems to have misread *e* as *en*. Read *and*.

200/17. *mid*: C *ou*; DM has mistaken *ou* 'where' for *o* 'avec'. Read *huer*. Cf. Wallenberg, p. 324.

200/18. *of hi*m / *ne uor hi*m: 'of itself nor for itself'. *Him* is the normal neuter reflexive pronoun.

200/19. *þes god*: C *cil don*; Wallenberg (p. 94, n. 1; 324) suggests that DM read *dieu* for *don*, since *god* is not usually masculine; but *þes* more probably reflects a French *cist*, the reading of all E manuscripts except G1, V, Ld, R1. The influence of the French often produces anomalous gender concord. Cf. discussion pp. 88 ff.

200/27–8. *þe zaulen. þet belongeþ*: C *les ames qui ap*artienent; *e les choses* should be provided before *qui* (P1, 2, A2, M, An, V, Ld, Ca1, Add1, R1). This is required to complete the sense. The English should read *þe zaulen and þe þinges þet* etc.

200/35–6. Acts 15: 9.

201/2. *uayrhede*: renders *purgacion*.

201/5–6. *yborȝinge*: C *sauuement*; we should expect *yberȝinge*. Wallenberg (p. 40, n. 2) suggests that the vowel may be due to the influence of the past participle but it may well be a scribal error. Cf. *bouore, bolongeþ, iocob, iorome* etc. and note to 17/32.

201/7–8. Matthew 5: 8.

201/8–9. *ine . . . is*: C *en present*; DM's translation makes good sense but does not represent the French, where the contrast seems to be between seeing God here on earth by faith and by the grace of the Holy Spirit, and seeing him in paradise.

201/9. *alyȝte*: this seems to be p.c. although the sense is predicative rather than attributive. Cf. 243/30, 250/12.

201/13. Cf. Hebrews 10: 22.

201/21–2. Wallenberg suggests (p. 324) that the second *þet* should be omitted and *he* inserted before *hine*. But the text makes sense as it stands; *to huam þet* means 'to whom' and the antecedent of *þet*[3] is *god*. *Man* is the subject of *heþ zuo uoryete* in lines 24–5.

201/21–7. The citation seems to be a free rendering of Psalm 48 (49): 13, 21 blended with Psalm 8: 5–9.

201/31. *of erþe*: C *de terre*; this reading, shared by G1, seems to be a corruption of *contraires*, the reading of E manuscripts except P1 and G1. The English should read *contrarie*.

201/32. *he tekþ*: C *i seme*; Wallenberg (p. 324) suggests that DM read *enseigne* for *seme*. He presumably read *i* as *il*.

201/36–202/1. Matthew 5: 8.

202/18–20. John 15: 3.

202/23–7. 4 Kings 5: 1–14.

202/29. *and* is not in C and is superfluous. Cf. Wallenberg, pp. 324–5.

202/31. *o*: seems to be an error for *a*. Cf. note to 17/22.

203/1–3. Bernard, *Epistolae*, 113 (PL clxxxii, col. 258).

203/9–13. Numbers 21: 9.

203/12. *his(e)*: C *le*; emend to *hit* in both instances.

203/18. Morris's emendation is required by the sense.

203/27–8. Perhaps a gloss on Proverbs 16: 27.

203/28–9. This seems to reflect a gloss on 1 Corinthians 15: 33: *corrumpunt mores bonos colloquia mala*.

203/36–204/2. Matthew 12: 34; Luke 6: 45.

204/5–7. *þe nase . . . ine guode smackes*: C differs from DM here in supplying a verb in these last two items; *les narilles de trop soi deliter . . . La langue de trop soi deliter* etc.

204/9. *ine*: C *e*; read *and* for *ine*.

204/9–10. Jeremiah 9: 21.

204/14. *fortin*: C *fortin*; *MED* (FORTIN adj.) records a Walterus Fortin in 1201; but the word is no doubt taken from the French and not evidence of an English loan.

204/20–1. *hem uledden*: C *sen foirent*; for the reflexive usage see *MED* FLEN v. (1) 1 (e).

204/25. *ine ʒenne*: C *en pecchie*; a number of early manuscripts (Pι, 4, V, Caι, Addι, Rι) read *empechie*. The English should read *wiþhyalde* as the reading *en pecchie* is clearly an error for *enpecchie, empechie*.

204/26. *of þe herte*: C *du cuer*; Gι shares the erroneous reading of C. Other early manuscripts read *pour ce (que)*. The reading of Gι and C may be a corruption of *du puer que*. In the English text, *of þe herte* should be omitted.

204/32–4. Galatians 5: 17.

205/3–4. Jeremiah 13: 7.

205/5. *þet*: is not in the French and should be omitted. *chasteté* is the subject of *uorrotede*.

205/8. *þe ilk*: read *þe ilke*. Cf. 211/33 where *þe ilk* is corrected to *þe ilke*.

205/8. *þe wyþdraʒinges*: C *par abstinence*; *þe* is an error for *be*.

205/11. *greate*: C *grosses*; *gros* here means 'coarse', 'plain'. Cf. note to 205/15. The reference is to *legumina . . . et aqua* of Daniel 1: 12.

205/10–12. Daniel 1: 5–16, Daniel 3. The sense requires 'and' before *nolden* in line 11. This reading appears in all E manuscripts except Pι, Addι, and Gι which, like C, omits the conjunction.

205/15. *greate*: C *grasses*; DM's text may have had the reading which appears in Pι, Addι, *granz* whence the rendering *greate*; or possibly he read *grosses* 'coarse'. Emend *greate* to *uete*.

205/17. *aliʒteþ*: C *alument*; the French verb is correctly plural since it connects the two parts of the subject by *e*; DM's connective is *oþer* and the verb should strictly be singular, *aliʒt*.

205/26–7. Cf. Psalm 17 (18): 26: *Cum sancto sanctus eris; et cum viro innocente innocenter eris*.

205/31–2. Ecclesiasticus 8: 20.

205/36–206/3. 2 Samuel (Kings) 13.

206/1. *Dauiþ is*: read *Dauiþis*. It is not clear in the manuscript whether the *-is* is separate or joined to *Dauiþ* but the form is likely to be the genitive case rather than an early example of the genitive compound with *his*.

206/3–5. Genesis 39: 1–20.

206/5–6. 1 Corinthians 6: 18.

206/10–11. Cf. Genesis 19: 15–17.

206/23. *stempe*: C *trebuche*; Wallenberg (p. 233, n. 2) points out that Morris is probably correct in connecting this word with the form *stumpe* in *The Owl and the Nightingale* even though the etymology is difficult. Wallenberg assumes an Old English **stympan* which he compares with Mod. Norw. *stympa* and *stumpa* 'stumble, trip', the sense here required.

206/24–6. Ecclesiasticus 33: 29.

206/26–7. Ephesians 4: 27.

206/29–30. *he is ydel* . . . *þet yefþ*: C *qui est oiseus* . . . *il done*; the reading of C gives the required sense. DM should read *he þet is ydel* . . . *yefþ*.

206/30. *to þe zaule*: C *a lame*; all other early manuscripts (except G1) read *a lanemi*. This gives better sense and the English should read *yuo* for *zaule*. G1 shares the erroneous reading of C.

206/30–2. Cf. Jerome, *Regula Monacharum*, Cap. xxxviii (PL xxx, col. 422).

206/34. *uor* is redundant; cf. Wallenberg, p. 325. The reference is to Ezechiel 16: 49.

206/35. *þet prede*: C *que orgoil*; DM's translation is a calque on the French. The *þet* is pleonastic. The Latin reads, *Ecce haec fuit iniquitas Sodomae, sororis tuae: superbia, saturitas panis et abundantia, et otium ipsius et filiarum eius.*

207/2–3. *deþ* . . . *lyeseþ* . . . *bezetteþ*: for the number of *uolk* see pp. 62–3. The number of the verbs should be regularized.

207/10. *he ne nimþ*: C *il ne prennent (pas)*; emend *he ne nimþ* to *hi ne nimeþ*.

207/13–15. Ambrose, *De Obitu Valentiniani Imperatoris*, 32 (PL xvi, col. 1369).

207/22–4. Mark 11: 24.

207/24–7. James 1: 6.

207/27–8. *yerninde and talyinde / ne þengþ naȝt*: C *coardant e contant ne pense riens*; there are a number of errors here; (i) unless it is a case of the rare sense 'be reluctant' (see *OED* YEARN v.[1] 6 b), *yerninde* cannot be right; DM's text may have read *courrant*; (ii) some early manuscripts read *doutant* for *coardant e contant* (so E except P4, V, R1, which omit, and G1 which reads as C); (iii) for *ne pense riens* in G1, C, other E manuscripts (except P4, V, R1, which omit) read *nempetre riens*. It may be that C's *contant* is a corruption of *doutant* as *ne pense riens* is of *nempetre riens*. The English should, perhaps, read *recreyd and dredinde / *receyueþ naȝt*. The passage seems to render James 1: 7: *non ergo aestimet homo ille quod accipiat aliquid a Domino.*

207/30–1. Cf. Psalm 27 (28): 7.

207/31–3. Psalm 32 (33): 22.

207/34. *zuo þet he*: C *cil qui*; DM has read *cil qui* as *si que*. The English should read *he þet*. Cf. 223/36.

207/34. *zayde*: C *disoit*; the correct reading is probably *dec(h)oit* as all E manuscripts except A2 (*desert*) and G1, An (*disoit*). V, R1 omit.

207/35–208/1. Matthew 7: 8; Luke 11: 10.

207/36. *clepeþ*: here and at 208/2 Wallenberg (p. 55, n. 2) derives from OE. *clæppian* as the sense requires; the form is irregular but may be due to confusion with *clepie*.

208/4. *skele*: C *reson*; DM has the wrong sense for *reson* which here means 'discourse'. Emend *skele* to *spekinge*.

208/5–6. *moche uolk acseþ*: see pp. 62–3.

208/7–9. James 4: 3.

208/10–13. Matthew 20: 20–1; Mark 10: 35–7.

208/11. *þe on*: C *que li uns*; read *þet þe on*.

208/15. *ansurede*: read *ansuerede*.

208/14–16. Matthew 20: 22; Mark 10: 38.

208/17. *yef he him lokeþ*: C *si se gart*; *gart* is best rendered as a jussive subjunctive and *si* as an adverb of affirmation (cf. Foulet, § 442); thus the English should read *zuo him loki* 'well, let him keep himself'. *Oþer* renders French *ou*.

208/19. Read *fariseu* as Morris suggests; the reference is to Luke 18: 10–14.

208/29. *libbinde*: C *uiues*; Cotton's *uiues* is an error for *uiles* (substantially the reading of P1, 4, M, G1, An, Ca1, Add1); read *uile* for DM's *libbinde*.

209/1–2. *Ne onderstand naȝt*: C *natent pas*; read *abid* for *onderstand*. Cf. note to 74/24. Ld reads *nentent*.

209/1–9. Cf. *Enn. in Psalmos*, Psalm, 62: 6 (PL xxxvi, col. 755–6).

209/9–12. Cf. Augustine, *Enn. in Psalmos*, 62: 6 (PL xxxvi, cols. 755–6). The attribution to Ambrose is perhaps a mistake.

209/10. *acseþ*: C *demande*; emend to imp. sg. *akse*.

209/10. *grat þing*: this should be plural as the French. Read *greate þing*.

209/14–16. John 14: 13, 14; 15: 16; 16: 23.

209/16. *Yef he*: C *Cil*; DM has misread *cil* 'he' as *s'il* 'if he'. Omit *yef*.

209/19–21. Matthew 6: 33.

209/21. *þou sselt habbe*: C *uous aurez*; emend to *ȝe ssole habbe*.

209/22–3. See Whiting M 215. The *Ayenbite* example is not cited.

209/32: *is þet lif eurelestinde*: C *cest la uie per-durable*; DM seems to have misunderstood the French, where *cest la uie per-durable* is in apposition to *reaume du ciel (þe riche of heuene)*. Read *þet is þet lif eurelestinde*; *bidde* is an imprecise rendering of *querre*.

210/2–3. Psalm 33 (34): 10.

210/5–6. *and mest him faileþ*: C *e plus li faut*; E manuscripts (except V, R1 which omit, and G1, which agrees with C) omit *e* before *plus* as the sense requires. In the English *and* should be omitted. DM's rendering of *faut* is imprecise.

210/7–8. *Epistola liii ad Paulinum* (PL xxii, col. 549).

210/10. *and acsi*: C *e demander*; the French should read *de demander* (so P1, 2, 4, A2, An, Ca1) and the English *to acsi*.

210/17. *be-tuene þine teþ*: C *entre tes denz*; Matthew 6: 6: *Tu autem cum oraveris, intra in cubiculum tuum, et clauso ostio, ora Patrem tuum in abscondito*. The phrase *entre tes denz* may have been thought to mean 'quietly', *sotto voce*. The Latin, however, suggests that the true reading is *entre dedenz*, the reading of P1, 4, A2, M, Ld, Ca1, Add1. The English should read *guo wiþinne*. G1, An share the erroneous reading of C.

210/20–5. Cyprian, *Liber de Oratione Dominica*, XXXI (PL iv, col. 557).

210/26–7. Isidore, *Sententiarum Liber*, III, viii (PL, lxxxiii, col. 673).

210/27–9. Cf. Augustine, *Tractatus IX in Joh*. (PL xxxv, col. 1464).

210/28. *beate*: C *debatre*; Wallenberg (p. 325) points out that DM has translated literally. But the French verb means 'move' not 'beat'. DM seems to have taken the phrase to mean 'babble'.

210/32. *betune*: read *betuene*.

210/33. *goth*: DM has other instances of the spelling *th* for *t* and there is no need to emend.

211/6. *opre speche*: C *ou uentre*; DM's text had the correct reading *un autre*. G1 shares the error of C.

211/7. *hit þe þingþ*: C *il te semble*; other E manuscripts omit *te* except V, R1, which omit the passage. Sense supports this reading and the English should read *hit þingþ*.

211/7–8. *zuych uolk . . . biddeþ*: for the number of *uolk* see pp. 62–3.

211/13–15. John 4: 24.

211/15–17. Psalm 140 (141): 2: *Dirigitur oratio mea sicut incensum in conspectu tuo*.

211/29–32. Probably a gloss on Psalm 129 (130): 2. At 211/31, *mid* renders French *du*.

211/32–33. Augustine, *Enn. in Psalmos*, Psalm 37: 10 (PL xxxvi, col. 404; *flagrantia charitatis, clamor cordis est*.

211/34. *uor to telle tales*: C *de paroles acontees*; read *of tales ytolde*. Cf. Wallenberg, p. 326.

211/34–212/2. For the citation from Gregory see note to 99/18–21.

212/2. *y-sliked ueleuold*: C *polies multiplier*; the French infinitive is substantival in function. The passage means 'not the multiplication of elegant and polished words'.

212/6–7. *þet he ous loki uram þo þyeues. and uram þe uer*: C *quil nous gart de ceus larrons e du feu*; the erroneous reading of C repeats a phrase from the previous sentence. Other E manuscripts (except P4, G1, V, R1) read *(en)contre le feu*.

212/10. *foles*: C *fous*; the reference is to Psalm 68 (69): 2: *Salvum me fac, Deus, quoniam intraverunt aquae usque ad animam meam*. It seems likely, therefore, that in line 10 the reading *foles* (French *fous*) is wrong and that the correct reading is *floz*; so E manuscripts except P4, V, R1, and G1, which shares the erroneous reading of C.

212/15. *of þe dyaþe*: C *de la mort*; the reading *de la mer* appears in all E manuscripts except P2, V, R1, and G1, which shares the error of C. The text should read *of þe ʒe*.

212/14–16. Matthew 8: 25; cf. Mark 4: 38; Luke 8: 24.

212/29–213/2. This passage does not appear in Cotton.

212/36–213/2. Matthew 6: 2, 5, 16.

213/12–13. *zeterday. Also byeþ þe festes principals*: VV (236/4) runs straight on: *Saterday and þe oþere hiʒe feste daies also*. Cotton has a paragraph mark between *sabat* and *ausi* but such a mark need not indicate a new sentence. Compare, for example, line 16 where Cotton has a para-graph mark after *recorde* (*recordeþ*) in spite of the fact that the *hou*-clauses are clearly the objects of *recordeþ*. It seems likely, therefore, that we should render *Also* as a conjunction 'just as' rather than an adverb 'likewise', 'in addition', which gives strained sense.

213/33. *ich guo playe. and solaci*: C *ie me uois deduire e iouer*; comparison with the French and with 213/34 suggests that *me* should be supplied before *solaci*.

214/11–12. Cf. Anselm, *Meditationes*, ii (PL clviii, col. 722).

214/14–15. 1 Corinthians 7: 29.

214/29. *man him ssel habbe / wel oneste*: C *on se doit auoir mout honestement*; DM's translation is a calque on the French *s'auoir* 'to behave' (see Gode-froy, Avoir). For *oneste* read *onestliche*.

214/33. Matthew 21: 13; Luke 19: 46.

214/35–215/2. Cf. Augustine, *Tractatus VII in Joh.* (PL xxxv, col. 1442).

215/15. com*munliche*: C *continuelment*; as Wallenberg points out (p. 326), DM has rendered *communalment*.

215/29–30. Psalm 21 (22): 7.

216/1–2. Cf. Bernard, *Sermones*, 12 *in Psalmum 'Qui Habitat'* (Leclercq, Rochais, iv. 459) and Job 13: 28.

216/3. Read *beyetinge* as Morris suggests. Wallenberg's comparison with *bleue* is dubious (p. 22, n. 2).

216/8–14. Esther 14 especially verse 16. At 216/14, *ine grat wlatiynge* renders *en grant abhominacion*, the reading of G1, C, Ca1. The text should, in fact, read *e en ai grant abhomination* as (P1), A2, M, An, Add1.

216/18. *payinges*: C *paiemenz*; Wallenberg (p. 184, n. 4) suggests that the French should read *paremenz*. This conjecture is confirmed by the reading of all E manuscripts except V, R1, and G1, which agrees with C.

216/19–22, 27, 31–3. 1 Timothy 2: 9.

216/27. *huiche byeþ*: C *queles soient*; Wallenberg (p. 326) points out that *queles* is for *qu'eles* and accordingly *huiche* should read *þet hi*. A sub-junctive should follow *huiche* as in the French. For *byeþ* therefore the text should read *ssolle by*.

216/30. *mid stondinde nhicke*: C *col estendu*; Wallenberg (p. 234, n. 4) suggests that DM has confused *estendu* 'stretched' with *estant* 'upright'.

216/34–217/2. 1 Corinthians 11: 5–15.

217/4. MS *ydift*: this may be an early example of the change from /xt/ to /ft/. See Jordan, §§ 196, n. and 294.

217/11. *of þan oþer of hire*: C *de celui ou de cele*; it seems that *þan* is to be taken as meaning 'him' in this context.

217/13. *ssol*: cf. note to 96/33.

217/19–20. Tobias 12: 8.

217/22–4. The reference is probably to Isaiah 1: 15–17.

217/31–2. Lamentations 3: 41.

217/33–4. 1 Timothy 2: 8.

217/35. *þe clene benen*: C *les nettes oeures*; DM's text may have read *eures* (cf. *euures* in M, Ca1) which he has rendered as 'hours', 'monastic prayers'. The correct reading would be *workes*. Cf. Wallenberg, p. 326.

218/1–3. Isaiah 1: 15.

218/9–10. *þe greate to mochelhedes*: C *les granz outrages*; *to* may be an error arising from the preceding *-te* of *greate*; or DM has coined the word *tomochelhede* 'excess'; *to* should be omitted or joined to *mochelhede*.

218/13–15. See note to 31/1–2.

218/20–2. The reference is to the parable of the talents (Matthew 25: 15–30).

218/26–9. Matthew 25: 1–13.

219/1. *poss[t]es*: no need to emend. See p. 49.

219/4–7. James 5: 15–16.

219/7. *uory[e]ue*: see note to 116/4.

219/8–9. Exodus 17: 8–13.

219/10–11. *more . . . biddinde*: C *plus uaut .i. saint e puet empriant*; the text appears to mean 'a holy man praying is of more worth and has more power etc.'

219/27–9. Matthew 18: 20.

220/3. *þet*: C *a ce que*; the reading of C shows that the meaning is 'in that'. Cf. Wallenberg, p. 326.

220/9. *amerreþ* renders French *honissent*.

220/9–10. *hare techinge þet kueade uolk*: C *leur enseignent les mauuais geus*; DM has rendered *geus* 'games' as *gens* and *enseignent* as *enseignement*. The English should read *kueade gemenes* for *þet kueade uolk* and *hise techeþ* for *hare techinge*. Cf. Wallenberg, p. 326.

220/15. *reherci*: the French suggests that this is intransitive but *hit* could be the object.

220/15. *kende*: C *nature*; the sense may be 'mode of action' (see *OED* KIND *sb.* I 8) but all other E manuscripts (except P4, which omits) have *matiere*. Cf. 127/24.

220/18-20. Proverbs 22: 6.

220/20-1. Perhaps a reference to Aristotle's Nicomachean Ethics: *Ex iuvene autem duccione recta sortiri ad virtutem, difficile non a talibus nutritum legibus* (*Aristoteles latinus* xxvi. 3 (Textus purus), ed. K. A. Gauthier (Leiden–Brussels, 1972), 79ᵇ31-2.)

220/22. *Huo þet tekþ colte endaunture*: C *qui aprent polein endanteure*; Wallenberg (p. 84, n. 1) suggests that DM has been confused by the use of *qui* for *que*. The French *en danteure* 'in taming' he has taken as a noun, possibly influenced by the existence of the English *endaunt* 'tame'. Read *þet þet colt lyerneþ ine taminge*.

220/30-2. *huo may . . . of hare zennes*: the French has *qui* for DM's *huo* which should be emended to *þet*. Translate 'which can prevent them from being married and who nevertheless are shriven themselves and repent of their sins'. The final member of the sentence is relative in implication although not in form.

221/10. *laȝe*: C *foi*; possibly a misreading of *foi* as *loi* as Wallenberg suggests (p. 326).

221/12. Genesis 2: 24; Matthew 19: 5, 6; cf. 1 Corinthians 6: 16.

221/18-22. Titus 2: 3-5.

221/35. Omit *bi*.

222/1. *scele*: C *raancon*; DM has read *raancon* as *raison*.

222/25. *he ofserueþ*: C *e desert*; supply *and*.

223/6. *zetnesses*: C *truies*; Wallenberg (p. 292, n. 4) suggests that DM, confronted with *truies*, substituted a word which seemed to him to make sense. As Wallenberg suggests, the original text probably read *termes*, a reading which appears in P1, M, V, Ld, Ca1, Add1, R1.

223/7. *yled mid scele*: C *sougiez a reson*; as Wallenberg points out (p. 326), the translation is very free and DM possibly did not understand the French.

223/15. *saren*: Wallenberg (p. 326) compares *euen, marþen, tobyen* and rejects Morris's proposed emendation to *sareu*. Cf. p. 51, n. 1.

223/15-23. Tobias 3: 7-8; 6: 16, 17.

223/22. *bote to hare lecherie to uoluelle*: C *fors a leur lecherie acomplir*; *uoluelle* is usually transitive and the first *to* should probably be omitted.

223/28. *ne oueryernþ*: C *notraie*; Wallenberg (p. 183, n. 1) is probably correct in suggesting that DM took the verb from *outrer* 'surpass'. A spelling such as that of P1, 2, A2, (*n*)*outroie* could have given rise to such confusion. The text should read *ne granteþ*,

223/36. *zuo þet he*: C *cil qui*; DM has taken *cil qui* as *si quil*. Cf. 207/34.

The English should read *huo þet*. The preceding clause goes with the sentence *þe oþer . . . naȝt guo*.

224/8. *manhod*: in view of the accusative *manhode*, this is probably for *manhode* by elision.

224/11. *hi alsuo abyde*: C *il sen doit souffrir*; DM has clearly had a different reading here.

224/18–19. *hit is þet . . . zenne*: C *se doit on souffrir de ce kon puet fere sanz pecchie*; the sense is evident from the context and from VV (249/5–7) which reads: *but oþerwhile schal a man forbere þing þat he may do wiþ-oute synne* etc. DM has mistaken the sense of *souffrir* which here must imply 'refrain from'. Cf. Wallenberg, p. 327.

224/28–30. Cf. *Physiologus*: *concupiscentiam fetus minime in se habet* (*Physiologus Latinus*, ed. F. J. Carmody (Paris, 1939), p. 57).

224/33. *þet*: C *que*; other E manuscripts read *il peche* after *que* (except P2, which omits, and G1, which shares the error of C). Read *he zeneȝeþ* after *þet*.

224/35. *yef hit is zenne*: C *que il pecche*; cf. Wallenberg, p. 327.

225/1. *is*: omit. The French text reads correctly: *Le tierz cas ou on puet* etc.

225/14–17. 1 Corinthians 7: 8–9.

225/34. *þo*: see note to 17/32.

226/2–5. *Physiologus*, ed. Carmody, pp. 49–50.

226/5. *he is*: read *hi* for *he*. The French has simply *est* which DM probably translated automatically as *he is*.

226/10–12. Judith 8: 5.

226/12–17. 1 Timothy 5: 11–14.

226/19–23. Luke 2: 36–7.

226/24–5. *ssarpnes of metes . . . þys spilþ ine lostes*: C *aspresce de uiandes. car sicom dist saint bernart ceste perit en delices*; various errors occur in this passage (i) all E manuscripts (except G1, which shares the reading of C) read after *uiandes*, *Car si comme dist sainz pole. La feme veve qui en delices maine sa vie ele muert par (pechie) delices.* (*Car si comme dist sainz bernarz*); (ii) most E texts share the reading *aspresce de uiandes* (P2, 4, A2, M, G1, An, Ld, Ca1); P1, Add1 read *aspresce de uie 7 soi abstenir de viandes* which may be correct; (iii) *ceste perit* is a weak reading and the correct reading, *chaste peri(s)t* appears in all E manuscripts except P2, C. The English text should read *ssarpnes of lyf and him wyþdraȝe uram metes. Vor ase zayþ saint pol. Þe wodewe þet ine delices let hare lyf hi sterfþ bi delices. Vor ase zayþ sain bernart chastete spilþ* etc. The Pauline reference is to 1 Timothy 5: 6: *quae (vidua) in deliciis est, vivens mortua est*.

226/31. *ase*: C *ausi*; the meaning is clearly 'also'. The correct reading is, perhaps, *alse*. Cf. note to 255/2–3.

226/31–227/4. Judith 8: 6–8.

226/34. *and more*: C *que plus*; read *þet more* as suggested by Wallenberg (p. 327).

226/36. *ledde*: C *amoit*; DM seems to have read *amenoit*. Cf. Wallenberg, p. 327.

227/10. *lokinge*: C *garde*; DM seems to have taken *garde* as a noun not a past participle. Emend to *yloked*.

227/15. *anlyke*: Wallenberg (p. 12, n. 2) assumes analogy from *anlikni* but this is unnecessary. The form probably derives from a case with a final back vowel.

227/24–6. Matthew 13: 44.

227/31–4. Matthew 22: 30; Mark 12: 25.

228/3. *chastete*: Wisdom 4: 1: *O quam pulchra est casta generatio cum claritate* whence the French *com est bele chastee lignee auoeques clarte*. DM has misunderstood the French and *chastete* ought to read *chaste*. The Latin further suggests that Wallenberg is wrong in supposing *lignee* to be a past participle. See p. 134, n. 2.

228/5. MS *castete*: there is no need to emend the manuscript here. The form occurs elsewhere in Middle English and is probably due to Latin *castitas*.

228/9–12. Cf. Jerome, *Epistola ad Eustochium de Custodia Virginitatis* (PL xxii, cols. 394–425).

228/16. *yzyenne*: C *apparant*; the English form is curious. The expected form would be *yzyene* (OE *gesione*). This form is probably due to confusion with the gerund. Cf. 238/19.

228/21. *y-queme god | and to his yuo*; C *plaire a dieu e a son anemi*; the double construction after *y-queme* may be due to French *a* and *to* should, perhaps, be omitted as Wallenberg suggests (p. 327).

228/24–6. 1 John 2: 15.

228/26–8. Galatians 1: 10.

228/27. MS *ichc* should be emended to *iche* or *ich*.

229/7. *And hi hise aliзteþ*: C *Eles reluisent*; DM seems to have read *e les* for *Eles*, namely, the daughters of Babylon. The verb *aliзte* is usually transitive in DM and we should, accordingly, emend to *hi ssyneþ*.

229/9. *ealde*: C *uiels* 'vile'; for this confusion see note 48/10.

229/10. *þe*: C *par*; read *be*.

229/11. *ham sseweþ*: C *se perent*; as Wallenberg (p. 327), points out, the verb is from *parer* 'adorn'. Read *agraypeþ* for *sseweþ*.

229/12–14. Psalm 44 (45): 14.

229/13. *þe kinges doзter of blisse*: a normal Middle English idiom for 'the king of bliss's daughter' and not an error as Wallenberg suggests (p. 327). Cf. 231/33–4, 241/25.

229/17. *me ssel wytye*: C *se doit on garder*; read *me ssel him wytye*.

229/19. *Iorome*: see note to 17/32.

229/30–2. 1 Corinthians 15: 33.

229/34. *y[e]fþ*: emendation is unnecessary; cf. note to 46/9.

229/34–5. *hi ham ssolle naȝt ssamie and afrounti*: C *il en deuient non uergoignex e affrontez* 'because of it they become shameless and bold'. DM has read *doiuent* for *deuient*, omitted *en*, and taken *non* as qualifying the verb instead of the adjective. Read *hi becomeþ þeruore wiþoute ssame and bolde*.

230/7–9. Canticles 2: 2.

230/9. *yloued*: C *ame*; DM has mistaken the noun *ame* 'soul' for the past participle of the verb *amer*. Emend *yloued* to *zaule*.

230/11. *specialliche more*: C *plus especiaument*; read *more specialliche*.

230/12–19. Cf. John, 13: 23; 19: 26, 27; 21: 7, 20; for John's virginity cf. Mombritius, *Sanctuarium* (Paris, 1910), ii, pp. 60–1.

230/23. *meniynges*: C *amouemens*; VV 255/17 *meuynges*; Wallenberg (p. 159, n. 1) suggests that DM read the French as *amone(s)temens* and translates 'admonitions'. The reading of VV, however, suggests that the correct reading may be *meuynges* 'impulses', a literal rendering of the French.

230/33–5. *Passio Sanctae Luciae*; see Mombritius, *Sanctuarium*, ii. p. 108, 41–2.

231/7–11. Bernard, *Sermones;* I, 5 *In Laudibus Virginis Matris* (Leclercq, Rochais, iv. 17).

231/7–8. *hit is . . . mid maidenhod*: C *cest mult bele chose* que *humilite auoeques uirginite*; DM has not really translated the idiomatic French *que*, *þet heþ* should, perhaps, be omitted. Cf. Wallenberg, p. 328.

231/16. *were y-woned*: C *solent*; the English means 'have been accustomed' rather than 'are accustomed' which the sense requires.

231/19–20. Luke 1: 29.

231/25. *þe ilke gates lokeþ* / *þe drede*: C *Ces portes gardent la paour*; the sense requires that *drede* be the subject.

231/28–30. *bisihede is specialliche . . . wordle*: C *curiosite especiaument de ueoir e de oir les uanitez du monde*; DM seems to have read *est speciaument* and lost the thread of the sentence. Read *bisihede, specialliche . . . wordle*.

231/30. *hy byeþ*: C *sont*; the subject is *bisihede* and both pronoun and verb should be singular.

231/31–4. Genesis 34: 1–2.

232/2–6. Matthew 25: 1–13.

232/6–7. *He clepeþ hier-ine þan of . . . holy cherche*: C *il apele ici endroit le reaume des cielz sainte eglise* 'herein he speaks of the kingdom of heaven, Holy Church. If DM is using *clepe* in the rare sense of 'speak of' (cf. *OED* CLEPE *v.* 4) then *þan of* is superfluous. But it may be that he did not understand the French *apele* and that *þan of* is the object of *clepe*. It should be omitted perhaps.

232/27. *þe bok of maydenhod*: Augustine, *De Sancta Virginitate* (PL xl, col. 412).

232/29–34. Augustine, op. cit., col. 412.

232/34. *we þe habbeþ y-zed uorbysne of þe lompe*: C *nous vus auons mis de la lampe essample*; *yzed* should, perhaps, read *yzet*.

232/35–6. Bernard, *Epistolae*, 322 (PL clxxxii, col. 527).

232/35. *Stude þou to bleue. uor hi*: C *estudiez vous . . . a perseuerance. car ele*; having translated *perseuerance* by a verb, DM has no antecedent for *hi*, which should read *bleuinge*. The reference is to Pseudo-Bernard, *Octo Puncta Perfectionis Assequendæ* (PL clxxxiv, col. 1184).

233/1. *Þise zix leues*: Cotton has, erroneously, *Ces .v. fuelles*. This error is shared by G1.

233/11–15. Augustine, *De Diligendo Deo* II (PL xl, col. 849): 'Diliges Dominum deum tuum ex toto corde tuo, *id est, ex toto intellectu*; et ex tota anima tua, *id est, ex tota voluntate tua*; et ex tota mente, *id est, ex tota memoria.*'

233/23 ff. Bernard, *Sermones super Cantica Canticorum*, XX, iii, 17–18 (Leclercq, Rochais i. 116).

234/1–3. 1 Timothy 1: 5.

234/2. *by*: the form *be* recorded by Wallenberg (s.v.) is an error. Cf. 247/32.

234/8. MS *hondraȝte*: the form *hondredaȝte* is assumed to be by analogy with *prittaȝte* (OE *þritiȝoðe*) etc. (*OED* HUNDREDAGHTE). It seems, therefore, possible that the form *hondraȝte* could be by contamination with the OE *hund*. In that case, Wallenberg is correct in suggesting that there is no need to emend (p. 125, n. 1).

234/9–12. Matthew 13: 23; Mark 4: 8.

234/13. *bouore, bolongeþ*: see note to 17/32.

234/27–8. *þe wyse maydynes: ham corounede*: C *les sages uierges corone*; the manuscript reads: *were mid ham ycorounede*. The words *were mid* and the letters *y* and the first *o* in *corounede* are subpuncted. *ham* and the final *e* of *corounede* are written above the line. Thus DM first wrote *were mid ycoroune d*. He then altered the construction but erroneously added an object *ham* which duplicates the object *þe wyse maydynes*. He should have written *þe wyse maydynes crouneþ*.

235/3. *and habbeþ ylete*: C *Eles ont laissees*; DM has perhaps mistaken the first letter of *Eles* as *e* 'and'. The text should read *Hi habbeþ ylete*.

235/6. Morris is clearly right here in suggesting that *tende* should be emended to *zixte*. None of the E manuscripts reads *disieme* for *sisieme*, which was presumably the reading of DM's manuscript.

235/12. *to chastete to loky*: C *a chastee garder*; cf. Wallenberg, pp. 333–4.

235/23–4. Leviticus 11: 44.

236/5–7. 1 Timothy 3: 2 and *passim*; but, more particularly, Titus 1: 7–9.

236/8–11. Exodus 12: 11.

236/12. *ham gerde | ope þe lenden*: C *ceindre leur rains*; Wallenberg may be right in suggesting (p. 328) that DM read *seur* for *leur* but the reading may be an early example of 'gird up'. Cf. 236/10.

236/13. *Þo*: C *dont*; DM would normally translate *þonne*.

236/13–16. Exodus 28: 40–2.

236/22. *And alsuo*: C *ausi*; omit *and*; *alsuo* is correlative with *ase* in line 20.

236/29. *ase moche ase scele berþ*: C *tant comme reson aporte*; as Wallenberg points out (p. 328), *aporter* means 'permit' (cf. Godefroy, Compl. APORTER). The text should read *graunteþ* for *berþ*.

237/3–4. Ezechiel 1: 18; 10: 12; Apocalypse 4: 6. The identification with the church is, of course, a gloss on the texts. Cf. Dante, *Purgatorio*, xxix.

237/13–17. *Ac huanne þe sseawere is briȝt . . . an dim*: C *Mais quant le mireor est cler* (so also G1) *on uoit bien sa tache e lordure qui est ou mireor. Mais cil qui en tel mireor ne se mire ne uoit mie la soe tache ne que len fet au mireor qui est lais e anubles*; this passage is confused. In the first place, lines 13–15 do not make sense. Many manuscripts read *la* for *sa* and *ors* for *cler*. This fits the argument, which is that as one cannot see one's own image in a dirty mirror but only the defects of the mirror, so when the clergy, the mirrors of Holy Church, are foul, their flock see not their own sins but only those of their pastors. In the second place, lines 15–17 should mean 'but, whoever looks in such a mirror, sees not his own defilement, any more than one does in a mirror that is foul and dim'. The negative in *ne se mire* (recorded only in C and G1) should be omitted. Thus, in line 14, we should read *uoul* for *briȝt* and omit *naȝt ne* in line 16.

237/16. *zikþ*: see p. 48.

237/21. *he*: renders French *on*. Cf. Wallenberg, p. 328.

237/23–5. Gregory, *Cura Pastoralis*, II, ii (PL lxxvii, col. 27).

237/25–6. Cf. Ecclesiasticus 34: 4: *Ab immundo quid mundabitur?*

237/28. *be þe ministre*: C *ou aministre*; Wallenberg (p. 328) rightly points out that the French means 'or administered'. Read *oþer iministred*.

237/31. *Vor*: C *Car*; this is an error for *que* 'than', the reading of P1, 2, 4, M, An, V, Add1, R1; G1 shares the error of C. *Hi* should, perhaps, be supplied before *hit*.

238/1. *þeruore þanne huam þet*: C *pour ce donc qu(e)*; DM has taken *que* as a relative. Omit *huam*.

238/5. *y-harmed*: C *puniz*; read *ipunissed*? Cf. Wallenberg, p. 329.

238/8. *zeuende*: C *sisime*; DM's reading is correct. It agrees with all the other E manuscripts.

238/13–14. *huo þet him . . . be spoushod ne ssel by naȝt*: C *sil se mariassent le mariage seroit nul*; read *yef hi* for *huo þet*; *ham doþ* for *him deþ*; *þe* for *be* and omit *ne*.

238/18–19. *þe uouler þet is þe spot*: *þe more he is yzyenne*; C comme *la tache est plus lede e plus apparant*; Wallenberg (p. 329) reads *ase þe spot is uouler and more yzyenne*. Cf. note to 228/16.

238/25, *ane*: the sense requires *one* for *ane*. Cf. note to 17/22.

238/27. *huanne*: the manuscript reading *þuanne* is, no doubt, a cross between *huanne* and *þanne* and is rightly emended by Morris.

238/28. *ane guodne man*: C *nus prodome*; DM clearly has the correct reading.

238/34. This tale is from *Vitae Patrum*, V, v, 39 (PL lxxiii, cols. 885–6).

239/15. *wer*: read *were*.

239/25–6. *moche uolk* ... *were yslaȝe*: for the number of *uolk* see pp. 62–3.

240/13. *uor him-zelue / to uiȝte*: C *pour soi* com*batre*; Wallenberg (p. 329) suggests reading *himzelf uor to uiȝte* but *uor himzelf to uiȝte* would be equally possible. The form *soi* appears to be for *soimeismes* but DM has taken it as reflexive.

240/34. *huerof*: C *dont*; *huerof* is clearly wrong. It should, perhaps, be emended to *hueruore*.

240/34–6. Cf. Galatians 2: 19–20; Romans 6: 11.

241/5–7. Galatians 6: 14. *MED* (CRUCIFIEN v. 2 (c)) interprets *ycrucifyed* as 'despised' but the biblical text supports the rendering 'crucified' with its specifically Christian overtones.

241/15–17. Philippians 3: 20: *Nostra autem conversatio in caelis est. Conversatio* is a rendering of the Greek πολίτευμα 'citizenship'.

241/18. *uor*: C *car se*; emend to *uor yef*.

241/21–4. Matthew 19: 21; cf. Mark 10: 21, Luke 18: 22.

241/25. *Mannes hord of religion*: 'a religious man's hoard'.

241/25–6. *Thesaurus monachi est voluntaria paupertas* (*Vitae Patrum*, V, vi, 14; PL lxxiii, col. 891).

241/28–9. Matthew 5: 3.

241/29. *sprit*: this form is probably genuine although it antedates the southern examples in *OED* (SPRITE *sb.*).

241/31. *no*: see *OED* No *conj.*[1]

241/34–6. Genesis 19: 17. Here, as at 242/2, DM uses the reflexive of *trosti* to render French *s'arester* 'stop, linger'. There seems no evidence of such a meaning for *trosti* and presumably DM did not understand the French.

242/5. *abide to*; C *entendre a*; 'give attention to', cf. note to 74/24.

242/6–8. Genesis 19: 26.

242/9. *ham*: C *ceus qui*; supply *þet*.

242/14–15. *byeþ þet uolk chealde*: for the number of *uolk* see pp. 62–3.

242/24–6. Luke 17: 32.

242/30–2. Luke 9: 62.

243/5–8. Philippians 3: 13: *Unum autem, quae quidem retro sunt obliviscens, ad ea uero quae sunt priora extendens meipsum* 'One thing (I can say) however, forgetting indeed what is behind me, reaching out of a truth for what lies ahead' etc. The translation of the second part of the quotation is not very exact. The French has *aloit tous iors auant soi* of which DM's is a literal rendering. VV (269/20) has more idiomatically *ʒede euere-more forwarde*.

243/9–10. *moche uolk . . . zetteþ*: see pp. 62–3.

243/25–7. Matthew 5: 8.

244/5–7. John 20: 29.

244/10–11. 1 Corinthians 13: 12.

244/12. *þet yzy*: C *que ueoir*; the infinitive is in apposition to *blissinge*. As elsewhere DM has rendered the idiomatic French *que* by *þet* but the sense would be better served by simply omitting it.

244/15–16. *mid . . . ham wondreþ/and ha*m *y-zyeþ*: C *ou li aignel e li saint se mirent e se merueillent*; as elsewhere in the text, DM has confused *ou* 'where' with *o* (*avec*). Emend *mid* to *huer*. DM has rendered the French verbs in the reverse order. The French text has 'where the lamb and the saints gaze and marvel'.

244/20–2. 1 Corinthians 2: 9.

244/22–34. Anselm, *Proslogion*, XXIV, XXV (Opera, ed. F. S. Schmitt (Edinburgh, 1946), I, 117–18).

244/29. *makinge*: C *fauture*; the form *faiture* appears in V, Add1, R1 and it is probably this form of the word which gave rise to DM's rendering. The sense is 'vague, crude shape' and the idiom should perhaps be compared with the phrase *mans wonder* in the Towneley *Noah*, 408. Thus *fauture dome* would mean 'thou shadow of a man' (Cf. Godefroy, FAITURE). It renders Latin *homuncio* 'manikin'.

244/29–30. *huet y-zyxt þou foleant uor to zeche*: C *que uais tu foleant por querre* 'why dost thou madly seek?'; DM has taken *uais* as *uois* and *y-zyxt* should read *gest*. He has also rendered *que* inaccurately as *huet* and may have mistakenly supposed it to be the object of *zeche*. It should read *hueruore*. The Latin reads *Cur ergo per multa vagaris . . . quaerendo*.

244/35. *nakede*: C *nue*; DM has mistaken *nue* 'cloud' for *nue* 'naked'; *uisage onwriʒe* represents an absolute construction.

245/4–5. *auoreye þane man þet he made . . . ine zaule*: C *uoir lome quil fist en cors e en ame*; there are a number of errors here; (i) Wallenberg (p. 329) pointed out that DM has rendered *uoir* as *uers*; (ii) for *quil fist* some E manuscripts read *qui tout (homme) fist 7 forma* (so P1 (rev.), 2, 4, A2, M, An, Ld, Ca1, Add1; V, R1 read *qui pour home fist e forma* (*toute creature* which is probably a corruption of the majority reading). The longer reading is probably to be regarded as the more original, referring as it does to the creative function of *þane man* namely Christ: (iii) all early manuscripts (except G1 which agrees with C) read after *forma*; *Car (Et) pourche uout diex deuenir homs que il feist en soi bieneure tout home en cors 7 en ame.* This completes the sense and is probably correct.

245/5. *y-ʒeʒ*: we should probably read *y-ʒeʒe* (C has *ueist*); *uor þan þet* here means 'in order that'.

245/6. *yziþ*: C *ueist*; read *y-ʒeʒe*.

245/7. *uand*: C *trovast*; *zuo þet* means here 'in order that', 'in such a way that' and we should expect *uounde*.

245/12. *yef hit onderstondeþ*: *þo þet lokeþ*: C *que cil attendent qui gardent*; Wallenberg (p. 329) reads *þet þo abideþ þet lokeþ*. No E manuscripts read *entendent*.

245/20–1. *ine him uor to likni*: C *en lui soi delit*er must mean 'to have pleasure in him'. Wallenberg (p. 149, n. 4) suggests confusion of the senses of *liki* and *likni*. But it would be simple to emend to *liki*.

245/27. *knaulechinge smackinde*: C *connoissance sauoureuse*; an elaboration of French *sapience* which is lost by DM's rendering *wysdom*. Cf. 106/16.

245/31. *be writinge*: C *par lescripture*; the reading of A2, Ca1, *par les creatures* gives better sense.

245/32–3. *lokeden . . . of*: C *regardoient*; as Wallenberg points out (p. 329), the French is transitive and means 'looked at'. Omit *of*.

245/34. *erþan þet hi*: C *en ce quil*; Wallenberg (p. 329–30) may be right in suggesting that DM has confused *en ce que* with *ancois que* and the English should, perhaps, read *ine þet hi*.

246/6. *ham yknewe*: C *le connoissent*; emend *ham* to *hit*.

246/10–11. *uayreþ | and clenseþ . . . and arereþ*: C *purge e nettoie . . . eslieue*; *purge e nettoie* are participles and the English should read *yuayred and yclensed*. *And* should be omitted before *arereþ*. The subject is *þe yefþe*. Cf. Wallenberg, p. 330.

246/18–21. Genesis 28: 12.

246/24. *to heuene*: C *ou ciel* 'in heaven' which DM has taken to mean 'to heaven'. Emend *to* to *ine*.

246/26–7. *huanne hi guoþ and profiteþ*: C *quant il uont profitant* 'since they continually progress'. Elsewhere DM translates the French idiom with *aller* by a participial phrase. For *quant* in the sense *puisque* see Godefroy, QUANT *conj.*

246/28. *herieþ*: C *laingent* 'love him'; DM has translated *loent*. Read *him louieþ*. Cf. Wallenberg, p. 330.

246/34–5. *þet trau . . . to þe grunde*: C *li arbre qui est chargiez de fruit tant sencline plus uers terre*; the reading of the majority of manuscripts indicates an omission. The correct reading supplies after *fruit*: *qui de tant quil est plus chargiez de fruit de.* In the same way, the English should read after *frut*: *þet þe more hit is ykarked mid frut.*

246/36–247/6. The main sentence appears to be *uor þe guode men . . . zuo ham behoueþ* 'because good men . . . indeed, must sometimes come down' etc. As Wallenberg (p. 330) points out, at 247/3, *his* is redundant. The French has simply *maine.* For *he* = 'one' see 237/21.

247/5. *iroted*: C *rauis*; Wallenberg (p. 330) suggests that DM has rendered a form of the verb *river*; but he may have had in his text the reading of An, R1, *ioins.*

247/8. *his*: C *ces*; DM has rendered *ses.*

247/9. *to þe workes* depends on *guo doun* in line 7.

247/11. *abide*: C *entendre*; cf. 242/5 and note to 74/24. No E manuscript reads *attendre.*

247/20. *þeruore*: C *dont*; the sense requires *þonne.*

247/27. *betake*: C *abandone*; cf. 198/20 where *betake* seems to mean 'set free', 'deliver'. The sense required here is 'overflowing'.

247/28. *þet god*: Wallenberg (p. 330) points out that *þet* is altered from *þe* and is probably an error.

247/30–1. Psalm 35 (36): 9. New Version.

247/29. *is*: C *est*; C's reading is clearly an error for *e*: *is* should read *and.*

247/30. *abandones*: DM has put a cross over this word and a cross in the margin but failed to replace it by an English word. The English verb *abandonen* means 'surrender', 'yield to' (cf. *MED* s.v.); but the sense required here is 'give fully, freely, overflow', presumably derived from the French. It may have been an uncertainty about the sense, rather than about the word itself, that decided DM, in the end, to leave it in the text.

247/31–2. *wylninge . . . solle*: C *li desirrer . . . seront*; read *wylninges.*

247/32. *by*: Wallenberg erroneously reads this as *be.*

247/32–3. Isaiah 48: 18; 66: 12.

248/8–9. *hire uor to wyne / and habbe*: C *por la quele gaaignier e auoir* 'to gain and possess which'; if we retain DM's rendering we must assume that a new sentence begins at *hire.* But *hire* could be emended to *huiche.* Read *wynne.*

248/11. *þet ne is dronke*: C *ne nest eniurez*; Wallenberg (p. 331) suggested that *þet* should be omitted. This is confirmed, not only by the reading of C, but by other E manuscripts (P2, A2, M, G1, An, Ca1). DM has rendered the erroneous reading *qui (ne soit) enyure* which appears in P1, V, Ld, Add1, R1.

248/14–16. Wisdom 8: 7.

248/20. *by þe cheake*: cf. note to 50/30.

248/24. *be skele*: C *a reson*; Wallenberg (p. 331) suggests reading *to* for *be.* For *to* 'on behalf of' cf. *OED* To *prep.* 30. For *loki to* cf. 93/9.

248/24–5. *hire . . . hire*: C *sa . . . li*; the first *hire* could be plural in which case the second should read *ham*. It seems that DM wrote *hire* as a rendering of French *sa* and thus put a feminine pronoun in line 24. But the pronouns should be plural as they refer to *skele* and *onderstondinge*.

248/28. *wyin*: read *wyn*. Cf. note to 131/6 and discussion p. 20, n. 2.

248/32–3. Philippians 3: 19.

249/2. *maked*: read *makeþ*.

249/3. *loki*: C *garde*; read *lokeþ*.

249/8. *gest*: C *oste*; Wallenberg (p. 331) pointed out that the sense requires *ost* 'host' for *oste*.

249/14. *of oure lhorde*: C *nostre seignor*; Wallenberg (p. 331) rightly points out that *nostre seignor* is not an appositive genitive but the accusative object.

249/19. *þet*: C *qui*; this may be an error for *car*, the reading of P1, 2, 4, A2, An, Ca1, Add1; or *qui* may be an error for *que* 'in that'.

249/21. *to*: DM has rendered French *a* as a preposition instead of as a verb. Read *heþ*. *Efter* is probably for *Efterward*; see note to 30/21.

249/29–30. Wisdom 11: 21.

250/5–6. *zet mesure . . . of sobreté*: C *met mesure tele comme reson aporte. la uertu datemprance e de sobrete*; the meaning is 'Moderation prescribes what reason demands, the virtue of temperance and sobriety'.

250/6–7. For moderation in virtue see *De Consideratione*, I, viii (Leclercq, Rochais iii. 404–5).

250/11. *outnime*: C *souz*; Wallenberg (p. 184, n. 2; p. 331) points out that DM has read *sauf*. Emend *outnime* to *onder*.

250/12. *a liʒte scele*: C *reson enluminee*; read *scele aliʒte*; cf. Wallenberg, p. 7, n. 4 and p. 331.

250/20–3. Cf. Augustine, *De Musica*, VI, xv, 50 (PL xxxii, col. 1189).

250/32–4. John 16: 33.

250/34–6. Augustine, *Confessions* I. i (PL xxxii, col. 661).

250/36. *of mares*: C *des mares*; Wallenberg translates 'marsh' but this does not fit the context nor the proverbial nature of the passage. The French is clearly plural and probably has the generalized sense 'waters'. DM did not understand the word. He left a gap in the text and wrote *mares* in the margin.

251/7. *y-clenzed uor*: C *purgie de*; read *yclenzed uram*.

251/8, 11. *y-zendred*: C *resise* 'calm'; DM seems to have mistakenly assumed that the French was from *reciser* 'cut off' (see Wallenberg, p. 291, n. 3). Read *smoþe*.

251/9. *hire y-knauþ*: C *si connoit*; the English should read *hire þer yknauþ*; *si* is for *s'y*.

251/14–16. *þe ilke welle . . . þe loue of god*: C *cele fonteine sus qui bon cuer qui se uoille sauuer se repose est lamour de dieu*; the passage means 'that well, upon which he who wishes to be saved rests, is the love of God'. DM's translation would run more smoothly if *he* were omitted before *þet*. It is not clear whether the manuscript reads *guod* or *guode*. The *e* in *guode* seems to have been partially erased and there is a cross over it. *guod(e)* and *herte* have been run together and separated by a vertical stroke.

251/29. *wyttes ys*: read *wyt ys*.

251/35. *is*: C *ie*; Wallenberg (p. 129, n. 2) argues that this is a genuine form and conjectures that the form was a sandhi development from *ich spek*.

252/14. *tornenoyment*: Wallenberg (p. 243, n. 2) correctly regards this as a scribal error for *tornoyment*.

252/28. *spacialliche*: this is probably an error for *specialliche* as Wallenberg suggests (p. 223, n. 1) unless it is by confusion with French *space* or its derivatives.

252/31. *misbylefde*: Morris's emendation is unnecessary. Cf. Mustanoja, p. 551.

252/35–253/1. Proverbs 3: 21.

253/1–2. *of zuo oȝene wytte*: cf. Proverbs 3: 7: *Ne sis sapiens apud temetipsum* 'Be not wise in your own conceit', The French has *de si propre sen*.

253/7–8. Romans 1: 5; 16: 26; *apeluchier* is taken over from the French *a peluchier* where *a* is a preposition. Cf. Wallenberg, p. 13, n. 2.

253/10–12. *zekȝ . . . þe resse*: C *quiert le moulle as ruissoles. ou celui qui quiert le peil en luef ou le nou el ionc*; of the three comparisons only the first, 'the meal in the cakes' has the support of the majority of manuscripts. For the second comparison, manuscripts read *le poil en loeil* (P1, 8, 9, 12, V, Add1, 2, R1); or *le poil en loeuf* (P2, 6, 7, 10, 13, 14, 16, A2, M, G1, 2, 4, 5, An, Ld, Ca1. Francis (VV note to 280/30–2) took *peil* (*poil*) as 'blade of grass' but it is more probable that it is a form of *peille* 'chicken'. (Cf. En2 *þe chickenen in þe eye*.) DM's reading seems to be due to a confusion of *poil* and *peil* 'skin'. The reading *peil* in G1, C is probably a form of *poil*. The third comparison appears as either *le feu en leau* (P1, 8, 12, 13, V, Add1, R1); *le nou el ionc* (P2, 6, 7, 9, 10, 14, 16, A2, M, G1, 2, 4, An, Ca1; *le poil el ionc* of Ld is probably an error; the reading *loef en le eaue* of P13 can probably also be ignored). Francis suggested that the original reading was either *le feu en jonc* 'the fire in the wick' or *loile en jonc* 'the oil in the wick'. But cf. Latin *nodum in scirpo quaerere*. The illustrations are designed to characterize the officious or over-anxious person who is concerned to find what is only potentially present. In line 10, *zikȝ* is for *zikþ* as Morris suggests. Cf. note to 40/5.

253/13. *ine* is a literal rendering of French *en*.

253/14. *mid*: C *ou*; DM has mistaken *ou* (*au*) for *o* (*avec*).

253/16–21. Ecclesiasticus 18: 30–1. *Post concupiscentias tuas non eas, et a voluntate tua avertere; si praestes animae tuae concupiscentias eius, faciet te in gaudium inimicis tuis.*

253/22. *uor . . . þe ilke þet*: C *ausi* com *cil*; both *uor* and *þet* should be omitted. The sentence runs: 'just as the man gives joy to his foe . . . when he concedes victory to him'. Cf. Wallenberg, p. 331.

253/24. *Yef he*: C *Cil*; read *þe ilke*. DM has taken *cil* as *s'il*.

253/25-7. 1 Peter 2: 11.

253/27-31. The changes of number are taken from the French.

253/35-254/1. Hebrews 11: 8-16.

254/4. *ofte*: C *uolentiers*.

254/5. *ine zikere guoinge*: *MED* (GOING(E ger. 6(a)) renders *guoinge* by 'demeanour', 'conduct', etc. but the French *en seur conduit* suggests that *ine zikere guoinge* means 'in safe conduct'.

254/6. *guoþ*: C con*duit*; the verb should be singular as is *let*. Read *geþ*.

254/22-3. *þe guode men and þe wyse*: Morris's emendation of MS. *man* to *men* could be supported by the French *li prodome e li sage*.

254/30. *þe*[1]: read *þet*. At 215/7, 242/33, 265/35 the form is unemended but cf. 59/9, 149/15, 153/2, 208/2 where Morris does emend; *þe* is often emended to *þet* in the manuscript but these cases missed the corrector's eye. For discussion see p. 82.

254/30. *wille*: C *uanite* and so other early manuscripts. DM's text probably had *uolente*.

254/33-4. Proverbs 17: 27.

254/35. *mid ueawe wordes*: C *au pois de paroles*; Wallenberg (p. 332) suggests that DM has mistaken *pois* 'weight' for *peu*. P1, 4, Add1, R1, however, read *pou*, *peu de paroles* and this was, no doubt, the reading of DM's manuscript.

255/2-3. *Vor ase*: C *ausi*; *vor* should be omitted. *ase* may here stand for *alse* 'likewise'. Cf. note to 226/31.

255/4. *aboue y-zawe*: C *seursemez*; as Wallenberg points out (p. 290, n. 2) *aboue y-zawed* is a literal rendering of the French *seursemez* 'ulcerated'.

255/4-6. Ecclesiasticus 28: 29.

255/8. *zome uolk byeþ*: for the number of *uolk* see pp. 62-3.

255/8-13. Whiting (M 555) regards this as proverbial.

255/9-10. *ne naȝt* ham *loki . . . by hit leazinge*: C *qui ne se gardent quil dient soit uoir soit menconge* 'who take no heed whether they speak truth or falsehood'. DM has taken the French to mean 'who cannot refrain from talking be it truth or falsehood'. Wallenberg (p. 332) emends to *þet naȝt ham lokeþ þet hi zigge zoþ oþer leazinge*.

255/16-17. *Yziȝ þet weter yerne*: C *ve leaue aler*; the French appears to mean 'Accursed be the flowing water' of which the English is clearly not a translation. G1 has the reading of C. Most manuscripts, however, have *ne* *lessier (lesse) pas aler leaue*. DM seems to have mistaken *ve* for part of the verb *veoir*. The reference is to Ecclesiasticus 25: 34: *Non des aquae tuae exitum*.

255/18–21. Proverbs 17: 14.

255/23–6. Ecclesiasticus 28: 29, 30.

255/26–8. Cf. Ecclesiasticus 28: 28, 29. This is not in the French.

255/33. *yef hi vyndeþ*: C *troeuent*; omit *yef hi*.

256/1–2. Psalm 38 (39): 2. The English is a literal rendering of *posui ori meo custodiam*.

256/3. *exameneþ*: C *examine*; the verb should be plural. DM's form is, of course, ambiguous.

256/24–7. Not in the French. Wallenberg points out (p. 332) that the reference is to Proverbs 25: 23: *Ventus aquilo dissipat pluvias, et facies tristis linguam detrahentem*.

256/27–9. Translate 'These great men should take good care what they hear and what they believe, for they find few who would tell them the truth'.

257/2. *help*: C *salu*; read *helþe*.

257/4–6. Ecclesiasticus 28: 28.

257/9. *mid þe drede*: C *de la pooir*; for *mid* read *of*. Cf. Wallenberg, p. 332.

257/17. *heruore*: C *por quoi*; read *hueruore*, as Wallenberg, p. 332. Cf. 118/20.

257/19–22. Cf. Psalm 57 (58): 5–6.

257/31. *stoppi*: C *il doit estouper*; read *he ssel stoppi*.

257/32. *uor to beþenche*: C *por remembrance*; read *uor beþenchinge*.

258/6. *zene*: is corrected from *zeneȝy* whence, perhaps, the single *n*. But cf. 118/8.

258/8. *hit is*: C *se*; read *yef* for *hit is*. It looks as if DM's text read *est* for *se*.

258/10–12. The reference is probably to the parable of Dives and Lazarus which opens with the words: *Homo quidam erat dives, qui induebatur purpura et bysso* (Luke 16: 19.)

258/22. *ham gledyeþ and predeþ*: C *se glorifient e sen orgoillissent*; the English should read *ham* before, and *þerof* after, *predeþ*.

258/29–30. Ecclesiasticus 11: 4.

258/30–1. 1 Timothy 2: 9.

258/32–3. *be þe stat/þet*: C *selom ce que lestat de*; Wallenberg (p. 332 emends to *be þan þet þe stat of* here and at 259/5.

259/22–3. Cf. Isaiah 65: 20.

259/25–8. 1 Corinthians 13: 11.

259/30–1. 1 Corinthians 14: 20; *lite* appears to be a rendering of *parvuli* and is, perhaps, plural. But it is to be noted that DM has rendered *pueri* by a singular *child*.

260/4–6. Luke 21: 34.

260/17. *ycontynent*: all the E manuscripts of the French read *contenues*. Cf. note to 39/15.

260/27. *charite: loue of god*: C *charite amour de dieu*; the correct reading appears to be *chiere amour de dieu* as all E manuscripts except Ld and G1, which reads *amur de dieu car* subpuncted after *par charite* and has *ke* supplied after *car*.

261/4–6. Matthew 5: 9.

261/6–8. Cf. Augustine, *De Genesi contra Manichaeos*, I, xx (PL xxxiv, col. 188).

261/10–11. 2 Corinthians 13: 11.

261/32–3. Philippians 4: 7.

261/34–6. Cf. 1 Corinthians 2: 9.

262/1. *bote a wlaffere*: C *fors baubier*; the normal meaning of *wlaffere* is 'a stammerer' but the sense here seems to require the meaning 'a fool'.

262/4. *lete wonie*: C *maint*; Wallenberg (p. 332) points out that DM has confused *mener* 'lead' with *manoir* 'dwell'. Read *lede*.

262/12. *zen*: the form is due to the exigencies of rhyme.

262/13. *wen*: Wallenberg (p. 275, n. 3) suggests derivation from *wen* 'thought, opinion'; but it is more likely to be *wen* 'blemish'. See *OED* WEN[1] 2.

262/14. *Huo ase god*: Michael means 'who is like God?'; see *OED* s.v.

262/24. *cominde*: Latin *adueniat*; perhaps an error for *by cominde*. Cf. note to 263/14.

263/12. *þis uorzoþe*: Latin *hoc* (Southern–Schmitt, 355/2); DM's text probably read *hoc autem* as OT.

263/14. *were comynde*: Latin *veniret* (355/4); the English, however, may be a rendering of *uenturus esset* (O); cf. 264/4 where *is comynde* renders *venturus est* and Visser, iii. 2, §§ 1830–2. At 267/16, on the other hand, *am wondrinde* renders a deponent verb, *miratus sum*.

263/15. DM agrees with OTLC in omitting *sed* (355/4) before *pater iste*.

263/16. *þe wyl of skele*: Latin *animus rationalis* (355/5); the English should read *þe wyt of skele*.

263/17–18. *his besteriinge*: Latin *motus sui* (355/6); the text should read *hire besteriinges*.

263/18. *wyt*: Latin *sensus* (355/6); *sensus* is probably plural and the English should read *wyttes*. The meaning is 'sensations, the senses'.

263/23. *earen. tonge*: Latin *lingua, aures* (356/2); DM has the same order as O.

263/24. *becomeþ*: Latin *insolescant* (356/2); DM seems to have taken the subjunctive for the indicative. The text should read *wolde become*.

263/26. *þet ilke zelue*: read *þet þet ilke zelue*.

263/27. *ac²*: O reads 7 for *quia* (356/5) in other early manuscripts. *Ac* may be a loose rendering of this.

263/27-8. *heȝlyche*: MED (HEIGHLI adv. 3 (c)) renders both as 'principally', 'especially'. But, at line 27, the Latin has *summopere* (356/4) and, at 28, *principaliter* (356/6). Thus the English should be translated 'with the greatest care' in the first instance and 'principally' in the second.

263/30-1. *þaȝles ȝef he ne were naȝt onlosti*: Latin *si tamen non negligens fuerit* (356/7) 'lest he should be negligent'; DM's translation is so literal as to be almost incomprehensible.

263/32-3. *ate uerste guoinge in . . . to by doreward*: Latin *prudentiam in primo aditu constituit* (356/8) 'Prudence he placed at the first entrance'; DM has attempted to clarify the phrase by the addition of *to by doreward*. He has misunderstood the meaning of *aditu*.

263/35-264/2. *Nixt þan . . . þet þe vyendes / þet sleȝþe zent to zygge / to keste out: strengþe wyþdroȝe. þet his uoule lostes wyþdroȝe: and wyþ-zede*: Latin *secus hanc fortitudo locatur, ut hostes, quos prudentia venire nuntiaverit, fortitudo repellat, Porro temperantia familiae intimae praeesse debet, ut eius coherceat ac cohibeat turpes appetitus* (356/10-13). The text is very confused here. The phrase *þet sleȝþe zent to zygge / to keste out* may mean 'whom Prudence sends to tell to cast out' but it is clearly not a literal translation of the Latin; nor is *strengþe wyþdroȝe* an adequate rendering of *fortitudo repellat*. In the second sentence something is clearly missing in the English. The text should read as in the Latin *Efterward mesure ssel loki þe mayne* before *þet his uoule lostes*.

264/4-5. *hueruore . . . ac eche tyme*: Latin *Et quia . . . omni hora* (356/13-14); read *þeruore þet . . . at eche tyme*. O omits *Et* as DM.

264/5. *Þise zuo y-diȝt* renders Latin *His ita dispositis* (356/14).

264/5-7. *naȝt longe to þe wakynde þe slep of zenne benymþ. Vor al þet lyf is to waky. Zome messagyers sleȝþe ssel lete in*: Latin *ne diu vigilantibus somnus peccati irrepat—tota enim vita vigilandum est—aliquos debet prudentia introducere nuntios* (356/15-16); DM has misunderstood the construction of the Latin sentence. He should have written *uor drede þet ate laste to þe wakynde þe slep of zenne cryepe—vor ine al þet lyf me ssel waky—zome messagyers sleȝþe ssel lete in* etc.

264/8. *þet me may a-waki myde*: Latin *quae ad exercitationem valeant* (356/17) 'which may serve to awaken'.

264/12. *heȝliche*: cf. note to 27/6.

264/14. *comyde*: emend, as Morris suggests, to *comynde*.

264/16. *is nou*: Latin *est* (356/22); DM's text corresponds to the reading *est modo* of POTH (L rev.).

264/23. *And huet*: POT supply *et* before *quid* (356/29).

264/25. *brengeþ*: like PO, DM's text omitted *ad hoc* before *ferunt* (356/30).

264/27–9. *þet þo þet byeþ to hare riʒte ouercomeþ: hire zaulen be strengþe: of þe bodye draʒeþ out*: Latin *ut quos sui esse iuris convicerint, eorum animas violenter extrahant* (356/32–3) 'in order that they may violently drag out the souls of those whom they have demonstrated to be under their jurisdiction'. DM's rendering does not make sense as it stands. The verb *byeþ* should be replaced by an infinitive; *ouercomeþ* should be replaced by *habbeþ yssewed* and *draʒeþ* by *hi moʒe draʒe*.

264/30. *comste*: Latin *venis modo* (356/34); POT omit *modo* as DM.

264/34. *wy-oute*: read *wyþoute*. Cf. p. 50.

264/34–5. *Vol of stenche* / *wy-oute comparisoun*: Latin *plenus fetore incomparabili* (357/2); DM's text, like PO, lacked the following phrase *plenus dolore innumerabili*.

265/4. *þet*: translates HL's *quae* not *quaecumque* (357/6).

265/6. *onþolyinde*: Latin *est intolerabile* (357/8); LC, like DM's text, omit *est*.

265/7–8. *ssolle by uorbernd . . . ssolle by y-wasted . . . ne ssolle wasti*: Latin *comburuntur . . . consumuntur . . . consummantur* (357/9); the sense requires a contrast between the first two tenses and the last, here indicated by the present subj. Some manuscripts have a future tense for the first two verbs (cf. (*con*)*cremabuntur* CHL and *consummabuntur* H) and this may explain DM's future in these cases; but the last verb should contrast with these by being in the present. For DM's use of verbs with *ssel*, however, cf. note to 265/9–10. For confusion between *consumo*, *consummo* cf. OED CONSUME *v*. 2.

265/9–10. *ssolle naʒt sterue . . . ne ssel neure by ykuenct*: Latin *non moritur . . . non extinguitur* (357/10). The English may depend on Latin futures (cf. *morietur* HLC); but similar renderings appear at 267/5 *ssel lessi*: Latin *minuitur* (358/25); 267/6 *ssel endi*: Latin *finitur* (358/25); 269/1 *ssel . . . nyme*: Latin *capit* (360/4).

265/12. *dyeules*; Latin *diabolici* (357/11); DM's text may have read *diaboli* as LC but cf. 43/4 and *men apostles* 267/23–4.

265/12. *to-gydere*: Latin *pariter* (357/12); an imprecise translation; the Latin means 'equally'.

265/14. *reste*: Latin *remedium* (357/13); DM's text seems to have had a different reading here.

265/17. *and zostren*: not in the Latin.

265/19. *youre bedes*: Latin *orationibus* (357/16); cf. *orationibus uestris* PO.

265/19. *porueynde guodes*: Latin *providentes bona* (357/17) 'giving thought to things that are good' (cf. Romans 12: 17). As Jensen pointed out (p. 33) *porueynde* is for *porueyynde*.

265/20. *alle men*: Latin *hominibus* (357/17); cf. *omnibus hominibus* (or rev.) in POTH.

265/20–2. *Do we to worke godes nebsseft | ine ssrifte | and ine zalmes: glede we hym*: the Latin (357/18) refers to a quotation from the psalms (Psalm 94 (95): 2): *Praeoccupemus faciem eius in confessione, Et in psalmis iubilemus ei. Do we to worke godes nebsseft* is a literal translation of *praeoccupemus faciem eius* 'Let us come before his presence'.

265/31–4. *þet we nolleþ . . . men*: DM seems to have had the reading of P: *Et quod nobis fieri non volumus aliis non faciamus, et quod nobis fieri volumus aliis faciamus* (cf. 357/25),

266/1–2. *þes ilke uerste: gratlyche*: Latin *iste prior* (357/29); POTH supply *ualde* after *prior* and this would seem to represent the reading of DM's text.

266/9–10. *Yef we longe godes drede | and be-þenchinge of dyaþe were stille*: Latin *si nos, dum timor et memoria mortis loqueretur, tacuimus* (358/3); DM's text probably read *si nos cum timore et memoria mortis tacuimus* as O. *Cum* here means 'in the presence of' but DM seems to have taken it to mean 'on account of'; cf. *OED* LONG *a*².

266/11. *þe spekinde*: Latin *te loquente* (358/4).

266/16–17. 1 Corinthians 13: 12. It may be noted that *ine ssede* is not a very close translation of *in enigmate* (358/7–8).

266/18–20. *þe ilke onspekynde | an on-todelinde magesté of þe holy trinyté*: Latin *ineffabilem illam individuae Trinitatis maiestatem* (358/8–9); the English should read *þe ilke onspekynde mageste of þe (holy an) on-todelinde trinyte*.

266/20. *Ac and*: 'but also'; cf. *sed et* PO for *sed quia* (358/9).

266/20–1. *lyʒt þer-inne woneþ*: Latin *lucem habitat* (358/9) (cf. 1 Timothy 6: 16). DM seems to have taken *lyʒt* as the subject. The text should read *woneþ ine lyʒt* etc.

266/21. *þo*: Latin *ipsa* (358/10); DM's rendering may represent *hac*, the reading of LC.

266/23. *uolnesse*: Latin *pulchritudo* (358/12); DM's text plainly had *plenitudo*.

266/24. *oure lhord iesu crist*: Latin *dominum Iesum Christum deum et hominem* (358/12–13); DM shares the omission of *deum et hominem* with O and supplies *nostrum* after *dominum* as POTHLC.

266/27. *ine him*: Latin *in eum* (358/15) 'at him'.

266/31. *zodes*: Latin *dei* (358/18); read *godes*.

266/33. *y-nemned*: is not an accurate rendering of Latin *nominandam* (358/19).

266/35. *ous*: DM's text may have had the reading of H *omnibus* for *hominibus* (358/21) of other early manuscripts.

266/35–6. *to huam hi is uol of merci*: Latin *cui vult miserentem* (358/21); DM's rendering is inexact. The Latin means 'on whom (mankind) she wishes him to have mercy'.

267/4. *eurelestinde holynesse*: Latin *coaequaeva beatitudo* (358/24–5); DM's rendering does not make the point; namely that the beatitude of the blessed spirits is commensurate with the vision and love of God. Cf. 268/24.

267/6. *wexe*: Latin *crescit* (358/26); read *wext*.

267/6. *þe ilke*: Latin *istorum* (358/26); read *hare*.

267/8–9. *no man uollyche þenche | ne naȝt ne may by ynoȝ to telle*; Latin *ullus hominum plene cogitare, nedum enarrare, sufficit* (358/27–8); DM's text probably had *nullus* (PH) for *ullus*. His rendering is, however, confused and hardly conveys the sense of the Latin. The English should read *no man ne may uollyche þenche ne telle*.

267/10. DM's text shared with POHL an omission after *gaudio* of the words *quod eam . . . obtinent* (358/29–30).

267/11–13. *þet ine longe anoy onderuynge | þet ouet of blysse wyþ-oute ende chongeden*: Latin *quod longae expectationis taedia percepto perennis gloriae fructu mutaverunt* (358/31–2) 'because they have exchanged the weariness of long expectation for the harvested fruit of perennial glory'. The text could be emended by reading *of longe weninge anoy* for *ine longe anoy*; supplying *uor* before *þet ouet*; adding *ygadered* after *ouet* to render *percepto* and omitting *onderuynge*.

267/13. *þe apostles*: DM's text, like POT, did not have *omnes* before *apostolos* (358/32).

267/14. *alle preste*: Latin *omnes iudicare paratos* (358/33); DM's text, like O, seems to have lacked *iudicare*. The words *uor to deme* should be provided after *preste*.

267/14–15. *of poure and of zyke*: Latin *de pauperibus et de infirmis* (358/33–4); this depends on *am wondrinde*.

267/15–16. *zuo blisuolle and holy . . . and zuo heȝe*: Latin *tam gloriosos tamque sublimes factos* (358/34); accordingly supply *ymad* after *heȝe*. DM may have intended *blisuolle and holy* to render *gloriosos*; or his text may have had a different reading.

267/15–16. *of oure lhord iesu crist*: Latin *a domino Iesu* (358/34); DM's text seems here to have had the same reading as O, *a domino Iesu Christo*.

267/16. *alneway*: Latin *superque hoc* (358/35); DM's *alneway* does not render *superque*. It seems that his manuscript, like POTHLC, lacked *hoc*.

267/19–21. *þet be þe pinen . . . hy come þerto*: Latin *qui passiones huius temporis, quas pertulerant, minimas reputabant ad illam gloriam, quas revelata erat in eis* (358/36–8) (cf. Romans 8 : 18). DM has not understood this sentence, perhaps because his manuscript, like PO, omitted *minimas*. The text should read *þet þe pinen of þise time huyche hi beren hilde uor lite to þo blisse* etc.; *hy come þerto* should be omitted.

267/21. *holynesse*: Latin *felicitate* (358/38); cf. 268/35 and 269/12 where *holynesse* again renders Latin *felicitas*. Cf. the notes to these lines.

267/21–3. *Hyre holynesse . . . Ich yzeȝ to þe blyssede heape*: Latin *Horum felicitate et gloria diu delectatus respexi ad gloriosam multitudinem* (358/38–359/1); DM has made two sentences of one. We might have expected *ine hyre holynesse . . . ich me lykede.*

267/27–8. *ine eurelestynde wy[þ]oute ende*: Latin *in perpetuas aeternitates* (359/4); *wyþoute ende* is here used as a noun.

267/28. *Monekes*: DM seems to have had the reading of P *monachi* for *et monachi* (359/5) of other early manuscripts.

267/31–2. *of alle zofthede / and nesshede*: a very imprecise rendering of Latin *omnique suavitate molliores* (359/7).

267/33. *wypeþ*: DM may have had the reading of LC *absterget* for *abstersit* (359/7) of other early manuscripts.

267/33. *and þane kyng*: DM may have had the reading, *regemque* of OTHL rather than *regem* (359/8) as in other early manuscripts.

267/33. *ssolle ysy*: is possibly a rendering of *uidebunt* (PO) rather than *vident* (359/8) in other early manuscripts; but cf. note to 265/9–10.

267/35. *sseppe*: DM has taken Latin *species* (359/9) to mean 'form'; but the sense here is 'beauty', 'splendour'. The English should read *uayrhede*.

267/36–268/2. *melodya . . . may zynge*: DM's rendering is closest to O: *melodia tanta est quam nulla hominum eloquentia digne enarrare potest 7 cantabant canticum quod alius nemo dicere poterat* (359/9–11). DM's sentence is an anacoluthon, however; *huyche* should read *is zuych þet.*

268/2. *þe zuete smel*: Latin *odor* (359/11); DM's rendering is perhaps a gloss on the Latin.

268/3. *zuo zuete ys: þet*: represents the reading of HLC *tam suavis est ut* for *tam suavis exuberat qui* (359/11–12).

268/4. *to hare benes: oure lhord arist*: 'Our Lord receives their prayers standing'; that is, pays special respect to their prayers.

268/7–9. *þet þou zigge ous . . . zay ous*: DM has rendered Latin *edicas* (359/16) twice.

268/11. *smackeþ*: Latin *sapiunt* (359/18); DM has rendered literally; cf. note to 268/22.

268/14–15. *Wylnynge . . . ende*: DM renders the reading of OHLC, *Desiderium vitae aeternae* for *Desiderium* (359/22) of other early manuscripts.

268/16. *be lyue*: Latin *vita* (359/22); DM's rendering is a loose reproduction of the Latin ablative.

268/18. *holy*: DM's text probably had *sancte* (HLC) for *beatae* (359/23).

268/18–20. John 17: 3.

268/20. *huam* renders Latin *quem* (359/25).

268/21. *and þeruore ylyche hy byeþ | uor hy y-zyeþ*: Latin *Unde et deo similes sunt, quoniam vident eum* (359/25–6); supply *god* before *ylyche* and *him* before *y-zyeþ*. Cf. 1 John 3: 2.

268/22. *Hy smackeþ þe redes and þe domes of god*: Latin *Sapiunt consilia atque iudicia dei, quae sunt abyssus multa* (359/26–7) (cf. Psalm 35 (36): 7). DM has omitted the last part of the sentence and, as at 268/11, 23, misunderstood the meaning of *sapere*, taking it in its original sense of 'taste'; hence the rendering *smackeþ*. Cf. 269/27–8.

268/25. *hy wyteþ huerto*: DM's text seems to have read *sciunt ad quid* (OH) for *sciunt unde et ad quid* (359/28).

268/27. *onzyginde*: Latin *ineffabiliter* (359/30).

268/27–8. *of zuo moche of hare oȝene holynesse*: Latin *de tanta sua beatitudine* (359/30) 'of their own so great beatitude'; DM's rendering is imprecise.

268/30–1. *þeruore by zyker | uor eurych*: Latin *Constat igitur quia singuli* (359/32); *by* should read *byþ* to render Latin *constat* and *uor* should read *þet* to render Latin *quia* which is used in the post-classical sense 'that'.

268/31–2. *and aseuele blissen to echen: ase his oȝene of alle*: Latin *et singula gaudia tanta sunt singulis, quantum proprium singulorum* (359/33–360/1); viz. 'and every joy is as great to each individual as is the particular joy of each'; *of alle* is a literal translation of *singulorum*. DM's text may have had the reading *gaudia tanta sunt singulis* (O) for *singula gaudia tanta sunt singulis*; *byeþ* is required after *blissen*.

268/32. *þeruore*: Latin *cum* 'since' (360/1); the English should read *þeruore þet*.

268/33–4. *þet hym and oþre made | þanne him zelue | and alle oþre*: Latin *quam se et alios* (360/2); DM's text seems to have had a reading more like that of O; *qui se et alios fecit* combined with that of the other manuscripts. It may be conjectured that DM's Latin read: *qui se et alios fecit, quam se et alios.*

268/34–6. *More hy byeþ glede wyþ-oute gessynge of godes holynesse:* . . . *myd hym*: Latin *plus gaudet absque estimatione de dei felicitate quam de sua et omnium aliorum (secum P)* (360/2–3). The Latin means 'each rejoices immeasurably more in the beatitude of God and of all others with him, than in his own'. *hy byeþ* refers back to *eurich* in line 32. It should, accordingly, be singular. The correct reading would be *he biþ*; *gessynge* is not a precise rendering of Latin *estimatione*.

268/36. *on*: *unusquisque* (360/3); DM's rendering is closer to P's *unus*.

269/2–3. Matthew 25: 21.

269/3–4. *naȝt þe blisse of þine lhorde | guo in to þe. uor hy ne may*: Latin *Non intret gaudium domini tui in te quia capi non posset* (360/5–6); DM's translation does not bring out the sense, which is that the joy of the Lord could not be received by the blessed rather than that it is incapable of entering into them.

269/5–7. Psalm 83 (84): 5.

269/11. *heryinge*: MED (HERIING(E ger. 1 (d)) renders 'honour', 'glory'. The Latin has *laude* (360/10).

269/12. *holynesse*: Latin *velocitate* (360/10); DM's text probably had *felicitate* (PO). Cf. note to 267/21.

269/25. *huet*: Latin *quid enim* (360/24); DM's text perhaps lacked *enim* as HLC.

269/26. *zede*: Latin *dixi quod dixi* (360/24); DM's text lacked *quod dixi* (PO).

269/26. *broþren and zostren*: Latin *fratres* (360/25).

269/27–8. Romans 12: 3. For the sense of *smacky* see note to 268/22.

269/28. *myd guode wylle*: Latin *et aequo animo* (360/26–7); supply *and*.

269/31. *let of*: Latin *loqui . . . cessaverit* (360/28); DM's text probably lacked *loqui* (POHLC).

269/31. *þus*: Latin *sic fratres* (360/29); DM's text probably lacked *fratres* (PO).

269/32. *eurich*: Latin *monachus* (360/29); DM's text perhaps read *homo* (O).

269/32. *uram*: Latin *et a* (360/30); *and uram* gives better sense.

269/34. Like PO, DM's text lacked the concluding lines of other early texts. Cf. Southern, 360/30–32.

270/20. *þe wordle þyestre*: the text should read *þe wordle is þyestre*.

270/25. *þu hest hueruore*: 'thou hast a reason to die'.

270/34–5. Translate 'And not because God puts (them) next to them'.

271/5. *yue wyl be wyþdraȝynge*: 'be resolute concerning abstinence'?

271/6. *clensy . . . arere*: the verbs must be regarded as passive or an object supplied.

271/11. See *IMEV*: No. 2034. DM seems to have adapted these lines from the first stanza of a macaronic prayer. Cf. Harley 2253 (f. 83a) and Carleton Brown, XIV, p. 256, note to No. 33.

THE GLOSSARY

THE order is alphabetical except that bracketed letters are not included in the alphabetical order. In the arrangement vocalic *y*, and *y* in the so-called diphthong spellings, are treated as *i*; consonantal *y* [ʒ] appears after *w*; consonantal *y* [dʒ] is treated as consonantal *i*(*j*) and appears after vocalic *i*; the *i*-prefix is ignored in verbs; ʒ is treated as *g* regardless of its phonetic value; þ follows *t*; *u* and *v* are separated according to function. Certain omissions in the citation of head-words should be noted. Thus *ai/ei* variants should be sought under *ai*; *be/bi* under *bi*; *c/k* under *c*; *cc/x* under *cc*; *ce*, *ci/s* under *s*(*e*), *s*(*i*); *cion/tion* under *cion*; *ck/kk* under *kk*; *des/dis* under *dis*; *on/oun* under *on*; *ku/qu* under *ku*; *s/z* in French words under *s* (except *zaint*); in native words under *z* (except *ase/alsuo*); *u/v* when a vowel under *u*; *u/v* when a consonant under *v*; *u/w* under *u* when *w* is part of a diphthong. It should be noted that, since *i* and *y*, and *u* and *v*, when purely graphic variants, are treated as interchangeable, the forms *writinge* and *writyngge* are indicated by *writing(g)e*; *zyʒþ*, *iziʒþ*, and *ziʒþ* by (*i*)*ziʒþ*; and so on.

The references are selective and do not necessarily indicate the first occurrence of a word. Except where forms have been deemed of special interest, they have been grouped together at the beginning of the entry. The swung dash stands for the head-word in any of its forms, although the full form is usually cited where the idiom is grammatical and the forms are therefore not interchangeable. Angled brackets indicate a form printed by Morris which requires emendation. Where a head-word is in question, however, an emended form is given and a cross-reference supplied. A double dagger indicates a form due to elision. Italicized references indicate an entry in the list of *corrigenda*.

Except in the case of the simplest entries, the semantic and grammatical sections are separated by a colon. It should be noted that, in such cases, the citations in the semantic section do not necessarily refer to the same grammatical category as the head-word. Where the meaning of a form is not indicated it is that of the immediately preceding form. In the order of entries phrases come at the end except in divided entries where they come after the semantic section. The grammatical analysis is not total. Thus the citation of a post-prepositional form in -*e* does not imply that the word in question does not exhibit a post-prepositional case in zero. In the same way, the plural of adjectives whose nominative singular ends in -*e* has not been separated from the singular unless the plural ends in -*s*. A bracketed grammatical analysis indicates that owing to the absence of a recorded form of the nominative, it is only conjectural.

Where Morris has indicated the manuscript reading, or where he has added a bracketed letter, this is indicated in the glossary by an asterisk. The manuscript reading is given in the glossary (i) when it cannot be inferred from Morris's bracketed form (ii) where Morris has tacitly emended. It has not been possible to indicate all the cases of inconsistent word-division. Thus Morris prints *asemoche* and *ase moche*; *domesman* and *domes man*; *into*, *in-to*, and *in to*; *þrisiþe* and *þri siþe* and so on. Only instances in which the reader may be misled are cross-referenced in the glossary.

The following abbreviations are used: *acc.* accusative; *adj.* adjective; *adv.* adverb; *comp.* comparative; *conj.* conjunction; *conj. adv.* conjunctive adverb; *dat.* dative; *def. art.* definite article; *dir. q.* direct question; *fem.* feminine; *gen.* genitive; *ind.* indicative; *indef. art.* indefinite article; *int.* interjection; *interr.* interrogative; *intr.* intransitive; *masc.* masculine; *n.* noun;[1] *neut.* neuter; *nom.* nominative; *num.* numeral; *ord.* ordinal; *pa.t.* past tense; *p.c.* prepositional case; *pl.* plural; *poss.* possessive; *pp.* past participle; *ppl. adj.* participial adjective; *pr.* present; *prep.* preposition; *pron.* pronoun; *pr. p.* present participle; *recipr.* reciprocal; *refl.* reflexive; *rel.* relative; *sg.* singular; *subj.* subjunctive; *superl.* superlative; *tr.* transitive; *v.* verb; *vbl. n.* verbal noun; *wk.* weak. The abbreviation *tr./intr.* is appended to verbs when the construction is ambiguous. Thus, where the construction *bidde to God* occurs, the collocations *bidde God*, *bidde him* defy analysis in traditional terms. The abbreviation *refl.* has been restricted to cases in which the expression in question is idiomatic from a modern point of view. Otherwise such verbs are simply listed as transitive.

A

a(n) *indef. art.* a 4/2, 131/5, (*before vowel or* h) **an** an 25/33, 45/32, 55/20, **ane** 142/31 *n.* a, **ane** *acc.* 14/31, 18/31, 53/24, 25 *n.*, 117/20 *n.* (*before vowel or* h) **an** 61/16, 84/12. **ane** *gen.* 239/2. *dat.* 178/31. a, **ane** *p.c.* 17/22 *n.*, 29/35, 32/2, 146/12 *n.*, 238/25 *n.*, (*before vowel or* h) **an** 171/23, 242/8; ~ *oþer* see **anoþer**.

a *prep.* see **an(e)**, **at**

a *int.* ah 51/5, 71/12

abandones (*French*) *pp.* overflowing 247/30 *n.*

abatye *v. tr.* diminish 28/25

abbayes *n. pl.* abbeys 30/28, 42/7

abbotte *n* (*dat. p.c.*) abbot 178/31, 219/24. *pl.* abbottes 67/30

abece *n.* ABC 1/19

abegge *v. tr.* expiate 73/28

abide *v. tr.* await, wait for 51/25, 113/9, 128/24; expect 169/28; endure 167/2, 176/8; *intr.* remain 13/1, 211/28, 247/11 *n.*; wait, delay 173/13, 15, 194/17, 224/18 *n.*; ~ *to* give attention to 242/5 *n.*:

abit *pr. 3 sg.* (*fut. sense*), 128/24, 211/28. **abideþ** *pl.* 72/13, 86/31, 176/8. **abyde** *subj. sg.* 224/11. **abyd** *imp. sg.* 173/15. **abod** *pa. t. 3 sg.* 173/13. **abyde** *pl.* 13/1. **abide** *pp.* 239/30.

abidinge *vbl. n.* delay 173/17

ablent *pr. 3 sg. tr.* blinds 16/25

abod see **abide**

abomynable *adj.* abominable 49/26

aboue *prep.* above 13/18, 108/15, 141/30; upon 248/4; over 15/33; over and above 35/7; *adv.* above 10/30, 15/32, 44/5; in addition 35/13; on top 236/27 cf. **þeraboue**

aboute *prep.* around 30/17, 96/23, 150/27 *n.* cf. **þeraboute**

aboutestondinges *n. pl.* circumstances 174/37, 175/24, 176/11

abstinence *n.* abstinence 236/28

abundance *n.* abundance 261/29

ac, ak(e) *conj.* but 6/26, 29, 55/6; however (*mais*) 68/8

accidye *n.* sloth 16/4

accombringe *vbl. n.* difficulty 182/35

[1] Or 'note'; it should be observed that this sometimes indicates a range of reference. Thus 175/14 *n.* refers to the note to 175/13–14.

accuseþ *pr. pl. tr.* accuse 43/35
acordi *v. intr.* agree 151/16. **acordeþ** *pr. 3 sg.* 60/35. **acordeþ** *pr. pl.* 151/11; *tr.* reconcile, make harmonious **acordeþ** *pr. 3 sg.* 147/19 *n.*, 153/1, 256/8. **acorded** *pp.* 153/15.
acorseþ *pr. 3 sg. tr.* curses 52/23. **acorsede** *pa. t. 3 sg.* 57/23. **acorsed** *pp.* accursed 66/22, 138/30. **acorsede** *pp. adj. pl.* accursed 189/28, 198/11
acounteþ *pr. 3 sg. intr.* gives an account 137/32
acsi *v. tr.* ask for, demand, request 99/11, 110/15, 208/29, **oxi** 114/1; require 13/29, 53/8, 154/14; ask (a question) 103/13, 151/20, 264/15; claim 222/23, 32; *intr.* ask 139/24, 180/2, 210/10; ask (a question) 178/31; require 223/27, 250/5, 258/33; inquire rationally 151/18: **acxy** *pr. 1 sg.* 101/15. **acsest** *2 sg.* 207/22, 208/8. **acseþ** *3 sg.* 54/18, 207/35, **okseþ** 6/18. **acseþ** *pl.* 89/15, 110/20, **okseþ**, **oxeþ** 54/11, 109/2. **acsi** *subj. sg.* 198/2, 207/24, 208/5. **akse** *imp. sg.* 184/14. **acseþ** *pl.* 209/10 *n.*, **ocseþ** 209/20 (*see note to* 209/21). **acsede** *pa. t. 3 sg.* 195/24. *pl.* 208/11. *subj. sg.* 222/31.
acsinge *vbl. n.* asking, request 197/36, 208/7, 209/14; (false) claim 39/17; **acsing(g)es** *pl.* questions, inquiries 129/9, 12
actiue *adj.* active 199/9
adaunteþ *pr. 3 sg. tr.* subdues 167/28
adopcion *n.* adoption 101/24, 102/15, 146/10
adoun *adv.* down 247/21
adraȝe *pp.* drawn 174/14, 218/18
adrenche *v. tr.* drown, inebriate, submerge 50/20. **adraynkþ**, a-drengþ *pr. 3 sg.* 92/32, 251/32. **adrencheþ** *pr. pl.* 50/22. **adreynten** *pa. t. pl.* 50/17. **adrayngt**, **adreynct** *pp.* 107/26, 239/20*, 248/27
aduersari(e) *n.* adversary 170/6, 238/21
aduersete, aduersite *n.* adversity 27/18, 30/5, 68/17. **aduersetes** *pl.* 84/6, 182/3

af(f)aited *ppl. adj.* elegant 212/1; disciplined 75/35
affeccioun *n.* emotion 151/11
afrounti *v. refl.* be affronted 229/35 *n.*
afterward see **efterward**
age *n.* age; *heþ* ∼ is of age 51/24–5
agelte *v. intr.* sin, offend 15/33. **agelt** *pr. 3 sg.* 5/7, **agelteþ** 6/5 *n.* **agelt** *pp.* 20/22; *tr.* transgress, sin against **agelt** *pr. 3 sg.* 19/24, 65/18, 125/7. **agelteþ** *pl.* 72/15 *n.*
aginne *v. tr*, begin 32/6, 168/35 (*passive sense*). **agonne** *pp.* 166/3; *intr.* 197/20
a(n)ginninge *vbl. n.* beginning, source 16/13, 31/9, 32/14
agraiþi *v. tr.* make ready, prepare 14/18, 76/3, 183/1; bedeck, adorn 125/23, 216/16, 32; dress (a wound) 148/17; *intr.* prepare 55/34: **agrayþeþ** *pr. 3 sg.* 28/25, 81/20, 119/17. *pl.* 125/23, 216/16. **agraypi** *subj. sg.* 183/1. **agrayþed** *pp.* 14/18, 56/2. *ppl. adj.* 94/34
agrayþinge *vbl. n.* adornment 228/30, 258/8, 267/35. **agraiþinges** *pl.* 176/28, 216/9, 226/33
aȝt *pron.* anything 137/34, 194/7, 21
ayder *pron.* either; **eyder** . . . **oþren** each . . . other 66/7 *n.*; ∼ **ayens oþren** opposed to each other 53/21
aye *n.* egg 253/11. **eyren** *pl.* 178/23
aymont *n.* adamant 187/24
akþ *pr. 3 sg. refl.* aches 51/12
al(le) *adj.* all, every 9/9, 39/18, 109/7. **al(le)** *acc.* 18/8, 56/35, 71/26, 110/33, complete 235/10. **al(l)**, **al(l)e** *p.c.* 15/6, 16/9, 49/22, 233/13 (see *note to* 9/13). **al**, **al(l)e** *pl.* 1/11, 9/13 *n.*, 68/28, 76/2; ∼ **ane lenten**, the whole of one Lent 91/6–7; *at* ∼ *þe times* every time 114/14; ∼ *day* always 75/30, 232/2; **al** *pron.* all, everything 15/16, 19/16, 73/12, 134/17; **alle** *pl.* all, everyone 12/36, 30/17, 80/25 *n.*, 119/10 *n.*, 11, 268/10, 32 *n.* ∼ *hit* it all 34/7, 71/13. **alle(n)** *p.c.* 145/36, 152/5, 188/5; *alþerworst/uerst* worst/ first of all 17/32, 27/7, 51/14; **al** *adv.* all, wholly, completely, quite (the) 1/4, 13/18, 19, 26/16, 56/27, 67/12; ∼ *alsuo/*

ase (*tout ausi que*) just as 66/3,87/27, 186/29; *of* ~ (*du tout*) completely 98/19, 106/32, 122/19; *of* ~ *in* ~ completely 163/27; ~ *to* (*iusqua*) right to, even to, to 13/19, 173/26, 246/'29; ~ *to þan þet* (*a ce que*) until 200/24 (cf. **alhuet**); ~ *þet is of ous* (*quant est de nous*) as far as we are concerned 117/18

alast see **laste**

ald *adj.* old 16/27 *n.*, 48/10 *n.*, 104/30 (*see note to* 104/26), 219/13; elder 102/11; of old, ancient 7/20, 124/27; long-established 166/7: **ealde** *wk. sg.* 102/11, **yalde** 7/20, **yealde** 97/13. **ealde** *pl.* 166/7, **yealde** 79/35, 184/20, **þe yealde** 184/18. **yealden** *p.c.* 184/16, **eldeste** *superl. wk.* 104/26 *n.*

aleft half see **ha(l)f**

alfpeny *n.* halfpenny 193/33

algorisme *n.* in *tellynge of* ~ numbering with Arabic numerals 1/17

alhuet, alwet *prep.* until 52/12; *conj.* until 26/10 *n.*, 19, 33/19, 36/21 *n.*, 197/35

aliȝte *v. tr.* illuminate 77/27, 105/27, 109/4; kindle 66/3, 205/1; *refl.* shine 229/7 *n.*: **aliȝt** *pr, 3 sg.* 66/3, 77/27, 121/35. **aliȝteþ** *pl.* 205/1, 16, 17 *n.* **aliȝt** *pp.* 105/27, 115/30, **aliȝte** *p.c.* 201/9 *n.*, *pl.* 243/30. *wk.* 250/12 *n.*

aliȝtinge *vbl. n.* incentive 221/23. **aliȝtynges** *pl.* 204/35

alyue *adj.* alive 93/34

allas *int.* alas 51/10, 53/35

al(l)one *adj.* alone 142/19, 206/4; *adv.* solely, exclusively 102/4, *250/21*

almiȝti *adj.* almighty 1/12, 5/2, 12/5

alneway *adv.* always 6/27, 18/12, 22; however, yet, nevertheless 20/2, 220/31, 225/25, 28

alosi *v. intr.* win praise 183/9. **aloseþ** *pr. pl.* 199/24 *n.*; *tr.* **alozed** *pp.* praised, esteemed 16/22

alouer *adv.* quite beyond 81/7 *n.*

alowe *v. tr.* praise 95/26 *n.* (*passive sense*); 227/13 (*passive sense*), 233/34 (*passive sense*)

alse, als(u)o see **ase**

altogidere *adv.* very 59/26

alþaȝ *conj.* although 19/18

alþeruerst see **al(le)**

alþerworst see **al(le)**

alwet see **alhuet**

am see **by**

amaistreþ *pr. 3 sg. tr.* masters, subdues 129/1, 149/29. *pl.* 149/29 *n.*

amang *prep.* among 41/32, 52/6, 62/23. *cf.* **þeramang**

amanzinge *vbl. n.* excommunication 189/25; *cf.* **manzinge**

ambicion *n.* ambition 17/26, 22/35

amendement *n.* improvement, progress 32/14; correction 148/7; satisfaction, performance of penance 171/1; rectification 83/24 *n.*

amendes *n. pl.* fines 37/21, 38/28; amends, penance 113/27, 180/6; correction 148/18 *n.*

amendi *v. tr.* make amends for, remedy 30/32, 39/33, 83/25. **amended** *pp.* 30/25; *refl.* mend one's ways 29/16, 74/23

amendinge *vbl. n.* improvement, progress 31/8; amendment 33/1; penance 179/11, 180/4

amerþ *pr. 3 sg. tr.* damages, destroys 205/22, 217/22. **amerreþ** *pl.* 130/23, 203/29, 205/1, 220/9 *n.* **amerd** *pp.* 124/14, 125/11, 217/23

ames see **mes** [1]

amesureþ *pr. 3 sg. tr.* moderates, keeps within measure 150/13, 252/3. **amesured** *ppl. adj.* moderate 258/1, 259/16

amid(d)e *prep.* in the middle of 97/28, 183/18; in the midst of 128/17 *n.*; in 143/16, 159/14 *n.*; *adv.* in the middle 95/14, 20, 264/3

amis *adv.* amiss; *gon* ~ go astray 160/6

amoner *n.* almoner 190/18

amonesteþ *pr. 3 sg. tr.* admonishes 8/4, 101/13

amote *n.* ant 141/24

ampayri, anpayri *v. tr.* harm, impair 10/9, 237/35. *cf.* **apayreþ**

an(e) *indef. art.* see **a(n)**

an(e), a *prep.* on 1/2, 12/29, 131/35; in 1/5, 52/25; at 51/12; **an** *adv.* on 14/22 *n.*, 167/25

an, and, ant, *conj.* and 1/2, 4/9, 65/14 *n.*, 68/15 *n.*, ⟨ande⟩ *13/24*, ⟨aud⟩ *88/36*, ⟨end⟩ *251/3*; but 165/17; ~

an, and, ant (*cont.*):
... ~ both ... and 22/7 *n.*, 30/13,
85/12; *adv.* also 149/11, 262/26
anche(a)(y)soun see encheyson
andzuerede see ansuerie
aneuen see euen
anfermi *subj. sg. intr.* affirm 152/7
angel, angle *n.* angel 16/15, 89/29,
185/4. angle *p.c.* 21/4, 100/30,
158/28. ang(e)les *pl.* 16/16, 20/21
anginnynge see a(n)ginninge
⟨angrice⟩ *n.* anguish 147/2 (*see note to
146/32*)
⟨angrisi⟩ *subj. sg. tr.* afflict 146/32 *n.*
anhaste see haste
anheʒi *v. tr.* elevate, exalt 23/10.
anheʒed *ppl. adj.* 266/34; *intr.* rise
42/23. anheʒeþ *pr. 3 sg.* is greater,
increases 49/14
anhet *pr. 3 sg. intr.* is aroused 108/22;
anhet *ppl. adj.* heated 131/5
anhyalde *ppl. adj.* withheld, con-
cealed 152/10
anhongeþ *pr. 3 sg. tr.* hangs 51/17.
anhonged *pp.* 241/11
anioynj *v. tr.* enjoin 172/20
anlich, anlyke *adj.* like, similar 186/
5, 227/15 *n.*
anliche *n.* like 145/19, 233/15
anlicnesse *n.* likeness 87/26, 88/28,
36
anlicni *v. tr. intr.* resemble 16/19,
32/1, 101/5; compare 157/4; *intr.*
~ *to* resemble 91/32, 261/12; *is* ~
to resembles 61/6, 29, 66/13, 17:
anlikneþ *pr. 3 sg.* 32/1, 91/32. *pl.*
32/9, 242/12. anlicned *pp.* 61/6, 29
anoy *n.* tribulation 267/12
anoylinge *vbl. n.* unction 14/9
anoyþ *pr. 3 sg. intr.* is odious 162/16
anon *adv.* at once 83/25, 155/24; ~
ase as soon as 81/11
anoþer *adj.* another 35/15, 122/35–
123/1, 247/13. anoþer, an(e)oþre
acc. 85/15, 110/5, 115/3, anoþerne
masc. 162/6. anoþer, ane oþre,
anoþre *p.c.* 159/2, 207/32, 228/16;
pron. 132/27, 184/3, 265/35, ano-
þre 25/34, 29/28. anoþer, anoþre,
anoþrene, ane oþrene *acc.* 53/25,
146/31, 155/25, 180/21. anoþres
gen. 197/21. anoþre(n) *p.c.* 40/11,
91/6, 186/11

anpayri see ampayri
ansuere *n.* answer 214/22
ansuerie *v. tr./intr.* answer 56/10,
141/35 *n.*; *intr.* reply 67/5, 6;
correspond 159/31; ansuereþ *pr. 3
sg.* 56/10. ansuerieþ *pl. 159/31.*
ansuere *imp. sg.* 194/10. ansue-
rede, ⟨ansurede⟩, andzuerede *pa.
t. 3 sg.* 89/15, 190/36, 208/15 *n.*
ant see an
antempred *ppl. adj.* temperate 224/
31
anticrist *n.* antichrist 182/6, 9
anuenymeþ see enuenymeþ
aouri *v. intr.* worship 135/30
apayreþ *pr. 3 sg. tr.* impairs 237/33.
cf. ampayri
aparceiuy *v. tr.* comprehend, per-
ceive 131/10. aparceyueþ *pr. pl.*
57/32
apeluchier (*French*) *v. intr.* criticize
253/8 *n.*
apert *adj.* manifest, overt 203/35.
aperte *acc.* 134/29. *p.c.* 11/3
aperteliche *adv.* plainly, clearly 13/
18, 26/15, 162/10
apocalipse *n.* Book of Revelation
14/31, 169/26, 174/8
apostate *n.* apostate 19/23
apostel *n.* apostle 41/29, 47/31.
apostles *pl.* 11/30, 12/3; *adj.*
apostolic 267/24 (*see note to 43/4*)
ap(p)ropred *ppl. adj.* set aside for,
appropriate to 40/30, 120/35, 225/
3; byeþ ~ *to* are the property of
41/18
aquayntonce *n.* acquaintance 143/6
aquencþ *pr. 3 sg. tr.* quenches 207/
18. aquench *imp. sg.* 130/4
aquyked *pp.* quickened 203/26
aquitti *v. intr.* pay, make amends
137/35 *n.*; *refl.* to be discharged
aquytteþ *pr. 3 sg. tr.* 36/13 *n.*
arbytres *n.* arbitress 154/7
arblast *n.* crossbow 47/20. arblaste
p.c. 71/15
archan[ǥ]le *n.* archangel 1/8 (*see
p. 50*)
archer *n.* archer 45/32
ardontliche *adv.* ardently 51/22,
102/11
are *poss. adj.* see he
aredy *adj.* ready 121/26

arere *v. tr.* stretch out, lift up, raise 31/34, 35, 123/17, 244/23; rouse, excite 23/10 *n.*, 61/35, 129/13 *n.*; enhance, exaggerate 28/4, 136/24; exalt 88/29, 200/14; *refl.* get up 179/26; *intr.* be uplifted 271/6 *n.*: **arere** *pr. 1 sg.* 178/36. **arereþ** *pr. 3 sg.* 123/17, 125/16. *pl.* 66/35, 136/24. **arere** *subj. sg.* 217/34. *pl.* 217/31. *imp. sg.* 156/15, 244/23. **arerede** *pa. t. 3 sg.* 203/11. **arered** *pp.* 24/24 *n.*, 239/9, 24. *ppl. adj.* 86/26

arȝnesse *n.* pusillanimity 31/14, 32/4

ariere (*French*) *n.* time past 165/9 *n.*

ariȝt aright, truly 18/32, 20/5, 70/29

ariȝthalf, see **ha(l)f**

arise *v. intr.* arise, rise up 50/24, 52/26, 268/4 *n.*; well up 248/4; rise from the dead 13/12; rise 133/22; rise in amount, increase 35/12, 49/2; come to pass, occur 30/18, 57/2; *refl.* to be aroused 47/34 *n.*; *tr.* raise 121/26 *n.*; *op* ~ rises above, surmounts 186/30 *n.*: **arist** *pr. 3 sg.* 50/24, 248/4. **arizeþ** *pl.* 52/20 *n.*, 56/18, 57/2. **aros** *pa. t. 3 sg.* 7/21, 173/12. **arise** *pp.* 24/27, 121/26

arizinge *vbl. n.* rising, getting up 52/16; resurrection 13/10, 14/13; up-surging (of an emotion), impulse 11/17, 147/3. **arizinges** (*moeuement*) *pl.* 9/12

armenþ see **armeþ**

armes *n. pl.*[1] arms 15/13

armes *n. pl.*[2] arms, weapons 162/8, 163/25

armeþ *pr. 3 sg. tr.* arms 111/24, 180/13; ⟨**armenþ**⟩ 125/22 *n.* **yarmed** *pp.* 83/15, 164/1

armure *n.* armour 170/30, 171/4

arn *n.* eagle 61/12

aros see **arise**

arowe see **ar(o)we**

arrogance *n.* arrogance 21/15

art *n.* art 83/22; cunning, trickery 65/3

art *v.* see **by**

article *n.* article of faith 12/4, 13/10. **articles** *pl.* 2/13, 13/25

ar(o)we *n.* arrow 46/2, 66/12

as see **ase**

as(s)ayleþ *pr. 3 sg. tr.* assails 17/14,

16, 158/1. **asayli** *subj. sg.* 170/6. **asaylede** *pa. t. 3 sg.* 249/16. **asayled** *pp.* 157/34

asaylinges *n. pl.* assaults 84/17, 117/20

asayþ *pr. 3 sg. tr.* tests, tries 170/2. **asayd** *pp.* 142/15; *ppl. adj.* proved 117/8

ascapie *v. tr.* escape, elude 39/1, 172/11. **ascapeþ** *pr. 3 sg.* 180/18, 209/31; *intr.* escape 56/11. **ascaped** *pp.* 166/9

ase *prep.* like 17/21, 18/24, 24/25; such as 27/17, 18, 78/24; as being 59/27

ase, als(u)o *adv.* thus, likewise, furthermore, in addition 1/14, 10/13, 28/16, 46/13, 103/30 *n.*, 226/31 *n.*; **ase** as if 121/6, 140/24, 199/15; as it were 15/21, 23/5, 28/15; as, for example 6/18, 25/17; ~ *be* according to 51/18, 180/8; ~ *to* in regard to 8/28, 12/7, 15; **alsuo** . . . þet so . . . that 247/3–4, 5–6; *for other correlative phrases see the next entry*

ase, alse, als(u)o (**ase**), **zuo ase** *conj.* as, just as, in the same way as 6/9 *n.*, 8/27, 15/7, 17/1, 19/24 *n.*, 28/8, 40/33, 74/33–4, 119/29, 213/13 *n.*, ⟨as⟩ 29/12 (*with ellipsis of verb*), 256/9‡; **ase** such as 9/12, 10/28; (**alsuo**) **ase** (**yef**) as though (*with subj.*) 30/14, 74/18 *n.*; 158/3, 166/33, 187/2; as being 62/27; since 271/16; so that 45/27; while 119/15; (**bote**) **ase**, (**bote**) **ase** (**moche**) þet, of **ase moche** þet, **a(l)se moche ase**, **ine zuo moche ase**, of **ase moche** þet (except) in so far as, (in) as much as 49/28, 59/15, 101/21-2, 103/34–5, 105/21, 136/33 *n.*; notwithstanding that 63/2 *n.*; *with correlative adverbs* (**al**)/**ase**/**alse**/**alsuo** (**ase**) . . . **alsuo** / **zuo** (*just*) as . . . so (likewise) 15/8–9, 12–14, 52/16–17 *n.*, 79/27–8, 121/32–5 (MS **ase** . . . **assuo**), 153/10–12, 186/29–30 (*with ellipsis of the second verb*), 241/7–9; **ase**/**alse**/**alsuo**/**zuo** . . . **ase** as . . . as 52/10–11, 89/6, 28–9, 107/3–5, 174/2; **ase**/**alzuo moche ase** . . . **zuo** (**moche**)

ase, alse, als(u)o (ase) (*cont.*):
alzuo in so far as, in as much as . . .
likewise 137/3, 138/9–11 *n.*, 169/
9–10; zuo . . . ase so . . . as if 74/18;
~ *moche* ~ *in him is*, ~ *moche is of
himzelue* by its own capacity, so far
as in him lies 19/15 *n.*, 200/33,
230/21–2; ~ *moche* ~ *may* as far as
possible 15/30–1 *n.*; ~ *moche* ~ (*he*)
can, ~ *moche he is* something or
other 130/19–21 (*see note to 130/
18–21*); ~ *moche* ~ (*combien que*)
however much 63/2; ~ *moche* ~ . . .
more the longer 174/9–10
aslaky *pr. subj. sg. tr.* slacken 253/14
aslepe *adj.* asleep 199/15
asoyli *v. tr.* absolve 172/19
asoyny *v. refl.* withdraw 242/3
aspiinges *vbl. n. pl.* ambushings,
plottings 117/35
aspis *n.* asp 257/20
aspiþ *pr. 3 sg. tr.* watches, lies in wait
for 173/28. **as(s)pieþ** *pl.* 253/29,
255/26, 32; notice **aspide** *pa. t. 3
sg.* 191/12; discover **aspid** *pp.* 142/
33
asse *n.* ass 141/15, 155/32, 156/1
assencion *n.* ascension 213/19
asterue *v. tr.* starve out 240/28.
asterued *pp.* 240/39, 32
astonie *v. tr.* astonish, 126/8;
terrify 257/33. **astoneþ** *pr. 3 sg.*
130/11 *n.*
astori *v. tr.* stock 136/4. **astoreþ** *pr.
3 sg.* 112/1
astrangli *v. tr.* strangle 50/27.
astrangleþ *pr. 3 sg.* 65/12. **astran-
glede** *pa. t. 3 sg.* 48/29
astruþ *pr. 3 sg. tr.* destroys 17/9
asummed *pp.* completed 168/34
at *prep.* at 20/29, 56/24, 213/18; on
14/24; in 103/6; from 184/14. **ate**,
aþe at the, to the 13/22, 14/20,
44/31, 242/31; of the 190/35; by
the 106/19; ~ *uerste* see **uerst** *adv.*
atamed *pp.* subdued 153/7
at(t)empre, *adj.* temperate, moder-
ate 254/26; well-balanced tempera-
mentally 153/8; mild 153/9
atempred, (*French*) **atempres** *ppl.
adj.* temperate 24/11, 259/10. *cf.*
antempred
atenende see **ende**

atrayt *adv.* leisurely 50/35
attwyte *v. tr./int.* reproach for 198/16.
atwyt *pr. 3 sg.* 66/28
atwytinge *vbl. n.* reproach 65/29,
194/25. **atuytinges** *pl.* 194/6
aube *n.* alb 236/34
aud see **an**
autorite *n.* authority, repute 147/23,
221/28
auarice *n.* avarice 2/1–8, 16/5
aue maria *n.* Ave Maria 4/7
auenture *n.* fortune 18/26, 27/18,
168/16; *par* ~, *be* ~ perchance
20/36, 129/26, 269/29
auer(e) *adj.* see **uer** *n.*
auer *adv.* see **uer** *adv.*
auerst see **uerst** *n.* and *ord. num.*
auocat *n.* advocate 127/26
auoerie, auouerie *n.* avowal, ac-
knowledgement 101/28, 146/11
auonci *v. tr.* advance, promote 82/30.
auonceþ *pr. 3 sg.* 68/1
auontage *n.* greater quantity: *don* ~
see **don**; *to* ~ in addition 209/21
auore *adv.* before, first 271/3; **auore
þet** *conj.* before 172/24
auor(e)ye, *prep.* against 1/3; in
regard to, towards 18/7, 26, 32/28;
in respect of 24/4, 6; ~ *god* in the
sight of God 172/16, 207/19, 234/
31
auoud *ppl. adj.* acknowledged 101/28
auouerie see **auoerie**
away(e) *adv.* away, off 4/9, 106/27,
108/5; *by* ~ to be gone 270/17
awaki *v. intr.* watch 264/8 *n.*; *tr.*
arouse, awaken **awakeþ** *pr. 3 sg.*
128/19, 28, 129/13 *n.* **awakede** *pa.
t. 3 sg.* 128/26; to be aware of,
aroused **awaked** *pp.* 31/29, 199/15
awarȝede *ppl. adj.* (*p.c.*) accursed
27/29
awynne *v. tr.* win 85/2
awreke *v. tr.* avenge 9/2, 59/23 *n.*,
76/1. **awrecþ, aw[r]ecȝþ** *pr. 3 sg.*
68/21, 70/5, 115/3, 147/3. **awreke**
subj. sg. 147/6. *pp.* 74/11, 83/25
awrekinge *vbl. n.* revenge 8/21
ayans see **toyeans**
aye *n.* (*p.c.*) egg 253/11. **eyren** *pl.*
178/23
aye(n) *prep.* against 1/1, 5/24, 170/1;
pertaining to, in regard to 24/3, 4,

188/10; to, towards 114/26, 115/22, 124/24*; *adv.* back, back again, again 36/17, 56/29, 252/12; back, backwards 159/25, 242/6; for **ayen comeþ** see **ayencomeþ**

ayeanward, aye(n)ward *adv.* the reverse, conversely 48/14, 49/4, 16, 56/28

ayenbite *n.* remorse 1/6, 5/15

ayencomeþ *pr. pl.* return 127/24

ayenyueld *pp.* see **uelle** *v. tr.*¹

ayens *prep.* against 6/25, 115/10; to, towards 125/31, 157/8 *n.*, 163/2; of 207/28; opposed to 98/26

ayenuallinge *vbl. n.* relapse 116/7

ayenward see **ayeanward**

ayenweȝe *v. tr.* re-weigh 57/15

ayenwyȝte *n.* counterweight 247/20

ayenyefþe *n.* return gift 120/24, 25

ayeward see **ayeanward**

aze see **ase**

azenkte *pa. t. 3 sg. tr.* sank 49/35

azet *pr. 3 sg. tr.* arrays 140/15

azide *adv.* sideways 216/31

B

baylyes *n. pl.* delegated authority, commission 26/9

baylifs *n. pl.* bailiffs 122/8

bayþ see **begge**

ybake *pp.* baked 112/1

bal *n.* ball 179/6 *n.*, 8

balance *n.* balance 91/13; jeopardy 30/35

bald, bold *adj.* bold 100/34, 105/2, 158/1. **bolde** *wk.* 170/16. **þe bolde** *pl.* 216/28 *n.*

barat *n.* fraud 39/19, 46/11, 82/29

bargayn *n.* (bad) bargain 9/27

baronage *n.* baronage, hierarchy (of heaven) 58/10

baronyes *n. pl.* baronies 38/32

barouns *n. pl.* barons 38/31, 85/27, 122/8

baselycoc *n.* basilisk 28/12

batayle *n.* battalion 249/12; battle, warfare 83/24, 116/23, 168/8. **batayles** *pl.* battles 91/5

baþeþ *pr. 3 sg. refl.* bathes 167/32 *n.*

be *v.* see **by**

beaȝ see **bouȝe**

beate *v. tr.* beat 236/22; *intr.* give the

---

accolade 116/17: **beat** *pr. 3 sg.* 30/13, 69/14, **byat** 100/19. **byet** *pa. t. 3 sg.* 175/15. **byete** *pl.* 156/8. *subj. sg.* 191/10. **ybeate** *pp.* 236/21, 239/15, **ybyate** 239/29; ~ **þe lippen** babble 210/28–9 *n.*

bebered *pp.* buried 263/4

beberkþ *pr. 3 sg. tr.* barks at 66/18

becaȝt *pp.* deceived 54/36, 125/25

becharmeþ *pr. 3 sg. tr.* puts under a spell, fascinates 257/24. *pl.* 60/27. **becharmed** *pp.* 257/27

beches *n. pl.* beech trees 23/26

beclepieþ *pr. pl. tr.* impede, delay 40/1 *n.*

becleppe *v. tr.* embrace, grasp 46/34 *n.*, 66/19 (*see note to 46/34*). **beclepþ** *pr. 3 sg.* 15/14, 88/30 (*see note to 46/34*). **beclepte** *pa. t. 3 sg.* 240/2. **beclept** *pp.* 15/15

becleppinge *vbl. n.* embrace 96/1 *n.*

become *v. intr.* become 93/3, 116/26. **becomþ** *pr. 3 sg.* 19/16, 43/10, 91/34. **becomeþ** *pl.* 78/1, 92/3, 263/24 *n.* **become** *subj. sg.* 98/34. *pl.* 139/13. **becom** *pa. t. 3 sg.* 16/18, 240/8. **become** *pp.* 144/12*, 201/26

bed, ybede see **bidde**

bed *n.* bed 31/14, 47/36, 171/12. **bedde** *p.c.* 52/20, 25, 177/16

bedeaweþ *pr. 3 sg. tr.* bedews 95/1, 116/24

bedeles *n. pl.* warrant officers 37/20, 39/10, 43/34

bedes *n. pl.* prayers 141/31, 265/19

begge *v. tr.* buy 17/13, 23/32; redeem 95/32, 266/29; *intr.* buy 44/14, 194/25; **bayþ** *pr. 3 sg.* 23/29, 76/34, **beggeþ** 44/20 *n.* **beggeþ** *pl.* 36/18, 39/13. **boȝte** *pa. t. 3 sg.* 133/11, 266/29. *pl.* 215/7. **yboȝt** *pp.* 145/23, 35, 194/24

beggeres *n. pl.* beggars 36/10

beggeþ *pr. 3 sg. tr.* begs 139/25

begginge *vbl. n.* purchase 38/14

begyleþ *pr. 3 sg. tr.* beguiles 16/28 *n.* **begyled** *pp.* 76/21

beginne *v. tr.* begin, start 65/34, 150/33; *intr.* begin, originate 119/22, 243/27: **biginþ** *pr. 3 sg.* 3/1, 51/4, 65/34, 142/29. **beginneþ** *pl.* 17/35, 66/31. **begonne** *pa. t. 2 sg.* 71/25 *n.*, 26

behat see behote
beheste *n.* promise 67/16, 225/25.
behestes *pl.* 98/22
behinde *prep.* behind 10/11, 136/32, 243/17; *adv.* behind 243/2; *beuore and* ~ in all directions 58/13; *þet beuore* ~ (*ce deuant deriere*) the other way round 45/29
behofsam *adj.* profitable 99/1, 192/4
behorewed *ppl. adj.* befouled 237/24
behote *v. tr.* promise 162/29; *intr.* 97/17: behat, behot *pr. 3 sg.* 64/9, 179/30, 261/3. behoteþ *pl.* 37/34, 65/11. behote *pp.* 13/3, 65/19* *n.*, 67/16
behotingge *vbl. n.* promising 207/34.
behotinges promises *pl.* 40/12, 42/4, 9
behoueþ *pr. 3 sg. impers.* (it) behoves, is necessary, is fitting 18/35, 57/15*, 160/34, 163/19 *n.*, 209/17*, 211/14; *with subject* must 148/24; befit 56/23*, are necessary 172/7: behoueþ *pl.* 172/7. behouede *pa. t. 3 sg.* 12/36, 128/14
beknaulechinge *vbl. n.* confession 32/35; understanding 77/27 *n.*
beknawynge *vbl. n.* knowledge 126/23
bekneu see byknawe
bekuydes see bequide
beles *n. pl.* boils 224/8
beleue *v. intr.* believe 151/35, 152/4. *pr. 1 sg.* 12/4, 13/28. bylefþ *pr. 3 sg.* 139/27; *tr.* 19/22, 24, 26, 151/36
beloke see beloukþ
belongeþ *pr. 3 sg. intr.* belongs, is a part or attribute 39/18, 43/11, 152/7 *n.*; pertains 11/31, 12/7, 15; *tr./intr.* befits 152/10, 195/30: belongeþ *pl.* 17/28, 37/28, 234/13* *n.*
beloued *ppl. adj.* beloved 104/27, 187/15. belouede *wk.* 230/14
beloukþ *pr. 3 sg. tr.* includes 99/22. beloke *pp.* 97/3
bench *n.* bench 130/3
bend *n.* bond 48/6. bende *p.c.* 220/30. bendes *pl.* 77/22
bene *n.* petition, prayer 3/3, 99/8, 35. benen, benes *pl.* 20/27, 25/17, 217/35
benefices *n. pl.* benefices 42/11; acts of piety, good deeds 96/13 *n.*

beneþe *adv.* beneath, (low) down 76/33, 108/12, 15 *n.*; below 126/1; *hier* ~ here on earth 232/7; *as a n.* this world below 250/23
benoteþ *pr. 3 sg. tr.* uses 90/21
ybent *pp.* bent 174/13
bequide *n.* testament, will 112/4. bekuydes *pl.* 38/25
berdone *n.* burden 84/15, 141/20
bere *n.*[1] bear 14/34, 15/11, 60/11
bere *n.*[2] barley 141/16
bere *v. tr.* carry, bring 56/30, 78/26, 215/35; have 257/7; bear (a likeness) 261/9; bear (a child, fruit) 12/18, 95/8, 97/2; bear (false witness) 64/35; sustain 254/7; endure 33/33, 141/20; show (honour or respect) 8/10, 21/9, 135/35; show (an emotion), manifest 8/30, 32/35, 48/17; wear 90/25, 217/12; urge 141/8; possess (a heritage) 101/29; *intr.* require 236/29 *n.*: bere *pr. 1 sg.* 64/18. berþ *3 sg.* 20/6, 37/30 *n.*, 195/4, 234/4; bereþ *pl.* 97/29 *n.*, 98/30, 231/18, 267/8. bere *subj. sg.* 221/10. *pl.* 217/17. berinde *pr. p.* 96/10. *ppl. adj.* 144/35. bere *pa. t. 2 sg.* 20/30. beren *pl.* 267/20. (y)bore *pp.* 17/22, 28, 221/33‡
bereblisse *n.* joy-bringer 72/21 *n.*
berede *v. refl.* bethink oneself, reflect 172/15
berȝe *v. tr.* save 197/9, 251/16, ⟨bouerȝe⟩ 134/16 *n.* (y)borȝe *pp.* 3/23, 11/28, 168/30; *ppl. adj.* safe 41/6
berieles *n.* tomb 12/29, 228/13. berieles *pl.* 26/2 *n.*
beringe *vbl. n.* birth 5/5, 130/28, 262/22; bearing, behaviour 259/9, 34
berke *v. intr.* bark 179/7
berne *v. tr.* burn 43/27, 229/28, 230/3; set alight 204/36; *intr.* burn, be burnt 173/23, 206/17: bernþ *pr. 3 sg.* 41/3, 64/12, 225/18. berneþ *pl.* 74/5. berne *sub. sg.* 163/21, 212/9. berninde *ppl. adj.* 49/32, 73/21, 107/1 (MS *bernide*), 211/19*. bernde *pa. t. 3 sg.* 242/7*. þe ybernde *pp. wk.* 116/2
bernes *n. pl.* barns 30/28
bernindeliche *adv.* ardently 31/12

berninge *vbl. n.* burning 205/7, 206/19

bernston, brenston *n.* brimstone 49/32, 73/21, 130/7

berobbeþ *pr. pl. tr.* rob 39/2

besme *n.* broom 172/1

besmet(ted) *pp.* defiled 32/26, 229/20

besnewed *ppl. adj.* snow-covered 81/9

bessette *v. tr.* shut, shut in, enclose 263/34. **bisset** *ppl. adj.* 94/29, 226/12; *pp.* 226/15, 231/24, 233/7; included 97/10

best *n.* beast 4/11, 14/32, 15/2. **beste** *p.c.* 14/33, 16/2. **bestes** *pl.* 36/28, 61/10

besteriinge *vbl. n.* affection, emotion 263/18 *n.*

bestrepþ *pr. 3 sg. tr.* extirpates 123/2, 127/32, 144/30. *pl.* **bestrepeþ** 127/27 *n.*

bet *comp. adv.* see **wel**

betakeþ *pr. pl. tr.* give, deliver 36/28 *n.*, 235/16, 20. **betoke** *pa. t. subj. sg.* 89/30. **betake** *pp.* 198/17, 20 *n.*; release 247/27 *n.*; *euele* ~ (*maubailli*) unfortunate 110/8; ~ (*ine*) *wed* give (as) security 36/12–13, 134/28

betere *comp. adv.* see **wel**

betocneþ *pr. 3 sg. tr.* signifies 1/19, 15/5, 202/29. *pl.* 15/29, 32, 232/10. **betoknede** *pa. t. 3 sg.* 236/9. **betokned** *pp.* 181/9, 199/28

betuene *prep.* between 30/18, 43/31, 261/19*; ⟨**betune**⟩ 210/32 *n.*; the difference between 4/11

beþ *n.* bath 74/4

beþenche *v. tr.* think, consider, reflect upon 101/3, 146/21, 172/27; remind, call to mind 100/24, 177/17; cause to consider 152/19 *n.*; *refl.* consider, recollect 174/18, 246/17; *intr.* remember, reflect 151/18, 152/19 *n.*, 257/32 *n.*: **beþenche** *pr. 1 sg.* 178/34. **beþengþ** *3 sg.* 18/11. **beþencheþ** *pl.* 38/29. **beþench** *imp. sg.* 130/3. **beþencheþ** *pl.* 242/25. **beþoʒte** *pa. t. 3 sg.* 156/1

beþenchinge *vbl. n.* reflection, deliberation 183/34, 184/25; recol-

lection, memory 88/32 *n.*, 105/25, 203/4, 233/14, 17; memorial 257/11; *maki* ~ see **maki**

beualle *v. intr.* befall, happen, 107/22. **biualþ** *pr. 3 sg.* 57/18, 20, 174/17. **bevil** *pa. t. 3 sg.* 191/10. **beualle** *pp.* 49/28; *tr./intr.* befall 118/13

beuelynge *vbl. n.* corruption 40/7

beuelst *pr. 2 sg. tr.* defilest 230/34. **beuelþ** *3 sg.* 178/18, 229/16. **beueleþ** *pl.* 228/18. **beueld** *pp.* 201/16

beulaʒe *v. tr.* flay, fleece 73/29 *n.* **beulaʒeþ** *pr. pl.* 38/26, **beuleaþ** 182/16, 218/5

beuliynge *vbl. n.* avoiding 121/20

bewepþ *pr. 3 sg. tr.* bewails 51/9

beyende *prep.* beyond 165/21

beyete *pp.* begotten 130/29, 147/29 *n.*, 224/5

beyetinge *vbl. n.* begetting 216/3 *n.*

bezeche *v. tr.* beseech 194/21; ask for 106/2, 12: **bezekþ** *pr. 3 sg.* 117/2. **bezecheþ, bezechiþ** *pl.* 98/9, 16, 115/11. **bezeche** *subj. pl.* 98/8

bezechinge *vbl. n.* petition, entreaty 98/12, 13, 116/23, 35. **bezechinges** *pl.* 98/15; pleas 39/23

bezenge *v. tr.* singe 230/4. **bezengþ** *pr. 3 sg.* 230/4

bezette *v. tr.* employ 46/5, 214/13, 26. **bezest** *pr. 2 sg.* 213/36. **bezetteþ** *pl.* 207/3 *n.* **bezet** *pp.* 102/6; spent 152/33

bezide *prep.* near, near to, in the proximity of, beside 131/26, 242/2; *adv.* in addition, as well 44/2, 196/20; of equal status 126/1; at hand 104/35 *n.*

bezide-zitteres *n. pl.* legal advisers, assessors 40/20

bezyinge *vbl. n.* circumspection 183/34, 184/25

bezuyke *pp.* deceived 76/21

bezuykere *n.* betrayer, traitor 171/17, 26

bezuyk(y)inge *vbl. n.* treachery, deceit 28/1, 5 (*see p. 98, n. 1*) 61/7, 21. **bezuykynges** *pl.* 23/12

bi *v. intr.* be 1/15, 49/21, 234/2, ⟨**be**⟩ 73/29 *n.* **to byenne** *infl. inf.* 131/24, 169/33. **am** *pr. 1 sg.* 1/13, 51/2. **art**

bi (*cont*.):
2 *sg.* 31/17, 32/21. **is** *3 sg.* 1/5, 6,
6/12, his 31/6. **bieþ** *pl.* 1/16, 77/3,
166/21, 195/36 *n.*, 242/14 *n.*, 242/
14 *n.*, **byet** 66/27 (*see p.* 97, *n.* 6),
bied 138/30 (*see p.* 97, *n.* 6), **byþ**
17/28 *n.*, 102/16, 208/28, **by** 142/
5 *n.* **bi** *subj. sg.* 1/3, 103/32, 107/11,
255/10. *pl.* 9/11, 216/32, be 16/9,
10. **bi** *imp. sg.* 54/30, 187/6, 188/14.
byeþ *pl.* 188/11, 235/24. wes *pa. t.*
1 sg. 259/26. were *2 sg.* 269/17. wes
3 sg. 7/19, 12/17. were(n), werin
pl. 5/4, 13/5–7, 71/15, 150/25, 239/
26 *n.* were *subj. sg.* 30/15, 39/14,
⟨wer⟩ 239/15 *n.* were(n) *pl.* 75/36,
196/35. (y)bi *pp.* 21/7, 167/12,
204/11; ~ *ine* see **ine**; *ne* ~ *naʒt to*
zigge ought not to be spoken 6/33–4;
~ *of* consist of, be made up of 35/
35, 37/19, 234/17. **byeþ** there are
78/4, 196/26 *n.*, 255/8 *n.*

bi *prep.* by, by means of 1/17, 6/16,
9/15, *238/14*, 249/11; from 63/31;
through 27/31, 131/17, 202/31;
(*depar*) amongst 12/26; by way of
32/1; in relation to 249/20; accord-
ing to 9/31, 10/2, 11/29; in regard
to, concerning 82/9, 221/15, 223/
33; for, on account of 31/10, 40/12,
240/7; *to form adverbs e.g.* ~ *his*
wytinde wittingly 6/23; ~ *red*
wisely 159/3; ~ *to moche* in excess
52/34–5; ~ *poʒte* deliberately 6/26,
63/11, 64/18; ~ *kueade/wyckede*
skele wickedly 9/24–5, 33; *in other*
phrases ~ *þe skele* of by reason of
35/22; ~ *spouse* as a spouse 10/34;
~ *þe morgen* in the morning 108/7;
~ *þer þet*, ~ *þan þet* see **þet** *conj.*;
~ *uourti daʒes* for forty days 13/14;
~ *zuo þet* (*with subj.*) on condition
that 36/26, 28
byad see **byet**
byam see **zonnebyam**
byat, ybyate see **beate**
bidde *v. tr./intr.* pray (to sb. for sth.),
entreat, ask for 1/3, 7/26, 29/1, 197/
35, 215/1; *tr.* bid, command,
admonish 116/20, 145/8; seek 209/
32 *n.*; *intr.* pray 99/18, 114/33,
266/30; ask, beg 194/26: **bidde** *pr.*
1 sg. 117/3. **bist** *2 sg.* 209/9. **bit** *3*

sg. 110/18, 21, 114/11. **biddeþ** *pl.*
99/16, 210/26, 211/8 *n.*, 268/7.
bidde *subj. sg.* 49/13, 114/5, 211/
15. *pl.* 98/8, 127/24. **bide** *imp. sg.*
210/20. **biddeþ** *pl.* 209/34. **bid-**
dinde *pr, p.* 219/11, 266/35. **bed**
pa. t. 3 sg. 191/16, 215/28. **ybede**
pp. 117/33
biddinge *vbl. n.* prayer, request 12/
28, 194/24. **bidding(g)es** *pl.* 38/20,
40/12, 42/4, 100/1
byet *pr. 3 sg. tr.* offers 181/25. **byad**
pa. t. 3 sg. 41/30
byet, byete see **beate**
byetinge see **beyetinge**
biginninge *vbl. n.* beginning 11/33,
70/12, 76/10, 119/25, 138/29. **be-**
gynnynges *pl.* 268/23*
byinge *vbl. n.* existence, essential
nature 82/35, 103/24
byknawe *v. tr.* acknowledge, confess
123/15–16 *n.*, 182/11 *n.* **beknaust**
pr. 2 sg. 100/7, 10, 14. **beknauþ** *pr.*
3 sg. 135/10. **beknaweþ** *pl.* 69/12,
132/19. **bekneu** *pa. t. 3 sg.* 215/30,
216/10
bylefþ see **beleue**
bileaue *n.* faith 2/14, 12/34, 19/23,
bileue 11/26, 207/25, **belyaue**
203/19, **byyleaue** 243/30 (*cf. p. 20,*
n. 2)
bynde *v. intr.* bind, bind fast together
97/15 *n.*, 172/17; *tr.* 15/13; limit,
fetter 86/12; commit, oblige, con-
strain 145/28, 220/3, 221/5, 235/12;
be entrenched, habitual 22/9: **bint**
pr. 3 sg. 33/9, 77/25. **byndeþ** *pl.*
97/16, 264/29. **ybounde** *pp.* 220/29
bynime *v. tr.* take away (sth. from
sb.), deprive (sb. of sth.) 32/12, 39/
30, 59/3, 77/15; take away, despoil
23/20, 41/16, 79/5, 86/26: **benimþ**
pr. 3 sg. 68/18, 79/6, 108/31 *n.*
benimeþ *pl.* 29/12, 39/32. **benome**
pp. 143/23, 190/15
byrie *n.* bier 258/19
bisemereþ *pr. pl. tr.* mock 22/21 *n.*
bisemer(e)s *n. pl.* taunts, mockery
52/31, 58/25, 63/7, 157/1
bisy *adj.* engaged (in an activity),
concerned 199/28, 216/32; active
199/33; solicitous 258/8; well-
calculated 58/15 *n.* **byzye** *p.c.* 199/

33, *wk.* 247/9. **bisye** *pl.* 58/15, 226/
14, **þe bysye** 253/9
bisihede *n.* concern, anxiety, pre-
occupation with worldly matters
55/29, 93/34, 228/31. **bisihedes** *pl.*
164/29, 165/4; curiosity 231/32, 36
bysinesse *n.* see **do**
bisiuol *adj.* elaborate 226/31
bisset see **bessette**
bissop *n.* bishop 189/22, 23, 236/14.
bissoppe *p.c.* 191/30. **biss(s)-**
oppes *pl.* 189/24, 235/8, 236/5
bissopriches *n. pl.* bishoprics 42/7
bist see **bidde**
byt *pr. 3 sg. tr.* bites 61/30, 66/17;
intr. 62/5; *ppl. adj.* pungent 143/34:
byteþ *pl.* 61/25, 70/4. *pr. p.*
bitinde 143/34
byte *n.* sting 61/20
biter *adj.* bitter 82/26, 35. **bitere** *pl.*
83/2, 107/14, **þe bitere** 150/6
biterhede *n.* bitterness 28/1, 3
biternesse *n.* bitterness 15/7, 172/29.
biterneses *pl.* 139/19 *n.*
byþ see **bi**
biualþ see **beualle**
byuealde *pp.* enveloped 188/29; *ppl.*
adj. enclosed 8/31
byuly *v. tr.* flee, avoid 9/13, 15/25,
60/15 *n.*, 134/6. **beulyჳþ, beulyჳt**
pr. 3 sg. 73/20, 75/22, 136/2.
beuleþ *pl.* 61/32. **beuly** *subj. pl.*
139/11. *imp. sg.* 205/29, 206/6.
beuloჳe *pa. t. pl.* 77/18, 78/9 (*see*
note to 78/9–17); *intr.* escape 173/16
byuore *prep.* before, in front of, in the
face of 21/6, 28/12, ⟨**beuor**⟩ 58/6 *n.*;
~ *him* forwards 243/8 *n.*; *adv.*
before, beforehand, already, 7/11,
49/13, 106/30, 182/13*, 195/9*;
foremost, first of all 119/30, 197/
20; in front 149/4; afore(men-
tioned) 15/31, 130/17, 234/13* *n.*;
forth 119/29, 150/35 *n.*; ~ *and*
behynde see **behinde**; *þet* ~
behinde see **behinde**; *conj.* before
194/21 *n.*
byzylyche *adv.* diligently 79/35
blake *adj.* (*pl.*) black 267/30
blame *n.* blame 23/10, 61/35
blameþ *pr. 3 sg. tr.* blames 17/3,
137/19. **blamyeþ** *pl.* 59/27.
yblamed *pp.* 27/20

blasfemeþ *pr. 3 sg. intr.* blasphemes
30/9
blasfemie *n.* blasphemy 57/30, 70/11.
blasfemies *pl.* 45/26, 69/24 *n.*, 25
blawe *v. intr.* blow 168/4. **blauþ** *pr. 3*
sg. 25/11. **blaweþ** *pl.* 24/26; hiss
pr. 3 sg. 32/11
bleche *adj.* pale 53/23
blechest *pr. 2 sg. tr.* injurest 147/36.
blecheþ *3 sg.* 40/28, 115/2
blefþ, blefte see **bleue**
blench *n.* trick: *makeþ his* ~ plays a
trick 130/1
blendeþ *pr. pl. tr.* blind 33/5. **yblent**
pp. 201/17, 223/10; *ppl. adj.* 72/30
yblessed see **yblissed**
blest *n.* blast of words 203/25
bleþeliche *adv.* gladly, willingly
20/27, 50/26, 203/32*. *comp.* **ble-**
þelaker 69/3, 140/8, 180/1 (*see*
pp. 16–17)
bleue *v. intr.* remain 91/2, 120/11,
172/33, 177/2 *n.*; be steadfast,
endure 232/35 *n.*, 267/6; dwell
47/2, 72/34, 245/21; ~ *in lyue*
survive 225/12: **blefþ** *pr. 3 sg.* 30/
20, 168/30, 172/31. **bleue** *subj. sg.*
262/13, 269/22. **blefte** *pa. t. 3 sg.*
12/21, 190/21. **bleften** *pl.* 189/10.
blefte *subj. pl.* 56/14. **ybleft,**
ybleued *pp.* 173/9, 176/5
bleuindeliche *adv.* perseveringly
141/21, 208/3
bleuinge *vbl. n.* homeland, dwelling
72/18; perseverance, tenacity 168/
22 *n.*, 215/18, 232/26; dwelling (of
thought) 47/4, 176/21
blind *adj.* blind 1/14. **þe blynde** *wk.*
270/18. **blynde** *pl.* 134/26, **þe**
blynde 56/25, 224/5
blisfolle see **blisuol**
blysce, blisse *n.* pleasure, joy, bliss
1/13, 14/14, 90/31. **blissen, blisses**
pl. 77/10, 93/13, 269/2; glory 59/3,
116/16, 18; *ydele* ~ see **ydel**;
ledinde ~ see **lede**
yblissed *pp.* blessed 167/22; **yblis-**
sed(e), yblessed *ppl. adj.* blessed
77/13, 93/32, 96/32, 168/22 *n.*,
⟨**yblisseþ**⟩, 162/32 *n.*, 163/15 *n.*
(y)blissede, yblessede *wk.* 70/2,
98/14, 172/26, 267/23. **yblissed(e)**
pl. 198/23 *n.*; sacred 41/2, 235/17

blyssedhede *n.* blessedness 97/5

yblisseþ see **yblissed**

blissinge *vbl. n.* blessing, blessedness 97/20, 133/30. **blissinges** *pl.* beatitudes 97/24, 98/21

blisuol, blisfolle *adj.* joyful, glad 75/4, 148/2; glorious, blessed 118/26: **blisuolle, blisfolle** *wk.* 118/26, 266/31. **blisuolle** *pl.* 267/15

blisuolliche *adv.* blissfully 94/7

bliþe *adj.* glad 87/27, 132/16; glad to do sth., compliant, obedient 85/19 *n.*

blod *n.* blood 1/2, 41/8. **blo(o)de** *p.c.* 107/4, 18, 111/35

blodi *adj.* bloody 46/2, 218/3, 4

blondere *n.* flatterer 61/1 *n.* **blonderes** *pl.* 60/8, 61/14

blonding(g)e *vbl. n.* flattery 10/16*, 57/28, 60/7. **blondingges** *pl.* 141/32

boc *n.* book 1/5, 42/19. **bokes** *pl.* 42/20, 61/9

bocherie *n.* slaughterhouse 64/31

bochouse *n. p.c.* library 1/6

bocle *n.* buckle 236/29

bodi *n.* body 14/33, 24/30. **bodie** *p.c.* 9/20, 10/24. **bodies** *pl.* 8/14, 61/24

bodilich *adj.* corporeal, physical 72/21, 200/21. **bodiliche** *pl.* 90/23, 119/12, **bodilich** 200/22

⟨**bodilich**⟩ *adv.* corporeally, physically 146/9 *n.*, 200/16‡, 240/36‡ (*see note to 146/9*)

boȝ *n.* bough, branch 2/1–8, 19/32, 21/15. **boȝe** *p.c.* 23/13, 59/8. **boȝes** *pl.* 2/20, 3/1, 26

boȝe *n.* bow 45/33, 174/12

boȝen see **bouȝe**

boȝsam *adj.* humble 59/34

boȝsamliche *adv.* humbly 70/23

boȝsamnesse *n.* obedience, humility 3/7, 33/1, 33; *by ine his* ~ *be obedient to him, under his authority* 250/17

boȝte, yboȝt see **begge**

boȝþ see **bouȝe**

boystoyse *adj.* (*pl.*) ignorant 103/24

bold see **bald**

bold(e)liche *adv.* boldly 34/27, 63/23

bonayrelyche *adv.* meekly 265/29, 31

bonteþ *pr. 3 sg. tr.* sifts 93/15 *n.*

bor *n.* boar 69/12

bord *n.* table 167/21. **borde** *p.c.* 235/35

(y)bore see **bere**

borgayse *n.* female burgess 216/26

borgeys, boryeis *n.* burgess 162/1, 3

borgeysye *n.* status of a burgess 161/35 *n.*

borȝeþ *pr. pl. intr.* receive credit, borrow 36/1

(y)borȝe see **berȝe**

yborȝinge *vbl. n.* salvation 201/5 *n.*

boryinde *ppl. adj.* piercing 66/12

boryeis see **borgeys**

bosyne *n.* trumpet 137/22

bosme *n.* (*p.c.*) bosom 163/21

bost *n.* ostentation, pomp 55/27, 71/13

bote *prep.* except 5/21, 12/11, 13/32; *conj.* than 142/19, 20; but 219/13; **bote (yef)**, ~ yef þet (*with subj.*) unless 7/31, 46/10, 85/34; **bote (yef)** . . . **ne** (*with subj.*) unless 6/31, 49/12, 109/20, 110/7; **ne** . . . ~ only 27/1–2, 31/28, 71/23*, *ne.* . . *botȝ* 72/2

bote *n.* satisfaction 4/5 *n.*, 180/3, 4

boterel *n.* toad 187/29

botme *n.* (*p.c.*) bottom 140/3, 264/33

botoun *n.* button 86/27

boþe *n.* market stall, shop 215/6

boue *prep.* above 251/15 *n.*

bouerȝe see **berȝe**

bougeren *n.* fine cloth made of linen or cotton 258/11

bougre *n.* heretic 19/22, 43/10, 63/21. **bougres** *pl.* 69/32, 134/19, 252/31

bouȝe *v. tr.* humble 78/15, 178/30; bow, incline 194/9; *intr.* bow, prostrate oneself 239/32; bow 246/34 *n.*; incline 154/15; condescend 157/12; submit, obey 8/14, 140/6, 143/33, 184/32: **bo(u)ȝ(þ)** *pr. 3 sg.* 20/8, 140/24, 141/21, 246/34 (*see p. 53*). **bouȝeþ** *pl.* 143/33, 147/10. **bouȝe** *subj. sg.* 68/29, 140/18. *pl.* 68/28. **bouȝ** *imp. sg.* 194/9. **bouȝinde** *ppl. adj.* 157/25. **beaȝ** *pa. t. 3 sg.* 239/32. **boȝen** *pl.* 84/34

bouȝinge *vbl. n.* inclining 153/21

ybounde see **bynde**

boundes *n. pl.* boundaries 206/11

boune *n.* limit 150/32 *n.*

bourdes see **b(o)urdes**

bourdedest *pa. t. 2 sg.* didst jest 20/ 30

boure *n. (p.c.)* bower 226/12

bouteþ see **bonteþ**

brayinde *ppl. adj.* roaring 73/22, 265/23

bread *n.* bread 38/2, 262/15, **bryead** 107/5, **bryad** 110/14. **breade** *p.c.* 110/23, 31, 111/19

brechgerdel *n.* loin-cloth 205/3. **brechgerdle** *p.c.* 205/5

brecþ see **breke**

bredale *n.* wedding 118/27, 166/34. **bredales** *pl.* 75/11, 128/25

brede *n.* breadth 105/5

bredgome *n.* bridegroom 233/9

breke *v. tr.* break, fail to observe 7/27, 51/35*; disrupt, destroy 16/21 *n.*, 116/30; *intr. ppl. adj.* brittle 82/13: **brecþ** *pr. 3 sg.* 8/8, 40/28, 41/3. **brekeþ** *pl.* 41/22. **brekynde** *pr. p.* 82/13. **brek** *pa. t. 3 sg.* 16/14. **breken** *pl.* 64/30, 213/ 10. **ybroke** *pp.* 65/21

brekinge *vbl. n.* breach 48/17, 261/4

bren *n.* bran 93/16, 210/31

brene *n.* burning heat 264/34

brenge *v. intr.* bring 118/25; *tr.* set (an example) 87/32; bring, lead 264/21. **brengþ** *pr. 3 sg.* 141/23, 160/6, 265/36*, **brengeþ** 33/27 *n.* **brengeþ** *pl.* 33/24, 83/29, 264/25. **bryng** *imp. sg.* 1/13 *n.* **brenge** *pl.* 1/10 *n.* **broȝte** *pa. t. 3 sg.* 118/31, 190/13, 215/35. **ybroȝt** *pp.* 261/21; ~ *ayen* restore 128/9; ~ *uorþ* exalt 268/25

brenston see **bernston**

bres *n.* brass 203/10, 13

bridel *n.* bridle 253/15, 254/27. **brid(d)le** *p.c.* 204/28, 254/29

bryest *n.* breast 175/15. **bryesten** *pl.* 247/8

briȝnesse see **briȝtnesse**

briȝt *adj.* radiant, clear 74/15, 159/10, 237/14. **briȝte** *pl.* 73/34, 108/19, 244/15

briȝte *adv.* clearly 72/28, 150/11, 156/20* (*see p. 50*)

briȝtliche *adv.* clearly 150/26, 157/ 15, 200/22

bri(ȝ)tnesse *n.* radiance 27/4, 81/24, 82/1 (*for this and following forms see*

note to 82/1), 121/32*, 142/4*, 266/ 23*; clarity, bright light 200/13, 32

bryng see **brenge**

brytnesse see **briȝtnesse**

broches *n. pl.* brooches 229/8

broȝte, ybroȝt see **brenge**

ybroke see **breke**

bronches *n. pl.* branches 9/11

brondes *n. pl.* fire-brands 205/8, 240/23

brotel *adj.* frail 129/24

brotelhede *n.* frailty 130/28

broþer *n.* brother 8/28, 12/23, 13/35. **broþren** *pl.* 101/34, 102/18

broþerhede *n.* brotherhood, frater- nity 110/21

broþerrede *n.* brotherhood, frater- nity 110/24

bulle *n.* bull, papal edict 62/21

buones *n. pl.* bones 64/30, 148/33

buoþe *adj.* both 265/6

b(o)urdes *n. pl.* jests 56/5, 58/22

busse *n.* bush 28/13

C

cachie *v. tr.* drive away 178/20. **cacheþ** *pr. 3 sg.* 171/33, 212/2

calices see **chalis**

calketreppen *n. pl.* snares 131/4

calouwemous *n.* bat 27/4

can see **conne**

candele *n.* candle 102/6. **candle** *p.c.* 206/16

caorsins *n. pl.* usurers 35/33

capiteles see **chapitele**

capons *n. pl.* capons 38/3

cardinals *n. pl.* cardinals 124/12

cardinal(e)s *adj. pl.* cardinal 3/25, 123/10, 124/1

carkeþ *pr. 3 sg. tr.* bears (crops) 230/ 21. **ycarked** *ppl. adj.* burdened 138/1, 142/5; laden 246/34. Cf. **chargeþ**

caroyne *n.* carcass 86/25

carten *n. pl.* carts 35/20

cartere *n.* carter 160/4

cas *n.* case, situation 46/12, 168/5, 190/22. **cas** *pl.* cases 42/22, 222/11, 34; categories 42/17; *be* ~ per- chance, as it happens 70/12, 266/1; by accident 115/3; *huet* ~ *yualle* whatever happens 36/24

castel *n.* castle 1/10, 57/5. **castele** *p.c.* 121/27, 231/23, 24. **casteles** *pl.* 38/32, 224/26

cat *n.* cat 179/32, 230/4, 5

catel *n.* capital 35/7, 36/25

cause *n.* reason, motive 42/34, 224/34; cause 176/10, 255/19. **causes** *pl.* causes 176/11, 268/23; legal cases 40/1

cedre *n.* cedar 131/34

celes see **sel**

cellen *n. pl.* cells 267/29

cerceaus (*French*) *n.* hoop 159/26 (*see note to 159/18*). cf. **quarteus**

chaynen, chaines *n. pl.* chains 264/22, 29

chald *n.* cold 139/19

chald *adj.* cold 74/4, 153/9, 170/18. **chealde** *pl.* 242/15 *n.*

chalenge *n.* false claiming 34/33

chalengeþ *pr. pl. tr.* slander 43/35 *n.*

chalis *n.* chalice 167/21, 235/17, 236/2. **calices** *pl.* 41/1

chambren see **chombren**

chancelier (*French*) *n.* flattering 243/34

chapele *n.* chapel 56/22

chapfare see **cheapfare**

chapfari *v. intr.* trade 162/3

chapit(e)le *n.* chapter, section (of a book) 136/29, 220/14, 255/21. **capiteles** *pl.* 1/16; ecclesiastical assemblies 43/31 (*cf. Wallenberg, p. 46, n. 8*)

chapman *n.* merchant 77/26, 158/25. **chapmen** *pl.* 76/24

chapuare see **cheapfare**

chargeþ *pr. 3 sg. tr.* instructs, directs 54/13; **ycharged** *ppl. adj.* burdened 127/15, 260/6; **chargeþ** *pr. pl. intr.* accuse 97/16. cf. **carkeþ**

charitable *adj.* charitable 145/4

charité *n.* charity 79/25, 83/16, 89/25; **charites** *pl.* graces 83/13 *n.*

charmere *n.* enchanter 257/22, 23. **charmeres** *pl.* 60/26, 69/33

charmeresses *n. pl.* female enchanters 19/27

charmes *n. pl.* charms 43/16

chast *adj.* chaste 202/13, 203/33. **chaste** *wk.* 204/29, 234/2. *pl.* **chast** 221/20‡

chasteté(e) *n.* chastity 4/1, 10, 181/17, 219/33*, 228/3 *n.*, 228/5* *n.*

chasthede *n.* chastity 230/34

chast(e)liche *adv.* chastely 221/17, 225/12, 238/10

chasti *v. tr.* chastise 8/12, 148/10. **chasteþ** *pr. 3 sg.* 17/3, 22/29. **chasti** *subj. sg.* 221/2

chastinge *vbl. n.* chastisement 68/35

chastisement *n.* chastisement 17/2

cheake *n.* cheek, jaw 248/20 *n.*

chealde see **chald**

cheap *n.* bargain. **cheape** *p.c.*; *guod* ~ cheaply 44/15; *to grat* ~ cheap 256/30; *to greate* ~ cheaply 36/19, 256/36

cheapfare *n.* commerce 36/4, **chapfare** 34/35, 44/11, 28, **chapuare** 120/18; formal compact 35/16; commodity 44/16, 90/32, 191/31 *n.* **cheapfares** *pl.* 36/20; **chapfares** commerce 45/4

cheas see **chiese**

cheaste *n.* contention 2/15, 65/24, **chyaste** 67/8. **cheastes** *pl.* 57/2, 139/19, 239/25

chef *n.* chaff 62/24, 137/28, 139/34. **cheue** *p.c.* 210/30

cheker *n.* chess-board 45/32, 46/2

chele *n.* cold 75/9, 265/6. **cheles** *pl.* chills, coldness 124/23

chenaille *n.* rabble 112/25 *n.*

cherche *n.* church 7/20, 29, 8/12, ⟨cherch⟩ 14/1 *n.*, 42/24 (*see note to 14/1*). **cherchen, cherches** *pl.* 30/27, 41/3

cherchtounes *n. pl.* churchyards 41/4

cherl *n.* ignoble person 76/4. **cherles** *pl.* 112/25

ches *n.* chess 52/30, 207/6

cheuuaille see **chenaille**

cheue see **chef**

chewynge *vbl. n.* chewing 111/4, 7

chyaste see **cheaste**

chide *v. intr.* quarrel 67/7

chidinge *vbl. n.* quarrelling 30/19, 65/28, 66/7

chiere *n.* countenance 256/26; *make uayre* ~ look cheerful 193/36; *makeþ uayr* ~ treats affectionately 155/35

chiese *v. tr.* choose 86/4, 101/26, **chise** 93/14; distinguish (one thing from another) 86/14: **chyest** *pr. 3 sg.* 126/33. **chieseþ** *pl.* 45/2, 165/16 *n.* **cheas** *pa. t. 3 sg.* 77/9. **ichose** *pp.* 42/6; **his/þe ychosene** *pl.* his/ the elect, the chosen of God 68/9, 96/15, 98/23

chyezinge *vbl. n.* election 42/8

chyewe *v. tr.* chew 111/11

child *n.* child 52/14, 58/31, 101/32* (*see note to 74/6*), 180/10* (see p. 49), 191/11 (MS. *chld*). **childe** *dat.* 208/32 (MS. *clilde*). **childe** *p.c.* 32/10, 74/3. **children** *pl.* 30/13, 29, 35/20, 77/1 *n.*

childbedde *n.*(*p.c.*) childbed 224/21* (*see p. 49*)

childhede *n.* childishness 82/3, 14* (*see p. 49*). **childhedes** *pl.* puerilities, childish ways 207/5, 259/28

childhedi *adj.* childish 259/13

childi *v. intr.* give birth 224/22

chinne *n.*(*p.c.*) chin 50/30 *n.*

chise see **chiese**

chomberier *n.* valet, servant 171/35 *n.*

chombre *n.* chamber 199/24, 206/3. **chambren** *pl.* 224/25

chonge *n.* change 104/14

chongi *v. tr.* transform 62/30, 129/1; exchange 42/13; gain in exchange 267/13 *n.*; *refl.* change 104/10: **chongeþ** *pr. 3 sg.* 141/18. *pl.* 42/13. **chongeden** *pa. t. pl.* 267/13 *n.* **ychonged** *pp.* 242/8

chonginde *ppl. adj.* mutable 104/11, 105/1, 120/5

ichose, ychosene see **chiese**

cipres *n.* cypress 131/34

cité *n.* city 49/33, 88/1. **cites** *pl.* 38/32, 43/28

clauen *n. pl.* claws 61/12

claustres *n. pl.* cloisters 267/28

clene *adj.* unpolluted, unalloyed, pure 5/13, 73/35, 131/11, 221/17, **clen** 159/13‡; seemly 42/10; wholehearted 141/4; mere 64/17, 176/29; ⟨**cliene**⟩ *pl.* wholesome 224/28* (*see note to 74/6*)

clene *adv.* purely 221/17, 223/31

clenlich *adj.* honest 42/33. **clenliche** *acc.* seemly 216/22. **clenliche** *pl.* honest 6/19 *n.*

clenliche *adv.* with purity 26/3, 48/32; solely, purely 120/14, 21* (*here*

and at 141/4 see note to 74/6), 27; **clienliche** completely 141/4

clennesse *n.* purity, innocence 49/22, 75/25, 205/28

clensi *v. tr.* cleanse, purify, clean, purge 108/30, 171/35, 237/26; *intr.* 246/10; be cleansed 271/6 *n.*: **clenzeþ** *pr. 3 sg.* 73/10, 74/10, 106/26. **clenzeþ** *pl.* 237/23, 238/1. **clensy** *pr. subj. sg.* 271/6. **yclenzed** *pp.* 73/33, 74/7, 107/11, ⟨**yclienzed**⟩ 74/6 *n.**

cleper *n.* clapper 58/14

clepie *v. tr.* summon 43/12, 190/35; call, name 9/10, 10/13; *intr.* ask 207/36 *n.*, 208/2: **clepie** *pr. 1 sg.* 42/33, 43/2. **clepest** *2 sg.* 100/6. **clepeþ** *3 sg.* 7/15, 17/25 *n.*, 61/11, ⟨**cliepeþ**⟩ 125/24* (*here and at 80/15, 104/13, 123/9; see note to 74/6*). **clepieþ, clepiyþ** *pl.* 58/2, 111/31, 194/5. **clepede** *pa. t. 3 sg.* 190/14, 27. **ycleped** *pp.* 3/19, 14/31, 16/7, 80/15 (MS *ycheped*), ⟨**yclieped**⟩ 104/13*, 123/9*

cler(e)gie *n.* learned speech 16/4, 5* (*see p. 49*), 18/3; knowledge 2/26, 71/35, 81/30, branch of learning 39/20. **clergyes** *pl.* 89/28

cler(e)k *n.* scholar 23/35, 71/30 *n.*; cleric 25/9, 41/10. **cler(e)kes** *pl.* 42/18, 20, 46/16, **clierkes** 78/32* (*see note to 74/6*)

clernesse *n.* radiance 95/2, **clyernesse** 109/1

cleuiinde *ppl. adj.* persuasive 54/35 *n.*, 98/14; persistent 107/29

cleuiyndelyche *adv.* persuasively 103/34

cliene see **clene**

clienliche see **clenliche**

yclienzed see **clensi**

cliepeþ, clieped see **clepie**

clier *adj.* bright, full of light 159/10; pure 159/16, 167/30; translucent 251/8; perspicacious 24/6, 78/25: **clyre** *pl.* 104/29. **clyerer** *comp.* 267/29

clierkes see **cler(e)k**

clierliche *adv.* distinctly 88/19, 155/12, 174/22

clyernesse see **clernesse**

clyre see **clier**

cliue *v. tr.* climb 32/3, 169/18; *intr.* climb, ascend, spring up 23/1, 89/3 *n.*, 127/10, 145/6: clifþ *pr. 3 sg.* 131/31, 159/28, 203/23. cliueþ *pl.* 164/6 *n.*, 246/23. cliue(n) *pa. t. pl.* 126/11, 246/21. ycliue *pp.* 24/25 (*see note to* 24/22–6), 26/11, 247/2

cloystre *n.* cloister 151/8, 242/11, 262/21 (MS. *choystre*)

cloystrers *n. pl.* monks 67/29

clom *n.* silence 264/12, 266/7

cloþ *n.* cloth 45/1, 3, 178/15; garment cloþe *p.c.* 133/17, 188/31. cloþes *pl.* 47/36, 128/31, 35

cloþeþ *pr. pl. tr.* clothe 229/5. cloþeþ *imp. pl.* 265/26. cloþede *pa. t. 3 sg.* 133/16. ycloþed *pp.* 236/15. *ppl. adj.* 61/30

cloþinge *vbl. n.* clothing 154/13, 165/31, 196/30

cloudes *n. pl.* clouds 108/6

coc *n.* cock 258/23

coccou *n.* cuckoo 22/8, 59/21

col *n.* a piece of coal 126/25, 205/25. cole *p.c.* 82/22. coles *pl.* 205/25

collacions *n. pl.* Collations (of Cassian) 155/21

(þane) colrik *adj.* choleric (person) 157/27

colt *n.* colt 185/34. colte *dat.* 220/22

col(o)ur *n.* colour 62/33, 81/25, 177/29. colurs *pl.* 15/9; ~ *of zenne* sinfulness 177/35 *n*,

colure *n.* dove 142/7, 11

coluerhous *n.* dovecot 142/6, 11

come *v. intr.* come 13/2, 22, 46/35, 179/27 *n.*; become 106/29; come to pass 67/6, 127/3; arise 168/5; *pr. 3 sg.* (it) results 31/12; attain 169/15; ~ *ayen* return 181/4; ~ *to* come by, obtain 23/11; attain to 156/13–14; ~ *uorþ* grow 119/16: to comene *infl. inf.* 106/29, 152/23 (*future*), 163/7(*future*), 167/3(*future*). come *pr. 1 sg.* 266/13. comst *2 sg.* 129/11, 239/32, 264/30 (*cf.* þou). comþ *3 sg.* 11/11, 180/22* (*see p. 52*), 232/33 (*future*). comeþ 155/33 *n.* comeþ *pl.* 15/26, 24/12, 25/6. come *subj. sg.* 33/21, 93/20, 107/35. com *imp. sg.* 137/23, 185/8, 194/13. comeþ *pl.* 198/23. cominde *pr. p.*

248/8 (*future*), 262/24 *n.*, 263/14, ⟨comyde⟩ 264/14 *n.* com *pa. t. 1 sg.* 259/27. come *2 sg.* 198/15. com *3 sg.* 14/32, 15/5, 26/34. come(n) *pl.* 130/25, 267/21. ycome *pp.* 56/5, 134/25, 262/6

comfort see confort

comynge *vbl. n.* coming 264/19; ~ *ayen* returning 87/11

commun *adj.* common, notorious 37/10; communal, in common 102/5, 120/33: commune *p.c.* 48/9, 147/31, *wk.* 151/3 *n.*

communliche see com(m)unliche

communy *v. tr.* share 102/34

comparer (*French*) *v. intr.* compare; *wypoute* ~ without comparison 243/33

comparisoneþ *pr. 3 sg. tr.* compares 94/25. ycomparisoned *pp.* 81/29

comparisoun *n.* comparison 81/22, 92/34, 235/18

compassion *n.* compassion 148/13, 156/24

compleccioun *n.* constitution 31/17; temperament 157/25

com(m)unliche *adv.* commonly, frequently 56/18, 211/27, 215/25; universally, equally 145/13, 35, 223/36

conceyueþ *pr. 3 sg tr.* experiences 136/7. y-conceyued *pp.* devised 58/28; conceived (a child) 221/35

condecendre (*French*) *v. intr.* condescend 157/8

ycondemned *pp.* condemned 113/34

condicion *n.* nature, quality, characteristic 173/11, 20. condicions *pl.* 172/7, 193/23; *mid* ~ *þet* in such a way that 195/32

condueþ *pr. 3 sg. tr.* guides 122/16

condut *n.* channel 202/31. condwys *pl.* 91/25

confermi *v. tr.* attach, make fast 121/17. confermeþ *pr. 3 sg.* strengthens 105/33, 106/14. confermy *subj. sg.* strengthen 109/23. yconfermed *pp.* confirmed 146/7; established 189/19

conferminge *vbl. n.* confirmation 14/7

confessour *n.* confessor, spiritual adviser 172/17. confessours *pl.*

confessors, those who avow Christianity in the face of persecution 267/23

confort, comfort *n.* comfort 72/19, 96/29, 260/31

conforti *v. tr.* strengthen, comfort 160/24. **conforteþ** *pr. 3 sg.* 111/20, 160/21, 161/19. **(y)conforted** *pp.* comforted 160/26, 161/18

confusion *n.* confusion 229/2, 3, 258/18

conioun *n.* fool 76/34

conne *v. tr.* know 11/23, 21/19, 57/14; know how to, be able to 57/15, 70/27, 158/23; *intr.* know 98/34; be accustomed to (*for this sense see note to 33/22*) 33/22, 77/33, 80/17, 103/26; ~ *þank* be grateful 58/31: **kanst** *pr. 2 sg.* 21/13. **can** *3 sg.* 21/20, 22/8, 23/ 35. **conne(þ)** *pl.* 24/20, 46/18 (*see p. 52*), 58/20, 249/27. **conne** *subj. sg.* 57/15, 72/1, 76/12. **couþe** *pa. t. 1 sg.* 89/28, 29. *3 sg.* 105/12, 133/3. **co(u)þe(n)** *pl.* 78/11, 12 (*see p. 15 and note to 78/9–17*), 98/12, 99/4, 126/10

connynge *vbl. n.* knowledge 90/4, 115/13, 122/29

consayle *n.* (*p.c.*) council 122/5, 10

consentement *n.* acquiescence, consenting 11/13. ⟨**consenteinens**⟩ *pl.* 19/3

consenti *v. intr.* consent 10/23, 73/30, 170/15; *refl.* consent 202/11: **consenteþ** *pr. 3 sg.* 253/25. *pl.* 38/15. **consenti** *subj. sg.* 202/10, 254/16. *pl.* 117/18. **consentede** *pa. t. 3 sg.* 249/18

consentinge *vbl. n.* acquiescence, consenting 117/26, 176/20, 202/14

conspiracions *n. pl.* conspiracies 23/12

constance *n.* constancy 167/34

contac *n.* strife 15/10, 40/7. **contackes** *pl.* 63/13

contacky *v. intr.* contend 57/1

contemplacion *n.* contemplation 204/27, 245/22, 247/2, 17

contemplatif, contemplatiue *adj.* contemplative 199/12, 247/22. **contemplative** *wk.* 245/18

ycontened, ycontined, ycontynent *ppl. adj.* contained, included, 12/17, 39/15 *n.*, 260/17 *n.*, **ycontyened** 12/2, 118/15

contenonce *n.* demeanour 259/8, 18, 34

contraye *n.* country 35/33, 86/34, 130/23

contrarie *n.* contrary, opposite 14/17, 69/3, 136/17 (*here and at 123/4, 7 and 261/13 see note to 28/29*), 261/13

contrarie *adj.* opposed, opposite 260/13. **contraries** *pl.* 123/4, 7

contrarious *adj.* contrary 28/29 *n.*

conuersacion *n.* citizenship 122/21, 241/17 *n.*; way of life 96/4, 268/8*; society 242/1

copereaus, coporeaus *n.* corporal 41/1, 235/18 (*see p. 49*)

coppes see **coupe**

corage *n.* heart 164/20

corde *n.* cord 58/27 *n.*

corn *n,* grain, corn 28/14, 35/8; germ 210/30. **cornes** *pl.* grains of corn 139/33; seeds 233/3, 11, 20; crops of corn 43/28

cornardyes (*French*) *n. pl.* follies 130/22

cornyeres *n. pl.* corners 124/19

coroune *n.* crown 168/28, 169/29, 230/35. **corounes** *pl.* 15/1, 116/15, 169/25

corouneþ *pr. 3 sg. tr.* crowns 72/22 *n.* **corounede** *pa. t. pl.* 234/28 *n.* **ycorouned** *pp.* 257/10, 267/19

corrupcion *n.* corruption 127/1, 227/11, 247/15

corruptes see **corupt**

corsinge *vbl. n.* blasphemy, cursing 27/36, 28/2, 97/19

cort *n.* court 39/27, 58/9, 99/30

cortays, cortoys *adj.* courteous, gracious 21/35, 100/36, 112/26

cortaysie *n.* courtesy, graciousness 18/10, 97/36, 98/11; good manners 118/23; favour 36/34; *pl.* **corteysyes**; ~ . . . *don* act courteously 162/7

cortaysliche *adv.* courteously, graciously 54/10, 106/5, 118/33. **cortayslaker** *comp.* 163/14

ycorumped *pp.* corrupted 140/12

corupt *adj.* corrupt 82/19. **corruptes** *pl.* 128/32

coruees (*French*) *n. pl.* socage-
services *38/27*
cos *n.* kiss 119/1
cosyn *n.* relative 89/14. cosynes *pl.*
89/16
cost *n.* expense 83/27; costes *pl.*
expenditure 40/15; *of grat* ∼ costly,
prize 58/3, 216/6, 31; *to gratter* ∼,
to litel ∼ at a higher rate of interest,
at a low rate of interest 36/1, 36/2;
zet grat ∼ spends much money
176/26–7 *n.*
costneþ *pr. 3 sg. tr.* costs 75/26,
121/4. costnede *pa. t. 3 sg.* 145/23
costningge *vbl. n.* expense 151/26*
costuolle *adj.* (*pl.*) costly 229/6
coþen see conne
cou *n.* cow 56/14, 191/19, 22. ken *pl.*
191/27
couche *n.* couch 171/12
ycountrefeted *pp.* deformed 15/4
coupe *n.* cup 167/20, 235/35, 236/1.
coppes, coupes *pl.* 30/14, 35/17
coustouse *adj.* (*pl.*) costly 216/8,
228/36
couþe see conne
couaitise *n.* greed, avarice 2/36, 16/5,
34/20, 137/4, *197/3**; (inordinate)
desire 11/11, 229/15, 243/6. couai-
tises *pl.* 125/9, 253/17, 254/27
(þe) couaytous *adj.* (the) avaricious
(man) 80/24. couaytouse *wk.* 136/
35. þe couaytous(e) *pl.* 154/31‡,
189/12, 209/30
couent *n.* assembly of the faithful,
church 110/26; monastic com-
munity 219/24
crayme *n.* chrism 41/1, 93/26, 27
crammeles *n. pl.* crumbs 253/10 *n.*
crane *n.* (*p.c.*) crane 56/13
credo *n,* creed 4/7, 12/2
creft *n.* trade, occupation 35/1, 36/3,
116/10; skill 90/17; art 19/28;
cunning 157/21: crefte *p.c.* 37/11,
45/11. creftes *pl.* 45/6, 178/25
crete *n.* cradle 137/6
cryepe *v. intr.* creep 107/24 *n.*
cristen *n.* a Christian man 93/26.
cristene *p.c.* 93/31; *adj.* Christian
11/27, 19/19, 182/11. cristene *p.c.*
∼ *cort* ecclesiastical court 39/27.
cristene, cristine *wk.* 2/13, 11/26,
29/21; þe cristene 182/10. (þe)

cristene *pl.* 64/25, 93/32, 145/20,
182/8
cristendom *n.* Christendom 64/34,
232/9; christening, baptism 93/27.
cristenedome *p.c.* 101/31, 145/20
cristesmesse *n.* Christmas 213/17
cristni *v. intr.* christen, baptize
107/7; *tr.* ycristned *pp.* 107/18
cristninge *vbl. n.* christening, bap-
tism 14/7, 74/1, 101/36
(þe) crokede *ppl. adj.* (*pl.*) the
deformed 56/25, 224/5
croki *v. tr.* crimp, curl 177/1 *n.*
crouche *n.* (*p.c.*) cross 111/34.
crouchen *pl.* crucifixes 41/1
ycrucefied *pp.* crucified 241/6 *n.*, 10
crueleté *n.* cruelty 15/16
curiouseliche *adv.* skilfully, ex-
quisitely 176/27

D

day *n.* day 7/5, 13/11, 41/23. dayes
gen. in the phrase eche ∼ daily
(*cotidien, cotidianum*) 112/11, 17–18,
262/25. daye *dat. in the phrase
eche* ∼ every day, daily 18/19, 112/
10 *n.*, 119/26, 156/3. *p.c.* 7/6, 13/22,
14/21. daзes, daies *pl.* 7/8, 13/14,
198/7; *of eche* ∼ (*cotidien*) daily
112/10¹; heþ ∼ is summoned (to
appear on a certain day) 172/36 *n.*;
adv. 71/33, 157/20
dayneþ *pr. 3 sg. intr.* deigns 18/16,
21/27. *pl.* 196/27. daynede *pa. t.
pl.* 126/13; *refl.* daynede *pa. t.
subj. pl.* 76/1
dame *n.* lady 39/20, 56/8, 80/7
damezele *n.* damsel 72/21
damni *v. tr.* condemn 137/25.
damneþ *pr. 3 sg.* 115/7. damnede
pa. t. 3 sg. 51/36. ydammed,
ydam(p)ned *pp.* 78/33, 90/20,
137/35
dan *n.* master 1/5
dane *n.* valley 160/32. danes *pl.* 59/24
dar *pr. 3 sg. intr.* dare 32/9, 33/34,
67/4. dorre(n) *pl.* 22/14, 32/6, 78/
17. dor *subj. sg.* 182/10 *n.* dorstest
pa. t. 2 sg. 73/29. dorste *3 sg.* 143/
29. *pl.* 163/35
de see þe
dead see dyad; deaþe(s) see dyaþ

deau *n.* dew 91/29, 136/3, dyau 144/
28. deawe *p.c.* 91/31
deceyui *v. tr.* deceive 82/28. deceyued *pp.* 79/34
decendi see descendeþ
deciple *n.* disciple 230/17. deciples, deciplis *pl.* 13/13, 17, 168/32, 230/17*
dedbote *n.* satisfaction, performance of penance 32/1, 33/2
dede *n.* activity 268/8; deed, act, action 10/31, 12/20, 21, 37/22 *n.*, 123/31 *n.* (*cf. MED* Dede 1 *a*(*d*)). dedes *pl.* 10/14, 21/29, 148/23 *n.*; *is ine ~* (*est en oeure*) is brought into play 21/30
dede(st), deden see do
defaced *pp.* obliterated 191/4
defayled *ppl. adj.* weakened 33/20
defaute *n.* lack 73/20; defectiveness, sinfulness 33/8, 132/6, 261/29; defautes *pl.* sins, defects 78/16, 108/9, 115/30; disfigurements 208/25
defendi *v. tr.* defend, protect 157/31, 175/4. defendeþ *pr. 3 sg.* 22/28, 61/1 *n.*, *pl.* 38/16, 69/12
defoulent (*French*) *pr. pl. tr.* trample on, oppress 182/16 *n.* defouly *subj. sg.* 221/2. defouled *pp.* 167/24
degre *n.* degree, stage 143/35. degres *pl.* 123/25; degrez ranks 267/7
del *n.* portion, part 17/5, 49/30; division, section, subdivision 165/7. dele *p.c.* 164/19; deles *pl.* 17/20, 50/9, ⟨delles⟩ 164/17 *n.*; *ine grat ~* to a great extent 86/15
dele *v. tr.* distinguish 76/14; separate 225/35; sever 148/25
delices *n. pl.* luxuries 24/21
delit *n.* delight 55/30
deliti *v. tr.* please 82/16, 91/27 *n.*; *intr.* deliteþ *pr. 3 sg.* is made happy 47/3
deliureonse *n.* deliverance 86/34
deliuri *v. tr.* save, set free 12/32, 13/3, 270/28; hand over, deliver 95/33: deliureþ *pr. 3 sg.* 128/28, 248/30. deliuri *subj. sg.* 103/11, 199/2. delyuri *pl.* 98/18. deliure *imp. sg.* 110/6, 118/3. deliurede *pa., t. 3 sg.* 128/27. deliured *pp.* 87/6, 99/24, 118/7
delue *v. intr.* dig 108/24; *tr.* dolue

pa. t. subj. sg. undermined 263/15. ydolue *pp.* 263/26
deme *v. tr.* adjudge 180/6, 269/29; judge, condemn 13/23, 85/17 *n.*, 263/7; *intr.* 217/11: demþ *pr. 3 sg.* 27/11, 28/6, 74/25. demde *pa. t. 3 sg.* 175/16. (y)demd *pp.* 12/27, 113/34, 137/24
demere *n.* judge 12/26, 62/17, 138/8. demeres *pl.* 39/24, 40/10
demynges *vbl. n.* judgements 27/29
denyes *n. pl.* deaneries 42/7
depe *v. intr.* immerse 107/7 *n.* depþ *pr. 3 sg.* 106/36; *tr.* ydept *ppl. adj.* 106/24, *pp.* 107/3, dyed 107/17
derie *v. intr.* do harm 84/35; *tr./intr.* harm 126/33, 166/17. deriynde *ppl. adj.* harmful 63/1
derne *adj.* secret 143/3
derrer see diere *adv.*
des *n. pl.* dice 45/16, 51/15
descendeþ *pr. 3 sg. intr.* descends 123/6. decendi *subj. sg.* come down 123/7
descriueþ *pr. pl. tr.* describe 168/21
deserited *pp.* disinherited 30/29
desert *n.* desert, wilderness 67/15, 131/3, 204/21
desertesoun *n.* desertion 48/19 *n.*
desgyzeþ *pr. 3 sg. tr.* disguises, transforms 158/3. desgised *pp.* 56/4; *~ uram* different from 97/14
desyr *n.* desire 106/6
desiri *v. tr.* desire 244/19
despayred *ppl. adj.* in despair 34/13
despense *n.* expenditure (see do). despenses *pl.* expenditure 55/22
despit *n.* contempt 19/35, 20/22, 69/35
desputede *pa. t. pl. tr* debated 79/35
desspendoure *n.* (*dat.*) steward 190/23
dest see do
destempringe *vbl. n.* imbalance 153/11
destorbeþ *pr. pl. tr.* destroy 179/1. desstorbed *pp.* impeded 212/35
destorbinge *vbl. n.* impediment 225/29
destrue *v. tr.* destroy 28/10, 22, 117/32. destrueþ, destruiþ *pr. pl.* 35/33, 36/10, 43/28. destrud *pp.* 30/28
detraccion *n.* detraction 10/13

dette *n.* debt 35/14, 115/21. **dettes**
pl. 113/19, 115/20
dettours *n. pl.* debtors 113/19
deþ see **do**
deuines *n. pl.* diviners 19/26
deuisi *v. tr.* describe 103/26, 144/22;
intr. imagine 73/6, 100/19
deuocion *n.* devotion, dedication 33/
17, 107/18, 136/8
deuout(e)liche *adv.* devoutly 134/9,
211/16, 212/24
dyacne *n.* deacon 176/1, 190/10,
225/33. **diaknen, dyaknes** *pl.*
190/5, 235/7
dyad *adj.* dead 12/29, 31/19, 72/
12 *n.*, **dyead** 79/27, **dead** 36/13
(*see below*), **a dyad** a dead person
258/20. **dyade** *p.c.* 35/9 (*see below*).
dyade *pl.* 13/7, 30/26, **deade** 86/29,
þe **dyade** 13/23, 263/7; ~ *wed*
mortgage 35/9, 36/13
dyadlich *adj.* mortal (sin) 8/17, 22, 32,
deadlich 47/8, 225/24, **dyeadlich**
170/14; subject to mortality 72/8,
244/20: **dyadliche** 6/31 (MS.
dyadlich), 7/17 (MS. *dyadlich*).
dyeadliche 200/26. **dyadliche** *pl.*
16/10, 41/33, ⟨dyadliches⟩ 9/11
dyadliche *adv.* mortally 5/23, 6/24,
34, **deadliche** 223/5
dyaf *adj.* deaf 1/14. **ane dyaue** *acc.* a
deaf man 211/8–9 (*see p. 65, n. 2*).
dyaue *wk.* 189/2, **dyeaue** 211/11.
dyaue *pl.* 189/3, þe **dyaue** 56/27,
224/6
⟨**dyamod**⟩ *n.* diamond 139/31 *n.*
dyaþ *n.* death 12/25, 23/11, **dyeaþ**
72/13, 79/5. **deaþes** *gen.* 130/2.
dyaþe *p.c.* 7/22, 12/32, **dyeaþe**
201/10, **deaþe** 87/8, 195/3. **dyea-
þes** *pl.* 72/11; *to* þe ~ mortally
132/29
dyau see **deau**
dyaue, dyeaue see **dyaf**
dich *n.* ditch 57/4
diciplines see **dissiplines**
dyead see **dyad**
dyep *adj.* deep 264/33. **dyepe** *p.c.*;
mid ~ *herte* from the depth of his
heart 171/14, 211/29. **dyepe** *pl.*
99/20
dyepnesse *n.* depth, profundity
105/6 *n.*, 152/2, 211/12, 31

diere *adj.* expensive 36/21, 68/17;
precious 79/32, 123/21
diere *adv.* expensively, at great cost
44/14, 194/24, 25; **derrer** *comp.*
36/8, 18; ~ *abegge* pay dearly for
73/27–8
dierþe *n.* scarcity 256/30
dieuel *n.* devil, 15/5, 9, 30, **dyuel**
49/34, 178/20. **dyeules** *gen.* 17/5,
19/28, 53/18. **dyuele** *dat.* 26/35,
62/25, 65/25. **dyeule** *p.c.* 1/1, 16/
28, **dyeuele** 118/4* *n.*, **dyuele**
189/30. **dyeulen** *pl.* 50/16, 53/20,
59/35; *adj.* devilish 43/4 *n.*, 265/
12
difference *n.* difference 10/30, 210/
29, 32
di(n)gneliche *adv.* suitably, worthily
20/35, 266/15, 267/36
di(n)gneté *n.* dignity 24/28, 215/20;
excellence, value 94/12, 99/9, 163/
29. **dingnetes** *pl.* excellent qualities
233/26; high offices 26/9, 12, 42/6;
be þe *ordre of hare* ~ in order of
merit 119/28–9
diȝte *v. tr.* dispose, order 7/12, 246/7;
array, adorn 14/32, 216/5, 217/
4* *n.*; put away, set aside 210/22,
235/14; instruct, direct, impel
147/22, 222/26; place 211/17 *n.*,
regulate 7/34, 124/31, 233/18;
dispense 147/25; prepare 20/35,
198/13; *intr.* ordain 270/31; **diȝt**
pr. 3 sg. 124/31, 147/22, 222/26.
diȝteþ *pl.* 7/34, 47/13, ⟨diȝt⟩ 11/
21 *n.* **diȝte** *subj. pl.* 147/25. *pa. t. 3*
sg. 7/12, 270/31. **idiȝt** *pp.* 198/25,
214/1, 217/4* *n.*, *ppl. adj.* 14/32,
47/12
diȝtere *n.* disposer 100/11
diȝtinge *n.* adornment 24/34, 47/20,
215/26. **diȝtinges** *pl.* divisions
17/27
diligence *n.* diligence 208/4
diligent *adj.* diligent 32/27, 220/7
diligentliche *adv.* diligently 70/21,
173/2, 208/2
dim *adj.* dim, lustreless 143/11, 159/
11, 12, 237/17
dingnelyche, dingnete see **di(n)g-
neliche, di(n)gnete**
dingneste *adj. superl. pl.* most
worthy of esteem 109/30

discord *n.* discord, dissension 43/30, 75/8, 157/28

discordance *n.* discordance 259/12

discrecion *n.* discretion, discernment 155/17, 156/17, 160/9

disete *n.* need 57/34

disordene *adj.* inordinate 34/26 *n.*, 46/21; irregular 48/24

disordeneliche *adv.* inordinately 55/7

dispendeþ *pr. 3 sg. tr.* spends, squanders 7/32, 19/4 *n.* **despendeþ** *pl.* 41/15, 187/22. **dispendede** *pa. t. 3 sg.* 128/13; *intr.* **despendeþ** *pl.* 55/19. **despendi** *subj. sg.* 53/33

dispoyly *v. tr.* rob 45/22

dissiplines, diciplines *n. pl.* mortifications 236/23, 240/25, 250/3

dissuol *n.* dishful 120/1

distemperance *n.* imbalance 153/14

distincti *v. intr.* distinguish 152/15, 158/23

diuers *adj.* perverse 68/26, 69/20.
diuers(e), diuerses *pl.* 162/2; various *15*/9, 44/19, 73/23, 124/26

diuerseþ *pr. 3 pl. refl.* vary 124/27

do *v. tr.* do, perform, commit, fulfil 7/7, 18/10, 31/20, 54/32, 67/34, 126/2 *n.*; inflict 164/2, 265/4; give, give over, confer 18/12, 47/19, 253/20; offer 115/11, 217/35; put, apply, add 36/30 *n.*, 72/22 *n.*, 142/7 *n.*, 148/20, 26 *n.*, 154/30 *n.*, 169/15, 270/35 *n.*; make (sb. do sth.), cause, bring to pass 9/1, 91/5, 170/21², 264/14; get 238/13; make 39/8, 123/21, 225/26; *ppl. adj.* perfect 87/12 *n.*; devote 140/8, 155/7, 199/13; *intr.* act 21/28, 31/5; *pro-verb* 15/14, 18/5, 40/33; ∼ *auerst(e)* delay 32/24 *n.*, 161/14; ∼ *auontage* give an increase 209/27; ∼ *beure* give priority to 243/12; proffer 181/25; ∼ *bysinesse* take trouble 56/1; ∼ *couaytise* be covetous 40/31; ∼ *diligence* make an effort 238/14–15; ∼ *do* (*age age*) well now 269/25; ∼ *dom* execute justice 37/11; ∼ *glotounyes* be gluttonous 52/3–4; ∼ *ham to* (*entendre a*) concern themselves with 198/19; ∼ *ine uoryetinge* forget 199/18; ∼ *in hare nyedes* see **nied**; ∼ *into sayzine* give possession

198/21; ∼ *laȝe* see **laȝe**; ∼ *manhode* do homage 19/13, 15; ∼ *merci* show mercy 199/1; ∼ *þi miȝte* do thine utmost 133/32; ∼*niede(s)* see **nied**; ∼ *op* put in safe keeping 232/22; ∼ (*oure*) *payne* do our utmost, take trouble 145/8, 238/14–15; ∼ (*hire*) *profit of* profit from 78/10 (*see note to 78/9–17*); ∼ (*hare*) *prou* take advantage 78/5; ∼ *prowesse* perform feats of chivalry 168/7; ∼ *red* decide on a course of action 57/11–12; ∼ *semblont* see **semblant**; ∼ *seruese* celebrate a church service 56/22; ∼ *to moche despense* be extravagant 21/32; ∼ *to naȝte* destroy 62/3; (*ham*) ∼ *to spoushod* enter into matrimony 235/13; (*him*) ∼ *to þe uelde* take to the field of battle 169/34; ∼ *to worke* see **work**; ∼ *þe herte ine* set the heart upon 155/6; ∼ *þet dyaue eare* turn a deaf ear 189/2; ∼ *þet . . . ne* prevent 232/31–2; ∼ *his wyl* do as one pleases 85/18, 179/26–7; ∼ *zouke* see **zouke**; ∼ *zuo moche* see **z(u)o**: **done** *infl. inf.* 8/16, 23, 170/21 *n.* **do** *pr. 1 sg.* 264/14. **dest** 2 *sg.* 54/32, 159/3. **deþ** *3 sg.* 18/10, 25/17 91/7* (*see note to 40/5*), 207/2 *n.* **doþ** *pl.* 40/5* *n.*, 72/23 *n.*, 74/12. **do** *subj. sg.* 32/25, 101/3. *pl.* 145/8, 147/29. *imp. sg.* 159/2, 194/31. **doþ** *pl.* 269/21. **doinde** *pr. p.* 194/35. **dede** *pa. t. 1 sg.* 259/26. **dedest** 2 *sg.* 21/5. **dede** *3 sg.* 29/5, 49/32, 50/27. **dede(n)** *pl.* 166/31, 181/14, 208/10. **dede** *subj. sg.* 89/31, 146/36, 270/31. **(i)do** *pp.* 9/20, 18/22, 45/12

ydobbed *pp.* dubbed 83/15

dob(b)leþ *pr. 3 sg. refl.* is doubled 22/11, 48/21; *tr.* double, make twice as large **dobbleþ** *pr. pl.* 60/20. **ydob(b)led** *pp.* 230/35; duplicated 249/21

dogge *n.* dog 66/17

doȝ *n.* dough 205/21. **doȝe** *p.c.* 111/31

doȝter *n.* daughter 17/5, ⟨doþter⟩ 142/31 *n.* **doȝtren** *pl.* 140/35, 229/1

dol *n.* portion 112/11. **doles** *pl.* parts 17/21

(y)dolue see delue

dom *n.* judgement, verdict 10/34, 27/15, 74/25; justice 124/7, 127/7, 222/18; legal procedings 6/18, 19, 10/7: dome *p.c.* 13/23, 14/21, 126/20. domes *pl.* 40/17, 152/2, 268/22

do(u)mb *adj.* dumb 1/14, 51/29, 210/29. þe do(u)mbe *pl.* 56/27, 224/6

domesman *n.* judge 115/9, 130/5. domesmen *pl.* 38/19, 44/3

dong *n.* dung 50/32, 61/33, 75/16. donge *p.c.* 81/9, 216/2

donghel *n.* dunghill 81/9, 230/21

dor see dar

dore *n.* door 174/8, 186/36, 255/27

doreward *n.* doorkeeper 121/23, 263/33

dorilot *n.* ornamental coiffure 177/2

dorre, dorste see dar

doþ see do; doþter see doȝter

doumb see do(u)mb

doun *dv.* down 17/7, 23/24, 67/12

dounward *adv.* in order of decreasing importance 119/18

doust *n.* dust 108/11, 26, 137/12

draf *n.* waste part of grapes or olives when the juice and oil have been extracted, dregs 93/17

dragoune *n.* (*p.c.*) dragon 174/1

draȝe *v. tr.* draw, attract, elicit, drag 58/27 *n.*, 77/3, 176/29, 186/7, 247/21; bring, lead 12/32, 13/8; apply 147/33; take (to witness) 64/15; treat 40/28, 32, 36, 239/15; *refl.* ~ to seek 79/34; ~ of treat of, discuss 155/22, 164/4; ~ smac to give flavour to 205/21-2; ~ uorþ rear, nourish 100/17, 185/34, 193/13; guide 185/20; draȝþ, draȝt *pr 3 sg* 15/20, 41/5, 174/12. draȝeþ *pl.* 43/24, 264/29. droȝ *pa. t. 3 sg.* 13/8. droȝen *pl.* 164/4. (y)draȝe *pp.* 1/15, 31/16, 132/35

draȝþe *n.* treatise 251/36, 260/11

draye *adj.* dry 137/16, 240/17, 18

drede *n.* awe, fear 3/31, 4/10, 17/27, 75/15 *n.*, dred 188/33‡; þet ne is non ~ there is no doubt 90/12; ne/ hit (ne) is no(n) ~ without doubt, there is no doubt 63/9, 65/25 *n.*, 105/13; wyþoute ~ doubtless 105/8, 133/23

drede *v. tr.* fear 78/13, 104/34, 189/34 (*passive*); *refl.* fear 34/14, 43/4, 125/17; *intr.* be afraid 207/26: dret *pr. 3 sg.* 26/24, 116/3. dredeþ 85/12 *n. pl.* 74/15, 84/5, 142/26. ydred *pp.* 104/31

dreduol *adj.* terrible 14/33, 15/5, 70/1 *n.*; dangerous, fearful, menacing 16/25, 22/23, 42/5; full of fear, reverent 116/5, 144/25, 150/10: dreduolle *wk.* 189/30. *pl.* 42/5, 10. dreduoller *comp.* 117/6

drench *n.* draught 130/2

dryfþ *pr. 3 sg. tr.* pursues 75/29. driueþ *pl.* 75/31; drive 171/32

drinke *n.* drink 9/16, 29/35, 50/7. drinkes *pl.* drink 207/4

drinke *v. tr.* drink 95/22; *intr.* 51/20, 93/2, 137/21; *ppl. adj.* intoxicated 75/14, 247/34, 258/7; soaked 107/4; *uol* ~ see uoldronke: drincþ, dringþ *pr. 3 sg.* 51/20, 245/30, 248/10. drinkeþ *pl.* 248/6. drinke *subj. sg.* 53/33. drink *imp. sg.* 54/25. ydronke *pp.* 51/13

drinkere *n.* drinker 52/5. drinkeres *pl.* 47/35

droȝ, droȝen see draȝe

dronkehede *n.* drunkenness 260/6

dronkenesse *n.* drunkenness 248/25

drope *n.* drop 75/13, 92/7, 189/6. dropen, dropes *pl.* 84/21, 92/12, 36

druȝþe *n.* drought 68/17

E

ealde see ald

ealdinge *vbl. n.* ageing 95/17

eare *n.* ear 179/16, 189/2, yeare 137/23, 177/23, 211/1. earen *pl.* 249/22, 257/1, 5, 257/33*, yearen 47/28, 154/20, yeren 257/9, 15

ech *adj.* each, every 5/6, 16/7, 131/35. eche *acc.* 70/17, 171/12. *gen.* 112/11, 262/25. eche *p.c.* 17/34, 35/13, 91/3; *pron.* each, everyone 12/3, 14/20, 19/14, 56/2. echen *dat.* 264/3. echen, echin *p.c.* 11/22, 58/6, 63/1, 119/15; ~ daye(s) see day; ~ oþer, oþren each other 115/5, 148/28, 268/26; ~ tyme always 264/5

ecko *n.* echo 60/34

eddre *n.* serpent 26/32, 61/16 *n.*, 151/2, 203/18* *n.* **eddren** *pl.* 61/21, 203/13

edefie *v. tr.* strengthen 197/1, 237/36

eft *adv.* again, furthermore, moreover 33/26, 71/35, 80/17

efter *prep.* after 5/5, 12/32, 13/4, 82/14 *n.*, 83/13 *n.*; on account of 225/24; *adv.* after 12/14, 22, 155/27 *n.*; afterwards 30/21 *n.*, furthermore 249/21 (*see note to 30/21*); ~ *þan* furthermore 20/25

eftertelleres *n. pl.* repeaters of tales 58/17, 18

ef(f)terw(u)ard *adv.* afterwards, and then, furthermore 20/18, 24/33* (*see p. 49 for this and 110/4, 184/4*), 30/20, 77/5 *n.*, 110/4*, 172/9* (*see p. 50*), 175/29 *n.*, 34* (*see p. 50*), 184/4*, 23 *n.*, ⟨afterward⟩ 28/15¹, following 105/22; ~ *þet* see **þet** *conj.*

efterwarde *n*, rearguard 118/1, 182/34

eftzone *adv.* thereafter, moreover 57/34, 73/15, 132/24

egypciens *n. pl.* Egyptians 79/34

eȝe *n.* eye 45/32, 75/30, 81/2. **eȝen** *pl.* 19/5, 45/31, 47/27

eȝte *num.* eight 45/24

eȝtende, eȝtinde *ord. num.* eighth 2/6, 10/3, 13/22

ey *int.* ahȝ 105/11

eyder see **ayder**

eyr *n.*¹ air 50/1, 62/32, 146/9

eyr *n.*² heir 48/20, 137/5. **eyrs** *pl.* 102/10, 107/21, 114/30

eyren see **aye**

eyse *n.* physical or material comfort 24/35 *n.*, 48/1; **eyses** *pl.* delights 204/36; *in/an* ~ at ease, comfortable 51/12, 93/36–94/1, 252/13

eysy *v. tr.* to make comfortable 82/16

elde *n.* maturity, adulthood 11/22, 259/21, 24, 27; old age 69/9, 220/20; life span 71/26

eldeste see **ald**

eldringes *n. pl.* ancestors 35/26; parents 118/32

eles *n. pl.* awls 66/12, 14

elifans *n.* elephant 224/29, **olyfont** 84/22

elles *adv.* otherwise 205/20

elleshuer *adv.* elsewhere; *he þengþ* ~ his thoughts are elsewhere 211/6–7

elmesse *n.* alms 4/8, 17/11, 76/12. **elmessen, elmesses** *pl.* alms 190/19, 194/35, 195/12, 13

emcristen *n.* fellow Christian 10/5, 66/21, 199/11

emeroydes *n. pl.* emeralds 77/1 *n.* (MS. *emerroydes*)

emne *adv.* level 151/3

emni *v. tr.* make equal 134/26, ⟨enmi⟩ 16/16

emparement *n.* deterioration 148/24 *n.*

emper(o)ur *n.* emperor 71/10, 85/16, 100/26. **emper(o)urs** *pl.* 78/32, 101/25

empire *n.* empire 85/15

empirete *n.* sovereign power? 85/25 *n.*

emteþ *pr. pl. tr.* make empty 58/4

emti *adj.* empty, vain 143/12, 144/11 *n.*

enchauntemens *n. pl.* enchantments 43/13

encheyson, enche(i)soun, anche(a)ysoun, anchesoun *n.* cause, reason, occasion 47/24, 25, 51/27, 217/2, 11, 258/6. **encheisons, encheysones, enchesons** *pl.* 68/3, 205/19, 33, 206/6, 9, 14, 17; *be þe* ~ *of* by reason of, because of 30/31, 47/17, 24

endaunture *n.* taming; *tekþ* ~ breaks in (a colt) 220/22 *n.*

ende *n.* end 1/4, 14/3, 33/21; purpose 162/4, 183/4, 25; *atenende* at the end, finally 128/15; *wy[þ]oute* ~ *n.* eternity 267/27–8 *n.*

endi *v. tr.* end, terminate 110/16, 113/25, 135/23 *n.*, 262/2; *intr.* come to an end 267/6; settle an account 115/19; (*with prolative infinitive*) stop (doing sth.) 130/8 (*future*): **endeþ** *pr. pl.* 70/15. **endi** *subj. sg.* 137/24

endinge *vbl. n.* ending 31/9, 71/8

englis(s) *n.* the English language 1/5, 211/5, 262/9. *adj. pl.* **englisse** 5/11

engrined *pp.* ensnared 154/33

eni *adj.* any 11/16, 16/22, 21/21. **enye** *acc.* 194/4. **enie** *p.c.* 49/6, 104/14,

eni (cont.):
  119/27. enie pl. 21/27; pron. any-
  one, any 43/8, 115/33, 182/10. acc.
  enye 49/8. enie p.c. any one 5/7.
  enye pl. any 68/35
enlefte ord. num. eleventh 14/10, 49/
  15
enne see o(n)
enmi see emni
ennelepi see onlepi
ententifliche adv. attentively 210/10
entremes n. entertainment between
  the courses of a meal 56/6
entremetti pr. subj. sg. intr. concern
  onself 152/9
enuenymeþ, anuenymeþ pr. 3 sg.
  tr. poisons 26/32, 27/6; intr.
  ⟨enueymeþ⟩ 62/14 n.: enuenimeþ
  pl. 257/7. enuenimed, anueny-
  med pp. 27/9, 50/2, 203/17
enuie n. envy 11/9, 75/9. 137/4
enuious adj. envious; þe enuious
  27/2, 7, 28/18. þe enuiouse wk.
  27/28
eppel n. apple 54/24, 82/11, 84/12.
  epple p.c. 82/9, 21
er(e) conj. (with subj.) before 130/3,
  167/21, 271/4; (with indic.) 194/
  21 n.; er þan conj. (with subj.) 33/
  21, 123/6, 167/20; (with indicative
  after a negative clause) 69/6; er þan
  (þet) see þet
ereges n. pl. heretics 40/33
(h)eresye n. heresy 69/23, 134/25,
  267/25
eretiks see heretike
erye v. tr. plough 227/28; intr. 214/
  20
(h)eritage n. inheritance, heritage
  36/12, 114/31, 253/34. (h)eritages
  pl. 39/13, 32
erl, n. earl 71/9, 86/28, 103/27. erles
  pl. 224/24
ermitage n. hermitage 239/33
errour n. error 69/22, 70/14, 233/13
erþe n. the earth, the world 2/34, 6/16,
  15/24, yerþe 8/3
erþlich adj. earthly, worldly, terres-
  trial 95/11. erþliche p.c. 106/28.
  pl. 6/4, 149/33, 214/21
esssse n. ashes 137/12
et(h)e v. tr. eat 51/5, 55/6, 7 n., 62/5,
  177/10 n.; intr. 110/31, 133/35,

183/17: et(h)ene infl. inf. 51/25,
  52/17, 146/21. est pr. 2 sg. 54/33.
  et(h) 3 sg. 51/20, 135/10, 137/21,
  eteþ¹ 61/25 n. et(h)eþ pl. 54/9,
  61/25², 62/5 n., 182/16. ete subj. sg.
  53/33. et(h) imp. sg. 50/35, 53/21,
  54/25. ethen þa. t. pl. 206/36.
  yyete pp. 13/17
eteres n. pl. eaters 47/36
etinge vbl. n. eating 56/12
eue(n) n. evening 113/11, 191/25;
  eve 262/19; an ∼ in the evening
  168/29
euel adj. evil 9/16, 23/12; wretched
  48/27; noxious 69/23: euele p.c.
  48/27, 69/23. wk. 115/32, 217/26.
  pl. 22/23, 66/35; ∼ wyl(les) see
  (y)wil; worse comp. worse (cf. p.
  69) 17/32, 76/6, wors 20/36‡,
  22/21‡, 31/9‡. pl. 27/29, 64/25; for
  worst superl. see alþerworst under
  al(le)
euele n. (p.c.) disease 202/36. eueles
  pl. 153/11, 208/24, 224/9; vices
  208/22; worse comp. in uram kuede
  to ∼ from bad to worse 48/5
euele adv. ill 20/23, 217/11, 239/15;
  ∼ telle (mesconter) miscalculate
  57/1; ∼ þonkeþ see þonki; worse
  comp. worse 213/8 (see p. 69)
euen see eue(n)
eu(e)re adv. ever 12/21, 68/13, 71/6,
  96/15 n.
euerte adv. yet 220/29
eurebleuinge vbl. n. everlastingness
  105/5
eurelestinde ppl. adj. everlasting
  93/4, 94/22, 97/3
euremo(r) adv. evermore 13/9, 220/
  24; always 55/10, 238/10
eur(e)ich pron. everyone 157/31,
  268/30, 32, 269/32. eurinne acc.
  sg. masc. 134/33, 136/26. eurichen
  p.c. 146/35
ewangelist n. evangelist 230/112,
  wangeliste 112/29‡
examini v. tr. examine 153/29.
  exameneþ pr. 3 sg. 184/29, 256/
  3 n. exaamened pp. 137/30
excusi v. tr. excuse 7/1. excuseþ pr.
  3 sg. 33/30, 61/2 (see note to 61/1-2),
  69/13, 136/21
exequitours n. pl. executors 38/24

exil *n.* exile 131/3, 215/34
yexiled *pp.* exiled 30/30

F

fable *n.* fable 155/31. fables *pl.* 156/
11
face *n.* face 88/8, 19, 244/10, 11
fa(i)li *v. tr.* fail 32/7, 117/22; *intr.*
195/10; be lacking, be defective
127/21, 186/32, 237/27; be ex-
hausted, cease, come to an end 33/
21, 81/16, 209/36; be at fault 173/4,
5; *impers.* be in need of (*Fr. faut*)
210/6; *ppl. adj.* incompetent 32/18
(*see note to 32/15*); ~ *of* fail to get
68/30: fa(i)leþ *pr. 3 sg.* 79/3, 80/10,
81/11. fayleþ *pl.* 80/10, 209/31
(*future*), 210/7 *n.* faly *subj. sg.*
173/4. failinde *pr. p.* 32/18.
yfa(y)led *pp.* 71/20, 187/3
fayntise *n.* deceit 26/16, 133/6
fayre *n.* fair 76/23
fallinde see fa(i)li
fanc *n.* mud 251/19
fariseu *n.* pharisee 208/10 *n.**. fari-
zeus *pl.* 175/13
fauour *n.* favour 230/11
fel *adj.* fierce, violent 66/14. felle *wk.*
66/17, þe felle 30/5. þe felle *pl.*
150/6. feller *comp.* 61/27. felliste
superl. wk. 61/23
felhede *n.* cruelty, violence 29/29,
159/33
fellaker *comp. adv.* (more) fiercely
174/11
felonie, *n.* violence, wrath, 67/35,
167/35, 150/16, ⟨felounye⟩ 30/4.
felonyes *pl.* calumnies 66/10
feloun *n.* cruel man 29/31, 30/3, 66/10
fer *n.* price, value 36/29 *n.*
feruent *adj.* fervent 121/18
feste *n.* feast 166/33. festes *pl.* 25/2,
128/25, 139/17; festivals 7/28, 33,
20/24, 41/22; makeþ greate ~ makes
a great fuss of 155/35–156/1
feure *n.* (*p.c.*) fever 29/35
fiaunce *n.* trust 164/10
fiebble, fyeble *adj.* feeble, fragile,
weak 31/12, 17, 82/14. fieblene
acc. masc. 227/20, þe fiebles *pl.*
148/32–3. þe fyebleste *superl. pl.*
148/30

fieblesse *n.* weakness, infirmity 33/
14, 69/9, 95/18
fyeþ *pr. 3 sg. refl.* trusts 136/16
figure *n.* geometrical figure 234/22,
23. figures *pl.* 234/23; forms 158/
14
filosofe *n.* philosopher 80/4, 120/23,
147/26. filosofes, philosofes,
philosophes *pl.* 72/6, 78/31, 124/3,
9
filosofie *n.* philosophy 97/8, 164/7
251/28
fineþ *pr. 3 sg. tr.* refines 106/27
firmament *n.* firmament 141/11
fisician, fisicien *n.* physician 172/14,
174/25, 180/9. fisiciane *p.c.* 132/
14. fisiciens *pl.* 143/35
fisike *n.* physic 53/7, 54/4, 6
flatour *n.* flatterer 257/24. flatours,
ulatours *pl.* 256/29, 35, 257/13
flechchi *v. tr.* waive, put aside 253/7;
intr. flechchi *pr. subj. sg.* be
deflected 253/3
(þane) fleumatike *adj. wk.* phleg-
matic (person) 157/29
flom, flum *n.* river 202/25, 28
flour *n.* flour 93/15, 111/32, 210/31;
flower 81/11, 95/28, 118/53.
flour(e)s *pl.* 61/33, 96/9, 118/25
flouri *v. intr.* blossom 95/10. flori-
sseþ *pr. pl.* 95/24, floureþ flourish
28/20. yfloured *ppl. adj.* flowery
136/2
flouringe *vbl, n.* flower 36/23
flum see flom
fol *n.* fool 77/9. fole *p.c.* 184/35. foles
pl. 26/6, 47/14, 210/10 *n.*, 232/12
fol(e) *adj.* mad, foolish 18/32, 21/31,
22/1, 68/15. fole *acc.* 25/20. *p.c.*
203/27. *pl.* 26/3, 218/27, 254/15*,
foles 212/20, 232/6
foleant (*French*) *ppl. adj.* foolish,
foolish one 244/30
folebayrie *n.* foolish ambition 17/25
folie *n.* folly 19/8, 70/13, 251/29.
folies *pl.* foolish words, follies
10/15, 16/32, 19/4
folliche *adv.* foolishly, rashly, im-
providently 23/6, 43/21, 64/3; sin-
fully, lustfully 141/2, 232/12
forest *n.* forest 131/4
fornays *n.* furnace 131/5. fornayse
p.c. 74/5, 205/12

fornicacion *n.* fornication 46/33, 47/ 32, 206/6
forré *see list of proper names*
forriers *n. pl.* servants preceding their master to arrange for food and lodging 195/11
fortin *adj.* the strong 204/14 *n.*
fortune *n.* fortune 76/31, 84/9, 181/ 20
foruions (*French*) *pr. pl.* go astray 155/3 *n.*
fourme *n.* image 87/26; shape 220/23
yfryd *pp.* fried 111/33, 35
friinges *n. pl.* fryings 23/2
froteþ *pr. 3 sg. tr.* strokes 155/35
fructefide *pa. t. 3 sg. intr.* fructified 234/10
fru(y)t *n.* produce, fruits 35/9, 10, 144/18; grain, seed 28/16; fruit 94/28, 98/30, 133/34

G

gabbeþ *pr. 3 sg. intr.* mocks 69/6 *n.*
gaderi *v. tr.* gather 133/34, 142/1 *n.*; bring together 137/16; win 120/28; *intr.* accumulate wealth or possessions 162/4: **gadereþ** *pr. 3 sg.* 263/25. pl. 101/34. **ygadered** *pp.* 191/13, 213/4
gaderinge *vbl. n.* acquisition of wealth 192/11
gamelos *n.* chameleon 62/31
ganglinde see **iangli**
gardin *n.* garden 94/31, 97/35, 232/ 18. **gardine** *p.c.* 94/27, 121/28, 130/17. **gardins** *pl.* 38/4
gardyner *n.* gardener 94/31, 95/19, 97/31
gate *n.* gate(way), door 72/25, 189/9, 218/25. **gates** *pl.* 154/23, 204/8, 218/34, 231/23
gauel *n.* usury 9/27; interest 35/12, 13
gauelere *n.* usurer 134/23. **gaueleres** *pl.* 35/6, 36/2, 135/22
gauelinge *vbl. n.* usury 34/32, 35/23, 28, 45/22
gauelockes *n. pl.* javelins 207/14
ȝefþe(s) see **yef(f)þe**
gelt *n.* guilt 30/27, 104/16 *n.* **gelte** *p.c.* 74/8 *n.* **geltes** *pl.* transgression(s) 15/29, 180/6
ygelt *pp.* gilded 233/20; *ppl. adj.* 26/2

gelti *adj.* guilty 70/22, 175/3, 11
geme *n.* game 34/17, 45/33, 46/4.
gemene *p.c.* 46/2. **gemenes** *pl.* 45/15, 207/7; pastimes 213/36
gememen *n. pl.* minstrels 63/6, 90/24
general *adj.* general 14/13, 94/16
generalliche *adj.* (*acc.*) universal 14/1, 263/8
generalliche *adv.* in general terms 9/10, 27/28, 94/11; universally 17/ 34; extensively 187/11
gentil *adj.* well-bred 75/32; noble, excellent 2/30, 75/34, 87/17. **gentile** *p.c.* 89/8. *wk.* 87/16. *pl.* 89/35
gentilesse *n.* good breeding 87/21, 89/2
gentyleté *n.* good breeding 89/7
gerde *v. tr.* gird 236/12 *n.* **gerten** *pa. t. pl.* 236/10. **ygert** *pp.* 236/15
gerdel *n.* girdle 236/11, 26, 31. **gerdle** *p.c.* 236/29, 34. **gerdles** *pl.* 236/16
gerlondes *n. pl.* garlands 71/19
germayn *adj.* germane 146/12
gernier *n.* granary 191/16. **gerniere** *p.c.* 191/13, **greynere** 140/1
gers *n.* vegetation, herbage 121/28; grass 111/12. **gerse** *p.c.* 28/13; *a/ine* ~ in blade 28/18, 36/22
gerten, ygert see **gerde**
ges *n.* jess 254/16, 19
gessynge *vbl. n.* guessing; *wyþoute* ~ assuredly 268/35
gest *n.* guest, intruder 249/8 *n.*
gest, geþ see **guo**
geus see **ieu**
gibet *n.* gibbet 128/24, 138/13, 171/ 17
gyewes see **ieu**
ȝigge see **zigge**
gyle *n.* deceit 40/6, 87/9. **gyles** *pl.* wiles 39/19, 63/12
gily *v. tr.* deceive 15/10, 62/30, 63/14. **gyleþ** *pr. 3 sg.* 77/25, 184/31. **ygiled** *pp.* 124/13, 150/19, 256/32
ginnes *n. pl.* snares 28/26, 54/21, 77/ 24
gin(n)inge, *vbl. n.* beginning, origin, source 12/34*, 14/4*, 16/9, 32/13, 198/13 (MS. *giniiynge*), 25
gyse *n.* guise 158/28
gled *adj.* cheerful, joyful 194/2, 238/ 23, 265/35. **glede** *acc.* 194/1 *n.*

gledye v. tr. gladden 266/1. refl. take pleasure, rejoice 27/21, 81/14, 258/ 22 n.; ppl. adj. intr. rejoicing, joyous 267/10: **gledeþ** pr. 3 sg. 81/ 14. **gledieþ** pl. 238/27, 258/22. ⟨**glede**⟩ subj. pl. 265/22 (see p. 99). imp. sg. 258/29. **glediynde** pr. p. 267/10

gledliche adv. joyfully, cheerfully 54/10, 59/14, 70/31. **gledlaker** comp. 113/10

glednesse n. joy 238/25, 30; **maki** ~ see **maki**

gles n. glass 76/34; piece of glass 82/ 11; a glass 245/29

glorie n. glory 87/7

glorifie v. intr. boast 215/26–7; tr. praise, boast (of), glorify 215/26. **glorifieþ** pr. 3 sg. 25/5. **glorefye** imp. sg. 270/3. **yglorefied** pp. 196/ 17

gloriouse adj. (pl.) glorious 96/18

glose n. gloss 187/27

glot(o)unie, glotonye n. gluttony 16/5, 55/20, 248/13, 260/6, 12. **glotounyes** pl. 52/4

glotoun n. glutton 50/31, 56/28, 248/ 31. **glotoune** p.c. 53/30. **glotoun(e)s, glotuns** pl. 50/18, 52/ 36, 55/29

glotounliche adv. gluttonously 111/2

glu n. glue 246/12

go see **guo**

god n. God 5/2, 6/1, 13/32. **god(d)es** gen. 2/3–12, 7/3, 77/9, **guodes** 40/ 30 (see p. 27, n. 1). **gode** p.c. 7/35, 31/34, 49/31. **godes** pl. 5/20

g(u)od n. good, good thing 79/22, 91/23 n., 136/25, 200/19 n., 244/ 25; wealth, possession 6/4, 7, 8/21, 41/30; good fortune 11/10, 11, 27/ 10; benefit 61/5, 113/2, 180/11; kindness, blessing 7/27, 13/31, 215/ 11; moral good, good deed, virtue 8/15, 26/28, 29/4; good, praise 60/ 32, 62/9, 123/27; uor ~ for the best 269/25: **guode** p.c. 2/24, 7/27, 74/29 n. **guodes** pl. 18/34, 63/15, 79/19, 265/19 n., **guod** 100/9 n.

goddoȝter n. god-daughter 48/33

godeleþ pr. 3 sg. tr. abuses 66/20, 21 **godelinge** vbl. n. abuse 65/29. **godelinges** pl. abusive words 66/19

godhede n. godhead 12/8, 111/9, 245/7

godliche adj.(pl.) theological (virtues) 123/9, 13

godmoder n. god-mother 48/33

godsone n. god-son 48/34

godspel n. gospel 96/23, 139/35, 211/ 13. **gods(s)pelle** p.c. 28/14, 103/2, 110/30

gods(s)pellere n. evangelist 2/16, 12/13, 13/26

godzyb n. god-father 48/34

godzybbe n. god-mother 48/35 n.

goye see **ioye**

igoyned see **ioineþ**

gold n. gold 6/4, 35/18, 74/6. **golde** p.c. 233/20, 22

gost n. spirit, (Holy) Spirit 3/17, 46/ 33, 211/13. **gostes** gen. 98/24, 265/ 28. **goste** p.c. 53/9, 54/14, 92/26 (MS. geste), 211/15. **gostes** pl. 119/ 11, 158/6, 30

gostlich adj. spiritual 27/19, 29/3, 42/35. **gostliche** wk. 93/14, 252/1. pl. 7/25, 8/10, 104/28, 200/27

gostliche adv. spiritually 7/12, 16, 146/9; in a spiritual sense 95/18

goth n. goat 210/33 n.

gouerneþ pr. 3 sg. intr. controls 122/26; tr. governs, controls 85/21, 124/10. **gouerneþ** pl. 122/9, 124/ 11, 161/28. **gouernede** pa. t. 3 sg. 125/3

gouernour n. ruler 100/11, 109/7, 126/3

goutes n. pl. gout 224/8

graate see **grat**

grace n. divine grace, spiritual endowment 13/31, 15/27, 25/10, 135/11, 178/15; natural endowment or ability 11/10, 12; good name, reputation 10/10; favour 101/29, 102/9. **graces** pl. endowments, gifts 20/13, 22/19, 119/12, 120/8 n.; spiritual endowments, graces 119/26, 33, 120/5; graciousness 68/10

graciouser adj. comp. more attractive, better endowed 24/10

grayne n. scarlet dye 107/17. **grayns** pl. seeds 230/27

gra(u)nteþ pr. 3 sg. intr. consents 225/18; tr. concedes 7/32.

gra(u)nteþ (*cont.*):
ygra(u)nted *pp.* granted 264/13;
given 65/19
gra(u)ntinge *vbl. n.* consent, con-
senting 10/32, 11/17, 47/6*, 212/
11. **grantinges** *pl.* 47/8
grat *adj.* great, considerable, big 8/27,
17/5, 183/34, 238/32; large, abun-
dant 19/10, 44/21, 185/8; many
18/17; lofty, elevated in rank, great
103/28, 164/17, 168/23, 209/10 *n.*;
very 156/20; grievous, harsh 128/
22; heavy 44/20; coarse 93/17,
205/11; obtuse, unsubtle 103/24;
ine ~ completely 111/7 *n.*; *þe* ~
the bulk 112/15; *þet* ~ sum total
245/21; *wel* ~ exceedingly 151/22,
155/5–6: **gratne** *acc. masc.* 238/32,
239/5. **greate** *acc.* 166/26, 179/15,
231/20, 240/9. *p.c.* 9/3, **graate**
133/19. **greate** *wk.* 15/16, 16/15,
93/17, **grate** 143/12, **grete** 23/24.
greate *pl.* 19/9, 21/22, 34/24,
greatte (*for forms with double
consonant see p. 42, n. 4*) 25/12, **grete**
77/8. þe **greaten** *p.c.* 139/12.
gratter *comp.* 36/2, 66/28, 176/2*,
grater 116/5, 164/18. **gratteste**
superl. wk. 80/12, 89/1, **gratteste**
pl. 44/20, 21, þe **grat(t)este** 41/33,
140/7, þe **gret(t)este** 67/14, 88/24
gratliche *adv.* greatly, gravely 47/15,
223/29, 266/1; loftily 196/28;
loudly 156/7
gratnesse *n.* magnitude 143/10;
greatness 164/15
greade *n.* lap 196/2
great(t)e(n) see **grat**
grede *v. tr.* proclaim 22/15, 60/4,
148/35; cry, call out 31/35, 212/33;
implore 115/19, 171/16; *intr.* cry
out (to), 211/29, 212/4, 6; cry out
56/8, 194/19, 212/9: **grede** *pr. 1 sg.*
211/31. **gret** *3 sg.* 56/8. **gredeþ** *pl.*
71/11, 148/35. **gredde** *pa. t. 3 sg.*
212/11. **gredden** *pl.* 212/15
gredinge *vbl. n.* clamour, suppli-
cation 211/32, 212/2. **gredynges**
pl. clamour 266/8
greynere see **gernier**
grene *adj.* verdant 116/26
gren(e)hede *n.* greenness, verdancy
28/12. 94/27, 97/33

greny *v. intr.* become green, burgeon
95/10, 97/32; *tr.* cause to burgeon
greneþ *pr. 3 sg.* 95/23
grese *n.* oil, grease 93/17, 205/17
gret see **grede**
grete see **grat**
greui *v. tr.* harm 39/26. **greueþ** *pr. 3
sg.* troubles, grieves, oppresses
254/8. *pl.* 142/28. **ygreued** *pp.*
weighed down 260/5, 171/3
greuousliche *adv.* grievously 47/17
griho(u)nd *n.* greyhound 75/28, 30,
155/29
gryn *n.* snare 47/22. **grines** *pl.* 77/22,
131/5, 157/15
grinde *v. intr.* grind 181/14
grindinge *vbl. n.* gnashing 265/5
grislich *adj.* terrible 49/29, 74/2
grochi *v. intr.* be resentful, complain
67/7, 68/20. **grocheþ** *pr. 3 sg.* 30/8,
34/3, 68/7
grochindeliche *adv.* grudgingly 193/
35
groch(ch)inge, grouchinge *vbl. n.*
complaint, resentment 34/1, 54/19,
67/23, 140/13, **grochinges** *pl.*
67/31 *n.*
gromes *n. pl.* servants, people of low
station 57/9, 112/24 *n.*, 210/7
grond *n.* ground 1/15. **gr(o)unde**
p.c. 246/35; earth 35/9; *a/to* ~ to
the ground 23/26, 91/33
groniynge *vbl. n.* groaning 264/36
grunny *v. intr.* grumble 67/8
guo *v. tr.* travel, go along 60/12, 78/
17; *intr.* walk, travel, go, pass 32/9,
46/30, 246/26 *n.*, 254/3; go 203/34;
þe **guoinde** those who pass by
196/29 *n.*; go away, depart 215/36,
226/14; pass away 9/2, 56/6; *ppl.
adj.* transitory 120/5; go and (do
sth.) 213/33; come 247/7, 13; grow,
issue 17/22; go about 216/29; arise
57/19; fall (into temptation) 117/
22; ~ *into* enter 42/14, 212/13; ~
ouer exceed 223/12; ~ *to* have
sexual relations with 223/34:
guonne *infl. inf.* 185/13, 226/14.
guo *pr. 1 sg.* 140/34. **gest** *2 sg.* 129/
12, 31, 130/6. **geþ** *3 sg.* 56/28, 206/
14, 235/2. **guoþ** *pl.* 34/22, 42/14,
52/20, 254/6 *n.* **guo** *subj. sg.* 73/18,
117/3, 254/28. *pl.* 117/17, 255/15,

256/4, **go** 117/26. **guo** *imp. sg.* 73/
1, 17, 74/35. **guoþ** *pl.* 52/20 *n.*,
189/28, 198/11. **guoinde** *pr. p.*
120/5. **iguo** *pp.* 71/27, 212/13,
242/7 (*for* **yede(n)** *see separate
entry*)
guoinge *vbl. n.* going; ~ *in* entrance
263/32; *ine zikere* ~ in safe con-
duct 254/5 *n.* **guoinges** *pl.* associ-
ation 231/28
guod(e) *adj.* morally good 14/20, 79/
23, 251/15 *n.*, ⟨**good**⟩ 60/1; (of)
good (quality) 26/6, 51/8, 168/3;
pleasing 16/17, 24/5–6, 177/12;
ample 53/26, 54/2; beneficial 98/14
(*see p. 64*), 168/5; þe **guode** the
good man 167/6; þet **guode** the
good 86/14, 121/21; þe **guode** *pl.*
good people 85/10; **guode** good
things 74/29 *n.*, 244/26, 261/30;
comp. of better standing 25/18:
guodne *acc. masc.* 238/28. **guode**
acc. 53/26, 54/2, 90/29, 207/23. *p.c.*
6/14, 11/16, 14/16. *wk.* 10/9, 24/5,
6 (*see p. 64*), 74/21. *pl.* 10/11, 17/10,
25/10, 254/22 *n.*, ⟨**guod**⟩ 100/9 *n.*,
þe **guode** 209/3, 6, 7. þe **guoden**
p.c. 72/31. **betere** *comp.* 25/18.
beste *superl. wk.* 113/21, 172/13.
pl, 142/21
guoddoere *n.* benefactor 135/8
guodhed(d)e *n.* excellence 79/33,
233/35; value, worth 233/21
guodnesse *n.* benefit, blessing 18/
29, 147/25; virtue, goodness 29/22,
96/20, 232/32, 244/17* (*see p. 49*);
worth, efficacy 94/12, 99/9, **guod-
nes‡** 191/33; prosperity (*pros-
peritee*) 131/29. **guodnesses** *pl.*
benefits 18/15, 19, 215/14; good
deeds 111/14, 175/9
guos *n.* goose 32/11

H

ha see **he**
habbe *v. tr.* have, possess 5/20, 7/1,
22/19, 130/19 *n.*, 156/9*, 245/20;
comprehend 244/26; get, obtain
9/18, 40/23, 156/9*, 198/31; hold
(in contempt) 196/34; consider
241/9; have, show (mercy, pity,
faith, etc.) 175/17, 197/14, 207/22;

suffer 186/35, 191/11; derive
(pleasure, etc.) 238/25, 30, 31; *intr.*
must, ought to 154/4; have (to do
with) 194/19; *with an adverb/pre-
dicative adjective* 36/24, 218/31,
226/27, 270/18; *perfect auxiliary*
7/10, 11/2, 58/28; *refl.* behave 214/
29 *n.*; **heþ** there are 105/15 *n.*,
122/2 *n.*; ~ *an* wear 14/22 *n.*, 267/
32; ~ *blisse* (*se glorifient*) glory 216/
16; ~ *drede* fear 84/6; ~ *hede* (*of*)
fear, be anxious (about) 166/14–15,
180/15, 257/26; take heed 99/17,
192/8, 230/24; ~ *honger* be hungry
198/13–14; ~ *leuere* would rather
31/30, 32/2; ~ *onworþ* disdain 35/
29, 270/25–6; ~ *ssame* be ashamed
50/1, 196/32; ~ *þorst* be thirsty
198/13–14; ~ *wyl* desire 231/2:
hab(b)e *pr. 1 sg.* 24/17, 51/10, 69/
16 (*see note to 58/28*). **hest** *2 sg.*
20/11, 194/29, 195/20. **heþ** *3 sg.*
9/29, 10/10, 145/25* (*see note to
40/5*), **het** 90/15, 174/3. **hab(b)eþ**
pl. 22/19, 27/24, 58/28 *n.*, 114/24
(*see note to 58/28*), **habbet** 126/14,
21 (*see p. 97, note 6*). **habbe**
subj. sg. 47/32, 81/33, 85/9. *pl.* 36/
24, 110/7, 150/2. **haue** *imp. sg.*
175/17, 197/14, 207/22. **habbeþ**
pl. 266/7. **heddest** *pa. t. 2 sg.* 58/32.
hedde *3 sg.* 14/35, 15/2, 193/29,
hed 241/9‡. **hedde(n)** *pl.* 51/8,
71/10, 189/8. **hed(d)e** *subj. sg.* 81/5
89/27, 190/16, 33 (*see note to 58/28*).
yhet *pp.* 40/23, 177/33, 198/34
ha(l)f *n.* side 1/18, 40/11, 72/17; part,
portion 13/5, 234/10–12. **halues** *pl.*
16/11; *ariʒt* ~ *and aleft* ~ in any/
every direction 23/3, 151/6–7*; *ine
þe guode* ~ in a good sense 152/13;
in þise ~ in this regard 154/11; *of
ech* ~ in every part 150/19; *of
oþer/oþre* ~ on the other hand 108/
13, 127/14, 162/18–19; *of þe* ~ *of*
from part of 49/10; *of/ane . . .* ~ *on
. . .* behalf 103/11, 190/13 (*see p.
49*); *to þe riʒt* ~ *and to þe left* ~ to
one side and to the other 152/12;
went (*in*) *to þe worse/guode* ~ looks
on the worst/best side 62/15, 136/
22–3
hayl *int.* hail! 262/29, 271/6

hald see healde

half *n.* see ha(l)f

half *adj.* half 173/14; *inflected in*: be þe haluedele by half 36/15; to þe haluedele according to the *métayage* system 36/28 *n.*

half *adv.* half 86/29, 211/4, 5

halȝen *n.* saint, holy man 214/4, 241/26, 256/23. halȝen *pl.* 6/32, 14/2, 20/20; the righteous 13/6

halȝy *v. tr.* consecrate, sanctify 106/21, 235/26, 237/31; dedicate 106/32; keep holy 7/4: halȝeþ *pr. 3 sg.* 106/25. *pl.* 237/23, 238/1. halȝi *pr. subj. sg.* 7/4. yhalȝed *pp.* 106/7, 235/17, 262/23, (y)halȝede *pl.* 40/30, 36

halke *n.* (*p.c.*) corner, secret place 210/20. halkes *pl.* 25/35, 37/14, 143/3

halle *n.* (*p.c.*) hall 102/7

halt see healde

halue(s) see ha(l)f

ham see he

hamzelue *emphatic pron. pl*, they themselves 175/11, 208/23; *refl. acc.* themselves 5/12, 16/26, 31, 40/11, 59/25

hand, hond *n.* hand 1/6, 19/13, 52/15, 131/17. honden *pl.* 31/35, 47/28, 148/19; *myd alle þe ~ (a tout les mains) þet hy moȝe* with alacrity 92/16-17; *for* nime an hand *see* nime

handleþ *pr. pl. tr.* handle 235/16

han(d)linge *vbl. n.* touching 46/28 (*see p. 49*)

handuol *n.* handful 77/35 *n.*

yhanged see hongy

hap *n.* fortune 24/2, 27/18, 76/31

hard *adj.* severe, harsh 67/33, 189/33, 240/17; difficult 33/30; hard, obdurate 68/26, 167/14, 242/14, 15; heavy, grievous 48/10, 218/11: harde *acc.* 189/34. *p.c.* 148/22. *wk.* 68/29. *pl.* 187/24

harder *adv. comp.* harder 174/12

hardi *adj.* bold 83/18, 84/22. *pl.* 83/27, 123/18; þe hardi 16/29

hardiesse *n.* boldness, courage 83/17, 162/30, 31

hard(i)liche *adv.* severely 208/15; boldly 143/27, 232/31; audaciously,

rashly 18/34, 60/6; vehemently 75/18 *n.* hardylaker *comp.* more confidently 60/12

hardnesse *n.* obduracy 29/14; cruelty 164/2; severity, rigour 221/2, 240/19. har(d)nesses *pl.* 181/2 (*see p. 49*), 236/23

hare *n.* hare 51/3, 75/27

hare *pron.* see he

harezelue see hirezelue

harkni *v. tr./intr.* listen to 63/9

harm *n.* injury, harm 8/34, 9/18, 128/6; loss 243/11; harmes *pl.* damage 30/31, 39/33, 43/29; damages 31/1; *mekeþ his ~* causes distress 27/13 *n.*

harmi *v. tr./intr.* injure, harm 9/1, 4, 10/8 (passive), 11/18, 63/14; *intr.* do harm 23/8: harmeþ *pr. 3 sg.* 52/33. *pl.* 79/7. harmi *subj. sg.* 146/32. yharmed *pp.* 238/5

harmuolle *adj.* (*pl.*) harmful 58/3

harneys *n.* domestic equipment 24/35

harnesses see hardnesses

harou *int.* help! 31/35

hassassis *n.* assassin 140/25

haste *n.* haste; *an ~* quickly, at once, forthwith 31/19, 60/16, 194/18; *an ~ huanne (tantost com)* when 149/3; as soon as 207/16-17

hasteliche *adv.* quickly, straightaway 65/12, 173/10, 194/12

hasti *v. tr.* make . . . hasten 174/9 *n. refl.* hasteþ *pr. 3 sg.* hasten 34/9 *n.* hastede *pa. t. subj. sg.* 174/6

hastif *adj.* rash 183/35, 184/3

hat, hatte see hote

hate *n.* hatred 8/26, 29/26, 114/10

hatie *v. tr.* hate 73/16, 74/27, 121/22. hatie *pr. 1 sg.* 216/12. hateþ *3 sg.* 8/28, 27/1, 141/5. hatieþ *pl.* 43/18, 72/20, 75/35 *n.* hatye *subj. sg.* 101/1. hateden *pa. t. pl.* 72/6. yhated *pp.* 76/16

hauberk *n.* hauberk 171/2, 180/13, 265/26

hauedliche *adj.* (*pl.*) capital 15/20

hauedzennes *b. pl.* capital sins 16/8, 105/18

hauene *n.* (*p.c.*) harbour 182/35, 183/2

hazard *n.* hazard, game of chance 171/23

he, ha *pron. masc.* he, one, it (*for cases in which the pronoun indicates grammatical gender see pp. 88–94*) 5/9, 6/34, 12/31, *128/9* (MS. hem), *131/12* (MS. *hi*), 134/28 *n.*, 147/2, 153/3, 237/21 *n.*, *245/8*, ⟨hi⟩ 87/12 *n.*, 139/15 *n.*, 144/14 *n.*, 181/2 *n.*, hine *acc.* 16/17, 31/23, 75/29. him *acc./dat./p.c.* 8/15, 16/19, 60/16 *n.*, 88/10, 164/22 (MS. *himm*), 196/15 *n.*, 211/1*; *possessive dative* 142/30, 167/11; *refl.* 5/7, 9/1, 97/34. his *poss.* his (possessions), his own, one's own *adj.* 1/5, 28/22, 132/5, 6, 175/14, 202/18*, is 206/1 *n.*; *pron.* 12/3, 22/13 *n.*, 54/3 *n.* hi *fem.* she, it 191/15, 216/9, 226/11, 228/11, ⟨huy⟩ *159/17*, ⟨he⟩ *228/6*. hi *acc.* it 95/10 *n.*, 151/9 *n.* his(e) her 10/22, 118/25, 206/3. hare, hire *acc./dat./ p.c.* 11/2, 64/33, 118/25, 191/26; *refl.* 216/10, 226/11, 260/22; hare, hire *poss. adj.* 37/32, 49/8, 226/12. hiren *pron. p.c.* herself 111/32 *n.* hit *neut.* it 1/3, 18/17, 27/23. *acc.* 8/25, 10/1, 2; *refl.* him (*see discussion p. 84*) 21/23, 134/3, 184/7. his *poss. adj.* 55/16, 95/15, 227/13; *anticipatory use* 12/36, 48/19, 53/1, 211/14; *pleonastic use* 164/28, 222/27; *subject of an impersonal verb* 27/10, 65/32, 184/4; *where the referent is expressed or implied in the preceding clause* (*cf.* OED It *I 1 c*) 1/4, 15/27. hi *pl.* 1/18, 5/11, 12, 6/6. his(e) *acc.* 5/5, 9/15, 85/29. ham *acc./dat./p.c.* 6/7, 8/11, 26/6. *refl.* ham, hem 5/13, 124/27, 193/15, 204/20 *n.* those who 242/9 *n. recipr.* togydere ~ 43/18, ~ togidere each other 139/10, 13. hare, here, hire *poss. adj.* 6/1, 22/15, 36/12, 132/25, 182/16* *n.* *pron.* hare, hyre 96/27, 144/16, *p.c.* hiren their property 38/30, their own 60/21

healde, hyealde, hyalde *v. tr.* obey, observe, keep (a promise) 5/6, 53/17, 54/16, 64/6, 65/11, 214/20 (*passive*); keep (oneself alone) 226/11; keep (company) 54/26* (*see p. 49*); contain 92/33; retain 220/22, 24; hold, grasp 15/13, 77/25; embrace 206/2; hold (in prison) 128/24; hold (a belief) 11/30 (*passive*); bind, oblige, commit 30/32, 69/8, 235/8*, 238/11; *ppl. adj.* obligatory 11/23; support, maintain, preserve 35/32, 53/15 *n.*, 154/28* (*see p. 49*), 196/8 *n.*, 249/32; harbour 8/31, 9/16, 147/7; consider, regard 23/7, 27/20, 54/28, 62/4* (*passive; see p. 49*), 132/8; *refl.* keep (quiet) 58/14, 255/9; adhere 134/22 *n.*; hold out 240/29, 31; remain 242/2; of healde see ofhealde; (*him*) ~ þet . . . ne (*with subj.*) refrain from 206/33–4; (*him*) ~ vestliche be resolute 166/1: halt *pr. 3 sg.* 18/31, 50/24, 59/7. healdeþ *pl.* 97/21, 123/16, hyeldeþ 124/16, hiealdeþ 134/30, 160/17. healde *subj. sg.* 154/3, hyalde 21/34, 130/24, hyealde 59/33, 154/28*, 166/1. hald *imp. sg.* 255/17. hild *pa. t. 3 sg.* 226/11, 241/8. hyelde *subj. sg.* 27/20 *n.* yhealde *pp.* 58/18*, 101/28, 235/8*, (y)hyalde 68/28, 132/32, (y)hyealde 8/31, 26/23, 259/14; *pl. adj.* 8/31, 9/16, 11/23

heap *n.* multitude 130/35, hyap 159/15, hieap 159/19. heape *p.c.* 267/23; hyeape heap 139/33, 205/25

heaued *n.* head 2/19, 16/1, heued 31/34, 64/13; end, conclusion 150/34 *n.*, 183/31; of ~ yet again 57/20 *n.*: heauede *p.c.* 62/14, 176/26, heuede 186/29, 258/29. heaueden, heauedes *pl.* 2/17, 14/35, 176/28, heuedes 15/26

hed, heddest, hedde(n) see habbe

hede, *n.* heed, note 89/34, 207/10, 208/24; care 172/9; him ne worþ non ~ he need not fear 74/26; huo þet nimþ wel ~ as observant people well know 32/26; for habbe ~ see habbe

hede *v. tr.* hide, conceal 44/32, 163/21. hedeþ *pr. pl.* 41/18, hedde *pa. t. 3 sg.* 129/7. yhed *pp.* 109/11, 139/2, 181/34

hedes see newehedes

hedinge *vbl. n.* concealment 196/8

heg *n.* hedge 232/18, 140/19

heȝ *adj.* high, tall 23/25, 60/34, 182/31; (of) high (rank) 25/8, 101/25,

heȝ (*cont.*):
102/19; high (court) 58/9; solemn 7/28; sublime, exalted 80/6, 88/2, 104/29; supreme, sovereign 64/16, 106/9, 133/25; high(way) 168/25; deep 182/36; profound 81/32; þe heȝeste the chief 120/14; *an ~* on high, aloft, up 45/33–46/1, 85/3, 119/23, 125/16; progressively 48/4–5 *n.*; upwards 95/2–3: heȝe *acc.* 81/32. *p.c.* 106/9, 118/17. *wk.* 58/9, 88/1, 168/25. *pl.* 16/28, 23/27, 43/32; þe heȝe 145/11. heȝere *comp.* 122/4 (*see p. 69*). *pl.* 176/2. heȝest *superl.* 244/32. heȝeste *wk.* 80/1, 6, 89/2, 247/2. heȝest *pl.* 124/8‡, þe heȝeste 25/12, 109/30, 122/4

heȝe *adv.* high 23/1, 24/25, 27, 26/8, 127/10. heȝere *comp.* 133/21; þe *~* at a higher price 44/16; heȝest *superl.* from the greatest height 238/20

heȝeþ *pr. 3 sg.* exaggerates (*hauce*) 136/20

heȝinge *vbl. n.* raising; *ine ~* at a profit? 35/16 *n.*

heȝliche *adj.* complete 264/12 *n.*; principal, chief 26/27 *n.*. *pl.* 27/6 *n.*

heȝliche *adv.* chiefly, principally 5/23 *n.*, 29/30, 263/28 *n.*; highly 73/12 *n.*; diligently 263/27 *n.*

heȝnesse *n.* noble birth, high rank 18/27, 137/7, 215/20; nobility 89/4, 97/4 *n.*, 123/24; loftiness 105/7 *n.*, 164/15. heȝnesses *pl.* dignities 24/21, 208/35

heȝþe *n.* top 24/24. heȝþes *pl.* interest 35/7

heyrone *n.* (*p.c.*) heron 193/13

hel *n.* hill, mountain 82/9, 182/26. helle *p.c.* 5/3, 96/22, 103/10. helles *pl.* 23/27, 59/24, 60/35. (*For 192/5 see Corrigenda*)

hele *v. tr.*¹ heal, make whole, complete 129/4, 217/27, 219/6; *intr.* heal 96/9: helþ *pr. 3 sg.* 129/3, 144/31. heleþ *pl.* 180/12 *n.* hele *subj. sg.* 174/29. helden *pa. t. pl.* 96/9. (y)held *pp.* 141/30, 148/6, 203/12; mended 232/25

hele *v. tr.*² conceal 175/4. yhole *pp.* 26/13, 139/2, 221/36

helle *n.* hell, limbo 2/29, 12/31, 73/8

helm *n.* helmet 265/27

help *n.* help 116/23, 117/21, 257/2 *n.* helpe *p.c.* 65/14, 98/24; *is ine ~* (*est en aide*) helps 9/1

helpe *v. intr.* help 79/6; *ppl. adj.* helpful 62/35, 63/4; *tr.* 42/23, 78/12, 79/13: helpþ *pr. 3 sg.* 117/23, 147/15, 187/1. helpeþ *pl.* 148/6. helpe *subj. sg.* 65/13, 86/20. *pl.* 213/27. helpinde *pr. p.* 30/33 *n.* yholpe *pp.* 184/12

helsny *pr. 1 sg. tr.* adjure 253/26

helt *pr. 3 sg. tr.* pours out 177/28 *n.*

helþ see hele¹

helþe *n.* health 18/24, 24/4, 53/2; salvation 30/35, 183/2, 265/27

hem see he

hennen *n. pl.* hens 38/3

her *n.* hair 181/11. here *p.c.* 176/31, 177/1 *n.*

herbe *n.* plant 153/8

herberȝeres *n. pl.* innkeepers 39/1

herberȝi *v. tr.* lodge, shelter 199/4. yherberȝed *pp.* 130/30, 195/15

here *n.* haircloth 90/25, 227/2

here *pron.* see he

yhere *v. tr.* hear, listen to 20/28, hihere 244/21, hyre 231/29, yhiere 202/17, 230/3; *intr.* yhere 132/30 *n.*, hiere 177/7: hierst *pr. 2 sg.* 210/25. yherþ *3 sg.* 25/16, 27/12, 56/31, hierþ, (y)hyerþ 62/8, 140/23 *n.*, 209/1, 256/23. (y)hereþ *pl.* 58/17, 178/10, 256/32, hiereþ, yhyereþ 122/18, 256/28 *n.* yhere *subj. sg.* 210/25, 257/22, yhiere 211/2. hyere *pl.* 257/23. (y)hyer *imp. sg.* 72/1, 211/30, 257/5. yhereþ *pl.* 266/13, yhyreþ 265/17. yhyerde *pa. t. 3 sg.* 191/19. yherd *pp.* 10/15, 97/27, 104/32, yhierd 20/27, 28, 211/14

heresye see (h)eresye

heretike *n.* heretic 9/23. (h)eretiks *pl.* 134/20, 182/8

herie *v. tr.* praise, worship 23/19, 55/11, 70/23, 246/28 *n.* hereþ *pr. 3 sg.* 59/33, 136/7, 18, 20. herieþ *pl.* 10/13, 92/10, 108/17. yhered *pp.* 23/17, 104/24, 196/14

heryinge *vbl. n.* praise, worship 23/16, 22, 134/6, 269/11 *n.* heryinges *pl.* 139/1, 267/7

heritage see (h)eritage
herkneres *n. pl.* listeners 58/21
hermite *n.* hermit 187/36
yhert *ppl. adj.* obdurate 29/14
herte *n.*[1] hart *216/30* (*MS. hert*)
herte *n.*[2] courage 83/32, 84/4, 8 *n.*, 127/13; intention, inclination 193/28, 198/2; heart 6/6, 127/25, 261/34. herten, hertes *pl.* 46/34, 127/25, 217/32; *do þe ~ ine* see do; *mid* ~ wholeheartedly 133/5–6
heruest *n.* harvest 86/32, 112/16. herueste *p.c.* harvest time 36/19
hes *n.* carrion 55/2 *n.*
hest see habbe
heste *n.* commandment, command 5/18, 19, 63/29, 180/10. hestes *pl.* 5/2, 11/20, 15/30
het,[1] yhet see habbe
het[2] see hote
hete *n.* heat, warmth 75/9, 95/7; ardour, burning desire 47/9, 55/24, 166/26. hetes *pl.* heat 124/22
hette(n) see hote
heþ see habbe
heued see heaued
heuene *n.* heaven 6/16, 12/5, 16/18, 227/30*. heuene *gen.* 262/7. heuenes *pl.* heaven 262/23, 263/5
heuenelyche *adj.* (*wk.*) heavenly 269/33
heui *adj.* heavy 44/27, 140/3; sluggish 31/28
heuinesse *n.* heaviness 271/3, 5; torpor, sloth 4/9, 31/27, 269/32
hewe *n.* servant 195/14
hi see he
hy(e)alde, hyelde see healde
hyane *n.* hyena 61/24
hyap see heap
hider *adv.* hither 140/34, 207/26
hidouse *adj.*(*pl.*) horrible 161/9
hidousliche *adv.* horribly 6/32
hieap see heap
hyeȝinges see lyeȝinges
hier *adv.* here 18/2, 59/34, 115/17, hiere in this world 137/25, 254/12
hyerbeuore *adv.* previously 59/3
hyerere *n.* hearer 256/24
hyereȝigginge *vbl. n.* hearsay 117/10
hierine *adv.* herein 232/6 *n.*
hyerof *adv.* concerning this 190/2
hierþe *n.* hearing 56/27, 91/24, 241/1

hihere see yhere
hild see healde
him see he
himzelf *emphatic pron.* himself 6/15, 49/34, 114/9; he himself 5/5, 100/13, 188/20. himzelue *refl. pron. acc./p.c.* himself, him himself *15/2*, 29/31, 48/26, 59/21; oneself 63/17
hine see he
hire(n) see he
hirezelue, harezelue *emphatic pron.* herself 97/15 *n.*; *refl. acc./p.c.* 231/19, 251/9
hiriaus *n. pl.* heralds 45/9 *n.*
his *pron.* see he
his *v.* see by
hise see he
hysians see hiriaus
hit see he
hoc see wyedhoc
hod *n.* holy orders, rank, status 235/9. hodes *pl.* 49/14, 176/2
yhoded *ppl. adj.* ordained 49/13, 235/7
hogges *n. pl.* hogs 89/6
hokes *n. pl.* hooks 264/22, 27
(y)hol *adj.* sound, wholesome, healthy 51/27, 128/30, 205/23, 251/22; whole, entire 62/5, 126/17; single 175/20; inviolate 12/22, 220/1; whole 171/2 *n.*: þe hole *wk.* 148/9. yhole *pl.* 220/1. þe holen *p.c.* 205/23. þe holer *comp.* 251/22
hole *n.* (*p.c.*) hole 142/11
yhole see hele[2]
holi *adj.* holy 1/2, 7/20, 29, *128/36* (*MS. hohi; see note to 74/6–7*).
holyiste *superl. wk.* 54/36* (*see p. 69*)
holyer *n.* fornicator 51/16
holyhede *n.* holiness, sanctity 247/1
holyliche *adv.* devoutly, piously 7/23, 74/17, 102/14. holylaker *comp.* 7/14
holinesse *n.* sanctity 25/32, 49/21, 105/23, 222/3* (*see note to 74/6*), 267/4 *n.*, 268/28 *n.*
(y)holliche *adv.* wisely, healthfully 29/34 *n.*, 94/6 *n.*; completely 109/25, 127/1, 175/2
yholpe see helpe
hom *adv.* home 155/33, 156/5, 191/25
hond(en) *n.*[1] see hand

hond *n.*² dog, hound 55/2, 75/33, 155/
32. hondes *gen.* 179/6. hounde
dat. 156/4. *p.c.* 155/32. houndes
pl. 70/4

hondred *num.* hundred 55/20, 75/18,
91/8

hondreda3te *num.* hundredfold 234/
8 *n.**, 12

hondreduald *num.* hundredfold 191/
21

honeste see (h)oneste

honesteliche *adv.* elegantly 47/14

honger *n.* hunger 73/22, 75/9, 163/
16; desire 183/8; *habbe* ∼ see
habbe

hongi *v. intr.* hang 57/4; be hung
31/2, 218/14; lean 151/6; *refl.*
incline 40/11; *tr. ppl. adj.* hung
203/14, hanged 241/9: hongeþ *pr.*
pl. 40/11. hongi *subj. sg.* 151/6. *pl.*
218/14. yhanged, yhonged *ppl.*
adj. 203/14, 241/9

hony *n.* honey 60/11, 136/1, 177/30

honur *n.* respect 21/9

hope *n.* hope 5/22, 6/6, 12/35

hopye *v. intr.* aspire 89/3 *n.* hopeþ
pr. 3 sg. trusts 207/33

hor *n.* filth 77/36, 137/15, 228/17.
hore *p.c.* mire 229/16

hord *n.* hoard, treasure 185/9, 241/21,
263/25

hordeþ *pr. 3 sg. tr.* lays up (treasure)
182/2

hordyer *n.* treasurer 121/28

hordom *n.* fornication 7/33, 9/7

hore-urostes *n. pl.* hoar-frosts 108/7

horling *n.* fornicator 52/5

hornes *n. pl.* horns 14/35, 32/10, 130/
22

hors *n.* horse 61/17, 140/32, 204/28.
horse *dat.* 179/17. hors *pl.* 35/8,
44/34, 210/6

ho(u)sebounde *n.* husband 48/22,
49/5, 239/27. hous(e)boundes *pl.*
48/29, 223/16

hosiinge *vbl. n.* hosiery 154/13 *n.*,
177/16

hot *n.* heat 139/19

hot *adj.* hot 66/24, 107/5, 170/19.
hote *wk.* 171/33

hote *v. intr.* command 143/32; *tr.*
enjoin, command 5/19, 78/6, 146/
7 *n.*, 186/24 *n.*; call 119/33, 199/8,

257/19; *pass.* be called 1/6, 5/14 *n.*,
124/28: hat *pr. 3 sg.* 50/34, 51/1,
54/18. hoteþ, hotiþ *pl.* 38/15,
122/11, 186/24 *n.* het *pa. t. 3 sg.*
5/5, 190/8, 236/9. yhote *pp.* 190/
32, 214/19. hatte *pass. pr. sg.* 61/16,
133/30, 141/10. hette *pass. pa. t. 3*
sg. 48/28, 129/10, 133/2. hetten *pl.*
67/20

hotere *n.* commander 109/7

hotestre *n.* mistress (*comanderesse*)
53/29

hotinge *vbl. n.* ordering 148/25

hou *interr. adv.* how 90/19, 219/12;
conj. adv. 5/12, 20/10, 64/34; *indef.*
however *90/15 n.*, 197/24; (*main*
clause not expressed) 3/32, 17/18; ∼
he ssolde vinde uayre notes what fair
notes he would find! 105/12; ∼ *þet*
hit by somehow or other 157/12;
however it be 103/29; ∼ *þis uerste*
word is zuete how sweet is this first
word! 101/12, *cf.* 93/8

hounde(s) see hond

houre see (h)oure

hous *n.* house 124/20, 136/4, 214/33.
house *p.c.* 30/2, 53/29, 113/21 *n.*,
172/30. hous *pl.* 41/4, 43/27

housebounde see ho(u)sebounde

huader *interr. particle* I wonder
whether 51/6

huam, huan see huo

hua(n)ne, huan *interr. adv.* when
264/16; huanne (þet) *conj. adv.*
6/25, 10/16, 26/22 *n.*, 36/23, 56/32
(*see note to 131/2*), 107/23*, 131/
2 *n**., 113/11*, 117/32*, 118/23*,
238/27 *n**.; since 11/28, 32/16,
246/26 *n.*; *indef.* whenever 35/21;
with ellipsis of the clause 19/7

huannes *interr. adv.* whence 129/11,
264/10, 30; *conj. adv.* whence 115/
15, 130/27

huas see huo

hue *interr. adv.* why 47/30 *n.*

hue3el *n.* wheel 24/23, 76/32, 181/
20

huer(e) *interr. adv.* where 129/8, 15,
264/15; *conj. adv.* huer (þet)
where 13/20, 14/22 *n.*, 56/21, 256/
13; in which 6/18, 244/31; to which
243/23; in whom 243/34

hueran *conj.* on which 176/26

huerbi *conj.* whereby, by which 22/5, 24/9, 43/24; on account of which 233/31; as a result of which 33/12, 107/12, 207/1; for what reason, on account of what 90/10, 135/9
huerin(n)e *conj.* in which 23/2, 31/ 15 *n.*, 44/11, 74/5
huermide *conj.* with which 23/28, 112/1, 266/29 *n.*; that with which, the wherewithal 115/18
huerof, hwerof *conj.* of which 11/20, 12/3, 17/31, 65/25 *n.*; concerning which, in regard to which 18/35, 126/28, 195/17 *n.*, 258/4; by means of which 16/28, 17/12; with which 32/25, 85/18, 119/8; from which 13/31, 23/34, 100/9; for which 23/ 19, 24/15; concerning what 172/10; whence 57/16; wherefore 204/20; in what regard 270/6; of this 65/ 25 *n.*; ~ *is þet heaued* to which that head belongs 149/13; *n.* the wherewithal 115/28, 194/29, 195/17 *n.*; that by means of which 55/20
hueronder *conj.* under which 221/34
hueroppe *conj.* upon which 251/2
huerout *conj.* out of which 215/6, 242/7
huerto *conj.* to which 79/33, 165/17, 169/15
huer(e)uore (þet) *conj.* for which, for which reason, on account of which 20/16, 61/5, 95/15 *n.*, 196/14, 264/ 4 *n.*, ⟨heruore⟩ 257/17 *n.*; *main clause not expressed* why 3/19, 21, 23, 80/15 *n.*, 118/20*; *habbe* ~ see **habbe**
huet *adj. sg. and pl.* what, what kind of 57/16, 68/20, 128/10 *n.*; *indef.* whatever 9/19; *interr. pron.* what (*introducing a dir. q.*) 51/5, 69/16 (*cf.* **misdo**), 71/12, 244/29 *n.*, wet 265/17; (*introducing an indir. q.*) 72/33, 80/1, 133/30; who 186/ 22 *n.*; *rel.* what, that which 115/14, 196/6, 208/8; **huet þet** *indef.* whatever 9/24, 20/16, 27/16; ~ *cas yfalle* see **cas**; ~ *þet hit bi* something or other 103/31–2
huet *adv.* however; ~ *hi is ydo* however perfect he is 87/12 *n.*; how; ~ *is uayr chastete* how fair is chastity 228/3 *n.*

huet *prep.* until 52/13
huete *n.* wheat 139/33, 141/16, 210/31
huetene *adj.* (*p.c.*) wheaten 82/21
huy see **he**
huich *adj.* which 100/29, 245/1, 263/ 26. **huyche** *acc.* what 56/1. **huiche** *p.c.* which, what 1/18, 151/21, 160/ 3. *pl.* which, what 87/11, 129/16, 130/32; *indef.* whatever *p.c.* 65/2; *pl.* **huyche huet þet** of whatever kind 45/17; **huych (þet)** *interr. pron.* that which, what manner of person/thing 101/14, 133/30. *rel.* which 107/24 *n.*, 154/5. **huychen** *p.c.* 263/24. **huiche** *pl.* whom 52/1, 122/15, which 85/17, 216/27 *n.*, 267/20 *n.* **huichen, huychin** *p.c.* whom 264/26, 267/4; whose 267/ 35; which 7/11, 91/22 *n.*, 175/2, 105/20; ~ *time* at what time 263/ 13–14; ~ *þet hit/hi by/byeþ* whatever /whoever it/they be/are 6/2, 38/2, 39/11; ~ *þet hit by* of what nature it be 57/16
huider *adv.* whither 115/15, 129/11, 30; wheresoever 235/2
huiderward, *adv.* whither 131/15
huile, huils see **oþerhuil, þerhuile, þerhuils**
huyt *n.* white 61/30
huyt(e) *adj.* white 81/8, 230/7, 236/20 **huite** *wk.* 181/17, 228/15, 18. *pl.* 236/16. **huyter** *comp.* 267/31
yhuited *ppl. adj.* made white, whited 178/16, 228/13
humours *n. pl.* humours 128/31, 129/2, 132/15
huo *interr. pron.* (*introducing dir. q.*) who 55/36–56/1 *n.*, 89/15, 269/18; *pl.* 218/4; **huam** *p.c.* 197/16; (*introducing indir. q.*) who 97/27 *n.*, 185/9, 264/10, 266/3. **huas (þet)** *gen.* 38/6, 8, 101/10. **huam** *p.c.* 172/9; *rel.* **huo** þet he who 5/14. **huam** *acc.* him whom 268/20 *n.* **huas** *gen.* whose 60/5, 131/17. **huam (þet)** *p.c. sg. & pl.* whom 16/34, 123/16, 196/22, 267/23; (that) which 21/30, 69/7, 96/3, 107/16, ⟨huan⟩ 17/15 *n.*; **huo (þet)** *indef.* whoever 5/7, 89/6, 137/32, 208/2*; those who 6/5 *n.*; ~ *moche* see **hou**

huose þet *indef. pron.* for whosoever 110/23

I

ich(e) *pron.* I 1/3, 139/1, 213/34, ⟨ichc⟩ 228/27 *n.*, ⟨is⟩ 251/35 *n.* **me** *acc. dat. p.c.* 1/2, 10, 115/25; *refl.* myself 175/6, 7. **mi** *poss. adj.* my 1/3, 14/30, 211/17; *(before* h, *vowel or in hiatus)* **min** 94/17, 101/16, 207/32. **mine** *acc.* 171/12, 211/30, 31. *gen.* 64/13. *p.c.* 89/16, 103/11. *pl.* 89/16, 171/11, 12

icinge *n.* avarice 16/4

ydel *adj.* idle 31/23, 142/20; frivolous, vain 58/2, 81/3, 83/1; empty 218/18, 28; devoid 131/12, 199/14, 218/20; ~ *blisse* vainglory 17/26, 23/15, 24, 195/32–3 *(see p. 63, n. 1)*; *in* ~ in vain 6/13: **ydele** *p.c.* 89/20. *pl.* 45/25, 58/2, 104/5

ydelhonded *adj.* empty-handed 218/21

ydelliche *adv.* vainly 80/26

idelnesse, ydelenesse *n.* idleness 31/21, 48/2, 206/24; futility, frivolity 58/1, 64/17, 104/5; vanity 176/32, 35, 177/3. **ydelnesses** *pl.* futilities, frivolities 74/13, 187/22, 231/29

yhende *adj.* near 212/34

yholnesse *n.* wholeness, integrity 230/28

yleaue *n.* permission 50/16, 19

yleaue-nymynge *n.* leave-taking 112/4

ilich *adj.* like 15/8, 64/14, 65/24, 87/31. **yliche** *pl.* 88/25, 155/24; alike 268/21

ilke *adj.* same 8/9; **þis ilke** this 236/33; **(þe, þet) ilke** the, that same 198/6, 263/20; this, that 22/5, 55/14, 73/26, 74/15, 224/11 *(see pp. 79–81)*. *pl.* those 5/7, 16/10, 23/35, ⟨þe ilk⟩ 205/8 *n.*; *pron.* **þes ilke** *(iste)* that man 266/1; **þe ilke** he, that man 5/22, 18/32, 24/27 *n.*, 32/1, 108/9 *n.*; she 81/4 *n.*; that 203/8. *pl.* those (people) 53/12, 57/31, 163/5; they, such people 54/7; ~ *and* ~ so and so 54/25–6; *for* ~ *zelue* see **zelf**

ymage *n.* image 81/21, 87/33, 242/8

ymaginacion *n.* imagination 158/16. **ymaginacions** *pl.* images 47/1

ympen *n. pl.* saplings 94/34, 35, 95/8

in *n.* inn, lodging 195/9, 10

in(e) *prep.* in 3/32, 6/17 *n.*, 7/20, 129/18, 171/22 *n.*, 253/13 *n.*; into 13/5, 6, 16/11, 29/35; to 260/27; on, upon 37/13, 41/10, 135/25 *n.*, 186/13; amongst 262/30; over 223/20; as, by way of 33/29, 36/12, 136/22; at 27/26, 54/9 (cf. **(h)oure**), 189/19, 203/19, 266/27 *n.*; against 68/13; between 175/20, 249/32, of 67/25, 107/3; with 55/23, 24, 216/14 *n.*, 224/34; under the heading of 42/17, 67/33; in regard to 44/17, 50/10; *bi* ~ indulge 217/1; *by* ~ *his boȝsamnesse* see **boȝsamnesse**; *is* ~ consists of 35/23, 36/31, 200/4; is to be found in 35/24, 42/12; *is* ~ *rede, helpe* advises, helps 9/1; ~ *kueade* see **kuead** *n.*; ~ *tokninge* as a sign 50/18; ~ *wytnesse* as a witness 10/9 *n.*; ~ *zuo moche þet* in so far as 49/11

in *adv.* in 75/4, 76/5, 155/1

ingnel *adj.* quick 141/6

ingratitude *n.* ingratitude 18/4

inguoinge *n.* entrance 72/25, 264/9; overture 105/11

inhoneste *adj.* unseemly 220/11

inhonesteliche *adj. (pl.)* unseemly 177/12

inne *adv.* within 203/34; in 225/8

innocence *n.* guilelessness 146/33, 181/17

innocent *adj.* innocuous 150/20

innumerable *adj.* incalculably great 267/17

ynoȝ *n.* sufficiency 187/7, 190/9; sufficient 22/18, 33/4; plenty 73/21; *more* ~ a greater abundance 137/28

ynoȝ *adj.* sufficient, enough, plenty of 22/18, 165/16; adequate 267/9;

ynoȝ *adv.* in abundance 46/15, 116/26; sufficiently 26/3, 31/29; adequately 112/33; ~ *hi trauayleþ* they work hard 143/17; *lesse* ~ inadequately 178/29 *n.*; *more* ~ in more abundance 85/9; considerably more 175/33 *n.*; *yet nou* ~ quite a few 68/3 *n.*

ynoȝbote *n.* see **bote**

ynoȝliche *adv.* sufficiently 55/21, 210/2

inpacience *n.* impatience 33/32, 67/34

into *prep.* into 15/22, 19/13, 22/32; up to, on to 126/11, 165/12; within 250/19; in 72/23

inwyt *n.* conscience 1/6, 5/15, 6/25. inwytte *p.c.* 33/6, 262/13; *ine* ~ conscious 7/16–17

ypocrisie *n.* hypocrisy 17/26, 25/27, 138/14

ypocrite *n.* hypocrite 26/23, 53/20. ypocrites *pl.* 25/29, 175/8

yqueme see kueme

irchouon *n.* hedgehog 142/4 (*see p. 28 n. 9*)

ire *n.* anger, wrath 8/27, 85/30, 101/32

yredy *adj.* imminent 173/28

yredliche *adv.* readily 1/17

is *poss. adj.* see he

is *pron.* see ich(e)

is *v.* see bi

yue see yeue

yuo *n.* enemy 170/29. (y)uo(n) *pl.* 77/16, 198/18, 255/26, 31, 32

ywer *adj.* sagacious, prudent 100/35, 182/33

yzen *n.* iron 139/32, 167/20 *n.*, 28, 217/2. ysnes *pl.* fetters 128/21

(þe) yzounde *adj.* (*pl.*) (the) sound 205/24

J

iangli *v. intr.* chatter 214/32. ganglinde *pr. p.* 226/14. iangledest *pa. t. 2 sg.* 20/29

ientilman *n.* gentleman 190/20

ieu *n.* Jew 43/10. ieus *pl.* 12/28, iewes 5/2, yewes 29/4, geus 213/10, gyewes 64/29

iogelour *n.* minstrel 172/31 *n.*

ioyaus, ioiax see iowel

ioye *n.* joy, pleasure 52/10, 75/7, goye 226/35. yoyes *pl.* 92/35

ioyel see iowel

ioineþ *pr. 3 sg. tr.* joins 79/31, 88/33 *n.*, 234/25. yyoyned *ppl. adj.* 260/26, ygoyned 247/3

ioisseþ *pr. 3 sg. refl.* rejoices 25/4

ioliuete *n.* pleasure 53/7, 15, 157/28

iornee *n.* day's work 113/9. iornayes *pl.* journeys 253/36

iowel *n.* jewel 112/6, ioyel 156/21. iueles *pl.* 77/1, ioiax 118/26, 30, ioyaus 216/13

ioustes *n. pl.* jousts 117/4

iuggi *v. tr.* jude 138/28

iurie *n.* Jewry 7/15

iustise *n.* justice 124/23, 127/4; judge 153/25

K

kachereles *n. pl.* catchpolls 263/30

kanst see conne

karoles *n. pl.* caroles 71/18, 207/6

kechene *n.* kitchen 171/33

kembe *v. tr.* comb 176/33, 36

kempe *n.* champion 50/23. kempen *pl.* 45/9

ken *n.*[1] see cou

ken *n.*[2] kindred 42/23, 66/30, 262/11. kenne *dat.* 37/32. *p.c.* 22/10, 49/1

ykend *pp.* conceived 12/17, 19, 263/2

kende *n.* nature 9/19, 18/24, 74/8, 127/24 *n.*, 157/2 *n.*, 220/15 *n.*; descent, lineage 101/19, kennd 189/24 *n.*; heritage, inheritance 17/6 *n.*, 84/13; right of inheritance 37/31; human nature 189/23. kendes *pl.* natures 268/23; *by* ~ (*par nature*) natural; *bokes of* ~ *of bestes* Bestiaries 61/9–10 (*cf. 185/32*); *habbe ine* ~ inherit 149/25–6

kendelich(e) *adj.* natural 47/30, 176/3 *n.*, 200/17, 246/3. kendeliche *pl.* 24/2, 90/17

kendeliche *adv.* naturally 24/9 *n.*, 186/10

kennd see kende

kenrede *n.* kindred, kinship 49/2, 228/3 *n.*; birth, rank 89/8, 11

kepe *v. tr.* keep aloof, conceal 226/7. kepþ *pr. 3 sg.* 180/34 *n.*

kertel *n.* kirtle, garment 191/9, 230/1, 236/20. kertles *pl.* 236/15, 19, 267/30

keruinde *ppl. adj.* cutting, sharp 66/11

kes(s)inge *vbl. n.* kissing 46/28, 29. kessinges *pl.* 46/25

kest *pr. 3 sg. tr.* kisses 161/20. keste *pa. t. 3 sg.* 240/2

keste *v. tr.* cast 108/30, 114/16, 115/31, 264/1 *n.*; shoot 66/16; bring 67/17; throw out (branches) 31/6,

lackeþ *pr. 3 sg. intr.* is lacking 210/2, 256/34

laȝe *n.* law 5/2, 7/21, 8/24; good faith, loyalty 221/10. **laȝes** *pl.* 97/14, 99/30, 101/25; *do* ~ do what is right 184/34

layde, ylayd, layþ see **legge**

layt *n.* flame 66/4

lamb *n.* lamb 232/29, 235/2. **lombe** *p.c.* 236/9, 244/15. **lambren** *pl.* 139/10

land *n.* land 19/12, 67/15, 90/9. **londe** *p.c.* 37/13, 38/18, 67/20. **londes** *pl.* 30/30, 36/12, 38/32

lang, long *adj.* long, lengthy 39/14, 24 *n.*, 99/7; slow 170/16. **longe** *p.c.* long 6/26, 99/17, 267/11; ~ *time* for a long time 267/22

langnesse *n.* length 105/4

langour *n.* sickness 93/34

lanterne *n.* lantern 195/4

large *adj.* liberal 21/34, 23/7, 100/35; ample 53/26, 54/2; **larger** *comp.* 24/10

largeliche *adv.* liberally 37/26, 77/15, 146/1

largesse *n.* liberality 102/1, 159/33, 188/4

last see **late**

laste *superl. adj.* (*wk.*) extreme 14/9; last 65/18, 245/16, **þe laste** 49/22, 70/11. *pl.* 13/27, 199/36; alast, ate **laste(n)** in the end, finally 69/10, 104/8, 239/30–1

late *adv.* late 52/17, 152/4, 174/15. **last** *superl.* last 17/15

latin *n.* Latin 145/1, 164/14, 257/20

laudes *n. pl.* lauds 51/7

launde *n.* glade 216/30

lauor *n.* wash-basin 202/22

lazre *n.* leper 189/5

lead *n.* plumb-line 151/5, **lyad** lead 141/16. **leade** *p.c.* plumb-line 150/31

leaf *n.* leaf 232/14, 26, **lyaf** 230/28, 36, **lyeaf** 62/6, 231/5, 14. **leave** *p.c.* 1/17, 20, **lyeaue** 1/18. **leaues** *pl.* 57/24, 59/8, **leues** 230/27, 233/1, **lyeaues** 57/26, 96/8

leas see **liese**

leat *pa. t. 3 sg. intr.* bowed 239/7, 16

leawede see **lewed**

leazinge *n.* falsehood, lying, decep-

tion 62/20, 255/10, **lyeasinge** 60/21, 175/19. **leazinges** *pl.* lies 2/13, 62/19, 27, **lezinges** 63/7, **lyazinges** 63/9, **lyeasynges** 45/25, **lyesinges** 10/17, 57/29, ⟨lea-ȝinges⟩ 61/34 *n.*

leche *n.* physician 129/1, 174/26, 28

lecherie *n.* voluptuousness, lechery 9/10, 16/6, 47/27; lust 63/27* *n.*

lecheries *pl.* sensuous pleasures 31/25

(**þe**) **lecherous** *adj.* the voluptuous 111/2–3

lecherusliche *adv.* in a profligate manner 128/13

lechurs *n. pl.* voluptuaries 55/31

lede *v. tr.* lead 51/13, 185/14, 199/4, 226/36 *n.*; treat 44/1 *n.* (*passive*); lead (a life) 76/9, 94/3, 246/24; develop 168/31; control, guide 53/27, 150/18, 232/11; drive (a plough) 242/33, 34, (waves) 207/26; bring 129/27, 28, take (to witness) 10/8 *n.*; set 115/9; *intr.* lead 165/12, 200/8, 206/7; ~ *blisse* rejoice 164/1; ~ *couaytise* be covetous 53/27 *n.*: **let(h)** *pr. 3 sg.* 34/15, 124/31, 200/6, **ledeþ** 75/26 *n.* **ledeþ** *pl.* 50/18, 53/27, 185/29. **lede** *subj. sg.* 183/27. *pl.* 98/20. **led** *imp. sg,* 116/9, 117/25, 262/27. **ledinde** *pr. p.* 164/1. **ledde** *pa. t. 3 sg.* 96/22, 191/26. **yled** *pp.* 223/7

ledinge *vbl. n.* guidance 189/12

ylefde see (**y**)**leue**

left *adj.* left 147/1, 196/6; *for* **ariȝthalf and alefthalf** see **ha(l)f** (**y**)**lefþ** see (**y**)**leue**

leȝe *n.* (*p.c.*) lye 145/22

l(h)eȝ(ȝ)e *v. intr.* laugh 58/21, 111/25, 161/20, 214/32. **lheȝþ** *pr. 3 sg.* 93/36

leȝers see **lyeȝere**

legge *v. tr.* lay down 149/11. **layde** *pa. t. 3 sg.* 149/8, 11; **layþ** *pr. 3 sg.* lays (hands on) 41/9; **ylayd** *pp.* staked 171/23; given 193/31, 32

leȝinge *vbl. n.* laughter 161/25. **lheȝinges** *pl.* jests 63/7

leme *n.* limb, part of the body 47/21, 115/1, 146/31. **lemes** *pl.* 102/22, 146/16; body 96/7

lemman *n.* beloved 94/29, 230/8, 9

lenden *n. pl.* loins 46/21, 236/11, 12
lene *v. tr.* lend, bestow, grant 35/6, 90/22, 147/25; *intr.* lend, give a loan 35/29, 30, 36/2; *ppl. adj. pl.* who make loans 35/6: **lenþ** *pr. 3 sg.* 6/7, 120/8, 135/13. **leneþ** *pl.* 35/6, 15, 25, 36/1. **lenynde** *pr. p.* 35/6. **lende** *pa. t. 3 sg.* 78/10. *pl.* 37/1. **ylend** *pp.* 19/10, 36/33, 79/18
lenere *n.* lender 35/15
lenge *v. intr.* delay 173/16. **leng** *imp. sg. tr.* 194/15 *n.* **ylengd** *pp.* prolonged 198/31
lenger see **longe**
leninge *vbl. n.* lending 35/23
lenten *n.* Lent 91/7, 175/32
lere *n.* loss 36/27, 46/4; diminution 120/10
lere *v. tr.* teach 121/3 *n.*
les see **litel** *adv.*
lesnesse *n.* remission 14/10, 263/9
lesse see **litel** *adj., adv.*
lessi *v. tr.* belittle 175/18. **lesseþ** *pr. 3 sg.* 28/3, 136/21; *intr.* diminish 267/5
lessinge *vbl. n.* diminution 268/17, 269/12
lessoun *n.* lesson 135/21. **lessouns** *pl.* 56/35
lest see **litel** *adv.*
leste see **litel** *adj.*
(y)leste *v. intr.* last, continue 68/13, 71/7, 73/25; live, survive 28/12, 148/9, 220/23; endure, be steadfast 84/17, 163/25; *ppl. adj.* enduring, lasting 84/23, 92/27: **ilest** *pr. 3 sg.* 168/24. **ilesteþ** *pl.* 209/10. **lestinde** *pr. p.* 84/23, 92/27
let, leth see **lede**
lete *v. tr.* let 56/11, 73/28, 264/7; cease, desist (from) 26/27, 197/4, 256/13; fail (to do sth.) 115/23; leave, leave behind, abandon 17/15 *n.*, 42/13 *n.*, 93/17, 243/17; bequeath 112/3, 6, 190/36; *intr.* ~ of cease 269/31: **lete** *pr. 1 sg.* 214/22. **let** *3 sg.* 26/22, 87/30, 181/7. **leteþ** *pl.* 6/7, 40/17, 98/28. **lete** *subj. sg.* 206/13, 253/4, 262/4. **let** *pa. t. 3 sg.* 78/18, 191/2, 226/32. **ylete** *pp.* 193/3, 235/3, 242/24
lettre *n.* handwriting 44/31; literal sense 99/4. **lettres** *pl.* writs,

credentials 39/25, 62/22; letters 1/7, 18, 211/22, ⟨lettre⟩ 105/16 *n.*; *zette to* ~ see **zette**
leuayne *n.* leaven 205/21
leuceruere *n.* female lynx 81/7 *n.*
(y)leue *v. tr.* believe, believe in 11/27, 14/10, 78/13, 184/26 *n.*; *refl.* have faith 182/20; *intr.* believe 11/34, 50/34 *n.*, 134/24, 253/3: **(y)leue** *pr. 1 sg.* 13/36, 89/23, 262/32. **(y)lefþ** *3 sg.* 22/30, 60/27*, 28, 135/13 *n.*, 152/4. **(y)leueþ** *pl.* 19/29, 60/20, 72/11. **leue** *subj. sg.* 13/29, 158/30. **ylefde** *pa. t. 3 sg.* 191/4. **yleued** *pp.* 244/6
leue see **lyeue**
yleued, leuede see **libbe**
l(h)euedi *n.* lady 47/20, 57/10, 76/31; supreme lady, queen 80/12. **lheuedyes, leuedis** *pl.* 47/11, 67/26, 215/19
leuele *n.* (*p.c.*) level 150/32
leuere see **lyeue**
leues see **leaf**
leuest, leueþ see **libbe**
leuinge *vbl. n.* remainder 73/33
lewed *adj.* layman 25/9. **leawede** *p.c.* lay 39/27. **lewede** *wk.* 237/13. *pl.* 262/10; lay folk 34/25, **leawede** 39/21, 42/19
lezere *n.* gleaner 86/32
lezinges see **leazinge**
lhade *v. tr.* draw up 98/28; bale 178/19
lhapþ see **lheape**
lhapwynche *n.* lapwing 61/31
lheape *v. intr.* leap about 89/32, 156/6; gush, spring up 27/33, 93/4; belch forth 66/3: **lhapþ** *pr. 3 sg.* 66/3, 155/34. **lheapeþ** *pl.* 140/24. **lheape** *subj. sg.* 27/33. **lhip** *pa. t. 3 sg.* 45/32, 240/1
lheddre *n.* (*p.c.*) ladder 246/19, 21
lhe33e see **l(h)e3(3)e**
lhe3inges see **le3inge**
lhene *adj.* lean 53/23; infertile 189/36
lheste *v. tr.* listen to 70/3, 229/29; *intr.* listen 61/22, 268/5: **lhest** *pr. 3 sg.* 61/22. **lhesteþ** *pl.* 268/14. **lheste** *pa. t. 3 sg.* 133/1, 199/31
lhestinge *vbl. n.* listening 258/1
lheuc *adj.* lukewarm 31/13

lheucliche *adv.* in a lukewarm manner 31/11
lheuedi see **l(h)euedi**
lhord see **l(h)ord**
lhordinges *n. pl.* lords 67/25
lhordssip *n.* mastery, authority 54/ 17, 68/22, 84/27. **lhordssipe** *p.c.* 84/32, 261/8
lhoude *adv.* loudly 212/34
lhoue *n. (p.c.)* loaf 82/21
lyad see **lead**
lyaf see **leaf**
lyazinges see **leazinge**
libbe *v. intr.* live 8/3, 28/17, 70/30. **leuest** *pr. 2 sg.* 194/30. **leueþ** *3 sg.* 54/6, 62/31, 74/32. **libbeþ** *pl.* 37/ 11, 53/6 *n.*, 268/11. **lybbe** *subj. pl.* 265/29. **libbinde** *ppl. adj.* 126/26, 208/29 *n.*; **þe lib(b)inde** the living 13/23, 75/1, 149/20; **libbende** 116/28 *n.*; *ine þine* ~ alive 73/18. **leuede** *pa. t. 3 sg.* 128/13. *subj. sg.* 71/5, 113/28. **yleued** *pp.* 130/34
libelles *n. pl.* documents setting out a charge 40/9
libinde see **libbe**
lyckestre *n.* female who licks 56/9 *n.*
licnesse image 49/21; similarity, likeness 92/34, 242/13
licuol *adj.* pleasing 217/15
lyeaf see **leaf**
lyeas see **liese**
lyeasinge see **leazinge**
lyeaue see **leaf**
lyeʒe *v. intr.* lie 22/15, 44/15, 56/36; *tr.* deceive 129/35; *ppl. adj.* forsworn 65/20: **lyeʒþ** *pr. 3 sg.* 63/2, 77/20, **lyeʒeþ** 129/35 *n.* **lyeʒeþ** *pl.* 52/9. **lyeʒe** *subj. sg.* 65/14 *n.*, 218/ 12. *pl.* 10/6. **yloʒe** *pp.* 65/20
lyeʒere *n.* liar 62/23, 27, 257/24. **lyeʒeres** *pl.* 58/18, 177/9, 256/29; ⟨leʒers⟩ falsifiers 19/25 *n.*
lyeʒinge *vbl. n.* lying, falsehood 2/14, 63/16, 143/19. **lyeʒinges** *pl.* lies 63/5 *n.*
lyerni *v. tr.* learn 2/18, 53/4, 135/29; *intr.* 34/23, 70/17, 122/10 *n.*: **lyernest** *pr. 2 sg.* 73/16. **lyerneþ** *3 sg.* 74/26, 75/3, 220/19. **lierneþ** *pl.* 36/ 3, 199/23 *n.*, ⟨lyernieþ⟩ (MS. *lyermeþ*) 122/10 *n.* **lierni** *subj. sg.* 74/31. *pl.* 209/7, **lyerne** 72/4 *n.*

lierne *imp. sg.* 70/26, 73/1, 74/33. **lyerneþ** *pl.* 133/27. **ylyerned** *pp.* 70/26, 28
liese *v. tr.* lose, waste 31/25, 40/3 *n.* (*causative*), 40/21 (*passive*), 214/10. **liest** *pr. 2 sg.* 214/2, 232/34. **liest** *3 sg.* 33/23, 49/10, 214/6. **lyezeþ** *pl.* 57/33, 149/34, 207/3 *n.*, **lyese** 40/3 (*see p. 52*). **lyese** *subj. sg.* 34/17. *pl.* 118/4, 242/27. **leas** *pa. t. 3 sg.* 85/1, **lyeas** 203/9. **loren** *subj. pl.* 235/29. **ilore** *pp.* 45/33, 46/13, 241/1
lyesinges see **leazinges**
lyeue *adj.* (*wk.*) dear 104/23, 117/24, **leue** 109/3. 113/18. *comp.* **leuere** (*see p. 69*); *habbe* ~ see **habbe**
lyexneþ *pr. 3 pl. tr.* contradict 66/7 *n.*
lif *n.* life 14/14, 50/18, 70/34. **lyues** *gen.* 1/4. **liue** *p.c.* 5/13, 7/22, 13/12. **liues** *pl.* 199/7, 238/34, 249/28
lyfnoþ *n.* livelihood 138/25
ligge *v. intr.* lie 31/28, 223/18. **liþ** *pr. 3 sg.* 31/32, 52/25, 224/21; is, exists 4/2, 83/26, 182/34; consists 55/32
liʒt *n.* light 121/33, 200/12, 270/16. **liʒte** *p.c.* 201/4, 266/21, 270/17
liʒt(e) *adj.* trivial 11/15, 250/12 *n.*; venial 11/19; easy 99/7, 170/16. **liʒter** *comp.* easier 78/19
liʒtbere *n.* Lucifer 16/14
liʒte *v. tr.* give light to 56/25
liʒthedes *n. pl.* frivolities 207/5, 7
liʒtliche *adv.* venially 6/29², 223/1, 4, 5* (*see p. 49*); readily 256/33; frivolously 6/29¹, 63/28; easily, quickly 9/3, 104/22, 151/29, 183/ 11 *n.*, 207/8* (*see p. 49*), 249/8* (*see p. 49*). **liʒtlaker** *comp.* 229/36
lykerous *adj.* delightful, seductive 95/11. **likerouses** *pl.* 47/36, 54/ 23
liki *v. tr./intr.* please 81/17, 119/21, 211/34, 215/2; *intr.* please, be pleasing 92/15, 176/29, 268/5; *refl.* delight in 127/23 *n.*, 177/11; *ppl. adj.* pleasing 63/5, 158/26, 214/ 25: **likeþ** *pr. 3 sg.* 81/17, 187/25, 202/8. **(y)liki** *subj. sg.* 109/4, 192/4, 215/5. **likinde, likende** *pr. p.* 62/ 35, 80/25, 159/16, 228/9. **lykede** *pa. t. 1 sg.* 267/22 *n.* **likede** *3 sg.* 256/22

likinge *n.* desire 253/14; pleasure, joy 81/26, 181/35, 248/1. **likinges** *pl.* 46/35 *n.*, 112/22
likni *v. tr./intr.* resemble 245/21 *n.* **likneþ** *pr. 3 sg.* 88/11; tr. **ylykned** *pp.* compared 234/2
lilye *n.* lily 230/6, 231/15, 233/1
line *n.* (builder's) line 124/32 *n.*, 150/31, 35, 153/23, 154/3; **be lingne** equitably 160/24 *n.*
line *adj. wk.* linen 178/15, **linene** 236/20 *n.*, 30. *pl.* 236/15, 16
lingne see **line**
lynx *n.* lynx 81/6
lio(u)n *n.* lion 15/16, 84/22, 164/16. **lyone** *p.c.* 173/36. **lyons** *pl.* 131/3
lipard *n.* leopard 14/34, 15/8. **lipars** *pl.* 131/4
lippen *n. pl.* lips 210/29, 211/9
litel *adj.* small, little 74/9, 84/2, 179/8; slight, inadequate 20/31, 52/9; feeble 32/4; petty 36/2, 38/1, 60/19; þe **litle** insufficiency 154/16; **lite** little (in quantity) 28/10, 36/33, 37/1; brief 71/17; few 32/26, 105/16 *n.*; *pl.* children 259/31 *n.*; *comp.* less 28/11, 74/7 *n. pl.* lesser 2/22, 90/6. *superl.* least 75/13, smallest 249/20; lowliest 140/7: **littlene** *acc. masc.* 238/32. **little** *acc.* 53/24. *p.c.* 135/7. (þe) **little** *wk.* 76/15, 179/6. **lit(t)le, lite** *pl.* 17/31, 37/15, 74/11, 79/21*, 259/31 *n.* (þe) **lesse** *comp.* 28/11, 71/32 *n.*, 210/4–5. *pl.* 78/22. **leste** *superl. wk.* 75/13. *pl.* 44/21. þe **leste** 140/7
litel, lite *adv.* little 29/10, 31/11, 78/7, 142/14. ~ *and* ~ little by little 119/15. **lesse** *comp.* more cheaply 36/15; less 20/17, 37/23, 237/29, **les** 118/22; ~ *ynoȝ* see **ynoȝ**. **lest** *superl.* 36/18; *ate* ~ at least 167/19 *n.* **lite** *n.* little 187/7, 244/19, **to lite** 249/33. **litle** *p.c.* 187/8; *a* ~ somewhat 56/19, 73/15, 263/22. **lest** *superl* 90/14
liþ see **ligge**
liue(s) see **lif**
lo *int.* lo! 269/13
loc *n.* lock 255/27. **lokes** *pl.* 151/16
lodesmanne *n. p.c.* pilot 140/23
lodliche *adj.* (*pl.*) hateful 203/35, 257/14. **lodlakest** *superl. sg.* 49/23

lodlichhede *n.* hatefulness 203/36
loȝ(e) *adj.* low 139/30, 140/5; (of) low (estate), lowly 102/19, 105/2, a **loȝer** a man of low estate 175/27; plain, humble 226/31, 34; *ine* ~ low down 119/23: þe **loȝe** *pl.* 145/11. **loȝer** *comp.* 175/27. **loȝest** *superl.* 122/4. þe **loȝeste** *pl.* 119/30, 122/11, 161/28
loȝe *adv.* low 182/31; *zet* ~ humbles 138/16–7
yloȝe see **lyeȝe**
loȝy *v. tr.* depreciate 28/25, 136/24; humble, abase 144/11, 216/10; *intr.* diminish 49/2, 14: **loȝeþ** *pr. 3 sg.* 136/21, 246/33. *pl.* 136/24. **yloȝed** *pp.* 144/11
loȝnesse *n.* humility 246/30
lokere *n.* guardian 21/4. **lokeres** *pl.* 220/6
lokes *n.* Whitsuntide 143/24, 163/33, 213/21
loki *v. tr.* observe, consider 77/32, 89/9, 176/20; see 7/4, 118/12; care for, have regard for 53/1, 223/30, 254/32; preserve, keep, reserve, observe 5/6, 7/19, 28 (*passive*), 93/9 *n.*, 151/9 (*passive*), 232/27; award 191/29 *n.*; protect, guard 38/27, 67/18, 128/14, 248/24 *n.*; look (at) 242/6, *intr.* 242/32 *n.*; *refl.* be careful, take care 6/31, 8/4, 256/27; keep (oneself) from, abstain, refrain 52/4, 162/12, 253/27, 255/9; *ham* ~ *moche* take great care 253/30; consider 73/15; look 43/13, 126/13, 216/31; **yloked to** concentrated on 250/21: **loky** *pr. 1 sg.* 195/29. **lokest** *2 sg.* 1/12, 93/9. **lokeþ** *3 sg.* 7/13, 21/4, 208/17. *pl.* 103/2, 227/9, 231/25 *n.* **loki** *subj. sg.* 53/34, 65/14, 117/17, 249/3 *n. pl.* 102/13, 253/27. **loke** *imp. sg.* 127/34, 129/20, 192/25. **lokeþ** *pl.* 242/26. **lokinde** *pr. p.* 232/30. **lokede** *pa. t. 1 sg.* 267/35. *3 sg.* 191/2, 242/6, 29. **lokede(n)** *pl.* 204/12, 235/28, 245/32. **lokede** *subj. sg.* 18/21. **yloked** *pp.* 20/24, 70/24, 117/15
lokin(g)ge *vbl. n.* guard, custody, care 8/13, 15, 227/10 *n.*, 256/1 *n.*, 263/11; penal custody 128/22; responsibility 8/11. **lokinges** *pl.*

vision 245/25; to þe ~ of in comparison with 108/35; with regard to 153/31

lombe see **lamb**

lompe n. lamp 186/27, 187/4, 233/5. **lompen** pl. 189/8, 218/28, 233/6

londe see **land**

lone n. (p.c.) loan 35/22. **lones** pl. 38/27

long adj. see **lang**

longaynes n. pl. filthy places 212/31 (cf. Wallenberg s.v.)

longe adv. long 8/30, 84/7, 206/16, ⟨long⟩ 32/22. **lenger** comp. 8/3, 56/14

longe prep. on account of 266/9 n.

l(h)ord n. lord 1/12, 6/14, 138/29; master 249/1. **lhordes** gen. lord 18/32, 170/28, 188/25. **l(h)orde** p.c. 6/22, 19/5, 235/19; owner 37/6. **l(h)ordes** pl. lords 16/31, 37/22, 38/25; masters 85/29

loren, ylore see **lyese**

los n. reputation, honour 10/9, 25/3, 23, 106/10; praise 26/5

lost n. desire, pleasure, lust 46/21, 47/4, 54/33, 83/31 n. **loste** p.c. 24/35 n., 80/2, 82/25. **lostes, lustes** pl. 24/30, 31/20, 247/6

losteþ pr. 3 sg. tr. enjoys 246/14

lostuol adj. pleasurable, delectable 80/18, 110/27, 261/31. **lostuolle, lostfolle** pl. 91/19, 92/10, 158/26. **lostuoller** comp. 92/25

lostuolliche adv. with pleasure 51/21

loue n. love 3/11, 9/31, 13/30; charity 116/21

louerede n. affection, friendship 3/12, 146/24, 149/5; adj. lovable 145/4 n.

louie v. tr. love 6/9. 31/12, 55/5; intr. 145/18: **louie** pr. 1 sg. 62/12. **louest** 2 sg. 205/29, 254/25. **loueþ** 3 sg. 27/1, 31/11, 50/33. **louieþ** pl. 6/3, 43/21, 52/18 n., 75/35 n. **louie** subj. sg. 87/17, 144/7 n. pl. 102/11, 139/10. **loue** imp. sg. 145/29, 203/2, 244/31. **þe louiinde** pr. p. 75/34, 145/4. ppl. adj. 75/34, 145/4. **louede** pa. t. 3 sg. 89/12, 95/31, 138/21. **louede(n)** pl. 52/10, 14. **yloued** pp. 104/31, 145/25, 230/9 n.; ppl. adj. 81/1

louieres n. pl. lovers 270/15, 20

lourinde ppl. adj. louring 256/26

lozengerie n. flattery 10/16, 23/6

lozeniour n. flatterer 22/12, 63/6

lustes see **lost**

luxurie n. lasciviousness 16/6, 157/29

M

made see **maki**

ma(i)denhod n. virginity 220/2, 227/23, 228/1

madines see **mayde**

magesté n. majesty 105/7, 123/24, 152/3

magnanimité n. magnanimity 164/9, 15

magnificence n. loftiness of purpose 164/11, 168/20

maȝe n. stomach 56/7

mai, moȝe v. intr. can, be able to 15/31, 20/4, 162/29, 232/20 (verb of motion understood); be capable of 21/20, 131/20, 142/15, 219/21; for use as an auxiliary see discussion pp. 106–7: **may** pr. 1 sg. 157/7, 169/11. **miȝt** 2 sg. 7/7, 27/27, 54/20, 114/34* (see pp. 49, 53 for this and the following entry), 141/25*. **mai** 3 sg. 6/30, 8/17, 222/9. **moȝe(n)** pl. 30/35, 86/9, 157/17*, 255/8. **moȝe** subj. sg. 7/1, 10/1, 15/25. pl. 79/5 n., 109/8, 232/20. **myȝte** pa. t. 1 sg. 115/24, 267/17* (see p. 50). **miȝtest** 2 sg. 104/22, 166/11. **miȝte** 3 sg. 85/2, 112/7, 204/26. **miȝte(n)** pl. 42/29, 80/2, 193/3. **myȝte** subj. sg. 31/26, 70/17, 116/19. **miȝte(n)** pl. 58/27, 162/14, 258/36

mayde n. maid, virgin 12/18, 15/27, 48/30. **maydenes, ma(y)dines** pl. 47/12, 98/28, 218/27, 234/31

maidenhod see **ma(i)denhod**

maimes n. pl. mutilations 135/27

ymaymed see **yma(y)med**

maine n. retinue, household 24/32, 30/12, 139/16

maister see **ma(i)ster**

maystresse n. mistress 34/21, 206/26

maystrie n. victory 91/5, 92/30, 169/30

make n. mate 226/3

mak(i)ere n. maker 251/10, 262/32, 267/8; author 269/31

maki *v. tr.* make, create 5/13, 50/31, 59/24 *n.*, 109/26; make sure 81/33; bring (it) about, cause 23/27, 26/27, 32/15, 44/35 *n.*; confer, grant 101/ 29, 249/2 *n.*; do 56/23, 109/27, 189/31; accomplish 110/3; *ppl. adj.* perfect 155/23 (*see note to 87/ 12*); commit 19/14, 39/11, 258/5; indulge in 22/20, 37/25, 40/14, 218/9; conform 88/28; tell (a lie) 62/27, 28; bear 189/36; turn 211/ 11; consecrate 237/28; undertake 162/25; *refl.* pretend to be 25/30; ~ *glednesse* be happy 27/26; ~ *greate feste* see **feste**; ~ *ham quaynte . . . of* pride themselves upon 89/4; ~ *his harm* create mischief 27/13; ~ *his miȝte* do his utmost 65/33; ~ *ioye* welcome, make merry with 156/3; ~ *markat* see **marcat**; ~ *memorie and bepenchinge* commemorate and call to mind 112/14; ~ *nyedes* carry on business 215/8–9; ~ *prou* derive benefit 85/11; ~ *ssame* act shamefully 50/31; ~ *strengpe* see **strengpe**; ~ *uayr* blandish 62/13; ~ *uayr(e) chiere* see **chiere**; ~ (*uayr*) *semblant* see **semblant**; ~ *ziker* confirm 64/15; ~ *zuo moche* see **z(u)o**: makest *pr. 2 sg.* 253/20. **makeþ** *3 sg.* 17/11, 25/28, 33/18, 155/35*, ⟨maked⟩ 249/2 *n. pl.* 6/1, 55/23, 194/18. **maki(e)** *subj. sg.* 127/11, 215/6, 260/9. **maki** *pl.* 107/15, 196/16. **make** *imp. sg.* 81/33, 116/32, 194/17. **maki(i)nde** *pr. p.* 35/16, 42/13. **madest** *pa. t. 2 sg.* 1/12. **made** *3 sg.* 5/19, 7/11, 13/ 20 *n. pl.* 12/3. **imad** *pp.* 7/10, 10/28, 145/35

makiere see **mak(i)ere**

maki(y)nge *vbl. n.* making 218/23; creature, creation 92/22, 244/29 *n.*, **makying** 1/13 *n.*

(þe) malancolien, melancolien *adj.* melancholy (person) 157/30, 253/10

malice *n.* malice 26/14

yma(y)med *ppl. adj.* maimed 135/26, 31, 141/30

man(n) *n.* (a) man 5/6, 8/20, 65/18, 151/3 *n.*, 246/33. **mannes** *gen.* 77/30, 86/7, 128/12. **manne** *dat.*

32/12, 60/24. *p.c.* 9/29, 12/36, 17/ 11. **men** *pl.* 5/11, 14/3, 16/26, 24/1, 254/23 *n.* **manne** *gen.* 9/8, 11/15, 27/10; **me** *pron.* one, a man 6/15, 17, 18, 7/22, 196/19, 231/22

maner, man(i)ere, manire *n.* way, manner 6/20, 9/19, 214/6; (a) kind, kind of 10/29 *n.*, 16/7, 18/2, 37/7; sorts, kinds of 23/31, 48/1, 91/21; (manner of) behaviour 177/32 *n.*, 259/14. **man(i)eres, maneris** *pl.* kinds 15/25, 39/22, 57/2; ways 13/14, 20/4, 23/3, 25/15 (MS. *maneneres*); ⟨*anone* ~⟩ on any account 132/21 *n.*; *ine guode* ~ with propriety 46/8; *of opre* ~ of some other kind 176/18 *n.*

manhede *adj.* humane 145/3 *n.*

manhode (*acc. sg.*) homage 19/13, 15; manhood 118/29. **manhod(e)** *p.c.* 12/15, 224/8‡ *n.*, 245/6, 9

manie *adj.* (*pl.*) many 9/12, 26/4, 31/ 25

mankende *n.* mankind 1/2

manne *n.* manna 67/19, 83/7, 181/34

manslaȝte, manslaȝþe *n.* manslayer 8/28, 54/30, 115/7; manslaughter 30/22. **manslaȝþes** *pl.* 57/3

manzinge *vbl. n.* excommunication 148/25, 189/21

marcat *n.* market 215/6. **markatte** *p.c.* 23/30; *maki* ~ strike a bargain 36/35, 42/12–13

marchons *n. pl.* merchants 36/26, 39/2

mares *n. pl,* waters 250/36 *n.*

mariage *n.* (state of) matrimony 220/3, 221/5. **mariages** *pl.* marriages 39/31, 48/20

marissi *v. refl.* marry 220/36; **ymarissed** *pp. tr.* 220/29, 30; *ppl. adj.* 48/15

mark *n.* mark 1/15. **marc** *pl.* 193/35

markes *n. pl.* boundaries, limits 206/ 13, 223/6, 12

martired *pp.* martyred 111/24

martirement *n.* martyrdom, great suffering 77/5

martires *n. pl.* martyrs 53/19, 74/3, 166/31; intense suffering 83/9

ma(i)ster *n.* master 65/24 *n.*, 76/26, 97/9, 160/21*, 164/7, 168/32 *n.*

maistre *p.c.* 97/36, 135/20, 140/26.
maistres *pl.* 40/6; scholars 200/
12; ~ *of workes* clerk of the works
150/29; *adj.* master 35/31; chief
249/4
mater(i)e, matire *n.* matter 49/26,
130/29, 262/3, ⟨matiere⟩ *136/12*;
material 152/30
matyn(e)s *n. pl.* matins 51/4, 7
maugre see **(y)wyte**
mawe *v. intr.* mow 214/21
me *pron.*¹ see **ich(e)**
me *pron*² see **man(n)**
mede *n.* payment, reward 14/23, 43/
24, 90/27. **medes** *pl.* 35/34, 169/26,
170/11
medecine *n.* medicine 69/18, 129/2,
173/25. **medicines** *pl.* 22/32 *n.*
medi *v. tr.* reward 146/1
medles *n. pl.* brawls 41/7, 66/32
melancolien see **malancolien**
mele *n.* meal 93/15
melk *n.* milk 137/9, 177/30
melle *n.* mill 24/25, 58/14, 141/15
melodie, melodya *n.* melody 151/
12, 267/36
melte *subj. sg. intr.* melt 171/14
memorie *n.* memory 107/29; *maki* ~
see **maki**
men *n.* see **man**
men *adj.* in the middle 122/4 *n.*; þe
men 122/7. **mene** *p.c. ine* ~ *time*
in the meantime 36/30 *n.*
ymende *imp. sg. tr.* take note 262/19
menestrals *n. pl.* minstrels 192/28
menet *n.* coin 241/27
mene-time see **men** *adj.*
ymengd *pp.* blended 196/10
meniynges *vbl. n. pl.* admonitions
230/23 *n.*
mennesse *n.* communion 14/1, 263/
9; *ine* ~ in common 268/8
mentel *n.* mantel 188/29, 221/34.
mentle *p.c.* 188/30, 221/36
merciuol *adj.* merciful 187/6, 188/
14, 195/20. þe **merciuolle** *pl.* 96/
31, 198/30
mere *n.* mare 185/34
ymered *ppl. adj.* refined 94/33
merite *n.* merit 134/12, 234/30; *to* ~
to his credit 222/9
mersi *n.* mercy 4/7, 5/8, 186/24, 189/
12* (*see p. 49*). *cf.* **do merci**

merss *n.* morass 251/20
mes *n.*¹ 'but', excuse 62/10 *n.*
mes *n.*² dish 56/11. **mes** *pl.* 55/28,
56/3, 4
mesayse *n.* distress 186/35, 191/11;
zetteþ to ~ see **zette**
messager, messagier, messagyr
n. messenger 211/22, 24, 264/9,
266/4. **messagere** *p.c.* 266/2.
messagyers *pl.* 195/9, 264/7
messages *n. pl.* errands 122/13, 189/
31
messe *n.* mass 20/29. **messen** *pl.* 31/
30
messedaye *n.* (*p.c.*) festival 175/32;
messedaȝes *pl.* 214/19
messinges *vbl. n. pl.* celebration of
festivals 71/19
mest(e) see **moche, moche(l)**
mesteres *n. gen. used adjectivally in*
~ *men* officials 39/11
mestier *n.* function, craft, occupation
187/36. **mestyeres** *pl.* 122/13, 167/
19, 27
mesure *n.* moderation 52/35, 53/1,
254/32; limit 119/27; measure
44/24, 54/1, 2, 84/3, 252/34.
mesures *pl.* 44/18, 21; *out of* ~
immoderately 51/21–2; *zette* ~ set
bounds 253/13
mesuri *v. tr.* measure 252/32, 33.
mesureþ *pr. 3 sg.* 254/34
met *pr. 3 sg. tr.* dreams 128/25
metal *n.* metal 26/7, 139/32, 152/30.
metals *pl.* 167/28
mete *n.* food 9/16, 29/34, 50/7. **metes**
pl. food 51/9, 54/23, 55/6
meteles *n. pl.* dreams 165/5
meteres *n. pl.* dreamers 32/8
metinge *vbl. n.*¹ measure 264/33
metinge *vbl. n.*² dream 92/4, 143/18.
metinges *pl.* 32/8, 77/21, 92/4
mezel *n.* a leper 202/25, 32. **mezels**
pl. 224/6
mi see **ich**
mid *prep.* by 5/4, 38/33, 167/19;
from 211/31 *n.*; with 10/26, 11/4,
44/24, 141/7 *n.*, 161/28 *n.*, 183/7 *n.*,
199/4 *n.*, 200/17 *n.*, 253/14 *n.*; by
comparison with 10/30; in 12/16;
mide *in postponed use* 50/13, 187/
12‡, 264/8 (*cf. pp. 76–7*); ~ *herte*
whole-heartedly 181/28–9; ~ *kueade*

mid (*cont.*):
maliciously 8/7; ~ *þan* in addition 234/19; ~ *wrong* unjustly 9/33, 39/ 4-5, 18, 41/17

mid(d)el *n.* mean 249/32; *adj.* median, in between 78/23, 122/23, 32, 136/21. *pl.* 79/21, 136/25 **midliste** *superl. pl.* midmost 122/8, þe **midleste** 122/31

midni3t *n.* midnight 173/12

midþolyinge *vbl. n.* compassion 157/1

mi3t(e), mi3test, mi3ten see **mai**

mi3te *n.* strength, power 15/2, 16/24, 80/32; substance 112/35; *be/efter/ mid . . . hare/his/þine* ~ to the best of (one's) ability 7/13, 47/10-11, 195/ 22; deliberately 146/32; *cf.* **do** *and* **maki**

mi3ti *adj.* strong 103/22

mi3tuol *adj.* strong, powerful, effective 83/19, 100/34, 130/6, 207/19*: **my3tuolle** *pl.* 269/9*. **mi3tuoller** *comp.* 112/34* (*see p. 49*)

milde *adj.* kind, gentle 100/17, 108/ 18; meek, humble 3/4, 59/31, 98/ 34; þe **mylde** 132/32, 134/35, 135/2. þe **mylde** *pl.* 96/27, 139/3, 149/29 *n.* **milder** *comp.* 204/15

mildeliche *adv.* humbly 110/12, 135/17, 175/15; gently 194/10

mildenes(se) *n.* humility 127/33, 130/14, 134/1*, 138/15* 231/8*, (*see p. 49*), 14, **myldenese** 132/17 (*see p. 41*); graciousness 65/9, 78/ 25 *n.*

mild(e)hede *n.* humility 132/1*, 133/8* (*for these forms see p. 49*)

mildi *v. tr.* humble 177/25, 215/16, 257/31. **ymylded** *pp.* 117/6

mimþ see **nime**

min(e) see **ich**

myny *v. intr.* mine 108/24. **ymyned** *pp.* 108/33

ministre *n.* priest 237/28, 29, 32. **ministres** *pl.* ministers 236/6

ministreþ *pr. pl. tr.* administer 238/2

miracle *n.* miracle 89/32, 134/29. **miracles** *pl.* 41/30, 56/23, 213/24

mirour *n.* mirror 158/10

(þe) **misbylefde** *ppl. adj. pl.* unbelieving 252/31 *n.*

misbileue *n.* false belief 13/7

(þe) **mysbyleuinde** *ppl. adj. pl.* unbelieving 69/32

misbeleuinge *vbl. n.* unbelief 134/25

misdede *n.* misdeed 115/16, 185/27, 241/11. **misdedes, misdedis** *pl.* 16/32, 113/17, 114/6

misdo *v. intr.* do wrong, err 136/27, 151/22; *tr.* wrong 113/17, 114/23, 146/32; *huet hab(b)e ich (him)* ~ what wrong have I done (him)? 69/ 17, 269/25: **misdeþ** *pr. 3 sg.* 94/23, 114/21 *n.*, 115/34. **misdoþ** *pl.* 100/ 20. **misdo** *subj. sg.* 146/32. *pp.* 113/ 18, 114/8*

misdoere *n.* wrong-doer 133/17. **misdoeres** *pl.* 8/23

misdoinge *vbl. n.* wrong-doing 157/7

mysfalles see **misual**

mysgeþ *pr. 3 sg. intr.* goes astray 94/ 24

misleueþ *pr. pl. intr.* disbelieve 180/ 26

misliki *v. tr./intr.* displease 257/35

misnimynge *vbl. n.* erring 109/27, 160/19

misnimþ *pr. 3 sg. intr.* makes a mistake, errs 83/23, 160/20. **misnimeþ** *pl.* 160/23. **mysnyme** *subj. sg.* 55/11

mispayþ *pr. 3 sg. tr./intr.* displeases 50/30, 211/1

misprayseþ *pr. 3 sg. tr.* dispraises 136/34, 143/13

misret *pr. 3 sg. tr.* advises badly 184/ 31

missayþ, missede see **miszigge**

misserued *pp.* served badly 20/25

missigginge *vbl. n.* slander 65/29. **myssigginges** *pl.* 66/8

misual *n.* misfortune 30/7, 86/28, 182/19. **mysfalles** *pl.* 84/19

misualle *subj. sg. intr.* fall out amiss 193/19

miswent *pr. 3 sg. tr.* turns aside 45/ 28; perverts 62/15. **miswendeþ** *pl.* 40/5, 67/1; deflect 22/24; abuse 52/22; misrepresent 136/25. **miswende** *imp. sg. refl.* turn aside 253/ 18. **miswent** *pp. tr.* perverted 18/32, 27/9, 82/19; *ppl. adj.* deranged 18/33

miszigge *v. tr.* slander 256/19 (*passive*); curse 189/27; *intr.* slan-

der, speak ill 23/9, 57/1, 69/29:
missayþ *pr. 3 sg.* 8/7, 28/2, 61/23.
misziggeþ *pl.* 10/11, 70/1, 194/5.
missede *pa. t. 3 sg.* 133/3
misziggere *n.* slanderer 61/8, 256/
24, 27. **misziggeres** *pl.* 61/20, 136/
24, 177/8
mo see **moche**
moche *adj.* much 9/15, 22/24, 28/23;
great 74/10, 163/24. *pl.* 258/5,
moche(le) 47/35; many 30/26, 53/
2, 207/2. **more** *comp.* more 25/31,
73/7; greater 63/17, 244/28; more
relevant 46/16; **mo** more (*in
number*) 68/3, 73/5, 24. **meste**
superl. wk. greatest 245/16, 256/30.
pl. 148/30, **mest** 210/6ỵ; *to* ~
excessive 39/7; in excess 259/1
moche(l), mochil *adv.* much, greatly
6/3, 9/14, 57/11; very 25/1, 68/14,
228/10; dearly 194/22 *n.*, 198/1*;
pre-eminently 110/11, 185/29, 226/
6; (*mout*) often 185/35; firmly 63/
18, 98/8; *ase* ~ *ase* see **ase**; *ase* ~
worþ (*ase*) see **worþ**; *ham lokeþ* ~
see **loki**; *to* ~ exceedingly 14/32–3,
49/26, 258/8, 11. **more** *comp.* more
2/32, 7/25, 32, 40/11, 230/11 *n.*;
even more 52/33; rather 136/15,
140/34; more particularly 7/24; (*to
form a comparative*) 7/14, 18/17,
24/9; ~ **uorþ** see **uorþ**; þe ~ þet
the more 140/2, 3 (*to form a
comparative phrase*). **mest** *superl.*
most 7/2, 23/28, 182/24, 261/12,
(þe) **meste** *wk.* (*to form a super-
lative*) 16/33, 112/5, 185/1 (*see p.
70*). *pl.* 25/13, 72/5; **moche(l)** *n.* a
great quantity 162/1; *ine zuo* ~ see
z(u)o; ~ *of* a great many 167/20;
to ~ too much, excess 154/15 *n.*,
207/4, 221/22, 249/32; *to* ~ *of* all
too many 30/30. **more** *comp.* more
43/32, 47/10, 56/15; **mo** more (*in
number*) 102/26, 135/24; *do/make
zuo* ~ see **z(u)o**, ~ *of* (even)
greater 98/10–11, 234/30; *wiþoute
mo(re)* only, merely 67/20, 107/16,
108/14; without more ado 110/15,
239/30. *zuo* ~ see **z(u)o**. **mest**
superl. 90/13, 139/27, 210/5¹
mochele see **moche**
mochelhede *n.* greatness 93/9; ex-

travagance 177/15; fullness 204/1;
cf. **tomochelhede**
moder *n.* mother 8/3, 5, 6, 20/20,
193/20 *n.* **modren** *pl.* 67/27
moʒe see **may**
moyrdrer *n.* murderer 171/23
molde *n.* soil 95/6
momenettes *n. pl.* idols 239/3,
momenes 6/1
monaye *n.* money 26/7, 62/22, 152/
28; price 145/23
mone *n.* moon 82/2, 7
monek *n.* monk 165/31, 239/1, 240/7.
moneke *p.c.* 219/25. **monekes** *pl.*
267/28
mongenel *n.* mangonel 116/30
mont *n.* mount 243/20
monþe *n.* (*acc./p.c.*) month 45/24,
128/33, 173/13
more see **moche, moche(l)**
morʒen *n.* morning 46/1, 51/1, 108/
7; *to morʒe* to-morrow 157/5, 179/
31, 194/13
mori *v. tr.* multiply, augment 45/25,
79/18, 176/12. **moreþ** *pr. 3 sg.* 28/
4, 62/2. **moreþ** *pl.* 60/20, 175/25
morsel *n.* morsel 248/21. **mosseles**
pl. 56/14 (*see p. 49*)
mortyer *n.* mortar 116/28
mosseles see **morsel**
mostard *n.* mustard 143/31, 33
mot *n.* mote 175/11. **motes** *pl.* 108/11,
12
mot *v. intr.* must 52/26, 137/36, 204/
35
mous *n.* mouse 179/33
mouþ *n.* mouth 27/8, 50/5, 66/24.
mo(u)þe *p.c.* 22/9, 27/30, 34* (*see
p. 15*), 42/32, 256/4 (*see p. 15*).
mouþes *pl.* 74/17
muekliche *adv.* simply 65/7 *n.*
mueknesse *n.* simplicity 65/4 *n.*
mule *n.* mule 223/23
multepliest *pr. 2 sg. tr.* multipliest
218/2. **multiplieþ** *3 sg.* 190/1
musi *v. intr.* marvel 47/14; amuse
oneself 231/32. **musy** *subj. sg.*
spend time 104/21 *n.*

N

naʒt *n.* anything 61/18 *n.*; naught,
nothing 6/14, 62/32, 127/21. **naʒte**

na3t (cont.):
p.c. 91/33, 104/7, 144/12; deþ to ~
see do; makeþ a ~ makes light of
59/30; of ~ in no way 156/4
na3t adj. worthless 165/6
na(u)3t, nat adv. not 6/28, 120/4 n.,
156/4* (for forms without t see pp.
49, 53), 175/21*, 222/9*; not at all
33/32, 90/11, 254/8; ne . . . na3t
not 9/4, 10/18, 45/11*, 196/27*,
197/17* (see note to 40/5); ~ wiþoute
more see moche(l); ne is ~ is void
49/9, 225/34; ~ uor þan (neporquant,
nekedent) nevertheless 81/1–2, 90/
34; nes ~ (ne fu pas) 71/16
na3ti v. tr. deny 9/14. ⟨na3t⟩ pr. pl.
39/28 n.
nay adv. no 190/29
nayle n. nail 43/14
ynayled pp. nailed 263/3
naked adj. naked 101/32, 128/1, 140/
20. nakede p.c. 244/35
nakediiche adv. openly 174/23
name n. name 6/13, 25/31, 99/35.
names pl. 103/16, 19
nameco(u)þhede n. renown, repu-
tation 25/21, 23 (see p. 16)
nameliche adv. especially, in particu-
lar 21/24, 44/13, 55/32
nanmore, nam(m)ore adv. any-
more 27/3 n., 49/7, 187/29, 269/27;
n. ~ ne is betuene there is no
difference between 270/1 n.; ~ ne is
of guodes there are no more good
things 89/19
nase n. nose 154/20, 177/11, 204/6
nat see na(u)3t
naturel adj. natural 18/25
naþemo adv. furthermore 41/16 n.
nawerelles adv. nowhere else 210/
27
ne adv. not 1/15, 5/20, 6/12; nor, or
1/15, 5/21, 8/5, 128/10, 141/22 n.,
241/31 n.; conj. ne . . . (ne) . . . ne
neither . . . (nor) . . . nor, either . . .
(or) . . . or 6/16, 10/7, 155/5, ne . . .
ne . . . no 241/31 n.; ne . . . na3t
see na(u)3t; ~ þet (ne que) any
more than 237/17
nebsseft n. face 265/21 n.
ne3(3)ebo(u)res, ne3ybores n. pl.
neighbours 30/16, 36/32, 38/3, 33,
ney3bores 10/22 n. Cf. p. 16

ne3en num. nine 45/23
ne3ende ord. num. ninth 10/20, 13/27,
35/1
ne3lecþ pr. 3 sg. intr. approaches
105/31 n.
nelle v. tr. will not, does not wish to
33/28, 69/2, 150/21; future auxil-
iary will not 173/5; nelle pr. 1 sg.
56/11, 218/3, 260/14. nele 3 sg.
8/14, 31/34, 65/11 n. nolleþ pl.
35/27, 38/6, 39/4. nolle subj. sg.
79/4, 139/21, 164/21. pl. 120/13,
209/31. noldest pa. t. 2 sg. 146/36.
nolde 3 sg. 116/13, 173/23, 222/29.
nolden pl. 64/26, 132/21, 192/29
nemeþ see nime
nemni v. tr. call, name, mention 49/
23, 26 (passive), 57/28, 164/14.
nemneþ pr. 3 sg. 103/34. ynemned
pp. 66/33, 79/13, 114/30
nenne see no(n)
nere, nes see nis; ne(s) . . . na3t see
na(u)3t
nesshede n. delicacy 267/32
nesssse adj. soft 153/20
nest n. nest 61/31, 178/22
net(t)len n. pl. nettles 156/28, 230/22
nette n. (p.c.) net 154/33, 170/25.
nettes pl. 77/22
neþ pr. 3 sg. tr. has not 84/7, 210/8
neuerte adv. never yet 99/3
neure adv. never 26/16, 28/32, 79/7
neuremo(r) adv. nevermore, never,
ever 71/29, 107/15, 142/18, 228/30;
no more 141/22
neuu n. nephew 48/28
newe adj. new, newly made 7/21, 97/
11, 101/11, 116/11. newene acc.
masc. 162/1. þe newen p.c. 99/5 n.
ynewed pp. renewed 107/17
newehedes n. pl. novelties 151/4
nhesseþ pr. 3 sg. tr. softens 94/32
nhicke, nykke n. neck 135/25, 138/1,
216/30 n. nykken pl. 56/13 n.
nhote n. nut 143/27
nice adj. stupid 59/7, 259/14
nied n. function 95/15; hardship
199/2; need, necessity 114/24*,
140/21 n., 168/22 n., 186/21, (nede)
255/25; pl. business, occupations
7/7, 31/29 n., 199/14, 214/1; ate ~
in time of need 149/1, 186/21–2; do
(ine) hare/hire/his ~ (set sb. to) work

for sb. 36/31–2 *n.*, 35–6, 39/6, 206/
23; take advantage 90/30–1; con-
duct business 90/34; *is* ~ is neces-
sary 42/21, 151/22, 156/20, ⟨niede⟩
201/5 (*see p. 57*); *ine* ~ occupied
142/19, 206/20; *out of* ~ beyond
what is necessary 48/1: niede *acc.*
90/31, 34, 95/15. *p.c.* 7/31, 30/34,
149/1. niedes *pl.* 52/12, 184/17,
215/12

nieduol *adj.* in need 36/7, 35; people
in need 193/8; needy 194/16;
necessary 112/18, 134/15, 151/21:
þe nieduolle *wk.* 194/16. *pl.* 95/4,
5, 110/9

nieȝ *adj.* close 49/2; near 224/21,
264/18. nier *comp.* 234/33. nixte
superl. pl. 122/6 *n.*; nixte *n.*
neighbour 148/11. *gen.* 11/7 *n. pl.*
30/17 *n.*, 78/12

nieȝ *adv.* nearly 51/10, 76/20, 87/
2 *n.*, 6. nier *comp.* more closely
261/15, 16

niȝt *n.* night 52/12, 22* (*see p. 50*),
71/31. niȝte *p.c.* 52/19; *of* ~ noc-
turnal 92/5; *adv.* 71/33, 157/20; *to*
~ see toniȝt

nykeren *n. pl.* sirens 61/9, 11

nykke see nhicke

nime *v. tr.* take 6/12, 37/4, 54/21;
undertake 166/25; take possession
of, possess 30/4, 133/31, 144/7;
overcome 248/26; catch, capture
37/12, 227/22, 238/31; *refl.* begin
68/19; *intr.* partake, receive 93/7,
207/35; ~ *a wycked wyl* be angry
108/28–9 (cf. wyl); ~ *þane dyaþ*
die 30/1; ~ *yeme* consider 24/16 *n.*,
54/32, 176/24: nimene *infl. inf.*
9/23, 165/11, 195/30. nymst *pr. 2
sg.* 110/35. nimþ *3 sg.* 24/16, 50/20,
207/10 *n.*, ⟨niymþ⟩ 68/19 (*see p.
20*), ⟨mimþ⟩ 22/3. nimeþ *pl.* 35/7,
38/31, 40/2, nemeþ 92/17. nime
subj. sg. 55/17, 148/11, 155/13. nim
imp. sg. 54/32, 89/34, 114/5.
nimeþ *pl.* 260/5, 265/27. nom *pa.
t. 3 sg.* 45/33, 118/28, 189/23.
nome *pl.* 87/23, 156/8. (y)nome
pp. 45/28, 80/4, 204/191; *ppl. adj.*
135/24

nimere *n.* consumer 248/32

niminge *vbl. n.* prowess 164/17

(*emprise*); undertaking, enterprise
21/31, 162/25. niminges *pl.* 183/
35; exactions 39/8; *yleaue* ~ see
yleaue-nymynge

nis *pr. 3 sg. intr.* is not 51/3, 64/8, 83/
14. nere *pa. t. 2 sg.* 20/34. nes *3 sg.*
26/15, 66/6, 71/16. nere *pl.* 73/33.
subj. sg. 86/9, 89/33, 98/13. *pl.* 52/5

nyteþ see not

niþing *n.* niggard 139/5. niþinges *pl.*
154/31

nixt *prep.* next to, close to 182/35,
263/35, 266/30

nixte see nieȝ *adj.*

no(n) *adj.* no, any (*for the distribution
of forms with and without* n *see p. 51f*)
6/20, 9/7, 11/16, 261/34. nenne *acc.
masc.* 8/19, 30/27, 48/6. none *acc.*
9/23, 10/5, 29/33. *gen.* 267/36, *dat.*
213/34. *p.c.* 64/26, 107/24, 124/13,
nenne 168/4, 256/15 (*see p. 73*).
none *pl.* 203/5, 211/22; *nenne
oþrenne* anyone else 175/5, 237/26;
~ þing nothing, anything 33/33,
65/23, 69/5, 125/17 *n.* none þinge
p.c. 125/7; ~ þing *adv.* not at all
12/20, 187/26; non *pron.* no one,
anyone, none 7/16, 20/21, 83/21.
nenne *acc. masc.* 10/8, 22/30, 48/12.
none *acc.* 49/8. nonen *dat.* 134/24.
p.c. 68/29, 120/6. none *pl.* 60/25,
218/3

no *conj.* see ne

noble *adj.* excellent, illustrious 25/1,
87/20, 112/21. nobleste *superl. wk.*
92/23

nobleliche *adv.* grandly 55/18

noblesse *n.* noble birth 20/14, 22/15,
24/5

noyse *n.* outcry 66/2. noyses *pl.*
clamour 215/8, 266/8

nolle, nolleþ, nolde see nelle

nom(e), ynome see nime

nombres *n. pl.* numbers 234/12

non *n.* noon 52/13

non *adj.* see no(n)

non *adv.* no 133/21, 262/2

norice *n.* nurse 161/18. noriches *pl.*
60/8

norici, norissi *v. tr.* nourish, foster
9/15, 154/5; *refl.* take nourishment
246/13: norisseþ, norisset *pr. 3
sg.* 21/22, 83/5, 89/6. norisseþ *pl.*

norici, norissi (*cont.*):
105/19, 204/25, 205/16. **norissy**
subj. sg. 127/28 *n.* **norissinde** *ppl.*
adj. 95/6, 112/36. **norissede** *pa. t.*
pl. 96/12. **ynorissed** *pp.* 130/33,
205/10

norissinge *vbl. n.* nourishment 112/
35

norture *n.* nourishment 113/2
norþ *n.* north 124/23
norþene *adj.* northern 256/25 (*see*
p. 49)

not *pr. 1 sg. tr.* know not 189/10,
218/29, 264/19. *3 sg.* 9/30, 25/5,
64/10, 129/18 *n.* **nyteþ** *pl.* 72/33

notaryes *n. pl.* notaries 40/8
note *n.* profit 159/26, 233/35, 247/11
notes *n. pl.* musical notes 105/13, 15,
118/10

noteþ *pr. 3 sg. intr.* flourishes 260/16
noty *v. tr.* set (to music) 118/10
noþer *conj.* neither 130/1, 269/20
noþing see **no(n)**
nou *adv.* now 20/10, 27/27, 53/24; *n.*
59/13

nouis *adj.* inexperienced 155/29.
nouices *pl.* 155/20

O

o(n) *adj.* one 12/1, 45/32, 46/7, 109/
11 *n.*, 202/31 *n.* (*for* on *before*
consonants see p. 51 f.). **enne** *acc.*
masc. 91/6, 145/9, 241/9. **one** *acc.*
52/7, 86/8, 145/9. **one** *p.c.* 40/11,
45/24, 55/17, 107/2 *n.*, 153/8 *n.*,
enne 249/22 (see p. *73*); **on(e)** *pron.*
one (man) 9/10, 41/33, 56/5, 66/9,
140/34; **þe on(e)** 17/32, 25/15,
86/2. **one(n)** *p.c.* 91/8, 102/4, 158/
11, 205/34, ⟨onenen⟩ 91/6 *n.*, **enne**
102/32, 129/9; ~ *to/wyþ* ~ tête à
tête 205/34, 206/2; **þe on . . . þe**
oþer/oþre(n) *recipr.* each other (i)
with antecedent pron. 186/17–18,
221/7 (ii) *without antecedent pron.*,
43/19, 114/32 (*see note to 114/31*),
147/28–9, 148/27

o(f) *prep.* of 1/7, *143/31* (MS. *os*), 33,
183/27; from 7/10, 46/26, 151/25;
to 60/10, 107/2; for, on account of
7/27, 27/20, 81/14; concerning 14/
28, 76/29, 78/22; on 55/17, 68/21.

72/16; in 38/12, 42/26–7, 54/3; in
regard to 24/15, 30/35, 199/14; at
47/11, 86/33; with, by means of
46/22, 50/2, 166/24; by 191/19,
203/10; *with infinitive* to 127/13,
133/32; anything of (*du*) 177/31;
some (*de*) 37/18–19; because of
17/6 *n.*

o *int.* oh! 93/8, 228/3
obedience *n.* obedience 140/28, 141/7
yobliged *pp.* committed 113/24;
constrained 238/11

ocseþ see **acsy**
ofacsed *pp.* investigated 152/8, 153/26
ofdret *ppl. adj.* afraid 266/2
office *n.* office, function 124/25, 155/
20, 235/14. **offices** *pl.* functions
50/6, 124/26, 148/2; duties, 122/
13; *ine* ~ officials 122/12

officials *n. pl.* officials 37/24, 67/30
offre *imp. sg. tr.* offer 194/29. **offrede**
pa. t. 3 sg. 193/30

offrendes *n. pl.* offerings 41/19
ofgoinge *vbl. n.* desert 215/24
ofguo *pp.* deserved 13/24, 14/15
ofhealde *v. tr.* retain, keep 24/8, 37/5,
38/9, **ofhyealde** 9/24, 78/21; re-
strain 254/29: **ofhalt** *pr. 3 sg.* 99/2,
178/1, 204/30. **ofhealdeþ** *pl.* 39/4*
(*see p. 49*), **ofhyealdeþ** 35/27, 38/5,
78/7, **ofhyaldeþ** 41/16. **ofhild** *pa. t.*
3 sg. 190/11. **ofhealde** *pp.* 254/18

ofhealdinge *vbl. n.* retaining 34/27
of(f)ringe *vbl. n.* offering 194/30,
229/20

ofserueþ *pr. 3 sg. intr.* is deserving
222/25 *n.*, 33; tr. **ofserued** *pp.*
deserved 171/17

ofseruinge *vbl. n.* desert, merit 101/
30, 114/26, 270/26. **ofseruinges**
pl. merit 209/33

oftake *v. tr.* detect 43/14
ofte *adj.* (*pl.*) many 20/23, 45/27, 249/
36

ofte *adv.* often 18/13, 20/10, 24/14
ofteziþes see **ofte** and **ziþe, ziþes**
oftyened *pp.* made angry 66/15
oȝe(n) *adj.* own 17/5, 48/23, 136/15;
personal, of one's own 109/24, 241/
20; (*substantival uses*) one's own
possession 9/27, 21/33, 39/30. *pl.*
one's own people 166/16; *his* ~
harm harm to himself 63/3; *of zuo*

GLOSSARY

~ *wytte* so self-opinionated 253/
1–2 *n.*: oʒene *acc.* 109/24. *p.c.* 253/2.
wk. 22/9, 28/33, 47/32. *pl.* 33/3, 139/
28, 179/14
oʒeneres *n. pl.* owners of property 37/
34
oʒninge *vbl. n.* holding of property
37/35
oʒþ *pr. 3 sg. tr.* owns 9/25
oyle, uile, vile *n.* oil 93/16, 21, 22,
oly 136/10 *n.*
oynement *n.* ointment 93/28
oksen see **oxe**
oly see **oyle**
olyfont see **elifans**
on see **o(n)**
onarmed *ppl. adj.* unarmed 170/31
onbynde *v. intr.* unbind 172/17.
onbynt *pr. 3 sg.* 97/16; *tr.* **onbyn-
deþ** *pl.* settle (a lawsuit) 40/14
onblissede *ppl. adj.* (*pl.*) unconse-
crated 41/13
onboʒsam *adj.* disobedient 21/7
onboʒsamnesse *n.* disobedience 8/
17, 33/28, 67/32
onchargeþ *pr. 3 sg. tr.* acquits 97/17
onclenlich *adj*, impure *42/33* (MS.
oimchenlich; see note to 74/6).
onclenliche *p.c.* 42/34
onclennesse *n.* moral impurity 203/
25
onconynghede *n.* ignorance 40/4
onconnynde *ppl. adj.* ignorant 59/32
onconnyndehede *n.* indiscretion 33/
11
onconnynge *vbl. n.* ignorance 131/10
oncouþe *adj.* unknown 253/28; (þe)
oncouþe stranger(s) 37/18, 193/10,
253/32
ondelfþ *pr. 3 sg. tr.* digs up 61/24
onder, under *prep.* under 12/25, 15/
13, *221/35*. cf. **þeronder**
onderbere *v. tr.* endure 84/16
onderlinges *n. pl.* subordinates 39/7,
182/16
ondernime *v. tr.* undertake 83/19,
123/18. **ondernimþ** *pr. 3 sg.* takes
onderstonde, understonde *v. tr.*
know, understand, understand the
nature of 74/24 *n.*, 28 *n.*, 90/10,
97/6 *n.*, 99/2, 123/28 *n.*, 147/5 *n.*,
245/12 *n.*; know how to 212/27;
intend 199/25, 215/9; comprehend

8/9, 14/5; interpret 57/24* (*see p.
49*); suppose 60/23; *intr.* under-
stand 24/7, 72/2, 209/1 *n.*; have
understanding 56/32; give thought,
attention 198/5, 199/10, 214/28;
þet is to ~ that is to say 6/25, 12/18,
13/5: **onderstonde** *pr. 1 sg.* 131/
30. **onderstanst** *2 sg.* 106/20,
270/10* (*see pp. 53 & 97, n. 4*).
onderstant *3 sg.* 65/5, 143/35,
196/4 *n.*, 211/2. **onderstondeþ** *pl.*
77/29, 146/33*, 148/7*, 160/27.
onderstonde *subj. sg.* 152/12. *pl.*
74/24 *n.* **onderstand** *imp. sg.* 108/
3, 127/34, 129/31, 160/15* *n.* (*see
p. 50*). **onderstode** *pa. t. subj. sg.*
138/2. **onderstonde** *pp.* 57/24* *n.*
(*see p. 49*), 99/33, 182/1
onderston(n)dinge *n.* understand-
ing, comprehension 4/9*, 56/33,
105/34* (*see note to 57/24*), 113/
5 *n.*, 120/25 (*see note to 74/24*);
memory 24/8 *n.*, 78/25; intention,
motive 25/24, 159/16*, 196/11,
222/16. **onderstondinges** *pl.* in-
tentions 152/11
onderuonge *v. tr.* receive 14/22, 32/
16, 68/35, 158/17*; accept 33/31,
39/35; undertake 127/13: **onder-
uangst** *pr. 2 sg.* 208/9*. **onder-
uangþ** *3 sg.* 18/16*, 19, 65/5, 100/
21*, 105/29, 111/16*, 158/7*.
onderuongeþ *pl.* 38/17, 42/16,
119/11. **onderuonge** *subj. sg.* 158/
31, 262/17. **onderuongeþ** *imp. pl.*
198/24, 265/36. **onderuinge** *pa. t.
2 sg.* 20/34, 21/1. **onderuing** *3 sg.*
5/3. **onderuinge** *pa. t.* 101/36, 267/
12. **onderuonge** *pp.* 115/26, 119/6,
235/10; *ppl. adj.* 120/19
onderuonginge *vbl. n*, receipts 37/
23, 173/1
onderuot *adv.* underfoot; *deþ* ~
despises 85/3 *n.*, 185/22, 204/33
onderzekþ *pr. 3 sg. tr.* examines 184/
23
ondo *v. tr.* separate 107/22. **ondeþ**
pr. 3 sg. opens 189/15; destroys
16/20 *n.* **ondo** *pp.* 136/8 *n.*; loo-
sened 106/15
one *adv.* alone 103/36, 142/29, 163/30
one(n) see **o(n)**
ones *adv.* once 73/17

(h)oneste *adj.* honourable, seemly, virtuous 45/11, 96/10, 214/29 *n.*, 222/7

onestete *n.* virtue 53/8, 54/7, 224/23

oneþ *pr. 3 sg. tr.* unites 88/33; *refl.* **oneþ** *pl.* 219/27

onhede *n.* unity 79/32; solitude 142/17, 29

oninge *vbl. n.* union, concord 65/26, 123/21, 135/19 *n.*; integrity 153/23.

onynges *pl.* unity 67/2

onioyni *v. tr.* detach 107/9

onkende *adj.* unnatural 77/14, 188/13

onknawyndliche *adv.* unwittingly 175/34

onleak *pa. t. 3 sg. intr.* opened 67/11

onlepi *adj.* singular 21/29; a single, one 13/31, 32, 71/6; only 263/1. **ennelepi** *acc. masc.* 75/13, 145/33. **onelepi** *acc.* 125/2, 155/18. *p.c.* 73/29, 104/9, 145/16

onlepihede *n.* singularity 21/25

onlepiliche *adv.* simply, only 55/26, 76/11, 109/24* (*see note to* 74/6), 114/35; with singleness of purpose? 153/22 *n.*

onlyche *adv.* only 265/19

onlosthede, onlusthede *n.* listlessness, *accidia* 31/4, 163/38, 206/25

onlosti *adj.* slack, listless 174/11, 263/31. þe onlosti 170/17

onlusthede see **onlosthede**

onneaþe *adv.* hardly, scarcely 15/21, 17/20, 28/28, **onnyeaþe** 174/16; reluctantly **onneaþe** 70/26, **onneþe** 152/27

onpayþ *pr. 3 sg. tr.* displeases 50/14

onriȝt *n.* unrighteousness 160/30; wrong 221/8

onriȝtuol(l)e *adj.* (*pl.*) unjust 39/8, 270/15

onspekynde *ppl. adj.* ineffable 266/18

onssriuel *adj.* negligent 32/17 *n.*

ontodelinde *ppl. adj.* indivisible 266/18

ontrewe *adj.* disloyal 18/7, 32/17 *n.*; dishonest 36/6, 37/20, 62/18

ontreweliche *adv.* dishonestly 44/23

ontrewþe, ontreuþe *n*, disloyalty 17/23, 18/3, 189/27

onþank *n.* ill-will 69/15

onþolyinde *ppl. adj.* intolerable 264/34; 265/6

onwyt *n.* madness 82/3, 27

onwythede *n.* madness 19/8

onwytinde *pr. p.* without the knowledge of 37/5

onwoneþ *pr. 3 sg. tr.* disaccustoms 32/22

onworþ *adj.* displeasing 49/31; contemptible, mean 132/24, 140/8, 215/32; *habbe* ~ see **habbe**

onworþhede *n.* disdain, contempt 17/24, 20/3, 63/33

onworþi *adj.* despicable 259/11

onworþi *v. tr.* despise 22/18, 93/12, 102/21; degrade 248/34; humble 215/28: **onworþest** *pr. 2 sg.* 20/12 *n.*, **onworþeþ** *3 sg.* 8/6, 34/3, 143/13. *pl.* 79/11, 161/32, 165/23. **onworþi** *subj. sg.* 195/33, 196/22. **onworþe** *imp. sg.* 196/23. **onworþede** *pa. t. 3 sg.* 175/14 *n.*, 189/5, 196/29, 208/19. *pl.* 72/7, 77/19, 126/5

onworþlych *adj.* contemptible 132/35

onworþnesse *n.* contempt, irreverence 9/2, 19/35, 20/22* (*see p. 50*), 20/23 *n.*, 21/2, 196/34* (*see p. 50*)

onwri *v. tr.* uncover, reveal 174/25, 32. **onwriþ** *pr. pl.* 58/1. **onwri** *subj. sg.* 174/29. **onwriȝe** *ppl. adj.* 88/17, 112/16, 244/35

onzaused *pp.* disintegrated 184/11 *n.*

onzyginde *ppl. adj.* ineffable 268/27

op *adv.* up 240/1, 246/21; ~ *arist* see **arise**; *ydo* ~ see **do**; ~ *let* see **oplet**; ~ *yerne* see **yerne**

oparizinge *vbl. n.* resurrection 213/18

opbereþ *pr. 3 pl. tr.* overpower 30/4 *n.*

ope *prep.* upon 15/1, 211/18, 212/15; over 54/17, 68/5, 118/10; against 34/16, 39/12, 58/26, ⟨opo⟩ 39/18 *n.*; in 39/15; ~ *his simple word* by his word alone 134/17; ~ *þe woke* of the previous week 7/24 *n.*

open *adj.* open 37/8, 188/2, 249/7. **opene** *pl.* 204/19, 231/26, 257/1

openi *v. intr.* open 130/9, 208/1. **openeþ** *pr. 3 sg. tr.* 129/14, 218/34, 219/12. **openede** *pa. t. 3 sg.* 96/24, 249/17

openliche *adv.* openly, plainly 65/2, 73/11, 80/20

ophebbeþ *pr. 3 sg. tr.* exalts 217/32

opinions *n. pl.* opinions 69/22
oplet *pr. 3 sg. tr.* wearies 33/12 *n.*
opnyme *v. tr.* undertake 83/34.
opnome *ppl. adj.* possessed 143/1
opniminge *vbl. n.* presumption 21/16 *n.*; undertaking 22/2, 83/26, 84/1. **opnymynges** *pl.* 83/28
oppe *adj.* open 255/33, 35
opriȝt *adv.* upright 56/29
oprisinge *vbl. n.* resurrection 227/32
opweninge *vbl. n.* pride 21/16.
opwexeþ *pr. pl. intr.* spring up 75/6 *n.*
ordayni *v. tr.* organize, regulate 94/19, 153/31, 155/1, 5 *n.*; control 263/21; direct 123/14; decide 29/17; make provision for 152/24: **ordayneþ** *pr. 3 sg.* 29/17, 153/1. *pl.* 125/22, 261/7. **ordayny** *subj. sg.* 263/21. **ordaynede** *pa. t. 3 sg.* 7/12. **yordayned** *ppl. adj.* 24/11, 153/15, 250/15
ordeneliche *adv.* in an ordered manner 125/29, 151/29
ordinance *n.* decree 124/34
ordine (*French*) *pp.* well-regulated 153/16, 259/16, 35
ordre *n.* (holy) orders 14/8, 48/7, 225/32; rank, order 16/14, 119/28, 124/17; state 48/24 *n.* **ordres** *pl.* orders 41/35, 266/34, 267/3
oreyson(e)s *n. pl.* prayers 51/5, 139/25
or(r)ible *adj.* horrible, terrible 43/5, 137/22
orped *adj.* valiant 183/6
os see **we**
ost *n.* host 67/14, 146/4, 204/20
oþ *n.* oath 64/6, 65/5. **oþe** *p.c.* 65/20. **oþes** *pl.* 64/14; promises 152/3
oþer *adj.* second, other 6/11, 72/28, 76/26; any other 6/16, 19 n., 8/21; secondary 209/29; *pron.* other 16/22 *n.*, 199/26, 257/21; the other 154/9; another 18/29, 24/10, 38/26; *pl.* other things 64/13, 107/15; *and* ~ etcetera 269/19; *of on and of* ~ from both 40/16–17; *þe* ~ *byeþ þet* there are those who 78/4: *adj.* **oþre** *acc.* 66/30 (*cf. p. 72*), 211/6. *p.c.* 38/20, 104/3, 108/13. *wk.* 30/3, 35/24, 44/21. *acc.* 89/9,

oþrene 87/14, 180/18. *p.c.* 180/16.
oþ(e)re *pl.* 23/13, 26/14, 224/7; *pron.* þe **oþre** 42/24, 62/5 *n.*, 67/24, 86/2. *acc.* 68/1, 147/19 (*see note to* 147/20), **oþren(n)e** 66/20, 175/5, 222/21. **oþren** *acc.*/ *dat.* 46/12, 61/35, 66/9, 68/18. **oþres** *gen.* 27/1, 136/16, 175/12. **oþere, oþre(n)** *p.c.* 40/16, 43/19, 225/11. **oþ(e)re** *pl.* 21/27, 97/16, 137/18. **oþren** *acc.*/*dat.*/*p.c.* 20/17, 27/3, 39/30, 235/20. *For reciprocal uses see* ayder, ech, on
oþer *conj.* or 6/18 *n.*, 8/7, 19/21, 21/19 *n.*, 217/11; ~ . . . ~ either . . . or 19/21–5, 25/8–9, 27/17–19, 30/6*
oþerhalf see **ha(l)f**
oþerhuil *adv.* sometimes 29/34, 30/4, 31/29; often 158/15 *n.*; at some time 269/31
oþerlaker *comp. adv.* otherwise 11/28, 94/9, 114/17; alternatively 81/6; ~ . . . ~ in one way . . . in another way 245/28–9
ouer *prep.* beyond 170/5; over 15/33, 182/22, 249/1; above 266/26, 271/8
oueral *adv.* everywhere, always 25/3, 77/27, 90/32; especially 141/14
ouercome *v. tr.* overcome, subdue 15/3, 84/1, 181/7 (*passive*), 249/11; win 170/15, 180/20, 21; *intr.* overcome 117/24, 170/11; *yelt . . . ~ to* admits defeat by 253/23: **ouercomþ** *pr. 3 sg.* 149/30, 167/6, 181/16* (*see note to* 40/5), **ouercomeþ** *180/20. pl.* 117/24, 170/11. **ouercom** *pa. t. 3 sg.* 169/35, 219/8, 249/16. **ouercome** *pp.* 124/15, 125/27, 252/14
ouercominge *vbl. n.* victory 15/32, 169/28, 235/1. **ouercom(e)ing-(g)es** *pl.* 169/24, 170/9*
ouerdede *n.* excess 55/11, 258/5, 260/2
ouerdoinge *vbl. n.* excess 258/32, 34, 260/7. **ouerdoinges** *pl.* 258/5, 260/9
ouergeþ *pr. 3 sg. tr.* excels 112/31; transcends 261/32; exceeds 252/29; overcomes 34/5. **ouerguoþ** *pl.* 212/10

oueryernþ *pr. 3 sg. intr.* transgresses 223/28 *n.*

ouerliche *adj.(acc.)* supreme 123/23, 24

ouerling *n.* superior 147/10; prelate 141/8. **ouerlinges** *pl.* 8/12, 122/19; overlords 182/15

ouermaistri *v. tr.* overpower 15/3

ouerþrauþ *pr. 3 sg. tr.* overthrows 168/12. **ouerþraweþ** *pl.* pervert 136/25. **ouerþrawe** *pp.* overthrown 15/15

ouerwenere *n.* arrogant person 21/26, 22/17* *n.*, 27. **ouerweneres** *pl.* 59/22

ouerweninde *ppl. adj.* arrogant 169/27

ouerweninge *vbl. n.* arrogance 17/24, 29/9, 253/2

ouet *n.* fruit 262/30, 267/12, 271/9

oule *n.* owl 27/4

(h)oure *n.* time 51/28; hour 19/8, 173/30, 219/14. **oures** *pl.* 112/12; *in time and in* ∼ at the proper time 54/9

oure *pron.* see **we**

ournemens *n. pl.* ornaments 140/15

ous see **we**

ousze(l)lue *refl. pron. p.c.* ourselves 265/30, 32, 33

out(e) of *prep. phr.* out of 6/18, 14/32, 18/31, 74/1* *(see p. 28, n. 9)*; outside 65/14; ∼ *nyede* beyond what is necessary 48/1

outguoinge *vbl. n.* escape 32/4; departure 190/4

outkestinge *vbl. n.* offshoot 22/16. **outkestinges** *pl.* 35/5

outnime *prep.* except 250/11 *n.*; **outynome** except for 221/6, 17

out(t)rage *n.* extravagance 54/18, 110/17; **outrages** *pl.* 19/5

oxe *n.* ox 111/12, 192/13. **oksen** *pl.* 243/10

oxy, oxeþ see **acsy**

P

paciense *n.* patience 33/34, 167/6, 13

paen *n.* pagan 114/28. **payenes** *gen.* 239/2. **paenes, payens** *pl.* 126/9, 19, 235/28; *adj.* 12/26, **payen** 165/9

paye *v. tr.* pay 39/4, 138/1; discharge 163/11, 169/13; satisfy 249/24; please 157/8 *n.*, 216/17; *refl.* be glad, take pleasure in 59/14 *n.*, 85/23; *intr.* pay 137/34: **payþ** *pr. 3 sg.* 36/16 *n.*, 51/17, 65/25, 26, **payeþ** 184/15. **payeþ** *pl.* 41/19, 223/32. **ypayd** *pp.* 50/13, 178/3, 187/12

payne *n.* trouble, endeavour 83/27, 88/5; *zette* ∼ *see* **zette**

paynest *pr. 2 sg. refl.* takest trouble, dost endeavour 100/32. **paineþ** *3 sg.* 28/18, 141/34, 238/22; *tr.* exerts himself 77/7 *n.* pains 66/9 *n.*

paynge *vbl. n.* payment 35/10. **payinges** *pl.* pleasures 216/18 *n.*

payre *n. pl.* pairs 258/35

pais *n.* peace 7/13, 43/33, 248/6. **paise, pese** *p.c.* 85/21, 94/2, 161/24, 250/13

paysible *adj.* peaceable 96/34, 261/5, 6

palme *n.* palm 131/33

paneworþes *n. pl.* pennyworths, bargains 23/29, 37/2, 90/33

panne *n.* pan 23/1, 111/33

pans see **peni**

papelard *n.* sycophant 26/23, 54/28

par see **auenture**

paradis *n.* paradise 14/15, 31/27, 50/28

parfit *adj.* perfect 185/6, 241/22, 246/31. **parfite** *wk.* 246/33. **þe parfite** *pl.* 247/10. **parfiter** *comp.* 238/29

parfitliche *adv.* perfectly 15/25, 107/28 (MS. *parfithliche*), 144/20

parosses *n. pl.* parishes 42/11

part *n,* part 102/35, 110/22

parteþ *pr. pl. intr.* participate 38/12

parti see **toparti**

parties *n. pl.* parts 155/3

partiner *n.* partner 256/19

pasi *v. tr.* pass through, pass over 72/12, 112/2; exceed, transgress 223/5, 258/4; surpass 99/8, 100/30, 112/30; last 191/14; *intr.* pass away 214/17; pass through, pass over 135/15, 252/1; be supreme 66/33; *ppl. adj.* transitory 209/5; past 59/10: **paci** *pr. 1 sg.* 252/1. **paseþ** *3 sg.* 81/35, 123/19, 247/18.

pl. 135/15. **pasinde** *pr. p.* 209/5.
pasede *pa. t. 3 sg.* 80/5. **ypased**
pp. 113/23, 152/21
pasindeliche *adv.* temporarily 172/31
paske *n.* Passover 133/20
passion *n.* passion 12/24, 107/3,
142/13
pater noster *n.* Pater Noster 2/35–6,
3/1–16
patremoyne *n.* patrimony 41/15
patriarche *n.* patriarch 137/11.
patriarkes *pl.* 267/10
patroyllart *n.* pidgin English 211/4
ypeynt *ppl. adj.* painted 26/2
peni *n.* penny 1/15, 23/28, 24/14.
pans *pl.* pennies, money 23/33,
42/3, 190/7
penonce *n.* penance 29/17, 33/29,
49/31. **penonces** *pl.* 26/4, 31/18,
181/3
pere *n.* pear 208/31
peregrinages *n. pl.* pilgrimages
187/17
perfeccion *n.* perfection 79/33, 98/21,
182/26
perfect *adj.* perfect 127/18
peril *n.* peril 16/34, 32/33, 83/27.
perils *pl.* 30/24, 77/32, 78/9
perilous *adj.* perilous 22/30, 28/28,
58/4. **peril(o)use** *wk.* 16/33, 112/3
perilousliche *adv.* perilously 254/19
perle *n.* pupil 158/18
perseuerance *n.* perseverance 168/
23, 208/4
perseuerantliche *adv.* perseveringly
210/11
persone *n.* person 12/11, 132/35,
259/5; **persones** *pl.* 12/1, 40/22,
48/4; *to hare ~* in their own
persons 35/25
pese see **pais**
pesen *n. pl.* peas 120/1
pette *n.* (*p.c.*) pit 207/9
peþ *n.* path 127/16, 185/13. **peþe** *p.c.*
32/9, 185/21
philosophes see **filozofe**
pic *n.* pick 108/23, 116/30
pietaille *n.* rabble 112/25 *n.*
ypiȝt *ppl. adj.* fixed 199/19, 253/2
pilgrim *n.* pilgrim 86/34, 253/28. **pil-
ȝrim(e)s** *pl.* 39/2, 253/29, 254/1
pine *n.* trouble 32/3; torment, pain
14/18, 53/13, 84/2. **pinen, pines**

pl. 73/23, 83/9, tortures 265/4;
mid greate ~ (*a grant peine*) with
great reluctance 190/10
pini *v. tr.* torment, torture 130/8,
263/3; *refl.* take pains 141/33 *n.*;
intr. 265/12: **pineþ** *pr. 3 sg.*
141/33 *n.* **pyneþ** *pl.* 265/12. **ypined**
pp. 213/9, 265/13
pite *n.* pity 116/24, 119/4, 122/30
pit(eu)ous, piteus *adj.* compas-
sionate 144/27, 150/10, 191/8
placebo *n.* placebo; *zingeþ ~* act the
sycophant 60/30
play *n.* play 143/16. **playes, pleȝes**
pl. amusements 92/18, 214/9
playe *v. intr.* play 45/17, 52/30,
179/32; gamble 46/12; disport
oneself 213/33, 34: **playe** *pr. 1 sg.*
213/34. **playþ** *3 sg.* 46/3, 51/15,
179/32. **yplayd** *pp.* 179/34
playeres *n. pl.* gamblers 69/35
playinges *vbl. n. pl.* amusements
71/19, 91/34
playneres *n. pl.* plaintiffs 39/23
playni *v. tr.* lament, regret, complain
of 132/12; **playneþ** *pr. 3 sg.* 128/3;
refl. complains 128/6, 181/1
playnte *n.* petition 99/34. **playntes**
pl. pleas 40/3, 91/4 *n.*; lamenta-
tions 99/20
plait *n.* legal pleading 39/20, 82/28
playtere *n.* advocate 98/11. **plaiteres**
pl. 39/25, 35, 44/4
playty *v. intr.* plead 99/31
playtinge *vbl. n.* pleading 163/23
plastres *n. pl.* plasters 148/20
pleȝes see **play**
plente *n.* abundance 24/34, 161/15,
plenty 206/36
plenteliche *adv.* abundantly 105/30
plentyuousliche *adv.* abundantly
51/22
plonteþ *pr. 3 sg. tr.* plants 123/3
poer *n.* fear 170/19 *n.*
poynt *n.* point 34/16 *n.*, 104/9;
moment 73/35; particular 252/29;
aspect, characteristic 33/32, 160/28,
164/8; circumstance 42/27; situa-
tion 171/30: **poynte** *p.c.* 104/9.
poyns *pl.* 33/24, 26, 34/10; *ine
no ~* at all 63/20
pokoc *n.* peacock 258/22. **pokoce**
p.c. 270/6

pole *n.* (*p.c.*) pole 203/11, 14
pond *n.* pound 1/15. **pond** *pl.* 91/8, 190/24, 26
popes *n. gen. sg.* pope's 62/21
porchaci *v. tr.* produce 9/15; obtain 162/9; cause, contrive 8/33, 34/12, 176/9; provide for 193/15; *intr.* obtain 55/34: **porchaceþ, pur-chaceþ** *pr. 3 sg.* 15/30, 25/23, 219/14. *pl.* 43/16, 30, 44/25, 105/17 *n.* **yporchaced** *pp.* 35/27, 117/31, 176/7
porche *n.* porch 135/26
porpos *n.* intention 220/33; *is ine* ~ intends 115/33–4
pors, purs *n.* purse 53/28, 31. **porse, purse** *p.c.* 53/30, 54/3, 91/3. **porses** *pl.* 188/1
port *n.* port 86/33
⟨**poruay**⟩ *v. tr.* foresee 152/23 *n.* **porueynde** *pr. p.* giving thought to 265/19 *n.* **poruayþ** *pr. 3 sg.* provides 138/25; *refl.* ensures 124/33; makes provision 19/6; *intr.* provides 145/36
porueynge *vbl. n.* provision 124/21
porueyonce *n.* foresight 83/21, 156/30*. **porueyonces** *pl.* 90/2 *n.*
porueyour *n.* provider 100/11
pos *n.* post 148/33 *n.*, 180/32. **posses** *pl.* 219/1 (*see p. 49*)
possession *n.* possession 149/27, 150/2, 261/25
post, postes see **pos**
pot *n.* pot 58/1, 177/28, 206/15. **potes** *pl.* 30/14
poty *v. tr.* put 135/34. **poteþ** *pr. 3 sg.* 107/6
poudres *n. pl.* powders 148/21
pouer *n.* power 71/12, 164/21, 172/19
pou(e)re *adj.* poor, poor people 36/32, 67/27, 78/1, 197/24; a **poure** 195/24; þe **pou(e)re** 35/36, 39/12, 188/24. **pouren** *p.c. pl.* 190/8
pouerte *n.* poverty 27/18, 43/8, 66/29
pou(e)rehede *n.* poverty 130/28, 131/14, 138/20
pouri *v. intr.* peer 177/1
pouringe *vbl. n.* peering 176/34
pourpre *n.* purple 229/5, 258/12
praye *n.* prey 75/31, 33, 142/9
praysi *v. tr.* praise, esteem, value 22/13, 135/34, 152/18 (*passive*);

refl. be of value 59/27 *n.*: **prayzest** *pr. 2 sg.* 20/16. **prayseþ, prazeþ** *3 sg.* 20/5, 143/26, 168/14, **prayseþ** *pl.* 78/7, 86/27. **praysi** *subj. sg.* 59/29. **prayzede** *pa. t. 3 sg.* 243/7. **ypraysed** *pp.* 16/22, 21/33, 138/8 *n.*
prayzinges *vbl. n. pl.* renown 25/4
precheþ *pr. pl. intr.* preach 42/2. **ypreched** *pp.* 141/29
prechinge *vbl. n.* preaching 191/20
precious *adj.* precious 57/33, 82/6, 112/21. *p.c.* 145/22. **preciouse** *wk.* 96/1, 3, 107/4. *pl.* 81/26, 96/7, 258/4, **preciouses** 76/27, 96/6
prede *n.* pride 16/2, 17/5, 18/2
prede *v. refl.* be proud 258/27. **prest** *pr. 2 sg.* 270/3, 4, 5. **predeþ** *pl.* 258/22 *n.*, **prodeþ** 79/11 *n.* **prette** *pa. t. 3 sg.* 258/23
predeþ, prette see **prede**
prekieþ, prikieþ *pr. pl. tr.* incite 230/23; *intr.* prick 257/16. **pre-kiinde, prikyinde** *ppl. adj.* prickly 66/14; stinging 148/22, 257/17
prekiynges *vbl. n. pl.* bites 203/13, 17
prelat *n.* prelate 175/27, 225/31, 237/20. **prelates** *pl.* 34/25, 39/6* *n.*, **prelas** 49/20
presense *n.* presence 161/15
present, presont *n.* present 189/16, 218/23. **presens** *pl.* 25/2
present, *adj.* present 10/18, 152/22, 270/18; *n.* the present 59/13
prest *n.* priest 191/23, 225/34, 236/14. **prestes** *gen.* 191/26. **preste** *p.c.* 172/35, 176/1, 191/19. **prestes** 40/34, 112/20, 235/8
prest, see **prede**
preste *adj.* (*pl.*) at hand 267/14
prestliche *adv.* readily 140/18
presum(p)cion *n.* presumption 17/25, 182/28, 195/35
preterit *adj.* past 59/9
preus, prous *adj.* brave 83/18, 28
pryente *n.* imprint 81/20. **prientes** *pl.* impressions 158/8
prikieþ, prikyinde see **prekieþ**
prikke *n.* instant 71/6, 17; point 207/9; pricker 150/32 *n.*
yprimsened *ppl. adj.* prime-signed 188/31
prince *n.* prince 71/9. **princes** *gen.*

231/34. **princes** *pl.* 38/31, 182/15, 239/6
principal *adj.* principal, chief 106/5, 13. **principale** *acc.* 35/14. **principal(e)s** *pl.* 17/21, 34/29, 209/29
principalliche *adv.* chiefly 26/4, 42/3, 50/9
priories *n. pl.* priories 30/28
priour *n.* prior 151/8. **priours** *pl.* 67/30
pris *n.* price 186/12, 234/1; *of* ~ costly, of value 19/1, 36/29 *n.*, 83/4, 258/8, 11–12
prison *n.* prison 32/2, 142/17. **prisone** *p.c.* 128/21, 166/9, 173/36; **prisons** *pl.* prisoners 86/33
priue *adj.* hidden, secret 25/18, 142/26; intimate 96/21; domestic 37/8, 17, 230/4; *n. pl.* **priues** members of one's domestic circle 37/18, 184/28
priueliche *adv.* secretly, privately 25/17, 205/34, ⟨**priuelyliche**⟩ 96/22 *n.*
priuilege *n.* privilege 15/26
priuite *n.* intimacy 143/6; mystery 221/36. **priuites** *pl.* secrets 89/30, 122/7
procuringe *vbl. n.* procurement 39/8
prodeþ see **prede**
prodigalite *n.* prodigality 21/32
proeue *n.* proof 134/19
profes *adj.* professed 238/13
profession *n.* profession 225/32
profete, prophete *n.* prophet 52/24, 93/21, 95/34. **profetes, prophetis** *pl.* 13/3, 267/9
profit *n.* profit, benefit 45/10, 99/21, 147/31; *do hire* ~ *of* see **do**
profitable *adj.* profitable, beneficial 89/26, 91/16, 94/5
profiti, profite *v. intr.* profit 70/17; (considered to) be beneficial 90/2, 217/28; flourish, prosper 28/17, 95/3, 97/33; progress 246/27 *n*: **profiteþ** *pr. 3 sg.* 119/17, *185/28 n.*, 202/5, 203/23. *pl.* 28/20, 97/29 *n.*, 160/7, 164/6 *n.*
prophete see **profete**
proposent (*French*) *pr. pl. intr.* propose 180/26 *n.*
propre *adj.* proper, appropriate 76/25, 103/17, 32 *n.*, 121/11; own 236/2
propreliche *adv.* strictly 55/30, 140/11; distinctively, particularly

34/30, 52/6, 88/3, 127/32; peculiarly, only 235/15, **properliche** 25/25 *n.*
prosperité *n.* prosperity 24/27, 125/19, 143/25. **prosperites** *pl.* prosperity 24/22
prou *n.* profit 120/17; *do, maki* ~ see **do, maki**
proud *adj.* proud 226/31, 231/6, 258/13; proud man 76/5. **proude** *wk.* 22/17 *n.*; þe **proude** 17/2, 22/5, 24/13, *pl.* 19/9, 134/20; proud people 16/20 *n.*, þe . . . **proude** 134/26
proudliche *adv.* proudly 168/15, 196/28
prouduol *adj.* ostentatious 217/10
prouendre *n.* food 112/15. **prouendres** *pl.* provisions 35/20; prebendaries 42/11, 25
prouesse *n.* prowess, valour 20/14, 22/11, 24/5, 166/18*. **prouesses** *pl.* prowess 59/11, 162/9
proui *v. tr.* try, test 116/11, 158/31; demonstrate, prove 13/13, 80/6, 163/24; *ppl. adj.* tested 152/29; proved 135/24; experienced 158/33, 184/17: **proueþ** *pr. 3 sg.* 151/5, 163/24. *pl.* 199/23 *n.*, **prouy** *subj. sg.* 158/31. **prouede** *pa. t. 3 sg.* 13/13. **yproued** *pp.* 125/21, 152/29, *199/33*, þe **yprouede** *wk.* 169/32
prouost *n.* provost 39/10 *n.*. **prouostes** *pl.* 43/34, **prouos** 37/20
prous see **preus**
prudence *n.* prudence 125/24, 126/32, 152/25
pub(b)lycan *n.* publican 175/14, 208/20
punissi *v. tr.* punish 148/11. **ypunyssed** *pp.* 74/10
purchaceþ see **porchaci**
pure *adj.* pure 93/17
purgatori(i)e *n.* purgatory 73/4, 31, 179/20
purgi *v. tr.* purge 132/16
purs(e) see **pors**
purté *n.* purity 202/9

Q

quaynte *adj.* see **maki**
quaynteliche *adv.* elaborately 47/13

quayntises see **que(a)yntise**
qualites *n. pl.* qualities 153/11
quarel *n.* arrow 71/14
quarteus (*French*) *n.* hoop 159/18; *cf.* **cerceaus**
que(a)yntise *n.* cunning 37/16; expertise 90/18 *n.* **quayntises** *pl.* ingenious ornaments 258/28
quereles *n. pl.* quarrels 83/23, debates 142/22 *n.*
querne *n.* mill 181/14
quit *adj.* free, quit 35/32, 137/33, 145/30. **kuytte** *pl.* 41/14, 176/35
quittinge *vbl. n.* remission of sin 114/1

R

rage *n.* raging wind 142/1 *n.*
raymi *v. tr.* plunder 44/1 n. (*passive*)
rayn *n.* rain 68/17, 84/21. **rene** *p.c.* 130/1 (MS. *repe*). **raynes** *pl.* 124/24, 256/26
rasour *n.* razor 66/11
raþe *adj.* early 52/16
raþe *adv.* soon 152/4. **raþre** *comp.* more quickly, sooner 61/19, 71/14, 179/29; rather 18/13, 69/2, 120/18; *þe* ~ on the contrary 90/28 *n.*
yrauissed *pp.* rapt 143/4; ravished 231/33
rearde *n.* voice 24/6, 60/34, 210/32; sound 265/10
yreaued *pp.* ravished 143/8, 23
rebel *adj.* rebellious 68/26, 32, 69/4. **rebels** *pl.* 68/34, 69/7
rebeleþ *pr. 3 sg. tr.* opposes 28/21 *n.*
rebours *adj.* stubborn 68/26. *pl.* 68/34
recorder (*French*) *v. intr.* recollecting 56/12
recordi *v. tr.* repeat 257/34; recall 21/10, 111/13, 208/27; *intr.* record 67/10, 213/16: **recordeþ** *pr. 3 sg.* 142/12, 203/6; *pl.* 59/11
recordinge *vbl. n.* remembrance 55/36
recouri *v. tr.* recover from 32/21
recreyd *ppl. adj.* exhausted 33/19; slothful 195/14
red *n.* plan 222/1; counsel, advice 4/6, 68/34, 109/20; decree 165/18; *is ine* ~ (*est en conseil*) advises 9/1; ~ *do* see **do**: **rede** *p.c.* 9/31, 10/2,

38/10. **redes** *pl.* 40/20, 89/30, 184/24
rede *v. tr.* read 44/7, 166/32; advise 69/1, 172/19; (*gouerner*) govern 154/17; *intr.* read 55/15, 70/21, 205/36: *rede pr. 1 sg.* 104/20. **ret** *3 sg.* 22/29, 56/35, 190/3. **redeþ** *pl.* 22/13 *n.*, 50/15, 186/24 *n.*, 251/12. **redde** *pa. t. 3 sg.* 184/8
rederes *n. pl.* advisers 184/13
refye see **resye**
reformeþ *pr. 3 sg. intr.* renews 81/19
refter *n.* beam 175/12
refu *n.* refuge 138/26
reg *n.* back 116/15, 189/17. **regge** *p.c.* 116/16, 133/12, 136/32
regyon *n.* region 268/2
regne *n.* kingdom 83/34, 85/6, 107/35. **regnes** *pl.* 85/28
regneþ *pr. 3 sg. intr.* reigns 67/24 *n.*
regnynde *pr. p.* 266/26
reherci *v. tr./intr.* repeat 220/15 *n.*
rekeni *v. tr.* consider, 214/3; *intr.* reckon, give an account 19/6, 35/11, 58/8, 79/16. **rekeneþ** *pr. pl.* 37/22
rekeninge *vbl. n.* reckoning, account 18/36, 19/6, 35/10
religion *n.* religion, holy or monastic orders 25/9, 37/33, 42/27* *n.*, 48/7, 12*, 241/25
religious *n.* religious 240/24, 241/3. *pl.* 34/25, 243/14
religious *adj.* of religion 34/25 (*see p. 68, n. 5*), 241/20
relikes *n. pl.* relics 64/22
remedie *n.* remedy 207/15, 240/21
remenont *n.* remainder 100/2
remue *v. refl.* move 104/10 *n.*
renable *adj.* moderate 95/7; rational 164/25
renay *n.* apostate, traitor 19/12, 21
renayrie, renoyrye *n.* apostasy 17/33, 19/11
rene see **rayn**
reneye *v. tr.* abjure 57/1. **renayþ** *pr. 3 sg.* 43/9; **reneyeþ** *pl.* 19/23; *intr. 3 sg.* is an apostate 19/19
renoyrye see **renayrie**
rentes *n. pl.* revenues 37/21, 24, 144/19; rents 41/19
repenteþ *pr. 3 sg. refl.* repents 238/26

repentonce *n.* repentance 202/30, 212/1

resembleþ *pr. pl. tr./intr.* resemble 61/16

resye *v. tr.* shake 116/22 (MS. *refye*); *intr.* 23/27 *n.*

respit *n.* delay 39/29

resse *n.* rush 253/12 *n.*

reste *n.* repose 7/15, 27/26, 142/3; peace 266/7

resti *v. refl.* rest 7/8, 119/2, 260/35; *intr.* 31/28, 250/35, 251/11; **resteþ** *pr. 3 sg.* 31/15, 142/4, 246/14. **restede** *pa. t. 3 sg.* 7/9, 251/14

rest(e)uol *adj.* contemplative 199/12, 200/4. **restuolle** *wk.* 199/33

ret see **rede**

reuen *n. pl.* bailiffs 37/20, 39/10, 43/34

reuerence *n.* reverence 20/7, 101/7, 118/16

reuerteþ *pr. 3 sg. refl.* calls to mind 128/10

reule *n.* rule 150/31, 151/2, 160/16 *n.* **ruieles** *pl.* 97/7

reuleþ *pr. 3 sg. tr.* regulates 124/32

reuþe *n.* pity 186/16, 187/1, 189/17

reuþeuol *adj.* compassionate 116/25, 186/15, 188/14. **þe rewþeuolle** *pl.* 198/19

reward *n.* regard; *to þe ~ of (au regart de)* in comparison with 74/4

yrewarded *pp.* regarded 136/6 *n.*

ribaud *n.* rascal 51/16, 127/35. **ribaus** *pl.* 192/28, 259/3

ribaudie *n.* debauchery 128/13, 203/25, 220/11. **ribaudyes** *pl.* 31/25

riche *n.* kingdom 66/23, 127/16, 198/21

riche *adj.* rich, powerful 37/25, 38/33, 55/27; **þe riche** 16/29, 67/28

richesse *n.* wealth 20/14, 59/20, 71/13. **richesses** *pl.* riches 18/26, 24/21, 75/15

ridinges *n. pl.* cavalcades 24/33, 139/16

riȝt *n.* right 222/25; justice, righteousness, equity 8/23, 38/21, 265/27; a claim 222/23; rights 110/22, 222/19; *pl.* dues 41/20; **þe riȝtes** justice 40/5; *be ~ rightly* 45/20, 65/15; *ne is no ~ is it right* 6/20;

to hare ~ under their jurisdiction 264/26–7: **riȝte** *p.c.* 100/15, 113/33, 137/29. **riȝtes** *pl.* 40/5, 41/20

riȝt(e) *adj.* true 80/16, 149/13, 207/21; pure 31/34; due, proper 51/28, 53/27, 124/17; strict 169/10; right 13/19, 146/36, ⟨ziȝt⟩ 39/29: *for* **ariȝthalf, alefthalf** see **half**; straight 127/16: **riȝte** *acc.* 126/22, 249/30. *p.c.* 28/28, 29/23, 31/34. *wk.* 53/27, 87/24, 111/16. *pl.* 65/3

riȝt *adv.* right, very 20/10, 74/15, 76/12; truly 59/27; *~ to þe uolle* see **uolle**

riȝte *v. tr.* straighten 56/26

riȝte *adv.* straight 160/1

riȝtnesse *n.* a balance, justice, equity 154/28, 264/2, 265/28* (*see p. 49*)

riȝtuol(le) *adj.* righteous, just 105/23, 131/17, 153/20, *196/20* (MS. *riȝuol*; *see p. 49*): true 269/23* (*see p. 49*); right 159/19; correct 44/22: **riȝtuolle** *acc.* 250/25. *p.c.* 135/18. **riȝtuolle** *pl.* 44/22, **þe ryȝtuolle** 269/22

riȝtuolliche *adv.* properly 20/8, 149/27; righteously 159/22, 265/29* (*see p. 50*); truly 196/35, 201/17; strictly 154/3; directly 185/20, 254/6

riȝtuolnesse *n.* justice, righteousness, equity 3/30*, 29/10, 13*, 125/28, 29*, 154/1*, 26*, 169/4*, 266/9* (*for forms with consonant loss see p. 49*)

yrymed *ppl. adj.* rhymed 99/18

rinde *n.* rind 96/4, 99/4

rine *v. intr.* rain 49/32

ryote *n.* rigmarole 99/17

riotouse *adj.* troublesome 170/17

ripe *adj.* ripe 28/16

ripe *v. intr.* reap 214/21

robbere *n.* robber 79/5. **robberes** *pl.* 39/1, 253/29, 270/15

robbi *v. tr.* rob, steal 212/4, 227/23. **robbeþ** *pr. pl.* 39/7, 254/10. **yrobbed** *pp.* 190/20, 199/18 *n.*

robbinge *vbl. n.* robbery 192/10. **robbynges** *pl.* 39/12

robe *n.* robe, garment 119/35, 133/12, 163/21. **robes** *pl.* 24/34, 35/18, 71/19

roberie *n.* robbery 9/26, 34/33, 38/23. **roberies** *pl.* 39/14
roche *n.* rock 142/2, 3, 168/2, 251/1
rocky *v. tr.* rock 116/22
rod(e) *n.(p.c.)* cross 1/2, 12/29, 64/29
romayns *n. pl.* Romans 12/27
romongours *n. pl.* dealers 44/34
rond *adj.* complete 1/14. **rounde** *acc.* round 234/22. *wk.* 234/23
ronsounes *n. pl.* ransoms 35/35
roppes *n. pl.* entrails 62/32
rote *n.* root 17/22, 31/6, 34/20. **roten, rotin** *pl.* 34/31, 35/2, 130/13 *n.*, 18, 153/17 *n.*
roted *ppl. adj.* rotten 205/23
iroted *pp.* rooted 26/13, 168/3, 247/5
rotie *v. intr.* rot 32/2, 205/24. **rotede** *pa. t. 3 sg.* 205/4
roþer *n.* rudder 160/5
rounde see **rond**
rubys *n. pl.* rubies 76/34
ruieles see **reule**
russoles *n. pl.* rissoles 253/11

S

sabat *n.* sabbath 7/5, 6, 15
sacrefice, sacrifice *n.* sacrifice 187/14, 192/13, 229/20. **sacrefices** *pl.* 187/16, 20
sacrement *n.* sacrament 14/7, 48/19, 110/35. **sacremens** *pl.* 14/6, 11, 40/35, 42/1, ⟨sacramens⟩ 222/4
sacreþ *pr. pl. tr.* consecrate 235/20. **ysacred** *pp.* 225/8
sacrilege *n.* sacrilege 34/34, 40/27
safir *n.* sapphire 82/12. **safyrs** *pl.* 77/1
saysyne *n.* possession 149/17, 23, 24; tenure 144/17 (*cf.* **do**)
salamandre *n.* salamander 167/31 (þane) **sanguinien** *adj.* (person) of sanguine temperament 157/28
sa(y)nd/t, sa(y)ny(n)t(e) see **zaint(e)**
sarasin *n.* Saracen 43/10, 64/26, 114/28. **sarasyns** *pl.* 79/2, 101/23
sarzineys *adj.* Saracenic 116/29
satisfacioun *n.* satisfaction 32/1
sauf *adj.* safe 36/25
sause *n.* sauce 55/9
saut(y)er *n.* psalter 91/9, 136/11,

142/5. **sautere** *p.c.* 27/36, 93/8
sauuour *n.* savour 138/26
scallede *adj.* scald-headed 224/6 (*cf. OED* SCALD-HEAD)
scarlet *n.* scarlet 167/25
scarse *adj.* (*acc.*) parsimonious 53/25, 54/3
scarsliche *adv.* parsimoniously 34/28
scarsnesse *n.* parsimony 159/34
sc(k)ele *n.* reason, cause 6/14, 17 *n.*, 19, 8/22, 54/16, 125/8 *n.*, 25*, 208/4 *n.*; account 18/36, 47/23, 171/21; reasonable 124/33, 198/32; *mochil is grat* ~ it is very reasonable 145/18; **sceles** *pl.* reasons, arguments 69/10, 80/6, 117/15; *by/uor* ~ *of* see **bi, uor**; *zette to* ~ see **zette**
sceluol *adj.* reasonable 51/28, 169/7. **sceluolle** *acc.* 250/7, 259/33
scin *n.* skin 81/5, 137/9, 230/4. **scinne** *p.c.* 44/9
sclondre *n.* slander 6/29. **sclondres** *pl.* 6/33
scluse *n.* sluice 255/11, 13, 17
scoffes *n. pl.* mockeries 128/34
scoldeþ *pr. 3 sg. tr.* scalds 66/25
scole *n.* school 34/22, 56/21, 61/8
scolers *n. pl.* scholars 39/20, 98/35
scome *n.* froth 44/24
scorn *n.* mockery 22/16. **scornes** *pl.* derisive comments 58/25, 74/13, 157/1
scorneres *n. pl.* mockers 63/6, 177/8
scornj, v. tr. mock 211/8. **scorneþ** *pr. 3 sg.* 22/21. *pl.* 211/8 *n.* **scorne** *subj. sg.* 54/27
scorpioun *n.* scorpion 62/13
scot *n.* payment, price 51/17, 218/11
scriueyns *n. pl.* scriveners 44/31
seconde *adj.* (*pl.*) secondary 209/29
secular *adj.* layman 175/27; **secu-lere(s)** *pl.* secular 215/9, 12
sel *n.* seal 62/21. **celes** *pl.* 40/9
sel *v.* see **ssel**
semblant, semblont *n.* appearance; *maky uayr* ~ be agreeable 27/26–7; *doþ/makeþ* ~ pretend, appear 137/1–2 *n.*, 211/9–10; *ssewy* ~ make it appear 257/18
sengle *adj.* single 48/13, 14, 175/36
sembleþ *pr. pl. tr./intr.* resemble 176/32

sentense *n.* opinion 69/21
serayn *n.* winged serpent 61/16 (*see* OED SIREN)
sercle *n.* circuit 141/12
sergont, sergond *n.* servant 133/2, 188/26, **seriont** 32/15. **sergonte** *p.c.* 33/21. **sergons** *pl.* 35/30, 39/5, sergeants 43/34
sermon *n.* sermon 20/29, 138/29. **sermons** *pl.* 20/28, 214/28
serui *v. tr./intr.* serve 5/21, 6/8, 84/28; *intr.* 33/22, 46/34, 236/36; *ppl. adj.* servant 93/10: **serui** *pr. 1 sg.* 156/3. **serueþ** *3 sg.* 24/32, 50/34, 75/27. *pl.* 218/30, 235/22, 34, **seruyeþ** 235/32 (*see p. 99, n. 8*). **seruinde** *pr. p.* 93/10. **seruede** *pa. t. 3 sg.* 226/22. **serueden** *pl.* 236/17. **yserued** *pp.* 115/28
seruise, seruese *n.* service 19/18, 52/27, 56/22, 151/12; task 140/8. **seruises** *pl.* 35/19 *n.*, 42/29; office, employment 40/21
seruons *n. pl.* officers 37/20
sest *see note to line 171/31-2*
symoniaks *n. pl.* simoniacs 41/31
symonie *n.* simony 34/34, 41/27, 42/30
simple *adj.* simple, modest 137/7, 142/8, 216/26; sincere 159/9, 13, 216/27; alone, only 134/14, 17, 246/2; not accompanied by any legal formalities 225/22, 25
simpleliche *adv.* with simplicity 134/8, 140/18, 151/36
simplesse *n.* simplicity 140/35
simulacion *n.* false pretence 23/6
sire *n.* sir, lord 89/14, 106/8, 212/16
skeluolliche *adj.* (*pl.*) reasonable 6/19 *n.*
slac *adj.* slack 32/17, 141/9, 263/20. **slacke** *pl.* 170/18
slacnesse *n.* sloth, slackness 33/7, 138/13, 159/33
slaȝe *v. tr.* slay 8/19, 89/31 *n.* (*passive*), **slea** 223/15, **sle** 48/26. ⟨**ssast**⟩ *pr. 2 sg.* 56/8 *n.* **slaȝþ**, **sslaȝt** *3 sg.* 34/13, 61/22, 192/17. **slaȝeþ** *pl.* 53/11. **yslaȝe** *pp.* 58/32, 171/25, 223/17, **ysslaȝe** 239/11
slaȝþe *n.* torment 90/3
sle(a) *see* **slaȝe**

sleauuol *adj.* slothful 32/30, 174/11, **sleawol** 206/22, **sleuuol** 32/17, 32, 67/34. þe **sleawolle** *wk.* 32/13, þe, þane **sleuuolle** 31/9, 34/17. þe **sleauuolle** *pl.* 170/17
sleawþe *n.* sloth 40/4, **sleauþe** 16/3, 34/15*, **sleuþe** 31/7, 32/23
sleȝe *adj.(pl.)* prudent 265/18
sleȝþe *n.* prudence 124/6, 12, 263/33; skill 18/25; cunning 124/13. **sleȝþes** *pl.* wiles 118/4
slep *n.* sleep 31/31, 264/6. **sslepe** *p.c.* 246/19
slepe *v. intr.* sleep 29/33, 31/29, 51/2; *refl.* 246/15: **slepþ** *pr. 3 sg.* 56/7, 121/27, 127/34. **slepinde** *ppl. adj.* 158/9. **yslepe** *pp.* 128/4
sleuþe, sleuuol *see* **sleawþe, sleauuol**
sleuuolliche *adv.* slothfully 32/25
ysliked *ppl. adj.* polished 99/17, 19, 212/2
slyt *pr. 3 sg. intr.* slips 149/2
smac *n.* inclination 33/17 *n.*; taste, flavour, savour 56/3, 82/21, 245/28, **ssmak** 83/10. **smakkes** *pl.* 112/23, 204/7 *n.*, 251/18; *out of* ~ insipid 106/29; *for draȝþ to* ~ *see* **draȝe**
smacky *v. tr.* savour, taste 247/24, 25, 251/25; *intr.* 106/16 *n.*, 269/27 *n.*, *ppl. adj.* savoury 245/27 *n.*: **smackeþ, smackyþ** *pr. 3 sg.* 106/18, 245/30, 247/25. **smackeþ** *pl.* 92/10, 268/11 *n.*, 22 *n.*, 23. **smacke** *imp. sg.* 269/28 *n.* **sma(c)kinde** *pr. p.* 245/27 *n.*, 260/23. **ysmacked** *pp.* 93/11
smal *adj.* small 74/28, 82/6, 102/18. **smale** *wk.* 136/1, 270/29, 32. *pl.* 17/29, 23/34, 30/18. **smaller** *comp.* into smaller pieces 64/31
smalliche *adv.* minutely 111/13
smech *n.* smoke 66/3, 137/15
smel *n.* smell, scent 95/28, 123/31, 177/30. **smelles** *pl.* 177/12, 204/6, 268/3
smelþ *see* **ssmelle**
smellinge *vbl. n.* smelling 91/24
smerieles *n.* ointment 187/29, 32, 217/26
smerieþ *pr. pl. tr.* smears 60/10. **smerede** *pa. t. 3 sg.* anointed 187/31. **ysmered** *pp.* 93/24, 28

smeringes *vbl. n. pl.* anointings 148/20

smertnesses *n. pl.* severities 181/3

smite *n.* stroke 140/23

smite *v. intr.* strike 116/17; *tr.* 149/3. **smit** *pr. 3 sg.* 30/13, 147/35. **ysmite** smitten *pp.* 203/17; ~ to *dyape* slay 48/27

smiþes *n. pl.* smiths 130/24

ysmoþed *ppl. adj.* polished 57/21

snaw *n.* snow 267/31

snegge *n.* snail 32/10

snode *n.* morsel 77/30, 111/4. **snoden** *pl.* 218/10

sobre *adj.* sober 221/20, 250/19, 252/2

sobreliche *adv.* soberly 248/9, 265/29, 30

sobrete *n.* sobriety 4/5, 159/34, 245/15

sodaynliche *adv.* suddenly 248/19; without premeditation 64/4

soffreþ *pr. 3 sg. tr.* suffers 139/18. *pl.* tolerate 38/19

soigneus *adj.* careful 155/4 *n.*; anxious 157/19 *n.*

solaci *v. intr.* amuse oneself 213/33 *n.*; *tr.* amuse 63/8. **solaci** *pr. 1 sg.* 213/34

solas *n.* solace 72/18, 77/2, 107/27

solemnete *n.* formality 225/27

solempne *adj.* formal 225/31. **solemnes** *pl.* solemn 224/14

somme, summe *n.* sum 97/10, 260/36

somoni *v. tr.* summon, call upon 87/30, 98/7. **somoneþ** *pr. 3 sg.* 100/3, 104/33

sophistrie *n.* sophistry 65/3

sopiere *n.* (*p.c.*) supper 133/19

sostyeni *v. tr.* maintain, support, sustain 56/30. **sostyeneþ** *pr. 3 sg.* 83/5, **sosteneþ** 111/28. **sostyeneþ, sustyeneþ** *pl.* 57/6, 66/34, **sosteneþ, sostinet** 38/16, 39/35. **sostyenede** *pa. t. subj. sg.* 104/7. **sostened** *pl.* 259/1

sostinonce, sustinonce *n.* sustenance 54/31, 85/8, 139/18

sotil *adj.* subtle 24/7, 25/34; difficult 99/7. **sotile(s), sotyls** *pl.* subtle 26/8, 157/19; delicate 105/15

sotylhede *n.* cunning 117/12

sotilliche *adv.* insidiously 26/8, 46/29; skilfully 58/20, 99/31

soucouri *v. tr.* succour 186/17

soudeurs *n. pl.* soldiers 146/5

soupi *v. intr.* sup 52/17

souerayn *adj.* sovereign 189/22

soui *v. tr.* save 98/2, 138/27, 162/15. **soueþ** *pr. pl.* 100/4. **soued** *pp.* 225/36

spacialliche see **specialliche**

spade *n.* spade 108/23

spari *v. intr.* abstain 224/12. *tr.* **spareþ** *pr. 3 sg.* spares 223/36. **spari** *subj. sg.* 157/34 *n.*

spearken *n. pl.* sparks 137/14

speche *n.* speech 21/24, 46/27, 50/8; language 110/5. **speches** *pl.* speech 142/27; languages 89/28, 90/4; epithets 103/22

special *adj.* special 15/26, 16/27, 230/9, 261/24. **speciale** *acc.* 234/34, 235/1; *in* ~ in particular 94/17

special(l)iche *adv.* particularly 7/35, 18/2, 69/28, ⟨spacialliche⟩ 252/28 *n.*

speke *v. tr.* speak, say, utter 58/15 *n.*, 110/5, 143/2, 211/4, *intr.* speak 33/34, 98/24, **sspeke** 154/21; say 20/3: **spekene** *infl. inf.* 94/17, 103/25, 110/12. **specþ** *pr. 3 sg.* 10/18, 27/35, 58/15 *n.*, 203/27. **spekeþ** *pl.* 18/1, 58/13, 60/5. **speke** *subj. pl.* 103/25 *n.* **spekinde** *pr. p.* 226/15, 266/11. **spek** *pa. t. 1 sg.* 251/35, 255/22, 260/11. *3 sg.* 183/15 **speke** *pl.* 70/7, 124/9, 201/30. *subj. sg.* 89/28, 258/9. **ispeke** *pp.* 27/24, 44/5, 75/20

spekeman *n.* spokesman 99/28. **spekemen** *pl.* 60/4

spekinge *vbl. n.* speaking 50/11

spelle *n.* (*p.c.*) gospel 5/5, 6/15, 11/1. **spelles** *pl.* discourses 202/18

yspended *pp.* expended 171/22

spendere *n.* treasurer 190/24, 27

spendinge *vbl. n.* spending 34/28; expenditure 21/31, 37/23. **spendinges** *pl.* expenditure 37/25, 173/1

sperringe *n.* fastening 53/1 *n.*

spilþ *pr. 3 sg. intr.* perishes 128/17, 182/35, 226/25; *tr.* destroys 254/20; wrecked 129/18: **spilleþ** *pl.* 212/16.

spille *subj. sg.* 212/11, 232/32.
yspild *pp.* 75/23
spirit see sp(i)rit
spirituellyche *adv.* spiritually 84/30
spiþre *n.* (*p.c.*) spider 164/31
sposayles *n. pl.* nuptials 189/9, 235/4
spot *n.* spot, stain 228/15, 229/16, 237/2. spotte *p.c.* 229/17, 27. spottes *pl.* 200/21, 228/17, 237/19
spotty *adj.* blemished 192/14
spousbreche *n.* adultery 37/30, 48/16
spouse *n.* marriage 10/34; spouse 118/24
spoushod *n.* marriage, matrimony 10/27, 14/8, 43/18, 49/7*
spousy *v. tr.* marry 118/28, 238/12; *refl.* 225/24, 28, 238/13; *ppl. adj.* 48/21, 175/35: spouseþ *pr. 3 sg.* 225/28. spousede *pa. t. 3 sg.* 118/28. (y)spoused *pp.* 231/2, 235/3
spousynge *vbl. n.* marrying 227/33
sprede *v. intr.* extend 29/9. spret *pr. 3 sg.* ramifies 17/19, 131/34; *refl.* spreads 23/2, 121/5
springe *v. tr.* shoot forth 144/33
sp(i)rit *n.* spirit 92/22, 131/24, 241/39
srifteuader see ssrifteuader
sriinges see friinges
sriueþ see ssriue
ssake *v. tr.* shake 4/9, 269/32; *intr.* tremble 130/12. *pr. subj. sg.* rock 168/3. *pl.* tremble 116/33
ssame *n.* shame 26/22, 49/30; humiliation, disgrace 8/34, 164/2. ssames *pl.* 21/5, 83/8; *habbe ~* see habbe
ssamie *v. refl.* to be ashamed 229/35 *n.*
ssamnesse *n.* modesty 142/31
ssamuest *adj.* bashful, modest, modest, humble 222/20, 231/17. ssamueste *pl.* 193/7, 216/28, þe . . . ssamueste 216/29 *n.*
ssamuol *adj.* shameful 117/1
ssamuolliche *adv.* shamefully 181/14
yssape see ssepþ
ssarnboddes *n. pl.* dung-beetles 61/32
ssarp *adj.* severe 165/11
ssarpnesse *n.* severity, austerity

142/6, 204/32, 232/17*, (*see p. 49*), ssarpnes 226/24‡. ssarpnesses *pl.* mortifications 187/17, 205/9
ssast see sla ʒe
ssat *pa. t. 3 sg. intr.* shot 45/33
sseawere *n.* mirror 84/12, ssewere 88/18, 158/6, 7. sseaweres *pl.* 177/1, ssewere 176/34
sseawy *v. tr.* show, reveal, exhibit 56/24, 73/9, ssewy 69/2 (*cf.* ureme); demonstrate 89/23, 94/11, 100/22 (*future*); display 44/30; *refl.* appear 218/21, 231/20; reveal 228/23; *intr.* appear 44/27, 35, 92/2 *n.*, 119/23 *n.*, 165/11; to be conspicuous 267/26; *~ semblont* see semblant: sseawy *pr. 1 sg.* 100/22 (*future*). sseaweþ *3 sg.* 21/23, 22/6, sseweþ 19/20. sseaweþ *pl.* 26/1, 47/13, 110/1, sseweþ 47/12, 103/31. ssewy *subj. sg.* 127/16 *n.*, 163/20. sseawede *pa. t. 3 sg.* 13/12, ssewede 96/19, 21, 103/9. ysse(a)wed 76/8, 79/20, 109/33
sseawynge *vbl. n.* vision 2/15, 14/28, ssewynge appearance 36/24; apparition 61/10; demonstration 163/22. ⟨sseawyinges⟩ *pl.* visions *14/30* (*see p. 98, n. 1*)
ssed *n.* shadow 71/14, 77/21, 137/15. ssede *p.c.* shade 97/1, 29, 142/2; *ine ~* obscurely 266/17 *n.*
sseddest *pa. t. 2 sg. tr.* sheddest 1/2. ssedde *3 sg.* 107/5, 186/13. yssed, ysset *pp.* 41/8, 239/11; spilt 177/29
sseduy *v. refl.* obtain shade 97/2
ssefþes see ssepþe
ssel *v. tr.* owe 54/31, 101/6, 115/18; *intr.* is entitled to 222/24; is to, must, ought to 2/20, 8/25, 9/7; shall, will, (*contingent future*) shall 8/3, 107/12, 118/7, 178/7 (*for modal uses see pp. 102–4*); ssel by *n.* 'shall be', future 104/16: ssel *pr. 1 sg.* 46/7, 51/12, 156/35. sselt *2 sg.* 5/20, 6/12, 73/4*, 5 *n.* ssel *3 sg.* 5/7, 7/22, 234/18* (*see p. 53*), sel 189/25 (*see p. 46, n. 2*). ssolle(n) *pl.* 5/12, 38/9, ssol (*see note to 96/31*), 96/31, 217/13, 236/18, ssole (*see note to 96/33*),

ssel (*cont.*):
96/33, 189/25. ssolle *subj. sg.*
51/6. ssolde *pa. t. 1 sg.* 64/19,
156/1. ssoldest *2 sg.* 20/17, 21/9,
31/19. ssolde *3 sg.* 17/12, 18/5,
19/22. ssolde(n) *pl.* 6/8, 38/27,
95/16. ssolde *subj. sg.* 33/3, 71/5,
75/13, 127/21* (*see p. 49*)
sseld *n.* shield 1/3, 167/8, 207/14
ssende *v. tr.* distress 126/8; revile
178/5; harm, corrupt 28/22, 148/9.
ssent *pr. 3 sg.* 125/11 *n.*
ssep *n.* sheep 137/7, 140/32, 192/13.
ssepes *gen.* 44/9. ssepe *p.c.*
50/27. ssep *pl.* 39/10
ssepe *n.* reward, prize 146/5, 168/29;
payment, wages 33/23, 40/2, 86/32.
ssepes *pl.* 39/5
ssepere see sseppere
ssepherde *n.* shepherd 140/33
sseppinges *n. pl.* created things,
creatures 64/11, 108/19, 200/27;
shapes, forms 158/13
ssep(p)ere *n.* creator 6/7, 7/9, 12/5
ssepþ, ssept *pr. 3 sg. tr.* creates,
gives form to 116/15, 17, 209/14;
sseppeþ imagines 92/2 (*see p. 98*):
ssop *pa. t. 3 sg.* 87/26. yssape pp.
87/33, 100/13, *ppl. adj.* 104/5
sseppe *n.* created things, creature,
creation 5/23, 6/16, 13/19; form,
shape 81/24, 152/30, 267/35 *n.*
ssepþes *pl.* creatures 64/17, 84/33,
85/13; forms, shapes 158/7, ssefþes
62/29 (*see page 48*)
sserte *n.* shirt 191/9
ssette *v. tr.* shut 179/5, 188/1.
sset *pr. 3 sg.* 218/24. ssete *imp. sg.*
210/18. ssette *pa. t. 3 sg.* 189/9.
ysset pp. 218/27; *ppl. adj.* secured,
shut 154/23, 257/2
ssetteles *n. pl.* bolts 94/30
ssette-pors *n.* shutter of purses
187/35
ssewy, ssewynge see sseawy
ssyetere *n.* archer 174/12
ssylde *imp. sg. tr.* shield 271/15
ssine *v. intr.* shine 188/6. ssinþ
pr. 3 sg. 64/12. ssyneþ *pl.* 267/27.
ssynynde *ppl. adj.* 76/34
ssip *n.* ship 112/1, 128/17, 178/19.
ssipe *p.c.* 129/18, 140/22, 160/5.
ssipes *pl.* 239/19

ssipmen *n. pl.* sailors 61/13, 140/22
ssla3t, yssla3e see sla3e
sslepe see slep
ssmak see smac
ssmelle *v. intr.* smell 154/20. smelþ
pr. 3 sg. 211/18, 20
sso *n.* shoe 220/23
ssofþ *pr. 3 sg. intr.* pushes 174/8 *n.*
ssoinge *vbl. n.* shoes 154/14, 177/17
ssolde(n), ssole(n) *etc.* see ssel
ssop see ssepþ
yssored pp. supported 207/19, 218/36
(cf. A. McIntosh, *Studies in Lan-
guage and Literature in Honor of
Margaret Schlauch, 1966*)
ssornede see ssoruede
ssort(e) *adj.* brief, short 71/4, 81/3,
98/14 (*see p. 64*), 99/6, *pl.* 99/22
ssorthede *n.* brevity 99/9
ssortliche *adv.* briefly 24/17, 79/20,
99/32. ssortlaker *comp.* 252/1
ssoruede *ppl. adj. pl.* scurvy (people)
224/6 *n.*
ssspeke see speke
ssrede *v. tr.* clothe 90/25. ssredeþ
pr. pl. 258/11. ssredde *pa. t. 3 sg.*
227/1. yssred pp. 188/31
ssredinge *vbl. n.* clothing 177/16,
258/3, 13
ssrewe *n.* wretch, evil man 32/2,
192/25
ssrewede *ppl. adj.* (*pl.*) wicked
224/9
ssrifteuader *n.* confessor 172/35,
174/21, srifteuader 158/32.
ssrifteuaderes *pl.* 38/10
ssrif(f)þe *n.* confession 20/35, 179/2,
ssrifte, ssriftte 4/4, 14/8, 137/32,
265/21* (*cf. p. 48*)
ssriue *v. intr.* confess 174/9 *n.*;
tr. confess 132/18; shrive 5/8,
32/31, 70/18, 173/29: ssrifþ *pr. 3
sg.* 174/24, 179/23 (*future*). s(s)ri-
ueþ *pl.* 132/21, 138/6, 174/16 *n.*
ssrof *pa. t. 3 sg.* 175/5, 178/31.
(y)ssriue pp. 70/21, 172/5, 174/19
ssriuere *n.* confessor 174/23, 177/23,
180/5. ssriueres *pl.* 175/21
ssroud *n.* garment, clothing 258/27,
30
stable *adj.* persistent, stable 83/20,
189/19
stablen *n. pl.* stables 210/7

stages *n. pl.* grades 122/2

stale *n.* stealing 9/26

stant *pr. 3 sg. intr.* stands 266/30.
stondeþ *pl.* 267/3. stondinde *pr.
p.* 170/22; *guoþ mid* ∼ *nhicke*
are stiff-necked, proud 216/30 *n.*

stape *n.* stage, degree 47/5, 132/5,
133/22. stapes *pl.* 46/33, 131/30,
132/1; steps 32/3; classes 219/35

starf see sterue

stat *n.* estate, status 25/8, 48/4, 49/19;
esteem 28/23; state, condition,
7/18, 122/17, 224/32. states *pl.*
122/15, 161/29, 219/34, stas 28/14

steaȝ *pa. t. 3 sg. intr.* ascended
13/18, 213/20, 263/5

stech *n.* bit 62/6, 8. stechches *pl.*
111/14

stede *n.* place 7/19, 36/30, 41/12;
occasion 206/28, 30. stedes *pl.*
40/30, 41/4, 45/2; (*finibus*) borders
269/24; *in oþre* ∼ elsewhere 210/16

stedeuest *adj.* steadfast, constant
84/23, 116/33; perfect 122/36
(*see note to* 86/35); earnest 142/24 *n.*:
stedeueste *p.c.* 166/14, 200/6.
þe stedeueste *pl.* 122/19

stedeuestliche *adv.* steadfastly 11/27,
233/27; completely 86/35 *n.*, 105/
23, 123/4

stedeuestnesse *n.* constancy 83/17,
164/11; perfection (*see note to*
86/35) 200/7, 8

stefhede *n.* firmness 263/21

stefliche *adv.* firmly 258/9

stele *v. intr.* steal 57/3; *tr.* 79/5 *n.*,
231/22, 232/21. stelst *pr. 2 sg.*
38/8. stelþ *3 sg.* 23/21, 37/32,
40/36. steleþ *pl.* 26/8, 37/13 *n.*,
38/1. ystole *pp.* 58/33

stempe *v. intr.* stumble 206/23 *n.*

stench *n.* stench 136/2, 137/15,
228/14. stenche *p.c.* 264/34

stene *v. tr.* stone (*passive*) 213/4

steple *n.* (*p.c.*) steeple 180/28.
steples *pl.* 23/25

sterie *v. intr.* prompt, incite 222/18,
229/30; *tr.* 173/29; move 185/31,
186/23, 210/28; *ppl. adj.* turbid
250/27: stereþ *pr. 3 sg.* 222/34.
ystered *pp.* 233/27

steriinges *vbl. n. pl.* impulses 250/10,
259/10, 261/7

sterne *adj.* stern 130/5

sterre *n.* star 141/10, 164/28. ster-
ren *pl.* 267/27

sterue *v. intr.* die 2/18, 70/27, 71/24;
ppl. adj. transitory 75/1: sterfst
pr. 2 sg. 71/33. sterfþ *3 sg.* 54/6,
71/2, sterf 70/26 *n.*, 75/2, 202/15.
sterueþ *pl.* 36/29, 53/3 *n.*, 71/32.
steruinde *pr. p.* 75/1. starf
pa. t. 3 sg. 165/21. storue(n)
pl. 12/34, 67/21

steruinge *vbl. n.* death 73/18,
95/16, 110/29

steues *n. pl.* staves 156/8

stille *adj.* silent 58/15, 115/9, 152/
26

stillehed *n.* silence 142/30

stilleliche *adv.* secretly 65/3

stinkinde *ppl. adj.* stinking 81/9,
189/29, 270/33

stocke *n.* (*p.c.*) trunk, stem 19/34,
22/16, 146/28

ystole see stele

stole *n.* (*p.c.*) stool 239/5, 8

ston *n.* stone 5/4, 63/30, 150/24.
stone *p.c.* 91/32. stones *pl.* 76/33,
81/26, 133/2

stonchi *v. tr.* quench, satisfy 73/23.
stoncheþ *pr. 3 sg.* 110/33

stondeþ, stondinde see stant

stoppi *v. tr.* stop 257/8, 31, 33.
stoppeþ *pr. 3 sg.* 257/20, 25.
stoppe *imp. sg.* 257/5, 15

stor *n.* incense 211/17, 18

storm *n.* storm 131/5

storue(n) see sterue

stoupi *subj. sg. intr.* incline 151/6

stout *adj.* terrible 130/5

strayny *subj. sg. tr.* restrain 263/21

strait *adj.* strict 54/5, 130/6. strayte
wk. narrow 78/16. straite *pl.*
267/29; parsimonious 187/18

straitliche *adv.* strictly, closely 7/19,
18/36, 34/28, 213/2*

strang *adj.* strong 16/27, 32/21,
51/11; fierce 168/9, 182/4, 24;
difficult 57/25, 78/19*, 104/19:
strangne *acc.* 227/21. stronge *p.c.*
168/2. *wk.* 181/9. *pl.* 83/35, 157/18,
204/11; þe ..... stronge 168/12,
13, stranger, strenger *comp.*
/5/20, 168/9, 204/14; *heþ more* ∼
to has more difficulty in 170/21 *n.*

strangliche, strongliche *adv.*
greatly, mightily 143/1, 233/26*
(*see page 50*), 28; firmly 15/13;
resolutely 127/3; vehemently 212/5:
stranglaker *comp.* 17/17* (*see
p. 49*), 25/11, 88/10. **stranglakest**
superl. 157/27

stream *n.* river, stream 72/26,
202/28, 31. **streame** *p.c.* 72/34,
streme 72/28 *n.* **streames** *pl.*
97/34, 98/29, **stremes** 248/11

strechche *v. refl.* extend 103/35

streng *n.* line; *ase* ~ as straight as a
die 159/14

strenger see **strang**

strengþe *n.* fortress 21/21 *n.*, 240/30;
power, strength 15/12*, 18/25,
126/12 *n.*, 141/24*; fortitude 3/29*,
111/23, **strengþ** 124/23‡; force,
violence 38/34, 46/12*, 149/31*,
182/6; *be* ~ in spite of himself
161/20 *n.*; *maky* ~ attach im-
portance 25/30–1, 107/15–16; *þerof
no* ~ it does not matter 51/36

strengþi *v. tr.* constrain 86/8 *n.*;
strengthen, fortify 105/1, 116/27.
strengþeþ *pr. 3 sg.* 111/20, 180/29;
nourishes 205/17*. **ystrengþed**
pp. fortified 201/9

strepe *v. tr.* extirpate 163/27.
strepeþ *pr. pl.* 105/18, 130/17.
strepe *subj. pl.* 98/19

strete *n.* (*p.c.*) street 143/17

strif *n.* debate 53/31; strife, conflict
22/2, 23/12, 65/7 *n.* **strifs** *pl.*
43/30, 57/3, 66/35

stryfinge *vbl. n.* strife 57/29

striui *v. intr.* quarrel 65/34. **striu-
inde** *pr. p.* in conflict 154/8.
ystriued *pp.* debated 164/33

strok *n.* blow 34/11, 167/11. **stroke**
p.c. 61/22. **strokes** *pl.* 167/20, 23;
claps 130/11

stronge, strongliche see **strang,
strangliche**

stude *n.* study 70/16 *n.*

studie *v. intr.* consider 24/19; en-
deavour 82/30, 155/5; study 94/19;
refl. 126/4: **studeþ** *pr. 3 sg.* 155/5.
studieþ *pl.* 34/24, 39/22, 56/21.
stude *imp. sg.* 232/35 *n.* **studede**
pa. t. pl. 126/4

subprior *n.* subprior 67/31

substance *n.* substance; *ope* ~ *adj.*
supersubstantial 113/4 *n.* **sub-
stances** *pl.* 112/31, 34 *n.*

substanciel *adj.* sustaining 112/30,
113/4, 5. **substancieler** *comp.*
113/1

sucre *n.* sugar 83/10 *n.*

sudyakne *n.* subdean 225/33. **suþ-
deaknes** *pl.* 235/7

summe see **somme**

suspect *adj.* suspect 205/34

suspiciouses *adj. pl.* of dubious
character 226/9, 231/28

sustyeneþ, sustinonce see **sostyeni,
sostinonce**

suþdeaknes see **sudyakne**

T

tabernacle *n.* tabernacle 236/17

table *n.* table 236/1. **tables** *pl.* slabs
of stone, tables (of the law) 5/4,
63/30; backgammon 45/16, 52/30,
207/6

ytaȝt see **teche**

tayl *n.*[1]. tail 61/12. **tayle** *p.c.* 61/6,
62/14, 257/21. **tayles** *pl.* 61/4

tayles *n.*[2] *pl.* taxes 38/27

take *v. tr.* give 171/27; take 220/23;
touch 22/31; *intr.* 56/19: **takþ**
pr. 3 sg. 175/22. **takeþ** *pl.* 36/26.
take *subj. sg.* 22/31. **tok** *pa. t. 3 sg.*
246/20. **token** *pl.* 36/36. **ytake**
pp. 75/12 *n.*

takynge *vbl. n.* touching 91/25.
takinges *pl.* 9/17, 10/29, 46/25

ytald see **telle**

tale *n.* number 11/29, 234/14, 16;
measure 108/11; denomination 152/
32; tale 4/2, 45/30. **tales** *pl.*
58/19, 99/17, 175/23 *n.*

talyinde *pr. p.* narrating 207/28 *n.*

tasteþ *pr. 3 sg. tr.* tastes 245/30,
247/25. **ytasted** *pp.* 93/11

tauerne *n.* tavern 56/18, 57/4, 128/1.
tauernes *pl.* 57/6

tauernyer *n.* tavern-goer 51/14.
tauernyers *pl.* tavern-keepers
44/24

te see **to**

tealde see **telle**

teares *n. pl.* tears 135/18, 171/12,
tyares 173/22, 226/19, **tyeares**

74/22, ⟨tyeaers⟩ *83/8*, **tyeres**
161/4; sap 96/5 *n.*

techches *n. pl.* vices 32/15, 136/23
teche *v. tr.* teach 8/11, 73/8, 118/18.
pr. 1 sg. 71/35 (*future*). **tekþ** *3 sg.*
6/9, 49/24, 54/15, 76/8 *n.* **techeþ**
pl. 8/15, 249/29. **teche** *subj. sg.*
127/26. **toȝte** *pa. t. 3 sg.* 96/19,
149/16, 187/5. **ytaȝt** *pp.* 267/27;
ppl. adj. euele ~ ill-bred 63/32;
pl. (**wel**) **ytoȝte** well-educated
254/34

techeres *n. pl.* teachers 267/24
techinge *vbl. n.* instruction, 17/1,
68/35, 69/20, 220/10* *n.* **techinges**
pl. instruction 220/18
tedraȝynge see **todraȝynge**
teȝele *n.* tile 167/14
telle *v. tr.* tell, proclaim 56/1, 73/25,
175/9; enumerate, number, cal-
culate 17/20, 23/35, 57/1 (*cf.* **euele**)
intr. 21/13; rehearse 178/26 *n.*:
telþ *pr. 3 sg.* 62/1, 71/21, 191/7.
telleþ *pl.* 58/16, 118/30 *n.*, 175/9;
tealde *pa. t. 3 sg.* 239/1. **ytald**
pp. 24/17, 70/10
tellynge *vbl. n.* see **algorisme**
temperance *n.* temperance 124/6,
22*, 126/34, 245/15
tempeste *n.* tempest 73/22, 142/1,
212/15. **tempestes** *pl.* 239/19
temple *n.* temple 175/15, 180/32,
193/30
tempreþ *pr. 3 sg. tr.* tempers 254/34.
wel ytempred *ppl. adj.* healthy
144/34; temperate 257/35
temptacion *n.* temptation 158/29,
252/7
ten *num.* ten 5/2, 11/20, 14/35
tende *ord. num.* tenth 2/8, 11/6, 13/
36
tendes *n. pl.* tithes 41/20
tendre *adj.* delicate, tender 31/18,
77/4, 148/33
teppe *n.* tap 27/31
terestre *adj.* terrestrial 50/28, 221/28
terme *n.* term, period of time 33/22,
35/13
testament *n.* will 191/1, 3
teþ *n. pl.* teeth 265/5; *be-tuene his/
þine* ~ quietly 67/8, 210/18 *n.*
teue *adv. phr.* yesterday evening
(= *to eue*) 51/11

tyares, tyeares see **teares**
tidyinges *n. pl.* tidings 58/16
tyeaers see **teares**
tyene *n.* disinclination 31/5, 14,
34/8; anger 64/4, 66/1, 69/34;
vexation 268/16
tyeny *v. tr.* weary 34/7; *refl.* become
weary 99/14; *intr.* pall 161/2:
tieneþ *pr. 3 sg.* 34/7, 161/3, 13.
tyeneþ *pl.* 142/28. **tyene** *imp. sg.*
73/15
tyeres see **teares**
time *n.* hour 117/20; time 12/26,
31/25, 39/24 *n.*, 56/7; extension of
credit 36/5 (*see note to 36/10*);
season 36/22, 68/17; world 267/19.
times *pl.* times 101/4, 114/14;
seasons 224/13; *ine* ~ see (h)**oure**;
none ~ never 90/33; *of* ~ temporal
154/29; *to* ~ on credit 44/28
time-zettere *n.* creditor 36/6 (*cf.
note to 36/5*)
time-zettinge *vbl. n.* giving of
credit 36/10 (*cf. note to 36/5*)
tim(e)lich *adj.* temporal, worldly
30/5, 44/12, 45/18. **timliche** *pl.*
2/21, 19/1, 52/12; *n. pl.* temporal
things 154/34 *n.*
tiront *n.* tyrant 230/34. **tyrans** *pl.*
182/7
to *prep.* to 1/4, 10, 13, 62/4 *n.*;
into 225/19; in 45/24 *n.*, 87/26 *n.*,
105/24 *n.*, 246/24 *n.*; at 12/28,
36/1, 119/14; by 106/20; from
139/2; with 48/9; against, towards
29/31, 108/23, 111/36; before
215/25; in accordance with, accord-
ing to 215/27, 243/16; in regard to,
as regards 26/3, 84/35, 252/28; in
comparison with 59/27; of 24/28,
25/3, 135/9; for 16/34, 42/21, 55/
30 *n.*, 89/3 *n.*, 93/9 *n.*, 248/24 *n.*;
as 91/33, 144/12; (*as an adjunct
of the infinitive in infinitival or
gerundial uses*) to, te 5/20, 31/13 *n.*,
82/24, 174/7, 204/25; in order to
22/15, 93/33; ~ **þan þet**, ~ **þet**
see **þet** *conj.* cf. **þerto**
to *adv.* too 6/3, 9/15, 16; all to
39/9; very 16/25, 18/19, 31/6;
excessively 258/11[1]; even 31/8; ~
moche see **moche**
toayans, toayens see **toyeans**

tobreȝþ *pr. 3 sg. tr.* dismember 6/33. **tobrekeþ** *pl.* 64/30, 70/1. **tobroke** *ppl. adj.* 206/15, *pp.* destroyed 30/27, broken up 239/19

tocleue *v. intr.* burst 56/10. *pr. 1 sg.* 56/9 (*future*). *subj. pl.* 50/21 *n.*

tocne *n.* sign, token 68/8 *n.*, 177/3 *n.*, 203/35, 222/20. **tocnen** *pl.* 2/17 *n.*, 10/27, 69/9 *n.*, 216/12

today *adv.* today 51/5

todele *v. tr.* divide, classify 2/20, 17/18, 164/4; distinguish 80/17, 83/16 *n.*, 123/25; separate 93/15, 235/29; distribute, give 122/27, 188/29; *refl.* be divided, separated 16/11, 221/15, 243/36; depart 81/12, 226/21: **todelþ** *pr. 3 sg.* 17/19, 23/33, 72/26. **todele** *subj. pl.* 72/5. **todel** *imp. sg.* 73/2, 74/34. **todelde** *pa. t. 3 sg.* 226/21. **todelden** *pl.* 164/4. **todeld** *pp.* 86/30, 106/16, 175/20

todelinge *vbl. n.* separation 72/2, 189/34; classification 3/28, 164/3

todiȝt *pr. 3 sg. tr.* distinguishes 164/14

todiȝtinge *vbl. n.* separation 72/14

todraȝþ *pr. 3 sg. tr.* tears to pieces 62/7

todraȝinge, tedraȝynge *vbl. n.* detraction 57/29, 61/7 *n.*, 62/7

togidere *adv.* together 48/35, 67/1, 111/9; united 14/4, 243/35; each other 146/2 *n.*, *for other reciprocal uses see* **he**

(y)toȝte see **teche**

toheawe *v. tr.* cut to pieces 178/7. **toheauþ** *pr. 3 sg.* 62/8

tok(en) see **take**

tokninge *vbl. n.* sign 50/18

tol *n.* toll 192/10

tomochelhede *n.* excess 248/13. **tomochelhedes** *pl.* 218/9 *n.*

tonge *n.* speeche, tongue 24/5, 50/11, 56/9. **tongen, tonges** *pl.* 22/23, 58/12, 142/2

toniȝt *adv.* tonight 51/10

tonne *n.* barrel 27/32, 167/23, 247/27. **tonnen** *pl.* 35/18

toparti *v. tr.* separate 107/8; *pr. 3 sg.* distinguishes 170/9

toppe *prep.* above 6/9, 106/9, 163/2

torment *n.* affliction 252/6; torment 29/32 *n.*, 79/15, 95/33. **tormens** *pl.* 73/6, 111/25, 161/9

tormenteþ *pr. pl. tr.* torment 53/20, 85/30 *n.*

tormentors *n. pl.* torturers 265/12

tornement, tornoyment *n.* tournament 46/14, 101/11, 252/11, ⟨**tornenoyment**⟩ 14 *n.* **tornemens, tornoymens** *pl.* 36/11, 117/4, 252/10

tornees see **coruees**

torni *v. intr.* deviate 152/11

toþrauþ *pr. 3 sg. tr.* disperses 256/25

toualþ *pr. 3 sg. intr.* falls 33/16, is ruined 184/11

toune *n.* (*p.c.*) town 162/5, 195/8. **tounes** *pl.* 30/27, 43/27

touor(e) *prep.* in front of, before 10/17, 13/17, 20/30; beyond 228/10; *adv.* afore (mentioned) 7/30, 97/23

tour *n.* tower 47/21, 151/6, 168/2. **tours** *pl.* 23/25, 116/21, 124/19

toyeans, **to(a)yens** *prep.* against 10/10, ⟨**to(a)yans**⟩, 6/23, 20/21, (*see p. 15*); opposite 158/10; towards 155/33, 156/6; ~ *wille* unwillingly 86/9

traysoun *n.* treason 37/15, 43/22

trauail *n.* suffering 130/33, 246/15; toil 251/12

trauayly *v. intr.* toil 33/15. to be in labour 74/3; *tr.* afflict 39/26; **trauayli** *pr. 1. sg.* 171/11. **trauayleþ** *pl.* 143/17

trauailinde *ppl. adj.* turbulent 167/32

trau *n.* tree 26/15, 57/22, 97/30 *n.* **traue** *p.c.* 95/24, 96/2, 35, **trauwe** 28/13. **traues** *pl.* 25/12, 94/27, 95/13

tresor *n.* treasure 57/35, 58/33, 96/24

tresoriere *n.* female treasurer 231/21

tretable *adj.* tractable 94/33; malleable 167/30

treteþ *pr. 3 sg. intr.* treats 142/22

trewe *adj.* honest 135/15, 153/20, 192/8; loyal 101/9, 103/21, 108/22. **treweste** *superl. wk.* 166/15

treu(e)liche *adv.* faithfully, truly 134/8, 135/3, 218/30, **trieweliche** 169/31; honestly 135/10 treuþe *n.* plighted word, loyalty 48/17, 65/19, 163/2; honesty 256/31; impartiality 153/24

triacle *n.* medicine, remedy 17/1, 61/18, 144/28

tribulacion *n.* tribulation 167/12, 269/19. **tribulaciouns** *pl.* 108/27

tribus *n. pl.* tribes 267/14

ytrid *pp.* tested 153/26

trieweliche see **treu(e)liche**

trinite *n.* Trinity 11/34, 105/24, 266/19

trobli *v. tr.* trouble, disturb 129/3, 150/16; *refl.* to feel emotion, be disturbed 104/9, 149/34: **tro(u)b-leþ** *pr. 3 sg.* 129/3, *250/24.* **troubleþ** *pl.* 149/34, 150/16

trone *n.* throne 181/31, 266/33. **tronen** *pl.* 267/13

trossinge *vbl. n.* binding up 176/34 *n.*

trosti *v. refl.* trust 242/2 *(see note to 241/34–6).* **trost** *imp. sg.* 241/35 *n.*

troubleþ see **trobli**

trufles *n. pl.* trifling tales, idle chatter 56/6, 58/22, 74/13; trifles 142/23

trufli *v. intr.* jest 214/32

truont *n.* beggar 174/30. **truons** *pl.* 194/5, 208/24

tuay(e), tuo *num.* two 1/18, 30/19, 32/30, 72/12‡ *(cf. p. 76)*

tuelf *num.* twelve 11/25 (MS. *tuels*), 26, 29, 24/26

tuelfte *ord. num.* twelfth 14/13

tuenti *num.* twenty 47/10, 239/21

tuies *num.* twice 35/11, 36/8, 112/1

tuyg *n.* twig 22/5. **tuygges** *pl.* 41/34, 43/7, **tuyegges** 17/29

tuysteþ *pr. 3 sg. intr.* bifurcates, divides 159/17, 24

tuo see **tuay(e)**

turle *n.* turtle-dove 226/2

þ

þa see **þe**

þaȝ *conj.* although *(with subj.)* 9/11, 20/1, 38/8; *(with ind.)* 56/10; if *(with subj.)* 32/24

þaȝles *adv.* nevertheless 6/17, 30, 8/22, 9/2

þan(n), þan(n)e *def. art. and dem. pron.* see **þe**

þan(n)e *adv.* then *(correlate with* **huan(ne))** 27/5, 36/7, 180/22; furthermore 11/31, 16/10; for, accordingly 7/14, 119/24 *n.,* 143/8 *n.,* 144/8 *n.,* 179/15 *n.,* 252/10; *conj.* when 20/33, 21/16, 179/15; than 12/12, *(with subj.)* 36/8, 193/30 *n.,* *(with ind.)* 168/10 *n.;* ~ þet because 100/14–15

þank *n.* grace 262/29; thanks 18/17; gratitude 159/23; *conne* ~ see **conne**: þonke *p.c.* 271/7. **þonkes** *pl.* 18/6, 55/12, 85/22

þannes *adv.* thence 12/32, 178/21, 263/6

þanoþrene *see* **þe** *and* **oþer** *adj.*

þe *def. art.* the 1/1, 3, 5/2, *185/16*[1], de 162/17 *(see p. 52),* ⟨þo⟩ 17/32 *n.,* 41/19, 47/4, 225/34. **þan(n)e** *acc. masc.* 7/5, 13/11, **þan(n)** 66/9‡, 72/32,‡ 87/14; *acc. of time* 213/5, 6; **þet** *neut.* 14/14, 15/7, 16/1; **þo** *dem. adj. acc. fem. (cf. p. 79, n. 1)* that 130/23, 225/6. **þo, þa** *p.c. (all genders)* 1/10, 33/16 *n.,* 50/25. **þo** *pl.* 71/20. **þet** *dem. pron.* that 16/12, 20/2 *n.,* 59/9*, 84/28 *n.,* 153/2*; ~ byeþ, *ssolle by* those are, will be, namely 154/29, 189/26. **þo** *acc. fem.* that 211/12 *(cf. p. 79, n. 1).* **þan(e)** *acc. masc.* he 61/22, 79/22. **þan** *dat. masc.* him 32/9, 217/11 *n.,* 253/10, 11. *p.c. (all genders)* that 30/31, 54/11, 154/29; him 23/11, 50/25, 85/24; *(hanc)* her 263/36. **þo** *pl.* those, them 9/13, 148/30, 158/24. **þane** *dat.* 64/13 *(see p. 52, n. 1).* **þan, þon** *p.c.* 11/31, 39/15, 122/10, 270/35 *n.;* *for mid* ~, *naȝt uor* ~ *see* **mid, na(u)ȝt**: *to* ~ þet for whom 22/32 *n.*

þe *pron. see* **þo(u)**

þe *adv.* the 8/3, 17/3, 21/34

þe *conj. and rel. pron.* see **þet**

þeawes *n. pl.* morals 259/21; *guode* ~ high moral principles, virtues, morality 78/29, **þeauwes** 131/32, **þewes** 79/30; *kueade, wyckede* ~ vices 17/8, 129/28, 149/29

þellich *adj.* this, of this nature, such 6/12, 7/4, 8/2; **þellyche** *acc.* 263/11. **þelliche** *pl.* 27/21, 266/14

þenche v. tr. think, intend 31/24,
57/34, 213/34; consider 184/24,
215/21, 257/29; think about 92/1;
conceive, imagine 55/14, 73/24,
81/28; intr. think 7/26, 47/1 n.,
204/25 n.; consider, 18/21, 173/3;
ppl. adj. intent 253/35; ~ elleshuer,
nawerelles (not) have one's thoughts
elsewhere 210/27, 211/6–7: þenche
pr. 1 sg. 213/34. þengst 2 sg.
214/3. þencþ, þengþ 3 sg. 24/22,
155/5, 257/28. þencheþ pl. 82/29,
210/27, 212/35. þenche subj. sg.
155/4 n., 203/20, 210/23. þench
imp. sg. 20/10, 92/4, 101/8. þen-
chinde pr. p. 212/29, 253/35.
þoȝte pa. t. 1 sg. 259/26. 3 sg.
191/28, 240/6. yþoȝt pp. 173/6

þenchinge vbl. n. intellect 270/8, 10;
thought 72/6; be ~ deliberately
6/26, 72/16. þenchinges pl.
thoughts 76/2, 212/10

þer(e) adv. there 13/1, 24/25, 208/27;
anticipatory subject 9/11, 195/35,
203/34; conj. where 1/11, 10/1, 20/7

þeraboute adv. round about 66/26

þeraboue adv. aloft 244/23

þeramang adv. among them 205/24

þerby adv. because of this 85/20

þerefter adv. afterwards, thereafter
267/9, 269/4

þerhuile, þerhuils (þet) conj. while,
as long as 7/18, 139/9, 194/30,
217/27

þerin(ne), þ(e)rin(e) adv. in there
56/31; into it 34/22, 58/2, 117/22;
in it 106/36, 167/23, 176/5

þerles n. pl. windows 204/9

þermide adv. as well 127/12, 15

þerne see þis

þerof adv. of it 5/7; of them 11/29;
for that 23/19; from this 23/5,
31/12, 89/19 n.; concerning this,
which 194/12, 220/13, 246/32;
because of this 34/4; ~ þet from
that from which 156/9; from the
fact that 161/9; of that of which
175/10 n.; from that which 192/7

þeronder adv. under it 226/26

þerteyens adv. contrary to them
11/23

þerto adv. to (do) it 8/25, 140/9,
169/15; to this 162/4; added to it

11/13; as well, in addition (to this)
57/12, 169/3, 239/26; ~ þet conj.
in order that (with subj.) 116/18–19,
172/6

þeruore adv. then, furthermore
178/30, 179/25; thus 193/15; there-
fore, for this reason 6/8, 14/24,
140/9, 268/32 n.; on account of
this 34/12, 90/27 n.; on account
of it 115/3; correlative with þer-
uore þet 50/8, 258/7; þer(e)-
uor(e) þet conj. because 50/5,
113/1, 149/22; in order that (with
subj. 21/34, 58/27, 137/28–9

þerwyþ adv. as well 140/27

þes(e) see þis

þet def. art. see þe

þet dem. pron. see þe

þet rel. pron. who, which, that 1/12,
5/24, 7/15, 150/33, ⟨þe⟩ 215/7 (see
note to 254/30); ⟨þeþ⟩ 228/20 (cf.
146/5 n.); as 254/3; him . . . who
159/7; whose 64/21; (with an ante-
cedent p.c.) 13/5, 20/8, 19, 64/8; (with
a following adverb) 18/1–2, 89/2–3n.;
225/7–8 (see pp. 81–2); that which,
what 9/29, 15/13, 151/20, 256/27; he
who 37/13 n.; those who 162/11;
huo þet . . . þet he who . . . he who
210/5–6; (governed by a preposition)
13/3, 24, 32/27, 59/27, 127/4;
interr. what (with subj.) 153/30

þet conj. that 12/19, 14/31, 15/2,
149/15*, ⟨þe⟩ 265/35 (see note to
254/30); (so) that 27/25, 33/5,
63/24; in order that (with subj.)
5/11, 125/25, 26, 27, ⟨þe⟩ 254/30 n.;
in that, because 20/23, 83/1 n.,
85/29 n., 211/31, 238/17¹, 256/28²;
provided that (with subj.) 196/20;
than 21/12 n., 24/20, 75/19 n.,
193/4 n.; ne ~ see ne; namely
244/12 n.; al to þan ~ see al;
(ase) be (þan) ~ according as 49/2,
175/3, 180/8; because 204/12;
be þan ~ . . . be þan ~ according
as . . . even so 119/17–18 n.; be
zuo ~ see bi; efterward ~ after
188/28–9; er þan ~ (with subj.)
before 158/31, 167/25, 245/34;
ine ~ , ine þan/þet ~ in that 18/13–
14, 55/23, 134/9; ine þet ~ (with
subj.) in so far as 20/34, 105/26;

ine zuo moche ~ see **in(e)**; *mid
þan* see **mid**; *naȝt uor þan* see
na(u)ȝt; ~ . . . *ne* but that,
without . . . -ing 27/10, 178/11–12,
226/29; unless 109/22 *n.*; *of* ~ from
the fact that 161/7; *to* (*þan*) ~
(*with ind.*) 106/20; (*with subj.*) in
order that 56/1, 170/32, 201/2–3;
uor þan ~, *uor* (*þet*) ~ (*with ind.*)
because 15/8, 51/20, 54/20 *n.*,
63/20; (*with subj.*) 224/16; *uor*
(*þan*) ~ (*with ind.*; *see note to*
23/7) in order that 26/5, 59/33,
60/17; (*with subj.*) 156/24; *uor* ~
. . . ~ 55/16–17; cf. **uor**; *uram* ~
from the time that 191/8; *wyþoute*
~ notwithstanding 220/35–6; *zuo*
~ (*with ind.*) with the result that
16/31, 67/16, 68/5; (*with subj.*)
in order that, in such a way that
113/8, 171/14, 174/23, 196/6–7;
zuiche/zuo . . . ~ such, so, to such
an extent . . . that 30/1, 61/18,
107/8, 176/31–2; *zuo* . . . *zuo* ~
so . . . that 33/12–14; *for þet as a
subordinating particle see the main
component*

þewes see **þeawes**
þi see **þo(u)**
þider *adv.* thither 140/34, 207/27
þief *n.* thief 37/8, 10 *n.*, 13, 51/16,
135/23. **þyeue** *p.c.* 263/29. **þieues**
pl. 37/7, 38/1, 57/4, **þyues** 254/9
þiefþe *n.* theft 9/23, 34/33, 37/4
þierne *n.* handmaid 129/10
þyester, þiestre *adj.* dark 45/2,
159/11, 18; in darkness 270/14, 19,
21
þiesterliche *adv.* obscurely 244/10
þiesternesse *n.* darkness 200/20,
264/35, **þyesterness** 189/29‡,
þyesternesses *pl.* darkness 108/8
þin(e), þinen see **þo(u)**
þezelue see **þizelf**
þing *n.* something 43/24, 59/9,
64/8; anything 165/6; reason 270/
24; matter, thing 39/14, 63/17,
138/34; possession 222/22; *uor no*
~ on any account 47/3: **þin(n)ge**
p.c. 23/18, 164/25, 222/30. **þing**
pl. 1/12, 103/5, 170/34, 209/10 *n.*,
þinge 83/19 *n.*, **þinges** 2/33, 6/4,
9/17, 40/36 *n.*

þin(n)gþ *pr. 3 sg. impers.* seems,
appears 18/15, 33/30, 80/31, 143/
16, 211/7 *n.* **þoȝte** *pa. t. 3 sg.*
187/32, 195/28, 208/14
þis *dem. adj.* this 1/5, 7/14, 48/9,
202/5. **þes** *nom. masc.* (*see pp. 85–6*)
23/2, 41/33, 43/7. **þise** (*see p. 70*)
146/28, 191/30, 250/9. **þerne**
acc. masc. (*see p. 73, n. 1*) 73/30,
86/5, 14. **þise** *acc.* 8/8, 53/4,
71/35, 98/35. (*all genders*) *dat.*
156/3. *p.c.* 5/13, 6/3, 8/9, **þese**
151/28. **þise** *pl.* 6/5, 12/2, 60/14,
þis (*see p. 74*) 73/12; **þis** *dem.
pron.* this 1/1, 25/32, 80/9. **þes**
nom. masc. (*cf. pp. 85–6*) this
man 53/26; this 62/4, 13. (*all
genders*) **þise(n)** *p.c.* 44/28, 45/7,
97/18. **þise** *pl.* these 1/16, 11/26,
25/6, **þis** 11/20 (*see p. 75, n. 4*);
these people 35/14, 36/2, 39/31;
þos *masc. pl.* (*see p. 75 n. 4*)
these people 10/18, 39/32, 242/12
þizelf *emphatic pron.* thyself 90/7;
þezelue, þizelue *refl. p.c.* 54/30,
73/1, 100/24, 145/30
þo *def. art.* see **þe**
þo *dem. adj. and pron.* see **þe**
þo(u), þu, þe *pron.* thou 1/2, 8/3,
20/10, 51/1, 148/4* *n.*; *suffixed in*
wyltou 166/10, **comste** 264/30.
þe *acc./dat.* 21/4, 71/27, 114/20,
196/8 *n.*; *refl.* thyself 7/8, 20/16,
179/26; **þi** *poss. adj.* 1/13, 21/10,
106/10–11, **þin** (*for use before
consonants see p. 51*) thy, thine
1/2, 106/10, 107/9 *n.*, 114/19,
146/36 *n.*, **þine** 159/9 *n.* (*see p. 70*).
acc. 5/22, 8/2, 54/34. *gen.* 11/7 *n.*,
10/22. *dat.* 10/8. *p.c.* 1/13, 20/10,
54/33. *pl.* 7/7, 156/15, 159/15;
þinen *pron.* 194/29 *n.*
þo *conj.* when 50/17, 70/6, 129/7,
236/13 *n.*
þoȝt *n.* thought, intent, intention
100/30. **þoȝte** *p.c.* 6/26, 11/4,
63/11*; **þoȝtes** *pl.* 9/16, 11/13,
27/14; solicitude 93/35; *ine* ~
thoughtful (*apensé*) 115/13
þoȝte, yþoȝt *v.*[1] see **þenche**
þoȝte *v.*[2] see **þin(n)gþ**
þolemodness(e) *n.* long-suffering,
patience 68/4, 182/19 *n.*, 215/31,

þolemodness(e) (*cont.*)
265/20; compassion 185/26, 30,
186/4, 8

þolie *v. tr.* suffer, endure 22/31,
68/35, 84/16; restrain 224/32;
permit 64/27, 34, 263/15; *intr.*
endure 33/33, 133/1, 167/4; *ppl.*
adj. patient 167/4: þoleþ *pr. 3 sg.*
125/19, 127/3, 132/34. þole *imp.*
sg. 117/25, 269/29. þolyinde *pr. p.*
167/4. þolede *pa. t. 3 sg.* 12/25,
78/18, 111/15. þoleden *pl.* 74/2.
yþoled *pp.* 182/30

þolyinge *vbl. n.* endurance 163/25,
164/10; *for mid* ~ see mid-
þolyinge

þon see þe

þondre *n.(p.c.)* thunder 130/11

þonke(s) see þank

þonki *v. tr./intr.* thank 6/8, 7/27,
24/12; *intr.* give thanks 134/8;
euele ~ express ill-will towards
30/8, 68/20: þonkeþ *pr. 3 sg.*
18/5, 9, 85/12. yþonked *pp.* 196/15

þonneliche *adv.* thinly 31/10 *n.*

þorз *prep.* through 81/7

þornes *n. pl.* thorns 142/6, 156/29,
230/9

þornhoз *n.* porcupine 66/13

yþorsse *pp.* struck 266/21; *ppl.*
adj. threshed 139/33

þorst *n.* thirst 73/22, 75/9, 96/30;
habbe ~ see habbe

þos *dem. adj., pron.* see þis

þos *adv.* see þus

þosend see þouzend

þoume *n.* thumb 43/14

þous see þus

þouzend, þouzond, þosend *num.*
thousand 67/17, 157/22, 190/34,
191/2, 264/20, þouzen 75/18 (*see*
pp. 15, 50, 52)

þrawe *v. tr.* cast, throw 17/7, 139/35;
thrust 179/6; pelt 133/2: þrauþ
pr. 3 sg. 23/24, 34/16, þrawþ
179/9. þrauwe *subj. pl.* 152/36.
þreu *pa. t. 3 sg.* 133/2

þreapni *v. tr.* threaten 84/20, 162/31;
intr. þreapneþ *pr. pl.* 97/17

þreapninge *vbl. n.* menace, threat
65/30, 121/24. þreapnynges *pl.*
38/28, 66/31

þrel *n.* serf, slave 19/16, 53/36,

86/18 *n.* þrelles *pl.* 67/28, 86/24,
149/36

þreldom *n.* bondage 87/4, 248/30,
253/7. þreldome *p.c.* 67/17, 86/23,
103/12

þreste *n. (p.c.)* throng 121/24 *n.*
þrestes *pl.* mêlées 183/7

þresten *pa. t. pl. tr.* thrust 204/25

þri *num.* three 7/34, 11/20, 25/33

þridde *ord. num.* third 7/3, 12/14,
13/11

þries *num.* three times 35/11, 36/8

þrin see þerin(ne)

þrittaзte *num.* thirty-fold 234/6, 11

þritti *num.* thirty 141/12, 234/12,
239/13

þriziþe see þri and ziþe, ziþes

þrote *n.* throat 14/34, 15/15, 50/24

þu see þo(u)

þus, þous, þos *adv.* thus 25/4,
46/29, 52/27; proportionately 227/
16

U/V (Vocalic)

uile see oyle

under see onder

understonde see onderstonde

vnonynge *vbl. n.* discord 65/30, 33

us see we

us *n.* use 37/33, 41/16, 55/35

usi *v. tr.* use 48/31, 120/8; indulge,
practise 55/23, 60/29 *n.*, 92/17;
intr. be accustomed 113/31; make
use 18/14 *n.*, 252/8: useþ *pr. 3 sg.*
53/25, 77/13, 185/19. useþ *pl.*
19/9, 55/9, 78/8. usy *subj. sg.*
79/14. *pl.* 79/10. used, *pp.* 115/27,
215/24

U/V (Consonantal)

uader *n.* father 8/2, 11/32, 193/20 *n.*
uader, uaderes *gen. sg.* 64/13,
263/20. uaderes *pl.* 8/10, 35/25, 26;
patriarchs 12/33

uaderlease *adj.(pl.)* fatherless 193/7,
uaderlyese 188/15

uair(e) *adj.* fair, elegant 16/17, 24/
31, 53/22, 57/21, 98/14, 144/35; gra-
cious 110/13, 139/1; excellent 190/2,
234/22; unblemished 88/8; *n.*
beauty 81/28 *n.*, 270/6; *maki* ~ *chiere*
see chiere; *maki* ~ see maki;
for ~ *semblant* see semblant:

uaire *p.c.* 36/23, 47/20. *wk.* 88/4, 98/13, 187/6. *pl.* 16/29, 23/29, 24/33, uayrer *comp.* 88/8, 146/23. uayreste, ua(y)riste *superl. wk.* 78/2, 81/23, 142/31 *n.*

uayr(e) *adv.* beautifully 47/12

uayrehede, uairhede *n.* beauty 16/15, 81/14, 228/31; purity 201/ 2 *n.*, 32, 246/25

uayreþ *pr. 3 sg. tr.* embellishes 231/11; *intr.* purifies 246/10; becomes fair 95/23: uayreþ *pl.* 233/1. yuayred *pp.* 107/12, 200/ 31

uayrliche *adv.* downrightly 59/26

(y)ualle *v. intr.* fall 42/29, 129/32, 204/29; decline 29/35, 33/14; start (*to do sth.*) 31/20; happen 15/21, 30/26, 54/5; result 48/19: *huet cas* ~ see cas: (i)ualþ *pr. 3 sg.* 15/21, 54/5, 66/24. ualleþ *pl.* 69/22, 176/9, 207/8. (y)ualle *subj. sg.* 36/25, 130/3, 206/34. ualle *pl.* 253/30. uil *pa. t. 3 sg.* 16/18, 46/2, 181/13. uille(n) *pl.* 67/12, 98/4, 204/16. yualle *pp.* 116/3, 135/22, 193/21

uallynge *vbl. n.* falling; ~ *doun* impairment 269/13

ualouweþ *pr. 3 sg. intr.* fades 81/11

uals *adj.* unjust, dishonest 22/2, 27/14, 40/8; false, counterfeit 19/21, 26/7, 40/8; erroneous 69/22; untrustworthy 171/4; *n.* deceiver 76/5: ualsne *acc. masc.* 24/14. ualse *acc.* 10/5, 26/7, 64/35. *wk.* 62/24. *pl.* 10/19, 27/29, 39/23

uals *adv.* falsely 6/23, 65/1

ualsere *n.* forger 62/23

ualseþ *pr. 3 sg. tr.* falsifies, forges 62/20. *pl.* 40/8

ualshede *n.* falsehood 10/17. ualshedes *pl.* deceptions 39/19, 40/10, 63/12

ualsliche *adv.* falsely 28/6, 64/35

ualsnesse *n.* falsehood 256/14

uand see (y)uinde

uanites *n. pl.* vanities 77/22

uanni *v. tr.* winnow 139/34

vareþ *pr. pl. intr.* fare; ~ *wel* prosper 1/11

yuarȝed *pp.* farrowed 61/29

uariste see uair

ueawe *adj. pl.* few 162/24, 254/35, 256/28

uede *v. tr.* feed 199/25, 29, 210/33 (*passive*); *refl.* 246/13: ueth *pr. 3 sg.* 246/13. uedde *pa. t. 3 sg.* 190/10. *pl.* 96/12. yued *pp.* 141/29, 199/27

uel *n.* skin 253/11 *n.* uelle *p.c.* 210/31

uelaȝe *n.* companion 21/3, 45/22, 52/ 1; partner 36/27 *n.*; accessary 256/ 20; opponent 50/23: uelaȝes *pl.* 57/ 6, 67/14, 139/14; *adj.* accessary 37/9

uelaȝest *pr. 2 sg. tr.* dost associate 101/16 *n.* uelaȝeþ *3 sg.* 102/12

uelaȝrede *n.* intercourse 9/8, 10/26, 43/19; company 16/19, 102/25, 139/7; partnership 110/22, 24; comradeship 38/13, 102/30, 33; communion 14/2; retinue 24/31.

uelaȝredes *pl.* friendships 220/9, 226/9; bands of companions, friendships 53/16 *n.* 139/17, 220/9, 226/9; *brek* ~ was disloyal 16/14; *þyeues be* ~ accomplices in theft 38/12

ueld *n.* field, battle-field 131/6, 227/28, 240/15. uelde *p.c.* 81/11, 109/11, 169/32. ueldes *pl.* 136/2, 156/27. cf. do

yueld, uelde see uelle

yuelde see uele

uele *adj.* many 5/20, 13/14, 16/11; *pron.* uelen *p.c.* 102/3; *to* ~ excessive 255/15

(y)uele *v. tr.* be aware of, feel 92/33 *n.*, 128/5, 132/12, 181/2, 204/22, 241/14; feel remorse for 132/11, 20; experience 106/18, 161/23, 245/26; touch 251/19, 22; *intr.* feel 154/22: (y)uelþ *pr. 3 sg.* 23/16, 31/32, 142/25 (y)ueleþ *pl.* 132/11, 20, 147/33. (y)uele *subj. sg.* 132/13 *n.*, 147/8, 240/34. yuelde *pa. t. pl.* 246/3*. yuelde *subj. sg.* 138/2

ueleuold *adj.* manifold 212/2 *n.*

ueleziþe see ziþe

uelinge *vbl. n.* awareness 161/16; touch 241/2

uelle *v. tr.*[1] fill, satisfy 55/20 *n.*, 77/30, 92/28, 110/33, 144/14 *n.*; *intr.* 92/6, 144/13 *n.*: uelþ *pr. 3 sg.* 55/15, 58/1, 5 *n.* uelleþ *pl.* 44/24. uelden *pa. t. pl.* 233/6. (y)ueld *pp.* 55/21, 143/23 *n.*, 199/27

uelle *v. tr.*² fell 130/25. uelþ *pr. 3 sg.*
25/12. yueld *pp.* 50/23; ~ doun
lay low 249/25
uelþe *n.* filth 56/35; 58/22, 61/31.
uelþes *pl.* filthiness 61/4, 108/30
uend see uiend
uendonginge *n.* vintage 36/19
uenial, veniel *adj.* venial 16/10,
73/10. uenial(s) *pl.* 74/11, 178/17
uenim *n.* poison 17/1, 22/32, 27/33
uenimous *adj.* venomous 203/17.
uenimouse *wk.* 27/27, 171/31.
uenimouses *pl.* 27/14, 35
uer *n.* fire 30/2, 49/32, 64/12; flame
186/27: uere *p.c.* 46/34, 74/6, 137/
17; auer(e) on fire 205/26; fiery
264/22
uer *adj.* distant 49/2 *n.* uerre *pl.*
remote 204/21; *adv.* far 89/3,
112/31, 133/9, 164/26; auer from
afar 91/32
uerliche *adv.* ardently 55/1, 6;
suddenly 130/1
uerlichhede *n.* ardour 55/3
uerlore see uorlyeseþ
uernyere *sb.* (*p.c.*) yesteryear 92/4
uerri *v. tr.* remove 178/20. uerreþ
pr. 3 sg. 178/21. yuerred *pp.*
240/33
uers *n.* verse 128/34, 198/7
uerst *n.* delay; auerst *adv.* tardily
32/24 *n.*; deþ auerst delays 161/14
uerst *adv.* first, in the first place
16/11, 24/28, 40/32; alþer ~ see al
uerste *imp. sg. intr.* procrastinate
173/16
uerste *ord. num. wk.* first 1/19,
17/14, 199/35; þe uerste, þes
ilke uerste 70/11, 207/21 (MS.
uesste), 239/16, 266/1. *pl.* 11/20;
ate uerste, auerst *adv.* in the
first place 5/16, 46/24, 127/11
uerþe *ord. num. wk.* fourth 8/1,
11/32, 12/24
uerþinges *n. pl.* farthings 193/30
uesseles *n. pl.* vessels 235/17
uest *adj.* enduring 189/18, stable
207/23; resolute 178/6, 220/33:
ueste *acc.* 207/25. *p.c.* 107/19.
pl. 116/33
uestliche *adv.* resolutely 166/1,
232/30; firmly, immovably 243/35,
251/4

uestnesse *n.* security 104/8 *n.*, 107/22
ueste *v. intr.* fast 50/34, 51/31, 52/8.
uesteþ *pr. pl.* 52/12. ueste *pa. t. 3
sg.* 227/2
uestemens *n. pl.* vestments 41/2
uestinge *vbl. n.* fasting 217/18,
224/15. uestinges *pl.* fasts 33/13,
51/35, 52/3
uestni *v. tr.* establish, confirm 105/28,
117/11 *n.*, 213/25; join 221/11:
uestneþ *pr. 3 sg.* 106/14, 107/7.
yuestned *pp.* 107/20, 21, 109/18
uet see uot
uet *n.* vessel 231/18. uete *p.c.* 203/34
uet *adj.* fat 53/22. uette *p.c.* fertile
190/1. *pl.* fat 35/19
ueteres *n. pl.* fetters 128/22
ueth see uede
uetteþ *pr. 3 sg. refl.* becomes fat
246/14
ueþeren *n. pl.* feathers 270/6
uice *n.* vice 18/3, 27/21, 152/6.
uices *pl.* 17/12, 19/9, 32/12
uictorie *n.* victory 167/16, 168/6*, 28
uyealdinde *ppl. adj.* folding 239/5
uiend *n.* enemy, fiend 157/17,
158/24, uend 1/3, 227/21. uiende
p.c. 19/13, 206/27. uiendes *pl.*
75/10, 114/32, 232/19
vif *num.* five 46/23, 49/33, 190/25
uifte *ord. num. wk.* fifth 8/18, 29/19,
227/8
uyftene, *num.* fifteen 190/24, 28, 32
uiȝt *n.* battle 169/23, 29, 219/9,
⟨uiyȝt⟩ 131/6 (*cf. p. 20*). uiȝtes
pl. 182/27
uiȝte *v. intr.* fight, struggle 15/3, 240/
13, wyȝte 131/7. viȝt *pr. 3 sg.* 169/
31, 181/3, 249/8. uiȝteþ *pl.* 117/23,
168/27, 255/33. uiȝtinde *ppl. adj.*
219/11. yuoȝte *pp.* 176/6, 7, 252/14
uiȝtinge *vbl. n.* violence 37/15;
battle 170/20, 180/15, 181/19.
uiȝtinges *pl.* 181/22, 182/23,
239/10
uiyȝt see uiȝt
uyl *adj.* vile, worthless 82/35, 83/2,
132/23. viles *pl.* 76/27. þe uileste
superl. wk. 92/22
uil, uille(n) *v.* see ualle
uilayn *adj.* contemptible 18/7, 59/1,
7. uyleyne *pl.* churlish 194/3
uile *n.* (*p.c.*) file 152/27

uileynie *n.* churlishness 18/10, 15; infamy 75/4, 87/18, 101/1, 125/18. uileynies *pl.* 31/24

uileynliche *adv.* infamously 64/24, 27, 69/35, 70/1. vileynlaker *comp.* 64/33

vilhede *n.* vileness 130/28

villiche *adv.* vilely 133/7, 18

(y)uinde *v. tr.* find 1/17 (*passive*), 33/3, 51/6; find narrated 195/23, 224/28; compose 105/12; invent 61/34; contrive 24/7, 82/28, 258/17; *intr.* find 207/36: vinst *pr. 2 sg.* 38/7. uint *3 sg.* 31/22, 62/10, 74/7 n., 8. uindeþ *pl.* 38/6, 61/9, 103/31, wyndeþ 108/10 n. uinde *subj. sg.* 206/28, 32. uand *pa. t. 3 sg.* 57/23, 181/36, 206/3, 245/7 n. (y)uo(u)nde *pp.* 83/24 n., 92/35, 186/1

uine, vyne *n.* vine 96/17, 156/27, 187/30. vines *pl.* 36/23, 38/34, 43/28

vingre *n.* (*p.c.*) finger 5/4, 63/30

uirtu(e) *n.* power, efficacy 12/20, *14/11*, 123/19; virtue 29/27, 83/15, 88/21, 160/16*. uirtues *pl.* 17/12, 18/28, 25/10; powers, capacities 19/2, 24/8

uirtuous *adj.* potent, efficacious 113/5, 237/30

uisaȝe *n.* face 45/29, 201/12, wizaȝe 201/11. uisages *pl.* forms 158/21

uisiteþ *pr. 3 sg. tr.* visits 128/7, 130/15

uiss *n.* fish 50/29, 110/17, 167/31. uisssse *p.c.* 61/12

vissere *n.* fisherman 50/28, 238/31

viþele *n.* fiddle 105/11

vlaȝe see beulaȝe

ulateri *v. tr.* flatter 61/3

ulaterie *n.* flattery 197/4

ulatours see flatour

uleaȝ see uliȝþ

uledde see uliȝþ

uleȝe *n.* insect, fly 136/1. uleȝen *pl.* 58/2, 270/4

yulemde *ppl. adj.* (*pl.*) fugitives 39/28

ules(s) *n.* flesh 47/34, 87/23, 181/4. ulesses *gen.* 271/3. ulesse *p.c.* 9/9, 13, 53/6

ulesslich *adj.* carnal 9/8, 10/26, 46/22, *146/14*. ulessliche *pl.* 92/18, 176/16; worldly 42/5; bodily 35/19

uleþ see uly, uliȝþ

ulexe *n.* (*p.c.*) flax 236/20

vly *v. intr.* fly 217/21, 254/17, 18. uliȝþ *pr. 3 sg.* 206/16, 254/19. vlyeþ *pl.* 58/2, uleþ 25/4, 61/17 n. vly *subj. sg.* 254/17. ulyinde *ppl. adj.* in flight 66/12, 71/14

uliȝþ *pr. 3 sg. tr.* avoids 181/28; *intr.* vanishes 165/3; flees 75/29. vlyeþ *pl.* 39/28, vleþ 41/5. uleaȝ *pa. t. 3 sg.* 129/10, 141/30, uledde 204/23, *refl.* fled uledde *sg.* 206/5. uledden *pl.* 204/21 n.

ulindre *n.* moth 206/16

ulyntes *n. pl.* flints 136/10

ulod *n.* river 247/33, 248/5. ulode *p.c.* 247/36

uo see yuo

uoȝel *n.* bird 71/14, 178/21, 185/32. uoȝeles *pl.* 105/14, 142/9

uoȝelere *n.* fowler 254/21

yuoȝte see uiȝte

uol *adj.* full 15/6, 27/32, 28/15; mature 259/24, 27; satisfied, satiated 183/20, 244/16: uolle *acc.* 259/24. *pl.* 19/9, 58/13, 96/20; ~ *a pot* a pot full 177/28 n.

uol *adv.* quite, full 1/14, 170/4; fully 26/11; ~ *dronke* see uoldronke

uolc *n.* people 15/11, 43/35, 220/10 n., 223/20. uolke *p.c.* 26/1, 35/2, 196/16 n. *pl.* 30/26, 189/25, uolc 53/2, 207/2, 239/25. (*For discussion see pp. 62–3*)

uoldo *ppl. adj.* perfect 28/11, 96/20, 146/7

uoldronke *ppl. adj.* intoxicated (*enyure*) 107/12–13; saturated (*abeure*) 247/34

uolȝi *v. tr.* follow 75/28, 235/1; observe 99/33; pursue, cultivate, frequent 22/4, 127/13, 177/34, 226/8; engage in 36/11; result from 45/20; *intr.* follow 1/1, 74/24; persevere 83/20 n., 166/26: uolȝeþ *pr. 3 sg.* 12/14, 24/31. *pl.* 261/14. uolȝe *imp. sg.* 253/17. volȝeþ *pl.* 232/29. uolȝinde *ppl. adj.*

uol3i (*cont.*):

1/16, 2/1. uol3ede *pa. t. pl.*
242/25. yuol3ed *pp.* 99/33

uolhede *n.* plenitude 119/10

uolkerede see uolc (196/16 *n.*)

uolle *n.* fullness 133/4; fill 247/26;
(*ri3t*) to *þe* ~ thoroughly, com-
pletely 156/9, 262/1; abundantly
160/8

uolleres *n. pl.* fullers 167/24

uolliche *adv.* completely 73/33,
78/31, 89/23; abundantly 119/27

uolmakeþ *pr. 3 sg. tr.* perfects
201/1. uolmad *ppl. adj.* 28/23,
260/32; complete 261/24

uolnesse *n.* plenitude 266/23 *n.*

uolserueþ *pr. 3 sg. intr.* serves fully
33/23 *n.*

uoluelle *v. intr.* succeed 166/27;
satisfy 223/23 (*see note to* 223/22);
tr. 85/32, 92/28, 261/28; fulfil
13/11, 145/28; perfect, consum-
mate 7/12, 166/2, 244/8; complete
253/36, 262/19; *ppl. adj.* sufficient
113/29; perfect 120/6, 149/5;
perfected 233/16: uoluelþ *pr. 3 sg.*
83/5, 88/23, 92/31. uoluelle *subj.*
sg. 166/2, 253/19. uoluellinde
pr. þ. 113/29. uolueld *pp.* 99/24,
136/9, 183/25. uoluelde *acc.* 149/5

uoluellinge *vbl. n.* fulfilment 260/36

yuonde see (y)uinde

uondere *n.* tempter 116/10, 14

uondi *v. tr.* tempt 15/11, 206/29,
238/22; *intr.* 25/14, 46/22: uondeþ
pr. 3 sg. 82/32 *n.*, 116/18. uondy
subj. sg. 170/5. uondede *pa. t. 3 sg.*
249/13 *n.* (y)uonded *pp.* 116/35,
117/5, 167/12

uondinge *vbl. n.* temptation 25/7,
107/25, 116/6, 212/21*. uondinges
pl. 1/1*, 31/32, 117/9 *n.*, 230/20*

uor *prep.* for 1/2, 15, 5/11, 45/23
(*see note to* 45/24), 197/22 *n.*,
251/7 *n.*, ⟨uore⟩ 7/31; on account
of 16/15, 30/5, 54/20; as 58/18,
59/7, 257/10; in regard to 251/7;
at 36/5; ~ *þe scele of* by reason of
225/6-7; ~ *þet* (*þet*) see *þet conj.*
uor *conj.* because 5/22, 6/24,
15/21, 67/8 *n.*, 121/2* *n.*, 167/12*;
na3t ~ *to* in order not to 9/15;
~ (*to*), ~ . . . *to*, ~ *te* (*with in-*

finitive) to, in order to 7/8 *n.*,
8/23, 9/27, 28/19, 209/13*,
257/32 *n.*; *cf.* touor(e)

uorbegge *v. tr.* redeem 78/11

uorbere *v. tr.* be patient with,
tolerate 148/31. uorberþ *pr. 3 sg.*
115/2, 146/31. uorbereþ *pl.* 148/
27; spare 64/32. uorbore *pp.* 189/
26

uorberinge *vbl. n.* forbearance 148/
30; abstinence 205/14, 236/28

uorberne *v. refl.* be consumed
225/21; *tr.* uorbernþ *pr. 3 sg.*
consumes 74/10. uorbernde
pa. t. 3 sg. 67/13. uorbernd *pp.*
30/28, 265/7

uorbyet *pr. 3 sg. tr.* commands
6/15, 8/20, 224/2; forbids 9/23,
10/25, 11/7. uorbode *pp.* 8/26, 9/9,
commanded 10/6

uorbisne *n.* proverb 47/20, 93/19;
parable, exemplary tale 128/15,
189/4, 191/30; pattern 87/33, 122/
14, 186/6; example 46/3, 49/21,
89/11, uorbisnen, uorbisnes *pl.*
167/26, 190/2, 237/35, 249/26

vord see word

uordeþ *pr. 3 sg. tr.* destroys 121/28

uore yzede see uor(ey)zede

uorespeche *n.* prologue 5/1, 98/31,
105/10

uorewerdes see uorwerde

uor3uelze see uorzuel3e

uorkest *pp.* exposed 186/2

uorlay *pa. t. 3 sg. tr.* violated 206/3
(MS. *uorhay*). uorlaye *pp.* 230/31,
231/34

uorleas see uorlyeseþ

uorlete *v. tr.* reject 263/33; leave,
abandon 126/5, 206/5, 259/28*;
fail 130/13; remit 262/26: uorlet
pr. 3 sg. 126/32. uorleteþ *pl.*
165/22, 178/9. uorlet *imp. sg.*
262/26. *pa. t. 1 sg.* 259/28*.
uorlet *3 sg.* 184/20, 206/5. uorlete
pl. 126/5. *pp.* 242/23

uorlyeseþ *pr. pl. tr.* lose, forfeit
57/34. uorleas *pa. t. 3 sg.* 181/10,
184/21, uorlyas 242/29. uorlore
pl. 67/15. *pp.* 56/33, uerlore
128/10; damned 13/8, 14/26; þe
uorlorene *pl.* the damned 13/6,
14/18

uorlyezinge *vbl. n.* perdition 156/26, 243/15

uorrotede *pa. t. 3 sg. intr.* rotted away 205/5. uorroted *ppl. adj.* rotten 229/25; gangrened 148/9

uorþ *adv.* forth 153/22; abroad 62/1; forward 135/34; *ynoʒ more* ~ quite a lot further 168/33; *more* ~ any further 168/31

uor þan þet see þe

uorþdraʒe *subj. pl. tr.* foster 98/20

yuorþed *pp.* fed 186/27

uorþenche *v. intr.* regret, repent 125/7, 171/10, 179/30; *ppl. adj.* repentant 178/27, 220/31; *refl.* repent 5/8, 29/18, 64/5, 174/19: *impers.* regret 62/13, 159/4, 184/6; *hit* ~ *of* is regretted 184/4: uorþingþ *pr. 3 sg.* 27/10, 29/1, 65/32, 180/1 *n.* uorþenchinde *pr. p.* 178/27, 220/31. uorþuʒte *pa. t. 3 sg.* 171/10

uorþenchinge *vbl. n.* repentance 20/35, 28/28, 29/23

uorþrawe *v. tr.* cast out 86/19 *n.*

uorwepinge see uor and wepinge

uorwerde *n.* agreement 36/24. uorewerdes *pl.* 215/8

uoryete *v. tr.* overlook, forget 46/7, 215/19, 243/17; *refl.* forget to do one's duty 56/7 *n.*; 243/17; *intr.* forget 32/30; *ppl. adj.* forgetful 32/17: uoryet *pr. 3 sg.* 18/9, 32/32, 92/14. uoryeteþ *pl.* 6/6, 75/32. voryet *imp. sg.* 73/17. uoryetinde *pr. p.* 32/17 *n.* uoryete *pp.* 115/23, 201/25, 215/28

uoryetinge *vbl. n.* forgetfulness 18/4*, 32/29, 33/5; oblivion 199/18, 260/28

uoryeue *v. tr.* forgive 113/16; give up 114/16, 115/32, 217/25; *intr.* forgive 114/7, 14, 179/36: to uoryeuene *infl. inf.* 114/19, 115/34. uoryeue *pr. 1 sg.* 114/14. uoryefþ *3 sg.* 28/35, 114/8, 116/7. uoryeueþ *pl.* 113/17, 19, 114/6. uoryeue *subj. sg.* 114/3* (*see note to 46/9*). uoryef *imp. sg.* 110/6, 113/19, 114/5. uoryaf *pa. t. 3 sg.* 114/21. uoryeue *pp.* 29/24, 70/8, 116/4* *n.*, 219/7* *n.*

uoryeuenesse *n.* forgiveness 32/34, 113/32, 114/1

uorzake *v. tr.* refuse 195/27. uorzakþ, uorzaʒþ *pr. 3 sg.* 222/21; repudiates 18/18, 43/9. uorzakeþ *pl.* refuse 48/12. uorzok *pa. t. 3 sg.* rejected 77/10

uor(ey)zede *ppl. adj.* aforesaid 190/21, 26

uorzoke *pp.* suckled 179/21 *n.*

uorzoþe *adv.* see zoþ

uorzuelʒe *v. tr.* devour, swallow up 56/15, 111/6, ⟨uorʒuelze⟩ 15/16. uorzuel(ʒ)þ, uorzuylþ *pr. 3 sg.* 17/9, 61/14 *n.*, 27. uorzuelʒeþ *pl.* 52/36. uorzualʒ *pa. t. 3 sg.* 67/11. *pp.* swallowed 111/12; *intr.* uorzuolʒe *pa. t. pl.* gourmandized 206/36

uorzuerie *v. intr.* swear falsely 44/16, 56/36; *tr.* perjure 10/7, 63/18. uorzuerþ *pr. 3 sg.* 6/23, 26; þe uorzuorene *pp. pl.* perjurers 19/25

vorzueriinges *vbl. n. pl.* perjuries 57/29

vorzuolʒe see vorzuelʒe

uot *n.* foot 56/30, 147/35. uet *pl.* 14/34, 15/11, 140/10

uoul *adj.* heinous, foul 22/7, 25/33, 32/2. uoule *wk.* 47/29, 56/4. *pl.* 25/34, 35/15. uouler *comp.* 228/15, 237/10, 238/18. þet uouleste *superl. wk.* 174/31* *n.*; uoul *n.* foulness 133/3

uoulhede *n.* filth 75/16; ugliness 81/27; moral turpitude, vileness 17/32, 33, 257/30. uoulhedes *pl.* vile deeds 25/35, 101/2

uoulliche *adv.* vilely 40/28, 132/34, 194/5

(y)uounde see (y)uinde

uour *num.* four 29/30, 31/20, 37/7

uourtaʒte *ord. num.* fortieth 13/16

uourti *num.* forty 13/14, 67/18, 128/33

uox *n.* fox 151/2. uoxe *p.c.* 61/6

uram *prep.* from 7/21, 12/33, 14/21, 194/16 *n.*, 204/5*; away from 224/25, 270/19

ureme *n.* benefit 43/6, 94/14; *hare* ~ *ssewy* show them what is to their advantage 69/1–2; *hit is oure* ~ it is for our good 102/24, 117/5

uremuol *adj.* profitable 80/19, 23; ~ *to guode* conducive to good 116/12

urend see **uriend**

urendrede *n.* friendship 149/7

urenss *n.* French 211/5

ureteþ *pr. pl. tr.* devour 39/9

ureþie *v. tr.* observe 7/23

uri *adj.* free 86/35, 87/11, 165/25

uri *imp. sg. tr.* deliver 262/28. **yuryd** *pp.* 86/22, 203/21

uridom *n.* franchise 41/23; freedom 85/34, *86/21*, 87/3, 14; **uridome** *p.c.* 87/5

uriend *n.* friend 117/13, 158/25, **urend** 149/2, 7, 8. **uriende** *p.c.* 194/32, **urende** 194/13. **uriendes** *pl.* 42/23, 142/21*, 244/22, **urendes** 30/6, 23, **urindes** 96/21

uriliche *adv.* in freedom 70/31; freely 86/5, 6

urindes see **uriend**

uriwyl *n.* free-will 86/4

urostes see **hore-urostes**

W

waggeþ *pr. 3 sg. tr.* moves 211/9

waȝe *n.* wave 207/26

way *n.* path, road 60/10, 78/16; way 32/11, 94/24, 189/13: **waye** *p.c.* 155/17, 160/3, 168/25. **wayes** *pl.* 77/5, 253/30, 254/10

waye *n.* balance 255/6, 7, 256/9

wayn *n.* gain 43/6

waynye see **wayuye**

wayte *n.* watchman 121/26

wayteþ *pr. 3 sg. intr.* lies in wait 263/28; *tr.* lies in wait for 179/28. **wayteþ** *pl.* 212/3, 255/32; keep a watch on 253/29, 254/9

waytinge *vbl. n. ine* ~ on the lookout 157/21. **waytinges** *pl.* ambushes 15/10

wayuerindemen *n. pl.* wayfaring men 39/3

wayuye *v. tr.* remove 88/7 *n.*

waki *v. intr.* sit up late, be awake 52/18, 137/22; keep watch, be vigilant 263/14, 264/7; *ppl. adj.* awake 158/9; þe **wakynde** vigilant men 264/6: **wakeþ** *pr. 3 sg.* 137/22, 263/27. **wakeþ** *imp. pl.* 265/18,

wakyeþ 265/22. **wakinde** *pr. p.* 158/9, 264/6

waki(i)nges *vbl. n. pl.* vigils 33/13, 232/17; late sittings 52/29. *cf. pp. 100–1*

wal *n.* wall 81/7, 151/3. **walles** *pl.* 116/29, 270/23

waleweþ *pr. pl. intr.* wallow 126/17

wangeliste see **ewangelist**

wanhope *n.* despair 29/12, 34/12, 87/9

wantrokiynge *vbl. n.* despair 265/1

warningges *vbl. n. pl.* warnings 148/20

wasti *v. intr.* be consumed 265/8;[2] *tr.* waste 207/7, 213/7; destroy 30/2; dispel 108/6, 7; devour 265/8[1]: **wasteþ** *pr. 3 sg.* 19/4 *n.*, 52/31. *pl.* 52/19 *n.*, 21, 55/19. **wastede** *pa. t. 3 sg.* 128/12. **ywasted** *pp.* 129/22

we *pron. pl.* 8/4, 10/6, 17/24 *n.* o(u)s, us *acc./dat./p.c.* 7/34, 68/11, 106/7, 118/3* *n.*; *poss. dative* 109/4; **ous** *refl. acc./p.c.* 8/4, 10/7, 98/4; **oure** *poss. adj.* our 6/14, 8/10, 11/21, 110/1* *n.*, 117/5; *pron.* ours 102/1, 111/31, 112/3

web *n.* web 164/31

wecþ see **weȝe**

wed *n.* security, pledge 36/13,[1] 113/21, 134/21: **wedde (dyade)** *p.c.* 35/9. **weddes** *pl.* 102/15 *n.*; dead wed see also **dyead**

weder *n.* weather 129/35

wedercoc *n.* weather-cock 180/28

wefde see **wyeued**

weȝe *v. tr.* weigh, weigh up 44/27, 57/14, 256/6; *intr.* weigh 91/14: **wecþ**, **weȝþ** *pr. 3 sg.* 140/2, 255/28. **yweȝe** *pp.* 152/28, 255/5

wel *adv.* well 1/11, 6/30, 20/10, 194/7 *n.*; very 16/27, 18/7; certainly, indeed 19/12, 51/3, 146/7, 178/9; rightly, truly 17/12, 117/4, 132/26; much 71/14, 107/25, 164/18; quite 93/36, 162/13; ~ *onneaþe* only with much difficulty 50/24; **wel wilynde** see **wel-wilynde**. **bet, betere** *comp.* better 7/8, 44/7, 198/3; rather 60/28; *by* ~ *mid* stand better with 25/18; ~ *byeþ worþ, is worþ* ~ are of greater worth, is more valuable 16/22–3,

146/13; ~ *he ssolde* he ought rather to 156/2; *him were* ~ it would be better for him 115/8–9. **best** *superl.* best 81/22; **wei** *n.* good 197/4

welle *n.* well 74/1, 91/30; fountain 131/26; source 28/30. **wellen** *pl.* 80/33

wel-wilynde *ppl. adj. pl. used substantivally* friends 112/11

wem *n.* defilement 267/26

wen *n.* blemish 262/13 *n.*

wende *v. tr.* convert 90/3, 109/22; deflect 29/15; turn, transform 28/6, 62/15, 76/31, 244/36; traverse 164/32; translate 262/8; *refl.* be turned, turn 180/28, 269/34; *intr.* go 13/4, 85/4 *n.*, 252/12; depart 71/2; turn, curve 6/30, 17/1, 159/25, 234/24; tend 201/19, 203/24: **went** *pr. 3 sg.* 22/32 *n.*, 69/18, 129/35. **wendeþ** *pl.* 60/32, 224/26, 242/10 **wende** *subj. sg.* 109/22. *pl.* 242/23. **wente** *pa. t. 1 sg.* 156/26, 267/2. *3 sg.* 12/31. **wenten** *subj. pl.* 13/1. **ywent** *pp.* 24/23, 71/2, 88/32

wendinge *vbl. n.* transit 70/34, 71/3; departure 133/21

wene *v. tr.* think, consider oneself, suppose 21/16, 26 59/12, 92/24; expect, intend 23/11, 210/24, 248/28; expect to have 139/26; *intr.* expect 179/29; expect to have 126/11 *n.*, 129/34: **wenst** *pr. 2 sg.* 129/25, 192/24. **wenþ** *3 sg.* 25/18, 128/3, 30. **weneþ** *pl.* 43/32, 47/15, 59/19. **wene** *subj. sg.* 80/22, 208/18. **wende** *pa. t. 3 sg.* 108/9, 156/9. **wenden** *pl.* 126/11 *n.* **wende** *subj. sg.* 228/32, 256/22

wenynge *vbl. n.* expectation 113/6

wepe *v. intr.* weep 115/19, 161/23. **wepþ** *pr. 3 sg.* 93/36, 137/6, 161/19. **wepeþ** *pl.* 71/11, 96/29, 160/25

wepindeliche *adv.* tearfully 192/20

wepinge *vbl. n.* weeping 93/22, 125/20 *n.*, 226/35. **wepinges** *pl.* weeping 73/24, 83/8, 161/1

werche *v. intr.* operate 174/26. **workeþ** *pr. 3 sg.* works 88/26. **wercheþ, workeþ** *pl.* 19/27, 168/28. **workinde** *pr. p.* 206/32

were(n) see **bi**

weri *adj.* weary 33/18, 84/24, 141/22

weri *v. intr.* become weary 155/31 *n.*

werie *v. tr.* protect, defend 124/21, 148/36, 170/22; excuse 99/13: **wereþ** *pr. 3 sg.* 17/4, 230/25, **werþ** 249/6. **weryeþ** *pl.* 69/21, **wereþ** 186/2. **werie** *subj. sg.* 129/29. **wereden** *pa. t. pl.* 267/25

werihede *n.* weariness 33/18

werynesse *n.* weariness 269/5

werm *n.* worm 215/30, 32, 270/30. **wermes** *pl.* 137/15, 216/4, 256/8. **wermene** *gen. pl.* 216/2

wermethe *ppl. adj.* worm-eaten 229/25

wernde *pa. t. 3 sg. tr.* denied 189/6

werre *n.* war, conflict 30/3, 43/33, 131/7. **werren, werres** *pl.* 43/31, 66/32, 239/10

werreres *n. pl.* warriors 29/30 *n.*

werri *v. tr.* oppose, fight against, persecute 18/13, 29/19, 57/5, 182/9; *intr.* fight 17/6, 102/31, 32: **werreþ** *pr. 3 sg.* 24/14 *n.*, 29/2, 3. *pl.* 182/6. **werrede** *pa. t. 3 sg.* 182/13. *pl.* 29/4

wes *n.* 'was' 104/15

wes *v.* see **bi**

wesse *v. tr.* wash 140/10, 171/11, 176/33. **wesst** *pr. 3 sg.* 202/33. **wesse** (*lauast*) *pa. t. subj. sg.* 202/25. **ywesse** *pp.* 107/16, 112/28, 145/21

wesseþ *pr. pl. tr.* wish 56/13

wessinge *vbl. n.* washing 178/16

west *n.* west 124/24

westen *pa. t. pl. intr.* wasted away? 72/8 *n.*

wet *adj.* moist 153/10

wet *pron.* see **huet**

weter *n.* water 66/24, 74/4, 96/7. **wetere** *p.c.* 93/3, 119/7, 167/32. **weteres, weteris** *pl.* 98/29, 119/7, 212/13

wetery *v. tr.* water 98/29. **wetereþ** *pr. 3 sg.* 97/31, 119/8. *pl.* 97/35. **ywetered** *pp.* 131/27

wetnesse *n.* moisture 242/16

weued see **wyeued**

wex *n.* wax 94/33

wexe *v. intr.* grow, increase 95/2, 97/32, 113/21, 267/6 *n.*; arise 67/

wexe (*cont.*):
31: **wext** *pr. 3 sg.* 3/32, 18/32 *n.*, 69/13. **wexeþ** *pl.* 23/5, 30/18, 34/29, 97/29 *n.*, 161/11 *n.* **uexe** *pp.* 26/11
wychche *n.* wizard 41/28. **wichen** *pl.* 19/27, 69/34; witches 40/33
wychecreft *n.* witchcraft 43/17
wycked(e), wykhed *adj.* wicked 1/3, 17/27, 35/1, 43/3; defective, bad 44/32, 159/11; cruel 124/22, 23, 24; ~ *wil* see **nime** and (y)**wil**: **wyckede** *p.c.* 9/25, 11/8, 229/11. *wk.* 8/22, 114/16. **wyckede** *pl.* 17/8, 108/27, 124/22, þe **wickede** 198/9
wyckedhede *n.* wickedness 43/2, 114/11, **wychkedhede** 43/3*n.*
wyd *adj.* wide 264/33
wyd- *prefix* see **wyþ-**
wyedhoc *n.* hoe 121/27
wyeued *n.* altar 236/1, **weued** 167/22. **wyefde, wyeuede** *p.c.* 14/8, 111/1, **wefde, weuede** 112/19, 235/15
wyf *n.* woman 181/5, 219/13; wife 30/13. **wyue** *p.c.* 30/11, 37/28, 49/4. **wyf, wyues** *pl.* 9/8 *n.*, 35/26, 48/11, 192/33
wifman, wymman *n.* woman 11/1, 48/22, 224/9. **wyfmanne** *dat.* 60/24. **wyfman(n)e** *p.c.* 31/16, 48/9, 49/6. **wyfmen, wym(m)en** *pl.* 10/26*, 33, 231/32, 262/30; female servants 67/26
wyȝte *n.* weight 44/25, 54/1 *n.*, 66/24 *n.* **wyȝtes** *pl.* 44/17
wyȝte *v.* see **uiȝte**
wykkednesse *n.* wickedness 31/31, 44/6, 192/29*; adversity (*aduersité*) 131/28
(y)**wil** *n.* wish(es), desire 9/25, 10/25, 11/7, 108/28; consent 37/6, 27, 86/8; ardour 111/5, 36; pleasure 86/19, 119/22, 122/27; will 18/14, 47/7, 243/29; striving 162/4; intention 94/17, 225/19, 232/26; *be his* ~ of his own volition 170/25; *by ine* ~ desire, intend 115/33, 117/31–2, 227/10; *do* ~ see **do**; *habbe* ~ see **habbe**; *in(e)* ~ *to* with the intention of 218/19, 222/14–15; *mid* (*guode*) ~ willingly, attentively 172/24, 195/31–2, 266/13, 269/28, 270/26, 27; *of grat/*

guode ~ resolute 100/34, 101/13–14, 105/3; *to* ~ (*a point*) precisely as desired 150/30; *euel/wycked* ~ (*mautalent*) bad feeling, ill-will, anger 66/1, 35, 108/29 (*cf.* **nime**), 114/16, 115/32; ~ *of skele* (*animus rationalis*) 263/16 *n.*: **wille** *p.c.* 8/29, 9/3, 11/17. **willes** *pl.* 19/3, 250/9, 29, ⟨**wyllis**⟩ 76/3 *n.*
wylde *adj.* wild 230/5; out of control, wayward 263/24, 271/14
wylhede *n.* purpose 164/16
wille *v. tr.* desire, want to, intend to 15/16, 23/8, 53/28, 262/2; be willing to 24/19, 29/16; be accustomed to 113/30; require 139/10; *future auxiliary* 16/12, 70/33, 110/4; *intr.* wish 101/18, 155/24 *n.*, 26 *n.*; *he* ~ *zigge* he means 209/4, 241/7; ~ *he/hi/we nolle he/hi/we*, ~ *him nolle him* willy-nilly 79/4, 120/12–13, 139/21, 164/21–2, 209/31; *for* **wel wilynde** *see* **wel-wilynde**: *for* **wylles uol** *see* **wyllesuol**: **wil(l)e** *pr. 1 sg.* 53/31, 101/18, 192/2, 262/8. **wilt** *2 sg.* 21/10, 70/31, 80/15 *n.*, 85/35, **wyltou** 166/10 (cf. þou). **wil(l)e** *3 sg.* 21/29, 61/3, 94/3, 210/9, ⟨**willieþ**⟩ 142/15 *n.* **wil(l)eþ** *pl.* 11/31 *n.*, 16/12, 21, 155/25. **wil(l)e** *subj. sg.* 109/4, 6, 113/16, 154/6. **wille** *pl.* 157/12, 209/31. **woldest** *pa. t. 2 sg.* 73/28, 210/9, 270/32. **wolde** *3 sg.* 13/4, 16/16, 41/29. **wolden** *pl.* 223/18. **wolde(n)** *subj. pl.* 22/27 *n.*, 52/4, 57/11, 132/28 (*for the distribution of forms cf. Wallenberg, p. 279, n. 2*; *for modal uses see discussion pp. 104–6*)
wyllesuol *adj.* wilfull 263/20
willieþ see **wille**
willinge *vbl. n.* desire 9/3
wylni *v. tr.* want, desire 36/21, 73/8, 244/19, 263/34 (*passive*); *intr.* aspire 156/13: **wilneþ** *pr. 3 sg.* 11/2, 23/4, 25/23. *pl.* 36/21, 72/21, 86/31. **wylne** *imp. sg.* 270/26. **wylnede** *pa. t. pl.* 72/8. **ywylned** *pp.* 76/16, 80/31, 133/20
wilning(g)e *vbl. n.* intention 47/9; desire 11/3*, 22/35, 72/16, 247/31 *n.*, 266/11, 268/9*. **wilninges**

pl. 85/31*, 176/19, 202/11*, 236/24, 253/27

wyluolle *adj. pl.* ambitious (*beeries*) 162/2

wiluolliche *adv.* willingly 140/19

wymman, wymmen see **wifman**

wyn *n.* wine 27/31, 35/8, **wyin** 248/28 (*see p. 20*). **wyne** *p.c.* 106/19, 235/35. **wynes** *pl.* 54/22

wynd *n.* wind 23/24, 59/5, 62/32. **wynde** *p.c.* 24/25, 180/29, 183/2. **wyndes** *pl.* 24/26

wyndeþ see **(y)uinde**

wyndowes *n. pl.* windows 154/24

wyngen *n. pl.* wings 217/17, 18

winne *v. tr.* gain, win 17/13, 31/26, 59/5, 160/19 *n.,* ⟨**wyne**⟩ 248/8 *n.;* *intr.* make money 40/34, 43/9, 162/3; ~ **ayen** see note to 178/28–9: **wynst** *pr. 2 sg.* 102/26. **winþ** *3 sg.* 46/8, 78/28, 183/15. **wynneþ** *pl.* 143/17, 169/25. **wynynde** *pr. p.* 108/20 *n.* **ywonne** *pp.* 71/27, 79/17, 97/22

wynnynge *vbl. n.* profit, winning 23/23*, 34/27, 36/27, 134/23 *n.*

wyntre *n.* (*p.c.*) winter 131/28

wypi *v. tr.* wipe 161/22. **wypeþ** *pr. 3 sg.* 161/19, 267/33; *intr.* wipe clean 106/26

wys *adj.* wise 81/32, 84/1, 100/35. **wise** *wk.* 72/4, 174/28, 186/25, 192/15. **wyse** *pl.* 72/6, 77/17, 92/8 (*see note to 92/8–10*), þe **wyse** 16/29, 72/27, 139/2. **wiser** *comp.* 204/14, þe **wyser** 253/4. **wyseste, wyziste** *superl. wk.* 54/36, 172/14

wisdom *n.* wisdom, knowledge 81/34, 83/11, 251/25. **wysdome** *p.c.* 96/3, 100/16, 119/2, 251/24

wyse *n.* manner 158/12. **wyzen** *pl.* ways 62/30, 158/3

wyshede *n.* wisdom 68/22

wisliche *adv.* wisely 94/7, 99/31, 172/23

wiste see **(y)wytie**

wit *n.* intellect, intelligence 11/28, 16/15, 18/25, 112/34 *n.;* wisdom, knowledge 71/30, 75/3, 81/35, 119/4 *n.,* 251/23, 29 *n.;* understanding 253/1, 259/30, 261/32, 263/18 *n.;* wits, mind 18/31, 30/13,

56/26; sense, significance 27/12, 65/5, 99/7; (*engin*) ingenuity 24/7; instruction 155/15, 156/29; *pl.* faculties 251/35, 266/22; senses 47/28, 74/18; *out of hare* ~ beside herself 191/15–16; *of zuo oȝene* ~ see **oȝe(n)**: **wyt(t)e** *p.c.* 22/10, 68/15, 115/14. **wit(t)es** 52/32, 91/25, 177/5, 251/29 *n.*

(y)wyte *v. tr.* know, understand 25/13, 26/18, 29/7; *þet is to wytene* that is to say 1/19, 13/10; *be hire/his/þine wytinde* (*a son escient etc.*) knowingly 6/23, 10/12, 21/1; *wypoute hare wytende* without their knowledge 37/27; *maugre hy* ~ they feel ill-will 69/15: **wytene** *infl. inf.* 14/7, 19/1. **wost** *pr. 2 sg.* 120/15, 216/11 **wot** *3 sg.* 10/1, 19/6, 64/16. **wyteþ** *pl.* 38/6, 65/10, 77/33. **wyte** *sub. sg.* 196/6. **(y)wyte** *pl.* 5/11, 196/1, 262/8. **ywyteþ** *imp. pl.* 263/13. **wytinde, wytende** *pr. p.* 10/12, 21/1, 37/27. **wiste** *pa. t. 3 sg.* 98/2, 173/33, 190/30. **wyste** *subj. sg.* 263/13. *pl.* 132/22. **ywyte** *pp.* 10/15

wytie *v. tr.* save, preserve 78/19 *n.,* 166/11, 197/11; keep 182/3 *n.;* guard 110/6, 122/9; *refl.* take care 186/25; *intr.* 229/17 *n.:* **wyteþ** *pr. 3 sg.* 182/3. **wytyeþ** *pl.* 122/9. **wytie** *subj. sg.* 174/15, 212/18. *pl.* 229/4. **(y)wyte** *imp. sg.* 110/6, 212/12, 241/36

wytindeliche *adv.* knowingly 8/5, 18/33, 23/17 *n.,* 65/1

wytlease *adj. pl.* lunatics 86/13

wytnesse *n.* testimony 10/5, 9, 163/23; witness 10/9 *n.,* 63/35. **wytnesses** *pl.* 10/19, 39/25, 44/4

wytnesseþ *pr. 3 sg. tr.* testifies, bears witness to 89/26, 188/20; *intr.* bears witness 138/22: **wytnesseþ, wytnesset** *pl.* 71/9, 108/17, 135/30, 219/4

wytuol *adj.* intelligent 150/13

wyþ *prep.* with 9/8, 11/3, 43/19; against 17/6, 7, 102/31; *face* ~ *face* face to face 244/10–11; ~ *wrong* wrongfully 12/28, 37/5

wiþbegge *v. tr.* redeem 186/14. **wiþboȝt** *pp.* 186/11

wyþclepie v. tr. recall 215/11. **wyþcleped** pp. withdrawn 189/20

wiþdraȝe v. tr. draw away, bring back, withdraw 58/28, 166/8, 192/35, 231/36; withhold 37/21, 240/27; restrain, subdue, control 9/14, 28/9, 236/28, 264/2 n.; refl. draw back, cease 206/19, 263/22; intr. abstain 52/7, 138/3; retrench 53/35: **wyþdraȝst** pr. 2 sg. 58/30. **wiþdraȝþ, wyþdraȝt** 3 sg. 151/25, 236/13, 254/14. **wyþdraȝeþ** pl. 37/21, 254/23. **wyþdraȝe** subj. sg. 53/35. **wyþdraȝ** imp. sg. 254/26. **wyþdroȝe** pa. t. subj. sg. 264/1, 2 n. **wyþdraȝe** pp. 236/28

wyþdraȝynge vbl. n. abstinence 271/5. **wyþdraȝinges** pl. abstinence 205/8

wyþdraȝþes n. pl. deprivation 240/32

wyþerweȝe v. tr. counterweigh 137/27

wyþhalt pr. 3 sg. tr. withholds 9/32; restrains 249/9, 254/27

wyþinne prep. within 27/11, 108/1, 116/27; adv. within 25/16, 99/6, **wiþine** 199/15, 212/33

wiþnime v. tr. condemn, blame 137/25, 27, 270/32; reprove, 22/28, 148/11; prevent 220/30 n.: **wyþnymene** infl. inf. 255/8 (passive), 270/35 (passive). **wiþnimþ** pr. 3 sg. 17/3* (see p. 50), 22/28, 69/11, 129/5*

wyþniminge vbl. n. error 82/34, 154/19; reproof 148/22; reproach 120/9. **wyþnymynges** pl. 66/27

wiþoute prep. without 9/3, 20/2, 37/34* (see p. 50 for forms without þ), 54/19*, 55/13 n., 94/7*, 120/25*, 230/30*, 231/14*, ⟨wydoute⟩ 95/7 (see p. 43, n. 1), **wiþout** 104/15‡; outside 10/7; except 150/7 n.; ~ mo and no more 67/20; naȝt ~ more see **moche(l)**; ~ þet see þet conj.; adv. without 10/27; in the modern sense external 20/13, 154/34

wyþscore imp. sg. tr. control 254/26

wyþsettinges n. pl. obstacles 39/29*

wyþstonde v. intr. resist 131/16, ⟨wydstonde⟩ 84/18 n. **wyþstant**

pr. 3 sg. 22/26. **wyþstondeþ** pl. 117/23; tr. intr. **wyþstondeþ** imp. pl. 265/25

wyþstondinge vbl. n. obduracy, recalcitrance 22/25, 29/13* (see p. 50), 57/30, 68/23; hostility 268/17

wyþþe n. halter 135/25

wyþwent pr. 3 sg. intr. bends 159/17

wyþzigge v. tr. deny 175/4. **wyþzede** pa. t. subj. sg. 264/2 n.

wiþzigginge vbl. n. opposition, reluctance 54/19, 109/28, 233/14

wyue see **wyf**

wyui v. intr. marry 225/17; refl. 225/20. **wyui** subj. sg. 225/16

wizage see **uisage**

wyze, wyziste see **wys**

wyzen see **wyse**

wlaffere n. stammerer 262/1 n.

wlatiinge vbl. n. aversion, distaste 178/12, 192/14, 216/14 n., 15

wlatuol adj. repulsive 241/8, 10

wo n. woe, anguish 75/15, 86/33, 265/11

wocnesse see **wotnesse**

wod adj. mad 18/31, 33. **(þe) wode** pl. 56/26, 70/4, 140/24

wode n. wood 95/28, 96/1, 213/5. **wodes** pl. 23/26

wodewe n. widow 48/14, 190/25, 226/10. **wodewen, wodewon** pl. 193/8, 225/14, 226/13

wodewehod n. widowhood 48/6, 185/18, 225/13

wodhede n. madness 17/33, 18/30

woȝ n. wall 72/15

woke n. week 110/18, 212/27; ope þe ~ see **op(e)**

wolde(st), wolden see **wille**

wolf n. wolf 50/26. **wolues** pl. 39/9, 139/11, 186/1

wolle n. wool 137/8

wombe n. womb 118/27, 271/9; stomach 50/33, 51/1, 53/11. **womben** pl. 248/32

wonde n. wound 174/27, 29, 217/27. **wo(u)nden** pl. 148/17, 266/28

ywonded ppl. adj. wounded 148/5, 12

wonder n. wonder 32/24, 34/17, 68/20; **wondres** pl. marvellous things 268/6; hit is ~ it is amazing 64/33-4

wonderliche *adv.* marvellously 14/32, 267/10

wonderuol *adj.* strange, marvellous 15/4, 92/32. **wonderuolle** *wk.* 266/33, 36

wondreþ *pr. pl. refl.* marvel 244/15; *intr.* **wondrinde** *pr. p.* 267/16 (*cf. note to 263/14*)

wone *n.* habit(s), custom 6/30, 22/17, 33/9, 258/16; use 210/2; way of life 85/8 *n.*; frame of mind 196/11 *n.*; **wones** *pl.* habits, customs 139/8, 166/7, 171/22 *n.*, 214/11; practices 38/28, 29 *n.* ~ *is* it is customary 118/23

wonie *v. tr.* accustom 220/17; become accustomed to 220/21 *n.*; *refl.* be accustomed 7/2; *intr.* dwell 49/12, 109/6, 266/20; (be) accustomed (to) 191/26, 231/16 *n.*, 260/10; **were/wes ywoned** used (to) 90/1–2, 156/11, 197/36: **woneþ** *pr. 3 sg.* 64/23, 247/15, 263/25. **wonyeþ** *pl.* 54/15, 87/34, 269/6. **ywoned** *pp.* 106/30, 169/33

woniynge *vbl. n.* dwelling 149/20, 21. **wonyinges** *pl.* 267/30

ywonne see **winne**

wop *n.* weeping, lamentation 71/18, 93/23, 265/5

word *n.* word 7/14, 42/2, 57/16, **vord** 101/3. **worde** *p.c.* 63/31, 99/11, 134/14. **word(d)es** *pl.* 10/28, 27/35, 57/31

word(d)le *n.* world 7/11, 12/34, 86/22* (*see p. 49 for this and other emended forms*), 142/16 (MS. *wordþe*), 164/27*, 165/7, 229/1, 241/12*. **wordles** *pl.*; *in* ~ *of* ~ for ever and ever 269/7

wordleliche *adj. pl.* worldly 164/22, 210/19, 22

work *n.* work 151/5. **worke** *p.c.* 31/23, 37/2, 119/20. **workes** *pl.* 14/16, 17/10; work 7/7; operations 124/27; *do to* ~ put in hand 153/35–6 (*mettre a oeure*); come before 265/20–1 *n.*

workeþ, workinde see **werche**

workman *n.* workman 86/32. **workmen** *pl.* 113/11, 167/27

workuol *adj.* active 199/9, 36

wors(e) *adj.* see **euel**

worse *adv.* see **euele**

worsi *v. intr.* deteriorate 33/18

wor(þ)ssipe *n.* respect, honour 8/9, 64/19, 135/35; glory 23/22, 151/32; reverence 48/32, 225/5; reputation 18/27, 75/6, 259/15. **worþssipes** *pl.* honours 75/16, 77/10, 78/1 (*for forms without* þ *see p. 50*)

wor(þ)ssipie, worþssipij *v. tr.* worship 5/21, 6/9, 78/13, 79/29 *n.*; honour, respect 135/34, 145/25, 193/18: **worþssipes** *pr. 2 sg.* 188/23, 24 (*cf. pp. 53 and 97, n. 4*). **wor(þ)ssipeþ** *3 sg.* 134/7, 9, 135/16. **worssipeþ** *pl.* 6/1, 148/27. **worþssipe** *imp. sg.* 8/2. **worssipede** *pa. t. 3 sg.* 89/12. **yworþssiped** *pp.* 104/27, 162/5; *ppl. adj.* 81/1, 31

worst *v.* see **yworþe**

worþ *n.* worth 76/25, 80/17, 112/33

worþ *adj.* worth 77/28, 82/34, 90/5; profitable, valuable 83/21, 90/7, 146/14; estimable, worthy 23/28, 117/7; *ase moche* ~ (beasts) of an equivalent value 36/30–1; *bi* ~ avail 54/24–5, 61/18–19, 257/2; *bi* ~ *to* be equal in value to 162/19 *n.*, 21; *is ase moche* ~ *ase* is equivalent to, signifies 7/15, 106/22–3, 118/35

worþ *v.* see **yworþe**

yworþe *v. intr. passive auxiliary with main verb understood* be (sold) 40/18; come to pass 262/24; *future passive auxiliary* shall be 189/26; *impers. him ne* ~ he shall not have 74/25, 90/28: **worst** *pr. 2 sg.* 270/5. **worþ** *3 sg.* 90/29, 189/26. **yworþe** *subj. sg.* 262/24

worþi, worþe *adj.* worthy 74/14, 76/4, 108/21; estimable 118/24; fit 94/34; appropriate 270/30

worþssipe see **wor(þ)ssipe**

worþssiphede *n.* status 49/15

worþssiplich *adj.* honorific 80/18

worssipliche *adv.* honourably 54/8

worþssipuol *adj.* honorific, honourable 80/23, 83/11, 259/32

worþuolle *adj. pl.* worthy of honour 16/30

wotnesse *n.* moisture 95/6 *n.*

wounden see **wonde**
woze *n.* clay 87/22, 89/8, 196/26; slough, mud 126/18, 179/24. **woses** *pl.* fluids 186/30
wraye *v. tr.* accuse 175/5. **wrayeþ** *pr. pl.* 175/10
wrang, wrong *n.* harm, injustice 86/7, 222/22. **wronges** *pl.* injuries, injustices 39/12, 40/5; *mid, wyþ* ~ see **mid, wyþ**
wrang, wrong *adj.* warped 159/17, 22; ~ *to* in conflict with 204/33
wrechche *adj.* wretched 70/29. **wrechchen** *pl.* niggardly 187/18
wrech(ch)e *n.*[1] wretch 25/5, 31/19, 52/32; niggard 210/8. **wrech(ch)en** *pl.* 188/1, 189/11, 270/15
wreche *n.*[2] vengeance 30/21, 45/28, 67/10
wrechide *adj. wk.* contemptible 109/22
ywreȝe see **wry**
wreke *v. tr.* expel 189/33. **wrek** *pa. t. 3 sg.* 215/7
wrekinge see **awrekinge**
wrench *n.* cleverness 129/35 *n.*
wrestlinge *vbl. n.* conflict 180/22, 35
wreþ see **wry**
wreþe *n.* rancour, wrath 8/27, 9/2, 16/3
wreþi *v. tr.* anger 60/2, 87/19, 232/2; *refl.* become angry 17/4, 34/2, 57/11: **wreþeþ** *pr. 3 sg.* 8/7, 45/27, 52/33. *pl.* 149/34, 35. **wreþþi** *subj. pl.* 8/5
(þe) **wreþuolle** *adj. wk.* wrathful 30/10 (MS. *wreþuollo*)
wry *v. tr.* cover, conceal 258/18. **wriȝþ, wrikþ** *pr. 3 sg.* 128/35, 167/10. **wryeþ** *pl.* 61/2 (*see note to 61/1*), 175/9, **wreþ** 61/4. **ywreȝe, ywriȝe** *pp.* 66/14, 210/34; *ppl. adj.* 96/25, 217/1; covert 37/8, 13
ywryȝeliche *adv.* covertly 37/14
writ *n.* scripture 57/24, 60/23, 77/20; document 173/3: **write** *p.c.* 191/4. **writes** *pl.* 42/30 *n.*, 65/4
write *v. intr.* write 112/33; *tr.* **writ** *pr. 3 sg.* 5/14 *n.* **wrot** *pa. t. 3 sg.* 63/29. **iwrite** *pp.* 5/4, 10, 103/8; *ppl. adj.* 126/9
writing(g)e, ⟨writing⟩ *n.* scripture

8/27, 31/22, 66/21, 93/20, 253/17*.
writinges *pl.* 13/12, 46/18, 87/29; writings of the fathers 76/17; literature 60/34
wrong *n.* see **wrang**
wrongliche *adv.* wrongfully 8/34
wroþ *adj.* angry 22/29, 66/15, 94/1. **wroþe** *pl.* 132/29
wroþe *adv.* badly 20/24

Y

yaf see **yeue**
yalde see **ald**
yalp see **yelpþ**
yarn see **yerne**
ye *pron.* ye 1/10 *n.*, 96/17, 189/10*, 28, 198/11*. **you, yow** *acc./dat./ p.c.* 198/12, 213/1, 218/28; *refl.* (yourselves) 242/26, 253/27, 265/26; **youre** *poss. adj.* 188/12, 213/1, 260/5; *pron.* 265/18
yeaf, yeaue, yef see **yeue**
yealde(n) see **ald**
yealdy *v. intr.* age 97/13. **yealdeþ** *pr. 3 sg.* 75/2
year(e) see **yer**
yeare, yeren see **eare**
yeast *n.* east 124/21
yede *pa. t. 3 sg. intr.* went 215/34, 231/32, 239/3. **yede(n)** *pl.* 67/19, 74/1, 166/32; ~ *ledinde blisse* rejoiced continually (*aloient menant ioie*) 164/1 *n.*
yef *conj.* if 5/8, 6/22, 9/30, 57/18 *n.* (*for* **yef** *in combination with other conjunctions, see the first component*); whether 184/25
yef(f)þe *n.* gift 13/30, 106/13, 200/2, **yefþ** 111/23‡, 144/27‡, ⟨ȝefþe⟩ 150/12; bounty 135/12; profit 35/12: **yefþes** *pl.* 3/17, 10/29, 24/11, 120/14 *n.*, **ȝefþes** 105/30, **yefþe** 3/21 *n.*, 120/30, 31 (*see note to previous entry*), 194/1
yelde *v. tr.* render, give 18/36, 79/16, 86/17; pay (a debt) 222/17, 32; return, reward, repay 9/29, 73/12, 191/29 *n.*, 215/24; make reparation for 31/1; give up, yield 35/28, 171/28; *intr.* return, render 13/24, 38/7; make reparation 31/2, 137/36, 218/14; *ppl. adj.* indebted

169/10: **yelde** *pr. 1. sg.* 139/1.
yelst *2 sg.* 38/7, 166/10. **yelt**
3 sg. 18/9, 19/16, 124/18, **yeldeþ**
18/6 *n.* **yeldeþ** *pl.* 42/26. **yelde**
subj. sg. 68/16. *pl.* 163/17. **yeld**
imp. sg. 253/19. **yeldinde** *pr. p.*
169/10. **(y)yolde** *pp.* 163/10, 171/
28; *ppl. adj.* 120/20
yeldere *n.* debtor 163/1. **yelderes**
pl. 262/27
yeldinge *vbl. n.* payment 115/29.
yeldinges *pl.* debts 262/26
yelleþ *pr. pl. intr.* howl 71/11
yelpþ *pr. 3 sg. refl.* boasts 22/10.
yelpeþ *pl.* 79/10, 89/7; *intr. pr.*
3 sg. 59/2. *pl.* 59/17, 18. **yalp** *pa. t.*
3 sg. 208/19
yelping(g)e *vbl. n.* boasting 22/6,
57/28, 58/35. **yelpinges** *pl.* 59/9
yelpere *n.* boaster 22/7, 12
yeme *n.* heed, see **nime**
yeme *v. refl.* give one's mind to
7/8 *n.*; *tr.* **yemd** *pp.* guarded
204/17
yemere *adj. pl.* miserable 215/13
yend *adj.* the other 256/10
yer *n.* year 35/11, 110/18, 191/14.
yeare *p.c.* 214/19, 262/21, **yere**
126/17, 258/35. **year** *pl.* 67/19,
113/29, **yer** 1/14, 128/33, **yeres**
172/29
yerd *n.* rod 95/34, 118/33
yere *n. (p.c.)* ear 28/15, 20
yerne *v. intr.* run, hasten 75/27,
111/24, 113/31; move, pass on
141/10, 177/5; *ppl. adj.* reluctant ?
207/27 *n.*; *ayen* ~ return 220/34;
~ *by* run through 176/13; ~
opo/op to attack 39/17–18, 61/28:
yernþ *pr. 3 sg.* 50/26, 61/16 *n.*,
75/27, 30 *n.* **yerneþ** *pl.* 74/9 *n.*,
140/24, 155/27 *n.* **yerne** *subj. sg.*
27/31, 202/31. **yerninde** *pr. p.*
207/27. **yarn** *pa. t. 3 sg.* 191/12.
yourne *pl.* 96/7
yerninge *vbl. n.* course 141/13;
running 255/11
yesteneuen *adv.* yesterday evening
51/8 (*see p. 49*)
yestre *n.* Easter 213/18
yet *adv.* still, yet 8/33, 33/26, 68/3,
209/6
yeue *v. tr.* give *14/15*, 40/20, 46/

9* *n.*, 93/3* (*see note to 46/9 for this
and all similarly emended forms*)
152/34*, 198/28*, 206/27; devote,
apply, give over 7/25, 33/10,
34/13, 165/20*, 197/33 *n.*, 229/
34*, 254/30; make 14/17, 83/3;
surrender 59/5, 107/28; *intr.* give
23/6, 76/32, 114/3*, 194/15; ~
of his pays 22/13; ~ *þane dyaþ*
slay 69/19; ~ *wyl* be resolute?
271/5 *n.*, *infl. inf.* 114/3*, 149/9,
195/30, 198/2. **yefst** *pr. 2 sg.*
93/10. **yefþ** *3 sg.* 14/11, 22/13 *n.*,
34/10, 46/4, 229/34*. **yeueþ** *pl.*
37/26, 40/20, 42/10. **yueþ** 45/8, 11;
yeue *subj. sg.* 98/17, 113/7, 118/6,
yue 271/5. **yeue** *pl.* 194/7, 217/2.
yef *imp. sg.* 101/17, 107/10, 110/6.
yueþ *pl.* 265/18. **yeaf** *pa. t. 3 sg.*
81/13, **yaf** 5/2, 50/16. **yeaue** *pl.*
140/6, 198/14. **subj. sg.** 190/23,
193/34, **yeue** 89/31. **(y)yeue** *pp.*
18/24, 20/13, 79/12, 188/36
yeuere *n.* giver 120/17, 121/15, 194/2
yeuynge *vbl. n.* giving 120/24
yok *n.* yoke 255/28
y-yolde, yolde see **yelde**
yolk *n.* yolk 96/3
yong *adj.* young 32/21, 179/26,
227/3. **yongne** *acc. masc.* 162/1.
yonge *gen.* (*see p. 66*) 48/30, 223/
16. *wk.* 155/29. *pl.* 220/17. (**þe**)
yonge 184/17, 21
you, yow see **ye**
yourne see **yerne**
yue, yueþ see **yeue**

Z

zay *etc.* see **zigge**
zayl *n.* sail 183/1
zain(t), saynd, sant *adj.* saint 1/7,
12/13, 23, *13/15 n.* (MS. *sanyt*), 20,
14/28, 15/1, 88/13, 99/18, 164/19,
170/19, 190/7*, *196/2* (MS. *sanyt*),
〈*sanyn*〉 14/30, 〈*sany(n)t*〉 121/2,
262/21, **zainte** *12/6,* 88/18, 121/6,
143/4*, 148/28*, 149/10, *170/4*
(MS. *zayte*), 8 (MS. *zayte*), 210/
7*, 221/18*, 244/11*, 253/25*,
〈*sanynte*〉 126/19, 〈*saynyte*〉 123/
22, **zante** 148/2, 〈*zayte*〉 253/8.
gen. 13/34 35. *p.c.* *41/29* (*for*

zain(t) (cont.):
discussion of the forms see note to
13/15 and pp. 53, 76)
zales n. pl. sales 91/3
zalmes n. pl. psalms 265/22
zalt n. salt 242/8, 13, 19. zalte adj.
pl. 119/8
zang n. song 60/10, 68/8, 105/12.
zonge p.c. 105/13, 16, 118/11.
zonges pl. 68/10, 71/20, 75/11
zante see zaint
zaule n. soul 9/18, 14/23, 19/17;
life 149/7, 11. zaulen, zaules pl.
souls, spirits 1/11, 8/13, 200/28;
lives 149/12
zawe v. intr. sow 214/21; tr. 227/28.
zaweþ pr. pl. 43/30. yzawe ppl.
adj. 255/4 n.
ze n. sea 14/32, 15/6, 37/13
ze (þet) pron. he who 117/8
zeayde see zigge
zech n. sack 81/9, 216/2, 3. zeche
p.c. 50/32
zeche v. tr. seek out, seek 22/12,
76/10, 93/33; inquire 80/1; con-
trive 38/29 n.; make for 57/32;
intr. seek 55/30 n., 75/26 n., 207/
36; ~ efter pursue 166/7: zecþ,
ze3þ pr. 3 sg. 25/23, 139/14, 143/2,
253/10*. (see note to 40/5). zecheþ,
zechiþ pl. 39/24, 55/27, 60/3.
zech imp. sg. 173/16, 184/9.
zeche subj. sg. 74/31, 94/3, 195/32.
pl. 147/31. zo3te pa. t. 3 sg. 175/16.
zo3ten pl. 80/1
zed n. seed 143/31, 189/36, 216/3
zed adj. resolute 83/20
zede, yzed see zigge
ze3e(n), yze3(e) see (i)zy
zelf emphatic pron. himself 93/25,
149/19, 248/3; itself 59/6; adj.
same zelue p.c. 45/24, 186/12.
wk. 41/21, 102/22; ilke ~ selfsame
263/26 n., 30; pron. same thing,
person 156/14, 190/30, 236/33
(forms with pronoun+zelf are listed
as compounds)
zelle v. tr. sell 41/32, 44/29, 33;
intr. 36/7, 44/23, 25: zelþ pr. 3 sg.
24/13, 36/4, 44/35, zelleþ 44/21 n.
zelleþ pl. 36/17, 40/17, 42/2.
zele imp. sg. 241/23, zel 185/7‡,
187/9‡. zyalde pa. t. pl. 215/7

zelleres n. pl. sellers 45/1
(ous) zellue see ousze(l)lue
zeluer n. silver, money 6/4, 35/6,
190/6. zelure p.c. 36/1
zen(e) see zenne
zent pr. 3 sg. tr. sends 68/11, 90/30,
135/12, 196/3 n. zende subj. sg.
262/7. zend imp. sg. 73/2. zentest
pa. t. 2 sg. 268/20. zente 3 sg.
67/13, 87/31, 190/26. yzent pp.
190/17, 33
yzendred ppl. adj. sundered 251/8 n.,
11
zene3ere n. sinner 60/12, 113/33,
127/34. zene3eres pl. 33/5, 114/
28, 128/16 n., 179/13
zene3i v. intr. sin 20/4, 44/27, 47/10.
zene3eþ pr. 3 sg. 5/23, 6/34, 7/2,
177/6*, 222/22*, 33* (see note to
40/5), ⟨zen3eþ⟩ 11/24. zene3eþ pl.
6/3, 19/29, 52/20 n., ⟨zene3þ⟩
155/3 (see p. 100, n. 3). zene3i
subj. sg. 225/27. yzene3ed pp.
11/2, 173/8, 176/14, ⟨yzene3d⟩
21/11 n.
zengþ pr. 3 sg. tr. singes 229/27
zenne n. sin 6/17, 7/17, 118/8 n.,
170/15, 258/6 n., ⟨zene⟩ 118/8 n.,
zen 262/12 n. zennen, zennes pl.
7/34, 9/11, 15/31
zenuol adj. sinful 136/12, a zenuol
132/26 n. me/þane/þe zenuolle
wk. 90/4, 113/22, 175/17. zenuolle
pl. sinful people 15/33, zenuol
59/32‡
zep n. sap 96/5 n.
zest see zette
(y)zet¹ see zette
zet² see zitte
zete n. seat 247/14
zeterday n. Saturday 7/5, 14, 213/2
zetnesse n. stability 104/8 n., 14.
zetnesses pl. laws 223/6 n.
zette v. tr. put, establish, set 84/30,
87/1, 243/35, 250/29; ppl. adj.
firm 116/20; plant, implant 94/31,
95/13, 97/28; locate 80/2; lay
down 149/6; prescribe, exercise
223/31, 250/5 n., 254/32; apply
155/28; assign 234/1; consign
260/27; associate 228/4; appoint
7/20, 214/31, 222/16; add 164/8,
12; set down 12/6, 155/31; arrange

119/27 *refl.* sit down 199/30, 251/14;
~ *grat cost* see **cost**; *him* ~ puts
himself out? 149/1 *n*; ~ *ine sorȝe*
makes sorrowful 250/25; *hou long
time he* ~ how long a time he had
taken 239/27–8; ~ *mesure* see
mesure: ~ *payne* strive 87/30–1;
~ *to lettre* teach to read 98/32; ~
to mesayse cause distress 58/16–17;
~ *to skele* (*mettre a reson*) call to
account 215/22: **zest** *pr. 2 sg.*
102/25. **zet** *3 sg.* 127/33, 248/13,
260/31. **zetteþ** *pl.* 6/5 *n.*, 67/8,
72/23 *n.*, 105/19, 243/10 *n.* **zette**
subj. sg. 127/28 *n.*, 252/27, 253/13.
pl. 87/30, 198/20. **zete** *imp. sg.*
158/10, 254/26. **sette** *pa. t. 1 sg.*
256/1 *n.* **zette** *3 sg.* 12/12, 13/34,
94/31. *pl.* 11/30, 80/2. **iset, yzet**
pp. 7/28, 24/24, 212/25, 251/4. *cf.*
bezette
yzeþ see (**i**)**zy**
zeþþe *prep.* since 14/4; *adv.* after-
wards 48/30; **zeþþe** (**þet**) *conj.*
since 47/30, 100/10, 261/33; after
177/31, 238/13, 242/9
zeue(n) *num.* seven 9/11, 11/21,
14/6, *35*, *15/26*, *16/6*
zeuend(e) *ord. num.* seventh 7/10,
9/21, *26/20*, 43/2
zeuenty *num.* seventy 1/14
zeueuald *adv.* sevenfold 268/11
(**i**)**zy** *v. tr.* see, perceive 21/10, 24/19,
200/22 (*passive*), 269/16; behold,
look at 161/35, 173/3, 267/17;
review 175/1; *infinitival adj.* visible
228/16 *n.*, 238/19; *refl.* gaze 244/
16 *n.*; *intr.* see 56/31, 155/13;
look 33/5, 130/10, 267/22: (**y**)**zy-
enne** *infl. inf.* 108/20, 158/17,
231/36. **izi** *pr. 1 sg.* 156/34, 164/35.
yzist, izixt *2 sg.* 73/27, 80/20,
121/33, 244/30 *n.* (**y**)**zicþ**, (**y**)**ziȝþ**,
(**y**)**ziȝt**, (**y**)**ziþ** *3 sg.* 11/1, 12,
27/16, 56/31, 60/29, 75/33, 91/32,
108/19, 120/18 *n.*, 123/32 *n.*, 143/
11, 160/36, 196/8, 237/16 *n.*, 245/
6 *n.* (**y**)**zyeþ** *pl.* 16/26, 46/4,
244/4*(*see note to* 40/5), **yzeþ** 36/34,
134/32. (**i**)**zi** *subj. sg.* 155/13,
156/17, 271/4. **yzy** *pl.* 134/22,
157/15. **ysy, yziȝ** *imp. sg.* 129/24,
185/9, 255/16 *n.* **zyinde** *pr. p.*

71/30 *n.* **izeȝ** *pa. t. 1 sg.* 156/28,
265/3, 267/9. **yzeȝe** *2 sg.* 20/33,
269/17, **yseȝeþe** (*with suffixed
pron.*) 264/32. **yzeȝ** *3 sg.* 2/16,
14/29, 187/36, 245/5 *n.* **yzeȝe(n)**
pl. 126/16 *n.*, 156/8, 203/12, 212/
15. (**y**)**zeȝe** *subj. sg.* 33/3, 173/23,
174/3. **zeȝen** *pl.* 204/26. **yzoȝe** *pp.*
173/6, 184/18, 264/11
zy (**þet**) *pron.* that (which) 102/7
(**y**)**zicþ** see (**i**)**zy**
zyalde see **zelle**
zicnesse *n.* sickness 16/33, 95/17,
132/14. **zycnesses**, *pl.* 53/3, 96/9,
224/7
zide *n.* side 87/23, 89/9, 151/16.
ziden, zides *pl.* 151/10, 11, 153/
14
zigge *v. tr.* say 52/8, 59/28, 63/32;
speak, utter 6/34 (*passive*), 52/31,
58/26, 63/10; mention 7/30, 10/31,
212/17; express, 69/15; tell 70/33,
175/21, 23, 34; enjoin 33/29;
proclaim, declare 132/25, 137/31,
164/33; call 112/17; name 176/13;
yzed so called 97/15; derived
93/27; 106/16 *n.*; interpreted 262/
14; *intr.* speak 16/2, 46/14; tell
191/18; ⟨**ȝigge**⟩ say *218/32*; *huet
is to* ~ what is meant by 106/21;
~ *ualse wytnesse* bear false witness
10/4–5: **ziggene** *infl. inf.* 134/21.
zigge *pr. 1 sg.* 40/34, 90/19, 213/1.
zayst *2 sg.* 71/28, 132/28. **zaiþ,
zayt** *3 sg.* 8/27, 122/3, 147/14,
248/16, 250/8*, 258/30*. **ziggeþ**
pl. 42/30, 69/15, 107/31. **zigge**
subj. sg. 104/23, 132/31, 143/2. *pl.*
50/12, 113/18, 256/29. **zay** *imp. sg.*
1/1, 103/10, 194/12. **zayde** *pa. t.
3 sg.* 103/13, 14, 118/32, 175/14 *n.*,
zede 89/14, 96/16, 103/10, **zeayde**
96/25 *n.*, ⟨**zayd**⟩ *137/13*. **zede** *pl.*
59/3. **yzed** *pp.* 70/6, 71/34, 137/19,
232/34 *n.*
ziggeres see **zoþ-ziggeres**
zigginge, ziggenge *vbl. n.* telling
49/30, 179/10; command 68/27;
discourse 135/5; **zigginges** *pl.*
speeches, sayings 58/19, 259/17;
be his ~ by his own account 19/19
ziȝt (39/29) see **riȝt**
(**y**)**ziȝþ** see (**i**)**zy**

ziȝþe *n.* sight 81/6, 91/24, 245/24; looks, looking 46/24, 47/11, 130/13 *n.*, 177/6; gaze 267/2; demeanour 216/27; regard 120/17; visions 150/24, 166/23; the Apocalypse 133/36; *to þe ~ of* in regard to, in comparison with 71/6, 81/27–8, 82/10

zik *adj.* sick 148/5, 173/26, 197/24. þe zike *wk.* 172/12, 174/25, 180/8. *pl.* 141/29

ziker *adj.* safe 124/20, 154/23; secure 144/17; sure, certain 13/2, 64/9, 86/19 *n.*, 93/19; confident, bold 83/19, 166/27; true 93/26, 112/29; *ine ~ guoinge* see guoinge; *maki ~* see maki: zikere *acc.* 93/19. *p.c.* 144/17, 254/5 *n.*, *pl.* 75/36, 102/16. zykeriste *superl. wk.* 78/2

zikerliche *adv.* safely 253/31, 254/4, 5; steadfastly 125/8; completely (*parfaitement*) 144/32; confidently, boldly 64/8, 10 *n.*, 94/6. zikerlaker *comp.* more reliably 195/5

zikernesse *n.* security 143/27, 144/15; intrepidity 164/10, 166/19

zikinges *n. pl.* sighs 99/20, 171/5, 15

ziknesse *n.* infirmity 257/30

zinge *v. tr.* sing 68/9, 268/1; *intr.* sing 22/8, 59/21, 105/15; bray 156/7: zyngþ *pr. 3 sg.* 68/7. zingeþ *pl.* 60/30, 61/13. zonge *pa. t. pl.* 261/20, 268/1

zinginge *vbl. n.* singing 59/16

zitte *v. intr.* sit 181/31, 240/3, 264/3. zit *pr. 3 sg.* 263/6. zittinde *pr. p.* 266/25, 267/13, 268/5. zet *pa. t. 3 sg.* 46/1, 96/23, 239/5. zete *subj. sg.* 208/12

ziþe, ziþes *n. pl.* times 20/18, 45/27, 59/32; often 21/11

zix *num.* six 7/10, 21/25, 29/7

izixt see (i)zy

zixte *ord. num.* sixth 9/5, 10/30, *13/10*, 16/5, ⟨zixt⟩ 164/11 *n.*

zixti *num.* sixty 71/28, 234/16

zixtiaȝte *ord. num.* sixty-fold 234/7, 11

z(u)o *adv.* so 15/24, 16/17, 27/9, 74/24 *n.*, 143/10*; such 19/1, 55/27, 204/17; thus, the case, so 17/35, 20/1, 30/15, 67/3; accordingly 100/17, 162/22, 179/22; likewise 27/2, 164/36; so (*as a particle of asseveration*) 65/13; indeed, however, yet again 15/8, 19/35, 25/15, 143/11, 247/6; *~ ase* see ase; *be ~ þet* see bi; *do, maki ~ moche* do sth. to such good effect, contrive 37/29 *n.*, 42/5, 44/26; *ine ~ moche þet* see in(e); *~ moche* 36/8, 17 (*see note to 36/8*); *~ moche . . . ~ moche* as much . . . as 91/10, 11; *for* zuo *in correlative phrases see* ase; *for* zuo *þet see* þet *conj.*

zobbinge *vbl. n.* sobbing 211/35

zofte *adj.* soft 47/36, 258/11; tender 144/34; bland 247/25; docile (*atempre*) 252/3

zofte *adv.* softly 31/16; gently 156/30

zofthede *n.* softness 267/31

zoȝe *n.* sow 61/29

yzoȝe see (i)zy

zoȝte(n) see zeche

zom *adj.* some 61/5, 62/8, 195/35 *n.* zome *acc.* 36/34, 168/7, 214/36 (*see p. 72*). *p.c.* 6/28, 7/31, 30/5. *pl.* 9/11, 20/13, 178/34; zom *pron.* someone, one person 24/9. zome *pl.* some 15/22, 27/20 *n.*, 28/16, 39/15

zomdel *adv.* to some extent 90/11, 268/13

zomere *n.* (*p.c.*) summer 131/28

zomtyme *adv.* once upon a time 71/10

zomþing *n.* something 33/29, 259/3, 266/15

zonday *n.* Sunday 7/20, 212/25, 213/6. zondayes *pl.* 41/22

zondes *n. pl.* messengers 87/29 *n.*

zone *n.* son 11/32, 12/7, 99/10. 122/15 *n.*, zones *pl.* 88/12, 96/34, 101/21

zone *adv.* soon, straightaway 42/29, 66/15, 81/10

zonge see zinge

zonge(s) see zang

zonne *n.* sun 27/5, 64/12, 81/25

zonnebyam *n.* sunbeam 108/11

zop *n.* sop 107/5

zorer *adv. comp.* more grievously 238/20

zorȝe *n.* grudging 194/10; grief, contrition 15/6, 27/25, 70/3 *n.*,

202/30* (*see note to 40/5*). **zorȝes**
pl. 27/30, 83/8; *zette ine* ~ see zette
zorȝy *v. intr.* grieve 171/13. **zor-**
ȝeþ *pr. 3 sg.* 28/27, 108/28. *pl.*
lament 71/11
zorȝuol(le) *adj.* careful 54/3; sorrow-
ful 148/4, 160/29; grievous 59/35,
181/8: **zorȝuolle** *pl.* 34/10, 132/20,
28
zoruollaker *adv. comp.* more griev-
ously 90/20 (*see p. 50*)
zoster *n.* sister 89/17, 94/29, 118/29.
zostren *pl.* 265/17, 269/26
zoþ *n.* truth, Christ 110/29. **zoþe**
p.c. 6/18, 211/15; *to* (*þe*) ~ (*a
certes*) in good earnest, assuredly
108/30*, 131/9, 143/13; *uor* ~ of a
truth 16/34, 57/7, 60/2; *for* **zoþ**
ȝiggeres see **zoþ-ȝiggeres**
zoþ(e) *adj.* true 64/9, 71/25, 83/12,
136/9 *n.* **zoþe** *acc.* 91/12, 93/23,
179/2. *p.c.* 12/34, 32/34, 185/21.
wk. 52/10, 76/14, 84/27; **þe(t)**
zoþe 103/23, 151/34. **zoþe** *pl.*
2/23, 77/12, 78/30
zoþ *adv.* truly 6/27 *n.*, 26/17, 51/33,
60/3
zoþhede *n.* truth 105/6
zoþliche *adv.* truly 74/25, 80/26,
87/7
zoþnesse *n.* truth 25/32, 29/20, 44/33
zoþuolliche *adv.* truly 133/13
zoþ-ȝiggeres *n. pl.* speakers of the
truth 256/34, 36
zouke *v. intr.* suck 91/27 *n.*, 136/10.
zoucþ *pr. 3 sg.* 136/3; *intr. don/
yeue* ~ suckle 60/9, 19, 247/9
zoure *adj.* (*p.c.*) sour 82/21. *pl.* 76/28
zoureþ *pr. 3 sg. tr.* ferments 205/21
zouteres *n. gen. sg.* shoemaker's
66/12
zouþ *n.* south 124/22
zueche see **zuich**
zuelȝ *n.* gullet 56/8; palate, taste
50/6, 82/19; *ate* ~ by taste, on the
palate 106/19
zuelȝe *v. intr.* taste 154/21*. **zuelȝþ**
pr. 3 sg. 123/32; *tr.* 106/17*
zuelȝynge *vbl. n.* tasting 91/24
zuere *n.* neck 155/34, 156/7
zuerie *v. intr.* swear 6/13, 7/2, 56/36.

zuereþ *pr. 3 sg.* 6/21, 30/9, 63/23,
zuerþ 6/24. **zuerieþ** *pl.* 65/10.
zuerie *subj. sg.* 6/15. **zuerieþ** *imp.
pl.* 63/26. **zuor** *pa. t. 3 sg.* 45/31.
zuore *subj. sg.* 64/27; *tr.* swear by
zuerye *pr. 1 sg.* 64/18
zueriinge *vbl. n.* swearing 63/33, 35
zuete *adj.* sweet 1/1, 68/10, 211/18,
þe zuete 76/27–8
zueteliche *adv.* sweetly, calmly,
gently, graciously 111/13, 112/13,
138/25, 147/2*, ⟨**zuetelich**⟩ 61/
12 *n.*
zuetnesse *n.* sweetness 55/13, 92/7,
106/18, **zuetness** 92/8‡; gracious-
ness, gentleness 93/9, 97/11, **zuyet-**
nesse 145/2; pleasure 162/20.
zuetnesses *pl.* 107/13, 251/18
zuich(e) *adj.* such and such 62/12 *n.*;
such (a), 8/30, 37/31, 210/32 (*see p.
70*). **zueche, zuiche** *acc.* 47/35, 53/
28, 244/27. **zuiche** *p.c.* 10/29, 25/24,
30/1; that 21/11; **zueche, zuiche**
pl. such, such things 5/24, 9/17,
83/27, 175/13 *n.*, ⟨**zuich**⟩ 128/35 *n.*;
pron. such a person, such 115/8,
203/34, 212/36; that man 157/5 *n.*
zuiche *pl.* such (people) 26/1,
99/2, 148/31. **zuichen** *p.c.* 37/12,
59/18, 212/36
zuift *adj.* swift 141/6. **zuyfte** *pl.*
268/12, 269/8. **zuyfter** *comp.* 66/11
zuyfthede *n.* swiftness 78/25, 270/4
zuyftliche *adv.* swiftly 140/19, 194/
26* (*see p. 49*)
zuykeþ *pr. pl. intr.* desist 157/20
zuin *n.* swine 64/31, 179/24, 255/3.
zuyn *pl.* 35/19, 50/17, 128/14
zuynch *n.* labour 83/8, 199/9
zuynke *pr. 1 sg. intr.* 171/11
zuynkeres *n. pl.* labourers 90/23
zuyþe *adv.* swiftly 111/1. **zuyþere**
comp. 61/71
zuo see **z(u)o**
zuolȝ *n.* plough 242/31, 33, 243/10
zuope *v. tr.* sweep 109/5
zuor(e) see **zuerie**
zuord *n.* sword 43/13, 148/24,
168/27. **zuorde** *p.c.* 43/25, 48/25,
218/17
zuot *n.* sweat 31/31, 96/7

INDEX OF PROPER NAMES